WRITING AS A HUMAN ACTIVITY: IMPLICATIONS AND APPLICATIONS OF THE WORK OF CHARLES BAZERMAN

PERSPECTIVES ON WRITING
Series Editors: Rich Rice, Heather MacNeill Falconer, and J. Michael Rifenburg
Consulting Editor: Susan H. McLeod | Associate Editor: Olivia Johnson

The Perspectives on Writing series addresses writing studies in a broad sense. Consistent with the wide ranging approaches characteristic of teaching and scholarship in writing across the curriculum, the series presents works that take divergent perspectives on working as a writer, teaching writing, administering writing programs, and studying writing in its various forms.

The WAC Clearinghouse, Colorado State University Open Press, and University Press of Colorado are collaborating so that these books will be widely available through free digital distribution and low-cost print editions. The publishers and the Series editors are committed to the principle that knowledge should freely circulate. We see the opportunities that new technologies have for further democratizing knowledge. And we see that to share the power of writing is to share the means for all to articulate their needs, interest, and learning into the great experiment of literacy.

Recent Books in the Series

William J. Macauley, Jr. et al. (Eds.), *Threshold Conscripts: Rhetoric and Composition Teaching Assistantships* (2023)

Jennifer Grouling, *Adapting VALUEs: Tracing the Life of a Rubric through Institutional Ethnography* (2022)

Chris M. Anson and Pamela Flash (Eds.), *Writing-Enriched Curricula: Models of Faculty-Driven and Departmental Transformation* (2021)

Asao B. Inoue, *Above the Well: An Antiracist Argument From a Boy of Color* (2021)

Alexandria L. Lockett, Iris D. Ruiz, James Chase Sanchez, and Christopher Carter (Eds.), *Race, Rhetoric, and Research Methods* (2021)

Kristopher M. Lotier, *Postprocess Postmortem* (2021)

Ryan J. Dippre and Talinn Phillips (Eds.), *Approaches to Lifespan Writing Research: Generating an Actionable Coherence* (2020)

Lesley Erin Bartlett, Sandra L. Tarabochia, Andrea R. Olinger, and Margaret J. Marshall (Eds.), *Diverse Approaches to Teaching, Learning, and Writing Across the Curriculum: IWAC at 25* (2020)

Hannah J. Rule, *Situating Writing Processes* (2019)

Asao B. Inoue, *Labor-Based Grading Contracts: Building Equity and Inclusion in the Compassionate Writing Classroom* (2019)

Mark Sutton and Sally Chandler (Eds.), *The Writing Studio Sampler: Stories About Change* (2018)

WRITING AS A HUMAN ACTIVITY: IMPLICATIONS AND APPLICATIONS OF THE WORK OF CHARLES BAZERMAN

Edited by Paul M. Rogers, David R. Russell,
Paula Carlino, and Jonathan M. Marine

The WAC Clearinghouse
wac.colostate.edu
Fort Collins, Colorado

University Press of Colorado
upcolorado.com
Denver, Colorado

The WAC Clearinghouse, Fort Collins, Colorado 80523
University Press of Colorado, Denver, Colorado 80203

© 2023 by Paul M. Rogers, David R. Russell, Paula Carlino, and Jonathan M. Marine. This work is licensed under a Creative Commons Attribution-NonCommercial-NoDerivatives 4.0 International.

ISBN 978-1-64215-180-0 (PDF) | 978-1-64215-181-7 (ePub) | 978-1-64642-391-0 (pbk.)

DOI 10.37514/PER-B.2023.1800

Produced in the United States of America

Library of Congress Cataloging-in-Publication Data

Names: Rogers, Paul M., editor. | Russell, David R., 1951– editor. | Carlino, Paula, editor. | Marine, Jonathan, 1983– editor. | Bazerman, Charles, honoree.
Title: Writing as a human activity : implications and applications of the work of Charles Bazerman / edited by Paul M. Rogers, David R. Russell, Paula Carlino, and Jonathan M. Marine
Description: Fort Collins, Colorado : The WAC Clearinghouse, [2023] | Series: Perspectives on writing | Includes bibliographical references and index.
Identifiers: LCCN 2023008549 (print) | LCCN 2023008550 (ebook) | ISBN 9781646423910 (paperback) | ISBN 9781642151800 (adobe pdf) | ISBN 9781642151817 (epub)
Subjects: LCSH: Authorship—Study and teaching. | English language—Rhetoric—Study and teaching. | Bazerman, Charles.
Classification: LCC PN181 .W76 2023 (print) | LCC PN181 (ebook) | DDC 808.0092—dc23/eng/20230417
LC record available at https://lccn.loc.gov/2023008549
LC ebook record available at https://lccn.loc.gov/2023008550

Copyeditor: Olivia Johnson
Designer: Mike Palmquist
Cover Photo: Paula Carlino. Used with permission.
Series Editors: Rich Rice, Heather MacNeill Falconer, and J. Michael Rifenburg
Consulting Editor: Susan H. McLeod
Associate Editor: Olivia Johnson

The WAC Clearinghouse supports teachers of writing across the disciplines. Hosted by Colorado State University, it brings together scholarly journals and book series as well as resources for teachers who use writing in their courses. This book is available in digital formats for free download at wac.colostate.edu.

Founded in 1965, the University Press of Colorado is a nonprofit cooperative publishing enterprise supported, in part, by Adams State University, Colorado State University, Fort Lewis College, Metropolitan State University of Denver, University of Alaska Fairbanks, University of Colorado, University of Denver, University of Northern Colorado, University of Wyoming, Utah State University, and Western Colorado University. For more information, visit upcolorado.com.

Land Acknowledgment. The Colorado State University Land Acknowledgment can be found at landacknowledgment.colostate.edu.

CONTENTS

Preface vii

Editors' Introduction 3
    David R. Russell, Paul M. Rogers, Paula Carlino,
    and Jonathan M. Marine

Part One. Academic and Scientific Writing

Chapter 1. New Cognitive Practices in a Master's Thesis Proposal
Writing Seminar. 31
    Paula Carlino

Chapter 2. Case Studies on Chance Encounters in Literacy
Development in Latin American Researchers 59
    Fatima Encinas and Nancy Keranen

Chapter 3. Changing Times; Changing Texts 79
    Ken Hyland

Chapter 4. Situated Regulation Writing Processes in Research
Writing: Lessons from Research and Teaching 101
    Montserrat Castelló

Part Two. Writing Pedagogy

Chapter 5. Writing at University and in the Workplace: Interrelations
and Learning Experiences at the Beginning of the Professional Activity. 125
    Lucía Natale

Chapter 6. Cultural Shaping of Standpoint and Reasoning in
Analytical Writing 143
    Liliana Tolchinsky and Anat Stavans

Part Three. Sociology of Knowledge & Organizational Communication

Chapter 7. Genre Change Around Teaching in the COVID-19 Pandemic . . 169
    JoAnne Yates

Chapter 8. Opening Up: Writing Studies' Turn to Open-Access
Book Publishing. 195
    Mike Palmquist

Contents

Chapter 9. Writing and Social Progress: Genre Evolution in the
Field of Social Entrepreneurship. 227
   Karyn Kessler and Paul M. Rogers

PART FOUR. ACTIVITY THEORY

Chapter 10. Two Paths Diverge in a Field: Dialectics and Dialogics
in Rhetorical Genre Studies 265
   Clay Spinuzzi

Chapter 11. Writing for Stabilization and Writing for Possibility: The
Dialectics of Representation in Everyday Work with Vulnerable Clients. . . 293
   Yrjö Engeström

PART FIVE. WRITING RESEARCH DEVELOPMENT

Chapter 12. A Review on Second Language Writing Research in China . . . 317
   Wu Dan and Li Zenghui

Chapter 13. Twenty Years of Research on Reading and Writing in Latin
American Higher Education: Lessons Learned from the ILEES Initiative. . 327
   Natalia Ávila Reyes, Elizabeth Narváez-Cardona, and Federico Navarro

PART SIX. NEW MEDIA AND TECHNOLOGY

Chapter 14. Rethinking Genre as Digital Social Action: Engaging
Bazerman with Medium Theory and Digital Media 351
   Jack Andersen

Chapter 15. What Writers Do with Language: Inscription and
Formulation as Core Elements of the Science of Writing 367
   Otto Kruse and Christian Rapp

Chapter 16. Genre Formation and Differentiation in New Media. 393
   Carolyn R. Miller

Chapter 17. Change, Change, Change—and the Processes that Abide 407
   Charles Bazerman

Chapter 18. What We Teach When We Teach Writing: A Big Picture
in a Small Frame. 415
   Charles Bazerman

Appendix. The Publications of Charles Bazerman in Chronological Order . . 423
   Jonathan M. Marine

Editors 441
Index 442

PREFACE

This book, conceived as a festschrift, is an edited collection of original chapters by international senior scholars who have been affiliated with the ideas and foundational work of Professor Charles Bazerman. The collection aims to account for Bazerman's shaping influence on the field of writing studies through scholarly engagement with his ideas, with Bazerman himself included as a contributor. Although a festschrift is defined as a collection of writings published in honor of a scholar, the editors envisioned this volume as more than a celebration of Bazerman's accomplishments. Rather, we propose this book as an extension and application of his contributions to the field in the spirit of committed scholarly discourse.

WRITING AS A HUMAN ACTIVITY: IMPLICATIONS AND APPLICATIONS OF THE WORK OF CHARLES BAZERMAN

EDITORS' INTRODUCTION

David R. Russell
Iowa State University

Paul M. Rogers
University of California, Santa Barbara

Paula Carlino
CONICET, Universidad de Buenos Aires, Universidad Pedagógica Nacional

Jonathan M. Marine
George Mason University

Modern scholarship, unlike the old rhetoric, values specialization. That value is reflected dramatically in festschrifts, which make the focus of a scholar's life's work the subject of a volume. With Bazerman the problem is that his specialization, writing, is about as general and ubiquitous an object as possible—second only to, well, rhetoric or communication in other media. And the goal of his research, teaching, and scholarly leadership has been to further broaden the study of writing, to move it beyond its usual disciplinary, pedagogical, and institutional confines (penmanship, literacy, orthography, grammar, rhetoric, linguistics, composition, and so on). He has taken writing in human life as the study of his lifetime.

In this introduction, we editors will not attempt to summarize his biography or contribution. Bazerman has over the decades recounted a number of moments from his life that figured importantly in his work, which we'll mention for reference.[1] Instead, we will attempt to put his contribution into context. David Russell will locate the seeds of his teaching and the research that grew out of it, in terms of developments in writing teaching during his early career. Paul Rogers will note his professional leadership during his mid and later career, particularly his service to what became writing studies. Paula Carlino will note aspects of his character and personality that allowed for his remarkable reach

---

1   He has conveniently collected his essays with biographical elements on his web page in the About section under the heading Biography and Overview: bazerman.education.ucsb.edu/biography-and-overview.

DOI: https://doi.org/10.37514/PER-B.2023.1800.1.3

Editors' Introduction

internationally. Finally, Jonathan Marine will explain our rationale for the organization and summarize the contents of the chapters.

FROM COMPOSITION TO WRITING STUDIES: SOME MOMENTS IN A LIFE AND A FIELD

Bazerman created—with the help of many, many others—what amounts to a new field: writing studies. In 2002 he proposed as an object of scholarly inquiry "writing in all its involvement in the world," in order to give writing "a serious home of its own" (Bazerman, 2002, p. 32). Throughout the 19th and 20th centuries, writing—defined in many radically different ways—had been studied in several disciplinary silos, with little talk across, most notably: in university education departments for teaching initial writing, as part of "literacy"; or in English departments for a very narrow but prestigious sliver of writing, high-end authorship of "literature," what he archly but accurately termed "the high end of the leisure entertainment business" (Bazerman, 1998, p. 19). In English departments, where he began to specialize in the late 1960s, the budding research on the process of writing was focused almost exclusively on first-year composition courses. There were no upper-level courses on writing (except those in technical communication, typically housed in business and engineering), no graduate programs in writing or composition, no professional organizations beyond the Conference on College Composition and Communication, which had little systematic research on writing. When he conceived writing studies in the 1990s, he did so on the pattern of other new university fields attempting to unite the work going in multiple disciplinary silos: American studies, women's studies, library & information studies, communication studies, cultural studies, and so on. But it was a long path from the late 1960s, when he began his career, to his proposing the field of writing studies.

EARLY STEPS TOWARD TEACHING WRITING AS INVOLVEMENT IN THE WORLD

In the mid-1960s, when he was an undergraduate at Cornell, the teaching of "English" was in upheaval—like the country itself. A meeting of British and American scholars of English in 1966, the Dartmouth Seminar, provoked a seminal rethinking among the Americans of writing teaching. They began to imagine writing not as a formal discipline like literature and grammar, but as a process of personal development through student-centered teaching and creative exploration. The federal government, under the National Defense Education Act (Strain, 2005), had begun to fund empirical research and curriculum reforms on writing under Project English, and more broadly, to fund a massive expansion of higher education, drawing in previously excluded groups. Cultural and political shifts during the Vietnam War brought massive increases in humanities enrollments. During his undergraduate years at Cornell (1963–1967), he was "switching majors every six months," (Bazerman, 2002b, p. 85) which exposed him to a wide variety of discourses and thus prepared him for his work on writing in the disciplines. He eventually landed on English and entered graduate school at Brandeis.

One of the federal education programs attracted Bazerman. In 1968, he entered a special program for graduate students to teach in low-income New York City elementary schools, which came with a deferment from the military draft for the war in Vietnam. Teaching first and third graders for two years at Public School 93K, in Brooklyn's Bedford-Stuyvesant, in the midst of a teachers' strike, taught him that "inner-city schools at that time, with their funding, social, political, and numerous other problems, made it nearly impossible to carry forward a progressive, student-oriented program," but also taught him "the pleasure of making a difference in other people's lives," through literacy. And the experience framed his future critical and political approach to literacy teaching (Bazerman, 1999, p. 19–20).

Back at Brandeis for the academic year 1970–71 to finish his Ph.D. in Renaissance literature (a literary period that attracted many other scholars of writing across the curriculum, incidentally, but perhaps not coincidentally), he was a world away from Bed-Sty. He wrote his dissertation on a seemingly esoteric genre: poems on the death of Queen Elizabeth I. But it emphasized (unusually for literary criticism in the late 1960s) the social as well as the aesthetic functions of occasional poetry in Elizabethan society (Jack Goody [1962] had previously taken up Ghanan funeral poems as a window into comparative sociology and anthropology). His dissertation, he said decades later, "foreshadowed my long-standing interests in rhetorical situation and genre" (Bazerman, 1999, p. 21).

The expansion of higher education to previously excluded people desiring to enter various professional worlds, lay behind his first tenure-track teaching position, at the open enrollment Baruch College in Manhattan. There he had many first-generation college students, whom he recalled were like his father, who was himself a first-generation college student during the Depression at the downtown business branch of City College (later to be called Baruch College). It was those students striving to better themselves that took his attention, not the esoteric call of great literature, viewed in the New Critical terms of the time as "verbal icons." Before tenure, he "gestured toward the kinds of publications my department would recognize" by writing some literary criticism, but after tenure, he "gave up the pretense of literary studies" to focus exclusively but broadly on writing, both in his research and his teaching (Bazerman, 1999, p. 21).

Editors' Introduction

HOW TO TEACH STUDENTS TO WRITE TO SUCCEED ON THEIR TERMS: FROM WAC TO WID

The massification of higher education, the rethinking of composition in English, and the budding of empirical research in writing begun in the 1960s converged in the 1970s to spark major innovations, led in part by faculty in the CUNY open enrollment colleges such as Baruch. The new focus on basic writing, begun by his CUNY colleague, Mina Shaughnessy, at City College, was designed to transition first-generation and underprepared students into first-year writing.[2] The CUNY Association of Writing Supervisors (CAWS) and the Instructional Resource Center she founded became central to reformulation of writing in higher education in another way, by helping students to transition into the university more broadly: writing across the curriculum (WAC).

The concept of WAC was just beginning to be developed nationally. As a young English professor teaching almost exclusively composition and developmental writing courses to open admissions students striving to enter various professional fields to better themselves and their families, Bazerman asked an obvious but then little-asked question: What are students reading and writing in their other courses? And he began to systematically investigate, through a survey, that most quotidian of school genres, the research paper. The name of the genre, he found, masked an immensely varied set of tacit teacher expectations, often tied to the discipline and thus to the universe of research, reading, writing, and social action in each field. That led him to study the relationship between reading and writing, what later came to be called intertextuality, before that term from Julia Kristeva (who used it rather differently) became current in the US (Eldred & Bazerman, 1995, p. 8).

WAC's focus was primarily on writing-to-learn, seen as a general cognitive accomplishment. But how does writing support learning? One way, Bazerman felt, is through deepening reading. He developed a teaching sequence for first year composition (FYC) based on the intertextual relationship between reading and writing across the curriculum. Out of that came *The Informed Writer* (1980), one of the first WAC textbooks. But his interest in disciplinary writing led him to look beyond WAC as writing-to-learn in general, to the specifics of writing in different disciplines. He wanted students—and writing teachers and researchers—to be aware of the differing methods, epistemes, and rhetorics operating in

---

2   In Shaughnessy, Bazerman saw a persistent and magnetic leader create a collaborative effort around writing, an effort that became an institution—with a name: basic writing. He would collaboratively found such institutions again and again himself: writing in the disciplines, The Research Network Forum, the Consortium of Graduate Programs in Rhetoric and Composition, Writing Research across Borders, Rhetoricians for Peace, the International Society for the Advancement of Writing Research (ISAWR), and of course writing studies.

the university. The second edition (1985) of his textbook, *The Informed Writer*, was subtitled "*Using sources in the disciplines.*" It included a section on reading and writing in various disciplinary areas, which marked out this new focus in WAC—from writing across the curriculum to writing in the disciplines, or WID, as he termed it (and the term stuck).

Whether WAC or WID, his pedagogy is based on treating seriously students who have chosen other disciplines, and their need to learn its discourse—without trying to convert or rescue them (Eldred & Bazerman, 1995, p. 19). He has always seen the critical power of writing teaching, in a political sense, but has been cautious about wearing his politics on his sleeves in the classroom (though he has been proud to wear it on an armband during a protest, as when he helped to found the Rhetoricians for Peace in the run-up to the second Iraq war) (Bazerman, 2019, p. 45). His writing teaching from his first years at an open admission university was about, as he put it:

> demystifying the class secrets of language and literacy. To my mind, teaching writing was such a political act that it never needed any overt political comment or political teaching. In fact, overt politics would distract us from the task of bringing new groups and individuals into positions of economic and social power and might even undermine the motivation of the students, who for the most part were more interested in the fates of themselves and their families than in any politics. (Bazerman, 1999, pp. 22–23)

He later said that textbook writing has been "as much a path of discovery and contribution for me as have been research and theory writing." It is motivated, for him, by "the practical problem of teaching underprepared college students for the reading and writing in their other courses. The payoff for solving the problem is both immediate and long term: the increased competence of writers as they move through the university and through their lives" (Bazerman, 1999, p. 23).

Had he done nothing but write his innovative textbooks in the 1980s and early 1990s, his place in the profession would be secure, but he went on to make pedagogy the driving force of his increasingly diverse research and theory. He said the uniqueness and reach of his research and theory was "not the result of individual characteristics or personal virtue . . . but precisely because I have become broadly conversant with the standard writing tools and the historical particulars of work within a range of academic disciplines" in order to develop his pedagogy of writing in the disciplines (Eldred & Bazerman, 1995, p. 89). Indeed, he conceived the first volume of his major theoretical work, *A Rhetoric of*

Editors' Introduction

Literate Action–Literate Action volume 1 (2013), as a guide for advanced writers, while the second volume, *A Theory of Literate Action–Literate Action volume 2*, lays out fully the theory behind the advice (2013b).

RESEARCH AND THEORY

To put Bazerman's contributions to theory and research in context, we might focus on 1978–1979, which was a crucial year. As a newly tenured associate professor, he waded into the controversies and contradictions out of which his research and theory emerged and continued throughout his career.

READING AND WRITING

The institutional separation of reading and writing after elementary school was and still often is a fact of American educational life. Literacy was mainly about reading—teaching young children to read initially or teaching "remedial" adults the "basics," as Bazerman did at Public School 93K and Baruch College, respectively. Writing was thought of as either the low-level skill of transcription of speech to text (again, in elementary or "remedial" schooling) or authorship of literary texts, "classics" studied in English classes. The great middle—where the vast majority of writing goes on—was not studied or taught, with a few exceptions such as "composition" in English classes or business and technical writing in a few university business or engineering departments.

Bazerman challenged that separation from the beginning. He published his first book in 1978, a textbook on reading, not writing, intended for study skills courses usually classified as "remedial" (Wiener & Bazerman, 1978). As we noted, he developed his reading-to-write-to-learn pedagogy in those years, which in 1981 became *The Informed Writer*—the writer informed mainly by reading. In 1978 he gave a paper that outlined a new theory of writing, one based on reading, "A Relationship Between Reading and Writing: The Conversational Model," which became his first major publication in the field of composition (1980). He was active in the CUNY Association of Writing Supervisors in the 1970s, and co-chaired it in 1978–1979. At their 1978 conference spoke on "The Role of Reading in the Kinds of Writing Students do in College," based on his survey research (Bazerman & Herrington, 2006).

WRITING AS A SOCIAL PHENOMENON

This focus on the kinds of reading and writing students do in college in different disciplines and majors, the movement from WAC to WID we noted earlier, required a serious study of those disciplinary differences, something that had rarely been done. This means, Bazerman said, that WID "tends to have more of a research orientation" than WAC (Eldred & Bazerman, 1995, p. 8). And from the late 1970s, he cast his net widely over a range of possibilities for research on the phenomenon of writing in the disciplines and professions. If writing is a conversation, then it is fundamentally social (though incorporating psychological, linguistic, and other factors). Thus, the social sciences, he reasoned, might offer ways of studying it—a radical idea in English departments then.

Divide Between Humanities and Social Sciences

In 1978 he joined a Columbia sociology of science seminar taught by giants in the field, Harriet Zuckerman and Robert Merton, which investigated science as a social institution (Bazerman & Herrington, 2006, p. 59) with systems of communication (mainly specialized reading and writing) through which knowledge is made in the disciplines. In doing so, Bazerman was crossing the great divide between what C.P. Snow called "The Two Cultures," the sciences and the humanities. Bazerman studied not texts as texts (or "verbal icons," as the phrase common in literary criticism held) but rather texts in human activity, the sociology and anthropology of writing. In 1979 he began attending meetings of the Society for Social Studies of Science (SSSS), where the rhetoric of science had started to be investigated, as well as the social history and anthropology of science and technology as institutions. The sociology of knowledge and the Project on the Rhetoric of Inquiry (POROI) also provided inspiration.

He could cross this great divide in the organization of knowledge because in 1978 he was tenured and no longer had to publish in literature (or pretend to). He got a Fellowship Leave and began publishing exclusively in composition and social science venues. His first scholarly publication was in a collection entitled *The University and the State* (Bazerman, 1978). His chapter was on grants—a genre with profound effects in the post-war world. Grants are about writing to learn (cognitive), he points out: "Grant writing, as any form of writing, helps to clarify and develop thought" (p. 222) But he emphasizes the genre has sociological effects as well, on "pecking order" (p. 225) power relations, self-perception, and also beyond: on the good of society and the state as well as individual good.

He chaired the CUNY Ad Hoc Committee for Graduate Business Writing in 1979, showing his interest in quotidian writing in the professions, an interest that would endure. The recently-organized Association of Teachers of Technical Writing (1973) and the Association for Business Communication (1935) provided other emerging research traditions for writing beyond the usual purview of English departments—and a window into the worlds of practical writing beyond academe. All these traditions of research touched upon writing and allowed him to explore how they could inform composition/rhetoric—and later writing studies (Bazerman & Herrington, 2006, p. 63).

RHETORIC FROM SPEECH TO ENGLISH

Another institutional split that shaped Bazerman's intellectual world was between the oral and the written. The social and political aspects of communication were traditionally the province of classical rhetoric, which was fundamentally oral. In 1915 professors interested in communication split off from English departments—which then as now was interested in aesthetics—and took rhetoric with it to form speech departments, where they added social science methods to the humanistic methods used to study classical rhetoric. In the 1960s, when some English professors became interested in studying written communication, they turned back to classical rhetoric for theories and pedagogies (though they pretty much ignored social science) (Russell, 2002).

In the summer of 1979 Bazerman attended Richard Young's NEH summer seminar on rhetoric and invention at Carnegie Mellon, where he met many future leading lights in the field who would champion rhetoric in composition—so successfully it came to be called "rhetoric and composition." Though he learned much from this tradition (his dissertation, after all, was on the communicative aspects of an ancient rhetorical genre, the eulogy), he found classical rhetoric inadequate to understanding the immense specialization of modern writing and life in the age of print (Bazerman & Russell, 1994).

CLASSICAL RHETORIC VERSUS COGNITIVE SCIENCE

The Carnegie Mellon community was then studying writing from a range of perspectives, from ancient rhetoric to cognitive psychology. There he met Dick Hayes from information-processing cognitive psychology and Linda Flower from English, who were pioneering empirical research on "the writing process," as they termed it. They were modeling in computer simulations the cognitive processes of "expert writers" (some members of Young's seminar even served as research subjects). Though Bazerman was impressed with the research and theory, he again turned to the social sciences—specifically social psychology—to understand the psychology of writing. His therapist, Tony Gabriele, introduced him to the work of Harry Stack Sullivan, an early 20th psychiatrist who focused on how the self is formed through the history of our social relations, mainly communicative. Sullivan looked not at "intrapsychic" but at "interactional"—especially interpersonal—sources of behavior, including psychotic behaviors. Sullivan's therapy is based on teaching a client to "engage in reflexive self-observations of language behaviors . . . monitor and examine the consequences of my own participation" (Bazerman, 1999, p. 20). And when, in the late 1980s, composition turned away from cognitive science to the old humanist rhetoric more congenial to those trained in English department humanities methods, Bazerman offered a third way, one that had a humanistic social psychology, using methods from the human sciences, such as sociology and anthropology, as well as the emerging "cultural psychology" of Vygotsky's circle, as we'll see (Cole, 1998).

WRITING AS LITERATE ACTION

Bazerman would continue to take several paths into social science research and theory adaptable to studying writing in human life—writing as an activity, a social action. In doing so he broke with extreme versions of "social construction," such as "deconstruction" from continental semiotics, which denied the possibility of a knowable reality. He published in 1979 a critical review of Latour and Woolgar's groundbreaking *Laboratory Life*, in which he took them to task for treating scientific discourse as fiction, even though science "has a commitment to ever more precise descriptions of ever more closely watched realities" (p. 20).

His path-making first article on WID, "What Written Knowledge Does" (1981) was published in *Philosophy of the Social Science*. It explored different kinds of social action that writing and reading accomplish in different fields. The article used not Kristeva's version of intertextuality, which emphasizes the play of referents, but rather a modification of James Kinneavy's theory, which emphasizes discourse as a tool for being responsible to others' descriptions of their observations of reality—though a final representation of reality may never be fully possible (see his chapter in this collection.) The author, the audience, and the object of discourse are mediated by language, Kinneavy said, but Bazerman adds that the literature in the field—the reading that the author and audience share about the object—is also mediated by the language, through intertextual reference.

On a consultation at the National University of Singapore in 1982 and then returning as a visiting Professor in 1985–86 he found, fortuitously, a complete run of the *Philosophical Transactions of the Royal Society* in the university library. That set him on the historical investigation that led to his first book, *Shaping Written Knowledge: The Genre and Activity of the Experimental Article in Science* (1988). The history of the experimental article, from its origins in letters circulated among gentleman scientists in the 17th century to modern research literature, offered a window on social and practical aspects of writing not much considered before.

Editors' Introduction

Genres as Forms of Life

The subtitle of *Shaping Written Knowledge* combines key elements for the field of writing studies that would emerge some 15 years later. People shape their knowledge and action in the activity of composing texts—writing is active in the world. Writing is shaped by genre, but genre as more than static form or conventions. Genres, as he would say later, are not only forms of words but forms of life (1994). And experimental articles, like other genres and texts, carry out an activity, in this case the activity of modern science. This insight he drew from a contributor to this volume, Carolyn Miller and her (1984) concept of genre as social action, in turn drawn from continental phenomenological sociology: Adolf Schutz' notion of typification. Humans classify the world so we can act in it, creating social facts (e.g., pieces of paper of a certain size printed a certain way by a certain government can be exchanged for goods and services because we agree they can, not because the pieces of paper have any intrinsic worth). Bazerman applied genre as social action to scientific communication: "The forms of scientific representation emerged simultaneously and dialectically with the activity of science and the social structure of the scientific community. Features of the experimental article developed as part of an agonistic social activity, arguing over experienced events. The experience is shaped by the argument just as the arguments exploit the experience in a public linguistic forum" (Bazerman, 1988, p. 155).

Language and Writing: A Theory of How Writing is Connected to the World

All aspects of writing, not just its genres, can be viewed as active engagement, and that includes language, which is in Bazerman's view more than a system of signs, to be correctly or properly arranged. Such a "code orientation" to language "hides the motive for writing," its role in the formulation of a complex social event. Bazerman applied Austin's theory of "speech acts" to writing and found in Swales' "move" analysis of scientific article introductions a version of applied linguistics that viewed scientific writing not as disembodied but as a solution to a problem of "establishing a place for one's work within a relevant literature" (1988, p. 149).

This emphasis on writing as social action in the world drew him to the American pragmatists, who explored the relation between mind, self, and society, especially Mead, but above all he drew on the Russian "troika" of Vygotsky, Leont'ev, and Luria. Vygotsky's viewed language as a cultural tool that allowed for coordinated activity, and transformed simultaneously cognitive capacities, the social world, and the material world in which humans act. Vygotsky gave Bazerman a way to get past both the naïve view of language as a direct description of reality and the cynical view of language as a socially constructed code without anything knowable beyond (Bazerman, 2013b).

Vygotsky's theory—combined with the social psychology of Leont'ev into "Activity Theory"—made the history of language use a crucial question. The theory sought to explain both individual learning and development, and social/institutional stability and change, as practices of using language and other tools in certain "stabilized-for-now" (Schryer, 1993) ways. Here Miller's concept of genre as social action became useful for seeing how written genres—and the practices they organize—develop over time, connecting thoughts and deeds, the past and the future. Bazerman would expand Miller's theory of genre to consider not just single genres but systems of intertextually connected genres, enacting social intentions and coordinating actions over time. After his book on the history of a genre in science, his research took up a series of activity systems mediated by systems of complex written genres: such as the patent system (1994), and the complex written systems that allowed inventions in the laboratory to move beyond it into the wider world. His second book of historical research, *The Languages of Edison's Light* (1999b), chronicles not only the documentary history of the invention of electric light, but also the documentary process by which this invention organized massive institutions, wielding vast power and organizing vast resources.

When Bazerman made his case for a discipline of writing studies two decades ago (2002), he did so by laying out three syntheses, each a charge for the study of writing: historical, theoretical, and practical. Together these "tell the same story, for the theory is an attempt to understand how we live our lives at the unfolding edge of history, using literacy in the ways that make most sense for us in our lives, to continually make a future from our own skills and choices as writers" (p. 38). He ultimately synthesized his theoretical insights in his two volume *Literate Action*—the phrase encompassing the connection between reading, writing, and human activity. And he would also in 2004, with Paul Prior and others, produce a manual for empirical research using a range of methods culminating in an activity theory methodology, which he used for several collaborative empirical projects. He organized scholarly efforts to provide other resources necessary to the existence and health of a field of study, such as handbooks, publishers, and bibliographic tools (Bazerman, [Ed.], 2008). And recently he launched a large-scale effort around the broad question of "lifespan" studies of writing, how writing develops and changes across the lives of individuals (Bazerman et al., 2018).

This brief sketch has pointed to his early and abiding interest in writing as the strategic exercise of agency and writing as purposeful action within "emergent structures of texts that conditioned the situation for future action." He concluded, "Even my professional service as editor, creator of professional forums, and departmental administrator are informed by these perspectives" (Bazerman, 2002b, p. 90). We now turn to Paul Rogers for an account of his leadership and service.

SERVICE TO WRITING STUDIES

Throughout his career, Bazerman engaged deeply with a number of professional organizations related to writing: the National Council of Teachers of English (NCTE), and its higher education branch, College Composition and Communication (CCC). In these organizations, and others, he contributed reliably as a committed member within the formal structures of these organizations' committees and subcommittees. At the same time, he consistently sought to advance the status of what was to become writing studies by instigating projects, programs, and entirely new organizations. The quality of his service across these activities, combined with the impact of his work and scholarly publication, ultimately positioned Bazerman as the recognized, international ambassador for writing studies, in the US, Europe, Asia, and South America, and as a serious cultural broker who was able to bring people together across disciplinary and geographical boundaries, as Paula Carlino's section explains.

His engagement with organizational structures, both those which he founded and those established organizations with whom he worked, were instantiations of Bazerman's vision of the social role of written texts in bringing about change, noting that "the best way to assure a text some enduring life is for it to gain a central role in an enduring institution, such as a church, university, or a government not troubled by coups, revolutions, or reconstitutions" (Bazerman, 2013, p. 52). In what follows I look briefly at some of the highlights of Bazerman's accomplishments in the service of writing studies, in particular his work as organizational leader in NCTE and CCC, as an activist for social justice and open access publication, and as a driving force in advancing writing research.

While Bazerman's service and leadership to NCTE and the CCC ultimately took place at the highest levels of these organizations—he served on NCTE's Executive Committee, and as Assistant Chair, Program and Associate Chair, and Chair of the CCC from 2007–2009—these preeminent roles came about after decades of service to both organizations as a member and active citizen. At what might be considered the pinnacle of his visibility and leadership in the CCC, as the program chair of the 2008 CCCC annual meeting in New Orleans, Bazerman used that platform to advance a broader vision of writing studies, as evidenced by the plenary speakers he invited to speak to the members of the CCCC. Notably, and in addition to prioritizing the voices of respected educators and journalists from New Orleans who spoke on the aftermath of the tragic handling of the Katrina hurricane disaster, he invited famed New Yorker journalist Seymour Hersh, who broke the stories on the My Lai massacre and the torture taking place in Abu Ghraib prison; archeologist and art historian Denise Schmandt-Bessarat, who published groundbreaking work on the earliest origins of writing; psychologist James Pennebaker, who documented empirically the medical impacts of trauma writing; feminist sociologist Dorothy Smith, whose work on textually mediated social organization and the documentary society revealed the ways in which writing and power relations permeate our daily lives; and, educational psychologist Charles "Skip" MacArthur, who presented work in a plenary session on the importance of explicit writing education from the earliest years of schooling. In reflecting on these plenary choices, Bazerman noted, "The speakers I invited were people largely from outside the world of composition which I thought the field would benefit from hearing to extend the vision of what is relevant to our work" (personal communication).

Bazerman's activity with NCTE and the CCCC resulted in his receiving both organizations' highest honors. In 2018, NCTE presented Bazerman with the James Squire Award, which is "given to an NCTE member who has had a transforming influence and has made a lasting intellectual contribution to the profession." Specifically, the award is given in recognition of "outstanding service, not only to the stature and development of NCTE and the discipline which it represents, but also to the profession of education as a whole, internationally as well as nationally." The Squire Award Committee Chair at the time, Doug Hesse, noted in his selection remarks, "Charles Bazerman not only meets this standard: he sets it for all of us." Two years later, Bazerman received the CCCC 2020 Exemplar Award which recognizes "a person whose years of service as an exemplar for our organization represents the highest ideals of scholarship, teaching, and service to the entire profession. The Exemplar Award seeks to recognize individuals whose record is national and international in scope, and who set the best examples for the CCCC membership." In Bazerman's service to NCTE and CCCC he sought to bring about change within existing systems while simultaneously opening up spaces for new activity.

Bazerman's Advocacy: Social Justice and Open Access

As reflected in his 2008 CCCC conference, Bazerman's leadership extended beyond his concern for the discipline to issues of social justice, as he has chronicled in his autobiographical piece entitled "The Work of a Middle-class Activist: Stuck in History." One particular example of this focus can be seen in his work in founding the Rhetoricians for Peace (RFP) in 2002, around the time of the buildup to the 2003 Iraq War, to which he was staunchly opposed. Designed to leverage the possibilities of new technologies, in particular listservs and social media, the RFP brought together and galvanized a geographically distributed group of colleagues who were a notable presence at the CCCC annual meetings, including during 2003, when the bombing of Iraq began. The RFP became a formal organization and accomplished a great deal of work in developing and making available pedagogical and scholarly resources to fight misinformation and doublespeak, and in standing in opposition to the rhetoric of continual war.

Another important contribution of Bazerman's has been his activism in support of open access publication (see Palmquist's chapter in this volume). His leadership in this area has involved an enormous amount of focused effort, demonstrated by his extensive body of editorial work (see Publications of Charles Bazerman in this volume) as well as his work with other key collaborators in breaking new ground in open access publishing, an area of work that was rife with complexity and difficult challenges (e.g., the implications of open-access online publication for tenure and promotion decisions; the stability, credibility, and visibility of online publications; and, the challenges associated with the financing and marketing of open access publications). Bazerman's work on open access began in the early days of the internet, when in 2003 he along with David Russell and Mike Palmquist published one of the first open access online scholarly publications *Writing Selves/Writing Societies*. Bazerman's investment and energy for open access publishing has been ongoing (as Palmquist recounts in his chapter) and has always involved him having "skin in the game," especially in his support and activity with the WAC Clearinghouse, but also in making easily accessible his considerable body of scholarship on his personal website (bazerman.education.ucsb.edu).

Advancing Writing Research

Bazerman's contributions to the field have been especially substantive in advancing writing research. For example, in 1988, Bazerman originated, organized, and chaired the Research Network Forum, whose ongoing mission has been to "mentor new and established researchers in rhetoric and composition studies." As Chair of the CCCC he also created the Research Impact Award and the CCCC Advancement of Knowledge Award. He was also an early founder and active member of the Consortium of Doctoral Programs in Rhetoric and Composition, which brought together graduate programs, faculty members, and graduate students to build research capacity and advance scholarly publication.

Perhaps Bazerman's most notable leadership activity, given its international reach, has been his work in founding the International Society for the

Advancement of Writing Research (ISAWR), an organization that embodies his multidisciplinary and complex view of writing and its role in human societies around the world. Dissatisfied with the lack of emphasis on empirical work in the CCCC conferences, Bazerman set out initially to provide a focused home for writing researchers. In 2003 Bazerman hosted a regional conference (i.e., California focused) at the University of California, Santa Barbara entitled "Writing as a Human Activity" from which this festschrift derives its title. And again in 2005, he hosted a national level conference "Writing Research in the Making," whose title reflected Bazerman's view that the field of writing studies was still in the early stages of grounding itself on an empirical foundation. The success of that conference led to the first Writing Research Across Borders (WRAB) conference in 2008. The title of this conference announced that there were indeed real boundaries in the activities associated with research on writing: methodological, epistemological, disciplinary, educational, political, and geographic. At the same, the conference encouraged the crossing of those borders by facilitating dialogue among researchers from various disciplines and research traditions.

Together with a distinguished "scientific committee" of leading writing researchers from around the world, Bazerman succeeded in gathering together writing researchers at all career stages and from across a broad range of research traditions and geographies to share empirical research on writing in multiple international venues. The quality of presentations and thoroughness of the conference planning helped to build momentum for the subsequent conferences in Washington, D.C. (2011), Paris (2014), and Bogota (2017). All of the WRAB conferences resulted in the publication of volumes of empirically grounded research, on which Bazerman served as lead editor: *Traditions of Writing Research* (2009), *International Advances in Writing Research* (2011), *Research on Writing: Multiple Perspectives* (2017), and *Knowing Writing: Writing Research across Borders* (2020). At the 2011 conference, the scientific committee gathered and voted to create the International Society for the Advancement of Writing Research (ISAWR). Bazerman was elected as ISAWR's inaugural chair.

Bazerman's scholarly reputation—as well as his rhetorical savvy, empathy, curiosity, and intercultural skills developed over many years —were essential in weaving together a global, international, and indeed interdisciplinary organization. Such an achievement in academia seems especially remarkable given the propensity for intellectual turf battles and the contentious nature of scholarly discourse across disciplinary and epistemological boundaries. Although Bazerman has cycled through the leadership of the organization (his term as immediate past chair ended in 2020), the organization remains vital and is scheduled to host WRAB VI in Trondheim, Norway, in 2023; and, at the time of this publication planning activities underway for WRAB VII to be held in 2026.

Editors' Introduction

It is important to note that Bazerman's global and national level leadership activity has been accompanied by a tangible and practical commitment to the faculty at his home institution, the University of California, Santa Barbara (UCSB). Bazerman served two terms as Chair of the Program in Education in the Gevirtz Graduate School of Education, and beginning in 2016, Bazerman created an endowment for an ongoing competitive faculty research award the "Bazerman Fellowship" for faculty in the UCSB Writing Program. The fellowship provides a sabbatical during which a faculty member can pursue research that will inform and enrich their teaching and advance knowledge in the field. Bazerman also sponsors lunches for the faculty where topics generated by the faculty are discussed in an open, scholarly, and convivial forum.

Bazerman has the ability to zoom in on the smallest details of organizational structure, governance, and finance and to zoom out to the broadest levels of theoretical framings and interdisciplinary discourse. His unique blend of strategic and organizational savvy, intellect, and willingness to get the work done underlie the effectiveness of his efforts. Bazerman's high standards of personal integrity have also undergirded his activity on every level and no doubt have contributed to the longevity of his influence and leadership legacy. In addition to deep commitment to high ethical standards, those who know him well have witnessed his deep empathy and humanity, his cross cultural and social emotional sensitivity, and his great ability to connect with people from around the world, to which Paula Carlino turns now.

PERSONAL CONNECTIONS: INTERNATIONAL REACH

Bazerman (whom I will refer to as Chuck in this final section on personal connection) not only disseminated his research on writing power, genres, disciplines, socialization, knowledge, writing anxiety, teaching, learning, and related issues. He also connected with others, especially his students (elementary, undergraduate, and graduate), but also with colleagues near and far geographically. One hallmark of these interactions was Chuck's curiosity and interest in understanding his students' and colleagues' points of view. Even as he made his own work known, he also wanted to know about his interlocutors and listened to their stories and ideas. Convinced that the construction of a field of study requires a collective work, he weaved numerous personal links. He stated, "I feel great pride in working with colleagues across the US and now internationally in bringing such enormous changes to the teaching of writing" (Bazerman, 2019, p. 43).

In Santa Barbara, for the first Writing Research Across Borders (WRAB) conference in 2008, he convened writing researchers from five continents, many of them the most widely read authors in the field. But he also made a point of including nascent scholars from peripheral regions on his roster and supported their travel with funding he specifically arranged (in partnership with his close colleague in the University of California system, Chris Thaiss). All participants felt welcome at this watershed event organized by Chuck, with his eagerness to include and integrate. Many retain the excitement of meeting their favorite authors "in person" and chatting with them at the welcome reception, or on the lovely school bus that Chuck provided to transport them. When an inexperienced scholar asked him if in his project to globalize writing research he considered that English would be the only language, he shared the concern with the organizing committee to accommodate the request, so that papers in source languages would be accepted, accompanied by some written support in English. Chuck was behind every detail of the conference: from personally writing the individualized mailings to providing memorable treats and snacks for the intervals between sessions. Many of us wondered where he found the time to do this.

Chuck had endearing exchanges with researchers from several continents. His relationship with Latin America, where his engagement was most extensive, illustrates his activism in favor of the democratic distribution of knowledge. Chuck always sought to know what was being done, researched, and discussed in Latin America. He traveled, participated, gathered, organized, and shared knowledge, academic initiatives, camaraderie meetings, *a cappella* singing (he has studied voice for many years), and warm affection in countless occasions and countries of the region. As in other continents, he organized joint research, stimulated exchange, hosted doctoral and postdoctoral fellows, reached remote points on the map, and paid his own travel expenses to be able to dialogue with local research groups. He agreed to work in the garages of private homes, because some public and free institutions in impoverished countries did not have better spaces. Carrying his leather briefcase crammed with resources, he generously distributed his books, CDs, and chocolates, offered comments on works in progress, took an interest in the history of Latin American dictatorships in the past and the struggles of their peoples, as well as interest in the local music. He asked to visit the Buenos Aires opera house, at the foot of which he indulged in a tuneful "O sole mio."

Chuck's written work goes hand in hand with his personal attitude and social deployment: "I wanted my scholarship to have the kind of power I sought in my own poetry—a power to articulate meanings important to me . . . a power to touch other people's minds and emotions as it gave shape to unarticulated experiences and feelings" (Bazerman, 2001, p. 183).

In Mexico, he became an expert on the flavors of pozole while leading research and making friends. At the SIGET's closing banquet in Caxias do Sul, Brazil, he connected colleagues from different countries: "You will understand each other, you have ideas in common." That introduction was the seed of numerous joint activities, and of an enduring friendship among those introduced to each other. He did the same in other cases. Chuck brought people together, helped them grow, valued the regional uniqueness, and gave a place as peers to those who were starting their careers. He shared his life stories, his family origins, his artistic tastes, and he listened to those who welcomed him in different countries. He did not fail to attend the final dance of a congress even when he had a broken leg.

Meeting Chuck has been surprising at first for many academics from diverse regions. In addition to his openness, curiosity, enthusiasm for sharing, lyrical singing, and willingness to bring researchers together, we are amazed by the breadth of his approach. When he talks about writing, he invites us into the myriad of angles with which writing practices can be considered:

> Research in writing across the curriculum, writing in the professions, writing in the workplace, and writing in the public sphere are far more than studies of instrumental exercises in the conventions of getting things done. They are studies in how people come to take on the thought, practice, perspective, and orientation of various ways of life ... and how we organize our modern way of life economically, intellectually, socially, interpersonally, managerially, and politically through the medium of texts. (Bazerman, 2002, p. 35)

Thus, when in interviews and in academic publications he refers to his origins, his personal journey, his motivations, his ethical and political stance, his psychotherapy, he does so in consonance with the idea that "writing is a major medium of participating in society and developing one's life with the contemporary complex literate world" (Biography and Overview).

For years now, in his emails at the bottom of his signature has appeared the following legend:

די פאראייניקטע שטאטן איז אַ קלאָפֿ ון אימיגראַנען

الولايات المتحدة هي أمة من المهاجرين

Los Estados Unidos es una nación de inmigrantes.

The U.S. is a nation of immigrants.

History will judge.

Those of us who have known him are not surprised. His academic activity and his work, at bottom, are part of the inclusive and democratizing political vision with which he avoided enlisting for the war and began his profession as an elementary school teacher with a disadvantaged population. In this sense, the broad view of writing as a human activity (and not as a form or as a norm) was motivated by the man who needed to expand his humanity in the expansion of the field of study to which he devoted a good part of his life.

The following chapters, introduced now by Jonathan Marine, celebrate and extend that broad view.

THE ORGANIZATION OF THE COLLECTION

As a part of the preparation for this volume, the editorial team reviewed many different examples of festschrifts including those written for Tony Dudley-Evans, James Kinneavy, and Jack Goody to which Bazerman had contributed. His contributions to these volumes were of particular interest to us in shaping the tone of the volume; in particular we noted that his chapters in those festschrifts stand out as clear examples of straightforward scholarly discourse and are devoid of hagiography. Thus, in crafting this volume we sought to emulate this approach.

Inviting authors to the festschrift was in many ways an easy task. Bazerman has worked closely with many scholars around the world, hosting many as visiting scholars at the University of California, Santa Barbara. He has also worked with a great many doctoral students, all of which provided for us a large pool of potential contributors. Our challenge was in narrowing that list to a group of scholars in a way that was somehow representative of Bazerman's global reach and disciplinary influence (and with apologies to the many scholars we had to leave out). Factors in our invitation process included considerations of gender, geography, and disciplinary specialization, which are reflected in the final list of contributing authors. Prior to inviting authors, we reviewed their published scholarship to identify the ways in which and degrees to which they had cited Bazerman in their own work.

Given that Bazerman's career and work were so multifaceted, we faced a special challenge of grouping the chapters in a coherent order that would capture the major themes in his scholarship. Fortunately for us, we had some assistance in that task as Bazerman himself has codified and categorized his own work on Researchgate, Google Scholar, and his own research website.[3]

We took all of this information into account as we began the process of organizing the contributions to this volume. As outlined in the earlier sections of this introduction, Bazerman's interests began with problems associated with the learning and teaching of writing in elementary school and college and writing

---

[3] These websites can be found, respectively, at researchgate.net/profile/Charles-Bazerman, scholar.google.com/citations?user=JIWTQUAAAAAJ&hl=en&oi=ao, and bazerman.education.ucsb.edu/research-themes.

across the curriculum, which were grounded in his own early experiences teaching students to write. Accordingly, we grouped together contributions focused on these types of phenomena in Section I: Academic & Scientific Writing and in Section II: Writing Pedagogy. In thinking about the typified conventions of the academic and scientific article, Bazerman became interested in social conceptions of genre which led him to explore varying applications of genre and activity. As a result, we clustered contributions in this regard in Section III: Sociology of Knowledge & Organizational Communication and in Section IV: Activity Theory. Bazerman's contributions to establishing research networks and a global community of writing researchers throughout his career are evidenced in Section V: Writing Research Development. We conclude with Section VI: New Media & Technology, which includes chapters on the emerging effects of media and technology on writing and composition subjects to which Bazerman has addressed in a number of his contributions.

OVERVIEW OF CHAPTERS

Paula Carlino—"New Cognitive Practices in a Master's Thesis Proposal Writing Seminar"

Carlino explores Bazerman's notion that genres shape the ways of thinking of those who participate in them, as genres influence cognitive activity according to the social practices that they help organize. The chapter analyzes videotaped classroom interactions in a master's thesis proposal writing seminar and identifies five types of specialized cognitive practices in which master's students engage. The chapter also characterizes an interactive pedagogy at the heart of the seminar, and in particular joint reviews, which were carried out in the context of the COVID-19 pandemic. These collective reviews are both a device for genre learning and a methodological resource that provides insight into the intellectual processes of those who write and talk about texts by exploring how genre-mediated writing not only transforms knowledge, but also the knower.

Fatima Encinas & Nancy Keranen—"Case Studies on Chance Encounters in Literacy Development in Latin American Researchers"

Encinas and Keranen illustrate the importance of the often-unacknowledged role chance encounters play in academic literacy and career development. As the role of chance encounters is rarely identified in career development strategies and research, the authors seek to fill this gap by examining and understanding the factors involved in chance encounters and their role in academic career development. Based on four case studies drawn from a cohort of science writers and research in Latin America, the authors explore the personal and environmental determinants which appear to have influenced, or led to, fortuitous chance encounters in order to speak to the potential pedagogical interventions which might positively contribute to academic literacy and career development.

Ken Hyland—"Changing Times; Changing Texts"

Building on Bazerman's contention that scholars construct a "stable rhetorical universe" within which their ideas make sense to others, and in particular how the research article as a genre was a response to a particular historical context, Hyland uses a corpus of 2.2 million words drawn from learning journals in four disciplines at three periods over the past 50 years in order to explore the ways the fragmentation and specialization of research has impacted knowledge construction practices in the disciplines.

Montserrat Castelló—"Situated Regulation Writing Processes in Research Writing. Lessons From Research and Teaching"

Using Bazerman's conception of writing regulation in the context of cross-disciplinary research on writing, Castelló argues for the significance and the role of situated writing regulation processes in research writing and discusses recent empirical results that validate the research on writing regulation from a socially situated approach. In reflecting on how teaching can increase our understanding of how research writing regulation works, the author argues that we can help students to intentionally decide on how, when, and why to use their resources, and suggests ways to facilitate and teach writing regulation to promote research writer development.

Lucia Natale—"Writing at the University and in the World of Work: Interrelationships and Learning in the Beginning of Professional Activity"

In the context of the expansion of the university system in Latin America at the end of the 20th century and into the beginning of the 21st, Natale explores how genres and the written production of specific texts confront college graduates as they enter into the professional contexts. By interviewing students as they enter into their careers, the author seeks to illuminate the relationships between genres and textual practices in the transition from academic to work environments. In doing so, Natale raises important considerations for teachers and researchers of writing as they design writing curriculum in higher education.

Liliana Tolchinsky & Anat Stavans—"Cultural Shaping of Standpoint and Reasoning in Analytical Writing"

Tolchinsky and Stavans foreground analytical writing as an important element in the activity systems which comprise the many educational and professional contexts which writers inhabit. Through investigating the relative dependence of textual organization on different rhetorical and cultural traditions, Tolchinsky and Stavans sketch the differing forms of reasoning which characterize Israeli and Spanish rhetorical traditions. By intervening in discussions surrounding the place of analytical writing in different rhetorical traditions, the authors are able to make a broader call for deeper investigations into the distinctions between how writers from differing cultural traditions carry on their social participatory performance.

Joanne Yates—"Genre Change Around Teaching in the COVID-19 Pandemic"

Yates acknowledges the role of Bazerman's work on genre in her own oeuvre before offering a lengthy and detailed narrative of instructional platforms, administrative decision-making, and Zoom/hybrid teaching in the School of Management at MIT during the COVID-19 shutdown. She draws on Zoom recordings, PowerPoint decks, administrative memos, and interviews, in describing the changes that faculty and administrators made in response to the pandemic emergency regulations imposed by the State of Massachusetts, MIT, and the Sloan School of Management. Her findings suggest that the pandemic shaped the varying genres of communication which educators and administrators drew upon to navigate and manage the impact to their teaching, and in doing so shed light on how the shift in MIT's genre repertoire can help us to better understand organizational change more broadly.

Mike Palmquist—"Opening Up: The Enduring Legacy of Chuck Bazerman's Turn Toward Open-Access Publishing"

Beginning with anecdotes of Bazerman's early involvement in and sponsorship of the WAC Clearinghouse, Palmquist sketches a picture of how scholars in the field of writing studies have long played a central role in exploring the use of technology to support writing and the teaching of writing. By showing how the field has changed in this regard over time, Palmquist makes the argument that new approaches to digital publishing resemble in many ways the decentralized networks which activity theory can help us to understand more deeply and offers a framework for the success of publishing collaboratives, using the WAC Clearinghouse as the central example.

Karyn Kessler and Paul Rogers—"Writing and Social Progress: Genre Evolution in the Field of Social Entrepreneurship"

Drawing on Bazerman's work on genre and activity, Kessler and Rogers present a case study of writing as a tool of mediation in human activity and in particular the genre of the profile and its role in establishing the field of social entrepreneurship. Drawing on interviews, surveys, and textual analysis of internal strategic documents from the world's 5th ranked NGO, Ashoka, the chapter focuses on the origin of the genre of the profile, the tensions between textual regularities and the need for genre change, and the impact of the genre on the development of a newly identified field of activity (social entrepreneurship) and a new set of actors (social entrepreneurs).

Clay Spinuzzi—"Two Paths Diverge in a Field: Dialectics and Dialogics in Rhetorical Genre Studies"

Arguing that Bazerman's synthesis of Vygotskian and Bakhtinian theory has had robust influence over the field, Spinuzzi explores the distinctions between dialectics and dialogics which respectively characterize the anchoring conceptions on which these two diverging theoretical perspectives are based. Because dialectics and dialogics provide different understandings of how meaning emerges, Spinuzzi contends that there is an underlying tension in Bazerman's work which has implications for our understanding of rhetorical genre studies more broadly.

Yrjö Engeström—"Writing for Stabilization and Writing for Possibility: The Dialects of Representation in Everyday Work with Vulnerable Clients"

Drawing on Bazerman's (1997) argument for understanding the foundational role of discourse in the structuring of professional activity systems, Engeström analyzes three types of representational instruments developed and used with vulnerable clients in order to provide a radically empowered new grasp of their future activity. Through discussing the possible transitions and iterative movement between the contextualized-emic, the decontextualized-etic, and the recontextualized-prospective modes of representation and writing, Engeström argues for a new model of the politics of deliberative shifts in representation.

Wu Dan & Li Zenghui—"A Review on Second Language Writing Research in China"

Dan and Zenghui present a review of L2 writing research in China in order to gauge the changes and trends of the work in CSSCI foreign language studies journals from 2001–2020. Through a rigorous selection process, they identified 601 empirical research articles. In the main, they found that L2 writing research in China is on the rise, with the proportion of empirical studies slightly decreasing over time as the range of methods and methodologies utilized expanded. With English writing research receiving more attention, Dan and Zenghui call on Chinese L2 writing researchers to continue to try new writing instructions methods and increase their communication and collaboration with international colleagues.

Editors' Introduction

Natalia Ávila Reyes, Elizabeth Narváez-Cardona, and Federico Navarro—"Twenty Years of Reading and Writing Research in Latin America: Lessons Learned From the ILEES Initiative"

This chapter traces twenty years of literacy and language research in Latin America in order to show the pioneering role of the ILEES organization in cohering the differing goals and focuses of writing research across the Southern Hemisphere. The panoramic view offered by this chapter helps to illuminate a more robust and interdisciplinary definition (and identity) of the institutionalization and professionalization of reading and writing research in Latin America. By giving more shape and form to this growing disciplinary community, the authors are able to present a clearer understanding of the configuration of reading and writing studies in Latin America, and in doing so, offer important considerations that strengthen its future scope.

Jack Andersen—"Rethinking Genre as Digital Social Action: Engaging Bazerman with Medium Theory and Digital Media"

Turning to media theory in order to understand digital forms of communication, Andersen discusses three of Bazerman's (1988, 1994, 1997) main works on genre in order to rethink genre as social action and contend that searching for information is a genre itself, a form of typified digital action. Arguing that digital media disrupt many traditional forms of communication, this chapter critically examines how to understand the role of genre and typified communication on and in activity systems and the people actively involved in them. If communication is transformed with and within digital media, and Anderson believes it is, then it is important to open a discursive space in which to examine the implications of understanding digital forms of communication.

Otto Kruse and Christian Rapp—"What Writers Do with Language: Digital Inscription Technologies Require a Fresh Look at Formulation Theory"

Attempting to match formulation theory to the new technological realities of digital writing, Kruse and Rapp draw on Bazerman's conception of the orderliness of language in order to frame a reconsideration of the role of inscription in digital and non-digital contexts in the construction of meaning. The chapter moves to a consideration of genre, audience, reader empathy, and then to words, lexicons, and word usage, connectives, phrases and multi-word-patterns, the need for grammar, the automaticity of text routines, and two kinds of language generation—with extended examples. Arguing that writers use certain linguistic units to accomplish their aims, the authors attempt to further clarify the role of language and the relation between language and thought with respect to operational units and in doing so account for the relationship between inscription and thinking.

Carolyn R. Miller—"Genre Formation and Differentiation in New Media"

Miller reflects and builds on Bazerman's work on genre theory and specifically *the medium* as an element of genres and their formation. Through drawing on media, she seeks to push beyond Bazerman's focus on the literate and discursive elements of genre formation into the auditory and visual so as to emphasize the multimodality of genre. Arguing that the particular affordances of the letter genre encouraged functional adaptations to new social circumstances and needs, and the functional utility and satisfactions of those adaptations in turn encourage replication and typification, Miller amplifies Bazerman's emphasis on the social grounding of genres by focusing on the interplay between social relations, exigence, and medium in the formation, and transformation, of genres.

REFERENCES

Bazerman, C. (1978). The grant, the scholar, and the university community. In S. Hook, P. Kurtz & M. Todorovich. *The University and the State* (pp. 221–226). Prometheus Books.

Bazerman, C. (1979). [Review of the book *Laboratory life: The social construction of scientific facts*, by B. Latour & S. Woolgar]. *Sage Library of Social Research, 80*, 14–20.

Bazerman, C. (1980). A relationship between reading and writing: The conversational model. *College English, 41*(6), 656–661.

Bazerman, C. (1981). *The informed writer*. Houghton Mifflin.

Bazerman, C. (1985). *The informed writer: Using sources in the disciplines*. Houghton Mifflin.

Bazerman, C. (1988). *Shaping written knowledge: The genre and activity of the experimental article in science*. University of Wisconsin Press.

Bazerman, C. (1994). Systems of genres and the enactment of social intentions. In A. Freedman & P. Medway (Eds.), *Genre and the new rhetoric* (pp. 79–101). Taylor and Francis.

Bazerman, C. (1998). Looking at writing: Writing what I see. In T. Enos & D. Roen (Eds.), *Living Rhetoric and Composition* (pp. 15–24). Erlbaum.

Bazerman, C. (1999b). *The languages of Edison's light*. MIT Press.

Bazerman, C. (2002). The case for writing studies as a major discipline. In G. Olson (Ed.), *The Intellectual Work of Composition* (pp. 32–38). Southern Illinois University Press.

Bazerman, C. (2003). Rhetorical research for reflective practice: A multi-layered narrative. In C. N. Candlin (Ed.), *Research and Practice in Professional Discourse* (pp. 79–94). City University of Hong Kong Press.

Bazerman, C. (2011). The work of a middle-class activist: Stuck in history. In S. Kahn (Ed.), *Activism and Rhetoric: Theories and Context for Political Engagement* (pp. 61–70). Routledge.

Bazerman, C. (2013). *A rhetoric of literate Action: Literate action volume 1*. The WAC Clearinghouse; Parlor Press.

Bazerman, C. (2013b). *A theory of literate action: Literate action volume 2*. WAC Clearinghouse.

Bazerman, C. (2019). The work of a middle-class activist: Stuck in history. In *Activism and Rhetoric* (pp. 190–200). Routledge.

Bazerman, C. (2020). What written knowledge does: Three examples of academic discourse. In *Landmark Essays* (pp. 159–188). Routledge.

Bazerman, C. (2021). The Ethical Poetry of Academic Writing. *Educação, Sociedade & Culturas*, nº 58, 183–192. https://doi.org/10.24840/esc.vi58.152

Bazerman, C. (Ed.). (2008). *Handbook of research on writing: History, society, school, individual, text*. Erlbaum.

Bazerman, C., Applebee, A. N., Berninger, V. W., Brandt, D., Graham, S., Jeffery, J., Matsuda, P. K., Murphy, S., Rowe, D. W., Schleppegrell, M. & Wilcox, K. C. (Eds.). (2018). *The lifespan development of writing*. National Council of Teachers of English.

Bazerman, C. & Herrington, A. (2006). Circles of interest: The growth of research communities in WAC and WID/WIP. In S. McLeod (Ed.), *Inventing a Profession: WAC history* (pp. 49–66). Parlor Press.

Bazerman, C. & Prior, P. A. (2004). *What writing does and how it does it: An introduction to analyzing texts and textual practices*. Routledge.

Biography and overview | Charles Bazerman. (n.d.). Retrieved May 10, 2022, from https://bazerman.education.ucsb.edu/biography-and-overview

Cole, M. (1998). *Cultural psychology: A once and future discipline*. Harvard University Press.

Eldred, M. (1995). Charles Bazerman: Writing is motivated participation: *Writing on the Edge*, *6*(2), 7–20.

Goody, J. (1962). *Death, property and the ancestors: A study of the mortuary customs of the LoDagaa of West Africa*. Stanford University Press.

Miller, C. R. (1984). Genre as social action. *Quarterly Journal of Speech*, *70*, 151–167.

Russell, D. R. (2002). *Writing in the academic disciplines: A curricular history*. SIU Press.

Schryer, C. F. (1993). Records as genre. *Written Communication*, *10*(2), 200–234.

Wiener, H. S. & Bazerman, C. (1978) *Reading Skills Handbook*. Houghton Mifflin.

PART ONE. ACADEMIC AND SCIENTIFIC WRITING

CHAPTER 1.
NEW COGNITIVE PRACTICES IN A MASTER'S THESIS PROPOSAL WRITING SEMINAR

Paula Carlino

CONICET, Universidad de Buenos Aires, Universidad Pedagógica Nacional

> Genres direct thinking and cognitive development by placing writers in defined problem spaces which give shape to the work to be accomplished.
> —Bazerman, Simon, Ewing, and Pieng (2013, p. 532)

Different authors have addressed the concept that writing can potentially function as an instrument to construct knowledge, challenging the idea that written language merely communicates already elaborated thoughts. Writing-mediated thinking tends to modify the thinking process, thus impacting the writer's knowledge. However, less explored is the notion that certain writing practices mold writers' cognition, beyond transforming their knowledge on the topics they are writing about. These uses of writing as a technology "allow [writers] to perform not only the same tasks more efficiently, but also to perform new tasks and new cognitive operations" (Salomon, 1992, p. 143). Charles Bazerman (2009) elaborates this concept through a sociocultural lens. He argues that framing our work under specific genres shapes not only our knowledge but human beings as knowledgeable subjects.

The hypothesis that "genres provide and scaffold highly differentiated communicative spaces" in which people "learn cognitive practices from specialized domains" (Bazerman, 2009) has received little empirical support since the effects of writing on cognition are hard to unravel because they take place over time and are embedded into different practices (Russell & Harms, 2010).

In this chapter, drawing from the previous hypothesis, I explore the experience that students attending a master's in teacher education program go through when they start writing their thesis proposal in a thesis proposal writing seminar. With this aim, I review the literature on the epistemic potential of writing, and the cognitive consequences of literacy. I focus on the notion of genres as tools that help organize social interactions while also shaping the participants' cognitive activity. Subsequently, I provide a description of the writing seminar from which I gathered data. I, then, analyze the participants' dialogue in online video lessons on Zoom and their written interchanges in the virtual classroom, which were collected during campus closure due to the pandemic. The question that guides my analysis is what specialized cognitive practices the students in this master's program start developing when they engage in writing their thesis proposals.

WRITING AND THE SOCIALIZATION OF THOUGHT

The writing to learn approach (Klein, 1999), related to the WAC movement (Bazerman et al., 2005; Russell, 1990), has spread the notion that writing not only communicates what is already known but also helps shape writers' knowledge. Many authors have fostered writing in all curricular areas so students can use writing to grasp and integrate knowledge of the contents they write about, both in higher education (e.g., Carlino, 2005; Chalmers & Fuller, 1996; Coffin et al., 2003; Gottschalk & Hjortshoj, 2004) as well as in primary and secondary education (Aisenberg & Lerner, 2008; Haneda & Wells, 2000; Lerner, Larramendy & Cohen, 2012; Tolchinsky & Simó, 2001; Tynjälä, Mason & Lonka, 2001). Although critical reviews by John Ackerman (1993) and Ochsner and Fowler (2004) alert on the data disparity on the relationship between writing and learning, numerous studies have shown that writing, under certain conditions, functions as a semiotic tool that affects knowledge construction. The notion that writing can serve as a thinking method challenges the widespread view that considers "writing as a textual product (rather than an intellectual process)" (Carter et al., 1998, p. 5).

Writing, as a technology of the word, externalizes thinking and makes it stable in time, thus enabling its critical revision (Ong, 1982; Young & Sullivan, 1984—in Klein, 1999). From a cognitive psychology viewpoint, knowledge is transformed by means of the interaction of the content space (what one has to say) and the rhetorical space (audience and purpose for writing) (Bereiter & Scardamalia, 1987; Scardamalia & Bereiter, 1992). It is the dialectic tension between both problem spaces that leads to deepening the reflective thinking mediated by writing. In this way, there is not an "automatic consequence" of writing in subjects' thinking processes, but its effect is relative to how writing is addressed (Scardamalia & Bereiter, 1985).

From a pedagogical stance, Judith Langer and Arthur Applebee (2007) concluded that the effect of writing on learning depends on the writing tasks set out in class. Subsequent studies in psychology have shown that it is decisive to consider what the writer does and what the task environment is like (Klein &

Boscolo, 2016; Klein et al., 2014). In a systematic review of published articles about writing in science, Gere et al. (2019) found that "specific components of writing assignments—meaning making, interactive processes, clear expectations, and metacognition—correlate highly with the greatest learning gains among students" (p. 129).

In the 1960s, from a macro perspective, historical, and anthropological studies examined the "consequences of literacy" in literate societies giving rise to the "great divide" thesis, i.e., the difference in the minds of people in oral and in literate cultures (Zavala et al., 2004). Nevertheless, ethnographic and intercultural research (Street, 1984; Zavala et al., 2004) contest the autonomous and decontextualized view of writing in these early anthropological studies. These authors show that literate practices differ from one community to another. The intellectual consequences of being literate depend on participating in some of these social practices, not on the effectiveness of writing itself (Scribner & Cole, 1981). Thus, specific uses of writing—inherent to particular socially organized activities—would influence the community members' cognition. Following Applebee's review of studies on the socio-cultural consequences of literacy (1984), the effects of writing vary according to "the functional roles that writing and literacy play in particular cultural or individual settings" (p. 581). So, what is socially done with writing (what writing helps do) is a determinant variable in considering writing as a transforming power of thought.

According to Bazerman (2006), the cognitive consequences of literacy have to be understood indirectly, in regard to the transformations that writing has contributed to producing throughout the history of societies and cultures, rather than to isolated individuals. The cognitive effect is framed within the cultural effect. In this sense, Bazerman draws on Goody's work to claim that, historically, writing has contributed to shaping institutions, whose social practices in turn shape subjects' attention and thought. These practices modify "the cultural and social environment within which each person experiences, thinks, and acts with available cultural tools and socially available responses" structured as genres (Bazerman, 2006, p. 219).

GENRES AND ACTIVITY SYSTEMS AS CHANNELS OF THOUGHT

In this work, I explore Bazerman's hypothesis framed within the Rhetorical Genre Studies (RGS) developed in North America and fertilized by Russell's contribution, which links genres with activity systems. Russell and Bazerman draw upon the Vygotskian tradition regarding the role of language in shaping higher psychological functions. From this perspective, cognitive functioning is not independent of the tools used. On the contrary, the specificity of culturally developed tools shapes individual mental operations. As a cultural tool, language structures human activities conveying social categories whose internalization reorganizes participants' perceptions and thinking (Bazerman, 2016a, p. 380).

My analysis below focuses on "what people are doing and how texts help people do it, rather than on texts as ends in themselves" (Bazerman, 2004, p. 319). For this reason, the RGS groundbreaking definition of genre, "typified rhetorical actions based in recurrent situations" (Miller, 1984, p. 159; Miller, 1994, p. 27), becomes relevant since it does not focus on the formal features of a kind of text, "but on the action it is used to accomplish" (Miller, 1984, p. 151; Miller, 1994, p. 20). In Bazerman's terms: "Genre is a sociopsychological category which we use to recognize and construct typified actions within typified situations" (1988, p. 319).

Following this perspective, genres contribute to the organization of activities and help the community members anticipate the expected modes to participate in reiterated social situations. In written communication, when the interactants do not share either time or space, the organization of the activity that genres provide helps mitigate misunderstandings. Even more, genres not only serve to organize social activity but also set purposes: "what we learn when we learn a genre is not just a pattern of forms or even a method of achieving our own ends. We learn, more importantly, what ends we may have" (Miller, 1984, p. 165; Miller, 1994, p. 32).

Thus, genres structure activities and "embody . . . social intentions" towards which participants can orient their energies (Bazerman, 1994, p. 69). In this way, people who write following the expectations created by the genres are shaped by "the roles and relationships open to us" within an environment of specific socio-cultural practices (Bazerman, 1994, p. 83). Given that genres differ from one domain to another, "disciplinary or practice-based thinking is differentiated according to the nature of the domain" (Bazerman et al., 2013, p. 532).

Russell links Bazerman's (1994) concept of genre system with Y. Engeström's notion of activity systems, rooted in the Vygotskian socio-historical theory (Russell, 1997, p. 505). Writing and genres are tools through which human beings carry out their purposes. Appropriating a new genre, learning the habitual and functional discursive uses in a particular situation and field, also means appropriating these instruments and the motives involved in the genre-mediated activity system. The process of learning to write in a new genre entails expanding the activity systems in which one can participate, and may bring about "subjectivity (identity)" challenges (Russell, 1997, p. 516).[1]

---

[1] Several studies examine the identity transformation and tensions when subjects join a new

Within this framework, researching the uses of writing in complex activity systems contributes to studying the higher cognitive functions, following the Vygotskian program. Thus, the modes of social organization of the activity, embodied in the genres, could be seen as shaping the formation of the collective and individual minds (Russell & Bazerman, 1997).

It should be noted that this perspective goes beyond the idea of writing as a tool to understand, learn, and construct *knowledge on the topic* we are writing about. Following Bazerman (2009), when we learn to write under an unfamiliar genre, we also develop new types of cognitive work according to the genre's social activity system. As writers appropriate the genre, they engage in novel thinking practices to carry out the purposes inherent in the new activity system and acquire the forms of attention and reasoning typical of the genre. Carter (2007) calls these thinking practices "ways of knowing" and "doing."

In this way, genres constitute a chain of transmission through which social practices shape individual cognition: "genres identify a problem space for the developing writer to work in as well as provide the form of the solution the writer seeks and particular tools useful in the solution. . . . Thus, in school and in the professions, the interaction between the group and individual cognitive development can be seen as mediated by activity system-specific genres" (Bazerman, 2009, p. 295). In this framework, Bazerman, Simon, Ewing, and Pieng (2013) studied prospective teachers' pieces of writing produced in a teacher education program over two years. Their study revealed that the writing carried out in their training helped them develop specific modes of thought of the domain in which they began to participate.

MY STUDY

The data I analyze in this chapter consists of oral and written exchanges between the graduate students and the instructor during the first part of the thesis proposal writing seminar in the Master's in Teacher Education at Universidad Pedagógica Nacional (UNIPE). This young, state, and tuition-free Argentine university mainly offers education for practicing teachers, who are, in turn, teacher educators.

The master's program entails two-years of coursework plus a thesis. The thesis implies carrying out a research project on an educator's activity. It presupposes observation and post-observation interviews. The master's program aims to train teachers to analyze teaching activity and help them develop a collaborative

---

activity system and the implied genres. See, for example, Carlino (2012) and Lundell and Beach (2003), on post-graduate writing. And see Gere (2019), Ivanic et al. (2009) and Thaiss and Zawacki (2006) on undergraduate programs.

attitude with the prospective teachers in the initial education program under their care. It seeks to promote shared reflexivity based on analyzing the traces of the classroom activities (e.g., video recordings).

The writing seminar is delivered in Spanish as it is usual in Buenos Aires, Argentina. It consists of 60 class hours divided into 15 monthly synchronous lessons on Zoom, 4 hours each, during three semesters. This schedule allows the instructors to follow the graduate students in their writing of a 7,000-word thesis proposal that should be submitted to an external board before they can start their research project. Framed within a situated pedagogy, i.e., non-propaedeutics (Carlino, 2012; Carlino, 2013), the seminar adopts Delia Lerner's concept (2001) that the core content in teaching writing is to teach *"los quehaceres del escritor"* (*"the writer's work"* or *"the writer's tasks"*). This notion entails what writers typically do when they write in a certain situation —in its social, rhetorical, linguistic, attitudinal, and cognitive dimensions. Lerner's pedagogical stance is consistent with Rhetorical Genre Studies' concept of genre as social action and with Bazerman's thesis that individual cognition is socialized through the activity the genres imply. Lerner, RGS, and Bazerman underline the pragmatic and practical nature of writing. They agree on highlighting the purposes, the context, the meaning, and the action rather than the formal aspects of language, the decontextualized norms, and the transmission of declarative knowledge. In this view, the seminar attempts to help the graduate students participate in social practices of specialized writing and avoids fragmenting them into decontextualized exercises that turn the activity meaningless.

The seminar syllabus outlines two types of content. The first type, "*The writers' work* that a thesis proposal entails (typical research writing and reading practices)," includes:

> Configuring a research problem that combines personal interests and a potential contribution to the debates in a field of study linked to teacher education. Arguing the relevance of the problem through integrating sources that are somehow contradictory, such as professional experiences, specialized literature, institutional regulations. Writing about the research problem as a research gap or disputed knowledge. Exploring, selecting and reading relevant literature to shape the problem and frame the intended study. Formulating research questions that follow from the research problem. (Taken from the writing seminar syllabus)

The second type of content consists of "Characteristics of the research proposal as a discursive genre." It encompasses, among others:

> The thesis proposal genre relating to the context of use: situational regularities, proposal functions, typical readers' expectations, and typical textual features. The socio-rhetorical situation in which a thesis proposal is written and read: audiences in different «rows», the asymmetry between author and reader, the writer's and the reader's purposes. (Taken from the writing seminar syllabus)

The seminar has been taught for six years with successive modifications.[2] At the beginning of the course, the instructor asks the graduate students to write an "autobiography as writers." Under her guidance, approved thesis proposals are analyzed. Students are given assignments that will help them advance progressively with writing each section of the thesis proposal and rework them recursively. In every lesson, students' inquiries are addressed, some students' drafts are collectively reviewed, so they receive multi-voiced comments from their peers and the instructor (Aitchison, 2003; Aitchison & Lee, 2006; Caffarella & Barnett, 2000; Carlino, 2008; Carlino, 2012; Dysthe, 2012; Lee & Boud, 2003). These collective reviews allow making explicit *the writer's work* involved in writing a research proposal, enabling participants' reflection upon it. Although students' initial knowledge is incipient, their participation contributes to developing it. They progressively learn the criteria to analyze their own production by discussing their peers' texts. Two or three times each semester, the students meet in small groups out-of-class time to review their drafts (Gere, 1987). On Moodle, they post questions arising from this self-managed work, which are later collected and discussed in the following synchronous lesson.

Students pass the seminar when the thesis advisor endorses the proposal, and by delivering a portfolio that shows their reflection on their learning process.

The students (N=30) are between 35 and 55 years old. Most of them are women, teaching secondary school classes and in non-university tertiary degree programs for pre-service teachers. They are highly experienced teachers with little or no research experience. They attend the master's program part time and do not have a scholarship. In the first semester of the seminar, they do not have a thesis advisor appointed.

The instructor, the author of this chapter, has long experience advising dissertations and leading research groups, and has been teaching research-writing seminars for two decades.

---

2   The seminar has been co designed by Liliana Calderón and Paula Carlino. In the 2020–2021 seminar, the students were grouped into two classes. Calderon and Carlino taught one class each. The data in this study was collected from Carlino's group.

DATA

Data was collected between August and November 2020. Due to the pandemic and the social distancing measures implemented in Argentina, universities turned their on-campus classes to remote teaching (Carlino, 2020). Consequently, the synchronous exchanges during the Zoom classes and the asynchronous exchanges in the Moodle classroom were recorded.

In this chapter, I analyze the exchanges that took place during the first semester of the seminar: the verbatim transcripts of 20 hours of video recorded lessons and graduate students' written participation on the Zoom chat and on Moodle. In this semester, students began to define their research topic and write the research problem statement, research questions, and a justification of the problem on both theoretical and educational grounds. The analysis of the interactions in the synchronous and asynchronous lessons to access the students' intellectual work during the seminar is a distinctive feature of this study.[3]

The transcript of the recorded lessons and the collected material was read and reread to identify the incipient cognitive practices prompted by the new genre. Progressively I constructed categories, shown in the following descriptive-interpretive analysis.

RESULTS

The analysis of the class oral interactions on Zoom and the written participation on the forums reveals that the graduate students engaged in new "problem spaces" in which they began to glimpse and develop ways of thinking aligned with social, disciplinary practices implied in the writing of the new genre (Bazerman, 2009). The need to produce a research proposal required them to start directing their cognitive and rhetorical efforts towards what researchers in the related domains do, unlike their usual professional activity as teachers.

At this starting point, they were far away from performing as expected at the end of the process. However, the task of developing a research proposal —that would be drafted, reviewed, and rewritten over three semesters— directed their attention to novel objects of thought. Writing was not the only driving force at play. Nevertheless, it became the axis around which an epistemic "talk about texts" (Wells, 1990b) developed throughout the seminar. Both the instructor's and the student's participation focused on what they had written or would write. The instructor intervened systematically to help raise awareness of the core

---

[3] This study draws near to the analysis of class transcripts made by Dysthe (1996), Haneda and Wells (2000), Lerner (2017), and Wells (1990b). My work differs from theirs because it attempts to identify the specialized cognitive tasks the genre mediates.

features of the genre and the activity system it represents. This reflection aimed at regulating the writing in progress.

Below, I present part of the oral and written interactions during the sessions in the first third of the seminar.[4] The aim is to display how learning to write in a new genre transforms the writer. I show that the process of writing the initial section of their thesis proposals implied beginning to perform novel "roles" for these students: *I. Writer, II. Epistemic contributor, III. Thinker of the disciplinary relevance of a research topic, IV. Producer of systematic knowledge,* and *V. Researcher focusing on the teaching practice*. These roles represent five categories of thinking practices implied in the *writer's work* driven by the writing of the thesis proposal in this master's program.

I. Writer: *Many graduate students began to think of themselves as writers for the first time. In their roles as teachers, they would consider themselves mainly as readers.*
A week before the beginning of the seminar, the instructor sent them a two-page narrative about her life experience in writing, and asked them to share their "autobiography as writers" on Moodle:

> To start this seminar, we decided to introduce ourselves by telling something about our personal history as writers. . . . Let me tell you something about my story as a "writer," and I make it clear that I call a "writer" any person who writes, although they do not write professionally. . . . (**Instructor**)

Students shared their written autobiographies before the first lesson; several expressed surprise at being called "writers," as these written excerpts show:

> Autobiography as a writer? First of all, I must say that the assignment surprised me. I have never thought of myself as a writer! (**Graciela**)

> My history as a writer (although I feel that the word is too big for me). (**Mariana**)

> I don't consider myself a "writer." (**Dora**)

> It would be easier for me to write an autobiography as a reader. (**Selene**)

---

4   Participants' pseudonyms go between brackets at the end when written excerpts come from the Moodle platform. Pseudonyms go at the beginning of the turn when they correspond to oral or written dialogues during Zoom synchronous sessions, for which the number of the session and the time of participation are shown between brackets to locate the pieces in a longitudinal process.

> Contrary to what can be expected from a language and literature teacher, I don't like writing . . . I've always found it much more interesting to read. . . . I feel more like a spectator than a protagonist. (**Naomi**)
>
> At first, I didn't see myself as a writer, and I think it's due to the burden this title carries for me. The picture I have in mind is of a person who writes very well, beautifully and cleverly, holds an academically celebrated order and says great or important things. (**Noelia**)
>
> These self-inflicted limitations of not being able to see ourselves as writers . . . [are due to the fact that] we were educated in the conviction that others write for us to read. (**Morena**)

The instructor responded to the autobiographical narratives on the written forum and emphasized the new role that the research proposal and the thesis require from writers:

> In several autobiographies, the emotion of surprise—and discomfort—at seeing yourselves as "writers" is repeated. . . . Actually, we tend to be more readers than writers. But writing a thesis places us on the way of becoming authors, without doubt, writing so others can read us, producing knowledge, and not only "consuming it." This transformation encompasses learning, switching the enunciative position and the subjective relationship with others. I emphasize this idea if it helps understand the step you took when enrolling in this master's program. And to help you develop patience because achieving it implies, for all of us, going through a very long process of personal transformation. (**Instructor**)

Many exchanges in the forums and during the Zoom lessons revealed students' struggle to develop their first research proposal. These exchanges also allow us to see that the instructor recurrently made explicit the costly process that writing implies (Carlino, 2012). Engaging in a graduate program that requires writing a proposal for empirical research leads to expanding the activity systems these students have, so far, been part of. The thesis proposal as a genre drives the process of beginning to see oneself as a writer, with the rights and responsibilities this entails.

II. Epistemic contributor: *In their attempts to draft the first section of their research proposal, graduate students began to think about epistemic problems, i.e.,* *issues needing to be understood, explained, etc. In contrast, as teachers, they were used to facing practical problems and solving them in practical terms.*

In the first lesson, the instructor started a conversation about the socio-rhetorical context of the research proposal and the final thesis. The students initially conceived that research directly provides a solution to practical issues:

> **Instructor**: What does the reader expect from my thesis? (1. 00:42:56)
>
> **Sonia**: I believe that they expect that it can give an answer to some problematic issues, . . . that it can improve a situation in a specific field. . . . [It] has to solve some problems in education, . . . I have to find a solution to something or improve something. (1. 00:46:12)
>
> **Mirta**: . . . that it could be an input, . . . a possible solution, in a territory, in a proposal even to the Ministry of Education. (1. 1:04:30)
>
> **Fabiana**: . . . a contribution to improve specific practices. (1. 1:05:25)
>
> **Morena**: Two small words would come to my mind: applicability, or practicality, . . . and I would also think it could be socially useful. (1. 1:06:16)

Meanwhile, some students wrote on the chat:

> **Dora**: Contributions to the field in which we are researching. (1. 1:03:06)
>
> **Mariana**: For me, it has to do with the context; it should be relevant here and now! (1. 1:05: 48)

Considering Dora's message, the instructor clarified that any research should contribute to knowledge. She highlighted that authors need to be aware of this issue when writing a problem statement as part of their research proposal. She also alerted that teachers tend to think of practical problems to be solved. In contrast, researchers aim to develop an understanding of an issue in the first place:

> **Instructor**: Exciting issues arose but let us examine them. . . . Any research implies an essential contribution. This is easily forgotten. . . . As teachers, we are always interested in improving something; we are interested in a practical purpose. We are eager to transform the world . . . But [in] research, . . . an

epistemic contribution is expected, a contribution to knowledge, not a contribution that transforms a phenomenon, it is not an intervention. (1. 1:08:00)

The chat board continued to reveal students' practical and epistemic perspectives. Mariana seemed to shift her view compared to her previous post:

Sonia: Contribution to curriculum designs. (1. 1:08:07)

Mariana: It may be a science advancement in the disciplinary field. (1. 1:09:22)

Finally, the practical relevance of a research project was discussed. A student grasped the difference between the epistemic (theoretical) and applied significance of a study:

Instructor: The second possible relevance of a research project . . . is a sort of practical or applied relevance. . . . But it presupposes epistemic relevance. In other words, if I construct knowledge that joins the discussions . . . in a theoretical field, it is probable that . . . someone can use it in practical terms to design educational policies, the curricula, teacher training programs, to improve something. Look! This is something practical, applied, but I will only be able to achieve it if my project, my thesis, meets the requirements of being epistemically relevant. (1. 01:14:08)

Juana: I think . . . that . . . the practical relevance . . . is beyond our scope. . . . [O]ur research might contribute and be taken into account, but our research may also contribute but it is not taken into account at that particular moment or in a particular context. (1. 01:14:20)

In the fourth session, two and a half months later, the instructor stressed the value of creating a research problem drawing from their professional experience (and not only from the literature). Again, she underlined the epistemic nature of the research problem, even if it emerged from a practical situation:

Instructor: What is the difference between a problematic professional situation and a [research] problem? A problem is something that is unknown to us and deserves research. The problematic professional situation is not an unknown issue. It is something that is not well resolved. It is a fact that is in an unstable equilibrium. . . . Now, turning it into a research

> problem demands raising questions, . . . expressing the desire to understand why this happens. . . . There is a problem of practical action that I have to transform into an epistemic problem, of knowledge. [When researching], I am not going to solve the situation in practical terms [but] I am trying to understand it. If later . . . the knowledge constructed on that situation is helpful or not to . . . solve that practical situation, ok, we will see. (4. 01:21:20—1:25:00)

Focusing on the problems of educational practice as a source of epistemic problems implies starting to build a previously uninhabited space of thought. The factual resolution is suspended to enable identifying what needs to be understood or explained. Only gradually, these students managed to perform this researcher's work implied in writing. Writing the first section of their research proposal began to orient their attention toward this new matter.

III. Thinker of disciplinary relevance for a research topic: *Graduate students began to ponder the potential significance of a research problem, i.e., its epistemic relevance for a field, instead of considering a topic that only interests them personally. This intellectual work was radically unfamiliar for them.*

In the first session, the instructor prompted students' discussion about the rhetorical context of a research proposal and the significance of a study. A student shared her emerging awareness of addressivity and the need to consider the disciplinary interest of any research:

> **Katia**: [Y]ou are introducing an element now with this socio-rhetorical approach, . . . I had not thought before, I had not included this in what interests me when I thought about the thesis project, in the assignment you gave us. I had not thought about who would be interested in reading it. I had only thought about what I was interested in producing. . . . I say, of course! How I did not take it into account! How I could not see it! . . . Now I would have to review my thesis topic because I was thinking about what interested me, but the truth is that I don't know who this might be of interest to. (1. 00:30:45)

In the following session, the instructor underlined that writing the first section of a research proposal implies linking the author's personal interest in a topic with its potential interest for a field of study, its responsiveness to ongoing disciplinary debates:

> **Instructor:** Because what Lola [a student whose draft is being reviewed] has to do is to construct a research problem that shows how . . . it not only responds to her interest, but it is also interesting for the disciplinary field. . . . Because what the reader expects is that I show them . . . why it is relevant and why studying it will contribute to knowledge. . . . What does "relevant" mean? . . . : That . . . it can dialogue with what is being discussed, what is being debated, in the disciplinary field. (2. 2:30:30)

In order to place their research problem in a pre-existing disciplinary conversation, the students were oriented to identify and read research papers related to the topics they wanted to investigate. This task, also unusual for them, required them to start developing new practices such as bibliographic search and the interpretation of unfamiliar texts to integrate them into formulating their research problem.

The topics chosen for their research projects were predominantly related to their professional teaching work (their teaching area). For example, in August 2020, Selene, a teacher in mathematics, started working on the topic: "Teaching activity at the primary or secondary level with students who have difficulties in learning mathematics and the professionals who work with them." In November 2021, she changed the proposal title to "The teaching activity in the interaction with students whose production in mathematics is far from institutional expectations."

In sum, considering both one's interests and a research territory to join the ongoing conversation is a typical *research writer's task*. It is a novel activity for those starting to write a thesis proposal. Beginning to think about a relevant research problem —with the instructor's guidance— does lead to developing the cognitive practice of harmonizing one's own interests with the disciplinary significance of a study.

IV. Producer of systematic knowledge: *Graduate students began to think that research questions—related to the knowledge they aspire to contribute—need to be considered in connection to a method that is able to provide empirical evidence to answer them. Before, as teachers, i.e., "communicators" of knowledge, they did not need to reflect upon the relationship between knowledge and method.*

In each of the five lessons analyzed, the instructor fostered considering the relationship between research questions and the appropriate method to address them. This issue was raised when discussing research questions whose answers could not be reached with the methodological approach required by this master's program.[5]

In the first session, when commenting on a draft, the instructor asked about the relationship between data and research question, and vice versa:

> **Instructor**: What data do I need to answer [this question]? . . . I am trying to align, ensure coherence . . . between questions and . . . methodology. . . . What data do I need to answer [this question]? (1. 2:45:38).
>
> **Noelia**: I would like you to repeat it . . . you've lost me. (1. 2:47:40) . . .
>
> **Instructor**: What data do I need, . . . to answer the question? (silence for 4 seconds) Can anybody risk an answer? (1. 2:49:00)
>
> **Sonia**: I need to have a film, a video recording of the lesson, to observe the interventions because . . . (1. 2: 49.07)
>
> **Instructor**: Sonia is saying that we need to observe a lesson. Because if I want to see the interventions, I need to observe the class. . . . Every time I wonder what the teacher does and how they intervene, I need to observe lessons and record them. Yes? I start relating questions with methodology.

Students mismatched research questions and methodological approaches several times. Several times, the instructor promoted similar reflections:

> **Instructor**: How can I answer the following question? [She reads:] "How does a teacher reflect on the gap between . . . what they planned and what they were able to do?" (1. 2:51:50)
>
> **Lola**: An interview, could it be?
>
> **Instructor**: What kind of interview?
>
> **Lola**: Self-confrontation?
>
> **Instructor**: There is it! . . . That question requires a self-confrontation interview to be answered.

---

5   This master's program basically requires graduate students to conduct an initial interview, then observe classes and later conduct a self-confrontation interview, i.e., an interview in which the researcher and the interviewee see and discuss a video recording of a part of a lesson.

The instructor described the new cognitive task (a typical activity in the research community) and called it "[looking for] coherence between research questions and method." An hour later, Katia wrote this phrase on the chat board, probably to metacognitively capture the mental task that they were performing in the collective review. At the end of the session, the instructor insisted on the need to achieve question-method coherence in every research proposal.

In the following sessions, a few students showed their incipient awareness of this relationship while commenting on a peer's draft:

> **Noelia**: When one thinks about the methodology [in this master's program], we think that we are going to observe a lesson, right? . . . I was wondering: if you think that your case is going to be a school principal, what are you going to observe? Where are you going to do the clipping to make the records observable? Because where are you going to get? . . . Are you going to record the conversation between teachers during a meeting? Or when they enter a classroom to participate in a class or meet parents? From there, I was thinking about what you are going to take away. What is going to be observable? (3. 2:18:44)
>
> **Mariana**: The questions [that appear in the reviewed draft] . . . cannot be answered with the methodology offered by Professional Didactics. (3. 2:49:28)
>
> **Mariana**: I don't grasp where [what data] you are going to look at the questions you are asking yourself. (4. 2:43:00)

Thinking about the relationship between research questions and methods remained a challenge for most students. The instructor returned to the question repeatedly:

> **Instructor**: I want us to think . . . for all the questions in other texts . . . what data and what methodology answer the research questions [you are formulating]. (4. 2:50:30)
>
> **Instructor**: Let's go to the question [in the text that we are working on]; how do you answer it? What data do I need to answer the first question? (4. 3:01:06) [No response for 20 seconds]
>
> **Sonia**: Observing it in the class. (4. 3:01:27)
>
> **Mariana**: It can also be prescribed in the teaching plan.
>
> **Student**: Planning . . .

Ensuring that method and expected data address research questions implies a relational, cognitive, unfamiliar task for these students. In line with Bazerman's notion that "to be able to produce [disciplinary texts], students must develop new ways of thinking and new ways of looking at the world" (2017a, p. 42), the writing of a coherent research proposal drives authors to consider how to generate the desired knowledge. Thinking of a method to address a knowledge gap is part of a social and cognitive practice triggered by writing a research proposal. As a member of a research community, the instructor noticed that the students were far from performing this practice and recurrently guided them to consider it.

V. Researcher focusing on the teaching practice: *The need to write a research proposal prompted that the graduate students shifted their attention from their students' learning to the teaching activity because the master's program requires them to observe an educator (principal, teacher, instructor) in a working situation and to reflect on it afterwards. Focusing on what an educator does and thinks was laborious for these participants since, in their teaching role, they were used to looking primarily at their own students.*

As the embryo of the research problem, the written assignment given by the instructor between lessons three and four suggested considering a problematic professional situation: some tension or practical disagreement that involved educators. However, several drafts were centered on students, and especially on students' shortcomings as learners, as these excerpts show:

> . . . We know the difficulty that it implies for students. . . . It is common to find students . . . who . . . encounter difficulties. . . . Some students do not succeed . . . (**Mariana**)
>
> . . . Students do not understand academic texts . . . (**Dora**)
>
> . . . Throughout these years working in higher education, in a teacher training institution for elementary education teachers, I see that first-year students are greatly heterogeneous . . . (**Ana**)
>
> . . . And here the following question arises, do the students actually have the necessary tools to carry out this work? . . . (**Irene**)
>
> . . . What idea of science do students construct? . . . (**Luana**)

To help the graduate students direct their attention to a teacher, the seminar instructor highlighted this issue repeatedly:

> **Instructor**: In the proposals, some of you focused on problematic situations, but looking at the students. Students

who ... lack specific expected knowledge, greatly heterogeneous groups.... However, I need a [research] problem that looks at the teacher. Yes? ... How can I turn a problem that is considered a students' problem into a teacher's professional problem? ... I have to talk about the challenge for the teacher.... Because I am going to interview teachers, and I am going to focus on observing what the teacher does. (4. 1:37:55)

More than once, the instructor indicated how to rephrase the wording of a draft to switch the focus:

Instructor: [to Ana] Try that the subject of the sentence in the problem statement be the teacher not the students. (4. 1:45:51).

In the following session, one participant mistakenly thought that a classmate's draft focused on the students instead of the teacher. In fact, the text mentioned the students as the background rather than the focus. However, it is interesting to consider her remark because it seems to show a "hypercorrection," which would reveal her recent awareness of the need to focus her research on what a teacher does and thinks:

Dora: Hi. In Fabiana's text, it seems that ... it is focused more on the student's side than on the teacher's side. (5. 1:28:10)

Instructor: Where do you see that it is more focused on the...? (5. 1:29:31)

Dora: student.... (She reads her classmate's text) "When the student is developing their practices in the classroom, the teacher is expected to..." (5. 1:29:40)

Two hours later, in a new cycle of collective reviews of a peer's draft, another participant pointed to a problem statement that did focus on students, and suggested how to change the research questions to shift the gaze to the teacher:

Katia: When I read [Irene's] text, ... I found something that ... had happened when you read mine.... [W]hen she asks, at the end of paragraph two, (reads) "[D]o the students have the necessary tools to do this job?" ... I would ask ... "[W]hat challenges or what problems does a teacher face in this situation?" ... It would help Irene look a little more at the teacher . . . and leave a little [aside] the student's problems. (5. 3:11:40)

In sum, the above analysis shows that writing the first section of their thesis proposal—mediated by the instructor's regulation—channeled the participants' thinking into issues that were unfamiliar to them as teachers. The new activity system in which they have begun to participate leads them to pay attention to an infrequent topic for these participants: the educators' professional tensions.

CODA

In the remaining two semesters of the seminar (in 2021), other sections of the thesis proposal were addressed. A preliminary examination shows that, as in the first semester, writing required engaging in new problem spaces, typical of certain domains. For example, having to write the "Background and theoretical framework" section, the participants started to grasp the difference between empirical studies and theoretical positions.

In summary, the set of results and the remaining data that exceed the scope of this article reveals that the classwork around successive students' drafts entailed not only a metalinguistic reflection on the formal features expected in the texts but on substantive aspects involved in writing. This reflection attempted to help perform *the writer's tasks* implied in a thesis proposal. Different discussions took place in this sense: about the enunciative options and their potential socio-rhetorical effects on the situation at stake, the content of the text, the methodological design of the participants' thesis, the writing practices and processes of a disciplinary community, and the emotions arising from the challenges that this experience posed.

DISCUSSION

The analysis of the above data shows that the process of writing a thesis proposal brought about the need to embark on certain thinking practices and play roles typical of members who belong to specialized communities. The socio-rhetorical situation that framed this writing (getting approval by the master's committee) demanded a response (Miller, 1994) (the written production structured according to the thesis proposal genre), and this, in turn, drove such practices (Bazerman, 2009).

The analysis reveals that the thesis proposal as a genre, and especially writing the section "Problem Statement" as required by this master's program, prompted the graduate students to orient their attention to new objects of thought: (1) seeing themselves as writers and not only as readers, (2) constructing knowledge problems (issues which need to be understood) and not only solving practical problems, (3) considering the potential disciplinary significance of a research topic (its relevance for a field of study) and not only the personal interest that it represents, (4) generating research questions aligned with the methods that could address them, and (5) focusing the professional tensions that educators face in a particular professional situation and not only the difficulties that the students show in their learning process. Engaging in these thinking practices proved challenging for students, unfamiliar with the genres used in educational research.

The results support the idea that the social "regulation of textual form" is "intertwined with regulating forms of material experience, reasoning" (Bazerman, 2017b, p. 26). They go beyond the claim that writing contributes to learning and transforming knowledge about the topic of writing. Writing in the new genre prompted the graduate students to start treading through unknown social and historically shaped "environments or habitats" (Bazerman, 1997b, p. 22) where they found themselves having to perceive and perform according to the social expectations embodied in the genre. Regarding the dialectical process proposed by Marlene Scardamalia and Carl Bereiter (1985; 1992), the data analyzed suggest that genre-mediated writing not only transforms knowledge but also begins to transform the knower.

Thus, the process of learning to write a text in an unfamiliar genre drives students to engage in specialized disciplinary work. This process requires them to go beyond their cognitive skills to align them with the ones developed by the community the students want to belong. In this way, genres as social interaction organizers shape the individual mind.

According to Bazerman, genres provide both the "tasks for their thought processes" (1997b, p. 22) and the "means of solution" (2009, p. 295), which are needed to participate in the new activity system. Now, was it only writing and rewriting the thesis proposal that drove students to assimilate the new "habitat?" Did the instructor's intervention and the collective reviews of the drafts contribute to the process? In my view, the genre governed a series of mediating gears, i.e., the activity of writing and rewriting the drafts, the exchanges during the joint reviews and in the virtual classroom, and the instructor's intervention. They all served as a testing laboratory that provided the graduate students with a safe environment to try once and again. While Bazerman (2016b, pp. 14–15) states: "[g]enres guide writers in understanding the situations they are writing for, who their audiences are, what form the texts might take, what material might be appropriately included, and what they may accomplish," my data suggests that it was these mediating gears that made visible for the students in the seminar the social expectations conveyed by the genre. Such gears also catalyzed and scaffolded the process so that the participants could articulate their individual thinking with the social expectations.

How did the instructor contribute? She planned the teaching process to enable the graduate students to start performing the *writer's work* concerning a thesis proposal. Following Lerner's pedagogical approach (Lerner, 2001, pp. 100, 143, 177), once students in the seminar began engaging in an authentic writing practice, their "action" was addressed as an "object of reflection" when the writer's decisions were discussed in the joint reviews. Their action was also considered as an "object of systematization" when generalizable features of the genre were abstracted from a particular draft—becoming relevant to all those who write a thesis proposal and not just the author of the text under review in class. The knowledge put into play during the reflection and the systematization helped students rework their written production.

While guiding the reflection and the systematization activities, the instructor promoted considering the textual and contextual features of the genre. She intervened "in situ, during the revision, . . . at the point of practical need" (Bazerman, 2009, p. 291), providing "explicit teaching to the task at hand" (Bazerman, 1997a, p. 1). This timely teaching orients the cognitive and discursive practices that students are undertaking. It provides an external regulation of attention and action that helps them set objectives, coordinate means, and understand functions. By contrast, writing seminars of a "propaedeutic" nature teach the overall features of a genre for future application, before and outside the point of need (Carlino, 2013).

Discussing their drafts throughout the seminar gradually leads students to start considering the problem spaces that the genre entails and encourages them to attempt perform the expected practices. At the end of the semester, the students' drafts are the products of an unfinished process that continues in the remaining two semesters of the seminar. The analyzed data shows that internalizing the tools provided by the genre and highlighted by the instructor cannot be achieved in the short term. Students start a gradual "mental knitting" process that may enable them to assimilate those tools. This fabric grows progressively as a result of students' work and bridges the gap between their current thinking practices and those needed to succeed in writing their thesis proposals. Students' participation, assimilating the tools at their own pace, enables their knitting of this cognitive fabric, which is neither received preformed nor internalized through the mere exposure to pertinent knowledge.

What did the graduate students' participation in the collective review activity contribute? Talking about the drafts helped them become aware of the thinking practices that the genre entails. This is in line with Gordon Wells' claim: to understand "the mental activities involved," students "need to participate jointly in . . . writing events with their teachers or more competent peers, in which these internal activities are externalized and thus made available for appropriation in talk about the text" (Wells, 1990a, p. 16). Collectively reviewing the drafts throughout the seminar became an opportunity to externalize and reflect on the *research writer's work* in crafting the thesis proposal. Also, the different readers' comments freed the graduate students from the habitual expert opinion given by a single evaluator. Unlike the instructors' or thesis advisors' suggestions, which students usually comply with by following the principle of authority, the joint review favors considering the comments without leaving aside their authorship.

Now then, in this activity, not only did the students see how their peers solved their writing problems, or how the instructor's guided them, but they also played the role of reviewers of their peers' drafts. This responsibility progressively led them to help their classmates to achieve what they might have not achieved in their own writing pieces yet. As an instructional device, the collective review goes beyond the zone of proximal development (ZPD) proposed by Vygotsky because, in a collective review, students learn not only from an expert but also learn "by acting as an expert," as they are empowered to play the role even before they are knowledgeable enough. While in the ZPD knowledge is constructed by interacting with a more advanced subject, in the collective review students who cannot still solve their own writing or research problems can gradually help each other.

The collective review throughout the seminar also deserves a methodological consideration. Its video recording allows researchers access to traces of the participants' mental activities at play, as Anne Gere and Andrew Abbott suggest: "Researchers interested in writing processes need to give more attention to writing groups as a source of information about what writers do when they write" (1985, p. 378). The analysis of collective review observations allows getting close to "the reasoning the writer used to produce the article" (Bazerman, 2017b, p. 25).

The methodological approach used in this study differs from other qualitative research that also observes classes to examine disciplinary enculturation or socialization processes but does not usually carry out a detailed analysis of the exchanges, only possible if the recordings are transcribed. In this sense, the longitudinal analysis of the transcribed collective review dialogues constitutes a privileged way to look into *the writer's work* that students begin to perform, and to observe how they are shaped by participant's interaction governed by the unfamiliar genre. This methodology helps glimpse the socialization process in a certain domain.

Unlike Bazerman et al. (2013, p. 531), which showed changes in thinking due to disciplinary training over two years, my analysis does not enable recognizing consolidated cognitive changes, which would have required extending the data collection over time. Neither did my study track some students' written progress as Bazerman et al. (2013) and other longitudinal research (e.g., Gere, 2019) do to identify intra- and intersubjective variations over time.

However, my study's methodological option of analyzing the oral and written exchanges in the seminar became a valuable tool to access the interactive cognitive processes. This option is congruent with the adopted theoretical framework: writing as an intellectual process rather than as a product (Carter et al., 1998), genre as a rhetorical action rather than formal features (Miller, 1984, p. 151), as well as an instrument of "what people are doing" "rather than as ends in themselves" (Bazerman, 2004, p. 319).

Thus, the main contribution of this study is twofold. On the one hand, it details the process of sociocultural shaping of cognition mediated by learning a new genre in a particular situation: it reveals the attentional objects and thinking relationships entailed in the writing of the first section of a thesis proposal in the context studied. It unfolds how the genre *requires* students' engaging in disciplinary cognitive practices. It sheds light on the socialization of cognition channeled by genres, on the "cognitive consequences of literacy" (Bazerman, 2006, p. 216). At the same time, it gives clues about the activity system that newcomers aspire to join, about "the cultural-historical activities that the texts mediate" (Russell & Bazerman, 1997, p. 23). Thus, those who are attempting to write a research proposal for the first time not only have to learn the formal features of discourse but also "the action it is used to accomplish" (Miller, 1984, p. 151). This makes the learning process more complex.

On the other hand, my study displays the design of a pedagogical intervention that scaffolds the learning process and mediates between the demands of the genre and its progressive individual appropriation. The exchanges during the lessons illustrate the type of writing seminars "that help to perform contextualized social actions," as opposed to those that "propaedeutically address partial attributes of language" (Carlino, 2013, p. 362). Given that appropriating a genre entails expanding the repertoire of available ways of knowing and doing, and not only the ways of saying, performing in-context writing seminars seem to fit the instructional goal of teaching new genres, i.e., teaching to participate in social practices that involve unfamiliar ways of specialized thinking.

ACKNOWLEDGMENTS

I would like to thank the graduate students for the opportunity to learn with them. I am also grateful to Lucia Natale, Ana Pereyra, Paul Rogers, and David Russell for their critical comments on a previous version of this article, and to Gabriela Di Gesú for her work in the English version of this article.

REFERENCES

Ackerman, J. (1993). The promise of writing to learn. *Written Communication, 10,* 334–370.
Aisenberg, B. & Lerner, D. (2008). Escribir para aprender historia. *Lectura y Vida, 29*(3), 24–43.
Aitchison, C. (2003). Thesis writing circles. *Hong Kong Journal of Applied Linguistics, 8*(2), 97–115.
Aitchison, C. & Lee, S. (2006). Research writing: Problems and pedagogies. *Teaching in Higher Education, 11*(3), 265–278.
Applebee, A. N. (1984). Writing and reasoning. *Review of Educational Research, 54*(4), 577–596.
Bazerman, C. (1988). *Shaping written knowledge: The genre and activity of the experimental article in science.* Madison University of Wisconsin Press. https://wac.colostate.edu/books/landmarks/bazerman-shaping/.
Bazerman, C. (1994). Systems of genre and the enactment of social intentions. In A. Freedman & P. Medway (Eds.), *Genre and the new rhetoric* (pp. 79–101). Taylor & Francis.
Bazerman, C. (1997a). Internalizing the field: Charles Bazerman on teaching writing in disciplinary classes. *Write Away! 3*(1), 1–3.
Bazerman, C. (1997b). The life of genre, the life in the classroom. In W. Bishop & H. Ostrom (Eds.), *Genre and writing* (pp. 19–26). Boynton/Cook.
Bazerman, C. (2004). Speech Acts, genres, and activity systems: How texts organize activity and people. In C. Bazerman & P. Prior (Eds.), *What writing does and how it does it.* Routledge.
Bazerman, C. (2006). The writing of social organization and the literate situating of cognition: Extending Goody's social implications of writing. In D. Olson & M. Cole, (Eds.), *Technology, literacy and the evolution of society: Implications of the work of Jack Goody* (pp. 215–239). Lawrence Erlbaum Associates.
Bazerman, C. (2009). Genre and cognitive development: Beyond writing to learn. In C. Bazerman, A. Bonini & D. Figueiredo (Eds.), *Genre in a changing world* (pp. 283–298). The WAC Clearinghouse; Parlor Press. https://doi.org/10.37514/PER-B.2009.2324.2.14.
Bazerman, C. (2016a). Interview with Charles Bazerman. In S. Souza & A. Sobral (organizers). *Gêneros, entre o texto e o discurso. Questões Conceituais e Metodológicas* (pp. 374–381). Market of Letters. https://bazerman.education.ucsb.edu/sites/default/files/docs/Bazerman2016INTSwederbookge%CC%82nero_entre_texto_e_discurso.pdf.
Bazerman, C. (2016b). What do socio-cultural studies of writing tell us about learning to write? In C. A. MacArthur, S. Graham & J. Fitzgerald. (Eds.), *Handbook of writing research, Second Edition* (pp. 11–23). Guilford Press.
Bazerman, C. (2017a). Equity means having full voice in the conversation. *Modern Languages, 50,* 33–46.
Bazerman, C. (2017b). The psychology of writing situated within social action: An empirical and theoretical program. In P. Portanova, J. Michael Rifenburg &

D. Roen (Eds.), *Contemporary perspectives on cognition and writing* (pp. 21–37). The WAC Clearinghouse; University Press of Colorado. https://doi.org/10.37514/PER-B.2017.0032.2.01.

Bazerman, C., Little, J., Bethel, L., Chavkin, T., Fouquette, D. & Garufis, J. (2005). *Reference guide to Writing Across the Curriculum*. Parlor Press; The WAC Clearinghouse. https://wac.colostate.edu/books/referenceguides/bazerman-wac/.

Bazerman, C., Simon, K., Ewing, P. & Pieng, P. (2013). Domain-specific cognitive development through written genres in a teacher education program. *Pragmatics & Cognition*, *21*(3), 530–551.

Bereiter, C. & Scardamalia, M. (1987). *The psychology of written composition*. Lawrence Erlbaum Associates.

Caffarella, R. S. & Barnett, B. G. (2000). Teaching doctoral students to become scholarly writers: The importance of giving and receiving critiques. *Studies in Higher Education*, *25*(1), 39–52.

Carlino, P. (2005). *Escribir, leer y aprender en la universidad. Una introducción a la alfabetización académica*. Fondo de Cultura Económica.

Carlino, P. (2008). Revisión entre pares en la formación de posgrado. *Lectura y Vida*, *29*(2), 20–31. https://www.aacademica.org/paula.carlino/98.

Carlino, P. (2012). Helping doctoral students of education to face writing and emotional challenges in identity transition. In M. Castello & C. Donahue (Eds.), *University writing: Selves and texts in academic societies* (pp. 217–234). Emerald Group Publishing.https://www.aacademica.org/paula.carlino/99.

Carlino, P. (2013). Alfabetización académica diez años después. *Revista Mexicana de Investigación Educativa*, *XVII* (57), 355–381. https://www.aacademica.org/paula.carlino/103.

Carlino, P. (2020). Reflexión pedagógica y trabajo docente en época de pandemia. In L. Beltramino (Ed.), *Aprendizajes y prácticas educativas en las actuales condiciones de época: COVID-19* (pp. 86–91). Universidad Nacional de Córdoba. https://www.aacademica.org/paula.carlino/271.pdf.

Carter, M. (2007). Ways of knowing, doing, and writing in the disciplines. *College Composition and Communication*, *58*(3), 385–418.

Carter, M., Ferzli M. & Wiebe, E. (2007). Writing to learn by learning to write in the disciplines. *Journal of Business and Technical Communication*, *21*(3), 278–302.

Carter, M., Miller, C. & Penrose, A. (1998). *Effective composition instruction: What does the research show?* Center for Communication in Science, Technology, and Management, North Carolina State University.

Chalmers, D. & Fuller, R. (1996). *Teaching for learning at university*. Kogan Page.

Coffin, C., Curry, M. J., Goodman, S., Hewings, A., Lillis T. & Swann, J. (2003). *Teaching academic writing. A toolkit for higher education*. Routledge.

Dysthe, O. (1996). The multivoiced classroom: interactions of writing and classroom discourse. *Written Communication*, *13*(3), 385–425.

Dysthe, O. (2012). Multivoiced classrooms in higher education academic writing. In M. Castello & C. Donahue (Eds.), *University writing. Selves and texts in academic societies* (pp. 201–216). Emerald Group Publishing https://doi.org/10.1163/9781780523873_012.

Gere, A. R. (1987). *Writing groups. History, theory, and implications*. Southern Illinois University Press.
Gere, A. R. (Ed.). (2019). *Developing writers in higher education: A longitudinal study*. University of Michigan Press. https://doi.org/10.3998/mpub.10079890.
Gere, A. R. & Abbott, R. D. (1985). Talking about writing: the language of writing groups. *Research in the Teaching of English, 19*(4), 362–385.
Gere, A. R., Limlamai, N., Wilson, E., MacDougall, S. K. & Pugh, R. (2019). Writing and conceptual learning in science: An analysis of assignments. *Written Communication, 36*(1), 99–135.
Gottschalk, K. & Hjortshoj, K. (2004). *The elements of teaching writing*. Bedford / St. Martin's.
Haneda, M. & Wells, G. (2000). Writing in knowledge-building communities. *Research in the Teaching of English, 34*(3), 430–457.
Ivanic, R., Edwards, R., Barton, D., Martin-Jones, M., Fowler, Z., Hughes, B., Mannion, G., Miller, K., Satchwell, C. & Smith, J. (2009). *Improving learning in college. Rethinking literacies across the curriculum*. Routledge.
Klein, P. (1999). Reopening inquiry into cognitive processes in Writing-To-Learn. *Educational Psychology Review, 11*(3), 203–270.
Klein, P. & Boscolo, P. (2016). Trends in research on writing as a learning activity. *Journal of Writing Research, 7*(3), 311–350.
Klein, P., Boscolo, P., Kirkpatrick, L. & Gelati, C. (Eds.) (2014). *Writing as a learning activity*. Brill.
Langer, J. A. & Applebee, A. N. (2007). *How writing shapes thinking: A study of teaching and learning*. National Council of Teachers of English. https://wac.colostate.edu/books/langer_applebee/. (Original work published 1987)
Lee, A. & Boud, D. (2003). Writing groups, change and academic identity: research development as local practice. *Studies in Higher Education, 28*(2), 187–200.
Lerner, D. (2001). *Leer y escribir en la escuela. Lo real, lo posible y lo necesario*. Fondo de Cultura Económica.
Lerner, D. (2017). *Leer para aprender historia: una investigación colaborativa protagonizada por equipos de docentes*. UNIPE y SUTEBA. https://editorial.unipe.edu.ar/colecciones/herramientas/leer-para-aprender-historia-detail,
Lerner, D., Larramendy, A. & Cohen, L. (2012). La escritura en la enseñanza y el aprendizaje de la historia. Aproximaciones desde una investigación didáctica. *Clío & Asociados, 16*, 106–113.
Lundell, D. B. & Beach, R. (2003). Dissertation writers' negotiations with competing activity systems. In C. Bazerman & D. R. Russell (Eds.), *Writing selves, writing societies: research from activity perspectives*. The WAC Clearinghouse; Mind, Culture, and Activity. https://doi.org/10.37514/PER-B.2003.2317.
Miller, C. (1984). Genre as social action. *Quarterly Journal of Speech, 70*, 151–167.
Miller, C. (1994). Genre as social action. In A. Freedman & P. Medway (Eds.), *Genre and the new rhetoric* (pp. 20–35). Taylor and Francis.
Ochsner, R. & Fowler, J. (2004). Playing devil's advocate: evaluating the literature of the WAC / WID movement. *Review of Educational Research, 74*(2), 117–140.

Ong, W. (1982). *Orality and literacy. The technologizing of the word*. Methuen.

Russell, D. (1990). Writing across the curriculum in historical perspective: toward a social interpretation. *College English, 52*, 52–73.

Russell, D. (1997). Rethinking genre in school and society. An activity theory analysis. *Written Communication, 14*(4), 504–554.

Russell, D. & Bazerman, C. (1997). Introduction. *Mind, Culture, and Activity, 4*(4), 223–223, https://doi.org/10.1207/s15327884mca0404_1.

Russell, D. & Harms, P. (2010). Genre, media, and communicating to learn in the disciplines: Vygotsky developmental theory and North American genre theory [Special issue]. *Signs Magazine, 43*(1), 227–248.

Salomon, G. (1992). The various influences of technology on the development of the mind. *Childhood and Learning, 15*(58), 143–159.

Scardamalia, M. & Bereiter, C. (1985). Development of dialectical processes in composition. In D. R. Olson, N. Torrance & A. Hildyard (Eds.), *Literacy, language and learning: The nature and consequences of reading and writing* (pp. 307–329). Cambridge University Press.

Scardamalia, M. & Bereiter, C. (1992). Dos modelos explicativos de los procesos de composición escrita. *Infancia y Aprendizaje, 58*, 43–64.

Scribner, S. & Cole, M. (1981). *The psychology of literacy*. Harvard University Press.

Street, B. (1984). *Literacy in theory and practice*. Cambridge University Press.

Thaiss, C. & Zawacki, T. M. (2006). *Engaged writers. Dynamic disciplines: research on the academic writing Life*. Boynton / Cook.

Tolchinsky, L. & Simó, R. (2001). *Escribir y leer a través del curriculum*. ICE/Horsori.

Tynjälä, P., Mason, L. & Lonka, K. (Eds.). (2001). *Writing as a learning tool. Integrating theory and practice*. Springer.

Wells, G. (1990a). Creating the conditions to encourage literate thinking. *Educational Leadership, 47*(6), 13–17.

Wells, G. (1990b). Talk about text: where literacy is learned and taught. *Curriculum Inquiry, 2*(4), 369–405.

Zavala, V., Niño-Murcia, M. & Ames, P. (2004). *Escritura y sociedad. Nuevas perspectivas teóricas y etnográficas*. Red para el desarrollo de las ciencias sociales en el Perú.

CHAPTER 2.

CASE STUDIES ON CHANCE ENCOUNTERS IN LITERACY DEVELOPMENT IN LATIN AMERICAN RESEARCHERS

Fatima Encinas and Nancy Keranen

Benemérita Universidad Autónoma de Puebla, Mexico

Most people can identify chance encounters or serendipitous moments which caused a life change. Chance encounters happen all the time. The effects they produce on people's lives vary from life changing, only slight effect, to no effect. In explaining the intensity of the influence of chance on lives, much of the literature on chance encounters cites Pasteur's comment (however, related to scientific discovery) that chance favors the prepared (e.g., Díaz de Chumaciero, 2004). This is the crux of our overall aim in this paper.

While the literature acknowledges the presence of chance encounters and their effects on professional development, very little seems to focus on chance in academic careers (Kindsiko & Baruch, 2019). Most academics, however, can point to instances of life changing chance encounters and fortuitous events in their career development. In spite of this, most infrequently, if ever, share these happenings with students—either in their writing or discussions (Goggin & Goggin, 2018). Kindsiko and Baruch (2019) in their study of doctoral candidates' career development regard this omission as a significant factor needing revision in current Ph.D. program design and recommend that future Ph.D. students "be made aware of the levels and impact of the possible chance events that may emerge during academic careers" (p. 136). Rice (2014) also notes the widespread lack of attention to chance found in traditional theories of career development. He goes on to develop a detailed review of newer career theories and how they have addressed the presence of chance in career development. Of the theories reviewed, only Krumboltz's Happenstance Learning Theory (2009) which is based on his earlier theory, Planned Happenstance, seems to offer any specific pedagogical strategies (Mitchell et al., 1999).

Before we can attempt to address this apparent lacuna, we need to look to theory to help us understand the role of chance in professional development and

DOI: https://doi.org/10.37514/PER-B.2023.1800.2.02

what characteristics people have which are seen to engage chance events, fortuitous encounters, or serendipity as a "catalyst for change" (Cabral & Solomone, 1990, p. 11). Thus, in this paper we seek to understand what the observed characteristics of a cohort of participants were (based on the theoretical models discussed below) which made them receptive to fortuitous chance encounters in their academic career development. With that knowledge, we attempt, in the final section of the paper, to suggest pedagogical interventions in incipient and novice academic researchers' professional development which could help them seek out chance encounters and use them for positive academic literacy and career development.

THE LITERATURE ON CHANCE ENCOUNTERS AND SERENDIPITY IN PROFESSIONAL DEVELOPMENT

What are chance encounters? The simplest definition is that chance encounters are an "unintended meeting of persons [or previously unknown symbolic objects, e.g., books and experiences] unfamiliar to each other" (Bandura, 1982, p. 748). Chance encounters are not necessarily good. Sometimes lives go wrong as a result of an unfortunate chance encounter (Bandura, 1982). However, for the purposes of this paper, we restrict our discussion to chance events which led to career changing / enhancing outcomes.

The most recent study we came across on chance encounters (Olshannikova et al., 2020) examines the influence and importance of incidences of "social serendipity" in knowledge workers' professional development. In Solomon's (2017) paper on temporal aspects of info-serendipity, the author summarizes the wide scope of studies in chance and serendipity carried out after the turn of the 21st century. Besides the obvious discipline of science, technology and medicine, the author cites studies in the areas of law, business, humanities and social sciences, and the topic of his paper—information sciences. Other researchers have looked at chance in the career development of female university graduates, non-professional workers, students, and workers and professionals in career transitions (comprehensively reviewed in Rice, 2014). More closely aligned with our study, we find some published research in the areas of career development (e.g., Bright et al., 2009; Kindsiko & Baruch, 2019; Mitchell et al., 1999; Rice, 2014), and rhetoric, writing, and literacy research (e.g., Mohammed & Boyd, 2010; White & DeGenero, 2016; Goggin & Goggin, 2016).

In spite of the established presence and importance of such encounters reported in the literature, very few studies on this phenomenon have suggested this feature of development could or should be explicitly taught as part of curriculum, training, or professional socialization strategies (with two notable exceptions discussed in the final sections of this paper). We argue that this could and should be done.

To do this, we first briefly review the literature on the mechanisms of enculturation and apprenticeship found in academic settings to understand what research has revealed about how academic careers are thought to be taught and learned. This is followed by a more extensive discussion of theories which set out to explain chance, serendipity, fortuitous events in career development.

THE MECHANISMS OF ENCULTURATION AND APPRENTICESHIP IN ACADEMIC SETTINGS

Charles Bazerman (2006, p. 223) describes enculturation and apprenticeship in academic settings as the "result of substantial [education] that makes these odd and particular forms of communication familiar, meaningful and intelligible in detail and nuance." This applies not only to forms of communication but to "the kinds of roles and stances one adopts, interpretive procedures, forms of contention, and uses to be made of the texts" (Bazerman, 2006, p. 223). For example, and in the case of our particular context, multilingual scientists have to communicate findings, discuss, and exchange the latest research developments in their specialties. To successfully carry this out, they need fluency in the full spectrum of knowledge and skills intrinsic to their particular specialties. In addition, they need to have written and spoken fluency not only in English, but the scientific English of their specialty which they can only fully acquire in immersive situations in their specialty (Bazerman et al., 2012).

Carrasco et al. (2012), in their study of students in Mexican doctoral programs, develop a theoretical framework for illuminating the kind of language learning Bazerman defined above. Relying on a number of frameworks, they see literacy academic development in both Spanish and English as situated, social, constructed, specifically dependent on context, and negotiated—learned through interaction, and requiring emotional engagement of everyone involved. This intense constructed learning leads to transformation from neophyte, to novice, then apprentice and ending as the target goal—independent researchers (Carrasco et al., 2012). During this trajectory or experience of a potential scientist intent on becoming a researcher in laboratory sciences, students acquire the role of author, reader, critic, editor, and local expert, by gradually participating in research processes and committees and review panels among other activities in their specialty (Carrasco et al., 2020).

Specific content knowledge of the discipline is, of course, explicitly taught. However, many language skills and practices leading to becoming independent researchers are not explicitly taught or learned. They are, for the most part, taken in via practice described as the "apprenticeship mechanism" which operates through the socio-cultural milieu of the learning environment. As Carrasco et al. (2012) explain, citing Delamont & Atkinson (2001, p. 100), this learning is *"caught* rather than *taught,* transmitted through personal experience rather than by systematic instruction. . . . It travels best where there is personal contact with an accomplished practitioner and where it is already tried and tested."

Thus, academic literacy development is believed to be implicit and constructed upon tacit insider knowledge (viz., Bazerman et al., 2012; Carrasco et al., 2012; Carrasco et al., 2020). In other words, this knowledge is passed on to learners *through* the social interactions carried out in the various contexts associated with the particular discipline.

Reflecting back on the first part of the paper, we bring back the notion that literacy in academic careers also develops from chance encounters happening within those same disciplinary contexts (and associated contexts). Whether someone benefits from those encounters is seen as an amalgam of a number of features. The question we raise at this point is: considering the clear importance and influence of chance, could those features be made explicit in career learning? And if so, what might that explicit knowledge and instruction look like? To answer those questions, we need to attempt to uncover the features and understand why some people are able to benefit from chance and, by inference then, why others do not.

THEORIES OF CHANCE ENCOUNTERS, FORTUITOUS EVENTS, SERENDIPITY IN ACADEMIC LITERACY AND CAREER DEVELOPMENT

The literature on this topic agrees—"chance plays an important role in everyone's career" (Mitchell et al., 1999, p. 116). Although it might seem like it at first glance and in spite of the common definition of chance, events of this nature do not happen from pure random chance. Certain elements, dispositions, interests, motivations were in place to enable the event. For a chance encounter to have an effect, a person needs to have at least some personal attributes (e.g., personality, cognitive, and affective factors). These need to express themselves in the target career/professional environments and will contribute to the likelihood and intensity of chance encounters within those environments. The factors are presented in the following section and summarized in Table 2.1.

FACILITATING THE LIKELIHOOD AND OVERALL EFFECTS OF CHANCE ENCOUNTERS

We all operate under a set of self-conceptions that form "prototypes" or "cognitive schemata" that are used as frames for our interpretations of the world. These interpretative frames also affect our behavioral choices and outcome evaluations which thus act as reinforcements to self-conceptions (Cabral & Salomone, 1990, p. 12). People who have established beliefs in their ability to cope with and take advantage of change are more likely to recognize and use chance encounters to change life path trajectories.

Emotional ties contribute to life changing effects of chance encounters. People will form lasting relationships if they like each other. Clearly, if a person finds qualities of others in an area disagreeable or if the person is deemed unlikeable by others in the milieu, lasting bonds are unlikely to be formed thus reducing the chances of life path changing effects from that particular association. This reinforces the notion of knowing oneself, being aware of personal standards and values, and being able to determine if those or compatible constructs are shared (Guindon & Hanna, 2002).

To these general characteristics White and DeGenaro (2016) offer some specific personal factors which they see as facilitating life changing events from chance encounters. The one that seems to particularly stand out is a willingness to engage in social interaction—to make "small talk" and have discipline related conversations, to have a willingness to make plans for collaboration, to take advantage of events like sharing a ride with a colleague or mentor and engaging in conversations about seemingly mundane matters such as hobbies—which can lead to discoveries of shared interests and values. Those kinds of interactions, if the interlocutors are willing, can lead to further and ongoing social occasions such as weekly social gatherings of likeminded peers and mentors. Even carpooling was regarded as an opportunity for collaboration and development—as a result of serendipitous meeting between scholars in similar disciplines.

To the factors presented thus far, Cabral and Salomone (1990, p. 10) add two personality factors, "locus of control" and "self-concept," to the explanation of the overall impact a chance event will have on life/career path direction. Locus of control has to do with an individual's conception of where the control in her or his life lies, more externally or more internally. Individuals who have a more external, deterministic conception of control are less likely to be "proactive" when chance encounters present themselves (Cabral & Salomone, 1990, p. 12). These features also appear in notions of agency (e.g., Bandura, 1989; Emirbayer & Mische, 1998).

To this framework, Wiseman (2003) adds affective factors such as the ability to control anxiety and, in a related vein, those who can control negative emotions by their use of counterfactual thinking. His studies related to chance, luck, and superstitions indicated that people who were generally more tense and anxious were less likely to notice an unexpected event. The heightened emotions caused participants in one of his reported studies to miss details and opportunities than less anxious people. Another feature of people who generally were able to recognize and benefit from fortuitous events was the tendency to use counterfactual thinking. Wiseman defines this as the ability to see barriers and setbacks not as problems and disasters, but as seeing these events as "not as bad as they seem," "to make the best of a bad situation"—to "soften the impact of the ill-fortune" (2003, p. 4).

Similarly, Rice (2014) cites a (rather small, $n=17$) study looking at professional careers of women which identified personal and environmental categories of factors which were seen to influence the overall strength of a chance event relative to the effect on career development. The personal class determinants consisted of "willingness to be flexible and take risks, competence, hard work, motivation, optimism, and being alert to opportunities" (p. 449). The environmental determinants identified were "maintaining a strong support system, [participation in] personal and cultural events . . . [and] freedom from external barriers such as being single or having few responsibilities" (p. 449).

As has already been implied in the above discussion generally focused on personal characteristics, the environment is also seen to play a role in the influence a chance encounter will have on life change. In fact, personal and social/environmental factors are tightly intertwined and are seen to work synergistically. The social/environmental factors identified in the literature work with the personal factors to further imbed the individual within the environments likely to promote academic success and provide opportunities for advantageous chance events.

Generally speaking, if the environment possesses desirable features, an individual is more likely to seek out membership in that environment. That will tend to increase the number and quality of chance events associated with it. So, if the environmental milieu rewards individuals sufficiently, they will be more likely to remain in the particular environment and be changed by the association. Likewise, the symbolic systems employed within the environment will also work to strengthen membership (and therefore lasting life path changes) of the members. Similarly, the "openness" or "closedness" of a milieu will determine the amount of life path effect on the individual. More open milieus will permit members contact with other environments and ideologies thus affecting life path trajectories. The more closed a milieu is the more direct affect it will have on the individual member and the ideologies they form (which further tend to influence life paths). Psychological closedness of the group members increases the overall strength of the group in turn increasing the likelihood of the long-term existence of the group. Generally speaking, the longer the time span, the more opportunities for chance and change (Bandura, 1982).

Thus, certain factors are seen to mediate the effects of chance encounters on life paths. To summarize, those factors fall within two larger reciprocal categories of personal and environmental factors. Personal characteristics mentioned are a cohort of personal attributes which work to maintain continued contact with an environment, along with emotional elements such as "likeability" and possession of shared values and behaviors. Environmental factors are more compelling if they provide a sufficient level of rewards, symbolic systems, if there is a psychological closeness between the members—shared interests, abilities, and beliefs, and whether the environments are more open or more closed (summarized in Table 2.1).

We see these and similar determinants in most of the literature we reviewed on this topic (summarized in Table 2.1). In the following sections we show what these determinants look like in our sample of data collected from mid to late career academic professionals working in a university setting (explained in detail further on).

METHODS

In order to complete the aims set out in the beginning of the paper, we seek examples of instances of chance reported by those who have been successful in their careers. Since chance is recognized as an element in everyone's career (e.g., Mitchell et al., 1999), we should find instances of it in our data related to career development. We draw the data from our studies carried out over a decade of research with a population of academics and researchers whose first language is Spanish, but who must write and publish their research in English. Our work with this group generated a rich collection of data associated with their development, practice, and psychological dispositions (explained in detail further on).

Participants—Successful Researchers Writing and Publishing in English

The well documented literature on science writers with native languages other than English highlights the challenges these writers face in their professional development. They not only need to achieve worldwide levels in their discipline knowledge, but they also have to communicate globally in the current language of science and technology, English (Bazerman et al., 2012). Yet in spite of these daunting challenges, many are able to participate and significantly contribute at the highest global levels. We feel these features make an interesting group to study and provide ample instances of how chance was seen to operate in their development as high level researchers and writers. To do this, we mined through our volumes of data and pulled out the instances of chance. With those we overlay the theories of career learning and chance and serendipitous events to help us make sense of the phenomena and then use these as "heuristics for action" (Bazerman, 1992, p. 103) as we propose in the final sections.

The research site was a large research university in central Mexico with a very high research rating in particle and nuclear physics, mathematical physics, and quantum and theoretical physics. Our participants, mid-career and late-career, were chosen because of their high levels of recognized academic output. They came from a number of specialties in physics, mathematics, medicine, economics, and psychology and also from a variety of national and linguistic backgrounds although most were native speakers of Spanish. In our various studies involving these participants, we used a variety of qualitative and quantitative data collection and interpretation methods. However, for the purposes of this paper, we will draw our data from the narrative interviews. From the larger group, we have selected to present the cases of four career successful researchers (defined as successful based on their affiliation in the *Sociedad Nacional de Investigadores*).

INTERVIEWS

The narrative interviews we chose for this followed the protocol found in Lieblich et al. (1998). The interviews, carried out individually, required only a standard sheet of paper for each participant which was divided into two numbered columns starting with zero and ending in most instances around 60, approximately 30 numbers per column, representing years of life. The interviewees were asked to fill in information related to anything that seemed important to them in any order they chose. They talked about the periods of their lives, important people, their personalities, and reactions to events as they filled out the years. Questions were asked only for the purposes of following up in more detail certain comments and to encourage them to think about their lives and experiences as those events related to their personal and career development. Analysis categories, codes, and procedures were developed after the interviews to ensure that no leading or biased questions would be asked or that the participants would be inadvertently led in any response direction.

The length of the interviews ranged from one to two hours or longer. Most of the interviews were conducted in Spanish. All of the interviews were digitally recorded and life story year sheets were kept as interview records. Permission was granted from each participant to record the interviews and all participants were assured of the anonymity and confidentiality of the interview data. All of the participants seemed to enjoy the interview experience, and a few recommended other colleagues as possible interview participants.

EXPLORATION OF THE DATA

Table 2.1 summarizes most of the characteristics identified in the literature reviewed above on chance which seem to influence the overall effect of such

Chance Encounters in Literacy Development

encounters or events. These qualities or characteristics are seen to work as a cohort rather than in isolation. The degree to which they are possessed or are perceived by a person tends to correlate positively with the level of intensity of personal change resulting from the chance encounter—i.e., whether the encounter changes their lives, has only a slight effect, or no effect.

Table 2.1. Personal and Social/Environmental Factors Associated with Overall Effects of Chance Encounters, Fortuitous Events, and Serendipity in Career Development

	Personal factors		**Social/Environmental factors**
1	Entry skills—substantial knowledge, experience, competencies	A	Milieu rewards—group benefits: actual and intangible
2	Emotional ties—liking the people met, or gaining other satisfactions from them	B	Symbolic environment and information management—what the environment looks like to the outside world. Does it invoke awe and reverence or hatred and disgust
3	Values and personal standards—possessing similar standards and worldviews	C	Milieu reach and closedness
4	Personal levels of self-conceptions & efficacy beliefs	D	Psychological closedness—belief strengthening ability of a group
5	Self-regulatory capabilities	E	Creates the possibly of a desired future
6	Beliefs in personal agency and locus of control orientation	F	Other intrinsic qualities of the field which provide interest and motivation to participate
7	Emotional control—i.e., levels of anxiety		
8	Willingness to accept variety and change		
9	The use of 'counterfactual thinking' when dealing with failures and barriers		
10	Levels of general optimism		

* *The number and letter designations were used as an analysis coding scheme (Collected from inter alia: Bandura, 1982; Cabral & Salomone, 1990; Mitchell et al., 1999; Wiseman, 2003).*

CASE STUDIES

White and DeGenero (2016) provide the structural model for the case study portion of our paper. They use case studies of individuals reporting on their chance encounters and fortuitous events which led to career and discipline changing moments. Below we present four cases in which we demonstrate what those events look like in our study population. We have used pseudonyms to identify the people participating in the interviews.

A number of interesting chance events directly supporting career paths were reported by the participants. Most of the interviewees identified these kinds of fortuitous encounters and events in the career development stage of their lives. This is probably due to the overall nature of the interview protocol which principally aimed to understand their literacy and career development as scientists, researchers, and research writers.

Jean Luc—Astrophysics, High Energy Phenomena, and Fundamental Physics

One of the clearest examples of a life changing chance event was reported by Jean Luc. The first thing he wrote on his interview form was regarding a school trip to the astronomical observatory near his school at the age of 12. He said that seeing the moons of Jupiter and the rings of Saturn through the observatory telescope set him permanently and single-mindedly on his chosen career course. "*Me incline por dedicarme esto de la astronomía y ya todo lo demás es consecuencia de eso*" [From this experience, I dedicated myself to astronomy and everything else after that is a result of this (observatory visit)].

However, it could be argued that sooner or later, there might have been other opportunities/incidents which his personality and abilities would have interacted with to result in a similar turn of events. From this point of view, chance might not seem to be as life-changing as it might appear at first sight, and single chance events are usually not evocative of change in themselves (Bright et al., 2009). In other words, besides the chance event(s), there are other predispositions and/or situations that will lead the individual to recognize and accept or reject the influence of the chance event.

Literacy development especially reading emerges as one of those cohorts of behaviors that made the interviewees particularly receptive to significant change from chance events. Jean Luc credited his love of reading to being punished as a child in primary school. He reported that he was not very sociable as a child which caused him to be punished for things he did to other children. Most of his punishment involved not being permitted to go to recess with the other children and having to stay inside and read or do some kind of schoolwork. He directly credited this punishment to his academic development that soon progressed beyond the level of his peers, an increase in his vocabulary, and his enduring love of reading. He said that the more he read, the more he wanted to read.

This literacy acceleration beyond that of his peers happened before the telescope event. We can see the strengthening of his academic self-efficacy beliefs, his beliefs in personal agency and locus of control orientations. Counter-factual thinking is also evident in that he came to regard his punishment as quite beneficial to his development and as a reinforcement or something that strengthened his self-conceptions (e.g., surpassing literacy levels of his peers). We can also assume a certain academic affinity with others in the astronomy milieu which would give him access to the rewards and benefits of acceptance into that environment.

Pavel—Social Sciences and Economics—Work, Knowledge and Development in Latin America

Pavel provides another example of the benefits from literacy development opening doors to life changing chance opportunities. He was from an extreme poverty background, from a very dangerous part of Mexico City. There were very few, if any, opportunities for children from these sorts of neighborhoods. According to Pavel, many of the schoolteachers treated all the children as already lost and basically not worthy of any effort. This attitude was one reason why Pavel said he had absolutely no academic interests and had no intention of going past the primary level. However, at the age of 10, his 16-year-old brother was murdered in the street. This unplanned and tragic event made him reassess his educational intentions.

In addition to growing up in a deadly impoverished environment, Pavel was one of the two participants who indicated physiological judgments related to somatic characteristics which, in his case contributed directly to his academic development. He reported that when he was young, he was very thin and weak. While he initially indicated no academic interest, he was at the same time assessing his physical abilities to survive, since the question of survival had now become a personal issue. He realized physically he could not survive, so he decided he should rely more on his cognitive abilities.

As a means of coping with their environments, many of the participants indicated strategies they employed that helped insulate themselves from the dangers in their surroundings. Reading created an escape, but also an unintended increase in literacy skills. As one of the strategies he engaged related to basic survival, Pavel tended to stay indoors reading, avoiding interaction with dangerous elements in his area. Complete isolation was of course not possible. Another strategy was to control or appease some of the more violent and dangerous adolescents by doing their school assignments for them. This also had the unintended effect of strengthening his academic efficacy beliefs while at the same time guaranteeing his importance in his immediate social milieu. He credited this interest in reading anything he could get his hands on as another factor contributing to his positive efficacy assessments regarding his academic abilities. He said he began to notice he knew more than his peers and that it was a result of his reading habits (and extra assignments).

We can see here another instance of chance events associated with literacy events. Like the others, as Pavel's self-conceptions and efficacy beliefs strengthened associated with his academic abilities, his access to environments which held more potential positive career enhancing events increased (e.g., higher education). We can also see the effects of an early environmental milieu which did not offer what he thought it should. This led to his engaging alternative strategies—demonstrating a willingness to change and to seek out other solutions. This is associated with his beliefs in personal agency and locus of control orientations, and counterfactual thinking.

Jonathan—Neuropsychology, Neuropsychological rehabilitation, Child neuropsychology

Jonathan said that before having a particular primary school teacher, he had no interest in school and had planned to quit after the primary level. In the fifth level of primary school, he had a teacher who inspired his love of academics. He said that up to that point he had no interest in school or studying and basically only did it because he was supposed to. This teacher was the first to pay any attention to the students. Jonathan said before that because of the backgrounds of the students (*de recursos muy bajos* [very disadvantaged]) many previous teachers had treated them as if they were all delinquents (echoing Pavel's opinion). Jonathan reported that for the first time, he had a high level of interaction with a teacher and it was apparent this teacher really cared about the learning outcomes of the students. He identified this teacher as a pivotal person in his life whom he very much identified himself with.

Jonathan talked about a group he formed of like-minded students during his university years which was fundamental in his development as a researcher. He had to quit his university studies because of the economic crisis of the 1980s. He started peddling clothing from house to house. He said that this barrier did not derail his goal of university study. He saw it as something he just had to get through and that eventually he would back on track. He credited that attitude to a high level of coping efficacy. Jonathan actually saw this job as a positive factor in his life. He enjoyed it because he came to know many people and he made enough money to support his family. When he finally returned to his undergraduate studies, he was in his 30s. Because of his age, he was put in the "*vespertino*" [afternoon] group with the other older students who were there because they generally worked in the mornings and then went to the university at night. Younger students were generally put in the "*matutino*" [morning] classes. So, he said it was very "good luck" he was put with the more mature students because they were very much interested in their studies and were very competitive in a way that they inspired each other to study and to really get involved in their education. Eventually with some of these classmates he formed a group dedicated to their field of study. The group produced publications, held seminars; they contacted researchers in their field, and were involved in curriculum changes in their own programs of study. The group, with varying numbers of members, was active all through his university and post-graduate years and was still active at the time of the interviews.

In Jonathan's case we see many of the dispositions identified in the literature. Several are particularly notable—his willingness to accept change, engaging in counter-factual thinking, and clearly a certain level of innate optimism. We can also see evidence of the effects of a variety of milieu rewards evident in his penchant for forming groups which led directly to a variety of chance events and other benefits from group membership. Almost all of the social/environmental factors are exemplified in his case.

Malcolm—Applied Optical Physics

Malcolm's established career is a product of the changes and vicissitudes of development articulated in Krumboltz (2009). Defining his career path took him a number of years. He first studied to become a Catholic priest. He then tried studying medicine in a military medical school. While preparing for the entrance exam, he realized he did not like biology or chemistry but was very interested in mathematics. So, he thought about studying a program in engineering in one or the other of the two most important engineering schools in Mexico City, but he had to revalidate his papers, which in Mexico implies a significant amount of time and trouble, and then present the specific entrance exam for the engineering program. All this would take about a year. So, his high school math teacher suggested he could register in the physics and mathematics department in his state university and then present the entrance exam for the other universities. He followed that advice. During that first semester he decided to stay in the field of physics. While he studied physics he worked as a janitor in the university in a place with an antique telescope. Intrigued and fascinated by that telescope, it was then that he decided to specialize in optics.

After 10 years of hard work, his team participated in an international project (more than 20 countries) on cosmic rays and they were invited to work with optic design. Malcolm's team designed the telescopes that were used to photograph a geographical zone with cosmic rays mainly because of their previous experience. Their telescopes later became crucial for the project and the team became very well known among the specialists in this field. As the head of the team, Malcolm received a number of invitations to meetings and conferences in other countries which were generally in English, of which he had almost no knowledge. Despite that apparent barrier, he used various compensating strategies centered around reliance on other group members. After almost seven years, one of Malcolm's papers, published in English, on laser waves started to be read and cited. He regarded that point as the final confirmation that he had finally achieved his career development goal.

We can see several instances of life changing chance in Malcolm's case. Besides his apparent willingness to accept change in his long search for the right career, we see evidence of environmental chance events that influenced his choices. He possibly initially viewed these as barriers, but in retrospect these were chance events which led to finding his true career passion—optics. We also see the element of chance in the advice of the teacher suggesting entering the undergraduate program in physics and mathematics. That chance factor is reinforced by his working as a janitor and coming in contact with the antique telescope which fired his imagination. And we can see examples of milieu rewards and psychological closedness of the group—their mutual belief strengthening and cooperation related to their group work and achievements.

CAN CHANCE BE RECOGNIZED, GENERATED, AND/OR INCORPORATED INTO ACADEMIC LITERACY DEVELOPMENT?

To some extent the case studies above seem to show that chance encounters with literacy and career changing events happened mainly in early academic and career path developmental stages. This would have been at a point where their younger selves did not recognize the importance of chance but were, in a way, deterministically in line for such events to happen. What about those who are beginning their careers without the benefit of those serendipitous events? Or what of those who have not had the opportunity to recognize the importance of chance in development? Or even those who have not, for example, developed similar coping strategies and resiliency demonstrated in the case studies? As discussed above, this is something that is often left unacknowledged in professional development settings. We feel this apparent gap provides a prima facie basis for suggesting interventions aimed at remedying this omission.

Nevertheless, the accepted definition of chance, seems that to suggest an explicit pedagogical approach in academic literacy preparation, acculturalization or apprenticeship is to deny the accepted nature of such events—i.e., what happens completely accidently and without planning cannot be taught. However, looking closely at the case studies highlighting chance together with the associated theories and studies we can begin to see that these events were not completely a result of pure random happenstance, chance, serendipity—or whatever we want to call it. Personal and environmental factors came together as a result of a connected string of dispositions, choices and events to create positive conditions for life changing events to happen. This opens the door to the possibility of explicitly preparing novices or incipient researchers and academics to increasing their receptivity to such events by helping them recognize personal dispositions and environmental/social situations that could produce positive and potentially life changing events.

Of the theories reviewed, only Krumboltz's Happenstance Learning Theory (2009), which is based on his earlier theory of Planned Happenstance, seems to offer any specific pedagogical strategies (Mitchell et al., 1999). The only other concrete framework for explicitly preparing people to recognize and seek out chance events we came across was in Wiseman (2003) with his description of his research-based "Luck School." Chance encounters, often associated with luck, was part of his analyses.

From our research and experiences with the Latin American scientists, we suggest a few features and strategies which might also be considered. The scientists we worked with reported being deeply engaged in their scientific fields and participating in "self-reinforcing and self-nourishing networks" (Keranen et al., 2012, p. 249). The recognition of the need to belong to their international communities was a central reported component of their success. Their immersion in these communities is both actual and virtual. It should be clear at this point in the discussion that immersion in the target environments is essential to exposure to positive chance events.

> In terms of the scientists' ability to successfully write in English and publish their work in high level journals, which is another reported essential feature of their careers, they found through their experiences that English language courses are limited in what they can accomplish. They often lack the ability to address each individual's actual practice in the writers' specific contexts. We learned that no general English course nor even a specialized one in scientific writing which uses authentic materials can provide enough depth in the language of their specialty or the hours required to develop fluency. Further writing practice and development must happen in context specific immersive environments (Bazerman et al., 2012). Again, we see the apparent importance of immersion into target environments.

There are diverse opportunities for these intense language experiences, even when participants are not in a face-to-face English environment. Digital communications have been increasingly used and could provide an immersive experience for these researchers interested in increasing their participation in their specialty. Facilitating supports, i.e., providing opportunities and raising awareness of the relevance of such opportunities, can be an important part of enabling researchers to understand the dynamics of participating and publishing in their specialty at a distance. These would be especially important for those who are still in the periphery of their specialty and have not yet acquired the communication skills and awareness to make connections and participate actively in the networks of their specialty. As Bazerman et al. observe:

> Situated practice in significant, immersive, accountable, and consequential activities leads to motivated problem solving and habituated use that advances fluency and accuracy. Thus, as language professionals, we ought to consider providing the means to engage in more regular and more intense language experiences, which will be rewarding, reinforcing, and part of a trajectory of deeper engagement. (2012, p. 247)

On the personal level, we suggest some specific approaches. The personal dispositions illuminated in the case studies and summarized in Table 2.1 suggest certain psychological approaches. Those would certainly involve strategies of literacy competence reinforcing, strengthening concepts of personal agency, identifying role models, and building coping efficacy. The evidence-based strategies found in Krumbolz (2009) and Wiseman (2004) provide specific strategies for carrying out these possible approaches.

We also suggest the utility of case studies (such as those presented in this paper) in academic literacy and career development. Such experiences can help scientists in the periphery connect the dots of chance occurrences through the development phases of a career to make a complete story of academic literacy development in their specialty. We see these as particularly useful if the students or novice researchers collected, analyzed, and presented the case studies themselves from experienced and successful academics. These studies could identify potential role models and also make chance enhancing connections in the target environments.

In spite of these discoveries and possible intervention strategies, at the core of the successful scientists is that *need* to fully participate. As one participant explained:

- La diferencia eso es, a lo mejor es un poco romántica pero yo creo que el secreto de una carrera exitosa digamos el plan de vida exitoso en el sentido de satisfecho y frustrado o insatisfecho es esa introspección, yo que quiero y ya al saber veo como es lo que quiero, en el caso este digamos de la investigación científica es yo quiero saber algo, no sé en

algún área del conocimiento humano y luego ya la otra es una cosa de consecuencia de la otra, pero es primero identificar si tengo esa sed de conocimiento esa necesidad de estar averiguando cosa, pues ya está la mayor parte de la carrera ganada.
- The difference is, perhaps this is a little romantic, but I believe the secret to a successful career, or a successful life in the sense of whether it is satisfying or frustrating or unsatisfying is this introspection. What I want and knowing what I want. Scientific investigation is "I want to know something." I don't know what area of human knowledge this is or what is a consequence of what, but first is to identify if you have this thirst to know things, this necessity to find things out, but then the major part of the career is won/achieved.

For those who have that inner drive interventions, strategies, instruction, immersive situations, and opportunities will place them in strategic locations for chance events to have lasting and positive effects on their literacy and career development.

FINAL THOUGHTS

As we learned from the histories and attitudes of the scientists who manage to publish regularly in English, chance events flourish into life and career path changing events. Considering the ubiquity and potential life changing benefits of such encounters documented in the literature and exemplified in the case studies, we propose that explicit strategies should be used to help novice academics/researchers recognize and understand the importance of chance encounters in their professional development. To support this assertion, we cast our argument within the larger theoretical models associated with chance encounters and serendipity in career development (inter alia, Bandura, 1982; 1989; Bright et al., 2009; Goggin & Goggin, 2018; Kindsiko & Baruch, 2019; Krumboltz, 2006) and the mechanisms of enculturation and apprenticeship in academic settings (e.g., Bazerman, 2006; Bazerman et al., 2012; Carrasco et al., 2012; 2020; Keranen et al., 2012). By examining instances of reported chance found in our case studies, we can see how the theories are actualized in the data. We can also see that what may initially appear as unplanned and happenstance is really a cohort of personal dispositions, environmental milieus, and events which can be retrospectively traced in career trajectories. As such these elements can be identified and made explicit with the aim of helping incipient academics and researchers increase their personal agency in seeking out and benefiting from chance events and encounters. How such instruction plays out in specific settings and academic disciplines is dependent on context and the imagination and creativity of leaders and instructors.

REFERENCES

Bandura, A. (1982). The psychology of chance encounters and life paths. *American Psychologist, 37*(7), 747–755.

Bandura, A. (1989). Human agency in social cognitive theory. *American Psychologist, 44*(9), 1175–1184.

Bazerman, C. (1992). Theories That Help Us Read and Write Better. In S. Witte (Ed.), *A Rhetoric of Doing: Festschrift for J. Kinneavy*. Southern Illinois University Press.

Bazerman, C. (2006). The writing of social organization and the literate situating of cognition: Extending Goody's social implications of writing. In D. Olson & M. Cole (Eds.), *Technology, literacy and the evolution of society: Implications of the work of Jack Goody* (pp. 215–240). Erlbaum.

Bazerman, C., Keranen, N. & Encinas, F. (2012). Facilitated Immersion at a Distance in Second Language Scientific Writing. In M. Castello & C. Donahue (Eds.), *University Writing: Selves and Texts in Academic Societies*. (pp. 235–248). Emerald.

Bright, J. E. H., Pryor, R. G. L., Chan, E. W. M. & Rijanto, J. (2009). Chance events in career development: Influence, control and multiplicity. *Journal of Vocational Behavior, 75*, 14–25.

Cabral, A. C. & Salomone, P. R. (1990). Chance and careers: Normative versus contextual development. *Career Development Quarterly, 39*(1), 5–17.

Carrasco, A., Méndez-Ochaita, M., Limón, R. & Encinas, F. (2020). Leer y escribir como interpretación de roles, aprender de experiencias de estudiantes de doctorado. *DIDAC, 75*, 32–39. https://ri.ibero.mx/handle/ibero/6278.

Carrasco A., Kent, R. & Keranen, N. (2012). Learning Careers and Enculturation—Production of Scientific Papers by PhD Students in a Mexican Physiology Laboratory: An exploratory case study. In C. Bazerman, C. Dean, J. Early, K. Lunsford, S. Null, P. Rogers & A. Stansell (Eds.), *International advances in writing research: Cultures, places and measures* (pp. 335–351). The WAC Clearinghouse; Parlor Press. https://doi.org/10.37514/PER-B.2012.0452.2.19.

Delamont, S. & Atkinson, P. (2001). Doctoring uncertainty: Mastering craft knowledge. *Social Studies of Science, 31*(1), 87–107.

Díaz de Chumaciero, C. L. (2004). Serendipity and pseudoserendipity in career paths of successful women: Orchestra conductors. *Creativity Research Journal, 16*(2–3), 345–356. https://doi.org/10.1080/10400419.2004.9651464.

Emirbayer, M. & Mische, A. (1998). What Is Agency? *American Journal of Sociology, 103*(4), 962–1023.

Goggin, M. D. & Goggin, P. N. (Eds.) (2018). *Serendipity in Rhetoric, Writing, and Literacy Research*. Utah State University Press.

Guindon, M. & Hanna, F. J. (2002). Coincidence, happenstance, serendipity, fate, or the hand of God: Case studies in serendipity. *The Career Development Quarterly, 50*, 195–208.

Holiday, R. (2021). Opening a Small-Town Bookstore During the Pandemic Was the Craziest Thing We Ever Did. *Texas Monthly*. https://www.texasmonthly.com/arts-entertainment/opening-small-town-bookstore-pandemic-craziest-thing-we-ever-did/.

Keranen, N., Encinas, F. & Bazerman, C. (2012). Immersed in the game of science: beliefs, emotions, and strategies of NNES scientists who regularly publish in English. In C. Bazerman, C. Dean, J. Early, K. Lunsford, S. Null, P. Rogers & A. Stansell (Eds.), *International advances in writing research: Cultures, places and measures* (pp. 387–402). The WAC Clearinghouse; Parlor Press. https://doi.org/10.37514/PER-B.2012.0452.2.22.

Kindsiko, E. & Baruch, Y. (2019). Careers of PhD graduates: The role of chance events and how to manage them. *Journal of Vocational Behavior, 112*, 122–140. https://doi.org/10.1016/j.jvb.2019.01.010.

Krumboltz, J. D. (2009). The happenstance learning theory. *Journal of Career Assessment, 17*(2), 135–154. https://doi.org/10.1177/1069072708328861.

Lieblich, A., Tuval-Mashiach, R. & Zilber, T. (1998). *Narrative Research: Reading, Analysis, and Interpretation*. Sage Publications.

Mitchell, K. E., Levin, A. S. & Krumboltz, J. D. (1999). Planned happenstance: Constructing unexpected career opportunities. *Journal of Counseling & Development, 77*, 115–124.

Mohammed, M. & Boyd, J. (2010). Realizing Distributed Gains: How Collaboration with Support Services Transformed a Basic Writing Program for International Students. *Journal of Basic Writing, 29*(1), 78–98. https://doi.org/10.37514/JBW-J.2010.29.1.05.

Olshannikova, E., Olsson, T., Huhtämaki, J., Paasovaara, S. & Kärkkäinen, H. (2020). From chance to serendipity: Knowledge workers' experiences of serendipitous social encounters. *Advances in Human-Computer Interaction*, Volume 2020, Article ID 1827107, 18 pages. https://doi.org/10.1155/2020/1827107.

Rice, A. (2014). Incorporation of chance into career development theory and research. *Journal of Career Development, 41*(5), 445–463. https://doi.org/10.1177/0894845313507750.

Solomon, Y. (2017). Temporal aspects of info-serendipity. *Temporalités: Revue de sciences sociales et humaines*. https://doi.org/10.4000/temporalites.3523.

White, E. M. & DeGenero, W. (2016). Basic writing and disciplinary maturation: How chance conversations continue to shape the field. *Journal of Basic Writing, 35*(1), 5–22. https://doi.org/10.37514/JBW-J.2016.35.1.02.

Williams, E. N., Soeprapto, E., Like, K., Touradji, P., Hess, S. & Hill, C. E. (1998). Perceptions of serendipity: Career paths of prominent academic women in counseling psychology. *Journal of Counseling Psychology, 45*(4), 379–389.

Wiseman, R. (2003). The luck factor. *Skeptical Inquirer: The Magazine for Science and Reason, 27*(3). http://www.richardwiseman.com/resources/The_Luck_Factor.pdf.

CHAPTER 3.

CHANGING TIMES; CHANGING TEXTS

Ken Hyland

University of East Anglia, United Kingdom

In *Shaping Written Knowledge*, Charles Bazerman opened a new world to many of us, demonstrating how scholars construct a "stable rhetorical universe" within which their ideas make sense to others. One of the key ideas in this book was how the research article is a child of its time; a response to a particular historical context which shapes both the forms of scientific writing and the communities that use them. Coming from applied linguistics and without Bazerman's unique ability to combine insights from rhetorical, sociological, and literary perspectives, this chapter nevertheless attempts to suggest how today's context has changed writing practices in the academy.

Since Bazerman published his book in 1988, the academic landscape is almost unrecognizable. There has been an explosion of journals, papers, and authors with the globalization of research and the encroaching demands of publishing metrics on scholars across the planet. We have also witnessed a growing imperative for authors to reach new audiences and sponsors and seen the fragmentation and specialization of research. Change has also been relentless in the ways that we communicate and consume research. New digital genres, new electronic platforms, new modes of access and new commercial models are transforming publication. Perhaps at no time since the invention of the printing press has the pace and extent of change been so rapid. How research is done, how collaboration is organized and managed, how the literature is stored and accessed, how texts are constructed and disseminated, how output is measured and rewarded, how claims are discussed and evaluated have all seen a complete transformation. It would, therefore, be surprising if these changes had not had an impact on academic writing, and here I attempt to track an important element of this change on disciplinary knowledge construction.

In this chapter, I explore a corpus of 2.2 million words from the same leading journals in four disciplines at three periods over the past 50 years. My goal is to trace changes in a number of key interactive features I refer to as stance and engagement.

DOI: https://doi.org/10.37514/PER-B.2023.1800.2.03

PERSUASION AND INTERACTION IN ACADEMIC WRITING

One of Bazerman's enduring insights, for me at least, is the idea that writing is social action: It does things in the world. While he may not have been the first to express this position, his work eloquently illustrates it, perhaps most strongly in a collection he edited with James Paradis in 1991. In the introduction of that book, they say:

> Writing is more than socially embedded: it is socially constructive. Writing structures our relations with others and organizes our perceptions of the world. By studying texts within their contexts, we study as well as the dynamics of context building. (Bazerman & Paradis, 1991, p. 3)

While they expressed this view in the context of a challenge to current literary criticism, it does, of course, apply equally to writing in the professions, and particularly to writing in the academy.

The idea that academic writing is an objective and faceless kind of discourse, dealing directly with observable facts, has been questioned since the 1960s. Work by sociologists of knowledge like Thomas Kuhn, Steve Fuller, and Bruno Latour questioned traditional Mertonian accounts of scientific truth that knowledge is built on experiment, induction, replication, and falsifiability. In the Mertonian view, scientific papers are persuasive because they communicate truths based on observing the social or natural world, so that a research article is just the channel through which these observable facts are reported. But this ignores the role of *interpretation* in the process —and the arguments used to support them.

The interpretation of observations depends on the assumptions that scientists bring to the problem. As the celebrated physicist Stephen Hawking one said, "A theory may describe a range of observations, but beyond that it makes no sense to ask if it corresponds to reality, because we do not know what reality is independent of a theory" (Hawking, 1993, p. 44).

Hawking and Mlodinow (2010) go on to talk about "Model-dependent realism" to describe how reality is seen through the lenses of our (sometimes conflicting) theories. In other words, there is always going to be at least one way of understanding data and the fact we can have these competing explanations shifts attention away from the observations to the ways academics argue their interpretations of them. We have to look for "proof" in textual practices for producing agreement—in writing. At the heart of academic persuasion, then, is the attempt to anticipate and head off possible objections to arguments. To do this, writers have to encode ideas, use warrants and frame arguments in ways their audience will find most convincing. They use the language and rhetorical devices of their disciplines. So this is where interaction comes into the frame as writers need to establish a professionally acceptable voice and a contextually appropriate attitude, both to their readers and their arguments.

The study of interaction has become important for those who study academic discourse for three main reasons:

1. It helps us see how persuasion is achieved through language.
2. It shows us how agreement is collaboratively achieved in particular contexts.
3. It shows us how writing is constitutive of context and vice versa.

Basically, interaction is important in academic writing as writers have to be familiar with a disciplinary audience and wider institutional influences to negotiate their knowledge claims. These language choices therefore tell us something about how writers understand their readers, their disciplines, and the times in which they work. But despite considerable interest in interaction, few studies address how it has changed, and this is the gap I seek to fill here.

INTERACTIVE PRACTICES: STANCE AND ENGAGEMENT

Bazerman and Paradis (1991) use the term "textual dynamics" to refer to the dialectical relationship between texts and context, the fact that written discourse both creates and is created by its context. We can see this operating in the changing milieu of scholarly publishing over the past 50 years, a time of unprecedented change for academics in their careers and working conditions leading to shifts in the ways writers rhetorically manage their interactions with readers and construct their disciplines. To explore this, I will examine diachronic corpus using my model which sees writers as taking a stance to convey their attitudes and credibility and engaging readers by explicitly bringing them into the discourse (Hyland, 2005).

Stance is a writer-oriented aspect of interaction and highlights authorial "positioning:" adopting a point of view in relation to both the issues discussed in a text and to others who hold points of view on those issues. Stance in this sense is a consistent series of rhetorical choices which allow authors to conduct interpersonal negotiations. It has three components: *evidentiality, affect,* and *presence.*

- **Evidentiality**—the writer's commitment to the reliability of information, either toning down a claim with hedges or ramping it up with boosters.
- **Affect**—the writer's attitude towards what is said expressed through attitude markers.

- **Presence**—the extent writers choose to intrude into a text using first person pronouns.

Engagement, on the other hand, is the ways writers recognize the presence of their readers in a text. It is an alignment dimension concerned with galvanizing support, expressing collegiality, resolving difficulties, and heading off objections (Hyland, 2005). By anticipating their background knowledge, interests, and expectations, a writer can seek to monitor readers' understanding and response to a text and manage their impression of the writer. It is more concerned with proximity to a community of readers than authorial positioning (Hyland, 2012). Engagement, then, turns on the degree to which writers present themselves as sharing attitudes with readers and manage affiliation. There are five ways in which authors make these connections.

- **Reader mentions** bring readers into a discourse, normally through second person pronouns, particularly inclusive we.
- **Questions** invite direct collusion because they address the reader as someone with an interest in the issue the question raises.
- **Appeals to shared knowledge** are explicit signals asking readers to recognize something as familiar or accepted (e.g., obviously, of course).
- **Directives** are instructions to the reader, mainly imperatives and obligation modals, which tell readers to perform an action or see things in the way the writer intends.
- **Personal asides** interrupt the argument to offer a comment on what has been said.

CORPUS AND METHOD

To see whether interactivity may have changed in professional academic writing in recent times, Kevin Jiang and I created three corpora to get a snapshot of four disciplines at three points over the past 50 years: 1965, 1985, and 2015 (Hyland & Jiang, 2019). We chose applied linguistics, sociology, electrical engineering, and biology as a cross section of disciplines and took six papers from each of the same five journals in each discipline with the top ranking in their field (according to their 2015 5-year impact factor). Two journals, *TESOL Quarterly* and *Foreign Language Annals*, only began in 1967 and so papers were chosen from issues in that year. This gave us a corpus of 360 papers of 2.2 million words. The most striking thing about the corpus is the massive increase in the length of papers over the period, which rose from some 600,000 words in 1965 to nearly a million in 2015. Figure 3.1 shows how papers in all fields, with the exception of biology, have increased.

Changing Times; Changing Texts

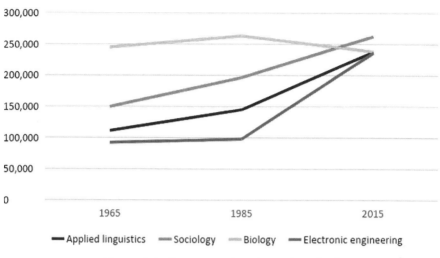

Figure 3.1. Corpus size (words per discipline)

We used *AntConc* (Anthony, 2019) to search the corpora using my 2005 list of most common interactive features in academic writing (Hyland, 2005), plus others we found in the corpus. Overall, 140 different items were examined and each occurrence was checked to establish that the feature was performing a function of stance or engagement.

OVERALL PATTERNS

Overall, we found 29,000 stance markers and almost 4000 engagement features in the 2015 papers, an increase of 54% in the last 50 years. However, when we take the fact that papers were much longer in 2015, this was a statistically significant *fall* of 9%. The figures normed to instances per 10,000 words are shown in Table 3.1 and indicate a steady decline in engagement and a heavy fall followed by a slight rise in stance.

Table 3.1. Distribution of Interactive Features Over Time (per 10,000 words)

	1965	**1985**	**2015**	**% Change**
Stance	324.3	291.6	304.9	- 6.0%
Engagement	46.1	44.4	40.3	- 12.7%
Total	370.4	336.0	345.2	- 9.3%

These falls are perhaps surprising given the increasingly competitive environment in which academics now work, where the rewards of publishing, both symbolic and financial, have become inseparable from the requirement to publish, secure funding, and gain the credit of citation. We can also see that stance features are about six times more numerous overall and that engagement has fallen more steeply. Interestingly, however, not all features have moved in the same direction.

Figure 3.2 presents the results for stance and shows that although markers of evidentiality and attitude have dropped by around 25%, self-mention has risen substantially. Writers seem less comfortable in marking their confidence in the accuracy or correctness of statements by boosting or hedging their claims and less likely to express an attitude to what they say. So, despite a greater personal presence emerging in academic writing since 1965, with self-mention rising by nearly 50%, there seems to have been a declining preference for strong authorial standpoints. Simply: writers are not getting behind their ideas or intervening as much as in the past while nevertheless ensuring that they are very present in their texts.

Engagement, features, which are used to grab readers' interest and address them personally, have also declined significantly (*log likelihood* = 29.82 p<0.001). But we can see in Figure 3.3 that while all other features have fallen, directives, which are used to steer readers to some action or idea, are up by 16%. Perhaps there are stronger reasons now to overtly push readers to agreement, but the overall declines in stance and engagement are puzzling. I will now turn to the disciplinary shifts to show the changes in more detail and to suggest some answers.

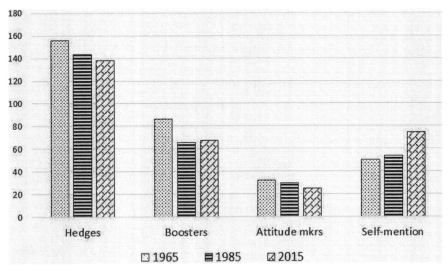

Figure 3.2. Distribution of stance features over time (per 10,000 words)

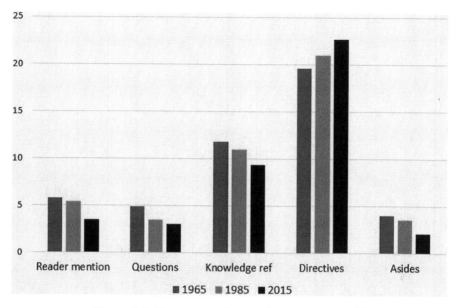

Figure 3.3. Engagement features (per 10,000 words)

CHANGES BY DISCIPLINE

The disciplinary changes turn out to be very surprising. The decline in the use of interactive features is unevenly distributed across fields and suggests that we are witnessing a modification, albeit very slowly, in academic writing conventions.

Figure 3.4 shows changes in stance over the three time points and we can see statistically significant falls in the use of these features in applied linguistics and sociology, although sociology has picked up a little since 1985. The science fields, especially engineering have risen significantly. Obviously, presenting a self is central to the writing process and we cannot avoid projecting an impression of ourselves and how we stand in relation to our arguments, discipline, and readers (Hyland, 2004). There is no "faceless" writing. But while writers in different disciplines represent themselves and their work in very different ways, how they do this seems to be converging. The soft knowledge fields, particularly in the past 30 years in the case of applied linguistics, have been slowly moving towards more "author-evacuated" prose; increasingly mimicking hard science practices. On the other hand, writers in the hard sciences, and spectacularly in the case of electrical engineering, are edging towards greater visibility, especially through self-mention to create a more explicit presence in the text.

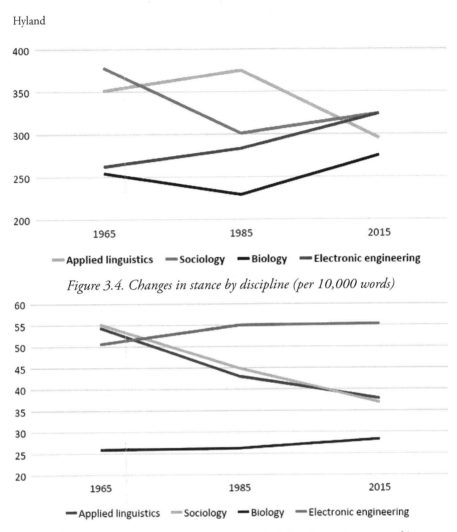

Figure 3.4. Changes in stance by discipline (per 10,000 words)

Figure 3.5. Changes in engagement by discipline (per 10,000 words)

Something similar is happening with *engagement*, with a statistically significant fall in the soft knowledge fields. Figure 3.5 indicates that writers in applied linguistics and sociology substantially reduced their use of engagement (LL = 86.60, p <0.001; LL = 110.06, p < 0.001). Biology and electrical engineering authors, on the other hand, have increased their use of engagement, particularly over the last 30 years, so frequencies in electrical engineering proportionately now exceed the other disciplines studied.

Overall, these trends are surprising as disciplines are distinguished as much by their argument patterns as by their epistemological assumptions or research topics (e.g., Bazerman, 1998; Hyland, 2004). Because the social sciences and humanities work with more interpretive, less abstract kinds of knowledge, writers put themselves into the text far more, with a stronger representation of self, and are also more likely to recognize alternative voices and appeals for solidarity. Their texts are therefore characterized by more extensive use of stance and engagement markers. In the hard disciplines, in contrast, we are used to seeing writers downplay their interactions and rely far more on arguments based on methods and procedures. The greater reliability invested in hard science procedures allows authors to step back from their texts and allow "fact to speak for themselves." This, anyway, is the traditional pattern, but it seems to be breaking down.

The soft-knowledge fields are moving towards more "author-evacuated" prose in a way which mimics the hard sciences with less overt intrusion and calls for solidarity. Hard scientists, however, seem to be edging towards greater visibility, spectacularly so in electrical engineering. Speculatively, we might attribute this to the social sciences adopting more empirical and quantitative studies which restrict opportunities for overt interaction. Alternatively, it may be due to the massive growth of second language writers publishing in English who have been schooled in objective writing styles. However, while plausible responses, we might suspect there is more to it than this. As Bazerman himself observes, "Regularized forms of writing are social institutions, interacting with other social institutions" (1988, p. 22). Creating public knowledge is conducted in a social and economic sphere which impacts on the how interactions are conducted and what is considered to be appropriate argument and we can see this more clearly by looking at some of the main changes, beginning with stance.

CHANGES IN STANCE MARKERS

Stance is the writer's positioning—towards the topic and readers—and the features which most explicitly convey this have dropped 7%, over 50 years, with only self-mention rising overall.

Table 3.2 shows the percentage changes in stance features over the period. Falls are shaded. The table indicates, among other things, that the biologists have become more measured in their stance expression but considerably more "present" in terms of self-mentions. The electrical engineers are, in general, taking a stronger stance, increasing their expression of attitude, presence, and evidentiality. In contrast, while the sociologists are projecting themselves into their texts with self-mentions, they are expressing their attitudes and epistemic judgments less frequently. The applied linguists are becoming more faceless overall, a directly opposite trend to the engineers.

Table 3.2. Percentage Changes in Stance Features 1965–2015 (per 10,000 words)

	App linguistics	Sociology	Biology	Electrical Eng
Hedges	- 36.0	- 20.8	14.0	7.6
Boosters	- 37.8	- 35.5	- 32.2	15.0
Attitude markers	- 26.2	-21.6	2.5	72.6
Self-mention	-27.2	37.7	163.1	62.5

Boosters and attitude markers show the steepest falls, and these are the most explicit ways writers can indicate their position to take a firm stance towards their arguments, conveying commitment and affective evaluations.

Attitude markers fell from a lower height as affect is relatively uncommon in academic writing. But because they are a marked choice, they are salient and so create greater impact when they do occur as these examples show:

4. This was an <u>extraordinary</u> moral position, given Christianity's (and other world religions) long tradition of almsgiving. (Sociology)
5. This was an <u>unexpected</u> result and provides <u>compelling</u> evidence for the <u>importance</u> of deltas based on their size alone. (Applied Linguistics)

By signaling an assumption of shared attitudes to material with an active audience, writers both express a position and seek to bring readers into agreement with it. There is, however, a decline in the explicit marking of affect with fairly dramatic falls in the soft sciences and, once again, an increase in electronic engineering. Frequencies for attitude were down by 26% in applied linguistics and 22% in sociology. So, writers here seem to be adopting stances which are less robust. The most common expressions of attitude are *important* and what I'll call *restrictive even*, which limits the extent of the claim with *even though* or *even if*. Both forms help writers to present a positive stance which aligns with community knowledge or what the discipline already accepts.

6. <u>Even though</u> ACC oxidase is usually considered as a constitutive enzyme, a growing number of recent studies indicate that. (Biology)
7. It is shown that in some particular case one can also estimate the thickness of the domain wall <u>even if</u> it is much smaller than the optical wavelength. (Electrical Engineering)

So, Statement 3 tells readers that the writer shares their position on the properties of ACC oxidase, it also sets up a contrary or unexpected position. Statement 4 highlights unexpectedness, comparing what the writer claims against what is assumed shared knowledge with readers. By categorically asserting statements which assume shared attitudes the writer constructs a relationship along with a text, but this is a relationship where the writer is firmly in the driving seat.

Boosters have also steadily declined in both soft knowledge disciplines and also show a trend towards more verbal uses. The most common form in 1965 and 1985 in both applied linguistics and sociology was *must*, the predominant modal of inferential certainty, but this had disappeared from the top 20 by 2015. Most interestingly, cognitive verbs such as *think, believe,* and *know* have been replaced by research verbs like *show, demonstrate,* and *find*. This represents a shift from commitments expressed as personal beliefs towards more objective, data-supported claims, from Statements 5 and 6 to those like Statements 7 and 8:

8. As promising as this approach seems, I think it fails. (Sociology)
9. That, I believe must be sought in an unhappy confusion in the minds of the teachers of composition. (Applied Linguistics)
10. We demonstrate that this inconsistency has resulted from inadequate control, . . . including the basis of norm comparisons. (Applied Linguistics)
11. In summary, we find that females are markedly superior to males in recalling social network information. (Sociology)

Writers in the soft knowledge fields are, then, appealing less to their personal convictions that something is true and preferring to attribute claims to their data.

Surprisingly, all stance markers have increased in electrical engineering. Attitude markers, for instance, have risen 73% in this field. Hedges and attitude markers are also up in biology, very much in contrast with the soft knowledge fields.

Hedges have also moved in different directions between the physical and social sciences. These devices allow writers to mark claims as provisional and pacify readers who may hold different views. They help authors to align their position with current thinking in the field, suggesting collegiality, reasonableness, and open-minded inquiry:

12. In this paper we show that a section of a corrugated waveguide may act in the same way. (Electrical Engineering)
13. This would seem to imply that these lamellae are non-planar in the melt, and undergo some form of shear, perhaps when crystallization is terminated by quenching. (Biology)

These writers are signaling a reluctance to be dogmatic and indicating that they are willing to entertain possible alternative views, that the waveguide may behave differently to their findings and that the lamellae do not have the characteristics the authors attribute to them.

The decline of hedges—by 36% in applied linguistics and 21% in sociology—therefore signals a shift in how assured writers wish to seem about their claims. *May* and *would*, always among the most popular hedges, remain the most common in both applied linguistics and sociology, but their frequencies fell by half. This seems to represent not only a decline in hedging but a shift away from forms which, according to Coates (1983), express assumption (*should* and *ought*), possibilities (*may, might,* and *could*) and hypotheticality (*would*) towards those which carry more speculative judgements, predicated on a reference to the uncertainty of human evaluation such as *suggest* and *likely*.

So, where writers *do* hedge, they seem to be making more speculative interpretations:

14. Humans might inadvertently be altering the relationships between plants and mycorrhizal fungi and so might be affecting the cost: benefit balances. (Biology)
15. It seems that Indo-European poetry must have been governed by isosyllabism, accentual patterns, and alliteration. (Applied Linguistics)
16. We speculate that HNF4oL and HNF4P may already function as transcription factors during oogenesis. (Biology)

In fact, these forms are often used to draw conclusions rather than comment on accuracy. They speculate about possible reasons for something rather than the reliability of the data or the veracity of interpretations.

However, with boosters also falling substantially (38% and 35% in applied linguistics and sociology respectively), this seems to represent a less intrusive stance overall rather than a strengthening of commitment. This fall may be related to what some see as an increasing scientism in the social sciences—with more or a hard science orientation in their methods and approaches. Methods are usually less established and open to question in the soft sciences so that in applied linguistics, for example, there has been debate around legitimate disciplinary methods for years. This has increased with the growth of more powerful and simple to use corpus analysis tools and statistical packages which make quantitative support for findings and more precise measurement of data possible.

Perhaps surprisingly, however, changes in the frequencies of evidential markers have moved in the opposite direction in the sciences. Hedging rose 14% (per 10,000 words) in biology and 8% in electronic engineering and even boosters were up in engineering, by 15%. *Show, must,* and *know* were the preferred forms in both disciplines over the entire period, although engineers have come to use a much wider array of expressions, especially *establish, prove,* and *clearly,* which are used to ensure readers are aware of the strength of results or claims:

17. We shall prove, however, that this is not the case. (Biology)
18. Clearly, the formation of thermal stresses in the monolith structure is a dynamic process, whose prediction requires. (Electrical Engineering)

19. We <u>have established</u> above that $(e(i)(t), \omega(i)(t))$ are bounded for all I = 1,..., j.. (Electrical Engineering)

The most dramatic change is in the rise in *self-mention*, where writers refer to themselves in the text. The use of *I* projects a personal stance and signals the writer's ownership of a claim. But while applied linguists now use this less than before, frequencies for biology are up 163%, electrical engineering 63%, and sociology 38%. All substantial rises. Personal reference is a clear indication of the perspective from which a statement should be interpreted, enabling writers to emphasize their own contribution and to seek agreement for it. As a result, this looks like a turn away from the convention of scientific objectivity—at least rhetorically. In the sciences it is common for writers to downplay their personal role to highlight the phenomena under study, the replicability of research activities, and the generality of the findings, subordinating their own voice to that of unmediated nature. Such a strategy subtly conveys an empiricist ideology that suggests research outcomes would be the same irrespective of the individual conducting it. In the humanities and social sciences, in contrast, the use of the first person is closely related to the desire to both strongly identify oneself with a particular argument and to gain credit for an individual view.

But there is a fine line to walk here. While impersonality helps authors show they are aware of the rhetorical conventions of their community, they must also stake out an individual position and strong persona as they argue for the originality of their claims. Thus:

- Impersonality helps authors display a disciplinary competence—indicating to readers they know how to argue using an appropriate community rhetoric, shaping their texts so readers find claims familiar and convincing.
- At the same time, they must create an independent voice and ownership of their claims.

This is the tension between what I have called *proximity* and *positioning* (Hyland, 2012), that is, the writer's relationship to the discipline and to what is being discussed in the text.

So self-mention, rather than disguising writer involvement, helps scientists to make their work more accessible and their role in it more visible. It is one way in which writers can respond to the growing imperative of "impact" as a measure in annual performance reviews and career assessments. A more visible presence is also a way of ensuring that their individual claims do not go unnoticed by university panels who judge applications for jobs, tenure, and promotion.

More specifically, while we find that *I* is increasing in most fields, *exclusive we* comprises nearly 60% of all self-mention overall. This form has doubled in electrical engineering and increased by four times in biology, making it the preferred marker of self-mention in the sciences. This is partly a response, no doubt, to the growing trend, driven by institutional pressures, towards collaborative writing and co-authorship. Data from *Thomson Reuters*, for example, shows the average number of authors in papers in the Science Citation Index grew by 50% between 1990 and 2010 (Hyland, 2015). Since then, of course, the free availability of collaborative writing platforms such as *Google Docs* or online tools like *Authorea* and *Overleaf* further facilitate co-authorship, as do lower costs of air travel and communication tools such as *Skype, Zoom,* and *WhatsApp* calls. The fact that disciplines have become more factionalized into areas of specialization, also contributes to co-authorship as researchers may need to cooperate with others to investigate questions and publish their research. Underlying all this, however, are the pressures on academics to increase their outputs, which can more easily be done by the division of labor.

Using exclusive *we* is also an alternative to anonymizing passive constructions and helps authors represent their ownership of claims and get credit for them. In this way it addresses the growing pressure on academics to sell their knowledge to readers outside their specialism—especially the commercial interests which funds its research. So, while *inclusive we* allows authors to create more distance between themselves and their reporting than *I,* it does not create the same anonymity. It is a halfway house of intrusion.

Sociologists have also increased their use of self-mention, but we expect this in the more discursive social sciences. Without the same kind of strong consensus on the explanatory role of experimental methods, the impact of writer intrusion can be crucial in gaining acceptance for statements. More surprising, however, is the 27% fall in the use of self-mention in applied linguistics. One explanation for this might be that linguists are more self-conscious about language and the strong claims that self-mention makes for agency.

There is, however, a more plausible reason. This fall is consistent with the decline in other interactional features in applied linguistics over this 50-year period and does not seem to be related to a more "author evacuated" style (Hyland & Jiang, 2019). In 1965, the earliest period of this data, applied linguistics was at an early stage in its evolution towards becoming a discipline. It was an emergent field with an undeveloped literature and a greater focus on personal accounts of language teaching. Since then, there has been a massive increase in empirically-oriented studies, a broadening of the discipline to include far more topics, and the growth of a dedicated literature (e.g., Hyland & Jiang, 2021). The Blackwell encyclopedia of applied linguistics (Chappelle, 2012), for example, has over 1000 entries covering 27 major areas while the SCImago catalogue lists 884 journals in the field (ca., December 2020). These advances have, of course, brought rhetorical changes in how claims are argued and accepted.

CHANGES IN ENGAGEMENT FEATURES

Now I turn to engagement and how writers step into the text to refer to readers directly, shaping the discourse to readers' assumed needs for involvement. It is concerned with galvanizing support, expressing collegiality, resolving difficulties, and heading off objections (Hyland, 2004; 2005) and has two main purposes:

20. To meet readers' expectations of inclusion. Readers are addressed as participants in an ongoing dialogue using reader mentions and asides, suggesting group membership and solidarity.
21. To rhetorically position the audience, predicting and responding to possible objections. Here the writer pulls the audience along to guide them to interpretations with *questions*, *directives*, and *references to shared knowledge*.

Engagement therefore highlights the dialogic role of discourse in predicting a reader's reaction and in responding to a larger textual conversation among members of a discipline. While it's far less frequent than stance, the fact engagement varies across disciplines shows how it reflects writers' assessments of what readers might know and expect. In other words, like stance, these features are markers of discipline and reflect current institutional priorities.

Table 3.3 shows percentages changes in engagement since 1965. Once again, falls are shaded and show that *asides* and *references to shared knowledge* have fallen steadily in all four disciplines. While *questions* have more than doubled in biology, most of these numbers are very low, just three questions per 10,000 words in biology in 2015 for example. It is, nevertheless, worth looking at those with the highest frequencies: reader mention and directives.

Table 3.3. Changes in Engagement (%)

	App. Linguistics	Sociology	Biology	Electrical Eng.
Reader mention	-38.2	-65.0	-50.0	65.2
Directives	-7.8	-0.3	8.6	35.3
Knowledge ref	-29.5	-28.6	-28.5	-22.9
Questions	-14.9	-36.8	146.2	-37.5
Asides	-71.7	-25.6	-29.6	-37.1

First, the table shows that *reader mention* has fallen significantly across all fields except electrical engineering. Explicitly referring to the reader is the clearest signal that the writer is thinking about an active audience. But while *you* and *your* are the most obvious acknowledgement of the reader, these are fairly rare in the corpus and almost non-existent in the hard sciences (Table 3.4).

Even linguists and sociologists have largely dropped the use of *you* over the past 50 years, with frequencies in sociology down from 5.0 to 0.5 cases per 10,000 words. This avoidance may indicate that writers may be reluctant to engage their interlocutors in such an explicitly direct and personal way, a trend we have seen above in the decreasing use of stance.

Table 3.4. Changes in Reader Mention Over Time (per 10,000 words)

Features	1965	1985	2015
you/your	1.7	1.3	0.3
one/reader	0.3	0.8	0.5
we/our/us	4.4	2.7	2.6

Where they are used, *you* and *your* rarely initiate a dialogue with a fellow specialist. Examples like Statement 17 from 1965, where the writer tries to engage readers as fellow professionals in a shared world, are uncommon in the 2015 corpus:

> 22. To evaluate the economics of retrofitting electrotechnologies into existing manufacturing processes, you should, of course, ask yourself: Is the existing process causing problems? If the answer is no, there is little incentive to change. However, if the answer is yes, you must define what the problems are, and you are likely to begin by determining if there is a bottleneck in the process." (Electrical Engineering)

Instead, we now see examples where *you* carries a more encompassing meaning, addressing the reader as an everyman scholar who is not a specialist but an intelligent person interested in the topic and able to follow the logic of the writer's argument, as in Statements 18 and 19:

> 23. For example, if you break the law, you can expect to be arrested, but if you go along quietly, you can, unless there is a special circumstance, expect to be treated reasonably. (Sociology)
>
> 24. That is, though you can see words, you cannot see ideas or content. If you cannot see content, you have no proof that it exists. What you cannot prove the existence of, they say, you have no business theorizing about. (Applied Linguistics)

The reader is thus pulled into the text as a partner, recruited by the writer to unravel a knotty problem together.

This usage functions like the indefinite pronoun *one,* which does the same job of impersonal interaction. *One,* in fact, has increased 4-fold in applied linguistics and is now over twice as frequent as *you:* Examples like these are common:

25. One cannot really see how a television channel could obtain large audiences by presenting news reports or shows in languages which are not understood by most of the people. (Applied Linguistics)
26. One can also expect similar attitudes and values relating to writing and writers. (Applied Linguistics)

This is still involving readers but has a less personally interactive tone than *you*. Writers are using these forms to express a collegial connection with their readers in order to head off objections to their arguments. So, the falls in the use of *you* may not only be because of its over-personal connotations, but perhaps because it fails to firmly build this kind of relationship. Instead, it seems to emphasize the differences between the writer and reader, establishing a contrast between them—*You* vs *I* rather than *you* and *I*. *Inclusive we*, on the other hand, stresses sharedness. It suggests that the writer and reader have the same interpretations and goals. But while it takes readers into account, it addresses them from a position of power, a superior, condescending *we* which attempts to lead readers through an argument and towards a preferred conclusion. In other words, pronouns claim authority as well as collegiality. They help create a dialogue in order to coax compliance with the author's claims and it may be the transparency of this manipulative strategy which accounts for its decline since 1965.

Electrical engineers have bucked this trend and substantially increased their use of reference to readers through use of *inclusive we*, which have risen considerably by over 65%. We are now more likely to see statements like this:

27. In the case of ti—**we** can obtain the expectation of E(diK). (Electrical Engineering)
28. So **we** can compute, from the device response (Fig. 7b), the external quality factor, Q, [3]. (Electrical Engineering)
29. These results broaden **our** understanding of bucket brigade devices and their potential role in new areas of application. (Electrical Engineering)

While the reasons for this are unclear, it may be related to the fact that engineers are under pressure to produce knowledge for wider fields of interest. They are increasingly reaching out to new audiences in only peripherally related areas, often outside academia itself, in the commercial world which funds much of its research. More interventionist engagement strategies, which seek to explicitly pull readers along towards particular viewpoints, may therefore help compensate for a less certain ability to rely on the persuasive efficacy of in-group understandings of methods, theories, and the significance of findings.

The final feature I want to mention are *directives*. These are typically imperatives or obligation modals and they instruct readers to perform an action or to see things in a way determined by the writer (Hyland, 2002; 2005). They are therefore a way of managing the readers' understanding of a text and are typically realized by an imperative (Statement 25); by a modal of obligation addressed to the reader (Statement 26); by a first person inclusive let-imperative (Statement 27); and by an adjective expressing the writer's judgement of necessity/importance with a complement *to-* clause (Statement 28):

30. ***See*** text for discussion of the statistical analyses and curve fitting. (Biology)
31. Such transformations ***should*** be studied in terms of the semantic and ideological transformations they entail. (Applied Linguistics)
32. For the sake of simplicity, ***let us*** consider a one port admittance element with a real pole-residue pair, p and k. (Electrical Engineering)
33. But ***it is important to*** recognize that institutional power is subject to competition and monopoly as well. (Sociology)

In each case there is a clear reader-oriented focus as the writer intervenes to direct the reader to some action or understanding.

Directives are extremely common and comprise about 56% of all engagement devices, having risen by 250% over the 50-years. One major change, however, has been the decline of obligation modals (*must, should, have to,* and *ought*), probably because of their potential interpersonal impact. These forms carry strong connotations of unequal power, claiming greater authority for the writer by requiring readers to act or see things in a way determined by the writer (Hyland, 2002). They therefore come close to violating conventions of democratic peer relationships in research writing, appearing to be explicit attempts to control readers:

34. It ***must*** be understood, however, that there are wide variations in applications that describe themselves as "interactive multimedia." (Applied Linguistics)
35. To calculate temperatures and heat capacities on the TI82, <u>one</u> <u>must</u> use lists instead of tables. (Electrical Engineering)

They have in many cases, been replaced by imperatives, which make less interpersonal impact on readers, especially those which are most frequent in the corpus: *note, let, see, consider, suppose, notice,* and *assume*.

36. <u>Notice</u> that by using the new algorithm the problems become easier with increasing capacities B. (Electrical Engineering)
37. <u>Assume</u> a medial axis as shown in Fig. 9. (Biology)

Essentially, directives bring readers into the text to move them in a particular direction. In fact, they direct readers to three main kinds of activity:

- ***Textual acts*** guide readers to another part of the text or to another text (e.g., Smith, 1999; refer to Table 3.2)
- ***Physical acts*** instruct them how to carry out some action in the real world (e.g., *open the valve, heat the mixture*)
- ***Cognitive acts*** position readers by leading them through a line of reasoning and steer them to certain conclusions (e.g., *note, concede,* or *consider* some argument).

The increase in directives over the last 50 years has largely been in textual and physical acts and, again, mainly in electrical engineering. Cognitive acts have fallen by half in the physical science texts. These are potentially the riskiest kind of directive as they explicitly position readers by telling them how they should understand something in the text:

38. The configuration <u>must be</u> understood as having almost normal reflection, and an external magnetic field along the z-coordinate. (Electrical Engineering)
39. <u>It is important to</u> recognize that social norms, as prescriptions serving as common guidelines for social action, are grounded in values and attitudes. (Sociology)
40. <u>One should be</u> aware that the identification of an MRNA as a maternal component does not necessarily prove the presence of the corresponding protein. (Biology)

The other categories of directives are less overtly manipulative and have declined less. The big rise in electrical engineering, in fact, has been in physical acts, which generally offer succinct experimental instructions:

41. It is important to prevent the front end bending at this point. (Electrical Engineering)
42. When s completes these parts, repeat the above procedure and adjust the value of ivi'j- 1 using (1). (Electrical Engineering)

Physical directives allow both precision and brevity—features valued by information saturated scientists, who often read rapidly for bottom line results pertinent to their own research (Bazerman, 1988). Increasingly, scientific papers are also read by those from the professional world looking for ideas with a potential commercial relevance. Like changes in stance, then, these falls in engagement reflect the growing heterogeneity of audiences. If, as a writer, you are less sure about who is reading your work, it is probably safer not to make assumptions about what your reader already knows and how they would prefer to interact with you.

DISCUSSION AND SOME CONCLUSIONS

In this paper I have traced changes in academic interaction over the past 50 years to discover if they can be explained by the seismic changes which have occurred in the institutional and social contexts of research publishing. The main findings are:

43. Stance and engagement have failed to keep pace with the increasing length of papers and show statistically significant falls.
44. Strong stances expressed through attitude markers and boosters have declined the most.
45. Self-mention and directives are the only markers to have increased overall.
46. Disciplinary changes show declines in sociology and applied linguistics and rises in biology and electrical engineering.

It seems, broadly, that research is now being reported more impersonally, with more subdued involvement and with less explicit effort to finesse the reader. This is not to say that writers are no longer crafting texts which take the processing needs and background knowledge of their readers into account, but that this is now being done with less obvious authorial intervention. These changes are relatively slow, but they seem to show a shift in argument patterns which have gone largely unnoticed.

In the hard sciences the cumulative nature of research and tightly structured procedures have generally allowed for succinct communication and relatively "strong" claims which can be attributed to observations in the lab rather than interpretations at the keyboard. The relatively clear criteria for establishing or refuting claims has allowed authors to remove themselves from the picture, but research papers in both biology and electrical engineering, and particularly the latter, display an increased deployment of stance markers, most noticeably self-mention. We also see the beginning of an authorial repositioning in terms of engagement, and particularly of directives and reader mention in electrical engineering. One reason for this may be the growing need of scientists to address audiences beyond an immediate group of informed insiders to promote both one's research and oneself.

In the more discursive soft knowledge fields there is a marked trend in the opposite direction, towards less explicit engagement and a less visible stance. The changes documented here minimize authorial presence and convey more cautious stances, directing readers to the persuasive strength of data or methodological practice rather than the convictions of the interpreting writer. Speculatively, this may be due to the increasing specialization of research in the social sciences for, as topics become more focused and the literature more concentrated, audiences are themselves becoming more specialized. Academic success ever more demands that professional academics carve out a very particular niche for themselves and make a contribution to a narrowly specific area. This means audiences are more familiar with issues and perhaps writers have less need for explicit engagement to persuade them. Another possible reason is the influence of style guides, writing textbooks and the massive growth of online writing advice. In a world where the majority of academics are writing in a language which is not their mother tongue, the influence of these sources of assistance may have a greater impact.

In the end, effective academic writing depends on rhetorical decisions about interpersonal intrusion which recognize and align with both disciplinary epistemologies and social practices and with wider political and institutional changes. The most significant of these in recent times would seem to concern the ways knowledge is constructed and disseminated to new audiences outside a traditional peer group, including commercial and industrial sponsors who might make use of the knowledge created and personnel boards who make high stakes decisions regarding the careers of academic writers. Academics are increasingly pushed to write for funders, commercial sponsors, grant awarding bodies, promotion and tenure committees, and other disciplinary outsiders. We are also being driven by career imperatives and an appraisal system obsessed by counting. Academics need to get their papers published, often in less specialized journals, to have their work recognized by more people, to be more widely noticed and cited by as many people as possible. New audiences, less specialized more results driven, and often looking for applications, are key factors which are driving, albeit slowly, how we write.

Overall, this study supports research which shows an inexorable growth in formality and authorial withdrawal since the inception of scientific writing some 350 years ago, a change which Atkinson (1999) describes as a move from a less "author-centered" rhetoric to a highly abstract and "object-centered" one. Bazerman (1988) himself traces this growing "collective intelligence" of the scientific community and the influence of contextual factors on its character as claims are increasingly separated from both nature and the individuals who perceive it. Just as the rhetorical style of articles has emerged over the centuries from the political establishment of a scientific community, the changes we see in these interactional choices similarly reflect changing audiences and material conditions.

REFERENCES

Anthony, L. (2019). *AntConc 3.5.8.* Waseda University. http://www.antlab.sci.waseda.ac.jp.
Bazerman, C. (1988). *Shaping written knowledge.* University of Wisconsin Press.
Bazerman, C. & Paradis, J. (Eds.). (1991). *Textual dynamics of the professions.* University of Wisconsin Press.

Chappelle, C. (2012). *The encyclopaedia of applied linguistics*. Willey Online.
Hawking, S. (1993). *Black holes and baby universes and other essays*. Bantam.
Hawking, S. & Mlodinow, L. (2010). *The grand design*. Bantam.
Hyland, K. (2002). Directives: argument and engagement in academic writing. *Applied Linguistics, 23*(2), 215–239.
Hyland, K. (2004). Patterns of engagement: Dialogic features and L2 student writing. In L. Ravelli & R. Ellis (Eds.), *Analyzing academic writing: Contextualized frameworks* (pp. 5–23). Continuum.
Hyland, K. (2005). Stance and engagement: a model of interaction in academic discourse. *Discourse Studies, 7*(2), 173–191.
Hyland, K. (2012). *Disciplinary identities*. Cambridge University Press.
Hyland, K. (2015). *Academic publishing: Issues and challenges in the construction of knowledge*. Oxford University Press.
Hyland, K. & Jiang, K. (2019). *Academic discourse and global publishing: Disciplinary persuasion in changing times*. Routledge.

CHAPTER 4.
SITUATED REGULATION WRITING PROCESSES IN RESEARCH WRITING: LESSONS FROM RESEARCH AND TEACHING

Montserrat Castelló
Universitat Ramon Llull, Barcelona

> We need to see when, how, and to what purpose [scientific writing] is employed in the concrete settings of human history.
>
> —Charles Bazerman (1988, p. 313)

My research on writing regulation is rooted in the disciplinary background of educational psychology, and specifically in the sociocognitive and sociocultural approaches to the field. More than fifteen years ago, when I started to focus on graduate and researcher writing, Charles Bazerman's pioneering historical and social account of scientific writing was an invaluable touchstone for my own disciplinary understanding of scientific language as a psychological, social, and linguistic tool, and of its effects on individuals and groups (Bazerman, 1988). The quote that introduces this chapter was a watchword, one that guided me in the reinterpretation and further elaboration of my conceptual framework, anchored in European interpretations of the works of Bakhtin and Vygotsky (Allal, 2020; Camps & Fontich, 2020). As a psychologist, I was (and am) above all interested in when, how, and why particular writers employ scientific language in the specific contexts of their research. Studies of how writers deal with research genres in real communicative situations and natural contexts were not predominant fifteen years ago in Europe, and this dialogue with voices from other contexts was crucial in my future work development.

This chapter chronicles the results of my own inner dialogue with Bazerman's contributions on scientific writing and regulation, a process that allowed me to expand the scope of my research on these topics and confront them from a different disciplinary background. As Bazerman himself wrote, "communication across [these] disciplines occurs only with tolerance and charity in respecting each other's conceptual domains" (Bazerman, 2012, p. 266). I trust readers to apply these attitudes to make such cross-disciplinary communication possible. In the first section, I characterize research writing as a socio-historical activity, crucial to researcher development, and I analyze the particular challenges early-career researchers face when dealing with—and learning to write in—specific research genres. I also examine the role of writing regulation processes in this characterization, while distinguishing between and problematizing the notions of self-regulation, co-regulation, and socially shared regulation, as well as their respective theoretical roots. In the second section, I consider some of the lights and shadows from our recent research on graduate and postgraduate students' cognitive, social, and emotional regulation writing processes, dealing with research genres such as theses, dissertations, and research articles. The focus is not only on results and knowledge contribution, but also on the methodological issues that underlie the study of regulation from a situated perspective. The potential of adopting a comprehensive unit of analysis—e.g., the regulation episode—is explored in contrast with a range of other traditional and innovative measures. Finally, the last section is devoted to a reflection on the role teaching plays in increasing our understanding of how research writing regulation works, and how it helps students make purposeful decisions as to how, when, and why to use certain resources and writing discursive mechanisms.

RESEARCH WRITING AS A DIALOGIC, HYBRID, AND SOCIO-HISTORICAL EPISTEMIC ACTIVITY

Research writing has been characterized as a particular kind of dialogic persuasive endeavor (Hyland, 2002; Tardy, 2012), one that involves not only the author(s) and the reader, but also the authors' and others' voices that are invoked in the minds of the author(s) (Bakhtin, 1986; Hermans, 2001). These additional voices may or may not be apparent in the final text (Bazerman, 1988; Prior, 2001). Thus, research writing is a highly rhetorical activity that involves the broader presence of the disciplinary research community (Bazerman, 2012) as well as the authors' identities and voices, all engaged in an asynchronous conversation (Castelló & Iñesta, 2012; Castelló, in press; Castelló & Sala-Bubaré, in press).

This particular conversation requires a combination of other literacy-related abilities, such as reading at different levels and with different purposes, talking about writing and texts, and discussing when, how, and why to communicate authorial voice and intentions. Though the relative importance of each of these abilities varies, it is impossible to think about research writing without accompanying it with intense and concurrent reading and with discussion of content and processes.

I have also argued that the hybrid nature of research writing implies producing different types of texts, usually invisible to students but necessary to manage complex research genres such as articles, theses, or research reports. These texts are *transitional* since they help writers to transition, to make the move, for instance, from ideas to assertions, from data to graphics, or from protocols to explanations. They are not mere drafts, since they have a different textual formulation than the final text, and because of that, they require writers to transition among diverse formats, modes, and formulations. The process of transforming raw data into graphics or tables and writing appropriate explanatory text in research articles is a clear example of the importance of such transitional texts (Castelló et al., 2007; Castelló, in press).

From a socio-historical perspective, research writing can be understood both as a psychological *tool* and as an *activity* in and of itself (Castelló & Sala-Bubaré, in press). It is well documented that writing is a psychological tool that, in the words of Vygotsky, allows us to manage, alter, and improve our high-order thinking (Bazerman, 2012; Vygotsky, 1980). Writers learn about their research topic, the genre and themselves as they write (Bazerman, 2009). Thus, research writing is an epistemic tool for knowledge construction and transformation, both for individual writers and for the disciplinary field as a whole (Castelló & Iñesta, 2012). This epistemic power connects with one of the primary purposes of research writing, to advance our reasoning and understanding of a given topic as individuals and societies.

At the same time, texts are also tools for cultural communication, transmission, and evolution (Bazerman, 2008; 2009; Bazerman & Bonini, 2009), since they embody ways of knowing and being in situated (social, cultural, and historical) writing contexts (Barton et al., 2000; Castelló et al., 2013; Bazerman, 2012). Researchers inevitably participate in a wide range of communicative situations, mediated by myriad research genres, which in turn are built and constrained by discipline-specific and historically evolving practices, values, and knowledge. In the framework of these practices, the presence of research genres varies from one discipline to the next, with new genres often emerging in most of them.

Research genres have multiplied and diversified dramatically over the past few years, as research purposes have gradually shifted to meet new social challenges. Researchers have been compelled to reinterpret their work and the overall paradigm of scientific contribution, and to gradually move from producing *science for society* to doing *science with society*, the latter practice involving the forging of new understandings and complicities with different stakeholders and societal agents (European Commission, 2018; Plieninger et al., 2021). While traditional genres such as research articles, dissertations, and theses are still pervasive and valued in most disciplines, new genres are emerging to address changes in research purposes and practices. For example, researchers are finding ways to face the need for greater and broader dissemination (e.g., through outlets such as Twitter, TED-talks, etc.), to increase multimodal communication (e.g., digital grant applications or continuous online reporting) and to respond to the pressures of globalization (e.g., research blogs, self-pre-publishing, social researchers' platforms). We do not know yet how, and to what degree, these new genres are making an impact and displacing traditional genres.

Nonetheless, research articles and master's or Ph.D. theses and dissertations often remain the main—or indeed the only possible—gateway into research communities in most disciplines. Consequently, most of our research has focused on how (early career) researchers write (or learn to write) in those common genres. Moreover, our studies have often been predominantly limited to research writing in social sciences, especially the fields of psychology, nursing, education, ecology, and sport sciences. The evidence I discuss in the following sections comes from those disciplines, I am aware that "each discipline and specialty have specific forms of argument that are sensitive to the changing social and conceptual structure of the field, as well as to the way in which evidence is linked to the conceptual terms and calculated upon" (Bazerman, 2012, p. 265). Consequently, any attempt to apply these results elsewhere or to use them to interpret writing in other disciplinary contexts should be undertaken with caution.

LEARNING TO WRITE RESEARCH GENRES— ARTICLES AND THESES—IN SOCIAL SCIENCES

Writing articles and theses during master's or doctoral studies constitutes a particular writing practice for social science students who find themselves halfway between academic and professional disciplinary communities. As part of their academic activity, students are used to producing texts to be read mainly by professors and/or tutors. Articles and theses partially share such characteristics, even at the doctoral level, since they are required, read, and assessed within the academic community. However, students are also expected to write such texts as professionals, with the objective of being published and thus read by the corresponding research and professional community (Russell & Cortes, 2012). This dual purpose explains why we appoint them as *academic research texts*.

Academic research texts' characteristics are dynamic, and they evolve along with contextual academic demands and cultural changes. In recent years, doctoral programs have been transitioning from content to competency-based curricula, though they are not yet abandoning traditional outputs and practices. Thus, while in some disciplines (e.g., economics, psychology, and nursing) it is increasingly frequent for students to write article-based theses instead of the traditional monographs, in other disciplinary fields (e.g., history, law, and philosophy), only traditional theses and dissertations are expected (Frick, 2019). These differences in the final outputs entail other more or less explicit changes in practices and research conceptualizations; among them, doing research (and writing) collaboratively within research teams, presenting and writing up preliminary results and advances for conferences, and developing international stays to collaborate with researchers at other institutions, often writing with them too. As a result of all of this, writing demands have increased and diversified, but without a corresponding shift in the kinds of support and training that students are given (Paré, 2019).

In all these cases, doctoral or even master's students are asked to position as professional writers while they are still students. They have to (learn how to) communicate with other researchers even though they are not yet full members of the research community (Lave & Wenger, 1991), and they are forced to contend with sophisticated genres (research articles, conferences proceedings, and papers) that are not usually required or taught at the undergraduate level and are thus largely unfamiliar to them. Moreover, when students are asked to write with other more experienced researchers, supervisors often fail to consider these asymmetrical relations or to take into account students' peripheral positions in these collaborative writing situations. This is especially disadvantageous to students from so-called peripheral linguistic contexts who aim to publish in English (Bazerman et al., 2012; Corcoran, 2019; Corcoran & Englander, 2016).

These constraints add layers of difficulty to the intrinsically challenging activity of research writing. Studies have shown that students find it extremely arduous to learn to write in research genres, especially articles (Berkenkotter et al., 1988; Lea & Stierer, 2000; Li, 2019; Li & Flowerdew, 2020), and that they tend to experience affective and cognitive contradictions when they attempt to bridge the gap between their previous practices and perceptions as writers and these new and more complex writing demands (Camps & Castelló, 2013; Castelló et al., 2013).

The available research results on how these contradictions impact students' writing processes and products point to several intertwined challenges. The first one is students' lack of strategies to effectively manage these highly dynamic and recursive writing processes and the cognitive burden that comes with them in a sustained way over time (van den Bergh & Rijlaarsdam, 2007; van den Bergh et al., 2016). The second challenge relates to students' scarce knowledge (and sometimes even naivety) about what genre is and does (Bazerman, 1988; Bazerman & Prior, 2003), and about how discourses develop within disciplines (Bazerman, 2008; 2012). This latter challenge adds rhetorical and social issues to the cognitive burden involved with the former. Finally, research writing is one of the central tools that allows students to position themselves as researchers, and this, in turn, requires them to develop their own voices and authorial identities (Aitchison et al., 2012; Matsuda & Tardy, 2007; Nelson & Castelló, 2012; Tardy, 2012; Wisker, 2013; Wisker, 2015). These challenges affect the writing process as a whole, from the text ideation and organization to the word choice level, and impact students' cognitive, affective and identity development. Learning how to regulate thoughts, emotions, and actions when facing research writing is crucially necessary for students if they are to resolve the contradictions originating from such challenges.

CHARACTERIZING WRITING REGULATION PROCESSES: SELF-REGULATION, CO-REGULATION, AND SOCIALLY SHARED REGULATION

According to our research writing conceptualization, we have defined writing regulation as a complex, recursive, and socially situated activity that involves cyclical thought-action-emotion dynamics (Castelló et al., 2013; Sala-Bubaré et al., 2021). Moreover, writing regulation processes take place at all the textual levels (from word to disciplinary discourse-levels) and throughout the writing process. It consists of both explicit decision-making processes and implicit adjustments (Iñesta & Castelló, 2012), which can serve different purposes and functions. This definition is embedded in a dynamic and socially situated approach to self-regulation that has not been frequent in writing research, especially in Higher Education (Sala-Bubaré & Castelló, 2018). While researchers have acknowledged the relevance of self-regulation, most of the studies addressing the socially situated dimension of writing have focused on other issues. The complexities inherent in this conceptualization pose methodological challenges to researchers seeking a fuller understanding of *cyclical thought-action-emotion dynamics* and *writers' ability to monitor their activity at varying levels of explicitness* when writing complex, lengthy research genres in specific disciplines (Iñesta & Castelló, 2012).

The first challenge arises from the approach to writers' thoughts and the actions they implement, which here cannot simply be categorized as "correct" or "incorrect," but must be viewed as more or less strategic or suitable to the writer's established goals. Such a perspective inevitably calls for a more carefully hedged and contextual analysis (Iñesta & Castelló, 2012; Castelló, 2002; Flowerdew & Wang, 2015).

The second challenge has to do with how we can understand and assess the writing process as a whole, from text ideation or planning and goal-setting to revising and sharing final products. The question, in other words, is how to analyze the processes responsible for the transition from thoughts (perceptions about writing, genres and strategies) to action. To unpack how this transition unfolds, we need to study writers-in-context and texts-as-artifacts of activity (Castelló, in press).

The third challenge derives from the conceptualization of dialogue as inherent to research writing. As mentioned above, this dialogue involves not only the writer(s) and the reader, but others' voices that are invoked in the minds of writer(s) such as those of colleagues, supervisors, or reviewers, among others (Prior, 2001). Accordingly, we need to identify those voices and examine their interplay with writers' writing processes in order to understand the extent to which writing regulation may be socially based (Castelló et al., 2010).

The last challenge refers to writers' development and appropriation of social, cultural, and historical practices associated with research writing (Bazerman & Prior, 2003). Examining this appropriation process requires clarifying the role of the individual and social dimensions of regulation. It is well-known that novice community members learn how to write and regulate their composition processes by participating in genuine discursive social practices. This participation is scaffolded by more advanced researchers, usually in a supervisory role, with the final aim of facilitating new researchers' appropriation of these tools, so that they will be able to use them autonomously and independently (Englert et al., 2006; Castelló et al., 2010). Through this *co-regulated activity*, supervisors and reviewers play an essential and indispensable role in the regulation process, as they offer new researchers different kinds of expertise and share the responsibility for their development (Järvelä et al., 2013; Hadwin et al., 2010).

Moreover, in collaborative professional writing scenarios, regulation is *socially shared* among all the voices that intervene at a certain level in text ideation, production, and publication (Castelló et al., 2010). Socially shared regulation is a collective regulatory activity, wherein processes and products are distributed throughout the group, and at the same time are the responsibility of each one of the individual subjects that make up the group. Research carried out from this perspective seeks to analyze both the shared regulation processes executed by a group and the self-regulation processes that the group members use to regulate other members or the group as a whole (Malmberg et al., 2017; Hadwin et al., 2017). Understanding the dynamics of socially-shared regulation, co-regulation, and self-regulation also means analyzing the interplay between individuals' positioning within the group—or disciplinary community—and their personal thoughts and actions in a particular writing situation.

Studies on writing regulation in higher education have increased in number and expanded in scope over the last twenty years (Sala-Bubaré & Castelló, 2018).

These studies mostly look at writers' activity through retrospective self-reports or text analysis, either separately or simultaneously. Researchers rarely observe online writing processes and their unfolding to understand how writers overcome challenges and difficulties that arise during writing and regulate their activity. In the few studies that have collected data on online processes, activity contexts are altered and participants write in controlled experimental conditions, in which the texts' length, purposes and rhetorical complexity are usually reduced. Other studies that do preserve activity contexts and genre complexity tend to rely on discursive data and writers' representations.

Each research writing situation (e.g., writing a scientific article) has its own history and it is situated within a particular constellation of contextual conditions that are both individual and disciplinary in nature, as Bazerman has astutely highlighted (1988; 2012; Bazerman & Prior, 2003). Consequently, any analysis should be anchored in these specific writing situations if it is to approach writing regulation as it truly develops.

STUDYING WRITING REGULATION FROM A SITUATED PERSPECTIVE: CONCEPTUAL AND METHODOLOGICAL ISSUES

Our team attempts to address the above-mentioned challenges in the study of writing regulation processes, with the aim of combining the analysis of writers' activity and their text development in communicative ecological situations in a range of contexts (Sala-Bubaré & Castelló, 2018; Iñesta & Castelló, 2012). Moreover, in line with current approaches on self-regulated learning that argue in favor of going beyond the analysis of isolated actions (Hadwin et al., 2017), we strive to identify the patterns in which actions are organized and given a situated meaning. To this end, we have tried to design our studies according to certain shared premises.

First, we adopt the notion of episodes—integrated by purposely in-context activities—as an alternative unit of analysis (Iñesta & Castelló, 2012; Castelló et al., 2013; Sala-Bubare et al., 2021), since we are interested in understanding the interplay between texts' development and writers' activity. This approach involves collecting and analyzing data simultaneously about what writers feel, do, and think (practices and conceptions) in an attempt to look at both the cognitive aspects and the social nature of writing. Second, we look for designs that guarantee individual interpretations and actions are not studied in isolation from the ecological conditions where they originate and within which they have meaning. Thus, we try to ensure that these designs combine qualitative and quantitative data in order to comprehensively integrate different analyses (of the social, textual, interactive, cognitive, and affective spheres). Finally, in light of the developmental nature of writing (Bazerman, 2013), and specifically its contribution to researcher development (Castelló, in press), whenever possible we have prioritized longitudinal designs in order to further our understanding of how research and writing conceptions, as well as practices and texts, intertwine and contribute to this development.

Awareness, Emotions and Stance (voice), Critical Components of Writing Regulation

Our earliest attempts to study writing regulation from a situated perspective took the form of two studies focusing on how doctoral students overcome difficulties when writing their theses (Castelló et al., 2009; Castelló et al., 2010). As in the other studies I refer to below, master's and Ph.D. students participated in a writing seminar that I designed and have been carrying out with other colleagues for more than fifteen years now. The writing seminar is peer review-based and encourages students to use drafts and intermediate texts as tools to drive co-regulation practice over a semester (Castelló, in press; Castelló et al., 2013). In our earliest studies, we collected data from individual interviews, writing diaries, and in-class pair discussion. These data provided information about the doctoral students' knowledge and conceptions about writing a thesis, as well as about their writing processes and their emotions. We also traced their writing activity by looking at series of drafts and revision strategies. Finally, we assessed the quality of the final text. The results showed text quality increased when students were able to explicitly associate their difficulties with specific problem-solving strategies. Notably, we observed that students' awareness of their writing processes correlated with their efforts to make their voices visible in their texts through the more or less strategic use of discursive mechanisms aimed at increasing authorial positioning and readers' engagement (Guinda & Hyland, 2012; Matsuda & Tardy, 2007). Moreover, those students who were more aware of their processes and difficulties tended to revise their texts at the structural and voice level. On the contrary, students that were less able to identify challenges and difficulties and were less aware of how these challenges interfered with their writing processes tended to revise their texts on a more superficial (lexical and grammatical) level. Those students who were less aware of their writing processes and strategies felt more anxious during that process.

From my perspective, the most relevant contribution of these first studies is they provided evidence regarding how co-regulation precedes—and in some cases is a precondition—for writers' self-regulation (Castelló et al., 2010). Peer discussion allowed writers to notice problems both in their texts and their writing conceptions, issues that in many cases had not been visible when revising their texts individually, nor even when reading peer reviews. As others also noted (Rogers, 2008; Negretti & Mežek, 2019), it was through interaction, when students in their reviewer role had to justify their comments, that writers were able to appropriate reviewers' suggestions. Even though in some cases they initially might not fully agree with those comments, when they reviewed their texts consistently and put the suggested strategies into action, they tended to realize that peer-review based discussions were key for them to understand the reasons underlying text improvement and that these interactions made writing self-regulation possible. This evidence challenges the naive idea of writing self- and co-regulation development as resulting from a unidirectional process of internalization, thus, in Bazerman's words *"creating a loop of individual and group development"* as I discuss in the final section of this chapter (2012).

A second contribution has to do with the methodological attempt to relate writing conceptions, perceived challenges or difficulties, and writing and revision strategies, which was the precursor of the regulation episodes notion we adopted later. We tried to perform a combined analysis of challenges and strategies used by particular groups of writers. Yet, in those studies, both challenges and strategies were treated as independent units of analysis, and our analysis of writers was not person-centered, but variable-centered. Moreover, except for looking at the evolution of drafts, we did not have any access to the online writing processes but relied instead on writers' retrospective reports and interactive draft-based discussions.

Writing Regulation as a Two-Layered System

The second study I want to refer to focused on how writing regulation occurs in real time (Castelló & Iñesta, 2012). We followed two expert writers while they produced an article in their field, educational psychology. Unlike the previous studies, in this case we combined the analysis of what the writers had planned and expected to do with what they actually did, the unfolding writing activity, through screen recordings of all the writing sessions until they finished the article, and for the first time we included the regulation episode as an integrated unit of analysis.

The analysis of these video-recorded actions revealed evidence of the explicit challenges identified by writers and the subsequent actions they took to solve each of those particular challenges. These sequences of actions were consistent with our definition of writing regulation episodes as both intentional and conscious. However, we also identified sequences of actions, which were aimed at reformulating or adjusting the written text, thus showing an intention to address a challenge, despite writers not making any explicit reference to it in the interviews or writing logs they completed during the writing process. We labeled such sequences of actions Implicit Regulation Episodes (IREs).

Consequently, we argue that writing regulation from a sociocultural perspective might be conceived as a two-layered system, with each level representing different types of episodes accounting for some particularities of the writing regulation activity dynamics. These two types of episodes differ mainly in their level of explicitness. Whereas in some cases writers mentioned facing more or less specific challenges and were aware of how they tried to solve them, in other situations they were not so conscious of this process. In those latter situations, recordings of their writing processes offered evidence of regulatory activity, yet this activity was implicit. This evidence of implicit regulation indicates that writers, especially those with extensive experience, might use some regulation strategies and mechanisms to adjust texts to disciplinary and research communities' ways of thinking without even being aware of them. Moreover, this implicit regulation seems to affect more local textual challenges (e.g., hedging sentences), whereas the explicit regulation episodes tend to address broader issues (e.g., organizing sections) (Castelló & Iñesta, 2012).

A second distinction between these two types of episodes relates to the significance of the time dimension in the dynamics of writing regulation activity. Our results revealed a morphological difference in both implicit and explicit types of regulation. In some regulation episodes, the challenge and the solutions are cited and implemented in the same writing session. We called these continuous regulation episodes. Meanwhile, discontinuous regulation episodes were those where the challenge and the solutions are cited and implemented over the course of multiple writing sessions.

Looking at these continuous and discontinuous episodes offers some new insight on the recursive nature of regulation. Even in the case of continuous regulation episodes, writers appear to implement actions associated with a particular intentionality at different times during the same writing session. Moreover, the interplay of continuous and discontinuous episodes also accounts for the writers' sustained efforts to fit their representation of the communicative situation with the evolving text during the writing activity, and how this representation is reviewed and recreated through time, specifically when dealing with complex texts such as scientific articles (Iñesta & Castelló, 2012).

CONTRADICTIONS AS DRIVERS OF WRITING REGULATION LEARNING

A major concern regarding researcher writing development is how to promote students' writing regulation, or in other words how to provide educational guidelines to help students and early career researchers appropriate the knowledge and strategies that more experienced researchers implicitly or explicitly display when writing complex texts. We have addressed this concern in two studies of Ph.D. students writing their first article. The students participated in a seminar, similar to the one described above, intended to help them to deal with this new genre (Castelló et al., 2013; Sala-Bubaré et al., 2021). One of these studies focused on identifying and explaining the contradictions students had to confront when writing and the efforts to connect such contradictions with their attempted solutions. As in the previous study, we brought together data concerning what writers thought and did in real time and under natural conditions, and we used regulation episodes as a comprehensive unit of analysis.

A significant contribution from this study is related to our understanding of how, when, and why certain regulation episodes affect texts and writers' development. Doctoral students reported feeling challenged when trying to manage the writing process without reducing its complexity, and when attempting to cope with genre uncertainty, specifically with their limited knowledge of article constraints and affordances. Those challenges were overcome via regulation episodes aimed at redefining the output, considering the text a tool to think instead of looking for a perfect final product. Only when students appropriated these regulation strategies and consistently modified their thoughts about the texts they were writing and research genres were they able to make substantial changes to their drafts and increase the quality of their final texts. We have evidence of how this appropriation is socially driven, again thanks to the socially shared-regulation practices wherein students acting as reviewers suggested strategies that they had been unable to generate by themselves previously when acting as writers and that through in-class discussions are further refined and transformed into authorial decisions (Castelló et al., 2013; Castelló, 2021).

Students felt also challenged due to their perception of themselves as on the periphery of the disciplinary community. They considered themselves outsiders or even impostors when trying to write an article as other consolidated researchers, who they referred to as "real researchers," would. These feelings and thoughts often remain implicit and regulating them appears difficult since this regulatory activity not only affects writing, but also has implications for other actions related to researcher development such as networking, publishing, and attending conferences.

The second study I want to refer to in this section features a methodological innovation aimed at complementing the previous analysis. We introduced the use of keystroke logging to achieve a more fine-grained micro-analysis of writing regulation processes (Sala-Bubaré et al., 2021). Though exploratory, the study may shed light on the socially-shared nature of writing regulation processes and how to address this social aspect empirically. Specifically, data revealed variations in writing processes after participants had received peer and expert feedback. These changes had to do with moving away from writing exclusively with the goal of text progression and toward much more problem-solving oriented writing, an approach that focuses more on strategic decisions in relation to anticipated problems and challenges. Before receiving feedback and thus before discussing the text, the student's writing showed a linear, text-driven path aimed at producing text heavily based on sources, mainly previous texts. After feedback, besides producing text, the focus was also on adjusting the text's progression to meet expectations and resolve issues raised by reviewers; thus, writing regulation processes increased. As other studies have highlighted, regulation takes place at all the textual levels and throughout each writing session (Castelló & Iñesta, 2012; Hadwin et al., 2010; van den Bergh et al., 2016). Despite individual variations related to topic and genre knowledge, what can be inferred from this case study is that once most of the text had been produced and reflective work could start, feedback acted to trigger more strategic, flexible regulation processes, promoting knowledge-transforming approaches.

Additionally, our data hint at a relationship between regulation processes and participants' positions as researchers, understood as an individual's attributes and conceptions about research (which may also be visible in the text through the writer's voice) and as the place the individual occupies in relation to other researchers, research groups and communities (Lave & Wenger, 1991; Kamler, 2008; Prior & Bilbro, 2012; Morton & Storch, 2019). That relationship can be traced when connecting students' perceived strengths and weaknesses as writers with their writing regulation processes. It appears that the less secure they feel about research writing, the more they rely on the sources and feedback, and the more likely they are to have trouble entering into a dialogue with other authors' voices and with readers. Thus, their voices are less apparent in their texts. These issues were present in writers' interactions with their peers' voices as they gave and received feedback, and these socially shared instances of writing regulation had a significant impact on their texts (Sala-Bubaré et al., 2021). These preliminary insights may be corroborated or contradicted in future studies with a larger number of participants with diverse profiles and characteristics.

FINAL REMARKS: LESSONS LEARNED AS TEACHERS

So although internalized thought and self-regulation may follow the Vygotskian path of intermental to intramental, the consequent path of

> expression is from intramental to intermental—creating a loop of individual and group development.
>
> —Charles Bazerman (2012)

In this chapter, I have argued that a sociocultural writing regulation approach is crucial for early career researchers to develop as writers and researchers, I have examined the conceptual and methodological challenges of this approach, and I have discussed some of our team's attempts to address them. This last section is devoted to reflecting on how lessons learned from research enlighten us as teachers as we develop educational proposals and guidelines that effectively contribute to early-career researchers' abilities to strategically regulate their emotions, knowledge and actions when writing and, ultimately, to develop as writers and researchers.

The statement heading this section is one of the drivers of this reflection since it inspired my research on writing regulation. According to Bazerman, research writing self-regulation may result from the internalization of thoughts and strategies that developed writers share with early career researchers, who are usually less developed writers. In these joint writing endeavors, co-regulation happens, tacit or explicitly, and personal development follows the path from intermental to intramental. Consistent with this path, Rogoff's notion of apprenticeship (1995) has been used to describe how, through this supervisory relationship and a one-to-one educational model, doctoral or master's students usually come to understand what research writing is and how it works. Supervisory dialogue helps students adopt disciplinary ways of producing knowledge and engage with the process of research writing (Dysthe, 2002, p. 499) through instances of co-regulation (Negretti & Mežek, 2019). While this model might explain some aspects of personal writing development, it does not account for early career researchers' socialization in their communities as writers and researchers, much less consider the potential of those newcomers to modify these communities through their texts and discourses. How writers put into action—that is, externalize—their skills and knowledge in specific challenging communicative situations is still unclear. As Bazerman claimed, "if the internalized concept has serious developmental consequences and interacts with other functional systems (i.e., structures of concepts, affects, and mental practices mobilized in addressing problems or challenges—or what might be called purposive structures of thoughts and feelings), it will likely be substantially transformed as it reemerges" (2012; p. 268). Such transformation, thus, follows an opposite direction of internalization processes, as it depends on the linguistic and conceptual development of the self and its positioning in a particular system of activity and communicative situation. When referring to writing regulation, we should account for decisions regarding linguistic, epistemic, and rhetoric choices and their articulation in a particular text are driven by writers intramental activity, fully aware of—and sensitive to—the characteristics, requirements, and constraints of their intermental landscape.

When it comes to research writing, the landscape is rapidly changing. Current concerns on doctoral education tend to focus on how to prepare the next generation of researchers so that they are able to conduct research in an ethical, responsible way that crosses disciplinary, national, and cultural boundaries, and to deal with relevant societal challenges. In the last ten years, the number of Ph.D. graduates working outside academia across different sectors and contexts has been increasing. In light of this, further questions have been raised as to whether present research education is effectively preparing graduates to truly enact science not only *for* but also *within* society. This generation of researchers will not only have to learn how to communicate their research; they will also need professional competencies to communicate with other professionals, disseminate their findings and convince funders. This wide range of communication competencies are necessary in the context of increasing diversity of genres and voices on multinational teams and in global settings (McAlpine et al., 2020; McAlpine et al., 2021; McAlpine & Castelló, in press).

Alternatives to the apprenticeship model have been proposed as additional ways of promoting early career researchers' appropriation of the aforementioned sophisticated researcher competencies and their writing development in socially situated settings. These models, anchored in the notions of community of practice and transformative learning (Castelló et al., 2013; Camps & Castelló, 2013), better account for the loop—in Bazerman's terms—of interpersonal and community or group development that characterizes researcher development. These teaching methods foster guided participation as a way of learning to write and publish in real-world conditions, while encouraging newcomers to adopt community and disciplinary tools and practices as they gradually take their own places within these communities.

Educational proposals based on these premises aim at promoting personal, interpersonal, and community writing development (Rogoff, 1995) while, in turn, requiring explicit efforts to navigate the social dimension of writing. Such an approach assumes that research texts are populated by several voices, even when they are written by a single author. In this context, it is critical that early career researchers confront authentic research writing situations in all their complexity. When it comes to research writing, as in other complex learning situations, the whole is more than the sum of its parts, and thus, simplifying writing situations as a pedagogical strategy to address novice writers' troubles might not be a good option (e.g., Castelló & Iñesta, 2012; Castelló et al., 2010; Castelló et al., 2013; Sala-Bubaré & Castelló, 2017; 2018).

From my perspective, fostering the development of strategic thinking when writing is one of the best ways to help students to deal with the complexity of research writing. Thus, I believe it is not only a matter of increasing students' knowledge about research writing, disciplinary content, and genre. What is relevant to learn is the interrelation of when, how, and why certain specific actions should be taken during the writing process, and how they contribute to the text and the writer's development. This is what writing regulation is about. Some key aspects of this regulation may be addressed by expert writers in an implicit way while affecting text production both at the macro (structural) and micro (local) levels, since it seems a huge amount of craftsmanship is involved in strategic text tailoring, though that craftsmanship usually remains invisible to the eyes of those who, like student researchers, would very much benefit from accessing and learning from it.

Finally, I would maintain that identity might be a useful articulating construct with the potential to address both individual and social issues and to promote individuals' harmonic development (Castelló & Iñesta, 2012; Castello et al., 2013). Though amorphous and elusive, the concept of identity has become central to the fields of writing development and researcher development in the last decade (Castelló et al., 2021). It is not currently possible—and perhaps not even appropriate—to provide a single, overarching definition of identity, considering the wide range of theoretical underpinnings characterizing research on identity. For educational purposes, the notion of identity trajectories might help to adjust guidelines and scaffolds to early career researchers' purposes, thoughts, and practices over time (past, present, and future) and to variations in writers' position in each researcher community. Moreover, considering that researchers have different positions of the self, according to the spheres of activity in which they act, educational proposals should adjust to how texts are used and mediate researchers' activity in each of these spheres (e.g., as teachers, as editors). Thus, we should help students to understand texts as artifacts-in-activity that evolve as they evolve as research writers and researchers. A scientific article is understood differently depending on whether the writer is using it as part of his or her thesis defense or is publishing it after graduating.

We still need to invest more research efforts in clarifying how reflection about authorial voice and the intentional use of mechanisms for constructing author identity through writing contribute to writing development. Still, I believe it might be a promising way to overcome some of the recurrent challenges students and early career researchers experience as they develop as research writers. Future research should also probably look at technologies and writing modalities throughout the lifespan and how they influence trajectories. Again, Bazerman is showing us the way forward for studies of writers' development: "How they are developing as writers is closely tied to how they are developing as people" (2019).

REFERENCES

Aitchison, C., Catterall, J., Ross, P. & Burgin, S. (2012). "Tough love and tears": Learning doctoral writing in the sciences. *Higher Education Research & Development*, *31*(4), 435–447.

Allal, L. (2020). Assessment and the co-regulation of learning in the classroom. *Assessment in Education: Principles, Policy & Practice*, *27*(4), 332–349. https://doi.org/10.1080/0969594X.2019.1609411.

Bakhtin, M. (1986). Speech genres and other late essays (V. W. McGee, Trans.; C. Emerson & M. Holquist, Eds.). University of Texas Press.

Barton, D., Hamilton, M. & Ivanič, R. (2000). *Situated literacies: Reading and writing in context*. Psychology Press.

Bazerman, C. (1988). *Shaping written knowledge: The genre and activity of the experimental article in science, 356*. University of Wisconsin Press.

Bazerman, C. (Ed.). (2008). Handbook of research on writing: History, society, school, individual, text. In *Handbook of research on writing: History, society, school, individual, text* (pp. xvii, 652). Taylor & Francis Group/Lawrence Erlbaum Associates.

Bazerman, C. (2009). Genre and cognitive development: Beyond writing to learn. *Pratiques. Linguistique, Littérature, Didactique*, *143–144*, 127–138. https://doi.org/10.4000/pratiques.1419.

Bazerman, C. (2012). *Writing with Concepts: Communal, Internalized, and Externalized. Mind, Culture, and Activity*, *19*(3), 259–272. https://doi.org/10.1080/10749039.2012.688231.

Bazerman, C. (2013). Understanding the lifelong journey of writing development. *Infancia y aprendizaje*, *36*(4), 421–441. https://doi.org/10.1174/021037013808200320.

Bazerman, C. (2019). Lives of Writing. *Writing and Pedagogy*, *10*(3), 327–331. https://doi.org/10.1558/wap.37066.

Bazerman, C. & Prior, P. (Eds.). (2003). Introduction. In *What writing does and how it does it: An introduction to analyzing texts and textual practices* (pp. 1–10). Routledge. https://doi.org/10.4324/9781410609526.

Bazerman, C., Bonini, A. & Figueiredo, D. (Eds.). (2009). *Genre in a changing world*. The WAC Clearinghouse; Parlor Press. https://doi.org/10.37514/PER-B.2009.2324.

Bazerman, C., Keranen, N. & Prudencio, F. (2012). Facilitated immersion at a distance in second language scientific writing. In M. Castelló & C. Donahue (Eds.), *University writing: Selves and texts in academic societies* (pp. 235–248). Brill Academic Publishers.

Berkenkotter, C., Huckin, T. N. & Ackerman, J. (1988). Conventions, Conversations, and the Writer: Case Study of a Student in a Rhetoric Ph.D. Program. *Research in the Teaching of English*, *22*(1), 9–44. http://www.jstor.org/stable/40171130.

Camps, A. & Castelló, M. (2013). La escritura académica en la universidad. *REDU. Revista de Docencia Universitaria*, *11*(1), 17–36 https://polipapers.upv.es/index.php/REDU/article/view/5590.

Camps, A. & Fontich, X. (2020). *Research and teaching at the intersection: Navigating the territory of grammar and writing in the context of metalinguistic activity*. PIE-Peter Lang SA Éditions Scientifiques Internationales.

Castelló, M & Iñesta, A. (2012). Texts as Artifacts-in-Activity: Developing Authorial Identity and Academic Voice in Writing Academic Research Papers [Special issue]. In M. Castelló & C. Donahue (Eds.), *University Writing: Selves and Texts in Academic Societies, Studies in Writing, 24* (pp. 179–200). Brill Academic Publishers.

Castelló, M. (2002). De la investigación sobre el proceso de composición a la enseñanza de la escritura. *Revista Signos, 35*(51–52), 149–162. https://doi.org/10.4067/S0718-09342002005100011.

Castelló, M. (Coord.); Iñesta, A., Miras, M., Solé, I., Teberosky, A., Zanotto, M. (2007). *Escribir y comunicarse en contextos científicos y académicos. Conocimientos y estrategias.* Graó

Castelló, M. (2022). Research writing, what do we know and how to move forward. In M. Gustafsson & A. Eriksson (Eds.), *Negotiating the intersections of writing and writing instruction* (pp. 89–122). The WAC Clearinghouse; University Press of Colorado. https://doi.org/10.37514/INT-B.2022.1466.2.04.

Castelló, M. & Sala-Bubaré, A. (in press). Research writing as a tool for doctoral students and early career researchers' development. In R. Horowitz (Ed.). *Handbook on Writing*. Routledge.

Castelló, M., Bañales Faz, G. & Vega López, N. A. (2010). Research approaches to the regulation of academic writing: The state of the question. *Electronic Journal of Research in Educational Psychology, 8(3)*, 1253–1282. 2010 (nº 22). http://repositorio.ual.es/bitstream/handle/10835/919/Art_22_474_spa.pdf?sequence=2.

Castelló, M., González, D. & Iñesta, A. (2010). Doctoral students' writing regulation: The impact of socially-shared revision in academic texts | La regulación de la escritura académica en el doctorado: El impacto de la revisión colaborativa en los textos. *Revista Espanola de Pedagogia, 68*(247).

Castello, M., Iñesta, A. & Corcelles, M. (2013). Learning to Write a Research Article: Ph.D. Students' Transitions toward Disciplinary Writing Regulation. *Research in the Teaching of English, 47*(4), 442–478.

Castelló, M., Iñesta, A. & Monereo, C. (2009). Towards self-regulated academic writing: An exploratory study with graduate students in a situated learning environment. *Electronic Journal of Research in Educational Psychology, 7*(3).

Castelló, M., McAlpine, L., Sala-Bubaré, A., Inouye, K. & Skakni, I. (2021). What perspectives underlie 'researcher identity'? A review of two decades of empirical studies. *Higher Education, 81*(3), 567–590. https://doi.org/10.1007/s10734-020-00557-8.

Corcoran, J. (2019). Addressing the "Bias Gap": A Research-Driven Argument for Critical Support of Plurilingual Scientists' Research Writing. *Written Communication, 36*(4), 538–577. https://doi.org/10.1177/0741088319861648.

Corcoran, J. & Englander, K. (2016). A Proposal for Critical-Pragmatic Pedagogical Approaches to English for Research Publication Purposes. *Publications, 4*(1). https://doi.org/10.3390/publications4010006.

Dysthe, O. (2002). Professors as Mediators of Academic Text Cultures: An Interview Study with Advisors and Master's Degree Students in Three Disciplines in a Norwegian University. *Written Communication, 19*(4), 493–544. https://doi.org/10.1177/074108802238010.

Englert, C. S., Mariage, T. V. & Dunsmore, K. (2006). Tenets of Sociocultural Theory in Writing Instruction Research. In C. MacArthur, S. Graham & J. Fitzgerald (Eds.), *Handbook of writing research* (pp. 208–221). The Guilford Press.

European Commission. (2018). Science with and for Society | Horizon 2020. In *Horizon 2020*. https://doi.org/10.2777/32018.

Flowerdew, J. & Wang, S. H. (2015). Identity in academic discourse. *Annual Review of Applied Linguistics, 35,* 81–99. https://doi.org/10.1017/S026719051400021X.

Freedman, A. & Medway, P. (1994). Introduction: New Views of Genre and Their Implications for Education. *Learning and Teaching Genre,* 1–22.

Frick, L. (2019). PhD by publication-panacea or paralysis? *Africa Education Review, 16*(5), 47–59.

Guinda, C. S. & Hyland, K. (2012). Introduction: A Context-Sensitive Approach to Stance and Voice. *Stance and Voice in Written Academic Genres,* 1–11. Palgrave Macmillan UK. https://doi.org/10.1057/9781137030825_1.

Hadwin, A. F., Oshige, M., Gress, C. L. Z. & Winne, P. H. (2010). Innovative ways for using Study to orchestrate and research social aspects of self-regulated learning. *Computers in Human Behavior, 26*(5), 794–805. https://doi.org/10.1016/j.chb.2007.06.007.

Hadwin, A. F., Järvelä, S. & Miller, M. (2017). Self-regulation, co-regulation, and shared regulation in collaborative learning environments. In D. H. Schunk & J. A. Greene (Eds.), *Handbook of Self-Regulation of Learning and Performance* (pp. 127–136). Routledge Taylor & Francis Group. https://doi.org/10.4324/9781315697048.

Hermans, H. J. M. (2001). The Dialogical Self: Toward a Theory of Personal and Cultural Positioning. *Culture & Psychology, 7*(3), 243–281. https://doi.org/10.1177/1354067X0173001.

Hyland, K. (2002). Authority and invisibility: Authorial identity in academic writing. *Journal of Pragmatics, 34*(8), 1091–1112. https://doi.org/10.1016/S0378-2166(02)00035-8.

Iñesta, A. & Castelló, M. (2012). Towards an integrative unit of analysis: Regulation episodes in expert research article writing. In C. Bazerman, C. Dean, J. Early, K. Lunsford, S. Null, P. Rogers & A. Stansell (Eds.), *International advances in writing research: Cultures, places and measures* (pp. 421–448). The WAC Clearinghouse; Parlor Press. https://doi.org/10.37514/PER-B.2012.0452.2.24.

Ivanič, R. (1998). *Writing and identity: The discoursal construction of identity in academic writing.* John Benjamins.

Järvelä, S., Järvenoja, H., Malmberg, J. & Hadwin, A. F. (2013). Exploring Socially Shared Regulation in the Context of Collaboration. *Journal of Cognitive Education and Psychology, 12*(3), 267–286. https://doi.org/10.1891/1945-8959.12.3.267.

Kamler, B. (2008). Rethinking doctoral publication practices: Writing from and beyond the thesis. *Studies in Higher Education, 33*(3), 283–294. https://doi.org/10.1080/03075070802049236.

Lave, J. & Wenger, E. (1991). Situated Learning: Legitimate Peripheral Participation. *Learning in Doing: Social, Cognitive and Computational Perspectives*. Cambridge University Press. https://doi.org/10.1017/CBO9780511815355.

Lea, M. & Stierer, B. (2000). *Student Writing in Higher Education: New Contexts*. Open University Press / Society for Research into Higher Education. http://oro.open.ac.uk/21798/.

Li, Y. (2019). Mentoring Junior Scientists for Research Publication. In P. Habibie & K. Hyland (Eds.), *Novice Writers and Scholarly Publication* (pp. 233–250). Palgrave Macmillan UK. https://doi.org/10.1007/978-3-319-95333-5_13.

Li, Y. & Flowerdew, J. (2020). Teaching English for Research Publication Purposes (ERPP): A review of language teachers' pedagogical initiatives. *English for Specific Purposes, 59*, 29–41. https://doi.org/10.1016/j.esp.2020.03.002.

Malmberg, J., Järvelä, S. & Järvenoja, H. (2017). Capturing temporal and sequential patterns of self-, co-, and socially shared regulation in the context of collaborative learning. *Contemporary Educational Psychology, 49*, 160–174.

Matsuda, P. K. & Tardy, C. M. (2007). Voice in academic writing: The rhetorical construction of author identity in blind manuscript review. *English for Specific Purposes, 26*(2), 235–249. https://doi.org/10.1016/j.esp.2006.10.001.

McAlpine, L. & Castelló, M. (submitted). What do PhD graduates in non-traditional careers actually do? Exploring the role of communication and research. *European Journal of Higher Education*.

McAlpine, L., Castello, M. & Pyhaltö, K. (2020). What influences PhD graduate trajectories during the degree: A research-based policy agenda. *Higher Education*. https://doi.org/10.1007/s10734-019-00448-7.

McAlpine, L., Skakni, I. & Inouye, K. (2021). PhD careers beyond the traditional: Integrating individual and structural factors for a richer account. *European Journal of Higher Education*, 1–21. https://doi.org/10.1080/21568235.2020.1870242.

Morton, J. & Storch, N. (2019). Developing an authorial voice in PhD multilingual student writing: The reader's perspective. *Journal of Second Language Writing, 43*, 15–23. https://doi.org/10.1016/j.jslw.2018.02.004.

Negretti, R. & Mežek, Š. (2019). Participatory appropriation as a pathway to self-regulation in academic writing: The case of three BA essay writers in literature. *The Journal of Writing Research, 11*(1), 1–40. https://doi.org/10.17239/jowr-2019.11.01.01.

Nelson, N. & Castelló, M. (2012). Academic writing and authorial voice. In M. Castelló & C. Donahue (Eds.), *University Writing: Selves and Texts in Academic Societies, Studies in Writing, 24*, (pp. 33–51). Emerald Group Publishing Limited.

Paré, A. (2019). Re-writing the doctorate: New contexts, identities, and genres. *Journal of Second Language Writing, 43*, 80–84. https://doi.org/10.1016/j.jslw.2018.08.004.

Plieninger, T., Fagerholm, N. & Bieling, C. (2021). How to run a sustainability science research group sustainably? *Sustainability Science, 16*(1), 321–328. https://doi.org/10.1007/s11625-020-00857-z.

Prior, P. (2001). Voices in text, mind, and society: Sociohistoric accounts of discourse acquisition and use. *Journal of Second Language Writing, 10*, 55–81.

Prior, P. & Bilbro, R. (2012). Academic Enculturation: Developing Literate Practices and Disciplinary Identities. In M. Castelló & C. Donahue (Ed.), *University Writing Selves and Texts in Academic Societies Studies in Writing, 24* (pp. 19–31).

Rogers, P. M. (2008). *The development of writers and writing abilities: A longitudinal study across and beyond the college-span* (Publication No. 3319795) [Doctoral dissertation, University of California, Santa Barbara]. ProQuest Dissertations and Theses.

Rogoff, B. (1995). Observing sociocultural activity on three planes: Participatory appropriation, guided participation, and apprenticeship. In J. Wertsch, P. del Rio & A. Alvarez (Eds.), *Sociocultural Studies of Mind*. Cambridge University Press.

Russell, D. R. & Cortes, V. (2012). Academic and scientific texts: The same or different communities. In M. Castelló & C. Donahue (Eds.), *University writing. Selves and texts in academic societies* (pp. 3–18). Brill Academic Publishers. https://doi.org/10.1163/9781780523873_002.

Sala-Bubaré A., Castelló, M. & Rijlaarsdam, G. (2021). Writing processes as situated regulation processes: A context-based approach to doctoral writing. *Journal of Writing Research, 13*(1), 1–30. https://doi.org/10.17239/jowr-2021.13.01.01.

Sala-Bubaré, A. & Castelló, M. (2017). Exploring the relationship between doctoral students' experiences and research community positioning. *Studies in Continuing Education, 39*(1), 16–34. https://doi.org/10.1080/0158037X.2016.1216832.

Sala-Bubaré, A. & Castelló, M. (2018). Writing regulation processes in higher education: A review of two decades of empirical research. *Reading and Writing, 31*(4), 757–777. https://doi.org/10.1007/s11145-017-9808-3.

Tardy, C. M. (2012). Current Conceptions of Voice. In K. Hyland & C. S. Guinda (Eds.), *Stance and Voice in Written Academic Genres* (pp. 34–48). Palgrave Macmillan UK. https://doi.org/10.1057/9781137030825_3.

Van den Bergh, H. & Rijlaarsdam, G. (2007). Chapter 9: The Dynamics of Idea Generation During Writing: An Online Study. In M. Torrance, L. van Waes & D. Galbraith (Eds.), *Writing and Cognition: Research and Applications* (pp. 125–150). Brill. https://doi.org/10.1163/9781849508223_010.

Van den Bergh, H., Rijlaarsdam, G. & van Steendam, E. (2016). Writing process theory: A functional dynamic approach. In *Handbook of writing research* (2nd ed.; pp. 57–71). The Guilford Press.

Vygotsky, L. S. (1980). *Mind in society: The development of higher psychological processes*. Harvard University Press.

Wisker, G. (2013). Articulate—academic writing, refereeing editing and publishing our work in learning, teaching and educational development. *Innovations in Education and Teaching International, 50*(4), 344–356. http://www.scopus.com/inward/record.url?eid=2-s2.0-84886419987&partnerID=40&md5=54bf0694d03122b6adf922bf625e6be3.

Wisker, Gina. (2015). Developing doctoral authors: Engaging with theoretical perspectives through the literature review. *Innovations in Education and Teaching International, 52*(1), 64–74.

PART TWO. WRITING PEDAGOGY

CHAPTER 5.

WRITING AT UNIVERSITY AND IN THE WORKPLACE: INTERRELATIONS AND LEARNING EXPERIENCES AT THE BEGINNING OF THE PROFESSIONAL ACTIVITY

Lucía Natale

Universidad Nacional de General Sarmiento, Argentina

Studies on academic literacy (Carlino, 2013) began in Latin America at the turn of the 20th century when universities from different countries created academic reading and writing workshops aimed at first-year university students. Implementing these courses responded to the need to integrate an increasing number of students who are mostly first-generation university students in their families (CEPAL, 2007). The expansion of the university system was particularly favored in Argentina with the establishment of twenty-nine new national public universities from the 1990s (Chiroleu, 2018). In this context, the initiatives on academic literacy have mainly focused on first-year students' "writing difficulties." Gradually, different research lines have been conducted, and new curricular spaces were dedicated to teaching and learning the different genres seen across the university curriculum (Carlino, 2013; Natale, 2013). Despite these advances, the processes university students in Latin America go through in their transition to professional life seem to be an incipient research problem (Natale et al., 2021). Yet, this issue has been addressed in the North American tradition for more than two decades (Artemeva, 2005; 2008; 2009; Bazerman, 1988; Bazerman & Russell, 2003; Berkenkotter et al., 1991; Dias et al., 1999; Ketter & Hunter, 2003; Russell, 1997).

To address this issue, in this chapter, we explore how students and graduates who start their activities in professional contexts approach genres (Bazerman, 1994; 2004a; 2004b) and the written production of specific texts. Likewise, we are interested in researching the writing knowledge built at university that both students and graduates put into practice and what new understanding and reflections on genres and writing they develop in professional contexts. To do this, we interviewed senior students and recent graduates from two academic programs at the National University of General Sarmiento (UNGS). These novices performed professional activities related to their study programs in different public institutions connected with the UNGS.

This type of inquiry is relevant for different reasons. Firstly, it can provide data on the typical genres and literate activities in the workplace. Secondly, it can gather meaningful information to include writing in the design of the curricula in professional academic programs. In the following sections, we contextualize the study and explain the methodology used and the concepts that support the analysis of the interviews. After examining how such issues are represented in the interviews, we offer some closing remarks.

CONTEXT OF THE STUDY

UNGS is an Argentinian public university created in 1992 within the framework of the expansion and diversification of higher education institutions in the country. It is located in Greater Buenos Aires, an area around the city of Buenos Aires, which is characterized by a series of economic and educational inequalities among the population. Most UNGS' students come from working families: eight out of ten are the first-generation university students in their families, while five out of ten are the first generation to complete high school.

UNGS is organized into four institutes: sciences, conurbation, human development, and industry. These institutes articulate education, research, and services to the community. Each of them addresses specific geographical, socioeconomic, and cultural issues. Their academic programs include degrees in technical studies and undergraduate programs such as engineering, diverse bachelor's degrees, university teacher education, and postgraduate courses, i.e., specializations, master's, and doctorates.

The analysis of the degree qualifications profiles (DQP from now on) from the different academic programs reveals that they equip students both for professional activities and scientific research. As an example, we can cite the bachelor's degree in ecology, as shown on the UNGS website. Graduates from the degree in ecology will be able to

> build knowledge on ecology through research and apply it in the specific field of land management in urban, rural, and natural ecosystems. Graduates will be able to carry out environmental diagnoses, design action proposals, and manage the implied ecosystems. They will identify the issues and necessary tools for sustainable management of natural resources

(renewable and nonrenewable). They will develop scientific and technological alternatives from a social perspective to minimize the ecological base of production's degradation and/or destruction and improve the human habitat conditions in their environmental component. (UNGS, 2018)

This DQP and others explicitly suggest that the course of studies prepares students to work in various fields, including scientific, technological, and institutional ones related to management. At the same time, specific genres are mentioned, such as environmental diagnoses and proposals for ecosystem management.

In short, this DQP and others articulate diverse settings and activities and foresee different genres for each of them. This observation corresponds with what a former faculty chair said in an interview for this study—the discussion about the academic programs included the negotiation about the genres that graduates should know to participate in different contexts. Such attention to graduates' and undergraduates' written production is present in the founding documents supporting the design of the academic programs at UNGS. Also, different devices aimed at working with academic and professional reading, writing, and speaking are implemented across the undergraduate curriculum.

Since its establishment, UNGS has offered two compulsory workshops for all first-year students. Spanish language instructors teach both courses in dedicated spaces, not integrated into other classes. These courses are aimed at first-year students and deal with general aspects of scientific and academic texts. They also address typical genres of the beginning of higher education studies, such as tests, monographs, reports. On the other hand, PRODEAC (Programa de Enseñanza de la Escritura a lo largo de las Carreras), a writing program integrated into and situated within the field of the disciplines, was implemented in 2005. It was of an interdisciplinary, progressive, and systematic nature across the study programs at the university (Natale & Stagnaro, 2013). Course instructors could optionally request PRODEAC assistance. This meant that a writing and reading specialist joined the team of course instructors. This specialist delivered the lessons that dealt with reading and writing texts framed in that specific course. Thus, the pedagogy adopted was grounded on collaborative work based on co-teaching (Natale, 2020).

In 2019, UNGS launched the so-called "Programa de Acceso y Acompañamiento a las Carreras de Grado y Pregrado." This program offers the two courses mentioned above, i.e., the reading and writing workshops, and a third space called "Acompañamiento a la Lectura y la Escritura en las Disciplinas" (ALED for its acronym in Spanish), which subsumes PRODEAC's operation and experience. The three courses are articulated and are mandatory in all academic programs at UNGS. ALED's work concerns two core subjects of the curricula—an intermediate and an advanced one. In this sense, students taking part in ALED are already oriented in their fields and are close to graduation. The activities usually consist of writing texts based on genres related to academic and professional life. As can be seen, the three curricular spaces aim to address literate practices and develop a sustained and gradual work across the curriculum with a progressive approach to the disciplinary genres.

METHODOLOGY

The study presented here is part of a research project that initially attempted to research the literate activities during the pre-professional practices (PPP) of different courses of studies at UNGS. It also looked into the genres used and the students' identity transformations at this stage in their academic programs. To achieve our objective, we initially planned semi-structured interviews with students in the period they were carrying out their PPP, among other research activities. We assumed that during the PPP, students had their first contact with work settings, considering a trajectory that begins at university and leads to students' labor insertion. However, the first interviews with senior students revealed that this path is not as linear as anticipated, but there are different situations. Given these first data, we reconsidered the students to be interviewed and included senior students and recent graduates already working in areas related to their studies (Natale et al., 2021).

We have collected 15 interviews with students and graduates with bachelor's degrees in public administration and ecology. In this chapter, we selected the interviews of four participants (Ivana, Andrea, Brian, and Agustina) who represent different trajectories between the university and the workplace. Ivana enrolled in the bachelor's degree in public administration because she was already working in an organization where graduates tend to work. Andrea and Agustina, who were finishing their bachelor's degree in ecology, had not had the opportunity to participate in work settings during their training. On the other hand, Brian began working as an employee in the environment department of a municipality shortly after starting the bachelor's degree in ecology.

At the time of the interview, the interviewees were carrying out professional activities in public institutions that have co-operative ties with the university, municipalities in neighboring areas, and a national organization dedicated to research and the provision of specialized services for water preservation. In this sense, we can say that these workplaces are highly organized and regulated by the state. Besides, we interviewed teachers who tutor students during their PPP and faculty chairs in order to delve into the meaning assigned to the students' participation in training activities in the world of work.

The research team members, who had taught the courses framed in ALED in the last stage of the academic programs, carried out the interviews. Thus, these instructors had been in touch with the students and graduates and had built up a degree of familiarity with them. The interview script aimed at exploring students' perceptions about the training that the academic programs provide for the professional practice in general and, in particular, for their participation in literate activities in the workplace.

THEORETICAL FRAMEWORK

From the activity theory perspective (Lave & Wenger, 1991; Prior, 1998; Wertsch, 1999), the interviewed students and graduates worked in highly structured public institutions. There, individuals and groups constituted the internal communities that performed social practices oriented to common goals. In these institutions, people perform social activities mediated by material artifacts, technology, and highly typified genres.

According to Carolyn Miller (1994), genres can be defined as typified rhetorical actions based on recurrent social situations. The recurrence of the situations gives rise to the recurrence in the forms of communication (Bazerman, 1994) due to the need to make the intended aims socially recognizable. As long as genres are related to activities performed in certain circumstances, they allow us to recognize individuals' intentions (Bazerman, 1994, p. 69). Thus, genres seem to be mediating artifacts to achieve the participants' objectives for an activity in a particular setting (Bazerman & Prior, 2005; Werstch, 1999).

Overall, playing a social role and its implied actions require a set of genres (Devitt, 1991), i.e., a group of textual genres related to specific situations and certain social systems. Each genre set, in turn, becomes part of a genre system (Bazerman, 1994) as long as it is related to a network with the genres employed by other participants of the social event. In a genre system, relationships are interwoven among the parts and the intervening genres in a situated social activity in a given setting. An activity system surges from the interrelation of such components, i.e., genres, participants, communities, activities, institutional settings (Russell, 1997).

The concept of activity system becomes central to consider the situation students and recent graduates face when joining the world of work. They must begin participating in new activities in unknown settings and interact with other participants using genres, tools, and devices they had not necessarily previously known. Novices learn to perform in new environments by participating in situated activities and relationships with other institution members. Such learning, thus, seems to be a social process since it takes place in a context, is mediated by other participants, and is related to the use of mediating tools to carry out the activity.

GENRES AND WRITING IN THE WORKPLACE

Before addressing the specific questions of interest, we will review some general questions about how the interviewees represent the genres of the workplace contexts where they are involved and how they carry out the expected written production.

We first include an excerpt from the interview with Ivana, who was studying public administration. This excerpt explores the completion of an assignment given to a team of students she belonged to while doing the PPP. Specifically, they were asked to present a project to improve an area of the municipality:

> **Ivana**: [To carry out the project,] we diagnosed the problem we found. In this case, we studied the municipal doctor's office: the demand, which was saturated; we saw the problems it was having, why it was saturated, why they did not get to see the people who went there. First, we started with a first approach. We did some interviews, not knowing what we were going to find, but, well, we started doing interviews. We aimed at pretty general things, and then we aimed at the main problem based on what we could interpret. And first was that: a status report. And then, yes, the assembly of the project. But we also made graphs, indexes, everything; we put everything together so they could know what problems they were having. And we gave them a set of recommendations to keep in mind too. Some were accepted, and others are still in process. We did more: a report that was for practice, for the university, and besides, we made the final diagnosis report for the municipality. For [the university] we made one and another for the institution.

As can be seen in this extract, Ivana and her peers put into play a series of textual practices learned at university. They aimed to complete a social action assigned to them in the municipality to improve some of its activities. The students had to prepare a project to introduce these improvements. Therefore, they previously elaborated a series of texts. They displayed a set of genres (interviews, situation report, diagnosis, graphics, indexes, recommendations) which constituted a set of actions necessary to achieve their goal. Thus, the project seemed to be a valuable tool for the municipality to introduce changes in an area. Still, it was also a mediating artifact to fulfill the students' intentions: to complete the assigned activities to pass their PPP.

In other interviews, the students mentioned other purposes, such as learning the professional tasks in the field, learning to operate in it, and doing a good job in the event there were future contracts. Thus, the action becomes guided by several objectives, which is a characteristic of all mediated action (Werstch, 1999).

On the other hand, in the above extract, students said they had to do another activity to pass the course that accompanies them during the PPP. They had to deal with another genre, i.e., a report on the carried-out tasks. In their dual role of student and intern, the interviewees reported different aims related to the activities they simultaneously developed in two different settings or "separate worlds" (Dias et al., 1999), which—as we will see in other examples—participants managed to articulate. To do this, they used typical genres of two complex institutional settings with established and regulated practices. Therefore, it seemed that they could be actively involved in two genre systems. In the intersections between the actions of the world of work and that of the academy, the complexity acquired by students' and graduates' participation in instances such as PPPs is revealed.

Next, to account for how textual production is repeatedly represented in the workplace, we analyze an extract from the interview with Andrea, a senior student in ecology who had no previous work experience. Based on the recommendation of her thesis tutor, she joined a national organization as an intern, where she worked as a professional. This institution produces specialized information for water preservation and disseminates it through periodic reports. Andrea was assigned the task of preparing these reports when she joined the organization. As we will see, producing reports seems to be a socially distributed activity in which different actors intervene:

> **Andrea**: For example, a provincial secretary of environment asks us for a report on the status of the rivers because there is a severe drought, and they have to make decisions. So, we prepare that report. We use data that the Argentinian Naval Prefecture usually gives us. They measure the rivers and pass the data on to us. Then, sometimes, drawing from that data, we produce other data. They give us raw data, and with that, we create others. For example, we make flow data modeled with models made by a colleague of mine. So, I do the following: I take the data, pass it through the model, and write the report. After that report, I send it to my boss, we discuss it together, and I adjust things. And usually, afterward, we

> discuss everything in meetings, with the help of others. . . .
> Those meetings are great; I learn a lot. There, we evaluate the objective (of the report) and adjust everything based on that.

In this extract, Andrea outlines a series of scenes that present writing a hydrological report as an activity situated in a particular context and motivated by a need. Likewise, as seen, performing the activity is distributed. It concerns the people who develop practices to fulfill the intention of providing the requested information (from the collection of raw data to the discussion on the textualization of the report). It also considers time, as it develops in different phases. On the other hand, various artifacts mediating the report preparation are also recorded, such as the models used for flow calculations. Besides, in the represented scenes, it is possible to see the links between different institutions (the government of a province, national organizations with varying types of participation) that come together to complete the activity. Thus, a literate activity (Prior, 1998) at a workplace within an institution is designed. As indicated by Prior, in these settings, the "documents cycle through a hierarchy of interlocking rings (internal and external)" (Prior, 1998, p. 142), which can be registered both in the vertical dimension of the hierarchical chain and in a horizontal axis, among the different groups involved. In addition, the characterization of this literate activity shows that the written production is not the only process taking place. Other subjective and social processes are also developed. Andrea begins to learn about the practices by participating in community activities. In her recount of the carried-out actions, we can understand that her participation goes beyond the elaboration of one first version of the text since it includes the interactions in which they offered her suggestions and other exchanges taking place in the meetings she attends.

BEGINNING TO PARTICIPATE IN THE WORKPLACE THROUGH GENRE PRODUCTION

After introducing the overall representation and production of genres arising from the interviews, we will focus on some specific aspects. We were interested in exploring how students and recent graduates face writing texts in the initial stage of their labor insertion. We wanted to know how they relate the knowledge and writing practices developed in the university training and what new knowledge on genres and writing they acquire.

To learn how they dealt with the text production of genres, we added questions in the interviews aimed explicitly at recovering those scenes. The following extract describes Andrea's experience in writing the requested hydrologic reports.

> **Interviewer**: Those hydrologic reports they asked you to make, did you know them from university?
>
> **Andrea**: No, they were nothing compared to the reports we worked on at UNGS. I had never handled this type of report. No. The truth is that I cried a lot because it was hard for me, really hard, as all of a sudden, they told me: "Well, you are going to write reports." I started reading previous reports, and on top of that, I did not like the way some of them were written. But I managed to write them because what they requested was important. . . . In the beginning, I found guidance in the previous reports that had been done, and later on, I started modifying some things, the things that I did not like. And well, that was how I managed to make it work.
>
> **Interviewer**: And did the institution regard them immediately as very good reports?
>
> **Andrea**: No, no, no. . . . They made a lot of suggestions when we had round table discussions. In those discussions, we read the reports, made suggestions, and they told me: "Look, maybe you can write this here, that there." And that's how I polished them. Now, luckily, they do not point anything out to me.

In this excerpt, Andrea describes how she faced the challenge of writing the assigned reports. As a genre, this report was unfamiliar for her, but it seemed to be a means to participate actively in the institution. Before this situation, through an analytical reading, she appealed to the recognition of the typified forms established in the institution. According to Andrea's point, reading the reports was not limited to identifying the report organization. It was a critical reading as she evaluated the aspects that she disliked so that she could then make changes. In this sense, Andrea adapted her statements to the typified forms that the genre adopted in the institution. Thus, the texts she produced are based on a strong relation of intertextuality, using forms, phrases, and expressions related to previous reports. It could then be a type of intertextuality internal to a system (Bazerman, 2004b, p. 90), as long as accepted forms are still respected. In this way, as a newcomer, Andrea showed signs of adaptation to the usual practices in the institution. Simultaneously, she introduced changes, which allowed her to gradually register her voice and creativity, in a tension between typifications and individuality. Thus, resorting to intertextuality seems to be the first step to learning to participate in the activities developed in the institution. However, her learning process was not passive; it did not arise from a mere reception of instructions. Instead, Andrea, still a newcomer, found room to get started in the genre and took the initiative to introduce modifications.

On the other hand, it seems clear that this process does not occur in isolation, but other senior employees and peers made suggestions so she could make the adjustments. The report was adapted to the objectives and the audience so that the final version of the text is "polished" in Andrea's words. In this sense, while learning was guided, it emerged as a collective enterprise since her experienced peers collaborated with the process. As Day et al. (1999) have found, it could be seen that the oldest members of the institution collaborated with the newcomers. Hence, they adapted to the situated practices and conventions. Likewise, these authors' findings are also confirmed—novices execute tasks considered essential for the institution and make substantial contributions to achieving institutional objectives, even though their productions are later reviewed by their superiors.

The newcomers' initiatives to generate changes in the typified forms can be seen in different interviews. In the following extract, Ivana recalled situations when she suggested modifications in the genre organization:

> **Ivana**: This year, a new manager came to the department. This person works with the council a lot. What the councils mainly do is present projects. He had seen that I worked on projects and asked me to help him. So I set up projects with him. In fact, I planned one, and it worked really well. I did carry it out; I did complete it. He shared a draft with me, and I changed and modified it so it looked like a professional project.
>
> **Ivana**: Perhaps, what I see is that this person, who is in charge, when he wants to plan projects, he makes a draft. But he does not have the perspective we have here [at university] regarding structure—what goes first and what to keep in mind. In fact, I gave him some ideas: "Look, it would be nice to include some data, some statistics, something to account for here." When they present you with the project and say: "Look, I have this idea," I wonder: what is the objective of this idea? Is it necessary? Is there a need to implement it? What I mean to say is: "OK, let's think about how to account for it so that it is more appealing and they want to take." You may present the project, but the question is: is it necessary? Who requests it? Is there an issue that it solves? That is the perspective of public administration: to see the state problems, to see the problems of the society, how the state can set up projects or proposals and solve those problems. It is

precisely that: to study the context, not to invest in something just because of it, but rather there should be a justification for executing it.

As in other interviews, we find that Ivana points out the differences in "perspectives" related to genres (a project, in this case) both in the academy and the municipality. She seems to identify herself close to the academic sphere since she describes the activity carried out from "the point of view of public administration." It includes the tasks of "looking at" and "analyzing" the problems of society. From such a perspective, the projects planned in the municipality appeared to be barely justified. That is why she emphasizes the need to strengthen the structure, the organization of the project's different parts. This means that she makes questions that cooperate in the reconstruction of the project. These questions somehow reflect those that the university instructors make students when they are writing a text with the same characteristics. In this sense, it can be said that the modifications Ivana introduced to the draft given by her boss show an intertextual relation with the projects she wrote for the university.

Following Artemeva's findings in a case study (2005; 2009), we can point out that the institutional project structure reveals the knowledge of genres the student had developed at university. The suggested changes are not only accepted, but they are soon repeatedly asked from her. In this sense, we could argue that the knowledge of genre developed in the two "separate" worlds (Dias et al., 1999) can be articulated to render a new shape to institutional genres. Thus, this interrelation shows that the genre-based training at the university contributes to revising the discursive practices of local institutions.

Therefore, the academic genres assigned at university and work seemed to be interwoven in the activities that students and graduates perform simultaneously in the two activity systems. This intersection is particularly true in a situation that Brian recounted. Brian, a senior student in ecology, had begun to work in a municipality. At the same time, he attended his first year at university, as he had applied for a job in a job bank before. He was hired temporarily to communicate a waste separation program to city dwellers. Once that contract expired, he became a permanent employee in the municipality's environment department, where he works as a middle manager. One of the first tasks he was assigned was to write a report on urban recyclers picking up waste at night. He was asked to gather information and interview them. At the same time, he was beginning to attend the methodology of qualitative research course at UNGS.

> **Brian**: It is a course where they teach us to carry out open interviews in which I have guiding questions, but they are not structured interviews. So, I was given a waste issue, and I had

> to do that for work. So, I worked on both things simultaneously. I proposed interviewing these urban recyclers from San Miguel. It was what I had to do for the municipality. And we conducted the interviews based on the bibliography of the course. The point is I did not work alone; I teamed with three classmates for the university assignment, they were reliable classmates . . . and well, we were going to work on it at night during my working hours. We went together, and together we asked the questions for the municipality and those that were useful for the course.

Once again, this excerpt reveals how two social actions in which Brian participated in intersected. One of them draws from the will to achieve a university goal: to complete the assignment, and with it, to pass the course. The other action is connected to his work assignment. Thus, we can see an intricate path where challenges surged, and Brian faced them strategically, binding the genres from both settings. In the two activities that Brian carried out simultaneously, the interview as a genre operates as a mediating tool of the activity. According to Brian, the tool designed with his peers is not used in the same way in the two contexts. We might suggest they are not using the same genre: they make questions "for the municipality" and "those that were useful for the course." Therefore, each subgroup responded to a specific objective, although some questions could be shared. In this sense, as the actions carried out are highly differentiated, we could conclude that they are two different genres. One is used as a source of information to produce an ethnographic work, and the other is a population survey interview. In this sense, Brian adopted different roles (student and employee) and thus participated in two different activity systems (academy and work). However, Brian managed to bind these roles by using the course literature to design the interview questions for work. Unlike the previous examples, he did not use accepted and recognizable forms for the institution, but he resorted to a validated supporting source (Bazerman, 2004b; 2015). In this point, it is remarkable how Brian, an inexperienced student coming from a working family, without an educational and social background that supported his performance, managed to articulate both actions with knowledge constructed solely at the university. Hence, without disregarding Artemeva's observations (2005; 2009) on the role that family-cultural capital plays in novices' professional development, we can argue that first-generation university students with good opportunities can advance in their careers developing their own strategies.

To conclude this section, we summarize some findings that arise from the interviews, exemplified through the selected extracts. Firstly, we found that resorting to intertextual relations is a frequently used resource. In general, students and fresh graduates tend to recycle knowledge acquired in the academy and critically examine the statements recognized as valid by the institution where they have their first professional experience. As newcomers, they avoid the passive reproduction of the typified forms and want to introduce changes that would improve texts in their opinion. Ivana's earlier excerpts show that the internal text structure is an aspect to improve in the documents of the administrative organisms. In this claim, the view of genres that seems to prevail is closer to the university's, as it is required in students' productions.

Another issue recurrently pointed out refers to the role peers and superiors of the institution play in the professional training. According to the interviewees, these participants acted as guides; they accompanied the activities that novices carried out and oriented textual practices through successive suggestions. They let novices display the knowledge acquired in the academy while newcomers get guidance from peers and superiors. Thus, work training for novices seems to be another social activity in the institutions where genres work as mediators.

LEARNING GENRES AT UNIVERSITY AND THE WORKPLACE

One of the axes of the interviews focused on exploring the learning of genres built in both contexts where students and graduates participate. The interviewees reported having developed new knowledge on texts and adapting them to different audiences and contexts. In Ivana's interview, we find the following reflections:

> **Ivana**: For example, writing this [intervention] project here [at university], is not the same as for the municipality, because maybe [the one for university] is more of an assignment. In the assignment, they give you the instructions, and in the municipality, you have more freedom, and you have to think how to put it together. That's why they differ a lot. . . . For that reason, [while we were doing the PPP] we have to know how to speak in two different ways. Here [at university], there is a mor' academic context, and there are concepts that we could not use in the municipality report because they are not related to the context. Considering these issues helped us decide what to say, what not to say, and to whom.

In this extract, we find that Ivana can differentiate the characteristics of the genre project in the two activity systems (the academic and the world of work) in which she participates while carrying out her PPP. As Dias et al. (1999) point out, the production of the university project is considered part of the academic genres. It aims to train students, as a characteristic that Ivana attributes: it was an "assignment." According to her, using concepts is a distinctive feature in this genre due to the professor's aim to evaluate the students' theoretical knowledge. On the other hand, academic textual production is constrained by the professor's definition of the task. Although it may work as a guide, it takes away some degree of "freedom," in Ivana's words. In the municipality, on the other hand, the activity requires a greater degree of autonomy: "It's you who has to think how to put it together." Thus, an essential difference surges, i.e., the degree of participation in the project design. The workplace is conceived of as a place for developing autonomy, always following the established rules and the tensions that arise among the different participants.

Ivana's thoughts on the relation between the shapes of genres in both spheres is also found in another extract:

> **Ivana**: They are two totally different products: what you prepare for university is academic-oriented, and you are prepared for that; you cite, and then you address an issue. Perhaps we did not know how to translate that, but we later realized we did not transfer it into another executive-level presentation. It was another product, we addressed it again from scratch: what the diagnosis was, the issues, the proposal, and that was it. [It was important] to be succinct and not to tire the reader, in this case, the organization. We discovered that back then, but we had not seen it before. I believe that it would be a significant difference.

From her participation in the work context, Ivana "discovered" an essential issue that "we had not seen before." The genre is not the same even though they have the same name: "project." Ivana understood that "they are two totally different products." That is why it was impossible to address them by treating them as a transfer problem. The contents or the issue addressed in the project seem to be the same. However, the purposes (pass a course/generate an improvement in an area of the municipality) and the audiences are different, leading to reorganizing the text to serve the essentials (diagnosis, problems, and proposals), to "be succinct and not to tire the reader." Thus, Ivana seemed to account for her awareness of the two audiences and the need to adapt her statements accordingly. She summarized this learning developed in the work context by saying: "it is necessary to know how to speak in two different ways." She elaborated on this idea later on, saying that understanding this issue helped her know "what to say and what not to say, and to whom." Through these comments, Ivana reveals that she has learned to consider her audiences and adapt her statements accordingly. In this instance, she begins to consider rhetorical aspects of the activity system in which she starts participating. In her own words, "I learned to be politically correct there [in the workplace]."

These learning experiences, from Agustina's point of view, a senior student in ecology, provided complementary training to the university's offer.

> **Interviewer**: What relationship do you find between the training offered by the municipality and that provided by the university?
>
> **Agustina**: I believe that the former complements the latter. And it complements it a lot in the sense that we have to suggest topics. Here one is immersed in a utopia of what management is like or needs or what one thinks it can obtain, while in a municipality one gets to see the constraints; one sees what to focus on. Delivering a presentation depends on the audience, so we try to use a language that everyone understands because not everyone knows what we know. I believe that it complements a lot more so that, in the future, we can continue growing [professionally]: we had to talk to other areas, talk to the neighbors and register their complaints. We gather information and presentations and process data. And working as a team, of course, also allows you to show your virtues. So, it complements it by taking all this into account. I think it enriches [university training] greatly.

In this extract, Agustina presents a sort of contrast between the learning process at university and that which derives from her participation in a work setting. Whereas the former is considered ideal or utopian, the latter allows them to experiment with issues connected to the reality of the organizations, the existing constraints, the audiences of the actions undertaken, and the statements made. Likewise, she highlights the fact that students have to participate in activities adopting different roles (interacting with other areas, listening to neighbors, registering complaints). Plus, they have to interact with diverse audiences and adapt their statements accordingly. Simultaneously, a new social intention appears: to show one's virtues and be eventually hired, as other interviewees have also said.

To summarize this section, it is important to consider, as stated in the previous section, the knowledge on genre the interviewees have built from their university training. One of them mentioned the organization of texts, the necessity to take care of the parts that they consist of. This emerged mainly in Ivana's testimony, who demanded the inclusion of data, arguments, and justification in the projects of the municipality.

Additionally, in this section, we have found that the students' participation in professional practice settings reveals dimensions of writing that the university does not show. Academic productions usually have a single audience, the professor, and one main objective: to account for the learning process (Dias et al., 1999). Thus, students' participation in work settings functions as complementary training. In these contexts, genres are no longer mere structures or parts to be included in a text but they operate as goal-oriented instruments to solve specific problems. Likewise, participants highlight the different audiences they address and their need to adapt their statements to the relationships established with them. Finally, another fundamental issue can be observed: students' participation in the two activity systems helps students gain awareness of the distinctions between the genres in both contexts.

CLOSING REMARKS

The findings that emerge from the analysis of the interviews have been presented, which are summarized below. As pointed out, students and graduates tend to solve the challenges given to them concerning the genres of the workplace by establishing intertextual relations between academic texts and those accepted in the organizations in which they start carrying out professional activities. Besides, it is seen that they adopt a critical perspective towards the texts of the organizations where their first professional practices are developed and remark on the necessity to introduce changes. These modifications they suggest are often based on the knowledge that they have developed from genres they have learned at university. Therefore, the characteristics of the academic genres that they retrieve appear when they produce new texts in the professional settings where they participate. On the other hand, the texts that students must make in the workplace are based on readings from the recommended bibliography in their courses. At the same time, the experiences they live in their jobs become input for academic productions. Thus, text productions, framed in both contexts, are connected through an intertextual relation. In these interrelationships, it can be seen that the research participants establish bridges between the two worlds in which they act: the academic and the workplace.

According to our interviewees, academic productions lead them to learn to pay attention to the internal organization of texts. On the other hand, it was found that the participation of students and graduates in the workplace generates new reflections and learning about writing and genres. Their involvement in the organizations where they started to work makes them aware of the importance of the rhetorical aspects and the goals that genres pursue.

Thus, learning about genres and writing built in both activity systems appears complementary. The systematic knowledge developed in the academy continues to be used since it is appreciated in public organizations. Simultaneously, the participation in the activities of those contexts highlights aspects of genre production that had not been considered so far. In this sense, we find a coincidence with Ketter and Hunter's (2003) claims: participating in social activities and using genres in two contexts enrich learning and encourage reflections on the textual practices in both contexts. Therefore, a pedagogical implication of this study is that the students' participation in actions that take place in work settings is extremely beneficial for the understanding of genres they gain and the learning of academic writing.

To conclude, we need to mention the limitations of the results found. Although they offer valuable information similar to those of international lines of research, we gathered them in a small-scale study. In this sense, future investigations intend to extend the number of participants and the research to other professional settings.

REFERENCES

Bazerman, C. (1988). *Shaping written knowledge: The genre and activity of the experimental article in science.* University of Wisconsin Press.

Bazerman, C. (1994). Systems of genres and the enactment of social intentions. In A. Freedman & P. Medway (Eds.), *Genre and the new rhetoric* (pp. 79–101). Taylor & Francis.

Bazerman, C. & Prior, P. (2003). *What writing does and how it does it: An introduction to analyzing texts and textual practices.* Routledge.

Bazerman, C. & Russell, D. R. (2003). *Writing selves, writing societies: Research from activity perspectives.* The WAC Clearinghouse; Mind, Culture, and Activity. https://doi.org/10.37514/PER-B.2003.2317.

Bazerman, C. (1994). Systems of genres and the enactment of social intentions. In A. Freedman & P. Medway (Eds.), *Genre and the new rhetoric.* Taylor & Francis.

Bazerman, C. (2004a). Speech acts, genres, and activity systems: How texts organize activity and people. In C. Bazerman & P. Prior (Eds.), *What writing does and how it does it: An introduction to analyzing texts and textual practices.* Lawrence Erlbaum.

Bazerman, C. (2004b). Intertextuality: How texts rely on other texts. In C. Bazerman & P. Prior (Eds.), *What writing does and how it does it. An introduction to analyzing texts and textual practices.* Lawrence Erlbaum.

Berkenkotter, C., Huckin, T. N. & Ackerman, J. (1991). Social context and socially constructed texts: The initiation of a graduate student into a writing community. In C. Bazerman & J. Paradis (Eds.), *Textual dynamics of the professions: Historical and contemporary studies of writing in professional communities* (pp. 191–215). University of Wisconsin Press.

Carlino, P. (2013). Alfabetización académica diez años después. *Revista Mexicana de investigación educativa, 18*(57), 355–381.

CEPAL. (2007). *Panorama social de América Latina.* CEPAL.

Chiroleu, A. (2018). Democratización e inclusión en la universidad argentina: Sus alcances durante los gobiernos. *Educaçâo em Revista, 34*, 1–26.

Devitt, A. J. (1991) Intertextuality in Tax Accounting: Generic, Referential, and Functional. In C. Bazerman & J. Paradis (Eds.), *Textual dynamics of the professions: Historical and contemporary studies of writing in professional communities* (pp. 306–35). University of Wisconsin Press.

Dias, P., Freedman, A., Medway, P. & Paré, A. (1999). *Worlds apart: acting and writing in academic and workplace contexts.* Erlbaum.

Ketter, J. & Hunter, J. (2003). Creating a writer's identity on the boundaries of two communities of practice. In C. Bazerman & D. R. Russell (Eds.), *Writing selves, writing societies: Research from activity perspectives* (pp. 307–329). The WAC Clearinghouse; Mind, Culture, and Activity. https://doi.org/10.37514/PER-B.2003.2317.2.09.

Lave, J. & Wenger, E. (1991). *Situated learning: Legitimate peripheral participation.* Cambridge University Press.

Miller, C. R. (1994). Genre as social action. In A. Freedman & P. Medway (Eds.), *Genre and the new rhetoric* (pp. 23–42). Taylor & Francis.

Natale, L., García, P. & Molina, M. L. (2021). De la vida universitaria a la profesional: Desafíos metodológicos para la exploración de las prácticas letradas en contexto. *Confluencia de saberes,* (3), 87–106.

Natale, L. (2013). Integración de enfoques en un programa institucional para el desarrollo de la escritura académica y profesional. *Revista mexicana de investigación educativa, 18*(58), 685–707.

Natale, L. & Stagnaro, D. (2013). Desarrollo de habilidades de lectura y escritura en la trayectoria académica del ingeniero: La experiencia de un programa desafiante e innovador. *Revista Argentina de Enseñanza de la Ingeniería, 2*(3), 45–52.

Prior, P. (1998). *Writing/disciplinarity: A sociohistoric account of literate activity in the academy.* Lawrence Erlbaum.

Russell, D. R. (1997). Rethinking genre in school and society: An activity theory analysis. *Written Communication, 14*(4), 504–554.

Universidad Nacional de General Sarmiento. (2017). *Estatuto.* Ediciones UNGS.

Universidad Nacional de General Sarmiento. (2019). *Primer censo de estudiantes de grado y pregrado.* https://www.ungs.edu.ar/wp-content/uploads/2019/12/Primer-censo-de-estudiantes-UNGS.pdf.

Universidad Nacional de General Sarmiento. (n.d.). *Licenciatura en Ecología.* Retrieved March 1, 2021, from https://www.ungs.edu.ar/carrera/licenciatura-en-ecologia.

Wertsch, J. (1999). *La mente en acción.* Aique.

CHAPTER 6.
CULTURAL SHAPING OF STANDPOINT AND REASONING IN ANALYTICAL WRITING

Liliana Tolchinsky and Anat Stavans
University of Barcelona, Spain, and Beit Berl College, Israel

Argumentation refers to the verbal expression of a reasoning—a process through which the reasons that inform our statements are explored (Underberg & Norton, 2018). It is a communication process whose product, an argument, is defined in logic as "a set of two or more propositions related to each other in such a way that all but one of them (the premises) are supposed to provide support for the remaining one (the conclusion)" (Kemerling, 2011). In ordinary language, words and phrases are used to construe statements that build an argument (e.g., claims, allegations, thesis) but what distinguishes an argument from a mere set of statements is the contrast between statements assumed to be true and others used to support them. This contrast results from the relation of inference that is supposed to hold between them. As explained by Van Dijk, "Hierarchically speaking an argument has a binary structure consisting of Premises and Conclusion, where the Conclusion contains information that is inferred from the information contained in the Premises" (1980, p. 117).

The ability to build a sound argument convincingly linking premises and conclusion in such a way that what is offered as true by the arguer is accepted as true by the addressee is a valuable skill in different contexts (at home, at the working place, in social contexts). In the educational context where argumentation is most often formally introduced, practiced, and assessed, it is through analytical text writing—a kind of prose in which the topic is the protagonist.

Analytical writing (i.e., reflecting on a topic and/or supporting claims with sound reasons) is not confined to a single subject area. It is as important to science as it is to language and history, and it becomes increasingly linked to academic success across grade levels. The prevalence of analytical writing embracing argumentative patterns has been shown in several studies (e.g., Zhu, 2001, as cited in Biria & Yakhabi, 2013). A long-standing debate in the study of academic writing is concerned with the effect of different rhetorical traditions on the properties of the quality of argumentation for academic purposes. With the establishment of Contrastive Rhetoric (CR) as a field of study in the late sixties (Kaplan, 1966) arguing for the culture-specificity of textual structures and argumentation patterns quite opposing positions were advanced. While some stressed the universality of academic discourse (e.g., Widdowson, 1979; Schwanzer, 1981), others consider reasonable to assume that different cultures would orient their discourse in different ways (Leki, 1991; Clyne, 1987) and still others argue that what is being identified as differing rhetoric might be merely non-skilled, developmental writing (Mohan & Lo, 1985).

Charles Bazerman (1988) added to the complexity of this debate highlighting the extent to which writers' plans, goals, and other process-based strategies are dependent on the particular purpose, settings, and audiences. By examining writing processes in different disciplines, he contends that the extent to which usages are universal or culture-bound relates to disciplinary knowledge and the relative stabilization of the disciplines. Recent developments pursue this direction tending to reject an either/or contrast—either universal or culture bound—in academic discourse, while stressing the role of educational systems on the rhetorical preferences of writers. On the one hand, it has been shown that rhetorical structures of scientific texts may show similar overall patterns of organization but different degrees of variation due to disciplinary (De Carvalho, 2001) and language differences (Suárez & Moreno, 2008). And, on the other hand, intercultural variation in the rhetorical decisions of writers due to topic content or level of schooling were found to be stronger than the similarities imposed by writers' being part of broadly defined cultural groups such as Oriental or Semitic (Clyne, 1987, Golebiowski, 1998). In her analysis of metatext use in research articles on economics written in English by Finnish and Anglo-American academics, Mauranen (1993), found that Anglo-American writers use more metatext than Finnish writers. She assumes that, despite a relative uniformity of academic papers obeying the requirements of genre in a particular discipline, there is significant intercultural variation in the rhetorical preferences of writers because "writing is a cultural object that is very much shaped by the educational system in which the writer has been socialised" (Mauranen, 1993, p. 112). In other words, we could argue that while there are some similarities across languages (perhaps rhetorical universals), there are different socio-cultural and socio-rhetorical aspects (perhaps rhetorical specific) that affect the composition process of well-organized and canonically tailored written texts.

This study aims to intervene in the debate on the relative dependence of textual organization on different rhetorical/cultural traditions as well as on the influence of instructional practices on the rhetorical choices of writers. Our main goal is to determine the effect of two contrasting rhetorical traditions, the Israeli—one strongly influenced by Anglo-Saxon rhetorical preferences, and the Spanish one—typically following the Romance rhetoric, on the structure and quality of the arguments deployed by Spanish and Israeli adolescents at the same grade level (10th-11th grade) producing an analytical essay on the topic of dress code. These students are at the last stage of compulsory education and, therefore, not yet acquainted with the conventionalized structuring of scientific texts that currently characterize publication (especially in higher education) in the different disciplines and professions. Thus, we expected that the essays produced by these adolescents will reflect culturally driven writing instruction practices rather than discipline-specific rhetoric grounded in crosslinguistic cannons of argumentative essays.

THE INFLUENCE OF RHETORICAL TRADITIONS ON WRITING

To be a proficient text-literate, one needs not only to be familiar with diverse types of texts, but also to command the writing patterns and procedures that better respond to the expectancies of readers that are part of the tradition in which these texts are nested. These texts implicitly broadcast the standards of text quality by translating knowledge into writing construed to fit a rhetorical tradition. Rhetorical traditions are grounded in the premise of bridging diverse voices through an act of persuasion as evident in the historical evolution of the field of rhetoric explained by Stroud as

> part of the challenge of coming to terms with difference is the confrontation with something, be it a tradition, a thinker, or a text, that challenges one's own way of understanding the world, possible accounts of it, and our structures of reasoning and justification. Moreover, bridging such differences either by recognizing or accepting them rather than rejecting or dismissing them is a great achievement for it forces our thinking and writing to move away from the all too comfortable and familiar and obscure our standard of judgement. (2019, p. 120)

Rhetorical traditions have been studied from different perspectives and disciplines. The almost inevitable perspective is CR which began as a text analysis of writers who were not native speakers of the language. The assumption of CR was that rhetorical traditions are anchored in cultural and linguistic conventions of the writer's first language (Soler-Monreal et al., 2011; Connor, 2002; 2014). Aligned with Bazerman's observation that "[w]riting is a complex social participatory performance in which the writer asserts meaning, goals, affiliations, and identities within a constantly changing, contingently organized social world, relaying on shared texts and knowledge" (2016, p.18), CR new directions have been on the process of composing quality written texts in meticulous description of the complexity of the cultural, social, situational, and contextual factors affecting writing (Connor, 2004, p. 292; Connor, 2008, p. 304). Although the initial impetus of CR was to compare written texts by native and non-native (particularly ESL writers), more recently the comparisons expanded to varieties of the same language ascribing to one of two CR approaches—either analyzing L1 texts in different cultures which are geared to professional audiences of native speakers and follow the rhetorical contexts into which they are inscribed; or finding textual criteria that characterize the successful or unsuccessful writer in that L1 (e.g., Pak & Acevedo, 2008; Leki, 1991) as well as between languages (e.g., Arvay & Tanko, 2004; Burgess, 2002; Loukianenko-Wolfe, 2008; Martín-Martín, 2003; Taylor & Chen, 1991; Suárez & Moreno, 2008).

A different perspective is the Rhetorical Structure Theory (RST) proposed by Mann & Thompson (1987) that has been applied to different areas of science in different languages over the years. From its very inception, it was conceived to characterize the text's rhetorical components and their relations in search for universal/cross cultural and language specific textual organizations. For example, Scott et al. (1999, as cited in Taboada & Mann, 2006) use RST to analyze realization of the components involved in generation and enablement (purpose, means, result, and condition for generation; sequence, purpose, condition, and result for enablement) in Portuguese, French, and English. They provided an interesting mapping of semantics to syntax using RST to show that the three languages use the rhetorical relations differently: for example, Portuguese does not use means for enablement; English uses condition and result for enablement, but Portuguese and French do not.

RST conceptualizes the overall text structure as hierarchically structured in which certain elements are foregrounded (nuclei) and others are backgrounded (satellites). Nuclear elements are genre-specific compulsory components. For example, the sequence of events is nuclear in narrative texts—there is no narrative without events—while evaluative components, although adding to text richness are taken as satellite and optional in a narrative. As we shall see, in argumentative texts, claims and supports are nuclear components whereas counterclaims, in contrast, although useful for fulfilling the communicative purpose of argumentation, are dispensable if they follow a claim. This distinction is particularly useful for examining texts produced by inexpert writers and serves to appreciate their awareness of genre constraints.

MAIN DIFFERENCES BETWEEN RHETORICAL TRADITIONS

Connor et. Al. discuss the origins of CR stating: "[a]s Diane Belcher puts it, "in the beginning was Kaplan" (2014, p. 59). His "doodles" article (1966), though controversial and even misunderstood, remains a ground-breaking study of student writing because it initiated the systematic analysis of the thesis that one's first language and culture influence the structure of discourse. Following in the footsteps of contrastive analysis (CA), which looked primarily at word- and sentence- level structures, Kaplan's work was the first to consider the above-the-sentence rhetorical structure of texts. Matsuda (2001) says that Kaplan's seminal work on CR was motivated by three different intellectual traditions: contrastive analysis, the Sapir-Whorf hypothesis, and the emerging field of composition and rhetoric at the paragraph level. Grounded in these traditions, Kaplan's pioneering work was criticized for both representing a deterministic view of culture and overgeneralizing findings based on essays written in English by students from different cultural/linguistic backgrounds disregarding other developmental and socio-cultural factors that influence writing (Casanave, 2004; see Kubota, 2010) such as the idea of culture as monolithic. Irrespective of the origin and historical evolution of CR, Kaplan's (1966) earlier model was concerned with paragraph organization. However, it advances—through rather sweeping overgeneralizations—useful categories of analysis to account for cultural differences in written texts especially those composed for academic purposes. According to Kaplan's model the following writing patterns can be identified across cultures.

47. In American (English) argumentative writing is linear, direct, and to the point, with the main thesis formulated at the beginning of the argument, and supporting arguments arranged hierarchically.
48. Semitic argumentative writing (Hebrew, Arabic, Aramaic) presents the argument in parallel propositions, or embedded in stories, not in hierarchical progression.
49. Oriental (Asian) argumentative writing approaches the argument in a circular, respectful, indirect, non-assertive, but authoritative way.
50. Romance (and German) argumentative writing favors a digressive style that requires readers to follow the argument to its conclusion.
51. Russian argumentative writing follows the Romance model, but with more freedom in dividing up parts of the argument as the author proceeds to the conclusion.

Forty years later, Rienecker and Jörgensen (2003), although going deeper into the major characteristics of each tradition, provide an account that pretty much coincides with Kaplan's in comparing the Continental (German-Romanic) with the Anglo-American traditions in scientific writing and coexist in the academic writing for higher education in the European context: The Anglo-American (problem-oriented) tradition and the continental (topic-oriented) tradition. The continental tradition emphasizes science as thinking, whereas the Anglo-American writing "emphasizes science as investigation and problem solving focusing on the empirically based study, and the systematically and updated literature-based research paper" (p. 104). These two traditions are imparted differently in the writing courses to the extent that they result in two different systems of thinking and knowledge making.

The globalization of communication and the homogenizing impact of the internet on people's habits of reading and writing could make us doubt the current validity of these distinctions, in spite the social presence of writing. Yet, writing conventions are taught in schools. While many children read outside school for entertainment, few write/produce written essays outside school. In other words, writing, for most schoolchildren, is nearly always a scholastic activity and inevitably reflects the culture of the school system and reproduces culturally preferred discourse styles. Conventions of writing are often shaped by and passed on to new generations through formal education in most societies (Leki, 1991; Connor, 1996).

Studies show that rhetorical traditions still have a strong impact on the teaching of writing in the school years and at college. Schleppegrell and Colombi (2005) describe the Anglo-American writing programs (so-called "Style and Comp" classes) as a fixed discourse structure (topic sentence expressing a standpoint, two or three paragraphs of arguments for and against, and a conclusion), providing a mnemonic scheme for overall text organization. Their Latin American counterparts, in contrast, emphasize motivation, functionality, and creativity even for academic writing.

THE USE OF ARGUMENTATIVE ESSAYS TO CATCH CULTURAL DIFFERENCES

In argumentative essays writers are expected to express their point of view on the topic and to use different strategies to persuade the audience of the validity of the point of view by the force of his argumentation (Tolchinsky et al., 2018). The audience are "[t]hose whom the orator wants to influence with his/her argumentation" (Perelman & Olbrechts-Tyteca, 1989, p. 55). Even though written texts are self-sustained/monological texts there is always a dialogical basis for persuasion to occur (Ramírez, 2010; Stavans et al., 2019). It is essential for the writer to think of the (potential) reader to choose the ideas to be presented (Chala & Chapetón, 2012; Bazerman, 2016). As any communication process, the quality of argumentation is subject to cultural differences. The strategies and linguistic means writers deploy to achieve their goals reflect the rhetoric of reference as a mode of "finding all available means" (Kaplan, 1966, p. 11).

Models of arguments (as well as of any other knowledge or skill such as reading or writing) are tools of thought that help organize phenomena even if they are imperfect (Galbraith, 1999). In the present study we use Toulmin's model (1958) considered to be a precursor of argumentation studies. His top-down approach focuses on identifying the different components of an argument and the roles they play within it. We provide here a short definition of the model components that will be elaborated in the next section. The two main elements are the *claim*, an assertion that the writer makes on the topic, and the *grounds*, that explicitly support the claim. The four other elements (*qualifier, warrants, backing,* and *rebuttals*) are not indispensable and help to further ground and limit the argument. Although Toulmin's model was criticized because it does not capture the dialogical dimension that he attributes to argumentation at a conceptual level (Leitão, 2000), it provides a solid basis to analyze rhetorical arguments and serves to compare argument structure cross-linguistically.

Applying Toulmin's model, studies showed that Chinese students use fewer rebuttal claims and data (Qin & Karabacak, 2010). American students prefer a practical orientation, supported by factual concrete evidence whereas Japanese students prefer a more humanistic aesthetic orientation with lesser degree of warrants and backing and with more subjective evidence (Okabe, 1983). Japanese students were also found to be more cautious and ambiguous in their writing. They use more frequently qualifiers, rhetorical questions, disclaimers and denials, ambiguous pronouns, and the passive voice compared to American students (Hinkel, 2005).

Studies have also attempted to characterize general patterns of reasoning based on the placement of the different components in the text. For example, the emplacement of the thesis statement has been assumed as indicative of deductive or inductive reasoning. In inductive writing the thesis statement is in the final position whereas deductive writing has the thesis statement in the initial position. Hinds explains that "deductive writing has the thesis statement in the initial position" (1990, p. 89). Non-deductive development can be of two forms: inductive, "having the thesis statement in the final position" (Hinds, 1990, p. 89) or quasi-inductive, "getting the readers to think for themselves, to consider the observations made, and to draw their own conclusions" (Hinds, 1990, pp. 99–100). In a native English argumentative writing, the paragraph begins with a clear thesis statement, followed by paragraphs containing relevant and adequate support of the thesis statement. As emphasized by Bain (2010, as cited in Hussin & Griffin, 2012), a deductive pattern, where the placement of thesis statement usually comes at the beginning of the paragraphs, is preferred by native English speakers "to indicate the scope of the text" (Kamimura & Oi, 1996) pointed out two major differences in the organization patterns in argumentative essays between American and Japanese writers, in which the former prefer the General-Specific pattern while the latter subscribe either to Specific-General pattern or the "Omission Pattern." Another difference they found is that the American writers organize ideas in linear way, while Japanese writers organize in a circular way (Torres & Medriano, 2020).

In a similar vein, Drid (2015) suggests that the organization of argumentation in essays, namely choosing to state the writer's claim early in the text or to postpone the statement of the point after advancing arguments, varies across cultures, engendering difficulties for learners of foreign languages. Delineating the senses of "induction" and "deduction" and scrutinizing their variants would make the comprehension of such cross-cultural disparities more lucid. Research indicates that induction and deduction, seen as two principal macrostructures of persuasive discourse, are end points of a wider continuum of argumentative text organizations with additional variants. Warnick and Manusov (2000), for instance, have investigated the variation of the justificatory macrostructures in relation to cultural beliefs and values in four cultural groups: African Americans, Asian Americans, Asians, and European Americans. Their study showed that the inductive and deductive modes of reasoning, which are the principal forms of argumentation known in the Western tradition, are not the sole patterns used in persuasion if one moves from one community to another.

Two new terms are introduced based on the extent to which the writing pattern places burden on the writer or reader to achieve text semantic connectedness: reader responsible as opposed to writer responsible texts, based on the division of responsibility between readers and writers, namely, "the amount of effort writers expend to make texts cohere through transitions and other uses of metatext" (Connor, 2002, p. 496; Hinds, 1987). McCool states that reader responsible cultures "emphasize flowery and ornate prose, subjects over actions, theory instead of practice, and an inductive or quasi-inductive line of reasoning" (2009, p. 2). Ferris and Hedgcock (2005) state that in English argumentation, statements of points of view are found to be explicit and are usually placed near the beginning of the text. In comparison, Japanese-speaking writers conceal their standpoints while presenting the different sides of an issue, with their position coming only at the end. Hinds investigated the two parties' evaluation of the others' style. He concluded that "Japanese readers found the linear, deductive argumentation style associated with English language texts to be dull, pointless, and self-involved. At the same time, English speaking readers perceived Japanese argumentative patterns to be circuitous, abstract, and occasionally evasive" (Ferris & Hedgcock, 2005). Other studies modeling Hinds' cross-linguistic typology are recorded. For instance, it is found that, unlike English texts which contain lucid, well-organized statements, German and Spanish texts put the burden on the reader to excavate for meaning (Clyne, 1987; Valero-Garces, 1996). This feature also characterizes writing in Hebrew (Zellermayer, 1988) and Arabic writers who tend not to use deduction in their writing (Almehmadi, 2012). Understanding the contrasts between English and Arabic in the rhetorical organization of argumentative texts is of relevance to predict "anomalies" in EFL writers' texts. Calling their divergences anomalies implies that they will fail to meet the expectations of English readerships if they happen to perform in English academic circles as international students.

THE STUDY

Our main goal was to explore the influence of two contrasting rhetorical communities on the superstructure of analytical essays aimed at developing an argument following a similar prompt. For this purpose, we examined a corpus of 60 texts, 30 produced in Spanish-by-Spanish native speakers and 30 produced in Hebrew by native Hebrew speaking students in secondary school. All the students attended the same school level (10th-11th grade), two years before the end of compulsory education. We assumed that students at this school level, while having acquired experience in text writing of different genres, are more dependent on the local tradition of the teaching of writing with little to no exposure or familiarity with the more international standard of Anglo-centric scientific writing.

Participants. The Spanish sample included native Spanish speakers from León, Spain, a Spanish monolingual community. Parents had secondary or university studies. Participants were involved in a bigger project in which they produced five texts about different topics. The present study is based on a subsample of 30 texts randomly selected among those produced in response to the prompt *"What do you think about the freedom of a dress code?"* Results of a pilot showed that the selected topic triggered varied and rich responses. Students produced their texts in the context of their regular classes using a computer. They had 30 minutes to complete the task.

The Hebrew sample consisted of 30 Hebrew speaking 10th graders from Kfar Saba and Raanana high school in northern-central Israel. The students come from mid-high SES homes. Children were asked to write a text in response to the prompt *"What do you think about instituting a school uniform?"* Texts were produced during the Hebrew language lesson using pen and paper and students were given 30 minutes to complete the task.

The teaching context. The Spanish curriculum introduces "texts typology," the explicit study of distinguishing features of different text types in elementary school. The typical structure of argumentative texts (thesis, different types of arguments, and conclusion) is described and illustrated by examples. Nevertheless, teaching of writing follows a communicative approach (Maqueo, 2006).

In light of this approach teachers emphasize the communicative objective of an argumentative text, richness of expression and topic content rather than text structure. Text production in class is not a frequent task but the texts analyzed for this study were produced in the contexts of a set of classroom activities in which both the communicative purpose and the readers were made explicit. The students were informed that their texts will be read by a group of future teachers and researchers to be acquainted with their opinions and ways of expression as part of their training.

The Israeli Hebrew writing curriculum of argumentative texts begins in middle school and lasts into the high-school years (7th to 10th grades). The teaching of argumentative writing is in context of other literacy related activities such as reading and responding to a text or discussing a controversial topic in class. Following these activities pupils engage in writing following the instructions regarding the structure of the argumentative texts as stating a claim to clearly establish a point of view, then the claim must be followed by supports in the form of facts, explanations, illustrations, and arguments, establishing a counterclaim and refuting it, and closing with a conclusion and a recommendation.

What Do We Look for in the Texts?

The topic we used and the instruction we gave were intended to elicit argumentation. The dressing code and the extent to which it should be controlled at school has been debated in the media both in Israel and Spain and is a highly relevant and authentic topic among adolescents. It is a topic of controversial nature that calls for considering both individual/personal motivations and social impositions. On the other hand, we invited the students to express their own thoughts; that is, to manifest their own point of view on a topic warranting that the interlocutor might think differently. We expected they will try to persuade the reader of their own rightful position. We were specifically curious as to whether they will resort to individual or social constraints to support their own point of view; and what kind of facts/evidence will be included in their reasoning. Moreover, we were interested in seeing whether students will invoke possible objections to their point of view in the form of counterclaims so as to appreciate the extent to which they are probing "internal" interlocutors.

To address these questions, we focus on the superstructural level of texts. The superstructure has been defined as a schematic structure, including "those functions of macro-propositions that have become conventionalized in a given culture" (Van Dijk, 1980, p. 108). As such, it is accepted by adult language users of a speech community and, therefore, learned mostly through formal instruction. Thus, given its conventionalized nature, we assumed that the functional categories the students include in their texts will reflect rhetorical socio-cultural differences. To interpret and characterize the functional categories in the text superstructure we followed Toulmin's model of argument structure and Van Dijk functional analyses and the distinction into nuclear and satellite components suggested in the RST theory.

We looked at the type of component, that is, the functional category realized by each macro-proposition in the text and the emplacement of the component meaning the location of the functional category in the text. In addition to establishing the functional category realized in the last macro-proposition, we analyzed which functional category was used as the first (opening) macro-proposition and which was used as the last (closure) macro-proposition in the text.

We assumed that the identification of the different functional categories included in a text (i.e., the specific articulation of the superstructure) will show the *general architecture* of the text. Concomitantly, the focus on the type of component that appears in the *opening* and *closure* emplacement in the text will cue the type or reasoning, whether deductive or inductive, and will frame (package) the general architecture of the texts. In what follows we elaborate on the types of components we distinguished to further clarify the above assumptions will be clearer.

Types of components. We distinguished two nuclear components (i.e., components that must be realized in the text) that are compulsory for building the argument structure: claims and grounds. Claims are the assertion that authors wish to prove to their audience while grounds are the reasons, fact or evidence that support the author's claim.

The nuclear components constitute what Van Dyjk defines as premises and conclusion (claims according to: Stavans et al., 2019; Toulmin, 1958) where the information of the latter can be inferred from the information of the former. The premises may often feature a certain setting (like the setting in narratives), in which the topic is introduced, who or what objects or notions are involved and what are the intention and the writer's point of view on the topic. Premises, accordingly, require facts which contain descriptions or assumptions about states or events that the speaker considers to be true or established and directly acceptable by the hearer. These are termed as *grounds* by Toulmin (1958) or *support* by Stavans et al. (2019).

The satellite components defined by Toulmin (1958) are the warrants, in charge of establishing the connection between claims and grounds. Accordingly, the warrant is a third important but dispensable component of the argument structure because it can be implicit (i.e., not realized in the texts but inferred by the reader). In his analysis, Van Dijk explains that to be able to draw a particular conclusion from particular facts, the argument needs a more general assumption about the relationship between these kinds of facts and claims. In Toulmin's analysis, backing refers to any additional support of the warrant (the connection between grounds and claims) but in Van Dijk's consequent analysis not only warrants but also facts (descriptions that support the premises) may need further motivation or backing. In many cases, the warrant is implied, and therefore the backing links to the claim by giving a specific example that function as warrant. Backing must be introduced when the warrant or the facts by themselves are not convincing enough to the readers or the listeners.

We also looked for the presence of counterclaims or rebuttals, in Toulmin's (1958) terminology. This category may increase the writer's probability to persuade the reader. The rebuttal is an acknowledgement of another valid view of the situation and would be equivalent to a counterclaim in Stavans et al. (2019) terminology introducing a greater degree of text autonomy with a multivoiced text that can invite dialogue with different potential readers (Leitão, 2003).

In Toulmin's model there is another component—the qualifiers, that restricts the instances the claim covers in cases where it may not be true in all circumstances. In this study we did not examine the use of qualifiers.

Given our special interest in the perspective from which the students define their point of view we further examined whether the claims that reflect the author point of view on the topic were based on individual-personal perspectives or on socially constrained perspectives. Claims as the one in (1a) produced by a Hebrew speaker student and in (1b) by a Spanish student were categorized as personal whereas claims as the one in (2a) produced by a Hebrew speaker student and in (2b) by a Spanish student, respectively were categorized as socially driven:

> (1a) ani xoshevet she'hayeldim tzrixim lakaxat haxlatot al ma lilbosh
>
> I think that the kid should make the decisions about what to wear.
>
> (1b) yo creo que todas las personas debemos poder llevar lo que cada uno crea conveniente
>
> I think that all the people (we) must be able to wear whatever one thinks (it is) convenient.
>
> (2a) lesikum,daati hi shanaxni tzrixim tilboshet axida bebeit hasefer bishvil hashayaxut vehabetixut shel hatalmidim
>
> To sum up, my opinion is that we need to use school uniforms for the unity and the security of the students.
>
> (2b) pero dentro de la ropa que te guste llevar tienes que adaptarte al sitio al que vas a ir

> [B]ut among the clothes you like to wear you have to adapt to the place you are going to go.

A third kind of claim contained a reflection on the topic but without personal evaluation whereby rather than expressing the student's point of view on the issue at stake either for individual or social reasons, these thematic claims reflected a generalization on the topic. Claims as the one displayed in (3a) produced by a Hebrew speaking student and in and (3b) by a Spanish student, respectively were categorized as thematic.

> (3a) haim ei paam xashavtem al hamashmaut belilbosh tilboshet axida bebeit hasefer?
>
> Have you ever thought about what it means to wear a uniform at school?
>
> (3b) La manera de vestir ha sido un tema de debate entre la gente en los últimos años
>
> The way of dressing has been a topic of debate among people in the last years.

We could make a similar distinction in terms of the individual or socially driven for the grounds students use to support their claims. Supports such as those expressed in (4a) and (4b) were considered as personal and those in (5a) and (5b) as socially driven.

> (4a) ledaati lilbosh tilboshet axida ze lo raayontov ki talmidim tzrixim lihiyot xofshii lilbosh et ma shehem rotzim
>
> In my opinion it is not a good idea to wear uniforms because students must be free to be able to dress as they want.
>
> (4b) siempre la ropa define, en parte, tu personalidad
>
> Always the clothes define, in part, your personality.
>
> (5a) ledaati ze rayon metzuyan. Reshit, kol hatalmidim shelovshim tilboshet axida margishim shyaxut lekvutza
>
> In my opinion it is a great idea. First of all, students who wear a school uniform feel a part of the group.
>
> (5b) lo más normal es que la gente se te quede mirando y hagan comentarios inadecuados e incluso falten el respeto a esa persona
>
> [T]he most normal (thing) is that people stare at you and make inappropriate comments and even disrespect that person.

According to the model of reference we used for characterizing and interpreting the text's functional categories, claims are to be supported by facts of empirical evidence of some kind. Thus, we also identified factual supports illustrated in (6a) and (6b) by Hebrew speaking and Spanish speaking students respectively.

> (6a) benosaf, harbe mexkarim her'u shetilboshet axida behexlet toremet lkesher bein hayeladim
>
> In addition, many studies have shown that a uniform definitely contributes to the connection between the children.
>
> (6b) este tipo de problemas suele ocurrir a la gente que viste de negro, a la gente que viste con ropa corta y a muchos tipos de personas
>
> [T]his kind of problems often occur to people who wear black, to people who dress in short clothes, and to many types of people.

Each of the authors independently divided the texts into macro-propositions and attributed a functional category according to the above explained criteria. Inter-rater reliability was achieved by parallel coding of 10% of the sample and reaching agreement on 92% of the coded macro-propositions.

What Do We Find in the Texts?

Israeli texts were shorter and contained fewer macro-propositions (M=8.43, SD=1.57) than those of their Spanish cohorts (M=11.47, SD=13.73). Under this rather trivial difference, we have found two rhetorical worlds. Israeli 10th graders' texts are *to the point*, they express in a short direct, and linear manner their claims and supporting grounds motivated mainly by personal preferences. They guide the reader to differentiate between opinion from conclusions and enumerating reasons. They relate to social equality, bullying, safety, and identity.

In contrast, Spanish texts appear as more convoluted reasoning mainly motivated by socially motivated constraints. The reader is challenged to distinguish between ought to be assertions, personal opinions and conclusions. At times, students resort to popular sayings as support to their claims and their digressions take them to include themes such as slavery, civilization, national freedom, and, in one case, suicide.

Despite this diversity, the two rhetorical worlds share two features which would be part of a robust and rich argumentative text architecture as would be expected in fully fledged scientific and academic texts. First, there is a substantial scarcity of counterclaims or attending to alternative views on the same phenomenon,

Cultural Shaping of Standpoint and Reasoning

rendering a biased and author-centric argument. Second, and equally surprising, there are fewer than expected empirical evidence as supporting grounds, rendering rather formulaic and prescribed and at times populist support to the claims.

Figure 6.1 showcases each group's distribution of the components in the texts including: claims (all three types summed up) and counterclaims (all types summed up), support (all types summed up), and warrants and backings (which constitute the general architecture of the texts).

Text architecture differs across the two group of participants. While half of the texts produced by Israeli students conform to the basic structure of an argument—including only claims and support, a similar number of texts produced by Spanish students include all types of components. Yet, texts containing claim, support, and warrant were produced only by Israeli students. Texts with counterclaims and support (CCS) were more frequent in the Israeli group than in the Spanish, whereas text constituting the architectures that include a counterclaim with a support followed by either warrant or backing (CCSW, CCSB) were more frequent among the Spanish texts than among the Israeli ones. The larger presence of counterclaims in the Spanish texts as compared to the Israeli ones may indicate that Israeli students are less prone to provide alternative views or anticipate objections to their own thoughts on the topic at stake. Rather, their basal architecture renders formulaic and somewhat shallow but felicitous argumentative texts.

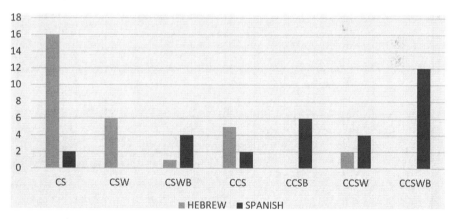

Figure 6.1. Texts "architecture" by number of texts in each group (Hebrew and Spanish) containing different combinations of components. Note: CS=Claim and Support; CSW=Claim, Support, and Warrant; CSWB=Claim, Support, Warrant, and Backing; CCS=Claim, Counterclaim, and Support; CCSB= Claim, Counterclaim, Support, and Backing; CCSW=Claim, Counterclaim, Support, and Warrant; CCSWB Claim, Counterclaim, Support, Warrant, and Backing

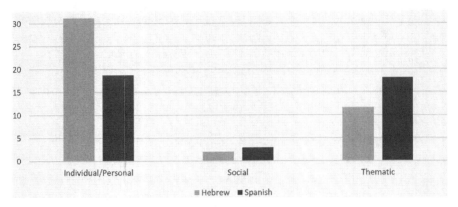

*Figure 6.2. Distribution of the proportion of the three types of **claims** (Individual/Personal, Social, and Thematic) in the texts of each group*

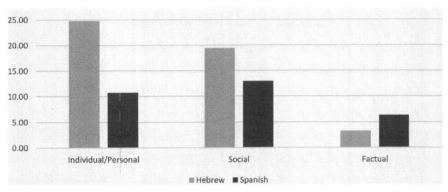

*Figure 6.3. Distribution of the proportion of the three types of **support** (Individual/Personal, Social/Moral, and Factual) in the texts of each group*

Our second concern en-route to deciphering the diversity of these rhetorical worlds was to look closely at the types of claims that were deployed by each group. Figure 6.2 displays the proportional distribution of the three types of claims (individual/personal, social, and thematic) in the texts of each group.

Nearly 30% of the texts of Israeli students frame their claim regarding their point of view on the school uniform as a dressing code on personal preferences such as their right to choose or their ownership on a decision that pertains to them as individuals, whereas almost 12% of their texts grounded their claims in a more general theme to justify their own perspective. Moreover, claims based on issues of socially driven constraints were scarce and negligible. In contrast, the Spanish students showed a balanced distribution (around 18%) of claims that uphold their standpoint on the topic resorting to personal rights and to

Cultural Shaping of Standpoint and Reasoning

reflections on general themes. Very few texts (around nearly 3%) include social considerations to defend their standpoint. In all, the main perspective taken by the Israeli students compared to their Spanish cohorts is one that centers more on the author's identity and thematic emphasis and much less on social considerations whereas the Spanish perspective is more balanced in the perspective taken by the author on the individual and thematic considerations and much less on the social ones, similar to that of the Israeli cohorts.

In a similar vein, we looked at the distribution of the different types of support/grounds components in each group as illustrated in Figure 6.3.

In general, both groups resort predominantly to two types of support—that of a personal nature and that of a socio-moral justification to their claims. Our findings show that Israeli students are more inclined to support their standpoint on justification of personal preferences (almost 25% of the texts) and slightly less on justifications of socio-moral reasons (less than 20% of the texts). To our surprise, about 3% of Israeli students resorted to facts or other kinds of empirical evidence to support their claims. Among the Spanish students, there is a slight preference for justifications of the socio-moral reasons (almost 13% of the texts) followed by personal motivations (almost 11%) and only about 6% of the texts included factual support to the students' standpoints. Like the immature albeit felicitous content of the claim component, the supports follow the very author-centered and shallow text in terms of its sophistication and quality.

Finally, we explored the distribution of the functional categories in the opening and closure emplacement to reveal a more culture-based rhetorical tradition (Table 6.1).

Table 6.1. Type of Component in Text Opening and Closure by Language

	Opening		Closure	
Type of component	Hebrew	Spanish	Hebrew	Spanish
Claim PoV Individual	23,33	16,67	83,33	33,33
Claim PoV Social	3,33	0,00	3,33	3,33
Claim Thematic	70,00	83,33	0,00	13,33
Counterclaim	0,00	0,00	0,00	10,00
Support Personal	0,00	0,00	6,67	6,67
Support Social	0,00	0,00	3,33	6,67
Support Factual	0,00	0,00	0,00	3,33
Warrants	0,00	0,00	3,33	3,33
Backing	0,00	0,00	0,00	13,33

We have found that in all the texts, by both Israeli and Spanish students, the macro-proposition in a text initial position (opening emplacement) is a claim. However, in the Hebrew texts 70% of the claims in opening position are of the thematic type and 23% advance a point of view of a personal preferences nature. The preferences for a thematic claim, that is the preference to start a text with a reflection on the topic, is more pronounced in the Spanish texts with more that 80% of the texts using this type of opening. In that sense the opening of the argumentative texts of both rhetorical worlds is similar. However, the distribution of the components differs in the closure emplacement. Although the preferred way of closure is still a personal claim, there are texts that close by means of other resources. Overall, the characterization of emplacement reflects on the reasoning that is recruited in construing an argument. As indicated earlier, an argument that opens with an explicit or implicit claim (individual, social, or thematic) and closes with any kind of support reflects deductive reasoning while a text where the claim is in the closure reflects an inductive reasoning.

Our results indicate that most of the students follow a deductive reasoning, moving from a thematic-driven assertion supported by personal justifications. To confirm this impression, we look *at each text* to examine the transition between the opening and the closure emplacement. Texts that open with a thematic claim and close with any kind of claim expressing the student point of view, a warrant or a backing were categorized as a deductive reasoning transition. Texts that open with any kind of claim expressing the student point of view and close with a thematic claim were categorized as displaying an inductive reasoning transition. Texts in which both opening and closure contained claims, or support of similar type were categorized as neither deductive nor inductive reasoning transition (Table 6.2).

Most Hebrew texts follow a deductive reasoning, moving from thematic claims in the opening macro-preposition to personal points of view claims followed by support. There is not such clear preference among the Spanish students, half of the texts follow a deductive pattern, but an almost identical number of students use the same type of claim at both the opening and the closure emplacement.

Table 6.2. The Distribution of Texts by type of Reasoning/Transition and Group

Type or Reasoning	Hebrew (n = 30)	Spanish (n = 30)
Deductive	21	15
Inductive	4	1
Neither/nor	5	14
Total	30	30

TWO RHETORICAL WORLDS

Both Israeli and Spanish students were able to build an argument, they could produce a set of statements they assume to express their own thoughts on the topic of a dress code, and another set of statements that supported these thoughts. They were able to create the binary structure that defines an argument (van Dijk, 1980). However, beyond this basic common ground the texts of these adolescents highlight two contrasting rhetorical approaches.

Texts differed in their overall architecture, in the perspective from which the standpoint was expressed, in the type of supports students offered, in the pattern of argumentation and in the quality of their prose. Israeli students' standpoint was mainly based on individual considerations while Spanish students' framing of their point of view was more diverse, some viewpoints were driven by individual concerns, others by social impositions. The texts also differed in the type of supports used to ground the standpoints, again basically personally grounded justifications to the claims in the Israeli texts, and socially constrained justifications in the Spanish ones. There was also a clear distinction in the general pattern of reasoning, with Israeli texts offering a deductive reasoning pattern whereas Spanish texts are diverse, half following a deductive the other half advancing a neither deductive nor inductive, both opening and the closure contained claims, or support of similar type.

These differences have implications in terms of the audience for which the texts are intended and as such, beyond the differences in features of the superstructure there were notable differences in the kind of prose. Israeli instructional material and curriculum, as previously described, advances a highly structured argumentative text. Thus, Israeli productions were easy to follow, and to interpret both in content and structure. In contrast, Spanish texts illustrate McCool's description of a reader-responsible culture in their emphasis of "flowery and ornate prose" (2009, p. 2), their appeal to sayings, and reference to big topics that sounded weird (and unnecessary) in relation to a discussion on the dressing code was rather disconcerting. We suppose that these extravagances result from students' effort to imbue their texts of relevant content, to escape from colloquial discourse attending to the requirement of formal uses of language.

These findings point currently at the relevance, albeit with limitations and old in its framing, of the validity of some of the gross distinctions made by Kaplan (1966/1980) and Rienecker and Jörgensen (2003). The basic distinctions were also observed and used to profile our texts as following either the Anglo-American or the Romance rhetoric. Still, our findings call for a deeper characterization of the argument structure. For instance, the kind of grounds students that belong to each cultural group used to support their claims and/or the use of qualifiers, which in turn reflect the writers' attitude toward the scope, certainty, or prescriptiveness of the state of affairs they used to justify their claims. These and other more fine-grained distinctions would complete the characterization of how writers from differing cultural traditions engaged in participatory text production carry on their "social participatory performance" (Bazerman, 2016).

In a more speculative vein, our findings point at the weight of pedagogical planning and practices exercised in the teaching of writing which is conservatively ordained by rhetorical conventions. There are different approaches to teaching writing taken by the Israeli as compared to the Spanish teachers. In the Israeli context, the teaching objectives in the writing of an argumentative text are highly structurally oriented but the practice of these objectives is embedded in multiple literacy activities around and towards the production of the texts, including reading, discussions, resource search, debates, and technologically grounded work in the classroom. These approaches and methods towards writing an argumentative text are eying the long-term expectations of the higher education system whereby the favored rhetorical tradition is the Anglo-American one. The outcome of such teaching practice suggests that the students shift away from the Semitic rhetorical features of Hebrew speakers' writing when producing a text in English as shown by Zellermayer (1988). While these observations illustrate the influence of the specific rhetoric in another language these may transfer when observing Israeli adolescents write in their first/native language. In contrast, the Spanish teacher's communicative approach, focusing on topic content, purpose, and motivation rather than on structural aspects seems to preserve many aspects of Romance rhetoric tradition.

To conclude, Bazerman and Prior stated: "To understand writing, we need to explore the practices that people engage in to produce texts as well as the way that writing practices gain their meaning and functions as dynamic elements of specific cultural settings" (2003, p. 2). Rhetorical structures are intricately related to cultural traditions for expressing, perceiving, and understanding the world. This relation as explored in this chapter, ascribes to the need to explore genre as well as text analysis in a sociocultural manner especially when the task at hand requires participatory writing in different languages, cultures, and rhetorical traditions, as a fundamental human need.

REFERENCES

Almehmadi, M. M. (2012). A contrastive rhetorical analysis of factual texts in English and Arabic. *Frontiers of Language and Teaching, 3*, 68–76.

Arvay, A. & Tanko, G. (2004). A contrastive analysis of English and Hungarian theoretical research article introductions. *International Review of Applied Linguistics in Language Teaching, 42*(1), 71.

Butler, D. B. (2010). *How L2 legal writers use strategies for scholarly writing: A mixed methods study*. [Unpublished doctoral dissertation] University of Maryland, College Park.

Bazerman, C. (1988). *Shaping written knowledge: The genre and activity of the experimental article in science, 356*. University of Wisconsin Press.

Bazerman, C. (2016). What do sociocultural studies of writing tell us about learning to write? In C. MacArthur, S. Graham & J. Fitzgerald (Eds.), *Handbook of writing research* (2nd ed.; pp. 11–23). Guilford.

Bazerman, C. & Prior, P. (2003). *What writing does and how it does it: An introduction to analyzing texts and textual practices*. Routledge.

Belcher, D. (2014). What we need and don't need intercultural rhetoric for: A retrospective and prospective look at an evolving research area. *Journal of Second Language Writing, 25*, 59–67.

Biria, R. & Yakhabi, M. (2013). Contrastive rhetorical analysis of argumentation techniques in the argumentative essays of English and Persian writers. *Journal of Language, Culture, and Translation, 2*(1), 1–14.

Burgess, S. R. (2002). The influence of speech perception, oral language ability, the home literacy environment, and pre-reading knowledge on the growth of phonological sensitivity: A one-year longitudinal investigation. *Reading and Writing, 15*(7), 709–737.

Casanave, C. (2004). *Controversies in second language writing*. University of Michigan Press.

Chala, P. A. & Chapetón, C. M. (2012). EFL argumentative essay writing as a situated-social practice: review of concepts. *Folios, 36*, 23–36.

Clyne, M. (1987). Cultural differences in the organization of academic texts: English and German. *Journal of pragmatics, 11*(2), 211–241.

Connor, U., Connor, U. M. & Long, M. H. (1996). *Contrastive rhetoric: Cross-cultural aspects of second language writing*. Cambridge University Press.

Connor, U. (2002). New directions in contrastive rhetoric. *TESOL Quarterly, 36*(4), 493–510.

Connor, U. (2004). Contrastive rhetoric: Old and new directions. In N. Kassabgy, Z. Ibrahim & S. Aydelott (Eds.), *Contrastive rhetoric: Issues, insights, and pedagogy* (pp. 1–24). The American University in Ciro Press.

Connor, U. (2008). Mapping multidimensional aspects of research: Reaching to intercultural rhetoric. In U. Connor, E. Nagelhout & W. Rozycki (Eds.), *Contrastive rhetoric: Reaching to intercultural rhetoric* (pp. 299–316). John Benjamins.

Connor, U., Ene, E. & Traversa, A. (2014). Intercultural rhetoric. In *The Routledge handbook of English for academic purposes* (pp. 294–306). Routledge.

Drid, T. (2015). Exploring the rhetorical and communicative impacts of native culture on the argumentative writing of Algerian Master students of EFL: Towards designing a university course for the teaching of argumentative essay writing. Unpublished doctoral thesis, Mentouri Brothers University, Constantine, Algeria.

Ferris, D. & Hedgcock, J. S. (2005). *Teaching composition: Purpose, process, and practice* (2nd ed.). Lawrence Erlbaum.

Galbraith, D. (1999). Writing as a knowledge-constituting process. Knowing what to write: *Conceptual Processes in Text Production, 4*, 13 9–164.

Golebiowski, Z. (1998). Rhetorical approaches to scientific writing: an English: Polish contrastive study. *Text, 18*(1).

Hinds, J. (1987). Reader Versus Writer Responsibility: A New Typology. In U. Connor & R. B. Kaplan (Eds.), *Writing across languages: Analysis of L2 text* (pp. 141–152). Addison Wesley Publishing Company.

Hinds, J. (1990). Inductive, deductive, quasi-inductive: Expository writing in Japanese, Korean, Chinese, and Thai. *Coherence in Writing: Research and Pedagogical Perspectives, 87*, 109.

Hinkel, E. (2005). Hedging, inflating, and persuading in L2 academic writing. *Applied Language Learning, 15*(1/2), 29.

Husin, M. S. & Griffin, K. (2012). The rhetorical organisation of English argumentative essays by Malay ESL students: The placement of the thesis statement. *The Journal of Asia EFL, 9*(1), 147–169.

Kamimura, T. & Oi, K. (1998). Argumentative strategies in American and Japanese English. *World Englishes, 17*(3), 307–323.

Kaplan, R. B. (1966). Cultural thought patterns in intercultural education. *Language Learning, 16*(1), 1–20.

Kemerling, G. (2011). *The philosophy pages.* http://www.philosophypages.com.

Kubota, R. Y. U. K. O. (2010). Cross-cultural perspectives on writing: Contrastive rhetoric. *Sociolinguistics and Language Education, 18*, 265–289.

Leitão, S. (2000). The potential of argument in knowledge building. *Human Development, 43*, 332–360.

Leitão, S. (2003). Evaluating and selecting counterarguments: Studies of children's rhetorical awareness. *Written Communication, 20*, 269–306.

Loukianenko-Wolfe, M. (2008). Different culture—different discourses? Rhetorical patterns of business letters by English and Russian speakers. In U. Connor, E. Nagelhout & W. V. Rozycki (Eds.), *Contrastive Rhetoric: Reaching to intercultural rhetoric* (pp. 87–121). John Benjamins.

Mann, W. & Thompson, S. (1987). *Rhetorical Structure Theory: A theory of text organization.* Information Sciences Institute.

Maqueo, A. M. (2006). *Lengua, aprendizaje y enseñanza: el enfoque comunicativo: De la teoría a la práctica.* Limusa

Martın-Martın, P. (2003). A genre analysis of English and Spanish research paper abstracts in experimental social sciences. *English for Specific Purposes, 22*, 25–43.

Matsuda, P. K. (2001). Voice in Japanese written discourse: Implications for second language writing. *Journal of Second Language Writing, 10*(1–2), 35–53.

Mauranen, A. (1993). Contrastive ESP Rhetoric Metatext in Finnish-English economic texts. *English for Specific Purposes, 12*, 3–22.

McCool, M. (2009). *Writing around the world: A guide to writing across cultures.* Bloomsbury.

Mohan, B. & Lo, W. (1985). Academic writing and Chinese students: Transfer and developmental factors. *Tesol Quarterly, 19*(3), 515–534.

Oi, K., Kamimura, T. & Sano, K. M. (1996). *Writing power.* Kenkyuusha

Okabe, R. (1983). Cultural assumptions of East and West: Japan and the United States. In W. B. Gudykunst (Ed.), *Intercultural communication theory: Current perspectives* (pp. 21–44). Sage Publications.

Pak, C. & Acevedo, R. (2008). Spanish-language newspaper editorials from Mexico, Spain, and the US. John Benjamins. https://doi.org/10.1075/pbns.169.09pak

Perelman, C. & Olbrechts-Tyteca, L. (1989). *Tratado de la argumentación*. Editorial Gredos.

Qin, J. & Karabacak, E. (2010). The analysis of Toulmin elements in Chinese EFL university argumentative writing. *System, 38*, 444–456.

Ramírez, R. (2010). *Didácticas de la lengua y de la argumentación escrita*. Universidad de Nariño.

Rienecker, L. & Jörgensen, P. S. (2003). The (im)possibilities in teaching university writing in the Anglo-American tradition when dealing with continental student writers. In L. Björk, G. Bräuer, L. Rienecker & P. S. Jörgensen (Eds.), *Teaching academic writing in European higher education* (pp. 101–112). Kluwer Academic Publishers.

Schleppegrell, M. J. & Colombi, M. C. (2005). *Developing advanced literacy in first and second languages: Meaning with power*. Routledge.

Scott, D., Delin, J. & Hartley, A. (1999). Identifying congruent pragmatic relations in procedural texts. *Languages in Contrast, 1*(1), 45–82.

Soler-Monreal, C., Carbonell-Olivares, M. & Gil-Salom, L. (2011). A contrastive study of the rhetorical organization of English and Spanish PhD thesis introductions. *English for Specific Purposes, 30*(1), 4–17.

Stavans, A., Seroussi, B. & Zadunaisky Ehrlich, S. (2019). Literacy-related abilities' effects on argumentative text quality structure. *Journal of Literacy Research, 51*(3), 315–335.

Stroud, S. R. (2019). Diversity in and among rhetorical traditions. *Advances in the History of Rhetoric, 22*(2), 120–124.

Suárez Tejerina, L. & Moreno A. I. (2008). The rhetorical structure of literary academic book reviews: An English-Spanish cross-linguistic approach. In U. Connor, E. Nagelhout & W. Rozycki (Eds.), *Contrastive Rhetoric: Reaching to Intercultural Rhetoric* (pp. 147–168). Amsterdam: Benjamins.

Taboada, M. & Mann, W. (2006). Rhetorical structure theory: Looking back and moving ahead. *Discourse Studies, 8*(3), 423–459.

Taylor, G. & Tingguang, C. (1991). Linguistic, cultural, and subcultural issues in contrastive discourse analysis: Anglo-American and Chinese scientific texts. *Applied Linguistics, 12*(3), 319–336.

Tolchinsky, L., Rosado, E. & Aparici, M. (2018). Escribir para pensar y persuadir de manera fundamentada. *Textos. Didàctica de la llengua i la literaturai, 76*, 14–21.

Torres, J. M. & Medriano, R. (2020). Rhetorical organization of Ilocano and Tagalog preservice teachers in their argumentative essays. *The Asian EFL Journal, 27*(2.2), 261–286.

Toulmin, S. (1958). *The uses of argument*. Cambridge University Press.

Underberg, L. & Norton, H. (2018). *Argumentation: The art of civil advocacy*. Sage.

Valero-Garcés, C. (1996). Contrastive ESP rhetoric: Metatext in Spanish-English economics texts. *English for Specific Purposes, 15*(4), 279–294.

Van Dijk, T. A. (1980). *Macrostructures: An interdisciplinary study of global structures in discourse, interaction, and cognition.* Lawrence Erlbaum.

Warnick, B. & Manusov, V. (2000). The organization of justificatory discourse in interaction: A comparison within and across cultures. *Argumentation, 14*(4), 381–404.

Widdowson, H. G. (1979). *Aspects of language teaching.* Oxford University Press.

Zellermayer, M. (1988). An analysis of oral and literate texts: Two types of reader-writer relationships in Hebrew and English. In B. A. Rafoth & D. L. Rubin (Eds.), *The social construction of written communication* (pp. 287–303). Ablex.

Zhu, W. (2001). Performing argumentative writing in English: Difficulties, processes, and strategies. *TESL Canada Journal, 19*(1), 34–51

PART THREE. SOCIOLOGY OF KNOWLEDGE & ORGANIZATIONAL COMMUNICATION

CHAPTER 7.

GENRE CHANGE AROUND TEACHING IN THE COVID-19 PANDEMIC

JoAnne Yates
Massachusetts Institute of Technology

As someone who has studied genre and genre change both historically and in contemporary, electronically mediated, organizational communication, I have long benefitted from the research of Charles Bazerman. Bazerman's *Shaping written knowledge: The genre and activity of the experimental article in science* (1988) was published a year before (and thus too late to influence) my *Control through communication: The rise of system in American management* (Yates, 1989), in which I studied the emergence of the genres of business communication (e.g., the memo) that dominated the 20th century. My colleague Wanda Orlikowski and I began our joint project on genre use in new media in the 1990s. Our first, theoretical paper (Yates & Orlikowski, 1992) drew on Carolyn Miller's (1984) "Genre as social action," Bazerman's *Shaping written knowledge (1988)*, and Anthony Giddens' (1984) structuration theory to propose genres of organizational communication as enacted structures with a socially recognized purpose and common characteristics of form (including the medium in which they were typically enacted). We then showed how, through the conceptual lens of these structures, we could understand changes in organizational communication over time, using the emergence of the memo as our primary example and Bazerman's experimental article as another.

Bazerman's influence on our work soon increased. Our first empirical paper on genre (Orlikowski & Yates, 1994) examined the early-1980s electronic communication of computer scientists at different firms and universities who were developing the Common LISP artificial intelligence language. Here, we also drew on Bazerman's (1994) concept of genre systems as we traced the evolution of three genres and a genre system that Common LISP participants used in what was then a new medium, email. His definition of genre systems as "interrelated genres that interact with each other in specific settings" (Bazerman, 1994, p. 97), along with Devitt's (1991) notion of genre sets encouraged us to focus on the relationships among genres in this piece. We introduced the notion of genre

DOI: https://doi.org/10.37514/PER-B.2023.1800.2.07

repertoire (an elaboration of Devitt's genre set) as a useful approach to understanding groups and organizations. Bazerman's genre systems also became the subject and inspiration of another piece in which we demonstrated their value for studying how people use sequences of typified communicative actions to coordinate their activity over time and space (Yates & Orlikowski, 2002). In that paper we identified six dimensions of genre systems[1] (which also apply to genres and genre repertoires) that can serve as heuristics for studying them: socially recognized purpose (*why*); typical content (*what*); form, including medium and format features (*how*); participants (*who*); timing (*when*), and geographical or virtual place (*where*). (I will draw on this heuristic in my analysis of teaching genres, below.) For over a decade Orlikowski and I studied how genres, genre systems, and genre repertoires evolved as they were enacted in new electronic media.[2]

At the same time, we introduced Bazerman's work to a new audience: scholars studying interactions between information technology (IT) and organizations in management and information schools. Bazerman (2001) contributed a chapter to a book I co-edited with John Van Maanen, *IT and Organizational Transformation: History, Rhetoric, and Practice*. Several other management and information scholars studying new media in organizations also adopted a genre approach. For example, Barbara H. Kwaśnik and Kevin Crowston edited a 2005 special issue of *Information Technology & People* on "Genres of Digital Documents." Bazerman has thus influenced the IT and organizations field, in addition to other fields from rhetoric to education.

In my contribution to this volume in his honor, I apply the notions of genre, genre system, and genre repertoire to a different content domain reflecting Bazerman's later academic home in an education school. What follows is an essay based on my participation in and observations of the changes in teaching genres, genre systems, and genre repertoires triggered by the COVID-19 pandemic in my academic home (the MIT Sloan School of Management) from March 2020 through January 2021. I draw on the recorded Zoom teaching and learning town halls (described later), PowerPoint decks for those gatherings and for a faculty retreat in May 2020, and a few administrative and teaching-related memos to faculty; in addition, I interviewed a few individuals.[3] Although my subject

---

1   Bazerman's (1994) discussion of the patent genre system considers, without naming, most of these dimensions.
2   Carolyn Miller's provocative contribution to this volume argues that medium and genre are inseparable when new media are initially introduced. I have always found it useful to differentiate them, at least analytically.
3   Interviewees include the teaching dean, staff director, head of Sloan Technology Services, and several faculty. I appreciate all my colleagues who helped me in this effort. I also thank Lori Breslow for pointing me to the few education papers I have cited.

matter is higher education, I examine it not from an education perspective (an area in which I have no expertise), but with the hope that my empirical case and analysis will be of interest to people in multiple disciplines that value Bazerman's work, including IT and organizations, media studies, rhetoric, and education. In it, I will use a genre lens (including the heuristic set of dimensions) to illuminate the changes that management faculty and administration instituted in teaching, as well as in discourse about teaching, in response to pandemic emergency regulations imposed by the state (Massachusetts), the university (MIT), and the management school (Sloan).[4]

On the most obvious level, in spring 2020 faculty had to adapt familiar genres of classroom teaching (e.g., the lecture, the discussion, the experiential exercise) to reach students mediated by Zoom, and in fall 2020 to reach masked students separated by 6 feet simultaneously with those in different locations and mediated by video or Zoom. Changes in the medium and form features (*how*) that Zoom offered initiated changes in other dimensions of genres. Encouraged by Bazerman's (1994) focus on interaction among genres, I also consider changes at the level of genre systems that coordinate a sequence of activities outside and within classes over an entire course. Further, the faculty's need to learn newly evolving teaching practices from each other spawned a new genre that was not part of a specific teaching genre or course genre system, but an addition to Sloan's previously limited community discourse about—and thus genre repertoire around—teaching: the teaching and learning town hall, which in turn catalyzed sharing of genre and genre system adaptations across the community. Finally, I reflect on these changes at different levels, and on how temporary or permanent they are likely to be.

TEACHING AT MIT SLOAN BEFORE THE PANDEMIC

First, some background on the MIT Sloan School of Management (Sloan) and its teaching in normal times is necessary to understand what follows. Sloan has an extensive portfolio of degreed educational programs. In the largest, flagship two-year MBA program, classes occur in the fall and spring semesters, with MBA students working in internships over the summer between the two years. Sloan also offers two mid-career MBA programs: the 12-month residential Sloan Fellows Program, and the part-time Executive MBA Program (EMBA) with employed students who often travel from a distance (or occasionally use Zoom) to attend weekend classes every three weeks. Beyond that, Sloan offers multiple

---

4 Throughout this paper I focus on teaching from the faculty rather than student side of the teaching and learning process.

specialized programs, many of which include classes in the summer as well as during the academic year. I will focus primarily on the teaching changes for the two-year MBA but will need to refer to other programs and formats when they became important in faculty sharing of new learnings about pandemic teaching.

Sloan faculty use a variety of teaching approaches, but below I briefly describe some common genres of classroom teaching enacted at Sloan and other business and professional schools. These classroom teaching genres may also be combined in a single class session. Some aspects of the six genre dimensions[5] are common to all of them: the medium (*how*) is face-to-face communication with the teacher and students (*who*), in the same classroom (*where*), during scheduled class time (*when*). In addition, teaching assistants (TAs)—more advanced MBA students or doctoral students—are present in most classes (*who*) to monitor student participation.

- Lecture:[6] A lecture's socially recognized purpose in the Sloan community (why) is the primarily one-way presentation of new content (what) by the instructor to the students (who), using PowerPoint slides or writing on the board (how). Lecture is frequently combined with discussion in Sloan classes.
- Discussion: In a discussion, students are assumed to have already received new content in a lecture or in pre-class reading, and the instructor solicits student reactions to the material and to each other's points to help students explore, apply, and understand the content and its implications (why and what). The professor often writes on a board or annotates slides to record student input (how).
- Case discussion:[7] A case class is a specific type of discussion teaching that pushes students to explore and extract more general principles from a concrete situation (why). It requires students to prepare for class by reading and analyzing a business case[8] built around a protagonist who must make a decision (what). The professor typically leads students through the case by asking them a series of questions and recording key points on the board (how).

---

5   In this paper I restrict my use of the dimensions to genres, not genre systems or repertoires, to avoid confusion.

6   I am focusing on genres as they are understood at Sloan, based on my own experience, but the lecture genre and others are more broadly recognized in academia and in education. For a classic exploration of the lecture, for example, see Bligh (1971, 2000).

7   Some business and professional schools have traditionally focused entirely on case classes, but Sloan uses a mix of genres.

8   The case itself is also a recognized genre used in business and professional schools; it is part of the case teaching genre system, which requires students to read it in advance, to participate in class discussion of it, and sometimes to write a case analysis due before or after class.

- Experiential exercise: Experiential exercises are used to help students learn a skill or gain deep understanding (why) through participating in a role play or other experience (what) and discussing it. The instructor typically divides students into groups (sometimes sending them out of the classroom to breakout rooms—where) to engage in the exercise; afterwards, the teacher leads a full-class debrief of it, often recording the learnings on boards (how).

Various additional form features may optionally be incorporated into multiple teaching genres. For example, faculty (especially in more qualitative courses) often pause a lecture or discussion and ask students sitting close together to form small *buzz groups*[9] to discuss a topic or raise questions among themselves for several minutes, then ask groups or individuals to report out. *Cold* and *warm calls* are questions posed by a teacher to a specific student (rather than to a volunteer), either with no warning (cold call) or with a warning earlier in the class (warm call).

The genre system around a course, which governs the dynamics of teaching and learning in it, includes many genres in addition to the teaching genres themselves. A website set up on the Canvas course management system contains the syllabus, assignments, readings, and cases for students to use as needed for each class, as well as places for them to submit their completed assignments (also genres in the genre system) and to receive feedback and grades from the TA or instructor. TAs interact with students outside of class, including holding office hours, responding to student questions, grading and returning assignments, and, in some courses, conducting scheduled recitations. Faculty also typically hold regular meetings with their TAs to coordinate these interactions and to discuss student participation. During class itself, the instructor instantiates the teaching genre in interaction with the students. These activities interlock across the entire semester as faculty, students, and TAs sequentially enact the course genre system.

Stepping back from specific courses to teaching more broadly, although good teaching is valued at Sloan (e.g., many teaching awards recognize it), discourse about and instruction in teaching (the part of Sloan's overall genre repertoire focused on teaching, which I will call the teaching repertoire) has traditionally been relatively informal and limited. Newly hired faculty attend an orientation which focuses more on research than on teaching. Most attention to teaching occurs within specific teaching groups (e.g., applied economics, accounting, organization studies). New faculty often learn to teach MBAs (a particularly challenging audience for those who earned their Ph.D.s in disciplinary departments

---

9   Buzz groups are related to the pair or small group activities that educational experts cite as ways to make lectures more interactive (Cranfield, 2016).

rather than in business schools) by talking to and sitting in on the classes of one or more senior faculty members in their teaching groups who have reputations as particularly good teachers. In classes with multiple sections, especially core (required) courses that are expected to be consistent across sections, all those teaching the course typically meet before each class to discuss *what* material will be covered and *how*, another source of learning about teaching. If newer faculty are struggling with teaching, they can also ask a senior faculty member or an in-house teaching coach to observe them teaching one or more class sessions and meet with them to give feedback and suggestions. Sharing *across* teaching groups around teaching is informal and relatively rare, occurring occasionally in workshops around new technology, in meetings for faculty in special programs, or in hallway conversations among friends.

With this background on pre-COVID-19 Sloan teaching, I now turn to the changes in classroom teaching genres, genre systems, and genre repertoires that were triggered by the pandemic and consequent restrictions. This period, from March 2020 to January 2021, included two phases of intensive change: the initial shift from in-person to fully online Zoom teaching halfway through the spring 2020 semester and the summer that followed, and the overlapping phase beginning in July 2020 when the school began preparing for simultaneously in-person and online instruction (which came to be called hyflex teaching) in fall 2020.[10]

PHASE 1: THE SHIFT TO TEACHING REMOTELY BY ZOOM

Initial changes occurred rapidly when MIT responded to the spread of COVID-19 and state restrictions by locking down in mid-March of 2020, sending students, faculty, and staff home and announcing that all classes would shift online. The lock-down was announced late in the week of March 9, and all MIT classes were cancelled for the following week; the week after that was MIT's scheduled spring break. Sloan faculty thus had two weeks to prepare for online teaching, a shift in the teaching medium (*how*), beginning the week of March 30. They immediately focused on learning technology basics to allow them to complete the semester from home, quickly migrating their teaching genres into Zoom, initially with as few other changes as possible.

During the two-week pause in courses, Sloan's administration and technical support groups disseminated considerable information related to teaching on Zoom. Within days, they sent faculty and staff a link to a Resource Hub for Online Teaching that Sloan Technology Services (STS) had just launched. The

---

10 Both online and hyflex teaching continued through the spring term of 2021, but I focus on the two periods of most intense change.

new Resource Hub signaled Sloan's initial approach in shifting to Zoom teaching with a statement that although teaching online might require faculty to rethink their classroom approach somewhat, most of their usual methods could be "interpreted" for use online. That is, they could enact their teaching genres live in Zoom with minimal changes beyond the new medium (*how*), as illustrated in a table with two columns—*Classroom Approach* and *Remote Alternatives*—and rows for teaching genres. An alternative to lectures, for example, was presenting using laptop and Zoom conferencing.[11] The table also suggested drawing or annotating on an iPad to replace writing on the board, a technique useful in multiple teaching genres. Similarly, alternative ways to conduct group work (for experiential exercises or for buzz groups in other genres) included using the Zoom breakout room feature to create virtual groups. These suggestions focused on importing form features (*how*) of existing teaching genres from the face-to-face classroom into Zoom (combined with Canvas, iPads, and other tools) as directly as possible. Formerly, STS had worked individually with faculty whose in-person courses included EMBA students who sometimes needed to Zoom into in-person classes, as well as with a few faculty who had created online courses on MITx (a massive open online course program using the edX platform developed by Harvard and MIT). Now, STS lacked the time and staff to work individually with every member of the spring teaching faculty before classes restarted in two weeks. STS and Sloan's administration immediately urged faculty, TAs, and administrative staff (admins) working with teaching faculty to take three newly created or revised live STS training classes via Zoom: Zoom Essentials, Canvas Essentials, and Best Practices in Online Teaching.[12] These live classes were offered multiple times during the next two weeks and recorded so those who could not attend them live could watch a recording. In the past, faculty were often reluctant to spend time attending STS training classes such as the earlier Canvas training, often sending their TAs and admins instead; now, however, facing imminent online teaching, many of them joined TAs and admins in taking the courses.

The class on Zoom Essentials demonstrated how to share screens, how to use Zoom breakout rooms, how to conduct a poll, and how students could put questions in Chat (unless it was disabled) or raise their blue Zoom hands to indicate

---

11   The table also included a few suggestions for asynchronous online classes (e.g., providing all pre-recorded lectures on Canvas), an approach adopted by some undergraduate MIT courses outside of Sloan to better accommodate international students who returned to their home countries, but these were never used at Sloan. Most MBA students stayed in the Cambridge area, and all Sloan constituencies (e.g., faculty, program administrators, students) preferred synchronous classes to allow interaction.

12   Because Sloan had shifted to Canvas courseware recently and not all faculty were fully comfortable with it, STS included and built on existing Canvas training to create Canvas Essentials, adding new elements linked to Zoom teaching.

they had a question. Trainers presented these many Zoom and Canvas features as ways to translate face-to-face teaching techniques such as recognizing student questions and putting students in buzz groups directly into the new medium through raised blue Zoom hands and Zoom breakout rooms. Nevertheless, this basic Zoom training made clear that change in *how* would necessitate other changes in the teaching genres, as the TAs would have to monitor the chat and raised hands for student questions, as well as set up and initiate breakouts and polls. This expanded role would involve them more critically in classroom teaching genres (a change in the participants or *who* dimension). Canvas Essentials, the second offering, taught how to use Canvas courseware, especially in conjunction with Zoom (e.g., timing the release of materials to students for use in experiential exercises, allowing outside speakers into a Zoom class via Canvas). The third new class, Best Practices in Online Teaching, was led by an instructional designer in STS; she suggested another unavoidable change: that faculty would not be able to cover as much content in an online class as in an in-person class (a change in the *what* dimension that was standard wisdom in MITx). These more-or-less involuntary changes in the participants (*who*) and content (*what*) of genres induced by the change in medium would become recurring themes in faculty discussion of the switch to Zoom.

Finally, the deputy dean (a faculty member who was scheduled to end his term as deputy dean[13] on July (1) sent an email before Zoom classes began that sought to reassure faculty: "The most important thing for the moment though is not technology but thoughtfulness. Remember: It's your course and you know the pedagogical goals of the course better than anyone" (email, deputy dean to faculty, 3/13/2020).

Faculty taught the second half of the spring term over Zoom, necessarily adapting the teaching genres by cutting back on content and working with TAs and admins in new ways. Meanwhile, recognizing the need to maintain an intense focus on teaching into the summer and following academic year, Sloan's dean persuaded the departing deputy dean, who was highly respected but better known for his research orientation than for his teaching, to take on a newly created position of associate dean for teaching and learning (teaching dean) beginning in July 2020. In preparation for a faculty retreat scheduled for late May, the soon-to-be teaching dean and the director of faculty and research services (staff director) organized a series of (Zoom) focus groups with faculty and a few students to extract learnings about online teaching from spring term that could be shared and incorporated into summer teaching. They reported their findings—based on 19 focus groups and 143 participants—during the (Zoom) faculty retreat.

---

13   The deputy dean is the top academic officer in the dean's office.

They judged that "Overall, this sudden transition went remarkably well" (PowerPoint slide from Zoom faculty retreat, 5/21/2020; subsequent quotations from the same source). Nevertheless, they also reported that faculty found Zoom teaching more stressful, exhausting, and not as much fun as in-person teaching. Faculty noted the importance of working as a team with the TA or a co-instructor in the classroom to manage questions, initiate polls, and put students in breakout rooms (a change in *who*). As the training had suggested, they found that the content they could cover in class was reduced (a significant change in *what* was covered in the teaching genres), for technology and other reasons. Faculty felt that student attention spans on Zoom were shorter and that "students need more interpersonal time . . . to maintain engagement," encouraging them to add additional form features (*how*) such as Zoom polls (which took time) to get student attention and gauge student understanding. Faculty also reported problems leading fluid discussions and getting good participation on Zoom, and the report mentioned one fairly common workaround: having students discuss questions among themselves in small Zoom breakout groups and report out (an adaptation in *how* the discussion and case class genres worked that also replaced cold calls with warm calls, since students knew who would report out). Other less common spring term workarounds were summarized on the retreat slides as follows: "Well-designed exercises—such as group presentations, pre-questions, polls and surveys, 'warm calling'—can increase participation." One instructor, for example, assigned brief reflection papers on cases or readings, due the night before class, to assure student preparation and to enable her to choose students to talk about specific points the next day in class, often with advance warning; another assigned open-ended surveys to be completed before class for a similar purpose.[14]

The report reflected a few, relatively small changes in teaching genre systems and in Sloan's teaching repertoire, as well. The added assignment and resulting reflection papers, for example, added faculty and student genres to the course genre system. Faculty also found that practicing Zoom teaching in advance with TAs was helpful, with practice sessions adding to the course genre system on the faculty and TA side. In terms of the teaching genre repertoire, they endorsed the importance of taking the STS workshops, which allowed some discussion of teaching methods, and took many more of these than usual in March. One faculty quote presented in the report pointed to a more interesting, though informal, development in Sloan's genre repertoire: "This experience has brought me closer actually to [other] faculty. Like we're comparing notes about how we each teach. . . . We've done more of that in the last six weeks than the entire

---

14   These techniques were later discussed during the teaching and learning town halls described below.

two-and-a-half years before that, just comparing notes and learning from and by each other." These informal conversations were still typically limited to those in the same teaching group or friends. Finally, the focus groups and retreat presentation summarizing them were new additions to the repertoire, sharing these learnings more broadly among faculty from all teaching groups.

Teaching migration into Zoom and modification to better suit the new medium continued during the summer for faculty who taught in programs that met then, including the mid-career Sloan Fellows program. Most faculty teaching online in the summer had not taught during the spring, but they could learn from conversations with their colleagues who taught in the spring and from the retreat presentation in May. In addition, they had more time to revise their courses. For example, three faculty teaching Sloan Fellows at the beginning of the summer all pre-recorded mini-lecture segments (5–10 minutes of slides and voice-over) on new technical concepts and assigned students to view them before class, then used class time for discussion and breakouts about applying the material to real problems. This video lecture technique was borrowed, one of them mentioned, from the flipped classroom model (she had taken a new STS training on the flipped classroom in May), though she noted that they had not adopted the whole model.[15] This modification to their normal lecture-plus-discussion teaching genre enabled them to make up some of the content loss in Zoom teaching by changing *how*, *where*, and *when* some content was presented; in addition, it changed *what* content was covered in class to make it more engaging to students. This new option significantly changed their use of teaching genres (reducing use of lecture and increasing use of discussion). Moreover, the videos themselves instantiated a new genre introduced into the course genre system.

Early in the summer, an organized opportunity for faculty discussion about teaching occurred between two groups of faculty teaching the mid-career Sloan Fellows students. The faculty and staff heads of the Sloan Fellows program convened a meeting (normally held face to face but now on Zoom) with three faculty who were currently teaching the newly matriculated class online and three who were preparing to teach these students later in the summer. Normally faculty and program administrators used the meeting (a very minor element of the teaching genre repertoire) to share information on the new class (e.g., identifying and discussing ways to help any international students struggling with English). This time,

---

15 This faculty member later told me that she had heard about the flipped classroom from colleagues in other parts of MIT, but when she participated in the STS course on it, she was overwhelmed by how extensive the recommended changes were. Since she only had a couple weeks before teaching the Sloan Fellows, she adopted only the idea of pre-recording video mini-lectures and decided to make them straightforward voice-over-slides lectures, rather than more elaborate productions with cartoons and animations as recommended in the course.

however, the meeting focused heavily on online teaching, expanding its role in the teaching genre repertoire. They discussed their use of the pre-recorded lectures and shared tips on making the best use of Zoom breakouts (e.g., creating a Google Doc for each room with instructions and open fields for students to complete) and on the value of Zoom's chat function (these students used chat to respond to questions posed by other students and provide examples from their work experience, thus supplementing classroom content or *what*). This meeting, by allowing them to share their learnings around these new teaching techniques with those who would teach the next set of Sloan Fellows courses, reinforced these modifications of classroom teaching genres and of the course genre systems across different classes delivered to this student population, as well as modifying the meeting itself, making it a more significant element of Sloan's teaching genre repertoire.[16]

More extensive changes in teaching genres and genre systems, and, most importantly, a major change in the teaching genre repertoire across the school, emerged in Phase 2, preparing for and teaching in fall 2020.

PHASE 2: PREPARATION FOR AND DELIVERY OF HYFLEX TEACHING IN FALL 2020

In June 2020, MIT determined that virtually all fall undergraduate teaching would take place via Zoom only, but decisions about graduate teaching were left up to MIT's schools in consultation with MIT. Meanwhile, Sloan's program directors and admissions officers were collecting input from current master's students with another year to go in their programs and from applicants who had been accepted into programs; many of these current and potential students were still deciding whether to attend or defer for a year. MBA students, especially, made clear that they considered in-person teaching and networking with classmates as key program elements, and that enrollment would fall dramatically if Sloan did not offer them such opportunities. Moreover, the many international students highlighted their need for in-person instruction to fulfill the requirements for F1 visas. On June 10, the deans met with faculty teaching group heads to explain why offering an on-campus fall experience was a priority for Sloan and to discuss how they could offer some simultaneous combination of in-person and online teaching, as well as some online-only teaching, in the fall.[17] This section traces the challenges and changes in teaching genres, genre systems,

---

16   The teaching dean circulated a link to the recording of this meeting to all faculty shortly afterwards and invited the participating faculty to present it in a teaching and learning town hall (discussed below) in the fall.

17   In addition, they committed to accommodating individual choices by students and faculty about whether to attend or teach in person or solely online.

and, most significantly, Sloan's teaching-related genre repertoire that emerged to enable and support this teaching mode.

Some additional important decisions were reached in the month following this meeting. To maximize the number of first year MBA students who could take core classes[18] in person, cohort sizes were decreased to 55 and the number of cohorts increased. Still, Massachusetts and MIT restrictions of all classrooms to 25 people at a time—22 students plus a teacher, TA, and audiovisual technician (AV tech)—meant that one classroom could not accommodate the demand for in-person learning. The faculty/staff MBA core planning group decided that if the classroom schedule could accommodate it, they needed to offer each core section in two classrooms of 22 students each, with another dozen students attending by Zoom. Subsequently, such a schedule was developed, in consultation with student leaders, by extending classroom teaching from 8:30 a.m. to 9:30 p.m. and moving some optional activities to Saturdays. By early July they had determined that they could accommodate two classrooms for all core courses (and a few popular electives) in the fall.

This 2-rooms+Zoom model created the simultaneously in-person and online teaching mode that became known at Sloan as *hyflex*.[19] The professor would preside in the main classroom and a TA in the second classroom (soon designated the *tandem* room and connected with the main classroom by video feeds controlled by audio visual technicians or AV techs in each room), while the remaining students were on Zoom (shown on a screen or monitor in both classrooms) from nearby apartments or from their homes in other countries.[20] This configuration created multiple teaching media or *how* (in person, on live video feed, on Zoom), locations or *where* (main classroom, tandem classroom, and Zoom), and student groups or *who* (students in each of the three locations and media).

Starting July 1, the new teaching dean, supported by the staff director, led an effort to adapt fall teaching to these conditions. They established new, bi-weekly, one-hour meetings on Friday mornings, called teaching and learning town halls (T&L town halls or town halls), to share information and learnings among teaching faculty. As the teaching dean announced:

> [W]e ([staff director] and I) would like to speak to the desires by many faculty teaching this fall, both to stay abreast of

---

18   During the first term of their program, MBAs took five required core courses in assigned cohorts.

19   Some elective classes would still be offered entirely via Zoom or in other hybrid configurations, but since the 2-rooms+Zoom hyflex mode was widely used and highly challenging, I will focus on it.

20   Initial visa problems were resolved more quickly than expected, and very early in the fall almost all students were settled at or near MIT.

progress on various relevant fronts and for opportunities for sharing knowledge and resources. To that end, starting **this Friday July 10 from 9–10am**, we will be hosting our first **Teaching & Learning Friday** town hall for faculty and for the staff who support faculty teaching. At this time, we will provide key updates (e.g., on classroom experiments, instructional technology, course support, pedagogy), and we will facilitate interactive conversations where faculty are talking to each other and sharing ideas. (Email from teaching dean to faculty, July 6, 2020).

These new Zoom meetings would regularly be attended by over 100 faculty and staff, with the majority faculty, throughout summer and fall 2020, a fact about which the teaching dean repeatedly expressed amazement and appreciation, since in the past teaching had never been the subject of so much faculty attention.[21]

Initially, anxiety about teaching in the unfamiliar hyflex mode no doubt drove high faculty attendance, but several other factors encouraged ongoing attendance. The staff director and teaching dean intentionally invited only faculty and the admins directly supporting their courses (plus a few STS leaders who could discuss technical issues), because they feared, based on past experience, that few faculty would come if attendees were primarily staff. They limited meetings to one hour on Friday mornings, a day and time at which very few faculty taught, to make attendance easy. The pandemic limitations also made personal and professional travel almost impossible, so faculty did not miss meetings because they were traveling. The teaching dean worked to make the topics of the meetings interesting, asking sets of different faculty to present at most Zoom meetings and then advertising who would be presenting and on what, to entice other faculty to attend. Attendees also got explanations of behind-the-scenes events that led to reversions to Zoom-only teaching a few times during the term.[22] In addition, attendance offered faculty a way to stay in touch with the community during COVID-19 isolation, as evidenced by the presence of

---

21 The attendance number is based on the teaching dean's statements about attendance at the beginning of the recorded meetings. No attendance records remain, so the statement about majority faculty attendance is based on my recollections. To put this number in context, the Sloan School has just over 110 tenure-line faculty and slightly more lecturers plus senior lecturers. I cannot estimate the proportions of tenure-line and non-tenure-line attendees, though there were significant numbers of both. I have considered them all to be faculty here.

22 Three times during the fall semester, Sloan's hyflex classes were moved entirely to Zoom for a few days pending testing, when evidence emerged of student get-togethers off-campus that broke MIT's and Sloan's rules. In each case, the teaching dean explained what had happened in town halls, information otherwise not readily available to faculty.

some on-leave and emeritus faculty. Although many attendees did not leave their cameras on, so their level of engagement was hard to judge, a tone of camaraderie in difficult conditions infused the presentations, questions, and interactions in chat. The T&L town hall soon became a well-recognized genre within Sloan, an addition to Sloan's previously limited genre repertoire around teaching.

The first T&L town hall meeting on July 10 set the stage for subsequent meetings. The teaching dean explained that although Sloan would continue to offer many fully remote Zoom classes, the new "'Hyflex' [classes]—with students both online and in-person—would be common" (PowerPoint slides shown at T&L town hall, July 10, 2020), especially in the MBA core and popular electives, and thus would be the focus of experiments and support efforts in coming months.[23] Given the challenges, he noted, faculty would need to prepare much earlier than usual for their fall term courses, and these meetings would help them do so. Most of the needed technology was already available in the classrooms and any needed updates or additions would be installed by fall. STS leaders reminded fall term faculty (many of whom had not taught in the spring and summer) to sign up for training workshops and practice teaching sessions and reassured them that STS would be able to support them in this mode as it had previously supported faculty who had a few EMBAs Zooming into their classes. The teaching dean noted that an additional TA would be needed (and funded) for classes taught in hyflex mode, and that teaching in this mode would require faculty to be part of a course or teaching team. Finally, a particularly good teacher who had been asked to coordinate work on the classroom experience (classroom experience coordinator) explained that he would conduct an initial classroom pilot in hyflex mode on campus later that same day and report back to the faculty on it and later pilots.

Subsequent summer town halls, supplemented by the teaching experience coordinator's email reports on three pilots, were used to assess and explain classroom technology, improve faculty understanding of the challenges of hyflex teaching, and share learnings from the pilots and from spring and summer Zoom teaching. The classroom experience coordinator focused on testing and standardizing classroom technology in the first pilot. The second pilot piggybacked on an ongoing, fully remote, summer course for one of the specialized master's programs; the professor and some students living locally agreed to don masks and move into

---

23   In a later meeting, he explained that he used the term *hyflex* rather than *hybrid* because he felt that hybrid was ambiguous because it sometimes refers to programs in which some courses are in person and some online. He defined his favored term, *hyflex*, as a combination of online and in-person simultaneously, within the same class. His definition could include just one classroom plus remote students on Zoom, but because in-person experiences were in such high demand, the school tried to include a tandem room whenever possible, making 2-rooms+Zoom the norm for hyflex teaching. In a few courses, students were in two classrooms, each with a TA, and faculty taught on Zoom from home.

a classroom for one class while the rest of the class remained remote on Zoom. A third pilot brought all the MBA core faculty (plus a few admins who volunteered to act as students) into classrooms or onto Zoom so each could practice and observe others practicing in the 2-rooms+Zoom configuration. These three pilots provided the major source of learning about hyflex teaching before the fall term began.[24] One summer town hall also hosted a panel of Sloan Fellows faculty who shared learnings from their summer Zoom-only teaching experience (discussed in Phase 1). As meetings continued into the fall, the teaching dean invited panels of faculty to speak at most meetings, describing their experiences and learnings, primarily in hyflex teaching.[25] Early town hall topics included technology, teaching teams and roles, and techniques for hyflex teaching.

The initial focus of pilots and town halls was getting the technology configured in the classrooms and figuring out how basic aspects of teaching could be handled in hyflex mode. The first pilot tested understandability of instructors through masks, adequacy of ceiling-hung microphones to pick up student comments made through masks, and the placement and use of monitors and screens.[26] Based on this pilot, by late August all classrooms were provided with adequate microphones and floor monitors visible only to the instructors (in addition to existing ceiling-mounted confidence monitors), allowing them to see students on Zoom and in the tandem classroom while facing the in-person students. Front and side screens were visible to the entire classroom and could show one (when the instructor projected PowerPoint slides on the other) or both the feed from the tandem room or the Zoom gallery view. The first pilot revealed that normal blackboard writing, a common form feature in all the teaching genres, was not readable by students on Zoom and in the tandem room; by August further pilots had shown that large chalk and fewer lines of text made board use possible, if not ideal. Other faculty substituted writing on and projecting from an iPad. Both techniques became common modifications to an existing form feature (*how*) used in many teaching genres.

Finally, the first pilot clarified that using breakout groups, which had worked well in Zoom-only teaching and had quickly become popular in all the teaching

---

24   MIT rules did not allow faculty to be in Sloan classrooms during the summer except in these pre-arranged pilots and, in the last two weeks before classes began, in pre-scheduled practice sessions.

25   A few meetings covered topics not directly related to hyflex teaching, but relevant to teaching more broadly, such as remote executive education teaching and the student experience in the programs during this period.

26   All classrooms had two screens for projection, a monitor built into the podium, and a ceiling-mounted confidence monitor visible only to the faculty. Some classrooms also had a floor-mounted monitor visible only to faculty that had been useful when EMBAs Zoomed into classes.

genres, was problematic in this new 2-rooms+Zoom configuration. Using random Zoom breakout groups (which required students in the classroom to have laptops open and to be signed onto Zoom) mixed the three student groups for equity, but students in the classroom needed to turn off their audio when not in breakout rooms to avoid feedback, then turn it back on when they entered the breakout room, potentially causing confusion and delay. They also needed large earphones (not the popular AirPods) to hear over the talking from nearby students in other groups. Another option was to put Zoom-only students into Zoom breakouts together and put students in each of the two classrooms into in-person breakouts with others in their rooms; the noise and required 6-foot spacing between students, however, made it hard to talk and hear within a group larger than three. Neither option was ideal, creating ongoing trade-offs around *who*, *where*, and *how* breakout or buzz groups met.

Another major focus in the pilots and town halls was the *teaching* (or *course*) *team*,[27] reflecting the increased number and broadened roles of those necessary to enact teaching genres in hyflex mode (*who*). The teacher role was discussed most. After the first pilot, the classroom experience coordinator reported that it was "an order of magnitude harder to handle three audiences than to teach on Zoom" (PowerPoint by classroom experience coordinator from July 17, 2020 T&L town hall meeting), and that he believed faculty would need not just one additional TA, but a TA for each of the three class locations (*where*)—main, tandem, and Zoom. For example, teachers could not see raised blue Zoom hands on the overhead or floor monitors showing Zoom attendees, nor could they keep track of raised physical hands in the tandem room, so they would have to coordinate with TAs in both locations. In the final, August pilot, each core instructor initially found the 2-rooms+Zoom configuration very disorienting. In the subsequent town hall discussion, one expert in-person teacher recited a litany of problems he encountered, including that chat was overwhelming, that cold calling was *terrible* because of the long pause before the unsuspecting student could unmute and answer, and that his laser pointer could not be seen outside the main room so he would need to learn to annotate slides on an iPad. He and others also highlighted the need to coordinate with TAs more closely (discussed further below). Summarizing the third pilot, the classroom experience coordinator emphasized that hyflex teaching was very different from Zoom teaching or in-person teaching and that each professor teaching this way should practice in the classrooms and on Zoom with the entire teaching team before the first day of class. At minimum, he noted, faculty needed to decide how they

---

27   These terms only came into common use at Sloan during this period, with *teaching team* focusing on those in the classroom and *course team* also including admins, who were not typically present in the classroom.

wanted to run discussions, another tradeoff. They could have every student sign into Zoom and encourage them to raise blue hands only (which was good for equity among the three sets of students but required laptops and Zoom open in class and demanded excellent TA coordination) or answer questions from students in the main room based on raised physical hands but pause at intervals to solicit questions from the other two sides (which allowed better flow in the main room but risked making the other students feel left out and still required coordination with two TAs to manage questions from the tandem room and Zoom students). Although all teaching involves some tradeoffs, experienced faculty are comfortable with the familiar tradeoffs, though novice teachers often find them stressful. Hyflex teaching, with its three media, locations, and student groups, required faculty to balance unfamiliar tradeoffs for every aspect of the class, making everyone a novice teacher in this new teaching mode.[28]

The expanded TA role was also discussed frequently in town halls. After the first pilot and the teaching coordinator's assessment that more TAs were needed, faculty teaching in hyflex mode were allocated resources for one extra *facilitator TA* (with a smaller appointment and less pay) for each additional side in the hyflex classroom, resulting in two facilitator TAs and a regular TA for the 2-rooms+Zoom configuration. The regular TA was responsible for normal out-of-class TA activities (e.g., office hours, grading, running recitations); in-class activities (e.g., monitoring chat for questions, alerting faculty to questions in the three locations, recording participation, managing polls or breakouts on Zoom) were divided among the regular and facilitator TAs. The faculty needed to train and coordinate with all the TAs in meetings outside of class, since a smooth-running class depended heavily on their skills. For example, faculty noted that if they were going to respond adequately to student questions, TAs sometimes needed to interrupt them, something that TAs hesitated to do without training and frequent reminders. The TA focus groups conducted after the fall term ended revealed that, even with additional facilitator TAs, the regular TAs thought their class preparation work had expanded enough that they deserved additional compensation.

AV techs, new additions to teaching teams, were mostly contract workers or new hires. In the main room they focused a camera on faculty, boards, PowerPoint slides, and students asking or answering questions, as appropriate, so students in the tandem room and on Zoom would be able to see what was going on in the main classroom (the tech in the tandem room needed to focus on students asking or answering questions in that room). To do that successfully, they needed to know what elements the class would include (e.g., lecture, discussion, breakouts, guest speakers) and when. Based on the pilots, the classroom

---

28   I'm grateful to my colleague Lori Breslow for this insight.

experience coordinator recommended that faculty share such information with AV techs before each class. During fall term town halls, faculty talked about huddling with the techs before class or sending them annotated class outlines ahead of time. In addition, the techs needed some in-the-moment coordination. For example, when teachers or TAs called on students in the main or tandem room based on raised blue Zoom hands, students needed to raise their physical hands before speaking so the tech would know where to point the camera.

Finally, faculty admins were part of the course team, broadly defined, though they were typically less visible to students. During the summer they compiled the reading lists and set up Canvas sites for fall courses as usual. Beyond that, their involvement in hyflex teaching varied greatly, depending on faculty desires and admin skills. On the high end of involvement, for example, the admin for the organizational processes core course played a critical role in a special, Zoom-only double class with a complicated experiential exercise that required non-random 6-person breakouts of almost 500 students in 6 sections and multiple teaching times, with different materials distributed to each student in a breakout room. She worked for several days in advance to set up breakout group assignments and to prepare Canvas to release the appropriate material to each student at the correct time. She was also on Zoom during all class times, fixing some minor glitches that occurred in some sections. Some tech-savvy admins regularly helped faculty manage the Zoom side of classes or substituted for TAs when needed. Admins, like TAs, formerly played more limited roles in teaching; now, faculty were dependent on them and on the added facilitator TAs and AV techs in new ways that were more visible to the faculty and students, requiring faculty to train and manage their teams if they wanted to enact any of the teaching genres successfully.

Other discussions in the T&L town halls addressed techniques for teaching in hyflex mode (*how*). Many faculty panelists spoke about their methods for calling on students (e.g., using all blue hands or calling on students in the main room by raised physical hands), making students in the tandem room feel more included (e.g., one professor always visited the tandem room during the class break), and using blackboards (e.g., one faculty member wrote on the board with regular, not large, chalk, but had a TA transcribe what he wrote onto an iPad so students in the other two rooms could see it).[29] Some faculty tried to escape particular tradeoffs of hyflex teaching by experimenting with alternative configurations. For example, faculty for the organizational processes core course led a case discussion with students in one room for the first 30 minutes of class while the regular TA led an experiential exercise in the other room;

---

29 In both the fall and spring semester, attendance in the tandem rooms fell off as the semester progressed with some students staying home and attending via Zoom.

then the professor and TA switched rooms and each did the same in the other room (Zoom participants were grouped with one of the rooms), followed by a concluding 10 minutes with faculty addressing both rooms and Zoom, a plan that required exact timing and skilled TAs. None of the faculty who spoke at the town hall meetings about their techniques claimed to have successfully solved all the challenges of hyflex teaching, but by sharing their experiences, they gave other faculty new ideas as well as reassurance that they were not alone in struggling with teaching in this mode.

After the fall term ended, the staff director organized another set of focus groups (of faculty, TAs, and students) to extract learnings to help those teaching in the spring 2021 term. In a January 2021 town hall he reported the findings, which covered Zoom-only and hyflex teaching. Overall, he summarized, "Those who felt good about what they accomplished" (staff director's PowerPoint slides, T&L town hall, January 15, 2021; subsequent quotations from same source) put a great deal of preparation into the effort and learned a lot. Efforts included everything from refining course objectives to learning that "Making minute choices—about what appears on which screen and which 'side' of the class you direct a question to in what moment—matters. Working out these choices is complex and iterative and can't be done by oneself." Faculty reported that they felt things went better than they initially expected, because of the additional training and resources (TA and AV), as well as the town halls. Faculty were generally less satisfied with the teaching experience than normal, even when they were satisfied with what they accomplished, because dealing with three sides "pushed the limits of manageability." Still, the staff director reported that at least one professor highlighted a long-term pedagogical gain: "Hyflex teaching forced us to be really crisp on our objectives and how we were allocating pre-class and during-class time to meet those objectives. So in many ways I felt that the hyflex situation forced us in very positive ways to be innovative in our pedagogy and I'm grateful for that opportunity." This quote suggests that at least some faculty refined and sharpened the *why* dimension of the teaching genres for their courses, as they shifted the distribution of material between classroom teaching and pre-class preparation (e.g., by creating video mini-lectures).

Beyond these general reactions, the focus groups revealed considerable variance in practices for the hyflex blending of Zoom with in-person teaching. Techniques around raised hands, chat, breakout groups, and use of pre-recorded lectures all varied, rather than converging on best practices enacted by all faculty. Consequently the report did not recommend any standard practices, instead simply summarizing what the staff director and teaching dean saw as four significant course adaptations: reduced content; the use of pre-recorded lectures; using techniques such as polls, chat, and breakouts to increase participation of and get feedback from students; and assigning student reflection papers on cases or readings, due before class, to guide the instructor in calling on students in class. The reduction of content (*what*) was common to most teaching faculty and genres, but not by choice. The significant course adaptation was how to manage that reduction, not the reduction itself. The use of classroom techniques such as polls and breakout groups (*how*) was a continuation of a trend that began in Phase 1, though these features were harder to enact in the hyflex than the Zoom-only classroom genres. Two of the listed Phase 2 innovations involved changes in the course genre systems as well as classroom genres. The summer Sloan Fellows faculty talked about creating pre-recorded lectures to replace some lost content as well as to improve student engagement in the classroom. This technique, an addition to the course genre system, had evidently spread to multiple courses, because student focus groups both praised the technique and complained that it was used in so many courses that cumulatively it added too much screen time to their out-of-class preparation. Assigning student reflection papers before class for faculty to use to improve in-class discussion, another change in the course genre system, must also have been adopted by additional faculty in the fall, since some students in the student focus groups complained about insufficient feedback on their reflection papers. These changes added to or substituted for other out-of-class preparation in course genre systems, with the ultimate intention of improving learning in and around the classroom genres.

The introduction of the T&L town halls to Sloan's teaching genre repertoire was probably the most significant change in Phase 2. These meetings drew faculty attendance from teaching groups across the school, and that attendance remained substantial (though certainly not universal) throughout the fall term, suggesting that many faculty found the meetings useful in their transition to hyflex teaching. The Town Hall genre's focus on and sharing of ideas about teaching among Sloan faculty was a major development in the community's teaching genre repertoire, perhaps signaling a change in its culture

REFLECTIONS ON CHANGES IN TEACHING-RELATED GENRES, GENRE SYSTEMS, AND GENRE REPERTOIRE

What does a genre perspective bring to this story of teaching and organizational change in a specific educational setting facing COVID-19 restrictions? And are the observed changes temporary, or will some become permanent? In this section I will focus on classroom teaching genres, course teaching systems, and finally Sloan's teaching repertoire as I reflect on each of these questions.

First, focusing on Sloan's teaching genres and their dimensions gives us a way of systematically viewing the changes in classroom teaching initiated by the pandemic. In Phase 1, faculty—with the support of STS training, TAs, and admins—migrated existing teaching genres into the new Zoom medium (*how*), initially with only the minimum necessary changes in other dimensions—less content coverage (*what*) and expanded TA and admin roles (*who*). The focus group report on spring term teaching demonstrated that some faculty members, recognizing that students were suffering Zoom fatigue and needed more engagement, made further changes in *how*, adding Zoom features such as polls and breakouts to the lecture and discussion teaching genres to keep students involved. The Sloan Fellows summer meeting revealed that a few weeks more of preparation time enabled additional faculty experimentation, most significantly taking lectures on technical concepts out of the combined lecture and discussion classes and putting them into video mini-lectures for viewing outside of class. This change allowed them to allocate more class time to discussing applications, a more engaging activity and a significant change in the *how* and *what* dimensions of their lecture and discussion teaching genres.

In Phase 2, the genre dimensions highlight why the move from Zoom-only to hyflex teaching was so challenging. Enacting classroom teaching genres required simultaneously using multiple media (*how*); interacting with multiple student groups (*who*) defined by their multiple locations (*where*); and coordinating even larger course teams (*who*). Hyflex teaching also reduced the content faculty could cover (*what*) and changed one aspect of timing (*when*) by extending the hours during which classes met into the evening. In enacting the genres in this new mode, only class purpose (*why*) initially remained the same. Hyflex teaching required the instructor to balance tradeoffs in all details of teaching.

The genre lens also enables us to look at changes in genre systems. By following Bazerman's (1994) emphasis on genre systems, and how multiple genres interact to coordinate actions over time and space, we can bring into focus changes in the course genre system, which coordinates teaching and learning over the semester and includes classroom teaching as just one element. For example, in Phase 1 a faculty member tried to improve her in-class discussions by requiring students to submit reflection papers a day before class and then using the information in them to improve in-class discussion. These new assignments not only changed the content and flow of the discussion teaching genre, but also added new assignments and student responses to the course genre system, pushing students to prepare more carefully and enabling faculty to improve class discussion quality by calling on students who had thought in advance about specific issues. Similarly, when Sloan Fellows faculty shifted conceptual material into short, pre-recorded videos that students viewed in advance, they added a new pre-class genre to the course genre system as well as improving the classroom teaching genres. They found that the tightly scripted video mini-lectures conveyed the conceptual content very efficiently and helped them limit the reduction of content in the classroom. In Phase 2, these video mini-lectures were added to more courses (hyflex and Zoom-only).

In the Phase 2 lead-up to fall term hyflex teaching, the teaching coordinator's strong recommendation to faculty to conduct practice sessions in the assigned classroom with the full teaching team added another genre, the practice class, to the course genre system. Faculty also had to coordinate with the AV techs, whether through annotated class outlines, huddles before class, or by other means, requiring more additions to the course genre system. Looking at the course genre system highlights that faculty out-of-class preparation increased significantly during this period, and student preparation in some cases increased (writing reflection papers) and in others shifted from reading to viewing (video mini-lectures). Changing the media of teaching genres induced changes in the more extensive course genre systems through which teaching and learning were enacted over a semester.

The changes in Sloan's genre repertoire around teaching more broadly were perhaps the most important changes of all. Before the pandemic Sloan did not have many regular venues for formally or informally discussing and sharing learnings about teaching, and most involved sharing between or among faculty in the same teaching group. This situation began to change slightly in Phase 1. A faculty focus group comment quoted earlier indicated that informal discussions about teaching between and among faculty increased greatly over the Zoom-only period. Moreover, the focus group meetings and the report itself were new additions to the teaching repertoire, with the report presented in the Zoom retreat where faculty across all teaching groups had the opportunity to discuss it further.[30] In addition, the summer Sloan Fellows meeting, an existing genre that took on an expanded role, spread teaching techniques and learnings among faculty across disciplinary lines but teaching in the same program.

The most significant change in the teaching-related genre repertoire was the teaching dean's introduction of the T&L town hall meetings in Phase 2, just in time to support the move into hyflex teaching. These meetings provided a venue for and encouraged faculty-to-faculty discussion of teaching. High faculty attendance throughout the year and since suggests that many faculty felt they benefited from learning about how others were managing teaching in the new media. The meetings also triggered further one-on-one or small group conversations (often suggested in chat at the end of faculty town hall presentations) as well as classroom experiments. This addition to the genre repertoire around teaching supported faculty during a difficult year and seemingly catalyzed a change in

---

30 In the past, Sloan retreats typically did not focus on detailed discussions of teaching.

Sloan culture around teaching during this period by making discussions about teaching common and accepted. This apparent cultural change showing that analysis of changes in an organization's genre repertoire can help us better understand organizational change more broadly (Orlikowski & Yates, 1994).

Will the changes in teaching genres, genre systems, and the genre repertoire survive the return to the classroom? Many of the new techniques developed specifically for teaching genres enacted in these media will undoubtedly disappear with a return to face-to-face teaching, but some may remain or evolve. For example, using breakouts in Zoom-only and hyflex teaching genres in almost all courses showed that breakouts could improve student engagement. In the future, we might expect faculty to continue to use them more broadly and extensively based on this experience. The faculty focus group statement that teaching during this period forced faculty to make objectives crisper, quoted earlier, suggests that some changes will improve teaching genres beyond the pandemic period because they refocused attention on the purpose or *why* dimension. In some cases we can already see evidence of ongoing influence. One faculty member who created video mini-lectures in the Sloan Fellows summer course so she could change how she used class time noted recently that faculty who teach the MBA core version of the same course are doing the same thing in fall 2021, even though classes are now face to face. They are all finding that this shift of lecture out of the classroom allows them to be more interactive (and thus to engage students more) in their in-class teaching. In at least some cases, changes in teaching genres adopted to deal with the exigencies of Zoom or hyflex teaching seem to be living on in face-to-face teaching.

We can ask the same question about changes in the course genre system. Practice teaching sessions with the (presumably reduced) teaching team seem unlikely to survive. In contrast, faculty who required students to write reflection papers on readings or cases before the class discussion and found that doing so improved class discussion seem likely to continue to use this assignment. Similarly, creating video mini-lectures for students to watch before class added an important new pre-class genre to the course genre system. In doing this, faculty rethought the distribution of in-class and out-of-class materials to achieve their goals over the course. Initial evidence that faculty are continuing to use this genre system modification in the return to in-person teaching suggests that it is very likely to survive.

Finally, and most importantly for Sloan as an organization, will the changes in the school-wide genre repertoire around teaching survive? The focus groups seem unlikely to continue with the return to in-person teaching. The seemingly culture-changing T&L town hall genre, which was critical to Sloan's successful adaptation to hyflex teaching and continued use of Zoom-only teaching, is a more important and potentially ongoing addition to Sloan's previously limited teaching repertoire. It provided an institutionally supported place for faculty to discuss teaching techniques and learn from each other at a time when they needed such support. It was also offered at a convenient time and (virtual) place. Gauging its odds of survival requires understanding this and other reasons it was so successful during the pandemic. In conversations and interviews, several people noted that the teaching dean's credibility and style of conducting the meetings (*who*) was another important factor in their success. He recognized that faculty, for better or for worse, were more likely to listen to and learn from peers than from educational specialists, and he made it easy for faculty to attend the meetings and to share their experiences without feeling that they had to be experts. He himself made no claims to expertise in teaching; rather, he recruited a classroom experience coordinator known for good teaching to organize the teaching pilots. He also assembled and introduced panels of faculty from different teaching areas, enthusiastically commented on the new methods and techniques they presented and expressed appreciation to them afterwards. Also important but less visible was the staff director, who suggested topics, did necessary behind-the-scenes work, and organized the two rounds of focus groups. As he summarized in his January 2021 focus group report, the town halls "have been invaluable for creating comfort with the craziness but more importantly for showcasing how our instructors can thrive and innovate with supporting resources in place" (staff director's PowerPoint slides presented in January 15, 2021 T&L town meeting).

What will happen to the town halls going forward? The genre has been well institutionalized over the past year, but circumstances around COVID-19 are changing and faculty are teaching students face to face again, albeit masked. The teaching dean announced during the summer of 2021 that the meetings will continue at least through the fall of 2021, and they have done so, in Zoom format, in the first month of the fall term, as I complete this paper. Attendance dropped from over 100 to a still substantial 70+ attendees at the first three meetings. The drop is not surprising since the return to in-person teaching reduced teaching anxiety and increased faculty travel and other faculty priorities somewhat. The content has also shifted away from teaching in the Zoom or hyflex configurations and towards more general teaching topics such as course development and Sloan teaching partnerships with international schools around the world. The teaching dean has made it easy for faculty to attend by continuing to have them in Zoom on Friday mornings, so faculty can stay home if they do not teach on Friday. Another test of the new genre's persistence in the repertoire will come when the teaching dean goes on sabbatical in January 2022, highlighting that *who* enacts this genre matters. Will another faculty member step into his role and continue the town hall meetings in a way that will encourage continued faculty attendance and focus on teaching? Will they evolve in a different direction under different leadership? Or will faculty attendance gradually decrease until the town hall meetings die out? The apparent cultural change that has made discussing teaching so important in this pandemic year makes me hopeful (though not confident) that the town halls will survive or other new genres will emerge to perform the same purpose of encouraging ongoing and Sloan-wide discussion of teaching.

Although the next chapter of teaching-related genres, genre systems, and genre repertoire at Sloan remains to be written, applying Bazerman's innovative ideas around genre to the school's pedagogical practices during the pandemic crisis yields valuable insights about the social and educational dynamics at Sloan. The same is, no doubt, true of pandemic teaching at other academic institutions. Bazerman's work on genres and their interactions is as relevant today as it was when I first read it over three decades ago.

REFERENCES

Bazerman, C. (2001). Politically wired: The changing places of political participation in the age of the internet. In J. Yates & J. Van Maanen (Eds.), *IT and organizational transformation: History, rhetoric, and practice* (pp. 137–154). Sage.

Bazerman, C. (1988). *Shaping written knowledge: The genre and activity of the experimental article in science.* University of Wisconsin Press.

Bazerman, C. (1994). Systems of genres and the enactment of social intentions. In A. Freedman & P. Medway (Eds.), *Genre and the new rhetoric* (pp. 79–101). Taylor & Francis.

Bazerman, C. & Paradis, J. (Eds.). (1991). *Textual dynamics of the professions: Historical and contemporary studies of writing in professional communities.* University of Wisconsin Press.

Bligh, D. A. (2000). *What's the use of lectures.* Jossey Bass. (Original work published 1971)

Cranfield, S. (2016). Teaching by leading and managing learning environments. In H. Pokorny & D. Warren (Eds.), *Enhancing teaching practice in higher education.* Sage Publications Ltd.

Devitt, A. J. (1991). Intertextuality in tax accounting: Generic, referential, and functional. In C. Bazerman & J. Paradis (Eds.), *Textual dynamics of the professions: Historical and contemporary studies of writing in professional communities* (pp. 336–357). University of Wisconsin Press.

Giddens, A. (1984). *The constitution of society: Outline of the theory of structure.* University of California Press.

Kwaśnik, B. H. & Crowston, K. (Eds.). (2005). Genres of digital documents [Special issue]. *Information Technology & People, 18*(2).

Miller, C. R. (1984). Genre as social action. *Quarterly Journal of Speech, 70,* 151–167.

Orlikowski, W. J. & Yates, J. (1994). Genre repertoire: Examining the structuring of communicative practices in organizations. *Administrative Science Quarterly,* 39, 541–574.

Yates, J. (1989). *Control through communication: The rise of system in American management.* Johns Hopkins University Press.

Yates, J. & Orlikowski, W. J. (2002). Genre systems: Structuring interaction through communicative norms [Special issue]. *Journal of Business Communication, 39*(1), 13–35.

CHAPTER 8.

OPENING UP: WRITING STUDIES' TURN TO OPEN-ACCESS BOOK PUBLISHING

Mike Palmquist
Colorado State University

For more than two decades, scholars in writing studies have explored and, with increasing frequency, embraced open-access publishing as a primary means of sharing scholarly work. While these efforts have most often been associated with scholarly journals, publishing initiatives focused on monographs, edited collections, and textbooks have grown to the point where their collective output rivals and in some cases exceeds that of traditional academic presses. In this chapter, I explore the development of open-access book publishing in our field, placing it in the context of early work with online open-access journals and, drawing on activity theory, consider the distributed, collaborative work typically involved in these open-access book initiatives, focusing in particular on how this work contributes to the quality and credibility of published books and the likely operational and financial sustainability of each initiative. [1]

THE RISE OF OPEN-ACCESS PUBLISHING IN WRITING STUDIES

Scholars in the field of writing studies have played a central role in exploring the use of technology to support writing and the teaching of writing. The field has contributed in important ways to the development of modern word processing programs; the design of communication tools such as chat, revision tracking, and commenting; the development and exploration of the potential uses of hypertext; and the early development and application of advanced writing environments.[2] These contributions have profoundly shaped how

---

1   Activity theory is discussed in detail later in this chapter. Key work includes Cole (1996), Engeström (1987, 1993, 1999a, 1999b, 2014), Leontiev (1978, 2005), Rubinštejn (1987), and Vygotsky (1978, 1986, 1989).
2   For representative work associated with word processing, see Bridwell et al. (1984), Collier (1983), Hawisher (1986, 1988), Kiefer & Smith (1983, 1984), LeBlanc (1988), and Sullivan

DOI: https://doi.org/10.37514/PER-B.2023.1800.2.08   195 writers compose, writing teachers work with students, and writing students learn to write.

With this attention to technology, it seems reasonable and perhaps even inevitable that our field has also included early adopters and innovators in the area of digital publishing. The work of these scholars—many of whom were graduate students or early career faculty members when they established the first open-access digital journals in the field—laid a strong foundation for making scholarly work available on the web. In 1996, writing in the first issue of *Kairos*, a journal that, with *RhetNet* and *enculturation*, set the direction for a still-growing collection of open-access journals in our field,[3] Fred Kemp considered the opportunities and challenges posed to scholars by the dissemination of scholarly work:

> Like medieval monks in the fifteenth century, many of us are facing displacement. A new breed of knowledge-makers is on the horizon, bringing a new breed of knowledge. The ACW [Association for Computers and Writing] and Kairos are searching out the all-important seam between the old and the new, that place where we can cross the divide without falling into a gap of self-absorbed, self-imposed, and futile isolation.

Kemp noted in his letter to the founders of *Kairos* that he foresaw a time when the internet would be "not be just an interesting gimmick, or even a flashy but shallow alternative to print sources, but the principal home to a 'knowledge domain,' that amorphous 'center' to the essential facts, opinions, and sheer ethos that holds an academic discipline together." He saw this happening relatively quickly, "Not because electronic text in and of itself reads better on a computer monitor. . . . Nor because the writing that appears in the electronic world is superior to that which appears in the print world. No one who loves the written

---

(1989). For work associated with the design of communication tools such as chat, revision tracking, and commenting, see Batson (1993, 1998), Day (1996), Kaplan et al. (1987), Neuwirth et al. (1987, 1988a, 1988b, 1990, 1993), Taylor (1993), Webb (1997), and Wojahn et al. (1998). For work associated with the development and exploration of the potential uses of hypertext, see Bolter (1991, 1993), Kaplan (1995), Moulthrop (1991, 1994), and Slatin 1990). For work associated with the early development and application of advanced writing environments, see Butler et al. (1988), Kozma (1991), Lansman et al. (1993), Neuwirth (1984), Smith (1987), Smith & Lansman (1989), Tuman (1993), and Wresch (1982, 1984).

3 *RhetNet* was established by Eric Crump in 1995. Its archive is available through the WAC Clearinghouse. *Kairos* (kairos.technorhetoric.net) published its first issue in spring 1996. Founding and early editorial staff members include Jennifer Bowie, Nick Carbone, Amelia DeLoach, Mick Dougherty, Doug Eyman, James Inman, Claudine Keenan, Elizabeth Pass, Michael Salvo, Greg Siering, Jason Teague, Jeff White, and Corey W. Wick. *Enculturation* (enculturation.net) was established in 1996 by Byron Hawk and David Rieder. Its first issue appeared in spring 1997. *Kairos* and *Enculturation* are both active journals.

word would make that claim . . . yet." Instead, he argued, the key advantage digital texts would have over printed texts "indisputably, is access."

Kemp's notion of access had more to do with increasing the number of voices that would be made available through the web than with open access to scholarly work—an observation that forecast the impacts of social media but which was grounded primarily in work with network-based communication and hypertext. Yet his focus on access continues to be relevant in both senses of the word. Within writing studies, certainly, open-access publishing has reshaped our scholarly work in fundamental ways, leading to a heavy reliance on open-access journals to support scholarly discourse within the field and, in what I will discuss in the following sections of this chapter, the early stages of a turn toward open-access book publishing.

Open-access publishing has become the norm for new journals in our field. Over the more than 25 years since Kemp made his observations, open-access journals have appeared with regularity. Some have been short-lived, while others seem likely to endure far beyond the tenure of their founders. Although established organizations have contributed to the growth of new journals, we have seen far more launched by scholars who have felt a need to fill a gap in our scholarly efforts. At the beginning of 2023, more than 115 writing studies journals were listed by the WAC Clearinghouse.[4] Of those, more than 80 are available in open-access formats. Most that are not available in open-access formats are published either by companies such as Elsevier or Sage or by professional organizations such as the National Council of Teachers of English, the Council of Writing Program Administrators, and the International Writing Centers Association—and this latter group of journals in some cases makes articles available in open-access formats after an embargo period. With some exceptions, the journals that do not release their work in open-access formats provide access to them in digital formats through library database subscriptions, typically through JSTOR or Project Muse. Notably, of 28 journals on the list that were established in the past decade, 27 have chosen to release their work in open-access formats.

PLACING OPEN-ACCESS PUBLISHING IN CONTEXT

Open-access publishing can be seen as a gift to readers of scholarly work—and arguably to the authors of that work, since they benefit from increased visibility for the information, ideas, and arguments they share. Open-access publishing

---

[4] The WAC Clearinghouse is a scholar-run publishing initiative established in 1997 that provides access to more than 185 scholarly books, more than a dozen journals, the CompPile database, and numerous resources for instructors who use writing in their courses (see wac.colostate.edu).

has extended the reach of journals and books beyond national borders. It has also contributed to increased availability of scholarly work over time—particularly work published in book form, since the digital nature of open-access publications and the low-cost of storage has allowed work to be available even decades after it was first published.

That said, open-access publishing can also be seen as a challenge to traditional academic reward structures, professional organizations, and academic publishers. As growing numbers of scholars in the field of writing studies have published in open-access venues, some of which lack the imprimatur of academic institutions or professional organizations, those engaged in merit, tenure, and promotion reviews have found themselves faced with the need to assess not only the quality of the journals and presses that publish this work but also the appropriateness of venues that do not align neatly with the long-recognized definitions of articles, book chapters, and books (see, for example, the discussion of *Intermezzo* later in this chapter).

Similarly, those engaged in leadership roles in our professional organizations have long recognized challenges associated with the rise of open-access journals and books. Simply put, the perceived value of membership in these organizations—and thus the annual dues they can charge—is tied at least to some extent to the value of access to an organization's subscription-based journals and discounted books. A similar challenge is posed to traditional academic presses, which rely on sales of books to ensure their continued operation. This is true even for presses that enjoy support from a professional organization, an academic institution, or a consortium of institutions. Open-access book publishing places pressure on both pricing structures and the ability to attract leading authors.

Equally important, open-access publishing represents a challenge to the scholars who work with open-access journals and book series. These challenges can be viewed as falling into two broad categories:

- *Quality and Credibility.* Scholars engaged in open-access publishing must consider how best to implement a high-quality peer-review process and devise appropriate and consistent oversight of that process. They must also determine how a journal or book series can be seen as a worthy home for work that advances current scholarly conversations.
- *Sustainability.* To ensure that an open-access journal or book series can endure, its leaders must consider how best to organize their efforts and whether funding is required for continued operation. In addition, they must consider how the work they publish can be situated within existing professional and institutional reward structures—or they must explore how to change those structures.

TURNING TOWARD OPEN-ACCESS BOOKS IN WRITING STUDIES

While open-access journals have become the norm in the field of writing studies, open-access book series publish only a fraction of books in our field. Even so, open-access book publishing has a relatively long history in writing studies, with the first peer-reviewed, open-access digital books published by *RhetNet* in 1996. Beth Baldwin's monograph, *Conversations: Computer-Mediated Dialogue, Multilogue, and Learning*, was released in July of that year, and a collection she edited with Tim Flood, *The Rhetorical Dimensions of Cyberspace*, was released a few months later. The next books would not appear until the early 2000s, and those would once again be released by a journal, in this case *Academic.Writing*, which was born out of efforts to establish the WAC Clearinghouse.

I've written elsewhere about the founding of the WAC Clearinghouse (Palmquist, 2022; Palmquist et al., 2012). Briefly, following a period of initial enthusiasm, it became clear that contributing to the development of a website was not widely recognized as worthy of consideration during annual merit evaluations or tenure and promotion reviews. To better address the rewards structures then in place at most higher-education institutions, those of us involved with founding the Clearinghouse decided to reshape it into an academic journal.[5] We believed that doing so would allow contributors to the project to receive credit for their work—in this case, as writers, reviewers, and editors—and that we could still distribute the resources that we had initially envisioned as the heart of the Clearinghouse. In mid-1998, we decided to create *Academic.Writing*, a scholarly journal that can be viewed at wac.colostate.edu/aw/. We released its first volume on March 6, 2000.

Within a few months, we were approached by scholars who wished to include their out-of-print books on the *Academic.Writing* website. Following RhetNet's example, we did so, releasing three books before the second volume of *Academic.Writing* was published: Susan McLeod and Margot Soven's edited collection *Writing Across the Curriculum: A Guide to Developing Programs*, Charles Bazerman's monograph *Shaping Written Knowledge: The Genre and Activity of the Experimental Article in Science*, and Toby Fulwiler and Art Young's edited collection *Language Connections: Writing and Reading Across the*

---

5   I initially approached William Condon and Christine Hult about the idea of developing a website that would provide access to scholarly work on WAC at the 1997 CCCC conference. By the end of 1997, we had been joined by Luann Barnes, Linn Bekins, Nick Carbone, Gail Hawisher, Will Hochman, Kate Kiefer, Donna LeCourt, Paul Prior, Martin Rosenberg, Cindy Selfe, and Richard Selfe, and a collection of resources had been published on the web.

Curriculum. During the same period, *Academic.Writing* also became home to the digital archives of three other journals: *Language and Learning Across the Disciplines*, *The WAC Journal*, and *RhetNet*.

Perhaps most important, a lengthy conversation with Bazerman a month after the publication of the first volume of *Academic.Writing* would eventually lead to a new vision for the Clearinghouse. Following our presentations at a WAC symposium at Baruch College, we embarked on a walking tour of Manhattan. At some point, our discussion turned to the publishing crisis that was then facing the field (see James McPherson's 2003 discussion of the crisis for a useful historical overview). Bazerman noted that books in a series he was then editing had been purchased by an average of 25 libraries nationwide, a significant drop from the hundreds of libraries that publishers had once counted on to purchase scholarly books. He told me that, for financial reasons, the publisher was considering dropping the series. As our walking tour progressed, we agreed to explore the idea of having the Clearinghouse publish the series in open-access formats. It would become the Reference Guides to Rhetoric and Composition series, which Bazerman continues to edit with Mary Jo Reiff and Anis Bawarshi and which the Clearinghouse co-publishes with Parlor Press (parlorpress.com).

Our discussion also led to two other agreements, one that would lead to a long-standing relationship with Bazerman and a second that would help set the direction for open-access book publishing in writing studies. First, we agreed to republish *Shaping Written Knowledge* on the Clearinghouse. This would be the first of seven original and five republished books that Bazerman would release through the Clearinghouse, and which collectively helped establish the Clearinghouse as a publisher of high-quality scholarly work. Second, we agreed to publish what would become the first original scholarly book released by the Clearinghouse, Bazerman and David Russell's edited collection, *Writing Selves/Writing Societies: Research from Activity Perspectives*.[6] Published in 2003, the book launched the Perspectives on Writing series, which to date has released more than 40 edited collections and monographs. It also served, to the best of my knowledge, as the first original open-access book published in writing studies since *RhetNet* had published Beth Baldwin and Tim Flood's books in 1996.

Within a decade, the Clearinghouse had published 25 original monographs and edited collections and had re-published 16 books on WAC and writing studies that had gone out of print.[7] During that time, several other open-access

---

6   A more detailed description of the discussion that led to publication of *Writing Selves/Writing Societies* can be found in Bazerman et al. (2008).

7   In the past eight years, that pace has accelerated. More than 100 original books are now available along with nearly 80 re-published books. See wac.colostate.edu/books/.

Opening Up

book series emerged, including the Computers and Composition Digital Press,[8] Writing Spaces,[9] and the Sweetland Digital Rhetoric Collaborative.[10] Two other initiatives, Intermezzo[11] and WLN Digital Edited Collections,[12] were subsequently established.

The leaders of these initiatives, like the leaders of the Clearinghouse, have wrestled with and, through a variety of strategies, succeeded in addressing issues related to quality, credibility, and sustainability. Notably, each initiative has established partnerships with established academic presses and, in some cases, with professional organizations. This includes the Clearinghouse, which counts among its partners the University Press of Colorado, Parlor Press, the National Council of Teachers of English, the Conference on College Composition and Communication, and the Association for Writing Across the Curriculum. The strategies used by the leaders of these open-access book projects, including decisions about whether and how to establish partnerships with other academic publishers and professional organizations, can be understood through the lens of activity theory.

DEVELOPING THE PUBLISHING COLLABORATIVE

---

8   The Computers and Composition Digital Press (ccdigitalpress.org) was founded in 2007 by Gail Hawisher and Cindy Selfe. It became an imprint of Utah State University Press in 2008, and published its first book, *Technological Ecologies & Sustainability*, a collection edited by Dànielle DeVoss, Heidi McKee, and Dickie Selfe, in 2009. Since its founding, CCDP has published more than 20 books, all of which are born digital.

9   Writing Spaces (writingspaces.org), which publishes open-access collections of peer-reviewed essays that are written by teachers for students, was founded by Charles Lowe and Pavel Zemliansky in 2009. To date, the complete volumes and individual essays have been downloaded more than 2.5 million times.

10   The Sweetland Digital Rhetoric Collaborative (digitalrhetoriccollaborative.org) was established in 2012, following the 2011 Computers and Writing Conference, as a collaboration between the Gayle Morris Sweetland Center for Writing and the University of Michigan Press. It published its first book in 2015 and has since published eight others. All of its books have a digital component, typically a website with embedded media. In addition to print editions, each book can be viewed through the Fulcrum publishing platform (fulcrum.org).

11   Intermezzo (intermezzo.enculturation.net), a digital book project associated with the journal enculturation, publishes works that are considered to be too long for a traditional journal article and too brief to work as a monograph. Led by editor and co-founder Jeff Rice and associate editors Casey Boyle and Jim Brown, Intermezzo published its first work in 2015, Bruce Horner, Cynthia Selfe, and Tim Lockridge's *Translinguality, Transmodality, and Difference: Exploring Dispositions and Change in Language and Learning*. It has since published 12 more longform works.

12   WLN Digital Edited Collections (wlnjournal.org/#resources) is supported by WLN: A Journal of Writing Center Scholarship. Its first book, *How We Teach Writing Tutors*, edited by Karen Gabrielle Johnson, Ted Roggenbuck, and Crystal Conzo, was published in January 2019. Two more edited collections have appeared since.

MODEL: A PERIOD OF TRANSITION

The impending publication of *Writing Selves/Writing Societies* encouraged the leaders of the WAC Clearinghouse to rethink its mission and organizational structure. In late 2002, the WAC Clearinghouse was relaunched as a publisher of journals and books, with *Academic.Writing* as one of its journals. Over the next several years, we would refine an approach to open-access publishing that I've referred to as the publishing collaborative (Palmquist, 2003; Palmquist, 2022). In a recent chapter in Greg Gibberson, Megan Schoen & Christian Weisser's edited collection *Editors in Writing*, I sketched the origins of my thinking about this approach:

> Drawing on activity theory, which I had been exposed to as a result of its central role in Bazerman and Russell's edited collection *Writing Selves/Writing Societies* (2003), I began thinking of the Clearinghouse as a useful example of the kinds of distributed, collaborative work that activity theory had been developed, in part, to interrogate and explain. (2022; pp. 118–138)

In their introduction to *Writing Selves/Writing Societies*, Bazerman and Russell (2003b) described the role activity theory might play in writing studies. Describing activity theory as "a set of related approaches that view human phenomena as dynamic, in action," they observed that it provides a productive means of understanding the production and use of texts:

> Human-produced artifacts, such as utterances or texts, or shovels or symphonies, are not to be understood as objects in themselves, but within the activities that give rise and use to them. Their meanings are found in these dynamics of human interaction… Texts—alphanumeric marks on surfaces—are one material tool or technology among many. But texts powerfully and pervasively mediate and re-mediate human activities. (Bazerman & Russell, 2003b, p. 1)

Activity theory—also referred to as cultural-historical activity theory (CHAT) and sociocultural activity theory—provides a theoretical framework that can help us understand cooperative work.[13] It emerged from work carried out by Soviet

---

[13] For more about activity theory, see Cole (1996), Engeström (1987, 1990, 1993, 1999a, 1999b, 2014), Engeström and Miettinen (1999), Kaptelinin (2005), Leontiev (1978, 2005), Rubinštejn (1987), and Vygotsky (1978, 1986, 1989). For more about its application to writing studies, see Bazerman and Russell (2003a, 2003b) and Russell (2009).

psychologists in the 1920s and 1930s to develop psychological theories that better addressed the work of groups, and in particular theories that could provide alternatives to Western theories that focused on the individual. Key voices in this effort included Alexei Leontiev, Sergei Rubinstein, and Lev Vygotsky. Jeanne Pau Yen Ho and her colleagues (2016) characterize activity theory as moving through three phases.[14] The initial phase is characterized by Vygotsky's three-part model of subject, object, and mediating artifact (see Figure 8.1).

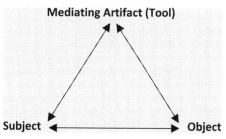

Figure 8.1. A model of the first phase of activity theory

Following the translation of their work, activity theory became a powerful framework for understanding the work of groups. Yrjö Engeström would play a central role in that emergence, drawing on Leontiev's work to expand Vygotsky's triadic activity model of subject, object, and mediator into a more complex model that is distinguished by its stronger focus on cultural and historical factors that shape the work of an activity system. His model, and more importantly his extensive efforts to explore the use of activity theory to understand complex, socially mediated actions and decision-making, marked a second phase in the development of activity theory (see Figure 8.2).

The most recent elaboration of activity theory focuses on the ways in which activity systems interact with each other or are embedded in larger systems of activity (see Figure 8.3). In this way, we might explore how the activity system associated with an academic journal and an open-access book series might interact with each or otherwise influence each other, perhaps through shared membership, shared goals (objects), similar rules (sometimes referred to as *norms*) or reliance on the same or similar tools. This third-stage approach might also be used to explore how an open-access book series is embedded within other (and perhaps overlapping) activity systems, such as academic publishing and professional communities.

---

14   Some scholars (e.g., Behrend, 2014; Ho et al., 2019) view Leontiev's elaboration of Vygotsky's model as a second phase in the development of activity theory. Since Vygotsky and Leontiev were not only contemporaries but collaborators, my sense is that their work might more reasonably be viewed as falling within the first stage.

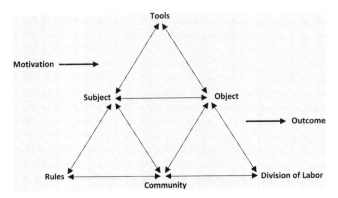

Figure 8.2. Engeström's model of activity theory

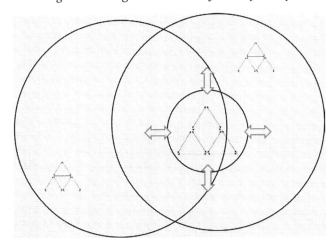

Figure 8.3. Interactions among embedded and overlapping activity systems

Over the past three decades, activity theory has been used to explore a wide range of complex systems. Scholars have focused on writing studies (Bazerman & Russell, 2003a; Russell, 1995; 2009), instructional technology (Behrend, 2014; Chung, 2019), distributed leadership (Ho et al., 2015; Takoeva, 2017), design thinking (Winstanley, 2019; Zahedi & Tessier, 2018), education (Abdullah, 2014; Al-Huneini et al., 2020; Carvalho, 2015; Pearson, 2009), human computer interaction (Draper, 1993; Kaptelinin & Nardie, 2012; Nardi, 1995), and software development (Dennehy & Conboy, 2017; Hoffman et al., 2020), to name only a few areas.

In the case of the WAC Clearinghouse, I found activity theory in general, and Engeström's model in particular, to be a useful framework within which to understanding how groups can collaborate on projects even in the face of limited communication and interaction. I had worried that, faced with a growing

Opening Up

number of journals, book series, and resource-development projects, the Clearinghouse would eventually collapse under its own weight. Drawing on activity theory, I began to understand how the Clearinghouse's loosely defined structure might be a strength rather than a weakness. Each individual member of the collaborative network—as I write this, a group of more than 180 scholars working as editors, publishers, reviewers, editorial board members, or project developers—contributes to one or more distinct projects. Communication occurs as needed, with the editors of book series and journals and the leaders of groups working on CompPile and various resource-development projects reaching out for support as needed—and otherwise acting independently to pursue a shared vision of the larger goals of the Clearinghouse initiative. Operating within the larger Clearinghouse mission of providing barrier- and cost-free access to scholarly work, each group sets its own goals and pursues them on its own timeline. The only limiting factors are financial support, individual expertise, the capabilities of the tools we use, and the time individuals are able to contribute to the project. I've tried to capture the nature of this activity as a set of overlapping spheres of activity (see Figure 8.4).

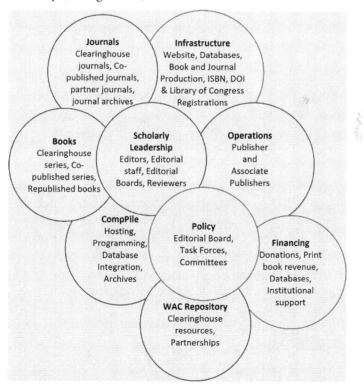

Figure 8.4. Overlapping activities in the WAC Clearinghouse

205

Eventually, I came to realize that the Clearinghouse mission, broadly shared among the members of the collaborative, was compelling enough—and sufficiently well situated in the rewards structures of the field and individual academic programs and institutions—that it could survive, and perhaps even flourish, as a decentralized project. For this particular project, the idea of a publishing collaborative, understood through the lens of activity theory, has provided a useful strategy for understanding how similar projects might develop and succeed.

THE GROWTH OF OPEN-ACCESS BOOK PUBLISHING AND THE EMERGENCE OF PUBLISHING COLLABORATIVES

Over the past decade, open-access book publishing has become more common in writing studies. This growth has been fueled by publishers, professional organizations, and the individual and collective efforts of writing scholars.

In some cases, these efforts have been undertaken by traditional publishers. During its acquisition by University Press of Colorado, for example, Utah State University Press placed PDF editions of books published prior to 2011 into Utah State's digital commons (digitalcommons.usu.edu). In addition to the books it co-published with the WAC Clearinghouse, Parlor Press has released several books in open-access formats. And the Conference on College Composition and Communication recently partnered with the WAC Clearinghouse to release some of the books in its Studies in Writing and Rhetoric series in open-access formats.

Individual scholars, often working with established publishers or organizations, have also released books in open-access formats. Cheryl Ball and Drew Loewe's edited collection *Bad Ideas About Writing* (textbooks.lib.wvu.edu/badideas/), for example, is widely used, as are two of Chuck Bazerman's textbooks—*The Informed Writer: Using Sources in the Disciplines* and *Involved: Writing for College, Writing for Your Self* (see wac.colostate.edu/repository/resources/writing/textbooks/).

In other cases, scholars in writing studies have written and released textbooks as part of the open-educational resources (OER) movement. Many OER textbooks have been supported by initiatives such as the Open SUNY Textbook Project (oer.suny.edu). Other OER textbooks have emerged through partnerships with organizations such as Lumen Learning (lumenlearning.com), and local institutional initiatives, such as *Open English @ SLCC* (openenglishatslcc.pressbooks.com).

In still other cases, open-access books have been published by initiatives similar to the earliest open-access journals. These can be characterized as publishing collaboratives that share, to a greater or lesser extent, the ethos of the WAC

Clearinghouse. Two of these collaboratives—the Computers and Composition Digital Press and Writing Spaces—were launched prior to 2010, while three others—Intermezzo, the Sweetland Digital Publishing Collaborative, and WLN Digital Edited Collections—were established in the past decade. While some of these initiatives grew out of established projects, such as the journals *enculturation*, and *WLN*, others were launched by scholars who saw a need for open-access books in a particular area.

Collectively, these publishing collaboratives rely on distributed, cooperative work that can be understood through the lens of activity theory. Their long-term success, as I will argue in the following section, will depend largely on how well they can establish themselves as credible sources of quality work, develop effective and efficient organizational structures, and obtain (or eliminate the need for) financial support.

BUILDING FRAMEWORKS FOR THE SUCCESS OF PUBLISHING COLLABORATIVES

Activity theory offers a robust set of tools for exploring the degree to which the publishing collaboratives discussed in this chapter have been able to ensure academic quality, establish credibility within the field of writing studies, develop effective organizational structures, and identify sources of support. While each of the publishing collaboratives discussed below has taken different routes to achieving success, and while some of them have not existed long enough to provide clear evidence that they can endure, the strategies they have employed offer insights about their quality, credibility, and sustainability.

Ensuring Quality

For serious scholars, a primary object of any publishing activity is ensuring that the scholarly work it produces and distributes is of high quality. Quality, in this sense, includes the scholarly argument or observations contained in a publication, the design of the publication, and design and content of the website used to access it. That said, for the majority of editors, the most important aspects of the publishing process are designing and managing a peer-review and manuscript-development process that is consistent with the highest standards of their field of study.

The work involved in producing a quality publication can be viewed through the lens of Engeström's model of activity theory as activities involving *subjects* (the editors and reviewers) using *mediating tools* (codified peer-review processes, digital communication systems, web-based submission systems, and digital production and design programs, among other possibilities) to accomplish the *object* of producing high quality scholarly publications. In the case of open-access publishing collaboratives, this activity is launched through the *motivation* to distribute scholarly work in ways that achieve an *outcome* that ensures access to all scholars (and other potential audiences) who can view work on the web. This work is shaped by the *rules* (norms and regulations, such as copyright rules and creative commons licenses) of the *community* (more specifically the group involved in a particular publishing collaborative and more generally the larger field of study to which the work will contribute) and the *division of labor* required to produce that work. Division of labor, for example, might lead some members of the collaborative to work primarily on developing a manuscript (see Figure 8.5) and others to focus on designing and distributing the final publication.

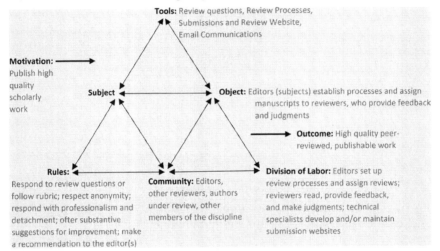

Figure 8.5. Depicting a peer review process via Engeström's model of activity theory

Quality can also be viewed in terms of embedded and overlapping activity systems. Critically, while the specific peer-review processes employed by a given publishing initiative—for example, a journal or book series—might be somewhat different from those employed by another initiative, those processes are shaped by larger activity systems. For example, the Perspectives on Writing book series, which is published by the WAC Clearinghouse, uses peer-review processes that are shaped by both Clearinghouse policies and the field of writing studies. Recent work on anti-racism, for instance, has affected reviewer and editor attention to citation practices, among other issues centering on equity and inclusion. In the case of the Perspectives on Writing series, Clearinghouse policies shape how peer-review is carried out. And those policies, in turn, are shaped by discussions in the larger field of writing studies.

Opening Up

The publishing collaboratives discussed in this chapter employ peer-review processes that are consistent with those used by all reputable publishers within the field: reviews are conducted anonymously, feedback that will lead to improvements in a document is expected, and reviewers are required to provide recommendations about the disposition of a manuscript. Only Intermezzo uses a modified system, notes editor and co-founder Jeff Rice, who explained that he has tended to depart from the more typical acquisition and development process associated with longer works. He does not, for example, require a proposal for a work. Nor does he require that work in the series make arguments in a traditional academic sense:

> I have not, as editor and publisher, worried about traditional approaches to scholarly writing that might include literature review, or specific citation practices (though we use MLA for style), or that have to make an argument, etc. I want authors to explore their ideas of interest in novel ways (personal communication, May 19, 2019).

In addition to peer-review activities, other activities that contribute to quality include the choice of and use of tools that support the design and distribution of published work. These tools can include software programs such as InDesign, Microsoft Word, Google Docs, Dreamweaver, Adobe Acrobat, Photoshop, and PressBooks; website management platforms such as WordPress and Mura CMS; web tagging tools such as HTML and CSS (Cascading Style Sheets); and database query languages such as SQL (Structured Query Language). Each of these programs, platforms, and languages is the focus of its own activity systems. To the extent that their use by publishers overlaps with other, often larger activity systems, including both the groups who define and extend them and users who employ them for purposes far different from publishing, the activities within those systems will shape the work—at least to some extent—performed in the service of open-access publishing. Beyond these tools, embedded and overlapping activity systems might also include various open-access publishing organizations—including the Creative Commons organization (creativecommons.org) and the Open Access Scholarly Publishing Association (oaspa.org)—as well as users of publishing systems such as Open Monograph Press (pkp.sfu.ca/omp/) and Vega Academic Publishing System (www.vegapublish.info/).

Quality, then, is influenced not only by the motivations of the subjects who work within a publishing collaborative to create excellent open-access publications but also by the larger activity systems in which their work is embedded and the numerous overlapping activity systems that are associated with the tools used to carry out their work.

Establishing Credibility

Credibility in scholarly publishing is largely earned by ensuring that publications advance existing scholarly conversations. Because judgments of credibility are subjective, however, the leaders of a publishing initiative might adopt strategies that signal competence and quality. The publishing collaboratives discussed in this chapter have adopted strategies such as aligning their book series with established presses and professional organizations, working to attract contributions of scholarly work from established authors, publishing work that departs in innovative ways from mainstream publications, seeking nominations for awards, and engaging in activities typical of established commercial publishers.

In 2001 and 2002, the leaders of the Clearinghouse faced challenges associated with credibility as they worked with *Writing Selves/Writing Societies*. While some of the initial work on the collection, such as solicitation of chapters and initial reviews of proposals, had been completed by the time Bazerman and Russell brought the book to the Clearinghouse, we found ourselves grappling with other questions, such as the formats to use for publishing, how best to incorporate video into the book, and how to obtain an ISBN and register the book with the Library of Congress.[15] Most important, we had to consider the impact of releasing the book in digital formats on the careers of the chapter authors, several of whom were untenured. In our communications with the authors, we explained our goals for the project, stressed the quality of our peer review process, explained that it would be registered with the Library of Congress, and called attention to the reputations of members of the Clearinghouse editorial board.

Eventually, the authors of all but two chapters agreed to continue with the project. One was a junior scholar who expressed concern about the reception a digital publication might receive from her tenure committee. Another set of co-authors did not respond to our message. During the editorial development process, other authors dropped out for a range of editorial reasons, such as missed deadlines, insufficient revision, and the outcome of final peer reviews.

Later, we would publish an article in *First Monday* (Bazerman et al., 2008) that reported that none of the contributors to *Writing Selves/Writing Societies* experienced difficulties and that, in fact, the chapters in the book had been cited at an unusually high rate. Since its publication in 2003, the book has been downloaded, in whole or as individual chapters, more than 500,000 times. Interestingly, despite the age of the book, it was downloaded roughly 8,000 times in the past year.[16]

---

15   ISBN is the acronym for International Standard Book Number, a unique identifier assigned to a book. To learn more, see isbn-international.org/content/what-isbn.

16   Because browsers typically download PDF documents in multiple concurrent streams,

Concerns about credibility were also expressed by the founders of the Computers and Composition Digital Press. In a 2009 email exchange with Gail Hawisher, Cindy Selfe, and the editorial team that produced the first book in the series, Selfe noted that she saw affiliation with a university press as a useful strategy for addressing concerns about pushing boundaries:

> Our effort has always been to publish projects that are 1.) innovative and creative (in terms of their digital instantiation) and 2.) recognizable as peer-reviewed, university press products *so that authors can use these projects in tenure and promotion cases with some confidence that they will be acknowledged by other scholars as publications characterized by rigorous review by specialist scholars in the field. This approach, we recognize, will entail walking a fine line between innovation and conventional values.* (personal communication, May 17, 2009; original emphasis)

The decision to align efforts with an established publisher or journal was made, either from the start or at a later time, by each of the publishing collaboratives discussed in this chapter. Computers and Composition Digital Press was launched as an imprint of Utah State University Press. Intermezzo and WLN Digital Edited Collections have operated since their founding within the structure of two leading academic journals, *Enculturation* and *WLN*, respectively. The Sweetland Digital Rhetoric Collaborative was launched in partnership with the University of Michigan Press. And Writing Spaces has partnered with Parlor Press and the WAC Clearinghouse since its founding. The WAC Clearinghouse has long partnered with Parlor Press, although that decision was made at a time when Parlor Press was still viewed as an experimental project. Later, the Clearinghouse would expand its publishing partnerships to include University Press of Colorado and the Conference on College Composition and Communication, both of which distribute print editions of its books.

Reflecting the influence of larger academic publishing activity systems, publishing collaboratives within the field of writing studies have also adopted practices associated with conventional publishing. Most assign ISBNs and register their work with the Library of Congress. And some assign DOIs (Digital Object Identifiers) to their publications.[17] A number of collaboratives engage

---

basing download statistics on "hits" can lead to inflated estimates. In contrast, I count how often a file is visited. Even so, just as there is a distinction between placing a print book on a shelf unread and spending time with it, opening a file and reading it are quite different things.

17   The Clearinghouse developed an automated, database-supported system that creates DOIs for each of its publications (books, book chapters, and journal articles). In 2020, it completed a two-year effort to assign and register DOIs for more than 2,500 publications.

in marketing, including the WAC Clearinghouse, which recently created the position of associate publisher for marketing and advancement. Most publishing collaboratives also seek nominations of their books for awards. In the past six years, for example, books published by the Clearinghouse have won seven awards from CCCC, the CWPA, and *Computers and Composition*.

Viewed within the context of activity theory, these efforts to establish credibility can be viewed primarily as aligning publishing activities with that of overlapping activity systems. Working with an established university press, for example, allows a publishing collaborative to benefit from previous efforts to establish workflows and productive division of labor, develop norms, and identify useful tools. Similarly, aligning efforts with norms, workflows, and tools used more generally within a discipline—and in other communities related to publishing, such as web developers and designers—provides important benefits.

Developing a Sustainable Organization

Organizational structure plays a critical role in the success and sustainability of an academic publishing initiative. While some journals and book series are launched with the expectation that, over time, they will cease publication, most are intended to enjoy long-term success. Within academic publishing, durable organizational structures typically provide clarity regarding individual and group responsibility, facilitate communication among members, and provide clear guidelines for growth and leadership transitions.

The organizational structures adopted by most of the publishing collaboratives discussed in this chapter resemble most closely that of an academic journal (see Table 8.1). These collaboratives have one or more lead editors, editorial team members, and editorial boards (most of which are working boards whose members both advise on policy and carry out peer review).

For these publishing collaboratives, the division of labor and the use of tools to support peer review, copy editing, design, and production follow a pattern similar to that of many open-access journals. Most of the publishing collaboratives operate in a hierarchical fashion, with roles falling into and expected duties being defined by a familiar pattern of a team of lead editors, editorial staff members, reviewers, and advisory board members. This organizational structure offers clarity through its reliance on long-standing norms regarding peer-review, copy editing, and design. Given a record of success within the field of writing studies, it seems reasonable to expect that this structure will contribute to the success of these initiatives.

Table 8.1. Publishing Collaborative Organization Structure

Collaborative	Lead Editors	Editorial Staff Members	Editorial Board Members	Fellows / Interns	Book Series	Autonomy
Computers and Composition Digital Press	3	4	66	4	1	Imprint of USUP, but operates autonomously
Writing Spaces	3	8	24	N/A	1	Autonomous
Sweetland Digital Rhetoric Collaborative *	3	N/A	8	1 or more	1	UM Press approves all contracts
Intermezzo	3	5	8	N/A	1	Autonomous, but under the enculturation umbrella
WLN Digital Editions	5	4	N/A	N/A	1	A production of the WLN journal
The WAC Clearinghouse	25**	14	47	1 or more	8	Autonomous

* Sweetland DRC editorial staff are drawn from the University of Michigan Press; reviewers are members of the computers and writing community.
** The Clearinghouse has a publisher, six associate publishers, and 18 series editors. Fourteen associate editors work with book series. Interns are usually given a title of associate editor for the duration of their work with a series. In addition to the series listed here, it republishes books from NCTE, USUP, and other publishers.

Equally important, the organizational structures adopted by each of the publishing collaboratives promote open and frequent communication—and they appear to reflect an emphasis on consensus-based decision making even in contexts that involve strong leadership from senior scholars. WLN Digital Edited Collections provides a good example of the interplay between a senior scholar and her fellow editors. "We have traditional titles, but no hierarchy in that we all have equal voices in decision-making and do a lot of emailing back and forth until we're comfortable with a decision," WLN editor in chief Muriel Harris wrote in response to my questions about their initiative (personal communication, June 4, 2019). Co-editor Lee Ann Glowzenski concurred, pointing out that "all of our decisions are made in conversation with one another" and explaining that "we all respect each other's ideas and strengths enough that if one member of the editorial team argues very strongly for or against a piece, the rest of us are very happy to listen" (personal communication, June 4, 2019). Anne

Ruggles Gere and Naomi Silver, who responded to my questions about their publishing collaborative, expressed similar sentiments, nothing that they "meet only rarely in person but share common goals and a non-hierarchical approach for the publishing we do" (personal communication, June 4, 2019).

It is unclear how well the organizational structures developed by each of the publishing collaboratives will support growth or leadership change. Since each of the collaboratives relies largely on volunteer labor (the Sweetland Digital Rhetoric Collaborative, which is an academic unit within the University of Michigan, is an exception), growth might lead to stresses on a collaborative and its members. Succession planning might be complicated by the volunteer nature of these initiatives, which depend on a level of enthusiasm that new members might not share. However, if the collaboratives employ strategies similar to those used by academic journals to select new leaders, successful transitions might occur.

The WAC Clearinghouse stands out as an exception to the organization structure typically adopted by the other publishing collaboratives, largely because it is the only collaborative that publishes more than one book series. To some extent, the organizational structure of the Clearinghouse resembles that of an academic press, with a publisher, several associate publishers, an editorial board, the editors of CompPile, editors of book series and journals, and a large number of editorial staff and reviewers for those book series and journals. It lacks, however, the hierarchical reporting structure typical of academic presses, where directors set priorities and manage staff workflow. Instead, the Clearinghouse employs a web-like structure in which volunteers take on work that is carried out as time becomes available. The primary function of the publisher and associate publishers is to provide coordination among and resources for the initiatives that fall under the Clearinghouse umbrella. In addition to funding, which is discussed in the next section, these resources include publishing tools (software and web-based tools that support book design, DOI creation and registration, and peer review of submissions), guidance on issues ranging from use of copyrighted materials to issues associated with human research, and the issuance of publishing contracts and memorandums of understanding. Certainly, allocating financial, technical, and other resources provides some degree of control over the activity of the collaborative, and in this sense the work done by the publisher and associate publishers resembles that of the director and associate directors of an academic press. Differences exist, however, in the lack of reporting lines between the publisher and the editors of Clearinghouse book series and journals, the lack of performance evaluations, and the ability of the editors to set their own publishing priorities within the framework of the larger Clearinghouse mission.

IDENTIFYING AND ACQUIRING SUSTAINABLE RESOURCES

Given enough funding, almost anything is possible. For the publishing collaboratives discussed in this chapter, however, concerns about funding typically take a back seat to those about volunteer time and expertise. It is possible, particularly in projects that publish only one or two books per year, to take advantage of institutionally-provided office space, computers and software, and web servers in ways that allow books to be published without significant—and in some cases, any—funding. Certainly, some costs cannot be avoided. If a book is to carry an ISBN and DOI, for example, costs will be incurred. However, by partnering with a university press or an established journal, as many of the publishing collaboratives discussed in this chapter have done, even those minimal costs might be avoided. Volunteer labor can be devoted to reviewing and developing manuscripts, carrying out copy editing, designing books, releasing them on the web, and publicizing their existence. And all of this can be done without the direct expenditure of funds, much as it is done with many open-access journals.

That said, more complicated projects—such as those carried out by the Computers and Composition Digital Press, the Sweetland Digital Rhetoric Collaborative, and the WAC Clearinghouse—often require time and expertise that cannot easily be obtained from volunteers. As websites grow larger and more complex, for example, institutional technical support might be required. If publications are to be listed by database vendors, librarians might be asked to provide support. If copy editors are hired, websites are hosted by vendors, or expenditures of any kind are to be charged to institutional accounts, university staff will be required to ensure that proper financial processes are followed.

The decision to partner with a publisher, which each of the collaboratives discussed here have made, albeit in different ways, can affect not only finances but also operations. For Writing Spaces, partnering with Parlor Press and the WAC Clearinghouse allowed it to focus on developing and reviewing its books, leaving production and design to its partners. For the Clearinghouse, partnering with Parlor Press and University Press of Colorado has not only helped it produce print editions at no additional cost but also has helped improve its production, design, registration, and marketing processes. In contrast, for the Sweetland Digital Rhetoric Collaborative, which works closely with University of Michigan Press, the relationship is more complicated. The UM Press played a key role in establishing the Collaborative, and it has helped it engage in an ambitious and successful set of operations. Unlike the other collaboratives, however, which operate largely independently, the Collaborative must gain approval from the Press for its book acquisition and development decisions. It also pays a subvention fee to the Press to cover some of the costs of designing and distributing its books. Gere and Silver noted that their publication process involves extensive communication between Collaborative team members and Press staff:

> Once [a book] has been accepted, it works its way through both a traditional print publication process and a process . . . to create and house digital assets. In the case of fully born digital projects, the authors work with the DRC website manager to house the project on the DRC site, and simultaneously work with the UM Press to create a print-based version that meets their criteria for accessibility and sustainability. The final publications may appear in print, e-book, open access linear digital publication, and open access interactive digital publication. (personal communication, June 4, 2019)

A key aspect of sustainability is identifying and responding to contradictions, which Engeström (1993) describes as conflicts that arise within an activity system. Within activity theory, contradictions are best viewed as opportunities for change, perhaps through refining motivations or redefining outcomes, perhaps through recognizing that a tool is ill-suited to a particular task, or perhaps through identifying conflicting rules or norms or challenges associated with how effort is distributed. The need to provide funding for the publishing activities of the Clearinghouse, for example, led its publisher to seek donations which, in turn, needed to be housed in a tax-free account. This led to interactions with the Colorado State University Foundation, which has worked with the Clearinghouse for more than a decade. More fundamentally, the contradictions between academic reward structures and "work on a website" led the Clearinghouse to reinvent itself in 1998, and subsequent contradictions with the norms associated with an academic journal led in 2001 and 2002 to yet another reinvention as an academic publisher. A subsequent contradiction occurred when Parlor Press was unable to serve as the publishing partner for an expanded set of book series, and the Clearinghouse established a partnership with University Press of Colorado. These changes were not without conflict—much discussion was involved before they were carried out—but they involved important changes in the organizational structure, funding, and operations of the Clearinghouse.

For the WAC Clearinghouse, two important contradictions remain. First, the motivation to expand its collection of open-access publications conflicts with its precarious funding stream. To date, funding has been provided from donations to a charitable account hosted by the Colorado State University Foundation, proceeds from sales of print editions of original books, and (until recently) internal funding made available intermittently during a 14-year period when the publisher served as an administrator at Colorado State University. While the amount of funding provided from institutional budgets was never large, the Clearinghouse no longer has access to this source of funding. Still, the question of the long-term viability of the Clearinghouse will likely focus on whether it can continue to cover its costs. In contrast, the more focused efforts of the other collaboratives suggest that funding issues will be less of an issue for their long-term success.

Second, like many other startups, the Clearinghouse has benefited from the energy and enthusiasm of its founders. As its leadership ages, the question of succession must be addressed. While efforts have been made to establish rules for succession, it is not clear whether a fully scholar-run, independent organization will be able to operate as effectively as it has when new leaders step in.

TAKING STOCK: THE IMPACT OF OPEN-ACCESS BOOK PUBLISHING

Since the mid-2000s, the number of open-access books produced by the publishing collaboratives highlighted in this chapter has grown steadily. By the end of 2005, six original open-access books had been released by the WAC Clearinghouse and *RhetNet*. In the next five years, a period which saw the founding of the Computers and Composition Digital Press and Writing Spaces, a dozen open-access books were published. In the next five years, during which the Sweetland Digital Rhetoric Collaborative and Intermezzo were established, 38 new open-access books were released. And from 2016 through 2020, a period during which WLN Digital Editions was launched, the number of new open-access books produced by the collaboratives grew to 65. This reflects both a growing number of publishing collaboratives and increases in the number of books published. Importantly, while the Clearinghouse makes up more than 60 percent of the books produced by these publishing collaboratives to date, its share has declined as more new collaboratives have been established (see Table 8.2).

Books published by open-access publishing collaboratives now exceeds the annual output of several of the traditional academic presses that focus on writing studies. For example, the catalogs at Southern Illinois University Press and the University of Pittsburgh Press indicate that, between the beginning of 2016 and the end of 2020, the two presses published a total of 29 books related to writing studies—not quite half as many books as were produced by the publishing collaboratives discussed in this chapter. Certainly, publishers such as NCTE and Utah State University Press have produced far more books in writing studies—and open-access book publishers are unlikely to surpass their output in the near to intermediate future. My sense, however, is that we are at a turning point in publishing in our field. The future will be kind to open-access book publishing, much in the way that the past two decades have been kind to open-access journal publishing.

Table 8.2. Original Open-Access Monographs, Collections, and Conference Proceedings by Time Period

	Pre-2006	2006–2010	2011–2015	2016–2020
RhetNet	2			
WAC Clearinghouse	4	9	26	35
Computers and Composition Digital Press		2	10	9
Writing Spaces		1	1	1
Sweetland Digital Rhetoric Collaborative			1	6
Intermezzo				12
WLN Digital Editions				2
Total	6	12	38	65

For several reasons, I believe this assessment is well founded. First, the technology that allows scholars to become publishers has become easier to use. Whether you are using open-source projects such as Open Monograph Press or Vega Academic Publishing System, or you are using commercial software tools such as Adobe InDesign or PressBooks, it is far easier to manage the technical processes of book publishing than it was even a decade ago. And while learning a program such as InDesign, for example, is not a simple process, it is one that can be accomplished with a modest investment of time—and that investment can be reduced by working with colleagues who have already gained some control over a particular program or publishing system. Improvements in publishing technology are making it increasingly attractive to consider launching new book series outside of (or alongside, in the case of the Clearinghouse, the Computers and Composition Digital Press, and the Sweetland Digital Rhetoric Collaborative) traditional academic presses.

Second, and with some exceptions, open-access book publishing is not influenced by many of the economic forces that shape the publishing decisions made by traditional academic presses. Some book projects are innovative and important, yet they are unlikely to result in enough sales to be practical for a traditional press to take on. This means that some worthy projects will not find a publisher. In contrast, open-access publishing collaboratives—which rely on volunteer, distributed labor and can take advantage of institutional infrastructure—can produce books for a lower cash outlay than traditional presses (largely because our salaries and benefits are already paid by our institutions, and because many of us can rely on our institutions' servers, workstations, software, office space, and technical support staff). Simply put, publishing collaboratives have strong economic advantages over academic presses, which must include in their calculation of the expenses associated with the publication of a book costs such as salaries, retirement and health benefits, computers and software, web servers, and rent, among other expenses.[18]

Third, much of the work of developing new books has long been done by scholars who serve as series editors and peer reviewers. The editors and reviewers working with publishers routinely engage in early discussions about book proposals, offer support for the development of calls for proposals for edited collections, engage in peer reviews, and provide advice about manuscript preparation. This work is largely "counted" during annual and promotion reviews. It seems reasonable to expect that what we now count will expand to include work associated with designing and producing scholarly work. And while this expansion is certainly happening too slowly for many of us (see the discussion of reward structures in Day et al., 2013), it is occurring nonetheless.

Fourth, open-access publications are as or more effective in shaping scholarly discourse than those published by traditional academic presses. The books produced by the publishing collaboratives discussed in this chapter have won several of our field's book-of-the-year awards. They enjoy high levels of citation—and thus impact. And because of this, increasing numbers of scholars are seeing open-access publishing not only as acceptable—even normal—but also as preferable, given its impact and connection to issues of equity and access.

Finally, open-access publishing appears to have far greater international reach than traditional publishing. In 2020, for example, the WAC Clearinghouse website received 3.1 million visits visitors from 1.4 million unique IP addresses and saw roughly 2.8 million downloads of books and articles. Of those visitors, more than 40 percent came from outside the United States. The site's logs recorded visits from more than 240 countries in six continents. Growing activity in the Clearinghouse's International Exchanges on the Study of Writing and its recently launched Latin American Section have certainly contributed to those numbers. A recent webinar by the Latin American Section attracted more than 1,400 registrants from 47 countries. Access to the web also plays a role in the numbers of visitors seen by the Clearinghouse, but it seems clear that longevity, a growing catalog of high-quality, peer-reviewed books and journals, the CompPile database, and efforts to promote the Clearinghouse

---

18 As one of the collection editors pointed out, it's important to avoid minimizing the amount of volunteer labor that goes into each Clearinghouse book. While the Clearinghouse pays only about $2,000 to produce a book (primarily for copy editing), the value of volunteer labor is significant. Typically, production and design for one of its book takes 30 hours. Some require far more.

through participation in and sponsorship of conferences outside the United States have made an impact.

Open-access book publishing, particularly that occurring through publishing collaboratives, will also have an impact on traditional academic publishers. As increasing numbers of books are released in open-access formats, traditional publishers will seek other ways to support their operations. Academic publishers are already participating in open-access initiatives such as Knowledge Unlatched (knowledgeunlatched.org), which uses funding from universities and foundations to release books from established university presses in open-access formats. Academic publishers are also exploring a model rooted in the 14th century that has great promise—shifting responsibility for publishing back to universities and colleges. Librarians have been engaged in these discussions for many years, and some academic presses have found new homes and more stable funding within libraries. This is an important shift, one that can sustain the knowledge and expertise of our academic presses in ways that allow them to continue the important work of sustaining scholarly discourse, work they have engaged in for centuries.

It is also a shift that would open the door to strong partnerships between academic presses and open-access book publishing, along the lines of those already established by the Computers and Composition Digital Press and the WAC Clearinghouse with the University Press of Colorado.[19] As the partnership between the Clearinghouse and University Press of Colorado demonstrates, sales of print books can be relatively high (and can exceed, in some cases, the average sales figures for traditional books) even when the book is being given away in open-access formats. And while the sales for any of the Clearinghouse's print editions only rarely generate enough revenue to cover their production costs, those that do suggest a path forward that includes a way for open-access publishing to be seen as a strategy that fits within the larger approaches taken by traditional academic presses.

Academic publishing is at an inflection point. I expect that, as a field, we will turn increasingly toward open-access book publishing. I expect that we will see university and college scholars taking greater control over the production and distribution of books. And I expect that we will see a growing recognition of the importance of work associated not only with writing books but also with developing, designing, and publishing them as well. These changes may take longer than the advocates of open-access publishing collaboratives might like, but they will happen. The role that traditional academic publishers will play in this process is uncertain, but regardless of whether they embrace it, resist it, or simply hope it goes away one thing is clear: change is coming.

---

19   The Utah State University Press, which supports the C&C Digital Press, is an imprint of the University Press of Colorado.

REFERENCES

Abdullah, Zaleha. (2014). Activity theory as analytical tool: A case study of developing student teachers' creativity in design. *Procedia—Social and Behavioral Sciences, 131*, 70–84. https://doi.org/10.1016/j.sbspro.2014.04.082.

Al-Huneini, Hamood, Walker, S. Aisha. & Badger, Rirchad. (2020). Introducing tablet computers to a rural primary school: An activity theory case study. *Computers & Education, 143*, 103648. https://doi.org/10.1016/j.compedu.2019.103648.

Baldwin, Beth. (1996). *Conversations: Computer-mediated dialogue, multilogue, and learning*. RhetNet. https://wac.colostate.edu/rhetnet.

Baldwin, Beth & Flood, Tim. (1996). *The rhetorical dimensions of cyberspace*. RhetNet. https://wac.colostate.edu/rhetnet.

Batson, Trent. (1993). ENFI research. *Computers and Composition, 10*(3), 93–101.

Batson, Trent. (1998). The ENFI Project: A networked classroom approach to writing instruction. *Academic Computing, 2*, 55–56.

Bazerman, Charles. (2000). *Shaping written knowledge: The genre and activity of the experimental article in science*. The WAC Clearinghouse. https://wac.colostate.edu/books/landmarks/bazerman-shaping/ (Original work published 1988 by University of Wisconsin Press)

Bazerman, Charles & Russell, David R. (Eds.). (2003a). *Writing selves/writing societies: Research from activity perspectives*. The WAC Clearinghouse; Mind, Culture, and Activity. https://doi.org/10.37514/PER-B.2003.2317.

Bazerman, Charles & Russell, David R. (2003b). Introduction. In Charles Bazerman & David R. Russell (Eds.), *Writing selves/writing societies: Research from activity perspectives* (pp. 1–6). The WAC Clearinghouse; Mind, Culture, and Activity. https://doi.org/10.37514/PER-B.2003.2317.1.3.

Bazerman, Charles, Blakesley, David, Palmquist, Mike & Russell, David R. (2008, January 7). Open access book publishing in writing studies: A case study. *First Monday, 13*(1). https://firstmonday.org/ojs/index.php/fm/article/view/2088/1920.

Behrend, Monica B. (2014). Engeström's activity theory as a tool to analyse online resources embedding academic literacies. *Journal of Academic Language & Learning, 8*(1), A109–A120.

Bolter, Jay David. (1991). *The writing space: The computer, hypertext, and the history of writing*. Lawrence Erlbaum.

Bolter, Jay David. (1993). Alone and together in the electronic bazaar. *Computers and Composition, 10*, 5–18.

Bridwell, Lillian S., Nancarrow, Paula Reed & Ross, Donald. (1984). The writing process and the writing machine: Current research on word processors relevant to the teaching of composition. In Richard Beach & Lillian Bridwell (Eds.), *New directions in composition research* (pp. 381–397). Guilford.

Butler, Wayne, Carter, Locke, Kemp, Fred O. & Taylor, Paul. (1988). *Daedalus instructional system* [Computer Software]. The Daedalus Group.

Carvalho, Maira B., Bellotti, Francesco, Berta Riccardo, De Gloria, Alessandro, Sedano, Carolina Islas, Hauge, Jannicke Baalsrud, Hu, Jun & Rauterberg, Matthias. (2015). An activity theory-based model for serious games analysis and conceptual design. *Computers & Education, 87,* 166–181. https://doi.org/10.1016/j.compedu.2015.03.023.

Chung, Ching-Jung, Hwang, Gwo-Jen & Lai, Chiu-Lin. (2019). A review of experimental mobile learning research in 2010–2016 based on the activity theory framework. *Computers & Education, 129,* 1–13. https://doi.org/10.1016/j.compedu.2018.10.010.

Cole, Michael. (1996). *Cultural psychology: A once and future discipline.* Cambridge University Press.

Collier, Richard M. (1983). The word processor and revision strategies. *College Composition and Communication, 34,* 149–155.

Day, Michael. (1996). Coverweb overview: Pedagogies in virtual spaces: Writing classes in the MOO. *Kairos, 1*(2). https://kairos.technorhetoric.net/1.2/coverweb.html.

Day, Michael, Delagrange, Susan H., Palmquist, Mike, Pemberton, Michael A. & Walker, Janice R. (2013). What we really value: Redefining scholarly engagement in tenure and promotion protocols. *College Composition and Communication, 65*(1), 185–208. http://www.ncte.org/library/NCTEFiles/Resources/Journals/CCC/0651-sep2013/CCC0651What.pdf.

Dennehy, Denis & Conboy, Kieran. (2017). Going with the flow: An activity theory analysis of flow techniques in software development. *Journal of Systems and Software, 133,* 16–173. https://doi.org/10.1016/j.jss.2016.10.003.

Draper, Stephen W. (1993). Critical notice: Activity theory: The new direction for HCI? *International Journal of Man-Machine Studies, 37*(6), 812–821.

Engeström, Yrjö. (1987). *Learning by expanding.* Orienta-Konsultit.

Engeström, Yrjö. (1990). *Learning, working and imagining: Twelve studies in activity theory.* Orienta-Konsultit.

Engeström, Yrjö. (1993). Developmental studies of work as a testbench of activity theory: The case of primary care medical practice. In Seth C. Chaiklin & Jean Lave (Eds.), *Understanding practice: Perspectives on activity and context* (pp. 64–103). Cambridge University Press.

Engeström, Yrjö. (1999a). Activity theory and individual and social transformation. In Yrjö Engeström, Reijo Miettinen & Raija-Leena Punamäki (Eds.), *Perspectives on activity theory* (pp. 19–38). Cambridge University Press.

Engeström, Y. (1999b). Innovative learning in work teams: Analyzing cycles of knowledge creation in practice. In Yrjö Engeström, Reijo Miettinen & Raija-Leena Punamäki (Eds.), *Perspectives on activity theory* (pp. 375–404). Cambridge University Press.

Engeström, Yrjö. (2014). *Learning by expanding* (2nd ed.). Cambridge University Press.

Engeström, Y. & Miettinen, R. (1999). Introduction. In Yrjö Engeström, Reijo Miettinen & Raija-Leena Punamäki (Eds.), *Perspectives on activity theory* (pp. 1–18). Cambridge University Press.

Fulwiler, Toby & Young, Art (Eds.). (2000). *Language connections: Writing and reading across the curriculum.* The WAC Clearinghouse. https://wac.colostate.edu/books/landmarks/language-connections/ (Original work published 1982 by National Council of Teachers of English)

Hawisher, Gail E. (1986). Studies in word processing. *Computers and Composition, 4,* 6–31.

Hawisher, Gail E. (1988). Research update: Writing and word processing. *Computers and Composition, 5,* 7–27.

Ho, Jeanne Pau Yen, Chen, Der-Thanq Victor & Ng, David. (2016). Distributed leadership through the lens of activity theory. *Educational Management Administration & Leadership, 44*(5), 814–836. https://doi.org/10.1177/1741143215570302.

Hoffmann, David, Ahlemann, Frederik & Reining, Stefan. (2020). Reconciling alignment, efficiency, and agility in IT project portfolio management: Recommendations based on a revelatory case study. *International Journal of Project Management, 38*(2), 124–136. https://doi.org/10.1016/j.ijproman.2020.01.004.

Kaplan, Nancy. (1995). *E-literacies: Politexts, hypertexts, and other cultural formations in the late age of print. Computer-Mediated Communication Magazine, 2*(3). http://www.ibiblio.org/cmc/mag/1995/mar/kaplan.html.

Kaplan, Nancy, Davis, Stuart & Martin, Joseph. (1987). *PROSE (Prompted Revision of Student Essays)* [Computer Software]. McGraw-Hill.

Kaptelinin, Victor. (2005). The object of activity: Making sense of the sense-maker. *Mind, Culture, and Activity, 12*(1), 4–18.

Kaptelinin, Victor & Nardie Bonnie. (2012). *Activity theory in HCI: Fundamentals and reflections.* Morgan and Claypool.

Kemp, Fred O. (1996). An open letter to Kairos. *Kairos: A Journal of Rhetoric, Technology, and Pedagogy, 1*(1). http://kairos.technorhetoric.net/1.1/binder.html?letters/kemp/kemp1.html.

Kiefer, Kathleen E. & Smith, Charles R. (1983). Textual analysis with computers: Tests of Bell Laboratories' computer software. *Research in the Teaching of English, 17*(3), 201–214.

Kiefer, Kathleen E. & Smith, Charles R. (1984). Improving students' revising and editing: The Writer's Workbench System. In William Wresch (Ed.), *The computer in composition instruction: A writer's tool* (pp. 65–82). National Council of Teachers of English.

Kozma, Robert B. (1991). The impact of computer-based tools and rhetorical prompts on writing processes and products. *Cognition and Instruction, 8,* 1–27.

Lansman, M., Smith, John B. & Weber, Irene. (1993). Using the Writing Environment to study writers' strategies. *Computers and Composition, 10*(2), 71–92.

LeBlanc, Paul. (1988). How to get the words just right: A reappraisal of word processing and revision. *Computers and Composition, 5,* 29–42.

Leontiev, Alexei N. (1978). *Activity, consciousness, and personality.* Marie J. Hall (Trans.). Prentice-Hall.

Leontiev, Alexei N. (2005). The genesis of activity. *Journal of Russian and East European Psychology, 43*(4), 58–71.

McLeod, Susan H. & Soven, Margot (Eds.). (2000). *Writing across the curriculum: A guide to developing programs.* The WAC Clearinghouse. https://wac.colostate.edu/books/landmarks/mcleod-soven/. (Original work published 1992 by Sage)

McPherson, James M. (2003, October 1). A crisis in scholarly publishing. *Perspectives on History, 41*(7). https://www.historians.org/publications-and-directories/perspectives-on-history/october-2003/a-crisis-in-scholarly-publishing.

Moulthrop, Stuart. (1991). The politics of hypertext. In Cynthia Selfe & Gail E. Hawisher (Eds.), *Evolving perspectives on computers and composition studies: Questions for the 1990s* (pp. 253–274). National Council of Teachers of English.

Moulthrop, Stuart. (1994). Rhizome and resistance: Hypertext and the dreams of a new culture. In George P. Landow (Ed.), *Hyper/text/theory* (pp. 299–322). Johns Hopkins University Press.

Nardi, Bonnie A. (1995). *Context and consciousness: Activity theory and human-computer interaction*. MIT Press.

Nardi, Bonnie, Whittaker, Steve & Schwarz, Heinrich. (2002). NetWORKers and their activity in intensional networks. *Computer Supported Cooperative Work, 11*, 205–242. https://doi.org/10.1023/A:1015241914483.

Neuwirth, Christine M. (1984). Toward the design of a flexible, computer-based writing environment. In William Wresch (Ed.), *The computer in composition instruction: A writer's tool* (pp. 191–205). National Council of Teachers of English.

Neuwirth, Christine M., Kaufer, David S., Chandook, Ravinder & Morris, James H. (1990). Issues in the design of computer support for co-authoring and commenting. *Proceedings of the Third Conference on Computer-Supported Cooperative Work*, Los Angeles, October 7–10, 1990. Association for Computing Machinery.

Neuwirth, Christine M., Kaufer, David S., Chimera, Rick & Gillespie, Terilyn. (1987). The Notes program: A hypertext application for writing from source texts. *Hypertext '87 Proceedings* (pp. 245–346). Association for Computing Machinery.

Neuwirth, Christine M., Kaufer, David S., Keim, Gary & Gillespie, Terilyn.(1988a). The Comments program: Computer Support for Response to Writing. Technical Report CECE-TR-3, Carnegie Mellon University, Center for Educational Computing in English.

Neuwirth, Christine M., Palmquist, Mike & Gillespie, Terilyn. (1988b). An instructor's guide to collaborative writing with CECE Talk: A computer network tool. Technical Report CECE-TR-8, Carnegie Mellon University, Center for Educational Computing in English.

Neuwirth, Christine M., Palmquist, Mike, Cochran, Cynthia, Gillespie, Terilyn., Hartman, Karen & Hajduk, Thomas. (1993). Why write-together-concurrently on a computer network? In Bertam Bruce, J. Peyton & Trent Batson (Eds.), *Network-based classrooms: Promises and realities* (pp. 181–209). Cambridge University Press.

Palmquist, Mike. (2003, March 19–22). New venues for academic publishing: From cooperative publishing ventures to collaborative web sites. *Plenary Presentation, Research Network Forum* [Conference presentation]. Conference on College Composition and Communication, New York, United States.

Palmquist, Mike. (2022). Opening a new chapter: Open access publishing in writing studies. In Greg Giberson, Megan Schoen & Christian Weisser (Eds.), *Editors in writing: Behind the curtain of scholarly publication in writing studies* (pp. 118–138). Utah State University Press.

Palmquist, Mike, Mullin, Joan & Blalock, Glenn. (2012). The role of activity analysis in writing research: Case studies of emerging scholarly communities. In Lee Nicholson & Mary P. Sheridan (Eds.), *Writing studies research in practice: Methods and methodologies* (pp. 231–244). Southern Illinois University Press.

Pearson, Sue. (2009). Using activity theory to understand prospective teachers' attitudes to and construction of special educational needs and/or disabilities. *Teaching and Teacher Education, 25*(4), 559–568. https://doi.org/10.1016/j.tate.2009.02.011.

Rubinštejn, Sergei L. (1987). Problems of psychology in the works of Karl Marx. *Studies in Soviet Thought 33*, 111–130. https://doi.org/10.1007/BF01151778. (Original work published 1934)

Russell, David R. (1995). Activity theory and its implications for writing instruction. In Joseph Petraglia (Ed.), *Reconceiving writing, rethinking writing instruction* (pp. 51–78). Erlbaum.

Russell, David R. (2009). Uses of activity theory in written communication research. In A. Sannino, H. Daniels & K. Gutierrez (Eds.), *Learning and expanding with activity theory* (pp. 40–52). Cambridge University Press.

Slatin, John M. (1990). Reading hypertext: Order and coherence in a new medium. *College English, 52*(8), 870–883.

Smith, John B. (1987). A hypertext writing environment and its cognitive basis. *Proceedings of HyperTEXT'87* (pp. 195–214). Association for Computing Machinery.

Smith, John B. & Lansman, M. (1989). A cognitive basis for a computer writing environment. In Bruce K. Britton & Shawn M. Glynn (Eds.), *Computer writing environments* (pp. 17–56). Erlbaum.

Sullivan, Patricia. (1989). Human-computer interaction perspectives on word-processing issues. *Computers and Composition, 6*(3), 11–33.

Takoeva, Vasilisa. (2017). *The re-appearing act of leadership: An exploration of leadership practice through the lens of cultural-historical activity theory* [Unpublished doctoral dissertation]. University of Birmingham.

Taylor, Paul H. (1993). *Computer conferencing and chaos: A study in fractal discourse* [Doctoral dissertation]. University of Texas at Austin. http://www.daedalus.com/downloads_public/dissertations/Taylor-Paul.pdf.

Tuman, Myron C. (1993). Campus word processing: Seven design principles for a new academic writing environment. *Computers and Composition, 10*(3), 49–62.

Vygotsky, Lev S. (1978). *Mind in society: The development of higher psychological processes.* Michael Cole, Vera John-Steiner, Sylvia Scribner & Ellen Souberman (Eds.). Harvard University Press.

Vygotsky, Lev S. (1986). *Thought and language.* Alex Kozulin (Ed. & Trans.). MIT Press. (Original work published 1934)

Vygotsky, L. S. (1989). Concrete human psychology. *Soviet Psychology, 27*(2), 53–77.

Webb, Patricia R. (1997). Narratives of self in networked communications. *Computers and Composition, 14*, 73–90.

Winstanley, Lisa. (2019, September 2). Mapping activity theory to a design thinking model (ATDT): A framework to propagate a culture of creative trust [Paper presentation]. International Association of Societies of Design Research Conference, Manchester, UK. https://iasdr2019.org/uploads/files/Proceedings/vo-f-1180-Win-L.pdf.

Wojahn, Patricia G., Neuwirth, Christine M. & Bullock, Barbara. (1998). Effects of interfaces for annotation on communication in a collaborative task. *Proceedings of CHI 1998* (pp. 456–463). Association for Computing Machinery.

Wresch, William. (1982). Computers in English class: Finally beyond grammar and drills. *College English, 44*(5), 483–90.

Wresch, William. (1984). Questions, answers, and automated writing. In William Wresch (Ed.), *The computer in composition instruction: A writer's tool* (pp. 143–153). National Council of Teachers of English.

Zahedi, Mithra & Tessier, Virginie. (2018, June 25). Designerly activity theory: Toward a new ontology for design research [Paper presentation]. Design Research Society Conference, Limerick, Ireland.

CHAPTER 9.

WRITING AND SOCIAL PROGRESS: GENRE EVOLUTION IN THE FIELD OF SOCIAL ENTREPRENEURSHIP

Karyn Kessler and Paul M. Rogers
University of California, Santa Barbara

To explore the role of writing as a tool of mediation in the formation and evolution of a newly recognized area of activity, we turn in this chapter to the field of social entrepreneurship—work that seeks to address the world's most intractable problems through entrepreneurial behavior and a commitment to the public good. Specifically, this study aims to examine the ways in which a particular genre—with genre defined here as social action (Miller, 1984) and as a typified and recognizable response to recurrent social situations or problems (Bazerman, 1988)—served as a primary driver in the activity of identifying a new category of social actors (social entrepreneurs) and building a new global field (social entrepreneurship). Taking Ashoka as a site of organizational analysis, this chapter tells the story of how one of the world's leading non-governmental organizations (NGO) prioritized, deployed, and evolved a written genre—The Fellow Profile—in order to organize around a vision, respond to changing needs, establish and scale up processes and organizational structures, grow its membership, and communicate its impact to multiple stakeholder groups including funders. [1]

We begin the chapter with a brief overview of rhetorical genre theory and Charles Bazerman's work on writing as a tool of mediation in human activity. We then turn our attention to describing the activity system of social entrepreneurship and, specifically, that system in its relationship to the organizational site of our study, Ashoka, including a comparison between the Ashoka Fellow Profile and a more commonly studied genre, the grant funding proposal. Next, we outline methods for this particular genre study and then present results of

---

1 Ashoka is the world's 5th ranked NGO according to the global ranking organization NGO Advisor. Ashoka has offices in 39 countries. Its global headquarters are in Arlington, Virginia, United States. Founded in 1980, Ashoka's mission is "to shape a global, entrepreneurial, competitive citizen sector, one that allows social entrepreneurs to thrive and enables the world's citizens to think and act as changemakers" (www.ashoka.org/about-ashoka).

DOI: https://doi.org/10.37514/PER-B.2023.1800.2.09

data collection and analysis. Following this, we discuss the ways in which the tensions between textual regularities and the need for genre change played a role in the development of the field of social entrepreneurship. We conclude with a reflection on the potential value a writing studies perspective brings to global and organizational efforts for social change and call for further genre research in organizations dedicated to advancing social progress.

WRITING AS A HUMAN ACTIVITY AND GENRE STUDIES

To look at the mediating role of writing in the activity system of social entrepreneurship, and in particular the written genre of the Fellow Profile as a driver in the development of the field, we draw on Bazerman's work which examines "how texts arise within and influence the living world of people and events" (2003, p. 309), and, in particular, his set of necessary conditions for "effective actions" (2013, p. 69) to occur:

> Each successful text creates for its readers a social fact. The social facts consist of meaningful social actions being accomplished through language, or speech acts. These acts are carried out in patterned, typical, and therefore intelligible textual forms or genres, which are related to other texts and genres that occur in related circumstances. Together the text types fit together as genre sets within genre systems, which are part of systems of human activity. (2003, p. 311)

In other words, writing—and thus, genres—provide those who write them with a means to regularize communication in specific types of circumstances, for specific purposes, and to specific audiences in ways that are recognizable to readers. Along similar lines, scholars of rhetorical genre theory have offered critical insights into the particular ways in which written genres can serve as important tools of social action (Miller, 1984) and for social action (Devitt, 2021) within activity systems, discourse communities, or communities of practice (Berkenkotter & Huckin, 1995; Beaufort, 1997; Bazerman, 2002). Genres of written communication can, for example, advance social change by "destabilizing existing social contexts, introducing new and competing alternatives, connecting new alternatives to what came before, and introducing and stabilizing new and emergent systems" (Faber, 2008). Further, genres can serve as important sites of distributed cognition where particular kinds of discursive knowledge are routinely gathered and shared, and which help orient and coordinate actions among writers and readers. As Spinuzzi notes, "genres are not simply performed or communicated, they represent the thinking out of a community as it cyclically performs an activity" (2004). In this way, from an organizational perspective, written genres serve both internal and external purposes.

Scholars have also identified the ways in which genres are formed and change over time (Bazerman, 1988; Orlikowski & Yates, 1994). As Bazerman notes, analyzing the formation and emergence of a genre (which is the focus of this chapter) illuminates "the forces to which textual features respond" (1988, p. 62) and "the kinds of problems the genre was attempting to solve, and how it went about solving them" (1988, p. 63). However, as the communities of practice and activity systems form and evolve, and as the external problems, needs, and forces to which a genre is responding change over time, so too must the genre and the infrastructure—defined in this chapter as social, programmatic, and material support (see Read, 2019; Grabill, 2010; DeVoss et al., 2005; Star & Ruhleder, 1996)— surrounding its production adapt if the genre is to remain relevant. The need for a genre's flexibility and adaptability notwithstanding, from a rhetorical genre theory perspective, textual regularities remain a critical feature for maintaining and ensuring the recognizability of the genre. As a result, this tension—the need for textual regularities and the need for variation and change—within a genre is said to be potentially productive; for, as these tensions play out within particular genres and within particular organizations, they provide a window into the internal and external needs and pressures to which a genre must respond while remaining "stabilized for now" (Schryer, 1994, p. 108).

INTRODUCTION TO THE ACTIVITY SYSTEM SOCIAL ENTREPRENEURSHIP AND ASHOKA

The activity system of social entrepreneurship has its origins in the work of a group of subjects or actors, social entrepreneurs, who introduce solutions to pressing social and environmental problems (e.g., poverty, human trafficking, climate change). The object of social entrepreneurs, broadly stated, is to improve the quality of life for people in practical ways. To make these improvements, social entrepreneurs use the tools of enterprise and business along with community engagement and the power of ordinary citizens to create novel solutions to what are typically localized problems. Examples of these innovative solutions include the development of micro-finance, community-sourced emergency preparedness social media platforms, greenscaping programs for heavily polluted urban areas, integrated systems to combat human trafficking, and much more.

While individuals fitting the description of social entrepreneur have lived throughout history (see Bornstein, 2007 for a history of the field), it is only in the past 40 years that social entrepreneurship has been galvanized into a recognized field of activity. In this sense, social entrepreneurship represents a deliberate reframing and destabilization of the narrative related to what we commonly refer to as the nonprofit sector; in principle, social entrepreneurs are individuals who play by a different and somewhat hybrid set of rules than that of either business or traditional non-profits as they apply "the mindset, processes, tools, and techniques of business entrepreneurship to the pursuit of a social and/or environmental mission" (Kickul & Lyons, 2016, p. 1).

This reframing and the establishing of social entrepreneurship as a recognized social fact has been successful, as in recent years and around the world, the community of social entrepreneurship and the work of social entrepreneurs has gained increasing recognition by governments, businesses, non-governmental organizations, and universities, as evidenced by:

- The development of hundreds of degree programs, courses and centers dedicated to social entrepreneurship at major universities around the world (e.g., SAID School of Business at Oxford, the Center for the Advancement of Social Entrepreneurship at Duke University, and the Center for Social Impact Strategy at the University of Pennsylvania).
- The rise of academic journals focused on social entrepreneurship such as the Stanford Social Innovation Review; Innovations Journal; the Journal of Social Entrepreneurship; and the International Journal of Social Entrepreneurship and Innovation.
- Increases in published research on social entrepreneurship in indexed, peer reviewed management journals (see Saebi et al., 2019, for a review).
- The emergence of multiple organizations championing frameworks of social entrepreneurship, including the Skoll Foundation, Ashoka, Acumen, the Schwab Foundation for Social Entrepreneurship, and Echoing Green.
- National, state, and local government involvement in social entrepreneurship. For example, in 2009, the U.S. White House under then President Obama created an Office of Social Innovation and Civic Participation (see Wolk & Ebinger, 2010, for examples of state and local government models).

How does Social Entrepreneurship Differ from Entrepreneurship and Government-Funded Work?

The word entrepreneurship is derived from a French word that means to "undertake," and involves the "shifting of economic resources into areas of higher productivity and yield" (Dees, 1998), which can lead to "creative destruction" (Schumpeter, 2013, p. 105)—the state at which new ventures effectively render existing products, services, and business models obsolete. While entrepreneurs and social entrepreneurs share similarities with regard to catalyzing and starting up new organizations and promoting new ideas, the greatest distinction between them is that, for social entrepreneurs, the primary end result of their activity is social impact (see for example, Porter et al., 2014), social value, or social good rather than financial profits.

Among the first organizations to sponsor the idea of social entrepreneurship and bring social entrepreneurs together as a network and community was Ashoka, whose founder and CEO, Bill Drayton, is credited with coining the term "social entrepreneur" (Thorpe, 2019). In simple terms, the work of the social entrepreneur at the individual level begins with one's ability to notice persistent and systemic problems in the local environment; then, beyond the individual's ability to identify the problem and the patterns contributing to its damaging effect, the social entrepreneur has an idea, a strategy, and a personal conviction to do something about it. As Drayton put it, the social entrepreneur is one who is able "to recognize when a part of society is not working and to solve the problem by changing the system, spreading solutions and persuading entire societies to take new leaps" (Drayton, 2005, p. 9). This bottom-up approach to social change, and the development and scaling of solutions that are rooted in the vision of individual leaders and grounded in local, community-based solutions are differentiating features of social entrepreneurship.

In significant ways, social entrepreneurs fill the gaps left when governments and markets fail to adequately address human and environmental needs—typically, basic ones. Where government-driven Calls for Proposals (CFPs) draw the attention and the efforts of researchers, innovators, and knowledge-producers through a top-down structure of soliciting, selecting, and funding the proposals that most effectively respond to the pre-selected, targeted areas of growth and advancement (e.g., war technology, medical technology, etc.), the field of social entrepreneurship depends on grassroots solutions that arise from local communities and are sponsored by local champions.

For the past 40 years, Ashoka has spread the idea of social entrepreneurship primarily through its rigorous process for identifying, designating, and supporting the world's leading social entrepreneurs in a network of "Ashoka Fellows." One example of an Ashoka Fellow is Bart Weetjens who created an organization, Apopo (www.apopo.org) to eliminate landmines left behind by war. The problem that Weetjens recognized was that landmines continue to pose danger to communities long after wars end as the hidden, underground explosives lead to ongoing risks for human death and injury. Weetjens, who is from Belgium, was named an Ashoka Fellow in 2006 for his innovative solution to this social problem—he and his team train giant pouched rats to effectively and safely detect explosives so that communities can safely clear the landmines across thousands of acres of land. The result—increased safety for people in war-torn neighborhoods around the world—allows communities to move beyond a basic concern for survival to reach higher levels of human potential. In this case, Weetjens was not responding to a government-driven CFP or a company's Corporate Social Responsibility (CSR) initiative to remove government-funded war technology left in the earth; rather, as a social entrepreneur, he, himself, had identified a persistent problem in his community, developed technology and processes for addressing the problem in a way that made use of the resources located right there in the same environment, formed teams with local community members to scale up the innovation, and, as a result, was found, selected, and funded by Ashoka as a fellow for his innovation and its potential to scale to other similar communities around the world.

How are Ashoka Fellows Selected?

To date, Ashoka's system for search and selection (the venture process) has led to the election of over 4,100 fellows in over 90 countries.[2] The dynamic system of activity follows five stages. First, on a rolling basis, Ashoka accepts and reviews nominations for fellowship from the social entrepreneurs themselves or from country representatives who are familiar with the work of the potential fellow. At the second stage, Ashoka's global team begins a conversation with the nominee in order to learn about their work. This may include site visits and input from other leaders in their field. Next is what Ashoka refers to as the "second opinion," which is when a senior Ashoka representative from outside the region interviews the candidate in-person, applying Ashoka's criteria, and probing a candidate's life history.[34] The fourth part of the process is "The Panel" for which Ashoka convenes a group of three leading social and business entrepreneurs from the nominee's country to assess the candidate's idea and potential impact in relation to the local context. The panel decides by consensus whether to recommend the candidate to the final stage of the Fellow selection process. Figure 9.1 captures the Ashoka Fellow selection process as explained on the Ashoka Netherlands website, ashoka.org/de/country/netherlands.

---

2 ashoka.org/en-tr/frequently-asked-questions
3 At each stage in the process, candidates are evaluated against Ashoka's core criteria: a new idea, creativity, entrepreneurial quality, social impact, and ethical fiber. This identification and review process (referred to internally at Ashoka as "venture" or "search and selection") begins with deep background investigations and multiple extended interviews with the candidate, and with outside references. If a candidate achieves the designation of Ashoka Fellow, they receive several years of significant financial support, and join a global network of peers. A major goal of Ashoka's work is to connect each fellow to the people, ideas, and resources they need to grow and deepen their impact.

Writing and Social Progress

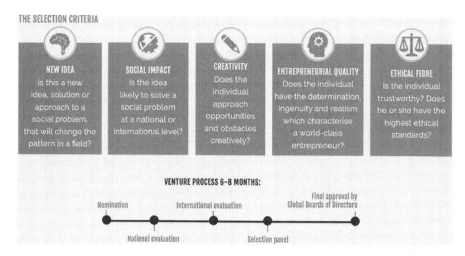

Figure 9.1. Ashoka's process of search and selection

The "data" gathered throughout this elaborate vetting process are captured and documented electronically and systematically along the way through an internal tracking system and culminates in the generation of a Fellow Profile. The developing profile advances with the candidate as they move through the venture process and is revised by Ashoka staff members as the candidate reaches new stages in the process. Finally, the candidate's profile is presented to the Ashoka Global Board of Directors for review, discussion, and vote. Candidates who are approved at the board meeting are then designated Ashoka Fellows. At that time, the Fellow Profile for the successful candidate is made public on the Ashoka.org website and in other publications and venues. Thus, the profile serves first as an internal case statement which contributes to the potential election of the fellow. Then, if the candidate is successful, the profile serves as an external record of the basis for their election as an Ashoka Fellow. (You can find Bart Weetjens' complete Ashoka profile online at www.ashoka.org/en-us/fellow/bart-weetjens.)

What is the Role of the Ashoka Fellow Profile as a Genre in this System of Activity?

Within the relatively nascent activity system of social entrepreneurship and the specific context of search and selection within Ashoka, one genre—The Fellow Profile—has emerged and persisted as the primary tool for internally organizing people, activity, ideas, and processes, as well as for presenting evidence for the existence and effectiveness of the impact and activity of social entrepreneurs. In this study, we report on the emergence of this new genre and how it has both remained stable and evolved throughout the formative years of an organization and a field.

233

Given the likely unfamiliarity of the Ashoka Fellow Profile as a genre to most readers, we pause here to consider some of the ways in which the profile relates to the more familiar genre of the funding or grant proposal. Grant funding proposals have been examined and recognized for the ways in which they—as a genre—traditionally respond to problems, are rhetorically persuasive (Conner & Mauranen, 1999; Myers, 1990), exist in a system of interacting genres (Connor, 2000; Tardy 2003), and are parts of larger genre sets (Bazerman, 1994; Devitt, 1991; Pare, 2000). While Myers notes that "the primary purpose of grant proposals is to persuade" and that "the various moves found in the proposals work toward the writer's aim of convincing the funding agency to provide financial support to the proposed problem" (1990, p. 8), for Ashoka and the profile, the surrounding context and the goals of the genre are markedly different. For example, a fellow is not invited into the process of writing their own "proposal." Instead, Ashoka staff members and country representatives are responsible for gathering and documenting evidence throughout a multi-stage system of search and selection. To further highlight this and other critical similarities and differences between these two genres, Table 9.1 focuses on issues of authorship, rhetorical effect, exigence, and implications.

Table 9.1. Comparison of Funding Proposals to Fellow Profiles

Attribute	Funding Proposals	Ashoka Fellow Profile
Authorship: Is the genre written by the person/people seeking funding?	Yes, the principal investigator is the author of the proposal and the person responsible for the outcome of the promised future work/results.	No, the Ashoka Fellow does not write or contribute directly to the Fellow Profile, but is responsible for the outcome of the promised future work/results. (A Fellow Profile is written and revised over months and even years by teams of people beginning with in-country Ashoka Venture Team members who are charged with the search, selection and nomination of potential Ashoka Fellows.)
Rhetorical Effect: Is the genre meant to be rhetorically persuasive with the end result being the funding of a promised/future project?	Yes, what makes a proposal successful is its approval by the funding agency; that is, the proposal has credibly convinced the funding agency and program officers of the merit of the proposal and the likelihood of the proposal writer(s) following through on the work.	Yes, the profile provides the basis upon which the decision is made as to whether or not a candidate becomes a fellow. If successful (i.e., persuasive), the individual is provided funding by Ashoka in order to focus exclusively on their social entrepreneurship work.

Attribute	Funding Proposals	Ashoka Fellow Profile
Exigence: Within the activity system, is the genre responding to a specific call for funding?	Yes, the process for awarding funding is top-down in that calls for proposals (e.g., in the United States, CFPs issued by the National Science Foundation or National Institutes for Health are meant to guide and focus researchers in particular directions to fill an identified need.	Yes and No. Ashoka has identified five primary areas of social entrepreneurship work—(environment, human rights, economic development, health, and education). However, the call for Ashoka Fellows is ongoing and bottom-up with a process that does not begin or end with an attempt to guide or focus those in the field to meet specific, identified needs. Rather, the call is to the general field of activity with a requirement that the locus of the idea and of the work stem from a potential fellow's ability and past proof of an ability to identify and systemically respond to the particular problems and needs of a community.
Impact: If the genre is successful at accomplishing its goal, is it designed to change the identity of the person who is funded?	No, proposals that are awarded do not intentionally change the identity of the recipient of a grant. Grants are more typically designed to produce the deliverables associated with the funding.	Yes, becoming an Ashoka Fellow itself is a designation, but more importantly, there is a good deal of evidence to suggest that becoming a fellow changes the identity of the recipient as he/she becomes recognized as a social entrepreneur and is now part of a network and organization that is committed to the field of social entrepreneurship.

Another genre to which profiles may be usefully compared is that of "capability statements," which, according to Van Nostrand's (2013) account, are ubiquitous in the research and development (R&D) activities of the military industrial complex. Specifically, "as every organization, vendor, and customer alike is obligated to explain itself and do so continually" (Van Nostrand, 2013, p. 171) it is commonplace for an organization to declare its credibility and make a case for its capability to succeed again in new contexts with new demands. As written texts, the main feature of capability statements is their "shared communicative purpose" of *positioning* an organization favorably within a particular industry segment. According to Van Nostrand, it is the "textual structure" that actualizes this purpose; namely, it is in a patterned "sequence of a few textual elements," that past performance is explicitly connected to future activity.

Overall, with regard to how the profile relates to this more familiar written genre of the Capability Statement, it can be said that the architecture and textual structure of the profile similarly links a fellow's credibility and past success to future potential and that, collectively, the profiles as a genre set fulfill a "shared communicative purpose" for Ashoka and for the field of social entrepreneurship. Specifically, profiles consistently provide evidence of the successful implementation of a fellow's new ideas through impact data—that is to say, the credibility which arises from the fellow's past performance is explicitly stated and connected to a claim of potentiality for the fellow's likely impact in the future. In this way, Ashoka is looking to effectively and efficiently identify people (with ideas and organizations) who will build on past learnings and have greater impact in the future in much the same way a venture capital firm might "bet" on a new business through early-stage investment. And, as is the case with capability statements in R&D activity, the textual structure or sequence of the profiles plays a critical role in shaping a narrative about the fellow—one that begins with the fellow's success with a new idea in a particular context and in response to a local, intractable problem before turning to the character of the social entrepreneur and their potential for greater future impact. The consistency of this narrative (i.e., the unchanging overall structure of the profile), positions Ashoka Fellows as field-level leaders who are worthy of the financial investment and attention of those who are interested in bringing about social change.

THIS STUDY

Ashoka Fellow Profiles as an Object of Study

As noted earlier, Ashoka Fellow Profiles (referred to as profiles and fellow profiles throughout) help systematically organize a complex and dynamic organizational process for selecting Ashoka Fellows. This activity takes place across writers, languages, countries, and fields of work. As an individual text, each profile is identically structured to provide an overview of the social entrepreneur's project and potential for wide-scale, positive social impact according to six content areas (see Table 9.2).

Beyond the function profiles play in the systematized process of search and selection within the organization, Ashoka Profiles offer a substantial resource to those interested in the field and provide a broad and historical view of social entrepreneurship around the world across many areas of work. Notably, and in this regard, fellow profiles have been utilized outside of Ashoka by social entrepreneurship scholars as primary data sources in a number of empirical investigations and peer reviewed journal articles that take up the fellow profiles as evidence and data (e.g., Meyskens et al., 2010; Chandra & Shang, 2017; Sunduramurthy et al., 2016; Nieuwenhuizen, 2020).

Analyzing Genre and Social Progress: The Mediating Role of Writing in Activity

As noted, a central framework for this study is the substantial body of scholarship which has demonstrated the importance of writing in shaping complex social activities and systems, as well as human identity and consciousness (Goody, 1986; Bazerman, 2006). This study further recognizes profiles as "a complex pattern of repeated social activity and rhetorical performance arising in response to a recurrent situation" (Pare & Smart, 1994, p. 122); in this particular case, the recurrent situation emerges from Ashoka's organizational vision and ongoing commitment to identifying leading social entrepreneurs around the world and advancing social entrepreneurship as a credible and defined field of activity on the global stage. The repeated social activity centers around the search and selection of leading social entrepreneurs, the Ashoka Fellows.

To capture these social and practical purposes in our examination of this now recognizable genre and the role it has played in the formation and evolution of the newly established field of social entrepreneurship, we set out to address three overarching research questions:

- What can we learn about genre as a mediating tool in activity systems by examining one genre (the Ashoka Fellow Profile) and following its origins and development over time?
- In what ways and to what extent has the Ashoka Fellow Profile as a genre supported the NGO's internal ability to organize itself and respond to emerging needs over time? And, how, if at all, have the tensions between textual regularities and the need for genre adaptation influenced the organization's overall activity?
- Externally-speaking, how, if at all, has the Ashoka Fellow Profile served as a tool for the early identification of social entrepreneurs while also shaping the growth of the field and a vision of a new global community?

METHODOLOGY

In our analysis of profiles as an object of study, we followed Bazerman's methodological guidelines (2003, pg. 324–326) for pursuing genre investigations. Further, in our study design, we responded to Pare and Smart who challenged writing scholars seeking to understand genres as sites of social action to look beyond the text toward other "observable constituent elements of a genre" (1994, p.122). Thus, in addition to conducting a detailed textual analysis of fellow profiles, we drew on three other sources of data beyond the profiles themselves:

- Interviews with senior Ashoka leaders and staff (n=6) who were knowledgeable of the history of the fellow profile, its role in the search and selection process over time, and profile writing processes and guidelines.
- Interviews with Ashoka Fellows (n=6) of whom the profiles were written and for whom the profile served as an evidentiary text at the point of election to fellowship and beyond.
- Analysis of over 50 internal Ashoka documents and guidelines related to profile writing which were written to both onboard new profile writers and to maintain consistency in the quality and features of the profile as a text over time, across countries and languages.

In selecting appropriate analytical tools to trace the genre of the profile, we applied Pare and Smart's (2004) four categories of analysis across our data sources. Specifically, we set out to trace the regularities of the textual features, social roles, composing processes, and reading practices associated with profile writing in order to more deeply understand both the internal work of the profile at Ashoka and the impact of the profile externally in the field of social entrepreneurship. (See Appendix A for more detail on research methods).

RESULTS

Textual Analysis of Ashoka Fellow Profiles: Form and Function

Sequentially, our analysis of the regularities among textual features, social roles, composing processes, and reading practices began with a close reading of the Ashoka Fellow Profiles and focused on the repeated patterns in overall structure, rhetorical moves, and common style. Table 9.2 presents an overview of the structure of Ashoka Fellow Profiles according to section.

Writing and Social Progress

Table 9.2. Structure of Ashoka Fellow Profiles

Fellow Profile Section	Textual Regularities
Year of Election Statement	Informs readers of the year of the fellow's election and the year the profile was written (Note: Profiles are not updated as the fellow's work changes over time.)
1–3 Sentence Overview	Introduces the fellow and their work in 1–3 sentences
The New Idea	Provides a layered and multidimensional description of each fellow's work
	Describes the local and/or regional context in which a fellow's work takes place
The New Idea (continued)	Builds credibility for the fellow in highlighting their innovative approach
	Appeals to readers' emotions by providing a window into the circumstances and populations being served
	Provides readers with a sense of the fellow's beliefs and values
	Frames the fellow's work as filling gaps and remedying failures in government services and public sector markets, or as catalysts for social movements
The Problem	Describes in detail and with some evidence the challenge the fellow's work is addressing
	Provides historical and national context
	Attends to the ways in which the problems have become normalized in existing systems (i.e., have become the status quo)
The Strategy	Details the Ashoka Fellow's work with a particular focus on the role of the organization that the fellow has launched
	Explains concrete "how-tos"
	Proposes potential replication and scale to other regions and populations
	Positions the fellow and their activation of local resources, organizational leadership skill, and rhetorical abilities at the center of the work
	Includes ways in which fellow's work addresses gaps in existing government services and programs which have left people underserved and in need

Fellow Profile Section	Textual Regularities
The Person	Positions the fellow as possessing deep and personal experience or having had powerful encounters that are often related to the specific problem being addressed
	Demonstrates fellow's past track record of success as a social entrepreneur, often highlighting influential experiences as a young person
	Describes the fellow as being on an entrepreneurial journey with the clear potential to have even greater impact in the future with the right support[4]

INTERVIEWS WITH ASHOKA SENIOR LEADERSHIP AND STAFF

Once the textual analysis of the 40 fellow profiles was complete, we turned to interviews with five senior Ashoka leaders and staff in order to explore the organization's memory of the profile as an emergent and, then, established genre.

History of Textual Features of the Ashoka Fellow Profiles: Origins

There is no way to tell the story of social entrepreneurship, Ashoka, or the mediating work of fellow profiles without considering the role of Ashoka's founder, Bill Drayton.[5] In our interview with longtime Drayton collaborator, Bill Carter, he explained the origins and exigence of the profile.[6] As Carter tells it, in the early 1980s, he and Drayton were having breakfast at the Yale Club when Drayton announced, "I figured it out! I figured out what the criteria are for selecting fellows and what the profile should be." In our interview with Drayton, he confirmed Carter's account and further contextualized the exigence of the profile, explaining, "We had been trying to figure out how to communicate the stories

---

[4] Ashoka founder Bill Drayton describes three major stages in a social entrepreneur's life: apprenticeship, launch, and maturity. Each of these stages contributes differently to the entrepreneur's efforts and is therefore treated differently within the Ashoka Fellowship.

[5] Drayton, whose Wikipedia profile identifies him as "a social entrepreneur," was a graduate of Yale Law School, a McKinsey consultant for 10 years, Assistant Administrator of the Environmental Protection Agency (EPA) during the Presidency of Jimmy Carter, visiting professor at Harvard and Stanford, and a recipient of the MacArthur "Genius Award" in 1984 for his work in founding Ashoka. (The story of the founding of Ashoka and Bill Drayton is chronicled in detail in David Bornstein's book "How to Change the World.") Drayton also was deeply involved in the civil rights movement as a teenager and spent time with Vinoba Bhave (a member of Mahatma Gandhi's inner circle) in India. Drayton conceived of the idea for social entrepreneurship in his days at Yale where he founded the Ashoka Circle.

[6] Carter worked closely with Drayton at the EPA, shared his background as a McKinsey consultant, later became a founding Board member of Ashoka and continues to serve in a variety of capacities within the organization.

of social entrepreneurs. It was a very practical experiment and we were thinking about the readers from the beginning." While it was at that breakfast meeting that the basic structure of the profile was codified and written down, as our interviews will show, it would take the next twenty years to develop the necessary infrastructure to fully support the consistent production of profiles across Ashoka's global organization. Forty years after the "back of the napkin" breakfast conversation, in our interview, Drayton provided a highly refined description of the genre features and an explanation of his vision for its intended effects, stating:

> We started with a teaser line that gives a taste of the person—where they were from, what problem they were working on and why, although the more elaborated person part comes at the end. Now, the new idea has been hinted at, and hopefully it draws people into the first paragraph. Like a newspaper story, you want to get across the basic and big idea. You want people to say, "That's an interesting idea. I see how that could work." You lose a lot of people if you don't have that impact right away. So, you are fleshing the new idea out, not at length but succinctly—at the level of the concept, then you go to the problems. For example, birds flying over Mexico are asphyxiating and falling to the ground. That's very concrete. You want the reader to say, "Now I see!" That's the second step. Then people can imagine telling their friends. Then you get to the third part. Well, lots of people have noticed the problem, but now, you've got this idea. "I've not heard this before. Where did it come from?" Then you get into the how. The vision. With feet on the ground. The how-tos. And, there you have the elements of the entrepreneurial story. Then you come to the person. And, please do not talk about awards or where they went to school, but what explains how this person's life led to this idea and this set of solutions. You need that life coherence. The hope is that it is designed to allow people to follow the unfolding of the idea. (B. Drayton, personal communication, March 29, 2021)

Drayton's original idea to create a genre that would tell "the entrepreneurial story" and present "the unfolding of the idea" led to the formalization of the Ashoka Fellow Profile structure which has remained in place for over 40 years. Further, Drayton's initial and ongoing consideration for the interaction between the text and the reader hint at his awareness of the profile's potential rhetorical impact. Thus, from the beginning, Drayton's vision for the genre included a sense of the social actions it could inspire (e.g., "That's an interesting idea," "Now I see!" and "Telling their friends").

In spite of the clarity with which Drayton could explain the work of profiles 40 years after their inception, Carter explained that in the early years of Ashoka, Drayton's propensity for history, detail and complexity threatened to undermine the simple structure of the genre. Drayton recognized the same need at that time and, therefore, another colleague, Michael Gallagher, was brought in to "crystalize the structure" of the fellow profile. In our interview with Gallagher, he echoed the same recollection, "While the fundamental categories of Problem, Idea, Strategy, and Person, were already clear in Bill Drayton's head, he did not *communicate* in clear categories when he talked about the early Ashoka Fellows."

Twenty-five years old at the time, Gallagher was brought in to solidify the genre of the profile. He recalled:

> In 1987, I had the good fortune to sit through 8 or ten lengthy interviews Bill Drayton had with an early cohort of Brazilian Ashoka nominees. As I sat through 4- to 6-hour interviews, light bulbs started to go off in my head and an Ashoka fog began to burn off. It quickly became clear to me, Bill Drayton has a clear methodology he is using, it just has not been written down and explained. To make myself useful on that trip to Brazil, I offered to write profiles of the candidates using the categories I observed Bill was using in interview after interview.

Gallagher's work in further standardizing the categories of the profile at this time was less about telling the story of the candidate social entrepreneur and more about formalizing Ashoka's search and selection process as an organization that needed to scale. Specifically, his work responded to what he referred to as "an important growth-related question for the organization: Can anyone other than Bill Drayton evaluate Ashoka Fellows?" If Drayton were needed to capture the story and evaluate the potential and determine the investment for every Ashoka Fellow, it would be difficult if not impossible for the organization to reliably expand and maintain the vision for a global movement and the rigor of the emerging processes at scale. To achieve these aims, more people needed to be brought into the process of selecting fellows and this included the writing of fellow profiles.

History of Textual Features of the Ashoka Fellow Profiles: Evolution

Though the fundamental structure of the profiles had become more formalized during the early years of the organization, interviews with Ashoka leaders further documented the ways in which the genre and the organization needed to adapt to both internal and external pressures as the organization grew and the genre matured. The most striking example of genre-relevant tension between stability and adaptability that emerged in our interviews centered around one particular section of the profile—The New Idea. Specifically, interview data pointed to the way that (1) the content of the new idea section needed to adjust to the increasing number of fellow elections over time, (2) the organization needed to reconsider and come to agreement regarding the criteria and evaluation of a prospective fellow's new idea, and (3) the new idea section and the profile as a whole needed to become better supported by Ashoka at the organizational level.

From the beginning, the structure of the genre placed priority on the fellow's new idea (i.e., the new idea section comes first before the problem, the strategy, or the person sections in the profile). In fact, interviews with leaders surfaced the widespread use of an internal and informal evaluation criteria known within Ashoka as the "knock out test." Namely, there was an absolute requirement that a prospective fellow possess an idea that would change the pattern in a field or a system of activity, and that the new idea had the potential for replication in other contexts or geographical regions. As interviewees explained, if a candidate did not have a truly "new idea," then they would be "knocked out" of the selection process.

This early emphasis on new ideas was and has remained important as it reflects Ashoka's founders' goal of creating a radically new process for funding people and their projects—a process that was focused on innovations for social good rather than the pedigree of a person or their personality. What was critical to Ashoka from the start, and thus central in the profile along the way, was the evidence-based and convincing presentation of a new, high-impact idea that was worth spreading. As Carter explained:

> What Bill [Drayton] was focused on was big ideas coming out of the global South transforming the hegemony of the development institutions and governments because, in his diagnosis, those elites had blown it at the World Bank. What they are doing is a waste of time and a waste of money. There are real people who have big ideas and the Muhammed Yunus's of the world are actually in the global South as opposed to relying on these elites at Harvard and places like that who are sitting there with their theories. [7] We just hated that. Instead,

---

7 In 2006, Bangladeshi Professor of Economics, Muhammed Yunus, was awarded the Nobel Peace Prize for his work in developing microfinance—the provision of small loans without collateral to people in poverty. The Nobel committee described Yunus's work as "an important liberating

we wanted to foster these people with the big ideas. (B. Carter, personal communication, March 22, 2021)

Thus, as social entrepreneurship began to spread and the process for fellow search and selection began to scale, our interview subjects described important tensions that emerged around the new idea section of the profile because there seemed to be a limit on the number of new ideas that were "as big" and as obviously system-changing as someone like Yunus's new idea—microfinance. While Ashoka's country representatives around the world were actively cultivating and nominating fellows who they believed were qualified, these candidates were being rejected for not meeting the new idea criteria and this became a point of organizational tension between the leadership and those in the field. As Carter explained, "We were too tight and it was keeping us from electing fellows. We were rejecting people in Asia and Latin America." (B. Carter, personal communication, March 22, 2021) He went on to describe how these tensions surfaced at a meeting in Virginia among Ashoka's global staff, recalling, "People were revolting. It was a riot, literally a riot."

The problem facing Ashoka at this point was not about the profile as a text type, per se; rather, the tension needing resolution had to do with the organization's staff being able to effectively and consistently apply the internal criteria for what constituted a new idea at the same time the definition for what counted as a new idea needed to shift, if the organization was to continue to accomplish its mission. The structure of the fellow profile in this way became a framework for the organizational members to come to terms with scaling up not only processes for coordinated activity, but also for scaling the social roles and material supports needed to align their activities and to share meanings in the face of changing demands and situations arising from the organization's growth.

Regularities in Social Roles: The Impact of Fellow Profiles in and Beyond Ashoka

In response to the need to grow the organizational capacity related to profile writing, Ashoka's leaders invested in the development of new positions, programmatic offerings, and textual supports (discussed in the next section), aimed at producing profiles that would meet the organization's high standards. Specifically, interviews with Ashoka staff pointed to a variety of human resources—people in positions—that emerged over time and that directly related to the

---

force in societies where women in particular have to struggle against repressive social and economic conditions" (The Nobel Peace Prize, 2006). This recognition from the Nobel committee brought increased visibility for Yunus's long-standing work in attempting to minimize poverty through the organization he launched, the Grameen Bank, as well as attention to the emergent field of social entrepreneurship in which he had become a major figure (Bornstein, 2005).

activity surrounding the profiles, (e.g., fellow nominators, profile writers, profile editors, board-level reviewers, and more). These positions became part of an expanding internal social network within the organization whose primary activity revolved around the activity of data gathering and profile writing within the context of searching for and selecting Ashoka Fellows. The expansion occurred geographically as the organization continued to scale its work and establish new offices (e.g., in Italy, Germany, Japan, as well as in the MENA region and in West, South, and East Africa) while it advanced the specialization of positions. Individuals, for example, became specialists within various aspects of search and selection, including, for example, individuals who became recognized as strong writers to serve as lead profile writers or the recognition of fellow nominators who had access to extended networks within the entrepreneurship and social entrepreneurship communities in particular countries and regions.

Internal Ashoka Documents and Guidelines

Regularities in Composing Processes: Further Development of Metagenres and Human Infrastructure

As Ashoka invested in human resources to stabilize and support scaling efforts, they also added material supports in the form of meta-genres that guided the production of the genre, "ruling out some kinds of expression, endorsing others" (Giltrow, 2002). With regard to the internal tensions related to the new idea, for example, such guidelines were introduced for the purpose of streamlining the thinking and better coordinating the activity, up and down the organization.

One of the individuals responsible for the development of these new guidelines was Chris Cusano, who recalled in his interview how, in November 2000, as a new staff member hired into the position of profile editor, he found himself needing to identify and resolve the tensions that had emerged around the profile. After Cusano had read the entire record of board meeting minutes "as case law," Cusano met with Carter and others to address the internal conflict related to the evolving standards for a big, new idea. They decided to create two documents to support the profile writing process: "Newness in Known Fields" and "New Idea Types."

The "Newness in Known Fields" document set out to address two problems for profile writers. According to Cusano, "First, Ashoka was looking for new ideas—the newer the better. Second, they knew that there were not many truly new, original, striking ideas. So, what then was the threshold for newness? How could Ashoka distinguish between the innovations they were looking for and merely incremental or derivative evolution, especially in well-established and well-known fields?" The solution presented to profile writers in the "Newness in

Known Fields" document was the identification of known fields like ecotourism, fair trade, and entrepreneurial training programs for youth, followed by distinctions (with examples) between common innovations in those fields and Ashoka's requirement for innovation that reflected "the next order of thinking altogether."

The "New Idea Types" document helped further by providing profile writers with archetypes of social entrepreneurs—the architect, the master organizer, the patient teacher, mentor or coach, and the visionary reformer—along with examples and definitions of four types of new ideas:

- Creating an entirely new field.
- Bringing citizenship to a strategically important group that has faced systematic discrimination.
- Changing the behavior of an important link in civil society.
- Inventing or re-inventing a routine process that citizens pass through.

Perhaps the most important section of the "New Idea Types" document was entitled "Yet is Not" (underline in the original) which describes in detail four counter-archetypes that did not meet Ashoka standards; namely, the (1) leading expert or professional, (2) the activist, (3) the dedicated social worker, or (4) the creative executive, enlightened bureaucrat, or consultant. Carter noted, "We handed [the Newness document] out to our country representatives and that was the breakthrough. What was a social entrepreneur and what wasn't." (C. Cusano, personal communication, March 29, 2021)

As detailed in his interview, Cusano's deeper diagnosis with regard to revisioning the new idea went beyond profiles as texts into the interconnected processes of search and selection and the surrounding culture at Ashoka. Beyond the establishment of guidelines to clarify the new idea sections of these document types, then, Cusano set out to address the broader issue of aligning the profile to the evolving social aspects of the search and selection processes in a number of ways, including the training of global staff members, the creation of additional supporting materials to guide profile writing and writers, and the hiring of people with backgrounds in writing. In his interview, he explained his plan to support profile writing by focusing first on training and developing profile writers:

> So, really what you're dealing with mostly is how people relate to each other and understand each other's roles and functions. And, so it was very important to me to turn away from focusing on the skill set of writing because what I realized is that Ashoka doesn't hire people because they could write. It's not fair to take an adult who you hire for other professional qualities, like entrepreneurship or whatever, to bring them in and

then start kind of criticizing them for not being a good writer. (C. Cusano, personal communication, March 29, 2021)

One of the documents Cusano created was called, "Six Principles of Profile Writing: And a Few Tips." The document focused not on the mechanics of writing profiles but on establishing a stronger culture of writing at Ashoka and on creating norms for the processes surrounding profile writing (e.g., the first principle in the document states: "Profiles are written in groups"). Later, however, Cusano and others did develop documents to address multiple features of the writing itself, including documents entitled: "Checklist for Profile Editing," "General Tips on Profile Writing," "What is a Profile," "What's Wrong with Jargon."

Jargon was a particular area in which Cusano sought to build capacity at the word level of profile writing. Remarking that one draft profile he read included the word community "56 times in three pages," Cusano created a document called "The Ashoka Jargon List" made up of 80 words which Ashoka writers "should watch out for" including: mobilize, operationalize, methodology, provide, focus, grassroots, capacity-building, institution-building, low-income, peri-urban, community, and disadvantaged. Cusano's guidance to profile writers regarding jargon was that adding these kinds of words for significance often had the opposite effect on readers. Cusano suggested that some words on the list "should be avoided altogether while others should cause readers and writers to pause and consider whether they mean something or not, whether they deliver the meaning they hope to, and whether what they mean can be said more clearly." (C. Cusano, personal communication, March 29, 2021)

In addition to beginning to explicitly standardize textual features by codifying structure, rhetorical moves, and style, the team also developed a one-page guide that covered the entire profile called "The Matrix." Carter explained that "the matrix guidelines took it even further by helping to focus on the most important area where the Fellow was making their big bet." (B. Carter, personal communication, March 22, 2021) In the matrix, the new idea presented a structure for capturing whether the fellow was developing a new field or was innovating within a known field. The matrix document divided the problem section into two categories as well—the material side of the problem (i.e., "how people feel the problem,") and systemic (i.e., the ways in which existing ideas, institutions and/or patterns "fail, fall short and need help"). In the strategy section, the matrix reads, "What is the principle that makes sense of the candidate's choices about how to succeed? Examples: To open markets; to create a new profession; to be first and open the way for others to follow." (B. Carter, personal communication, March 22, 2021)

Below these general guidelines are open text boxes where Profile writers—in many cases, the reviewer or country representative—are provided space to take notes. For example, the boxes under the problem section read, "systemic problem explained" and the boxes under the strategy section read, "systemic solution applied," thus encouraging clear connections between the problems and the solutions in each case and furthering the profile writers' overall conceptual understanding of the important relationship between problems and solutions in all cases. The person section explicitly invites the reviewer to identify one of two pathways to explain the origin of the fellow's idea. For example, the profile writer can focus on the fellow's "Evolution," that is, a chronology from childhood, or on an "Epiphany" a life changing event. In the document, both of these pathways leave space for the writer to include an "Anecdote," which Carter described as "a note of grace, where the reader can have the voice of the fellow right in front of them." (B. Carter, personal communication, March 22, 2021) Taken together, these guidelines—a representation of Ashoka's investment in meta-genres—provided a layer of material support to the goal of stabilizing and scaling the genre of the Fellow Profile over time.

Regularities in Reading Processes: Profiles as Catalysts for Individual and Societal Transformation

While readers of the profile were on the mind of the founders of Ashoka from the beginning, our interviewees drew on a variety of metaphors to capture the particular ways in which the genre has aimed to influence readers in recurring ways. Drayton, for example, focused on the role of readers and their engagement with the profiles, connecting this activity to the broader goal of the organization to spread social entrepreneurship. He presents the profile as an invitation to shift or sway public thinking and mindset around the potential of the field, stating, "In the profile we have the paradigm. Every time someone reads a profile, they in effect read a paradigm statement that defines social entrepreneurship."

Another senior leader, Cusano, referred to the profile as a tool for transportation or movement and, like Drayton, focused on the reader's ability to better understand and thus spread social entrepreneurship as a result, stating:

> The profile is a vessel for the new idea, it's an exemplar, that delivers another instantiation of the paradigm. Not only are we saying here is the person who works with manual scavengers in Dubai, but we're explaining that the way this person works with manual scavengers in Mumbai, is yet another instantiation of the thing we call social entrepreneurship. (C. Cusano, personal communication, March 29, 2021)

In fact, and in alignment with Drayton's and Cusano's comment on the impact of the profiles on readers, Ashoka's consistent production and distribution of fellow profiles in the aggregate is by design a method for providing a strong evidence base which in effect establishes the field itself as a social fact. As Cusano further noted:

> To build the field [of social entrepreneurship], it's not the individual instances that matter, for what you need is a big undeniable chunk of evidence to show that you've been productive. And, I've heard that same thing echoed by other social entrepreneurs working on other issues where data is important, for example, in the human rights field. Just reporting about one case of disappearance isn't enough, you need to have 150 cases documented in a big thick report that you can smack down on someone's desk and say, you can't deny this, this is real. (C. Cusano, personal communication, March 29, 2021)

In addition to the work of establishing the social roles to ensure the stability of the profile across a global organization, in his interview, Drayton shared his perspective on the ways profiles influenced the lives and identities (i.e., the social roles) of the candidate fellows themselves. Drayton stated:

> One of the most important effects of Ashoka's fellow selection process is that it helps all the candidates understand who they are. Being able to say out loud for the first time that one *is a social entrepreneur* is very powerful—and hugely empowering. Thus, the first impact of the profile is on the candidates themselves. I've heard a good many say that the profile has given them a perspective that they didn't have before or that they didn't have consciously before. (B. Drayton, personal communication, March 29, 2021)

The hope for Drayton and Ashoka was that the genre of the profile would support a process that was beneficial to the candidates along the way (even if they were not ultimately chosen as a fellow); if the process was ultimately successful, the published profile would stand as the evidentiary case which led to the official naming of an "Ashoka Fellow." As a genre, the profile and its surrounding activity facilitates a process and is, in the end, a speech act which transforms the identities of real individuals who can, from that point on, take on a truly novel and globally-recognizable social identity, or role, with all of the benefits and expectations attached.

Interviews with Drayton and former Ashoka President, Diana Wells provided additional anecdotal evidence to describe other ways in which profiles are taken up by readers including the sharing of knowledge of innovative practices across fields of work and geographical regions; as sources for journalists and researchers investigating some of society's most pressing issues; and, in fundraising (sometimes involving dramatic sums of money) for the social entrepreneurs themselves and for Ashoka.

Interviews with Ashoka Fellows

Regularities in Reading Processes

Finally, in seeking to gain a more complete picture of the role(s) of the profile, we invited the subjects of the profiles—Ashoka Fellows—to take part in interviews as a special class of readers. To begin, several fellows noted that they had not read their Ashoka Profile in several years. For example, Fellow Aaron Pereira, 2004, France, indicated that he hadn't read his profile in 17 years, commenting, "So this feels so so so distant to me!" He went on to say, "There's a part where I love the historical record of it. However, I do wish that it had the ability to be more profoundly updated alongside the historical record. That's been a bit of a strange thing for me with my Profile as it's pretty far off from what I'm doing now."

Similarly, Jane Leu, 2005, United States, remarked:

> I never gave much thought to the profile itself and no one has really ever referenced it to me, at least not in a long time. I got elected in 2005, so it's possible that I've just forgotten a lot of these things. But my assessment is that it has stood the test of time. The small details have changed but the overall case statement, problem, and strategy has remained the way Ashoka described it. Not bad! Especially since UpGlo (the name of her organization) recently celebrated being a twenty-year-old organization that has helped 18,000 foreign-born professionals pursue their careers in the US. (J. Leu, personal communication, April 25, 2021)

Greg Van Kirk, 2008, United States, mentioned the potential for profiles to become quickly outdated as was his experience, whereas Aleta Margolis, 2000, United States, felt "the wording I would write is exactly the same today." And, like Margolis, David Castro, 2009, United States, said:

> The profile was, to the best of my understanding, a recapitulation of the case for why I should be a fellow, that's what it was, it was the case statement, and it was highly congruent with my work, it was how I explained my fundamental work. And, that has not changed that much in the sense that the profile captured some of the big drivers of my work. For me, it's always been about community empowerment that's the driving force behind the work that I do. (D. Castro, personal communication, April 26, 2021)

Overall, fellows expressed in different ways the value of the search and selection process, and in particular, the framing of their work within the sections of their fellow profile. Margolis remarked, for example, that although she had been leading her organization, The Center for Inspired Teaching, for five or six years when she became a fellow, the question-and-answer sessions that took place during her election process provided her with lasting value in identifying and articulating her strategy which then was captured in the strategy section of her fellow profile. She noted, "The process of being, and I will use the word, *forced* to articulate what it is, I do, and why was incredibly important, not only in talking about how Inspired Teaching works, but in doing it."

Lennon Flowers, 2016, United States, also remarked on how structuring her story in the format of the profile held real value for her work, "The framing of the problem statement first, followed by the strategy to address the component parts of that problem, and the big idea underlying all of it, all had a big influence on how I shaped The Dinner Party (the name of her organization) from Day 1."

David Castro also pointed to the ways in which the search and selection process, captured and reflected in his fellow profile, had a powerful influence on his identity, stating:

> I think, for me, one of the highlights of the whole process even to this day, is to imagine myself as a social entrepreneur. I didn't see myself in the entrepreneur paradigm, I might have seen myself as a change maker. I saw myself as a leader. I didn't necessarily think of myself as an entrepreneur and that framing made me really think deeply about what entrepreneurship is and what social entrepreneurship is, and that has been a lasting and powerful impact on my work. The other thing that the profile does is put you in the mind of the community of other people who are profiled along with you.

> And, if you bring the right energy to that which is to think of yourself as being part of a community, you can benefit enormously from the relationships that come out of it. (D. Castro, personal communication, April 26, 2021)

Castro went on to describe his sense of the role of profiles in the Ashoka Fellow global community:

> Profiles are interesting in the sense that they're archetypes and patterns and descriptions of inspirational work. I think of them like sonnets as they do have a certain form, and they capture an essence of the work, but when you get into the work the cases are always more involved. The profile is a map, not the territory. When you get into the territory, you're going to see that maybe it wasn't exactly the way it was described in the profile because Ashoka is working to make the work fit into a paradigm and nobody's work totally fits the paradigm it's an approximation. But another important element is the solidarity, the sense of motivation that comes from knowing that you're not alone in your work and that's something that is really important, because people get burned out. People get tired and especially when they run into obstacles which we all do. So, knowing that there are other people out there who are inspirational keeps you going when you run into hard spots. (D. Castro, personal communication, April 26, 2021)

Castro and the other Ashoka Fellows' perceptions of the ways in which profiles work and are part of a larger sphere of social activity add additional support to earlier findings in the study; namely, the search and selection process and the structure the profile provided for that process had a relatively immediate impact on the fellows, including the funding of their ventures. Interviews with Ashoka leaders, staff and fellows underscored the central mediating role of profiles for organizing Ashoka's global activity. Internally, the fellow profile plays a pivotal role throughout the search and selection process, as even the initial notes taken in the first opinion interviews become data for what will become the final profile presented to the board and, ultimately, a new fellow's public-facing profile.

It would be, however, an oversimplification to reduce the complex search and selection process to the profile itself; for, while the profile is central, it is embedded in a growing set of genres and increasingly broader systems of activity. Cusano hinted at the interconnection of the dynamic social process to the profile as genre (i.e., social action) stating, "the profile is only one data source by which the board of directors makes their decisions, as they rely also on notes, their own subject matter expertise, and their confidence in the people in the room." In this way, we can identify profiles as part of an internal genre set aimed directly at supporting the primary activity of electing fellows and building the field of social entrepreneurship, including the board minutes of the profile decisions which are sent to all 450 staff members across Ashoka's global organization. Wells remarked on this point, "Board comments regarding profiles are made public to all staff. Those minutes are Ashoka's pedagogy, not whether they passed or not, but why."

DISCUSSION

In significant ways, what we know today about the field of social entrepreneurship and of social entrepreneurs has been influenced by Ashoka and the genre of the fellow profile which they developed. By studying the exigence and evolution of the profile over time, we can appreciate the birth and growth of an entire field through one organization's intentional efforts to create and maintain a genre (and the social action associated with that genre), as well as the genre set and system that has evolved through productive tensions between the genre's remarkable stability and the need for change and adaptation over time. Beginning with a leader who first noticed something different, sought to identify what it was, and then developed a process to encourage others to do the same, Ashoka spread and scaled the idea of social entrepreneurship such that it has now matured from a social movement into an established, recognizable field of activity around the world.

In this study, we set out to explore what we, as writing researchers, could learn about genre as a mediating tool in activity systems by examining this one genre—the Ashoka Fellow Profile—and following its origins and development over time. Interviews with Drayton and Carter pointed toward the very beginnings of an origin story—a focused moment in time, a kairotic moment in which the problem of identifying the qualities of a social entrepreneur was answered by the creation of criteria and a framework for the search and selection of other people and projects possessing the same caliber of impact and innovation for social good. Whether they knew it or not, unidentified social entrepreneurs were doing the work of changing systems and mindsets and locating connected resources in the environments of problems. Rather than a top-down funding model that called for these professionals to pause their efforts and mold their activities into the shape of a CFP, Ashoka's radical approach to funding disrupted this pattern by heading into the field itself and cultivating individual social entrepreneurs through a process that would, according to the fellows interviewed in this study, be of great value to the fellows themselves.

Drayton's prioritization of written profiles from the very start of Ashoka's work was intentionally designed to destabilize the narrative of international aid and to critique the mediocrity of the non-profit sector as a whole, both of which he perceived as languishing in uninspired, inefficient practice. By relabeling the non-profit sector as "the citizen sector," and infusing both the discourse of development and the work of nonprofits with the energy of entrepreneurship, he was able to enlist others in stabilizing a new model of activity centered in the local yet scalable ideas of social entrepreneurs, and normalizing all of this as a new field of work. Ashoka accomplished this in part through their consistency and attention to detail in the work of searching for and identifying leading social entrepreneurs (at an average of 100 per year for 40 years), an activity that was organized around the structure and process of the profile.

As a mediating tool in the activity of social entrepreneurship, then, the fellow profile became not only a text and evidentiary case for an election decision, but also a reflection on an internal system-wide and global process for that election. Further, beyond the internal impacts, the fellow profile has generated, over years, the social fact of the social entrepreneur and a textual record of the existence of a field and a way for those outside of the field to recognize, understand, and support it. In the case of Ashoka as the site for this study, the fellow profile was described in interviews as a tool for documenting social entrepreneurs' activity; a paradigm for a how to understand and engage with the world; a criteria for fellowship; a lengthy process for maximizing a social entrepreneur's potential for impact; a system of interconnected genres, meta-genres, people and positions; an invitation to funding agencies to support the work of social entrepreneurs; a sonnet; and, a framework that is actively changing the world. In short, findings from this study suggest that the mediating roles of this particular genre are dynamic and multi-dimensional such that no one metaphor (e.g., tool) accounts for all that it accomplishes, internally or externally. In fact, the genre of the profile is so intertwined to the origin and growth of the organization and the field that it is difficult to know whether the birth and growth of the field influenced the real and metaphorical roles of the profile or if the profile—through all of its maturation—was the primary object to influence the direction of the field.

More narrowly, the Ashoka Fellow Profile as a genre supported the NGO's internal ability to organize itself and respond to emerging needs over time. Interviews with Ashoka leaders and review of supporting materials pointed to particular decisions made early and throughout the organization's history to utilize the profile and its regularized textual features to:

- coordinate activity systematically
- develop and distribute meta-genres to guide profile writers and writing across countries and languages
- create personnel positions to regularize organizational and composing processes
- reconcile internal conflicts over terminology, concepts, and criteria

A close reading and analysis of the 40 selected Ashoka Fellow Profiles showed how consistent the textual features of the genre have been applied and reinforced over time. Though the summarizing activity inherent in the textual analysis of the profiles does obscure many of the unique and individual features of individual profiles, the analysis does showcase their uniformity in content areas, focus, style, and intended rhetorical impact (i.e., persuasive force). These regularities, associated with the profiles for over 40 years, are arguably one of the main forces behind the success of Ashoka in contributing to the establishment of the field of social entrepreneurship and the establishing of the identity of social entrepreneurs and social entrepreneurship as a "social fact." Further, the analysis points to a consistent yet broad audience for the profiles, with the primary audiences being the Ashoka board members and the candidate fellows and secondary audiences including funders, Ashoka staff members, other fellows, and those interested in the field of social entrepreneurship.

The greatest example of tensions arising between textual regularities and the need for genre change was evident in interviewees' recalling of the internal, organizational conflict over what constituted the new idea. A byproduct of organizational and field growth, the emergence of divergent interpretations of a big, new idea led to sincere efforts on behalf of the organization to develop infrastructure—through human and material resources—to stabilize and regularize the genre while adapting to new shifts in the field of social entrepreneurship. As the profile encountered new social contexts and situations, and as the field of social entrepreneurship and Ashoka grew, elements within the profile required adaptation and change, even as the overall structure of the profiles remained the same. This tension between the stable aspects of the genre and the need for evolution were absolutely necessary if the genre of the profile was to stay relevant to Ashoka's mission and vision. We find these tensions instructive and generative in considering the processes, complexity, and nature of what constitutes, what Bazerman referred to as, "a successful text" (2003, p. 311).

With regard to the profile as a genre that operates somewhat similarly to R&D capability statements, our research made clear the ways in which profiles consistently link a fellow's past success with a new idea in a particular context to their future potential impact on a greater scale. Beyond this positioning of individual fellows, it is worth considering the way in which profiles in the aggregate—the entire set of fellow profiles—serve as *a kind of capability statement for Ashoka itself*; specifically, the profiles are evidence of Ashoka's successful 40-year record. As Ashoka does the organizational work of operating and scaling itself, the success of its process and of its fellows establishes its credibility to continue and do more.

As a collection, profiles reveal Ashoka as an organization that is not only skilled in identifying leading social entrepreneurs but also in building a professional community that is in possession of highly specialized forms of valuable knowledge, including: a deep understanding of and network of relationships in a variety of regions around the world (e.g., Ashoka has over 400 fellows in India) and subject matter expertise that is focused on a variety of global problems and solutions (e.g., Ashoka has over 200 fellows working on issues of crime and corruption around the world). New ideas derived from fellows in the election process are, as we have seen, required to show promise of scalability and replicability; thus, Ashoka as a global network possesses a great deal of knowledge which it can and does share. Further, the profiles generate new knowledge as the body of fellow profiles (now over 4000) are used in a variety of empirical studies. In these ways, the collection of profiles does not only reflect the capability of the organization or its members at any given point, but also the evolving breadth and depth of the field of social entrepreneurship over time.

However, beyond their use as a knowledge source in research on social innovation, more importantly is the degree to which profiles provide a site of learning for Ashoka itself. As an early and evolving organization committed to establishing and sharing a vision of a particular kind of actor (the social entrepreneur) and a new field (social entrepreneurship), the profiles have provided a dedicated space to answer two key questions—"What is social entrepreneurship?" and "Who are social entrepreneurs?"

Finally, this study also set out to examine if and how the Ashoka Fellow Profile has served as a tool for the early identification of social entrepreneurs while also shaping the growth of the field and a vision of a new global community. In this regard, interviews and textual analyses document how, in the process of electing fellows and building their global presence, Ashoka has produced many texts, and many social facts. These facts as construed in the profiles themselves would not have existed without Ashoka creating them. And, although Ashoka's accountability ultimately is to its funders, board of directors, and other stakeholders, it has emerged as a highly credible organization known for its high standards. In Ashoka's production of text and activities, we have seen increasingly refined systems that lead towards predictable sets of outcomes, which are most apparent to those who are familiar with the work. Here then is another example of highly typified genres embedded in highly typified systems of activity within which the social facts that are created lead to consequences in the real world.

CONCLUSION

The Ashoka Fellow Profiles tell a special kind of story. They communicate a paradigm of action to be shared—portraits of a group of global actors who are working to solve difficult environmental and social problems, along with details of their strategic initiatives and approaches. In the aggregate, the stories communicate a vision of a field in which these actors are exemplars. From its inception, Ashoka's leaders shaped the profiles purposefully to resonate with readers in order to communicate something new and persuasive, which would inspire rational optimism and foster imaginations of new possibilities. The production, circulation, and use of these stories (that is to say, writing as a mediating tool in activity), in part, constitutes the very activity of Ashoka, and has contributed to the creation of a new field, social entrepreneurship, and of a new identity, the social entrepreneur.

The genre analysis of Ashoka and the profile suggests that writing studies researchers may gain a great deal through investigating the role of writing in organizations that are working to foster social change. Understanding more clearly the discursive practices of organizations who have proven effective in advancing social progress can be a promising knowledge source for others interested in advancing social justice and environmental sustainability, disrupting, and changing antiquated and oppressive systems, and "providing the tools for thinking about social creativity in making new things happen in new ways" (Bazerman, 2003, p. 311).

REFERENCES

Ashoka. (2014). *Form 990: Return of Organization Exempt from Income Tax*. Ashoka: Innovators for the Public, Guidestar.

Ashoka. (2018). *The Unlonely Planet: How Ashoka accelerates impact* (2018 Global Fellows Study). https://www.ashoka.org/it/il-nostro-impatto.

Ashoka. (n.d.). *Ashoka envisions a world in which everyone is a changemaker: Ashoka: Everyone a changemaker*. Retrieved April 21, 2021, from https://www.ashoka.org/en-gb/about-ashoka.

Bazerman, C. (1988). Shaping written knowledge: The genre and activity of the experimental article in science. University of Wisconsin Press.

Bazerman, C. (1994). Systems of genres and the enactment of social intentions. In A. Freedman & P. Medway (Eds.), Genre and the new rhetoric (pp. 79–101). Taylor and Francis.

Bazerman, C. (1997). Discursively structured activities. Mind, culture, and activity, 4(4), 296–308.

Bazerman, C. (2003). Speech acts, genres, and activity systems: How texts organize activity and people. In What writing does and how it does it (pp. 315–346). Routledge.

Bazerman, C. (2006). The writing of social organization and the literate situating of cognition: Extending Goody's social implications of writing. Technology, literacy and the evolution of society: Implications of the work of Jack Goody, 215–240. Psychology Press.

Bazerman, C. (2013). *A rhetoric of literate action: Literate action volume 1*. The WAC Clearinghouse; Parlor Press. https://doi.org/10.37514/PER-B.2013.0513.

Bazerman, C. (2019). The work of a middle-class activist: Stuck in history. In *Activism and rhetoric* (pp. 190–200). Routledge.

Beaufort, A. (1997). Operationalizing the concept of discourse community: A case study of one institutional site of composing. *Research in the Teaching of English, 31*(4), 486–529.

Berkenkotter, C. & Huckin, T. N. (2016). *Genre knowledge in disciplinary communication: Cognition/culture/power*. Routledge.

Bornstein, D. (2005). *The price of a dream: The story of the Grameen Bank*. Oxford University Press.

Bornstein, D. (2007). *How to change the world: Social entrepreneurs and the power of new ideas*. Oxford University Press.

Chandra, Y. & Shang, L. (2017). Unpacking the biographical antecedents of the emergence of social enterprises: A narrative perspective. *VOLUNTAS: International Journal of Voluntary and Nonprofit Organizations, 28*(6), 2498–2529.

Connor, U. & Mauranen, A. (1999). Linguistic analysis of grant proposals: European Union research grants. *English for Specific Purposes Journal, 18*(1), 47–62.

Connor, U. (2000). Variation in rhetorical moves in grant proposals of US humanists and scientists. *Text & Talk, 20*(1), 1–28.

Dees, J. G. (1998). *The meaning of "social entrepreneurship."* Social Entrepreneurship Founders Working Group, Center for the Advancement of Social Entrepreneurship, Fuqua School of Business, Duke University. http://faculty.fuqua.duke.edu/centers/case/files/dees-SE.pdf.

Devitt, A. J. (1991). Intertextuality in tax accounting: Generic, referential, and functional. In C. Bazerman & J. G. Paradis (Eds.), *Textual dynamics of the professions: Historical and contemporary studies of writing in professional communities* (pp. 336–357). University of Wisconsin Press.

Devitt, A. J. (2021). Genre for social action: Transforming worlds through genre awareness and action. In S. Auken & C. Sunesen (Eds.), *Genre in the climate debate* (pp. 17–33). De Gruyter Open Poland.

DeVoss, D. N., Cushman, E. & Grabill, J. T. (2005). Infrastructure and composing: The when of new-media writing. *College Composition and Communication*, 14–44.

Drayton, B. (2005). Everyone a changemaker. *Peer Review, 7*(3), 8–11.

Faber, B. D. (2002). *Community action and organizational change: Image, narrative, identity*. Southern Illinois University Press.

Faber, B. D. (2008). Writing and social change. In C. Bazerman (Ed.), *Handbook of research on writing: History, society, school, individual, text* (pp. 269–280). Erlbaum.

Faber, B. D. (2013). *Discourse, technology, and change.* Bloomsbury.

Giltrow, J. (2002). Meta-genre. In R. Coe, L. Lingard & T. Teslenko (Eds.), *The rhetoric and ideology of genre: Strategies for stability and change* (pp. 187–205). Hampton Press.

Goody, J. (1986). *The logic of writing and the organization of society.* Cambridge University Press.

Grabill, J. (2010). Infrastructure outreach and the engaged writing program. In S. K. Rose & I. Weiser (Eds.), *Going public: What writing programs learn from engagement* (pp. 15–28). Utah State University Press.

Gupta, P., Chauhan, S., Paul, J. & Jaiswal, M. P. (2020). Social entrepreneurship research: A review and future research agenda. *Journal of Business Research*, 113, 209–229.

Kickul, J. & Lyons, T. S. (2016). *Understanding social entrepreneurship: The relentless pursuit of mission in an ever changing world.* Routledge.

Meyskens, M., Robb-Post, C., Stamp, J. A., Carsrud, A. L. & Reynolds, P. D. (2010). Social ventures from a resource-based perspective: An exploratory study assessing global Ashoka fellows. *Entrepreneurship theory and practice*, 34(4), 661–680.

Miller, C. R. (1984). Genre as social action. *Quarterly Journal of Speech*, 70(2),151–167.

Myers, G. (1990). *Writing Biology: Texts in the social construction of scientific knowledge.* University of Wisconsin Press.

Nieuwenhuizen, C. (2020). Innovation and social value creation of female social entrepreneurs in Africa. In *ECIE 2020 16th European Conference on Innovation and Entrepreneurship*. Academic Conferences Limited.

Nobel prize organization. (2006, October 13). *Nobel Peace Prize 2006* [Press release]. https://www.nobelprize.org/prizes/peace/2006/press-release/.

Orlikowski, W. & Yates, J. (1994). Genre repertoire: The structuring of communicative practices in organizations. *Administrative Science Quarterly*, 39(4), 541–574. https://doi.org/10.2307/2393771.

Paré, A. & Smart, G. (1994). Observing genres in action: Towards a research methodology. In A. Freedman & P. Medway (Eds.), *Genre and the new rhetoric*, 146–154. Taylor & Francis.

Paré, A. (2000). Writing as a way into social work: Genre sets, genre systems, and distributed cognition. *Transitions: Writing in academic and workplace settings*, 145–166. Hampton Press.

Porter, M. E., Stern, S. & Green, M. (2014). *Social progress index 2014.* Social Progress Imperative.

Read, S. (2019). The infrastructural function: A relational theory of infrastructure for writing studies. *Journal of Business and Technical Communication*, 33(3), 233–267.

Saebi, T., Foss, N. J. & Linder, S. (2019). Social entrepreneurship research: Past achievements and future promises. *Journal of Management*, 45(1), 70–95. https://doi.org/10.1177/0149206318793196.

Schumpeter, J. (2013). *Capitalism, socialism, and democracy.* Routledge.

Schryer, C. F. (1994). The lab vs. the clinic: Sites of competing genres. In A. Freedman & P. Medway (Eds.), *Genre and the new rhetoric* (pp. 105–124). Taylor & Francis.

Spinuzzi, C. (2004). Describing assemblages: Genre sets, systems, repertoires, and ecologies. *Computer Writing and Research Lab*, 1–9.

Star, S. L. & Ruhleder, K. (1996). Steps toward an ecology of infrastructure: Design and access for large information spaces. *Information Systems Research, 7*(1), 111–134.

Sunduramurthy, C., Zheng, C., Musteen, M., Francis, J. & Rhyne, L. (2016). Doing more with less, systematically? Bricolage and ingenieuring in successful social ventures. *Journal of World Business, 51*(5), 855–870.

Tardy, C. M. (2003). A genre system view of the funding of academic research. *Written Communication, 20*(1), 7–36.

Thorpe, D. (2019, September 13). *Father of Social Entrepreneurship says 'society is at a profound turning point'*. Forbes. https://tinyurl.com/yc2u9s7c.

Van Nostrand, A. D. (2013). *Fundable knowledge: The marketing of defense technology*. Routledge.

Wolk, A. & Ebinger, C. G. (2010). Government and social innovation: Current state and local models. *Innovations: Technology, Governance, Globalization, 5*(3), 135–157.

APPENDIX A (MORE DETAILS ON RESEARCH METHODS)

Data Sources

Textual Analysis of Ashoka Fellow Profiles

To manage the number of profiles included in this genre analysis, we followed Bazerman's directive to identify a point of diminishing returns plus a couple more (2003, p. 327). First, we were interested in the profiles' ability to showcase the scope of the Ashoka Fellows as social entrepreneurs and also of Ashoka as a leading organization for orchestrating this global work. Second, we were interested in tracing possible changes to the profile as a text type over the organization's 40-year history. To accomplish these inquiry goals, we conducted a close reading of the regularities in textual features for a selection of 40 fellow profiles which were chosen according to the following criteria:

- Scope over time: one profile was selected from each year since the organization's founding.
- Scope of global representation: as a collection, the profile data set included 26 countries.
- Scope of gender representation: as a collection, the profiles reflected ½ male fellows and ½ female fellows.

Once selected, each profile was coded for three broad rhetorical dimensions of textual regularity (following Pare & Smart, 2004, p. 123):

- Repeated patterns in structure
- Rhetorical moves
- Common style

Interviews of Ashoka Leaders and Fellows

To understand the social roles, composing process and reading practices associated with the fellow profiles, we personally conducted semi-structured interviews with Ashoka's senior leadership, key staff members and Ashoka Fellows.

Interviews with Ashoka leadership and senior staff (n=5) focused on the following categories of inquiry:

52. The origin of the profile.
53. Changes to the profiles over time.
54. The influence of profiles on the processes and people involved in search and selection.
55. The kinds of knowledge and discourse embedded in the profiles.
56. Evidence of external impact of the profile for Ashoka.

Interviews with Ashoka Fellows (n=6) differed in that we asked each individual to read (prior to the interview) their own profile and to consider it retrospectively. Interview questions included:

- What can you say about how the profile was developed at the time of your election as an Ashoka Fellow?
- What, if any, was the impact of the profile on your work at that time?
- How do you view the durability of the profile for your work over time?
- Can you explain the relevance of the profile to your work today?
- Do you have any evidence of the impact of the profile individually or on the field?

Internal Ashoka Documents and Guidelines

Examination of Ashoka documents and guidelines followed closely the methodological work of Paré and Smart who, in their analysis of predisposition reports (as an example of genre as social activity that embodies a shared, repeated, and observable strategy), identified the important role of organizational guidelines (if provided) in making clear the essential components (structural, rhetorical, and stylistic) of texts so that the strategy can be intentionally enacted by a collective group (e.g., professionals, organizations) over time, across contexts, etc. with regularity.

Such guidelines, they say, "do more than prescribe the sequence and function of the report sections, they also provide a set of rhetorical moves" (1994, p. 124). They also pointed out the ways in which generic restrictions ensure regularity, for example, the types of evidence that can or cannot be employed.

Thus, as a part of our analysis of the profile, we reviewed over 50 instructional and supporting documents, which had been developed to guide or inform multiple aspects of the profile writing process. Specifically, we looked for evidence of the organization guiding its writers to ensure regularities in textual features and to consider ways in which these documents reflected changes in elements of the profile. A selected list of these guideline documents include:

- "What is a Profile?"
- "Checklist for Profile Editing"
- "General Tips on Profile Writing"
- "Ashoka Jargon List"
- "The [Profile] Matrix"
- "Ashoka Board Minutes"

PART FOUR. ACTIVITY THEORY

CHAPTER 10.

TWO PATHS DIVERGE IN A FIELD: DIALECTICS AND DIALOGICS IN RHETORICAL GENRE STUDIES

Clay Spinuzzi
University of Texas, Austin

Few have impacted rhetorical genre studies (RGS) more than Charles Bazerman. His careful textual studies and theorization have helped RGS to develop the critical concept of genre, in which writers learn an activity in part through learning genres "Writers find in existing models the solution to the recurring rhetorical problems" of the activity in which they engage, and "[a]s these solutions become familiar, accepted, and molded through repeated use, they gain institutional force," becoming a "social reality" (1988, p. 8). In learning genres and producing genre instances, writers take up and participate in a cultural heritage, one that involves conceptualizing, orienting to, and applying values to a recurrent situation (cf. Rogoff, 2003, p. 276). Put differently, in genre, the gains of human cultural development are preserved across generations, activities, groups, and cultures.

How are these gains preserved? In his subsequent work (Bazerman, 2004; 2013b), Bazerman draws on a synthesis of Vygotskian and Bakhtinian theory (and has led many of us in writing studies to similarly do so). Yet these two strands of theory are anchored by two (related but different) paths for understanding cultural heritage: dialectics and dialogics. Although they look and sound similar, they have fundamentally different understandings of how meaning emerges. Dialectics understands meaning as emerging through the unification of opposites, leading to a more thickly mediated unity (Wegerif, 2008; cf. Matusov, 2009). In contrast, Bakhtinian dialogics understands meaning as emerging through persistent difference. Ultimately, Bazerman has taken the path of dialectics, approaching genre developmentally, and interpreting dialogics through the frame of dialectics by drawing from Bakhtin's colleague Voloshinov, who also framed dialogue as dialectical (Bazerman, 2013b, chapter 9).

Here, I retrace the steps of these two paths, dialectics and dialogics, with special attention to how Bazerman has developed his understanding of genre by drawing on the Vygotsky Circle and the Bakhtin Circle, or, as Bazerman styles it, the Voloshinov Circle (Bazerman, 2013b, p. 151). I conclude by discussing the implications of this underlying tension in Bazerman's work and in RGS more generally, considering the question of whether we might take the other path.

But first, a personal note. When I was a graduate student at Iowa State University in the 1990s, my dissertation director, David R. Russell, suggested I read a research report by a Finn named Yrjö Engeström. He gave me a stack of paper—a photocopied book—and told me I could make a third-generation copy of it. It felt like *samizdat*. I wondered: Where on earth had David gotten it? Then, on the first page of the stack, I saw the handwritten name of the original's owner: "CHUCK BAZERMAN."

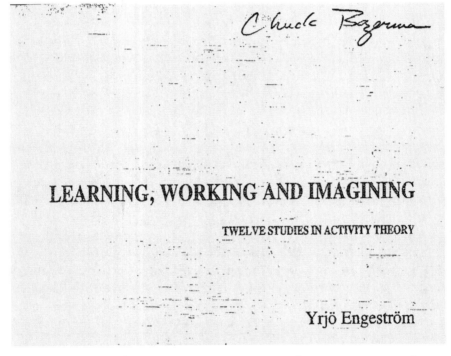

Figure 10.1. *One vector of Engeströmian activity theory into writing studies (Engeström 1990, modified by Charles Bazerman, unknown date)*

At the time, writing studies was having a bit of an identity crisis. It was only in the previous decade, the 1980s, that writing studies had truly separated from English and begun to build itself as a distinct field, and it was still trying to establish a research paradigm on which to build empirical studies (see Spinuzzi, 2021b). The quirky Finnish work that had passed from Chuck to David to me—activity theory—was part of a broader sociocognitive paradigm that writing studies would adopt throughout the 1990s and 2000s. That paradigm also included other frameworks with plenty of disagreements but enough of a family resemblance to interact: Vygotskian theory, situated and distributed cognition, communities of practice theory, actor-network theory, and genre theory. These frameworks were monist, materialist, and focused on providing an account of how human sociocultural efforts were made durable through materials—in other words, how the gains (broadly defined) of human cultural development are materially developed, preserved, and reproduced across generations, activities, groups, and cultures. As Rogoff puts it:

> Artifacts such as books, orthographies, computers, languages, and hammers are essentially social, historical objects, transforming with the ideas of both their designers and their later users. They form and are formed by the practices of their use and by related practices, in historical and anticipated communities. . . . Artifacts serve to amplify as well as constrain the possibilities of human activity as the artifacts participate in the practices in which they are employed. . . . They are representatives of earlier solutions to similar problems by other people, which later generations modify and apply to new problems, extending and transforming their use. (Rogoff, 2003, p. 276)

As one leading contender for describing such families of meaningful artifacts, genre theory had already been developed considerably in the previous decade. In 1984, Carolyn Miller wrote the pivotal article "Genre as Social Action," which theorized genre based on Schutz. Bazerman took up Miller's conception of genre as social action, applying his own readings of Vygotsky and Voloshinov (see Bazerman, 2004, p. 59) to yield his extended examination of genre in *Shaping Written Knowledge* (1988). In that book—among other cases—he used archives of the Royal Society to examine how the genre of the experimental article developed over long periods of time as a repeated response to a repeated rhetorical situation. In this account, genres *develop* as they are applied repeatedly to similar rhetorical situations, changing in concert with those situations. That is, they exist in a dialectical relationship as part of a larger unity. Their development forms a cultural heritage that presents relatively durable resources for those who pick up these genres: a neophyte who seeks to publish an experimental article can imitate the moves of its genre, producing a successful instance of the genre—even if they do not fully understand the rhetorical moves, their purposes, or how these purposes could be accomplished in alternate ways. Put crudely, the solutions have been embedded in the genre, and the author can tap into them just by taking the genre up. In doing so, the neophyte accepts the consensus and builds on it.

Also during the 1980s, M. M. Bakhtin's works were translated into English (1981; 1984a, 1984b; 1986). Even though he was a literary critic, his essentially social understanding of genre had direct implications for a sociocognitive approach to writing studies. But genre theory, although a theory of social action, did not in itself offer an account of sociocognitive development. So, as the decade turned, Bazerman was one of the first in writing studies to synthesize genre theory with activity theory (Bazerman, 1997; 2004; Artemeva & Freedman, 2001; Berkenkotter & Huckin, 1995; Haas, 1996; Russell, 1995; 1997a, 1997b; Schryer & Spoel, 2005; Spinuzzi, 1996; Winsor, 1999). This genre+activity theory synthesis has sometimes been termed "Rhetorical Genre Studies" (RGS; e.g., Artemeva & Freedman, 2001; 2007) or "Writing and Genre Research" (WAGR; Russell, 2009; cf. McNely, 2019; Read, 2016; Spinuzzi, 2010). Furthermore, Bazerman has sustained his focus on exploring the antecedents and branches of these relevant theories, diving deeply into the works of the Vygotsky Circle (Vygotsky, Leontiev, Luria) and the Bakhtin Circle (Bakhtin, Medvedev, Voloshinov; see Bazerman, 2004; 2013b; Bazerman et al., 2003).

Later, Bazerman (2013b) lucidly explained a fact that had become increasingly obvious to many of us who had enthusiastically embraced a genre+activity synthesis over the prior couple of decades: Bakhtin's and Vygotsky's ideas were not entirely compatible. Specifically, Vygotsky applied dialectics as his core account of learning and development. But Bakhtin—Bakhtin had a different view, as he expressed in a terse note in one of his fabled notebooks:

> Dialogue and dialectics. Take a dialogue and remove the voices (the partitioning of voices), remove the intonations (emotional and individualizing ones), carve out abstract concepts and judgments from living words and responses, cram everything into one abstract consciousness—and that's how you get dialectics. (Bakhtin, 1986, p. 147)

That is, for Bakhtin, dialectics was not the best way to understand utterances or genre. Bakhtin's perspective was informed by the fact that, like Vygotsky, he had to operate under Stalinism, but unlike Vygotsky, he could not find unity in Stalinism. Living in the USSR, "on this barren ground, under this unfree sky" (quoted in Bocharov & Lupanov, 1994, p. 1012), Bakhtin insisted (quietly, mainly in private notebooks) that *meaning emerges not from unity but from difference*. Rather than understanding genre as dialectical, he understood it as dialogical: genre still serves as a cultural heritage, but one in which "the word is half someone else's" (Bakhtin, 1981, p. 293) and meaning emerges from the clash of unmerged voices (1984a, p. 6, 30). In taking up a genre, the individual does tap into the cultural heritage from which it emerged but populates it with their own intentions. Put another way, genre is not a *thing* that evolves and develops, but a set of cross-referenced *enactments* that evoke, resonate with, and sometimes violate previous ones.

Thus, both dialectical and dialogical understandings of genre understand it as a cultural heritage, but they understand the function of cultural heritage differently. The tensions between these two understandings were not well discussed when they were taken up in writing studies in the 1990s and 2000s, but Bazerman recognized that these two paths diverged (or as Prior put it, this "dual orientation to discourse and development:" Prior, 2009, p. 28) and sought a way to reconcile these competing ideas. He found it in the work of Bakhtin's collaborator, V. I. Voloshinov (Bazerman, 2004; 2013b). Voloshinov wrote about dialogics far more lucidly than Bakhtin; applied the question of dialogue to language more broadly, not just to literary works as Bakhtin; and, most saliently for our discussion, interpreted dialogics within the frame of dialectics.

A *path* is itself a form of cultural heritage: when you find a path, you find that the labor of others before you have made this way easier than (say) crashing through the woods. You know that the path leads somewhere and that people before you have found it useful to get there. In fact, the pursuit of a path (in Greek: *methodos*) gives us the term *method*: like a path through the woods, method lets us move faster and farther than we could on our own, but at the cost of following someone else's lead and accepting the destination they have selected. Because Bazerman's interest has been in learning and development, he selected that destination and trod a path to it: the path of dialectics, a path that has led him in recent years to examine how individuals accumulate competence and expertise in writing across their entire lifespan (Bazerman, 2013a; 2018). We might characterize this latest work as the study of a "mind in society," to use a phrase associated with Vygotsky (1978): an examination of dialogic possibilities framed within dialectics.

But other paths exist—to recall a certain over-quoted poem by Robert Frost—and unlike Frost's narrator, we can actually retrace our steps, consider why we took one path, and explore other paths as well. And that is what I'll do in this chapter: I'll discuss dialectics, dialogics, Voloshinov's attempted rapprochement of the two, and how Bazerman takes up Voloshinov's rapprochement in RGS. I end by proposing how to further address this tension in RGS by exploring the other path: dialogics.

PATH 1: DIALECTICS

Dialectics can be traced back to the ancient Greeks, then through Hegel and Marx, then curdling into the universal rules of Engels and the dialectical materialism of Lenin and Stalin. The latter two are the most salient for us, since Bakhtin began his work, and Vygotsky both began and finished his work, between the 1917 Revolution and the Great Purge of 1937–1938.

Dialectics in the USSR

In his 1938 *Dialectical and Historical Materialism*, Stalin glosses the history of dialectics:

> Dialectics comes from the Greek *dialego*, to discourse, to debate. In ancient times dialectics was the art of arriving at the truth by disclosing the contradictions in the argument of an opponent and overcoming these contradictions. There were philosophers in ancient times who believed that the disclosure of contradictions in thought and the clash of opposite opinions was the best method of arriving at the truth. This dialectical method of thought, later extended to the phenomena of nature, developed into the dialectical method of apprehending nature, which regards the phenomena of nature as being in constant movement and undergoing constant change, and the development of nature as the result of the development of the contradictions in nature, as the result of the interaction of opposed forces in nature. (2013, p. 139)

Although Stalin's writings are generally propagandic, this gloss is a good starting place for understanding dialectics as it developed from ancient Greek discourse to the Stalinist dialectical materialism that underpinned the Soviet state—and to Vygotsky's theory of mediation and Leontiev's activity theory. See also Dafermos (2018, pp. 244–248), who provides a much fuller list of types of dialectics: spontaneous (naive), Sophistic (eristic), Platonic, Aristotelian, Stoic, Kantian, Fichtean, Hegelian, and Marxian—but not Engelsian or Stalinist.

For the ancient Greeks, dialectics was an approach to establishing truth through discourse among opposing sides. This approach was exemplified in the Socratic dialogues, in which the interlocutors advanced opposing ideas and queried each others' propositions until arriving at a truth. As Matusov argues, these Socratic dialogues were dialectical, but not in a Hegelian sense: they did not address unities with mutually constituting oppositions (2009, p. 19). For Hegel, dialectics provided a way to discuss the question of unity in change. As Beiser argues, for Hegel, "the point of the dialectic will be to remove contradictions by showing how contradictory predicates that seem true of the same thing are really only true of different parts or aspects of the same thing" (2005, p. 162). Beiser adds:

> The dialectic arises from an inevitable contradiction in the procedures of the understanding. The understanding contradicts itself because it both separates things, as if they were completely independent of one another, and connects them, as if neither could exist apart from the other. It separates things when it analyzes them into their parts, each of which is given a self-sufficient status; and it connects them according to the principle of sufficient reason, showing how each event has a cause, or how each part inheres in a still smaller part, and so on ad infinitum. Hence the understanding ascribes both independence and dependence to things. The only way to resolve the contradiction, it turns out, is to reinterpret the independent or self-sufficient term as the whole of which all connected or dependent terms are only parts. (Beiser, 2005, p. 164)

For Hegel, dialectics detects how development involves opposing elements, leading to the disintegration of the current state and the creation of a relatively stable new state (Singer, 1983).

Marx adapted Hegel's idealist dialectic into a materialist method, particularly in using the notion of contradiction in opposition to formal logic (Wilde, 1991, p. 277). As Wegerif argues, "a key feature of dialectic in both Hegel and Marx is that it attempts to integrate real dialogues and struggles into a logical story of development, leading to unity either in the 'Absolute Notion' of Hegel or the truly rational society under global communism of Marx" (2008, p. 350).

Yet Marx alluded to and applied dialectics rather than explaining the method thoroughly (Wilde, 1991). It was Engels who most influentially codified the method—changing it drastically: "In writings published after Marx's death in 1883, Engels extended the dialectical method to encompass nature and in doing so transformed dialectic into a set of three 'laws.' This work had nothing to do with Marx's own dialectic, which . . . was quintessentially a social scientific method" (Wilde, 1991, p. 291).

Engels' three laws included: "The law of the transformation of quantity into quality and vice versa," "The law of the interpenetration of opposites," and "The law of the negation of the negation" (Engels, 1954). Engels insisted that these were not "mere laws of thought" but rather "really laws of development of nature, and therefore are valid also for theoretical natural science" (1954, pp. 26–27). That is, dialectics was a materialist science of development and interconnections, one that established unity in difference, and its laws were universal. According to Engels, "objective" dialectics, which "prevails throughout nature . . . [is] the motion of opposites which asserts itself everywhere in nature, and which by the continual conflict of opposites and their final passage into one another, or into higher forms, determines the life of nature" (1954, p. 280). This science of interconnections provided a unified theory that would explain the dynamic workings of people, economies, societies, biology, physics, and chemistry with equal insight, predicated on the continuous interactions among parties rather than on rigid cause-effect relations or essentialist understandings of things-in-themselves.

Engelsian dialectics fit the bill for Vygotsky, who was attempting to develop a psychological theory that would transcend other theories and become universally applicable (1927). According to Cole, "When Engels' *Dialectics of Nature* appeared in 1925, Vygotsky immediately incorporated it into his thinking" (in his epilogue to Luria's biography: Luria, 1979, p. 204). But Dafermos argues that Vygotsky did not realize the difference between Marx's understanding of "dialectic as the peculiar logic of the peculiar object" and Engels' "dialectic as a general world outlook" (2018, p. 252).

Dialectics of Nature also influenced Stalin, whose 1938 *Dialectical and Historical Materialism* (as a chapter in the *Short Course*) was made mandatory reading in all schools and universities in the USSR (Toassa charges that Stalin "quotes Engels, but sacrifices these interactions for the sake of a purely 'progressive' dialectic;" 2019, p. 5.). In this work, Stalin lays out the four major tenets of what he characterizes as Marxist dialectics, characteristics that all sanctioned theory in the USSR had to follow:

- **"Nature Connected and Determined:"** Marxist dialectics understands each phenomenon as part of a dynamic system that must be understood as a whole (2013, p. 9).
- **"Nature is a State of Continuous Motion and Change:"** (p. 9) "The dialectical method therefore requires that phenomena should be considered not only from the standpoint of their interconnection and interdependence, but also from the standpoint of their movement, their change, their development, their coming into being and going out of being" (p. 10).
- **"Natural Quantitative Change Leads to Qualitative Change:"** (p. 9) Citing Engels, Stalin argued that Marxist dialectics understands change in terms of incremental (quantitative) changes that reach a tipping point, resulting in qualitative changes. "The dialectical method therefore holds that the process of development should be understood not as movement in a circle, not as a simple repetition of what has already occurred, but as an onward and upward movement, as a

transition from an old qualitative state to a new qualitative state, as a development from the simple to the complex, from the lower to the higher" (pp. 10–11).

- **"Contradictions Inherent in Nature:"** (p. 13) "Dialectics holds that internal contradictions are inherent in all things and phenomena of nature" (p. 13), specifically contradictions between past and future versions of a phenomenon undergoing continual development. "The dialectical method therefore holds that the process of development from the lower to the higher takes place not as a harmonious unfolding of phenomena, but as a disclosure of the contradictions inherent in things and phenomena, as a 'struggle' of opposite tendencies which operate on the basis of these contradictions" (p. 13).

Stalin used this account of natural interconnected change, proceeding inexorably from lower and simpler to higher and more complex, to justify the inexorable progression from capitalist to socialist and communist economic organization (cf. Lenin, 1987). To the members of the young Soviet Union, this claim of certainty was heartening: they were on the right side of history, and nature herself was their ally.

This claim of certainty was bolstered by Stalin's insistence that Marxist philosophical materialism implies an objective reality whose laws are fully knowable, yielding objective truth (2013). Individuals may have different *perspectives*, but through continued dialectical engagement, they should develop a *unity* converging on objective reality. White (2014) characterizes this tendency as "a quest for one-ness" (p. 222), while Wegerif (2008) argues that dialectics strives toward a more complexly mediated unity (p. 350).

To return to RGS for a moment, we can consider how dialectics has influenced Bazerman's understanding of how writing competence and expertise accumulates (2018, p. 327), as do repertoires and strategies (2013b, p. 421), across an individual's lifetime. More broadly, we can see how a genre (the term being used as a noun, a thing) develops over time by similarly accumulating repertoires and strategies, rhetorical solutions that generally work: a path that develops by being traversed over and over by generations of writers, shaping the written knowledge of participants (Bazerman, 1988).

This developmental orientation is evident in Vygotsky and Leontiev, whose work underpins activity theory's account of development.

Vygotsky

Vygotsky argued that thought is not just internalized speech, speech is not just expressed thought, and they meet their potential when they enter a predictable, developmental, dialectic relationship. At that point they irrevocably change each other's character, though they never entirely merge. Lower mental processes become higher mental processes by becoming verbal, by being mediated with signs.

Vygotsky explained that concept formation happens in three stages. The first is when the child solves problems by placing items in unorganized heaps: "At this stage, word meaning denotes nothing more to the child than a vague syncretic conglomeration of individual objects that have somehow or other coalesced into an image in his mind. Because of its syncretic origin, that image is highly unstable" (2012, p. 118). The second stage is what he calls "thinking in complexes:" "In a complex, individual objects are united in the child's mind not only by his subjective impressions but also by bonds actually existing between these objects. This is a new achievement, an ascent to a much higher level" (Vygotsky, 2012, p. 120). He adds: "In a complex, the bonds between its opponents are concrete and factual rather than abstract and logical" (Vygotsky, 2012, p. 120). Vygotsky and his colleagues identify five types of complexes: associative, collections, chains, diffuse, and pseudo-concepts (2012, pp. 121–128).

The pseudo-concept is termed a "germinating seed" that leads to the third stage, the concept: a unifying theme (Vygotsky, 2012, p. 132) that allows the language user to transcend complexes and transcend the given language to form her own understandings and groups. Complexes, Vygotsky says, characterize not only children's thought but also the thought of "primitive people" as well as in etymologies of common words; he posits a "ceaseless struggle within the developing language between conceptual thought and the heritage of primitive thinking in complexes"—a struggle that is not so ceaseless after all in terms of individual words, since the concept usually wins (2012, pp. 138, 140, 141). In Vygotsky's understanding, development systematically leads from specific uses to general principles (though some peoples may not get all the way to the abstract stage of concepts).

Compare Vygotsky's discussion of concept formation with his discussion of dialogue: "Dialogue implies immediate unpremeditated utterance. It consists of replies, repartee; it is a chain of reactions. Monologue, by comparison, is a complex formation; the linguistic elaboration can be attended to leisurely and consciously" (2012, p. 257). In other words, dialogue is unfinished, not well thought out, rough-hewn, reactionary; monologue is in comparison finished, detailed, and *higher*. For Vygotsky, as we've seen, complex formations are preferable to simple ones and abstract, general concepts are preferable to associative chains; monologue is more developed than dialogue. Dialogue is the raw source that becomes refined in monologue. No wonder Vygotsky saw monologue as the true form of inner speech: "Written and inner speech represent the monologue; oral speech, in most cases, the dialogue" (2012, p. 254).

Not that dialogue is to be shunned. Vygotsky found it to be interesting as well. He used Dostoevsky's story of "a conversation of drunks that entirely consisted of one unprintable word" to illustrate his statement that "dialogue always presupposes in the partners sufficient knowledge of the subject to permit abbreviated speech and, under certain conditions, purely predicative sentences" (2012, p. 255).

Leontiev

Similarly, Leontiev used the concept of *crystallization* to describe how the development of psychological functions could be passed along, not just biologically, but culturally: once society developed, progress in the sphere of man's psychological abilities was established and transmitted from one generation to another in a unique form, one that was esoteric, that expressed itself through the phenomena of objective reality. The new form of accumulating and transmitting phylogenetic or, more precisely, historical experience emerged because of certain features which are typical of human activity—namely, its productive, creative aspect, which is most apparent in the basic human activity that work represents. (Leont'ev, 1960/1969, p. 425)

Here, Leontiev's discussion of crystallization sounds a bit like the cultural knowledge that is shaped and accumulated in genres: "By effecting the process of production, both material and cultural, *work is crystallized or assumes final form in its product*" and thus "the conversion of human activity into its product appears to be a process whereby *man's* [sic] *activity*, the activity of human qualities, is *embodied in the product produced*. The history of material and cultural development thus appears to be a process which, in its external objective form, gives expression to the growth of human abilities" (1960/1969, p. 425, my emphasis; cf. Leontyev, 2009b, p. 116). Thus the use of tools and instruments "can be thought of as expressing and consolidating the gains man has made with respect to the motor functions of the hand" (1960/1969, p. 425). Like a well-worn path through the woods, this cultural heritage transcends individuals (1960/1969, p. 425). In this way, Leontiev collapsed Vygotsky's distinction between physical and psychological tools (i.e., labor tools mediating the object of labor vs. signs mediating the self). As Leontiev argues elsewhere, a tool is a "*social object*," "*a socially developed means of action, namely the labour operations that have been given material shape, are crystallised, as it were, in it*" (2009b, p. 192, my emphasis; cf. Leontyev, 2009a, p. 102). Here, crystallization is a dialectical process: Over time, labor operations are "given material shape," a shape that is "developed socially in the course of collective labour" (Leontyev, 2009b, p. 192), allowing for the "accumulating and transmitting" of "historical experience" (Leont'ev, 1960/1969, p. 425) within that collective labor. That is, we could develop a cultural heritage, one that transcended individual development because it was invested in tools. And these tools developed dialectically, with new iterations incorporating new and modified operations (i.e., proceeding from simpler to more complex tools), while standardizing (i.e., developing toward unity). In taking up tools, humans could also take up their cultural heritage, benefiting from the dialectical development of their predecessors.

DRAWBACKS OF THE DIALECTICAL ACCOUNT

As I alluded earlier, we can see how the Vygotskian dialectical account links to early RGS, and especially Bazerman's work. Here, scholars were concerned with how individuals—often students—*learned* their disciplines by learning the genres at play in them (e.g., Artemeva & Freedman, 2001; Bazerman, 1997; Berkenkotter & Huckin, 1995; Freedman et al., 1994; Haas, 1996; Russell, 1995; 1997a, 1997b; Winsor, 1999). Traversing this path gets us to a certain destination: we can examine development and learning over time. This path helps teachers (and managers) to understand how those individuals develop, taking on prescribed cultural knowledge as well as the objectives implied in that knowledge, *accumulating* it as they more effectively inhabit their roles within a cultural system. The path slopes upwards, moving learners to a higher level of cultural functioning, and studies on this path often focus on key transitional moments such as classroom simulations (e.g., Freedman et al., 1994; Paretti et al., 2007), internships (e.g., Artemeva, 2008; 2009; Winsor, 1996; 1999), and undertaking new jobs and careers (e.g., Schryer & Spoel, 2005; Spinuzzi, 2008). Perhaps these are weighted to the concerns of pedagogy and the population (students) to which their authors had most ready access.

Yet we do not just *master* cultural systems; we also *resist* them, and (perhaps this is another way of saying it) we inhabit and help to enact different cultural systems simultaneously. Thus, although the dialectical account seems plausible in closely bounded activities, outside those stage-managed bounds, it encounters problems. For instance, we find that the same artifact can be mobilized in very different ways across activities and cultures (cf. Rogoff, 2003, p. 6). Similarly, artifacts must often be localized in order to make sense in a given milieu and to avoid the missteps of colonialism (Sun, 2020; cf. Escobar, 2017). That is, accounts of crystallization typically do not discuss *whose* cultural heritage is crystallized and reproduced—a symptom of the cross-cultural blind spot to which Engeström (1996) alluded in his discussion of Leontievan activity theory. This question was not especially pressing to Leninists and Stalinists, who expected to move toward a unified world in which Communism would eventually sweep across all nations, yielding a unified (monological) future (Reed, 1919; McAuley,

1992). But in the post-Soviet, post-Cold War era, we are instead coming to grips with a culturally, politically, economically, and professionally diverse world—one in which a single master ideology is no longer on the horizon and in which the withering away of the state seems utterly implausible. In this world, we must recognize the *double consciousness* that W.E.B Du Bois evocatively described (1897) and that Wertsch (2002) explored in the wake of Soviet-era internal exile. In this world, we are generally suspicious of the prospect of development toward a more complexly mediated unity—even in education (see Young, 2002).

Consequently, we turn to a different path: Bakhtin's competing understanding of dialogism, which offers an account of cultural heritage based on difference.

PATH 2: DIALOGICS

As mentioned earlier, dialogics is often either subsumed under dialectics (e.g., Engeström, 1987/2014; Roth, 2009) or characterized as coexisting with dialectic (e.g., Daniels, 2008, pp. 123–124). Bazerman draws on Voloshinov (1973) to validate this move. But others argue that they are fundamentally different, resting on different premises of how meaning emerges. For Bakhtin, utterances gain meaning in relation to each other, in difference rather than in unity (as dialectics would have it). In this section, we will review dialogics; trace the discussion of dialogics and genre in activity theory and related areas; and examine the limits of genre as an account for cultural heritage.

Dialogics According to Bakhtin

Bakhtin was Vygotsky's contemporary, born one year before him. As Vygotsky rode the wave of the Revolution, rising from marginalized Jewish atheist to respected psychologist, Bakhtin was dragged under. Born into a minor aristocratic family, and a Christian, he initially was excited about the possibilities of the Revolution. But in 1929, just as his book *Problems of Dostoevsky's Art* was published, Bakhtin was arrested and sentenced to ten years in a labor camp. On appeal, he was instead sentenced to exile in Kazakhstan, where he served as a bookkeeper for six years (meanwhile writing essays, including his now-famous "Discourse in the Novel;" Bakhtin, 1981).

Like Vygotsky, Bakhtin was trained as a literary scholar, and like Vygotsky, he focused on language and its role in consciousness (not as a psychologist or educator but as a language philosopher and literary theorist). He spent much of his life thinking through this issue, developing many pieces of writing, the majority of which were left unpublished until long after Stalin's death. Yet Bakhtin was skeptical of dialectics as a mechanism for understanding how people develop meaning. Indeed, Morson and Emerson argue that "Bakhtin's contempt for dialectics was a constant, and appears in writings of the 1920s as well as of the 1970s" (1990, p. 57). Across Bakhtin's life works, he expressed the concern that Hegelian dialectics ultimately implied a single authoritative consciousness, one in which disagreement and difference could not survive. As Matusov argues, for Bakhtin, *dialectics* implies monologism, in which a final word could silence disagreement (2011)—a final word such as the scientific concept that Vygotsky describes as the highest stage of development (Vygotsky, 2012). In contrast, *dialogics* implies that no final word is possible. This difference can be graphically illustrated in the two scholars' visions of human development. Vygotsky sought, through educational revolution, to develop the New Man, who would exceed the capabilities of contemporary humans just as humans exceed the capabilities of apes (Vygotsky, 1994). Bakhtin, on the other hand, examined prosaic change rather than revolution, finding meaning in daily life and everyday disagreements among ordinary people (Morson & Emerson, 1990, p. 280). As Matusov (2011) argues, a dialogic approach is characterized by *interproblematicity*:

> It involves the participants' genuine interest in the problem here and now . . . genuine interest in what the other participants have to say about it (i.e., their dialogic interaddressivity); seriousness about their own contributions; readiness, if not desire, to hear other participants' judgments of them (i.e., their responsibility); persuasiveness based on the discourse rather than an authority, tradition or prejudice (i.e., internally persuasive discourse); and acknowledgement of equal rights for the participants to define the problem and engage in and disengage from the communication about it (i.e., mutual respect). (Matusov, 2011, p. 104)

Dialogics can be understood as Hegelian dialectics inside out. Whereas Hegel sought unity in difference, Bakhtin sought differences even in superficially identical utterances: meaning proceeds from relationships (1986, p. 125). As Wegerif (2008) argues, in dialectic, meaning is grounded in identity, so contradictions are to be overcome; in dialogue, meaning is grounded in difference, so it makes no sense to overcome the difference. This is a different path indeed, with implications for how we understand genre.

Bakhtin contends that "dialogue is possible only among people, not among abstract elements of language" (Morson & Emerson, 1990, p. 131). These people jointly own the dialogue. Like dialectics, dialogue is an interactionist understanding of concrete interrelations; but in contrast with dialectics, dialogue is value-laden and allows infinite shades of meaning (Morson & Emerson, 1990, p. 132). Bakhtin tells us that "In Dostoevsky's world even *agreement* retains its *dialogic* character, that is, it never leads to a *merging* of voices and truths in a single *impersonal* truth, as occurs in the monologic world" (Bakhtin, 1984a, p. 95, his emphasis). Even when two people accept the same logical proposition, they accept it within their own orientations and social worlds. This is why no two utterances can be considered the same (Bakhtin, 1984a, p. 183)—a position that denies dialectic unity because it takes away the abstract unity of a statement.

Thus, two speaking subjects may say the "same" thing while conveying very different meanings. This, Bakhtin says, is a dialogic relationship. And he contrasts it with the clash between two different statements—thesis and antithesis—that can "be united in a single utterance of a single subject, expressing his unified dialectical position on a given question" (1984a, p. 183; cf. Bakhtin, 1986, p. 125). A dialectical statement does not contain an argument; it fits neatly into one consciousness, one utterance, and one position. As Eun summarizes, Bakhtin and Vygotsky:

> differed in that Vygotsky sought to organize the incoherent nature into a system by means of the dialectical method, which results in one prevailing truth (although this truth is born of rational discussion rather than by force), whereas Bakhtin preferred to leave things as they are, namely, messy and disorganized. The chaotic multiplicity of consciousness that forever refuse [sic] to merge is what Bakhtin saw as the essence of human consciousness." (2019, p. 10)

Morson and Emerson argue that "Bakhtin considered it conceptually disastrous to think of dialogue after the model of the script . . . where one speech simply follows another" (1990, p. 138). When Vygotsky discussed the spoken dialogue of the drunks in Dostoevsky (2012), he interpreted the dialogue as a chain of reactions, inferior to the more finished and unified monologue that can be found in "complex formations" such as written and inner speech—complex formations that reflect the abstract monologism of dialectic. But this understanding of dialogue as a chain of reactions misses the point, in Bakhtin's understanding: "The complexities created by the already-spoken-about quality of the word, and by the listener's active understanding, create an *internal dialogism* of the word. Every utterance is dialogized *from within* by these (and some other) factors" (Morson & Emerson, 1990, p. 138). Dialogue does not become more abstract or evolve into a complex formation that can be summed up in a single utterance by a single consciousness. That is, unlike dialectic, dialogue is unfinalizable. To revisit a quote above, dialogue "never leads to a merging of voices and truths in a single impersonal truth, as occurs in the monologic world" (Bakhtin, 1984a, p. 95).

This contrast extends beyond the phenomena of speech and writing. Bakhtin sees dialogue as internal as well, that is, thought itself: "But again we repeat: *the thinking human consciousness and the dialogic sphere in which this consciousness exists*, in all its depth and specificity, cannot be reached through a monologic artistic approach" (1984, p. 271, his emphasis). That is, our very consciousness is dialogic—a striking contrast to Vygotsky's understanding of scientific concepts as a dialectically formed, finished monologue. So, although Wertsch is correct in noting that Bakhtin and Vygotsky both understand thought as a form of inner speech (1991), they conceived of this inner speech as having different ends.

To sum up: In Bakhtin's analysis of Dostoevsky—and, it appears, in his analysis of language as a whole—a permanent, necessary gap exists between speakers, resulting in a permanent dialogue, a permanent array of differences that are discussed and negotiated but never finalized, synthesized, or eliminated. Oppositions are never canceled out; they are not seen as contradictions to be overcome; every utterance expects an answer; differences are taken seriously. The truth, he says, is born between people searching for truth—it is not ready-made and waiting to be discovered: "Two voices is the minimum for life, the minimum for existence" (1984a, p. 252). The "voices of the mind" (Wertsch, 1991) are voices of different participants interacting, perhaps never coming to a permanent agreement that would produce a unity of consciousness (Bakhtin, 1984a, p. 30). These voices are best understood as enactments, performances, that gain meaning in tension with other performances.

Where does that leave the genre+activity theory synthesis that our field adopted in the 1990s and 2000s, and that Bazerman seeks to strengthen in *A Theory of Literate Action, Vol. II* (2013b)? Eugene Matusov argues that a tension exists between dialogue and activity: "activity is responsible for the monologicity aspect of discourse" because "joint collective activity is about accomplishing something." In activity,

> the subject of such an activity is a unified, shared, common understanding—one consciousness, as Bakhtin would say. A joint activity becomes problematic when shared understanding is not achieved, partially achieved, or achieved about wrong things. Although heteroglossia can be viewed as a productive force in the activity at its initial and intermediary stages, at the final phase, it has to be eliminated. From this point of view, activity is essentially anti-dialogue (anti-heteroglossic). However, as Bakhtin showed, this unifying,

> centripetal force is an important aspect of any discourse defining one's voice, the recognized unity of consciousness. The problem starts when the other complementary and necessary aspect of discourse—namely dialogicity—is either ignored or attempted to actively exclude from the analysis (and design) or eliminate from the discourse, when a voice becomes the voice. In the latter case, there becomes a tendency to establish a regime of excessive monologism. (Matusov, 2013, p. 383)

Yet

> Monologicity has to be appreciated and recognized as an important and necessary aspect of discourse. For example, although Bakhtin criticized dialectics in many of his writings, he also acknowledged that dialectics can produce "a higher-level dialogue," "dialectics was born of dialogue so as to return again to dialogue at a much higher level (a dialogue of *personalities*)" (Bakhtin et al., 1986, p. 162) [The] activity approach has to be complemented by focus on dialogicity (Engeström et al., 1999). (Matusov, 2013, p. 385)

But this leaves us with the question of how to preserve dialogism if activity is ultimately monologic. How can cultural heritage be conveyed in a dialogical world? One answer that Bakhtin provides is that of *genre*.

Genre according to Bakhtin

Bakhtin discusses the notion of genre in several publications across his scholarship, but most specifically in his late essay "The problem of speech genres" (1986). There, he argues that although "each separate utterance is individual . . . each sphere in which language is used develops its own *relatively stable types* of these utterances," which he calls "*speech genres*" (1986, p. 60, his emphasis). Such genres include not only literary genres (Bakhtin's interest), but also military commands, business documents, social commentary, and scientific statements (1986, pp. 60–61). These genres can be characterized as primary (which are "simple" and "have taken form in unmediated speech communication") and secondary (which are "complex" and "ideological," having taken in primary genres and interrelated them (1986, p. 62).

At the base of speech genres, Bakhtin argues, are "spheres of human activity" (1986, p. 65). Speech only exists in the form of concrete utterances performed by real, individual speakers (Bakhtin, 1986, p. 71). These utterances typically follow a "speech plan" (Bakhtin, 1986, p.77), a cultural heritage that underpins the enactment. And by using relatively stable, recognizable, normative patterns of speech—speech genres—we can reveal and implement our individual speech plans (Bakhtin, 1986, p. 80). He adds: "Genres correspond to typical situations of speech communication, typical themes, and consequently, also to particular contacts between the *meanings* of words and actual concrete reality under certain typical circumstances" (Bakhtin, 1986, p. 87, his emphasis). In providing relative stability, genres allow their users to draw on cultural heritage while still producing unique utterances. As Bakhtin argues elsewhere, "a genre lives in the present, but always *remembers* its past, its beginning" (1984a, p. 106; cf. 1984a, p. 121). A genre possesses its own organic logic (Bakhtin, 1984a, p.157). Language, he argues, is never unitary, but represents a multitude of concrete worlds; these worlds are stratified through genres, in which "Certain features . . . will knit together with the intentional aim, and with the overall accentual system inherent in one or another genre" (Bakhtin, 1981, p. 288). This stratification includes professional stratification ("the language of the lawyer, the businessman, the politician, the public education teacher and so forth"), and these often correspond to the stratification of genres (Bakhtin, 1981, p. 289).

For Bakhtin, then, genre is understood as fundamentally dialogic. In providing relatively stable, and thus recognizable, patterns for utterances, genres represent a stratified worldview within which individuals can arrange their speech plans and relate their unique utterances. That is, genres represent cultural heritage; in taking up and *enacting* a genre (understood as a verb, not as a noun as in Leontievan crystallization), individuals ground themselves in that heritage. In this view, we do not *acquire and produce* a genre; we *do* genre.

Unfortunately, a Bakhtinian approach does not give us a satisfactory understanding of development. Yes, genres may be understood as cultural resources that have developed over time, but Bakhtin is uninterested in this development: he is more concerned with the fact that the word is half someone else's, that people use these cultural resources in tension with their own unmerged voices to produce meaning through difference. This approach is suitable for understanding instances of language use, and especially differences and resistance in language use, but not for understanding how genres provide a developing cultural heritage. Whereas the path of dialectics slopes upwards to greater heights of development, the path of dialogics does not really slope at all, instead meandering through a level field; it did not lead to the concerns that were critical to Bazerman and others in RGS. Thus Bazerman (2013b) turns to another member of the Bakhtin Circle: V. I. Voloshinov.

Bazerman's Path: Dialectics and Dialogics in Voloshinov

Up to this point, we have discussed the diverging paths of dialectics and dialogics, and we have alluded to how Bazerman followed the former path, framing dialogics within dialectics. He followed this path, in part, by way of V. I. Voloshinov, who was a member of the same circle as Bakhtin and whose two books (1927/1976; 1929/1973) are sometimes attributed in part or whole to Bakhtin (cf. Clark & Holquist, 1984). Unlike Bakhtin's books, Voloshinov's two books are well-structured and lucid, and they are explicitly positioned as language philosophy rather than literary criticism (see Prior, 2009 on this point). For these and other reasons, Bazerman actually characterizes the Bakhtin Circle as "*Voloshinov* and his circle" (2013b, p. 151, my emphasis) and praises Voloshinov for his more *sociologically* oriented understanding of genre compared to that of Bakhtin, who focused specifically on *literary* questions. Ironically, in 1929, the same year Voloshinov (1973) was originally published, sociology was banned in the USSR (Osipov, 2009, p. 83).

For those who prefer the destination of a developmental, dialectical understanding of genre, like Bazerman, Voloshinov has a lot to offer. Critically, he neatly characterizes dialogics as a kind of dialectics—a stance that provides a rapprochement between these two lines of thought. This rapprochement comes as a relief to researchers who want to draw on both lines to support a genre+activity theory synthesis. Specifically, Bazerman prefers Voloshinov's account of dialogics as "grounded in human interchange" and responding to prior utterances (2013b, p. 152). Utterances are thus co-produced: actively produced and actively received. Voloshinov's account has direct implications for genre, since "genre, by shaping the roles . . . also frames the addressivity of those texts that realize the genre" (Bazerman, 2013b, p. 155).

Yet Voloshinov and Bakhtin were not quite on the same page. As Morson and Emerson argue:

> Voloshinov changes Bakhtin's theories by accepting his specific descriptions of language but then accounting for language so described in historical-materialist terms. Bakhtin describes language as not systematic; Voloshinov agrees, but argues that this asystematicity only leads us to look for an external system to explain it. That system is Marxism as Voloshinov understood it. Indeed, the reformulation of Marxism was central to Voloshinov's whole enterprise, as it was not for the non-Marxist Bakhtin. (1990, p. 125)

In terms of system, Voloshinov focuses on structure and process, and looks for an ideological system with ideological laws that govern language (1973, pp.

33, 38, 96–97). And, like Vygotsky, he frames language development as a dialectic generational process in which modern language emerges from primitive ones—although he manages not to be as teleological as Vygotsky sometimes sounds (1973, p. 106). As Morson and Emerson argue, "Voloshinov's ultimate purpose is to link a dialogic approach to language to a dialectical view of history, a purpose completely at odds with Bakhtin," and this was done through the sign (1990, pp. 162, 207). For Voloshinov, the sign is given, but "changeable and adaptable" (Voloshinov, 1973, p. 68); as Bazerman comments, the "individual when confronted with an actual communicative situation adapts and improvises to convey a meaning directed toward the addressee" (2013b, p. 153). Prior states that while Voloshinov is concerned with signs and semiotics, Bakhtin—whose concerns are narrowly literary—is simply not (Prior, 2009, p. 19, 20).

Thus, unlike Bakhtin, Voloshinov and Vygotsky both explore the sociocultural question of how such signs are developed internally (mediating the individual's own behavior) and externally (mediating their interactions with others). Both postulate a "sea of inner speech" (Prior, 2009, p. 20, referring to Voloshinov), a well of signs that are dialectically transformed through being internalized and externalized (Vygotsky, 2012). That is, both understand these signs as originating culturally, then being taken up and transformed by individuals operating within that culture, then being enacted again in a social setting. Vygotsky (1978) provides a classic example of how internalization and externalization work: an infant reaches vainly for an object that is then handed to her by a parent. Eventually the infant's attempt to control the environment directly becomes *pointing*, a sign that directs the parent's actions. The sign thus qualitatively transforms the character of the child's activity, and in learning and taking up a culture's mediators, the child becomes acculturated (Luria, 1976). This dialectical understanding of signs, explored so well in Bazerman's 2013 book (chapter 2), connects directly to his account of Voloshinov's understanding of signs (chapter 9), on which Voloshinov builds his interactionist, reciprocal understanding of genres.

Yet despite their similarities, Voloshinov and Vygotsky do part ways in terms of dialogue. To illustrate: Voloshinov uses the same example Vygotsky does in *Thought and Language*—Dostoevsky's drunks—but Voloshinov rereads the dialogue in terms of active reception involving value judgments (1973, p. 103). As he argues, "*Multiplicity of meanings is the constitutive feature of word*" (p. 101, his emphasis). Whereas Vygotsky thinks of dialogue as a chain of reactions, Voloshinov understands it as always occurring, even when the person is not speaking. Thus, they part ways when it comes to written language, which Vygotsky sees as monologic and Voloshinov sees as "vitiated dialogue" (p. 111). Monologic utterances, in Voloshinov's understanding, are vitiated (spoiled) because they do not allow an active response (p. 78; cf. p. 117). He regarded "the finished monologic utterance" as an abstraction (p. 72). For Voloshinov, true understanding is dialogical, involving a word and a counterword (p. 102).

Voloshinov also diverges from Bakhtin's understanding of dialogue in several ways. First, he understands utterances as agreeing with or negating each other (Voloshinov 1973, p. 80)—a stance that Bakhtin rejects in *Problems of Dostoevsky's Poetics*, where he subtly critiques dialectics for conceptualizing utterances as simply agreeing or disagreeing, theses and antitheses. In Bakhtin's understanding, utterances can be identical yet diverge in meaning and import; that divergence is usually partial or in shades, not opposed. As Morson & Emerson argue, "whereas Bakhtin celebrates intense dialogization and double-voicing, Voloshinov, writing as a Marxist, describes such phenomena disapprovingly" (Morson & Emerson 1990, p. 124). Second, as we've seen, Voloshinov speaks almost entirely of the sign, something that Bakhtin rarely mentions. Like Vygotsky, Voloshinov sees the word as an inner sign (1973, p. 14), and he sees every outer sign as engulfed by inner signs (1973, p. 33); as Morson and Emerson (1990) argue, sign is a way for Voloshinov to bridge dialogue and dialectics by framing the responsive interactions of dialogue within dialectic's developmental understanding of signs.

In short, we can see why Voloshinov offers a dialectical path for Bazerman, who attempts to "recover Voloshinov from Bakhtin" (1994, p. 54) to develop an understanding of genre. Since Voloshinov's understanding of genre (and dialogics more generally) is grounded in dialectics, it provides a ready account of genre development, one that integrates well with broader theories of human and cultural development such as the work of Vygotsky, Leontiev, and Luria. This upward-sloping path gets us to the destinations that many of us in RGS, including Bazerman, have set out to reach: developmental understandings of how people join and enact durable activities, how they learn and develop the cultural resources that sustain such activities, and how they accumulate repertoires and strategies throughout their lives so they can navigate those activities with competence and expertise. As Prior says, North American versions of genre theory have oriented to both discourse and development (2009, p. 28), and Voloshinov's (and Bazerman's) path allows us to have both by framing discourse (dialogue) within development (dialectics).

And yet this elevated destination implies a trust in the activities—really, the *institutions*—we envision people joining. But as the *annus horribilis* of 2020 made manifest, institutions should not always earn our trust. For all its virtues, the upward-sloping path we have taken, in focusing on *developing and accumulating* repertoires, has not prepared us well to examine the *contrastive* meaning-making that emerges from tensions within, across, and outside of such institutions.

RETRACING OUR STEPS: UNDERLYING TENSIONS IN RHETORICAL GENRE STUDIES

Earlier I noted that Matusov identified a tension between Bakhtinian dialogism, which finds meaning in difference, and the monologic tendency of the Vygotsky-Leontiev approach, which presupposes that the activity's participants strive for unity. This underlying tension remains in RGS. In using genres, we learn the orientation and cultural logic (see Sun, 2020) of the sphere of activity in which we participate. Yet, as discussed above, we can also bring in different orientations and cultural logics, partially because a genre evolves through its performances (i.e., we take up and enact genres). This distrust of unidirectional development has begun to reassert itself in genre theory, especially as we have grappled with another concept that Bazerman discussed early on: *genre systems* (Bazerman, 1994; cf. Andersen et al., 2014; Prior, 2009; Spinuzzi, 2004), in which multiple genres that have developed in different cultural milieus become associated with each other. In such situations, *cross-genre development cannot be understood unidirectionally*, since genres and their relationships tend to develop multidimensionally, in relation to each other (and each others' cultural heritages) as well as to a rhetorical situation (or collection of interdependent rhetorical situations). Activity theorists have argued that learning is not a linear arrow but more like a spiral; but in learning and applying multiple genres from multiple source activities to a target activity, we may find that learning takes multiple directions at once, oriented toward many activities and many lines of development. Russell (1997a) illustrates this point well in an early discussion of how students participate in multiple activities, often not in alignment, and mobilize genres grounded in each of them. That is, these situations are more multiply oriented than the teacher-student dyads that Vygotsky, Luria, and Leontiev often investigated, in which the learning institution validated and underwrote a specific line of development.

That multiple orientation is not unique to RGS. More broadly, as activity theory has been applied to inter-individual, inter-organizational, and public cases, fewer mechanisms exist for enforcing or incentivizing agreement (Spinuzzi, 2020). For instance, Engeström's Change Laboratories methodology is designed to host dialogues across different people with a special focus on higher-level epistemic questions such as "why" and "where to?" (Engeström, 2007; Engeström et al., 2006; cf. Bødker & Iverson, 2002; cf. Bødker, 1997, the "why," "what," and "how" layers). Yet the tension between dialogue and dialectics remains, since Change Labs are meant to eventually develop a consensus solution, i.e., a unity on which an institution can agree (see Engeström & Sannino, 2021; Spinuzzi, 2021b). In subordinating dialogue to dialectics, activity theory research has tended to presuppose that the goal of dialogue is to develop a synthesis. Thus, we see what is sometimes characterized as a managerial approach, one that acknowledges multiple perspectives but uses interventionist methodology to foster mutual agreement across actors.

When Vygotsky characterized development dialectically, in terms of height (as we saw earlier), the metaphor was unidirectional, reflecting the teleological Marxist-Leninist understanding of history. In contrast, Bakhtin understood forces of language as centripetal and centrifugal (1981, p. 272), i.e., as being tugged between a centrist monologism vs. flying away from it in all directions. Others who have criticized dialectics in the intervening years have used other metaphors to escape its monologism, such as rhizomes and lines of flight (Deleuze & Guattari, 1987) or translation (Latour, 2006).

In RGS, we have similarly started to think of genre assemblages in terms of enactments or networks in which differing cultural heritages compete or engage in dialogue without merging (Edenfield, 2016; Jones, 2016; Hashimov & McNely, 2012; Read, 2016; 2020; Spinuzzi, 2008; Swarts, 2010). And that question of multidimensional development becomes even more pressing when considering intercultural communication. For instance, Sun (2020) draws on rhetoric, practice theory, social justice theory, and decolonialist methodology to analyze how social media design has been taken up differently in North America and Asia, attending to the ideological and discursive affordances required by different users in different positionalities, situations, and cultures. Beyond helping us to understand cross-cultural social media use, Sun argues for better designing and localizing social media by sensitively attending to the ideological and discursive affordances required by different users in different positionalities, situations, and cultures. To address these issues, Sun moves away from activity theory's dialectical developmental approach in favor of dialogism, heteroglossia, and epistemic diversity (2020, pp. 52, 71–72). Similarly, Fraiberg examines translinguistic and transmodal practices across regimes of practice in Israeli soldiers and entrepreneurs (Fraiberg 2013; 2017a; 2017b).

In short, the question of cultural heritage becomes more fraught when we have to ask: *whose* culture? *Whose* heritage? How do different cultures intermingle and when do voices need to remain unmerged? What have we accepted as cultural "gains" that are not really gains to our interlocutors (e.g., Hawkins, 2016, which makes uncomfortable reading next to Luria, 1976)? The dialectics of Vygotsky, Leontiev, Luria, and Voloshinov is poorly equipped to answer these questions, questions that were central to the dialogics of Bakhtin. Although the path we have followed has taken us a long way, and has provided tremendous insights, it has also led us away from such questions. Perhaps it's time to retrace our steps and take the other path as well.

REFERENCES

Andersen, J., Bazerman, C. & Schneider, J. (2014). Beyond single genres: Pattern mapping in global communication. In E. M. Jakobs & J. Perrin (Eds.), *Handbook of Writing and Text Production* (pp. 305–322). De Gruyter.

Artemeva, N. (2008). Toward a unified social theory of genre learning. *Journal of Business and Technical Communication, 22*(2), 160–185.

Artemeva, N. (2009). Stories of becoming: A study of novice engineers learning genres of their profession. In C. Bazerman, A. Bonini & D. Figueiredo (Eds.), *Genre in a changing world* (pp. 158–178). The WAC Clearinghouse; Parlor Press. https://doi.org/10.37514/PER-B.2009.2324.2.08.

Artemeva, N. & Freedman, A. (Eds.). (2007). *Rhetorical genre studies and beyond*. Inkshed.

Artemeva, N. & Freedman, A. (2001). "Just the boys playing on computers": An activity theory analysis of differences in the cultures of two engineering firms. *Journal of Business and Technical Communication, 15*(2), 164–194.

Bakhtin, M. M. (1986). *Speech genres and other late essays*. University of Texas Press.

Bakhtin, M. M. (1984). *Rabelais and his world*. Indiana University Press.

Bakhtin, M. M. (1984). *Problems of Dostoevsky's poetics*. University of Minnesota Press.

Bakhtin, M. M. (1981). *The dialogic imagination: Four essays*. University of Texas Press.

Bazerman, C., Farmer, F., Halasek, K. & Williams, J. M. (2005). Responses to Bakhtin's "Dialogic Origins and Dialogic Pedagogy of Grammar: Stylistics as Part of Russian Language Instruction in Secondary Schools": Further responses and a tentative conclusion. *Written Communication, 22*(3), 363–374. https://doi.org/10.1177/0741088305278032.

Bazerman, C. (1988). *Shaping written knowledge: The genre and activity of the experimental article in science*. University of Wisconsin Press.

Bazerman, C. (1994). Systems of genre and the enactment of social intentions. In A. Freedman & P. Medway (Eds.), *Genre and the new rhetoric* (pp. 79–99). Taylor & Francis.

Bazerman, C. (1997). Discursively structured activities. *Mind, Culture, and Activity, 4*(4), 296–308.

Bazerman, C. (2013). *A theory of literate action: Literate action, Volume 2*. The WAC Clearinghouse; Parlor Press. https://doi.org/10.37514/PER-B.2013.4791.

Bazerman, C. (2004). Intertextualities: Voloshinov, Bakhtin, literary theory, and literacy studies. In A. F. Ball & S. W. Freedman (Eds.), *Bakhtinian perspectives on language, literacy, and learning* (pp. 53–65). Cambridge.

Bazerman, C., Little, J. & Chavkin, T. (2003). The production of information for genred activity spaces: Informational motives and consequences of the environmental impact statement. *Written Communication, 20*(4), 455–477. https://doi.org/10.1177/0741088303260375.

Beiser, F. (2005). *Hegel*. Routledge.

Berkenkotter, C. & Huckin, T. N. (1995). *Genre knowledge in disciplinary communication: Cognition/culture/power*. Erlbaum.

Bocharov, S. & Lupanov, V. (1994). Conversations with Bakhtin. *PMLA, 109*(5), 1009–1024.

Bødker, S. (1997). Computers in mediated human activity. *Mind, Culture, and Activity, 4*(3), 149–158.
Bødker, S. & Iversen, O. S. (2002). Staging a professional participatory design practice—Moving PD beyond the initial fascination of user involvement. *ACM International Conference Proceeding Series, 31*, 11–18. https://doi.org/10.1145/572020.572023.
Clark, K. & Holquist, M. (1984). *Mikhail Bakhtin.* Belknap Press.
Dafermos, M. (2018). *Rethinking cultural-historical theory: A dialectical perspective to Vygotsky.* Springer.
Daniels, H. (2008). *Vygotsky and research.* Routledge.
Deleuze, G. & Guattari, F. (1987). *A thousand plateaus: Capitalism and schizophrenia.* University of Minnesota Press.
Du Bois, W. E. B. (1897). Strivings of the Negro People. *The Atlantic.* https://www.theatlantic.com/magazine/archive/1897/08/strivings-of-the-negro-people/305446/.
Edenfield, A. C. (2017). Power and communication in worker cooperatives: An overview. *Journal of Technical Writing and Communication, 47*(3), 260–279. https://doi.org/10.1177/0047281616641921.
Engels, F. (1954). *Dialectics of nature.* Moscow: Foreign Languages Publishing House.
Engeström, Y. (2007). Enriching the theory of expansive learning: Lessons from journeys toward coconfiguration. *Mind, Culture, and Activity, 14*(1–2), 23–39.
Engeström, Y. (2014). *Learning by expanding.* Cambridge University Press.
Engeström, Y. (1996). Developmental work research as educational research: Looking ten years back and into the zone of proximal development. *Nordisk Pedagogik, 16*(3), 131–143.
Engeström, Y. (1990). *Learning, working, and imagining: Twelve studies in activity theory.* Orienta-Konsultit Oy.
Engeström, Y., Pasanen, A., Toiviainen, H. & Haavisto, V. (2006). Expansive learning as collaborative concept formation at work. In K. Yamazumi, Y. Engeström & H. Daniels (Eds.), *New Learning challenges: Going beyond the industrial age system of school and work* (pp. 47–77). Kansai University Press.
Engeström, Y. & Sannino, A. (2020). From mediated actions to heterogenous coalitions: Four generations of activity-theoretical studies of work and learning. *Mind Culture and Activity, 00*(00), 1–20. https://doi.org/10.1080/10749039.2020.1806328.
Escobar, A. (2017). *Designs for the pluriverse: Radical interdependence, autonomy, and the making of worlds.* Duke University Press.
Eun, B. (2019). Two diverging paths toward a common destination: The dialogism of Vygotsky and Bakhtin. *Culture and Psychology, 25*(4), 484–502. https://doi.org/10.1177/1354067X18820635.
Fraiberg, S. (2013). Reassembling technical communication: A framework for studying multilingual and multimodal practices in global contexts. *Technical Communication Quarterly, 22*(1), 10–27. https://doi.org/10.1080/10572252.2013.735635.
Fraiberg, S. (2017). Pretty bullets: Tracing transmedia/translingual literacies of an Israeli soldier across regimes of practice. *College Composition and Communication, 69*(1), 87–117.
Fraiberg, S. (2017). Start-up nation: Studying transnational entrepreneurial practices in Israel's start-up ecosystem. *Journal of Business and Technical Communication, 31*(3), 350–388. https://doi.org/10.1177/1050651917695541.

Freedman, A., Adam, C. & Smart, G. (1994). Wearing suits to class: Simulating genres and simulations as genre. *Written Communication, 11*(2), 193–226.

Haas, C. (1996). *Writing technology: Studies on the materiality of literacy*. Erlbaum.

Hawkins, S. (2016). *Writing and colonialism in Northern Ghana: The encounter between the LoDagaa and "the world on paper."* University of Toronto Press.

Hashimov, E. & McNely, B. (2012). Left to their own devices: Ad hoc genres and the design of transmedia narratives. *30th ACM International Conference on Design*, 251–259. https://doi.org/10.1145/2379057.2379105.

Jones, N. N. (2016). Found things: Genre, narrative, and identification in a networked activist organization. *Technical Communication Quarterly, 25*(4), 298–318. https://doi.org/10.1080/10572252.2016.1228790.

Latour, B. (2006). *Reassembling the social: An introduction to actor-network-theory*. Oxford University Press.

Lenin, V. I. (1987). *Essential works of Lenin*. (H. M. Christman, Ed.). Dover.

Leont'ev, A. N. (1969). On the biological and social aspects of human development: The training of auditory ability. In M. Cole & I. Maltzman (Eds.), *A handbook of contemporary Soviet psychology* (pp. 423–440). Basic Books.

Leontyev, A. N. (2009). *The development of mind*. Marxists Internet Archive.

Leontyev, A. N. (2009). *Activity and consciousness*. Marxists Internet Archive.

Luria, A. R. (1976). *Cognitive development, its cultural and social foundations*. Harvard University Press.

Luria, A. R., Cole, M. & Cole, S. (1979). *The making of mind: A personal account of Soviet psychology*. Harvard University Press.

Matusov, E. (2013). *Journey into dialogic pedagogy*. Nova Science Publishers.

Matusov, E. (2011). Irreconcilable differences in Vygotsky's and Bakhtin's approaches to the social and the individual: An educational perspective. *Culture and Psychology, 17*(1), 99–119. https://doi.org/10.1177/1354067X10388840.

McAuley, M. (1992). *Soviet politics, 1917–1991*. Oxford University Press.

McNely, B. (2019). Under pressure: Exploring agency-structure dynamics with a rhetorical approach to register. *Technical Communication Quarterly, 28*(4), 317–331. https://doi.org/10.1080/10572252.2019.1621387.

Metraux, A. (2021). Alexander Luria: Marxist psychologist and transnational scientific broker: A personal account. In A. Yasnitsky (Ed.), *A history of Marxist psychology: The Golden Age of Soviet Science* (pp. 156–190). Routledge.

Miller, C. R. (1984). Genre as social action. *Quarterly Journal of Speech, 70*(2), 151–167.

Miller, C. R. (2016). Genre innovation: Evolution, emergence, or something else? *The Journal of Media Innovations, 3*(2), 4–19. https://doi.org/10.5617/jmi.v3i2.2432.

Morson, G. S. & Emerson, C. (1990). *Mikhail Bakhtin: Creation of a prosaics*. Stanford University Press.

Osipov, G. V. (2009). The rebirth of sociology in Russia. *Russian Social Science Review, 50*(6), 80–108. https://doi.org/10.1080/10611428.2009.11065377.

Paretti, M. C., McNair, L. D. & Holloway-Attaway, L. (2007). Teaching technical communication in an era of distributed work: A case study of collaboration between U.S. and Swedish students. *Technical Communication Quarterly, 16*(3), 327–352.

Read, S. (2020). How to build a supercomputer: U.S. research infrastructure and the documents that mitigate the uncertainties of big science. *Written Communication*, *37*(4), 1–36. https://doi.org/10.1177/0741088320939541.

Read, S. (2016). The net work genre function. *Journal of Business and Technical Communication*, *30*(4), 419–450. https://doi.org/10.1177/1050651916651909.

Reed, J. (1919). *Ten days that shook the world*. International Publishers.

Rogoff, B. (2003). *The cultural nature of human development*. Oxford University Press.

Roth, W. M. (2009). *Dialogism: A Bakhtinian perspective on science and learning*. Brill.

Russell, D. R. (1997). Writing and genre in higher education and workplaces: A review of studies that use cultural-historical activity theory. *Mind, Culture, and Activity*, *4*(4), 224–237.

Russell, D. R. (2009). Uses of activity theory in written communication research. In A. Sannino, H. Daniels & K. D. Gutierrez (Eds.), *Learning and expanding with activity theory* (pp. 40–52). Cambridge University Press.

Russell, D. R. (1995). Activity theory and its implications for writing instruction. In J. Petraglia (Ed.), *Reconceiving writing, rethinking writing instruction* (pp. 51–78). Lawrence Erlbaum Associates.

Russell, D. R. (1997). Rethinking genre in school and society: An activity theory analysis. *Written Communication*, *14*(4), 504–554.

Schryer, C. F. & Spoel, P. (2005). Genre theory, health-care discourse, and professional identity formation. *Journal of Business and Technical Communication*, *19*(3), 249–278. http://jbt.sagepub.com/cgi/content/abstract/19/3/249.

Singer, P. (1983). *Hegel: A very short introduction*. Oxford.

Spinuzzi, C. (2010). Secret sauce and snake oil: Writing monthly reports in a highly contingent environment. *Written Communication*, *27*(4), 363–409.

Spinuzzi, C. (2021). What's wrong with 3GAT? In C. Donahue, K. Blewett & C. Monroe (Eds.), *The expanding universe of writing studies: Higher education writing research*. Peter Lang.

Spinuzzi, C. (1996). Pseudotransactionality, activity theory, and professional writing instruction. *Technical Communication Quarterly*, *5*(3), 295–308.

Spinuzzi, C. (2008). *Network: Theorizing knowledge work in telecommunications*. Cambridge University Press.

Spinuzzi, C. (2003). *Tracing genres through organizations: A sociocultural approach to information design*. MIT Press.

Spinuzzi, C. (2020). "Trying to predict the future": Third-generation activity theory's codesign orientation. *Mind, Culture, and Activity*, *27*(1), 4–18. https://doi.org/10.1080/10749039.2019.1660790.

Spinuzzi, C. (2004). Four ways to investigate assemblages of texts: Genre sets, systems, repertoires, and ecologies. In *SIGDOC '04: Proceedings of the 22nd annual international conference on Design of communication* (pp. 110–116). ACM.

Spinuzzi, C. (2020). Scaling Change Labs: A Response to "From Mediated Actions To Heterogenous Coalitions: Four Generations Of Activity-theoretical Studies Of Work And Learning." *Mind Culture and Activity*, *00*(00), 1–8. https://doi.org/10.1080/10749039.2020.1840594.

Stalin, J. (2013). *History of the Community Party of the Soviet Union (Bolsheviks): Short course*. Prism Key Press.

Sun, H. (2020). *Global social media design: Bridging differences across cultures*. Oxford University Press.

Swarts, J. (2010). Recycled writing: Assembling actor networks from reusable content. *Journal of Business and Technical Communication, 24*(2), 127–163.

Toassa, G. (2019). Leontiev about matter and consciousness: His critique of Vygotsky in the Soviet context Leontiev sobre Matéria e Consciência : Sua crítica a Vigotski nos Anos 1930s *. *Psicologia: Teoria e Pesquisa, 35*, 1–10.

Trotsky, L. (2005). *Literature and revolution*. Haymarket Books.

Voloshinov, V. N. (1976). *Freudianism: A Marxist critique*. Academic Press.

Voloshinov, V. N. (1973). *Marxism and the philosophy of language*. Seminar Press.

Vygotsky, L. S. (1994). The Socialist alteration of man. In R. van der Veer & J. Valsiner (Eds.), *The Vygotsky reader* (pp. 175–184). Blackwell.

Vygotsky, L. S. (2012). *Thought and language* (3rd ed.). MIT Press.

Vygotsky, L. S. & Luria, A. R. (1993). *Studies on the history of behavior: Ape, primitive, and child*. Erlbaum.

Vygotsky, L. S. (1997). *The collected works of L.S. Vygotsky Volume 4: The history of the development of higher mental functions*. Plenum.

Vygotsky, L. S. (1974). *The psychology of art*. MIT Press.

Wegerif, R. (2008). Dialogic or dialectic? The significance of ontological assumptions in research on educational dialogue. *British Educational Research Journal, 34*(3), 347–361. https://doi.org/10.1080/01411920701532228.

Wells, G. (2001). *Dialogic inquiry: Towards a socio-cultural practice and theory of education*. Cambridge University Press.

Wertsch, J. V. (2002). *Voices of collective remembering*. Cambridge University Press.

Wertsch, J. V. (1985). *Vygotsky and the social formation of mind*. Harvard University Press.

Wertsch, J. V. (1998). *Mind as action*. Oxford University Press.

Wertsch, J. V. (1991). *Voices of the mind: A sociocultural approach to mediated action*. Harvard University Press.

White, E. J. (2014). Bakhtinian dialogic and Vygotskian dialectic: Compatabilities and contradictions in the classroom? *Educational Philosophy and Theory, 46*(3), 220–236. https://doi.org/10.1111/j.1469-5812.2011.00814.x.

Wilde, L. (1991). *Logic: Dialectic and contradiction*. Cambridge University Press.

Winsor, D. A. (1999). Genre and activity systems: The role of documentation in maintaining and changing engineering activity systems. *Written Communication, 16*(2), 200–224.

Winsor, D. A. (1996). *Writing like an Engineer: A rhetorical education*. Erlbaum.

Yasnitsky, A. (2016). Unity in diversity: The Vygotsky-Luria circle as an informal personal network of scholars. In A. Yasnitsky & R. van der Veer (Eds.), *Revisionist revolution in Vygotsky studies* (pp. 27–49). Routledge.

Young, V. A. (2010). Should Writers Use They Own English? *Iowa Journal of Cultural Studies, 12*(1), 110–118.

Zavershneva, E. & Van Der Veer, R. (Eds.). (2018). *Vygotsky's notebooks: A selection*. Springer.

CHAPTER 11.

WRITING FOR STABILIZATION AND WRITING FOR POSSIBILITY: THE DIALECTICS OF REPRESENTATION IN EVERYDAY WORK WITH VULNERABLE CLIENTS

Yrjö Engeström
CRADLE, University of Helsinki

About 25 years ago, Charles Bazerman (1997) put forward a powerful argument for understanding the foundational role of discourse in the structuring of professional activity systems. As if to drive the point home, in the same journal issue, Carol Berkenkotter and Doris Ravotas (1997) published a paper in which they showed how in psychiatric consultations the client's initial oral account—which the authors characterize as emic—is transformed into a decontextualized etic record, replacing active verbs with nominalizations that allow the classification of the case in accordance with the American Psychiatric Association's Diagnostic and Statistical Manual of Mental Disorders, to be turned into a billable diagnostic category.

Similar shifts from accounts and narratives expressing clients' personal concerns to official records have been analyzed by Hugh Mehan (1993) in the handling of school students' learning disabilities. I have called the outcome of this shift *stabilization knowledge* (Engeström, 2007), indicating that it involves the representation and classification of an unruly idiosyncratic bundle of problems in terms of well-known categories that allow the formation of a *case* as a bounded and relatively stable entity that can be handled according to standard guidelines and procedures. Stabilization has been aptly characterized by Brian Smith:

> Stabilization is not just a process of standing back in order to let the object quieten; it also involves reaching out and bashing the object into shape, so that it will be stable enough to register. . . . The stuff of objects is by nature unruly. It is a collaborative achievement for them to hold, or be held, still enough to be brought into focus. (1996, p. 300)

DOI: https://doi.org/10.37514/PER-B.2023.1800.2.11

So stabilizing category knowledge is used to turn the problematic into a closed phenomenon that can be registered, calculated, and pushed around rather than transformed. Stabilization is unavoidable, but stabilizing categories such as diagnostic labels tend to become stigmatic stamps. What is missing in the pioneering studies of Berkenkotter and Ravotas and Mehan on the shift from emic to etic is the possibility of going beyond stabilization.

Much of my work in the past 25 years has been focused on designing and implementing ways and instruments for making another shift, from stabilization to *possibilization*, or possibility knowledge (for a philosophical discussion of possibilization, see Epstein, 2019). The shift to possibilization means that the client's needs are examined by means of collaborative negotiation, against the background of their history and emergence. The critical component is the use of *representational instruments* that allow the client and the professional to depict the client's possible *movement* from his or her past and current positions toward a radically empowered position in which the client and the professional as well at times has a qualitatively different grasp of their activity. This is a shift toward recontextualized and prospective modes of representation, writing, and action.

In what follows, I will first summarize the characteristic features of the shift from emic to etic representations in encounters between professionals and vulnerable clients. I will then discuss the available literature on possibilization and possibility knowledge. This leads me to introduce three types of representational instruments developed and used for possibilization in my own studies and those published by others. These three types are *written agreements, four-field models,* and *pathway representations*. I will show how each one of these types of representation can work to open up and support discursive and practical re-orientation toward dynamic possibilities in professional-client interaction. I will conclude the chapter with a discussion of possible transitions and iterative movement between the contextualized-emic, the decontextualized-etic, and the recontextualized-prospective modes of representation and writing, arguing for a politics of deliberative shifts in representation.

FROM EMIC TO ETIC

The conceptual pair of emic and etic was initially coined by Pike (1954). He pointed out that the study of phonemics involves examination of the sounds used in a particular language, while phonetics attempts to generalize from studies of individual languages to universals covering all languages. By analogy, emic categories are culturally specific while etic categories are culturally universal.

The shift from the client's contextual and emic account to the professional's decontextualized and etic record may be summarized with the help of Figure 11.1.

	CLIENT'S *EMIC* ORAL ACCOUNT	⟹	PROFESSIONAL'S *ETIC* WRITTEN ACCOUNT
LINGUISTIC PREFERENCE	ACTIVE VERBS		NOMINALIZATIONS, INCLUDING NUMERALLY BASED CATEGORIZATIONS
PURPOSE AND FUNCTION	EXPRESSION OF CONCERN		STABILIZATION
GENERAL QUALITY	CONTEXTUALIZED, EMIC		DECONTEXTUALIZED, ETIC

Figure 11.1. The shift from emic to etic (Berkenkotter & Ravotas, 1997)

Berkenkotter and Ravotas (1997) showed that that nominalizations, such as names of diagnostic categories, play a critical role in the professional's move into the decontextualized mode of etic representation. Mehan (1993) pointed out also the frequent use of numbers, such as test scores, along with and as justification for nominalizations.

The shift summarized in Figure 11.1 serves the purpose of stabilization or "blackboxing controversies" (Berkenkotter & Ravotas, 1997, p. 258). It turns the client's idiosyncratic worries into a billable diagnosis that can be quickly and efficiently referenced and included in statistics.

It is also fairly common that professional communities develop sweepingly general "insider" categories to label problematic cases. Examples include the category "GROP patients" (Getting Rid of Patients) observed by Terry Mizrahi (1985) in hospitals and the category of "heartsink patients" (O'Dowd, 1988; Moscrop, 2011) widely used among general practitioners in the UK.

POSSIBILITY KNOWLEDGE AND POSSIBILIZATION

There is little literature on possibility knowledge or possibilistic thinking. A recent paper by the management scholars Matthew Grimes and Timothy Vogus (2021) is an exception. These authors define possibilistic thinking as "a cognitive practice which . . . involves the systematic deconstruction and interrogation of the assumptions upon which existing solutions are based as well as the subsequent development of new 'worlds'" (Grimes & Vogus, 2021, p. 2). As this definition does not clearly distinguish possibilistic thinking from other kinds of creative thought, it needs to be elaborated and specified further.

In interactions between professionals and clients, possibility knowledge or possibilization as a mode of representation depicts the client's possible movement from their past and current positions toward a radically empowered position in which the client has a qualitatively different grasp of their activity. This emphasis on putting the object (client's situation or position) into movement stems from the object-oriented stance of cultural-historical activity theory and from Lev Vygotsky's dynamic conception of the zone of proximal development as a zone of possibilities (Sannino & Engeström, 2018). The first step toward possibilization understood in this way often requires breaking away from a closed category whose inhabitants are doomed to stigma, stagnation, and marginality (Engeström, 1996).

To achieve possibility knowledge, one needs a new instrumentality, or a new politics of representation, to use Mehan's (1993) terminology. The core of such a new instrumentality consists of representations of transitions across the past, the present, and the future. The transitions are understood as actions taken by the client and by those involved in shaping the client's services. Tracing and projecting transitions destabilizes knowledge, puts it in movement, and opens up possibilities (Engeström, 2007). This concept of possibility knowledge has subsequently been utilized by Martin Kramer (2018), Kristiina Kumpulainen et al. (2018), Anna Rainio and Riikka Hoffman (2021), Helena Thuneberg et al. (2014), and Keiko Yasukawa et al. (2014), among others.

Transitions and projected actions can be depicted in multiple ways. In the following, I discuss three alternatives. The first type is written agreements negotiated between the professional and the client. An example of this is the mobility agreement developed in the home care services for the elderly in Helsinki, Finland. The second type is four-field models that depict zones of proximal development for an activity. An example of this is the recent interventionist research on expansive learning among preservice bilingual teachers conducted in New York. The third type is pathway representations. The example is homelessness pathways developed in ongoing interventionist studies on the eradication of homelessness in Finland, conducted by Annalisa Sannino's RESET research group.

WRITTEN AGREEMENTS

Among elderly home care clients, the loss of physical mobility is a central factor behind the erosion of agency and increasing social exclusion. Interventions aimed at maintaining and improving the clients' mobility are therefore very important as possible sources of revitalized agency. However, maintaining and improving the physical mobility of the client is commonly not part of the daily tasks of home care services. The elderly home care client's possibilities of improving their physical mobility are thus usually left unexplored.

Within our project "Preventing social exclusion among the elderly in home care in the City of Helsinki," researchers and practitioners developed a new instrument named the Mobility Agreement (Nummijoki & Engeström, 2009). The Mobility Agreement is aimed at contributing to the home care client's functional capacity and physical mobility through physical actions planned and executed with the support of the home care worker. Jointly negotiated and approved by the home care client and the home care worker, the Mobility Agreement facilitates the initiation, follow-up and evaluation of regular physical exercises embedded in the daily chores of the client's life at home. As an artifact, the Mobility Agreement is a printed form which the client and the worker together fill with an assessment of the client's condition and a plan of specific mobility exercises to be performed by the client either jointly with the worker or alone. The agreement is supported by an illustrated booklet that graphically displays and explains a variety of possible exercises. Today the Mobility Agreement is systematically implemented in the municipal home care services of Helsinki, and its implementation has been analyzed in a number of studies (Engeström et al., 2012; Engeström et al., 2015; Nummijoki et al., 2018).

I will examine the possibilization potential of the Mobility Agreement with the help of two cases. In the first case, the client was an 86-year old woman. The client felt that her mobility had deteriorated, and due to dizziness, and she did not dare to walk alone outside her home. The client had a Mobility Agreement according to which her mobility was systematically supported by means of taking the trash out together with the visiting home care worker. In this visit, the client and the home care worker took the trash out together. After that, the client and the home care worker had a lengthy conversation about the client's life and care. Toward the end of the conversation, the home care worker took up the taking out of the trash.

> **Home care worker**: Yes, and then there is the taking out of the trash bag every time the home care visits you. Do you at least in that situation go out and move? Each time when home care visits, do you take out the trash bag with them?
>
> **Client**: No, I don't. They have taken it themselves.
>
> **Home care worker**: Oh really. Somebody has taken it out for you?
>
> **Client**: Yes.
>
> Home care worker: Well, well.
>
> **Client**: Many of them have taken it out. The other day I accidentally asked a young guy who brought me the food, I asked if he would take out the trash bags. He said that it is not their job. It might not be, indeed.

Home care worker: No, it is not their job, they just take care of the meals.

Client: I said sorry about that.

Home care worker: But it would be good for you to always go with them to take [the trash bags] out. It does not take a long time.

Client: Yes, I have taken it occasionally, then some relative may come to visit and ask if I have any trash. I say look around if there is any.

Home care worker: Well, . . . we have agreed that we won't go and take out just one old newspaper. But it would be good to keep it regular, so that even if the home care worker offers to take out [the trash bag], you just say that let us go together.

Client: That is right, yes.

Home care worker: So you get to go out a little.

The exchange was important in that the trash bag triggered a critical examination of the actual practice in relation to the mutually accepted Mobility Agreement. The critique concerned both the home care workers and the client who had failed to implement the regularity principle of the agreement: "even if the home care worker offers to take out [the trash bag], you just say that let us go together" (home care worker). In other words, the worker and the client revitalized or "rewrote" the agreement so as to become a practically effective tool instead of perpetuating a challenging rule This volitional action of joint commitment was grounded in the preceding joint physical action of actually taking out the trash bag together.

In my second case, the client was a 75-year old woman. She felt that her condition was relatively poor, whereas the home care worker saw her condition in more positive terms. The client took care of smaller daily chores but needed help in bigger tasks. The client had a Mobility Agreement, constructed to support the client's volitional actions to maintain and develop her mobility. The visit was focused on the assessment of the implementation of the agreement as well as to further planning and introduction of useful mobility exercises.

Home care worker: Well, right. Now that you have made this Mobility Agreement, you have agreed . . . that you will try to take care of washing clothes, washing dishes, and cooking yourself also in the future. Isn't that so? . . . You didn't agree to conduct other exercises besides these everyday chores?

Client: No.

> **Home care worker**: Right. So this is based on the idea that we won't wash dishes for you. Is that so?
>
> **Client**: Yes.

The home care worker asked the client to test if she could stand up from the chair five times. The client was able to complete the exercise two times. The home care worker then introduced the exercise booklet to the client.

> **Home care worker**: Did you discuss with Sarah [another home care worker] these exercise programs [shows the exercise booklet attached to the Mobility Agreement]?
>
> **Client**: No, we did not.
>
> **Home care worker**: The idea of these is that we try to repeat on a daily basis these exercises, and that way to maintain and improve your mobility. Are you interested in this?
>
> **Client**: Yes, I am interested. But I cannot carry out all of them.
>
> **Home care worker**: Yes, and probably it would not be wise either. And it is by no means a good idea to start doing them alone. But would you be ready to add a few of these [into your Mobility Agreement]? So that when you have a good day and you feel energetic, we will do a few of these to improve your balance and the strength of your arms.

The home care worker and the client proceeded to test physically some of the other exercises. At the end of this, the home care worker asked if the client would like to keep the exercise booklet.

> **Home care worker**: Would you like me to leave this [the exercise booklet] with you?
>
> **Client**: Yes.
>
> **Home care worker**: Well, I leave this with you, so you can study it yourself. But this contains also these [exercises] which ask you to stand and move your feet, don't do them yet at this point because your balance may not hold. These can be taken into your program later, these in which you do not really lean on anything.

In this encounter, the Mobility Agreement was revisited, assessed, amended, and tested in volitional physical actions. The previously constructed written agreement was now extended to include the printed exercise booklet that the client could use at her own convenience. The home care worker made a focused effort at conceptualizing the idea of the Mobility Agreement practice.

Home care worker: And now you of course wonder what this is and what is the purpose of all this. The purpose is to try and maintain your mobility, perhaps even improve it a bit, but above all so that you can live in your own home as long as you want, and get by in your own home. Of course we would wash your dishes faster, but the point is to maintain the mobility and control of your own hands.

This case further exemplifies the importance of continuous critique, renegotiation, and rewriting of the agreement. Clearly possibilization is not a one-off event, and the representational artifacts that serve possibilization are not static or closed. Future is a moving target, not a fixed end point.

The mobility agreement is built on explicit written *commitments* to perform concrete actions. In the first case, the home care worker and the client revived the commitment to regularly take out the trash in a collaborative way so that the client would also take a walk outside the home. In the second case, the worker and the client committed to expand the client's mobility exercises by studying the exercise booklet and selecting appropriate exercises to be included in the Mobility Agreement.

The cases also indicate that writing for possibilization may be best understood as a multimodal achievement. Ed Hutchins (2005) points out that multimodal representations are likely to become more robust than single-mode ones. Multimodal integration may be accomplished by embedding the representations in durable material media, or "material anchors" (Hutchins, 2005, p. 1555), such as the trash bag in the first case and the illustrated exercise booklet in the second case. Another way to accomplish multimodal integration is to enact representations in bodily movements, turning such bodily movements into "somatic anchors" for concepts and texts (Hutchins, 2010, p. 445).

FOUR-FIELD MODELS

We conducted an intervention study at a public primary health care center in Finland in 2004–2005. The center was new, and its chief physician wanted to do something about the care of difficult patients. He suggested that the staff should aim at working with "two pipelines," one for common one-problem patients, the other one for difficult patients, such as those with multiple chronic illnesses, addictions, multiple medications, mental health problems, etc. Patients put into the second pipeline should be investigated, conceptualized and new tools for their care should be developed. My research team began to follow patients identified by the practitioners as potentially difficult. We interviewed these patients, observed their consultations, and eventually brought them into so-called laboratory sessions with the staff, to discuss their needs and services. All these interactions were recorded.

One of our initial findings was that the patient and the professional caregiver often saw the situation in radically different light. What was a "heartsink case" for the practitioner may have been a first ray of hope for the patient.

> **General practitioner**: She is a red flag to me, and I'd rather hand her over to someone else, redirect her elsewhere, for example to the psychiatric clinic. But they won't take her because she wants medicine but not therapy. She needs more and gets less; she is the last one I'd like to talk with.
>
> **Patient**: This personal general practitioner of mine, she really cares for me. This is the first time I get this feeling that she not only renews my prescription but also demands that I come to consultation and says it firmly. Now of course even more firmly, but it does help me!

It became clear to us that the construction of the patient is a two-dimensional achievement. On the one hand, the client or the patient herself may be active or passive in helping herself. On the other hand, the network of professional caregivers may be active or passive in collaborating and coordinating their efforts. With these two dimensions, we put together a four-field diagram in which we could depict the possible movement of the patient. Figure 11.2 depicts this co-constructed movement. The upper arrow represents the movement of the professionals as seen by the patient; the lower arrow represents the movement of the patient as seen by the professionals.

The use of this representation had consequences when patients began to reflect on their life and care with the help of this instrument. Here is an example from such a session with a patient who was initially considered very difficult in that she would cling to the practitioners and become dependent on their constant attention.

> **Family guidance worker**: Well, I'd like to ask if it is useful to meet again in this combination, or shall we continue each one? So that we'll carry on with Vera in the Family Guidance Clinic, and—
>
> **Patient**: I think probably no. At least now I don't feel that this is necessary. Because *everyone* has now been in a couple of these meetings and knows where we stand. So I can be in touch, tell you if something big and radical happens. And how each one of

you can help if it is close to your profession. This sounds funny, but this is how I think. Or what do you think?

Child welfare supervisor: Your idea sounds good to me, that you don't want to cling to us after all.

Patient: Exactly. Because it helps me forward this way.

Family guidance worker: These are big issues, yes.

Patient: About that model, if you want my comment, it seemed pretty utopian when you started making it. But now that I look at it, it kind of pulls me better into life. I mean, this is how it goes, or how it must go, normally. It's been a long time, about ten years, since I've been working, so I've lost touch with development. I have adapted, accepted things as they are. I haven't realized that there may be something else. I mean, normal work and life and such. So that was a pretty good move. When you see it there in front of us, it makes things concrete. It sticks. It would be good to get a copy.

Researcher: Yeah, I'll take a photo and send it to you by email. And a copy will be delivered home to you [the patient].

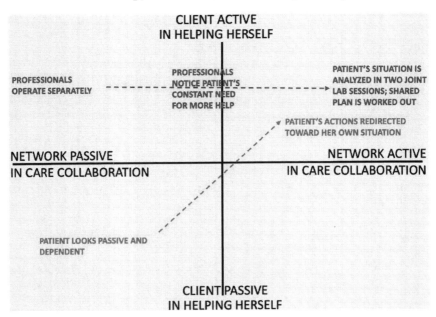

Figure 11.2. Four-field model for depicting the zone of possibilities for the patient and her caregivers (Engeström, 2007, p. 274)

Four-field models have subsequently been used in many formative Change Laboratory (CL) interventions around the world (for the theory and methodology of CL, see Sannino et al., 2016). Sharon Chang's recent work on Chinese and Korean preservice bilingual teachers provides an interesting example (Chang, 2021; see also Chang et al., 2021). In her study, the preservice bilingual teachers had the position of clients as broadly understood in the present analysis, while the instructors of the bilingual teacher education program represented the professionals. In the four-field model co-constructed in Chang's study, the horizontal axis represented a continuum from teacher as assimilator to teachers and students as advocates (in terms of bilingual teacher beliefs and philosophical stance). The vertical axis denoted a continuum from decontextualized learning to contextualized learning (in terms of bilingual curriculum design and pedagogical decisions). The CL participants visualized their growth as both teachers and learners by moving within the four quadrants and using their experience to collectively form new concepts and discover potential solutions together. Chang characterizes the functioning of the four-field model as follows:

> The four-field model allowed the CL participants to express their understandings regarding their experiences in their day-to-day practice and articulate the ways this situated activity was tied to the historical contradictions and structural barriers in bilingual education. The participants then considered how they could respond to their own conflicting motives. In this context, the four-field model provided a visual-spatial heuristic scaffolding tool that allowed the teacher educator to understand the preservice teachers' future-oriented actions. (Chang, 2021, p. 227)

Each student teacher produced an individual four-field model by reflecting on one's experiences of teaching in bilingual classroom placements. Each student-teacher marked their own position in the diagram once a week for six times. This way each student's completed four-field depicted a trajectory of movement and development over time. Each week the marking in the model was complemented by written comments in a four-field model worksheet. These reflections were shared and discussed among the participants:

> The CL participants demonstrated movement in their individually-generated four-field model away from blaming the existing challenges and restrictions and towards creative and active problem solving in bilingual education to better meet the needs of English language learners. Using the individually-generated

four-field model, the CL participants collectively reflected on how to transform their current circumstances to become culturally responsive bilingual teachers. (Chang, 2021, p. 233)

Figure 11.3 depicts the completed individual four-field model of one student, Joy. The numbers indicate the dates of the weekly markings. Chang points out that Joy moved back from November 4 to November 18 on the horizontal X-axis before reaching the upper right-hand quadrant on November 25, focusing on making bilingual learning more equitable for her English language learners.

Joy herself commented on the zig-zag movement depicted in Figure 11.3 as follows:

> At first, when I saw that I stayed at the same spot after a week in the field, I was panicking and I thought: "Why didn't I make any change (or even [went] back) for this week?" and I felt really bad. But after [the professor] said that it is totally okay to be back and forth, I got the point. Learning is never a direct path, and in the way of being a good teacher, it is OK to come across some rubs. Therefore, the four-field model and trajectory are like a guidance for me, to make me reflect on myself at a certain part of time, thinking where I can be better. I think that's the meaning of it. (Joy, Four-Field Model Worksheet)

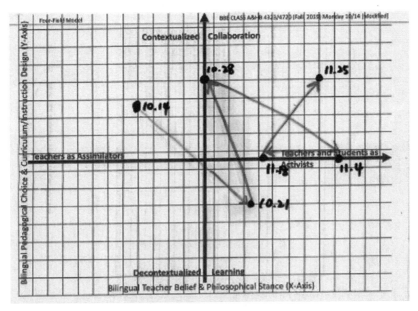

Figure 11.3. Joy's individually generated four-field model (Chang, 2021, p. 239)

The two examples discussed in this section show that four-field models require and serve the purpose of *envisioning* the direction of development needed to break out of a paralyzing conflict of motives (Sannino, 2015). At the same time, these models and the written reflections attached to them allow both clients and professionals to trace the stepwise and typically non-linear progression of opening up a new field of possibilities.

The axes of a four-field model are attempts to capture societally critical dimensions of development in an activity. The stepwise movement depicted in the four-field reflects individual and collaborative efforts to understand the past and design the possible future of an individual client and the practitioners working with her or him. Thus, a four-field model is aimed at bringing together the political and the personal.

PATHWAY REPRESENTATIONS

Pathway representations are prominent in health care. The term "care pathway" or "clinical pathway" is internationally accepted in healthcare management. A clinical pathway is a method for managing the care of a well-defined group of patients during a well-defined period of time. Aimed at increasing efficiency in the use of resources by coordinating the roles and sequencing the actions of the different caregivers, a clinical pathway explicitly states the goals and main steps of care. Deviations from the pathway are documented and evaluated as variances.

As *normative* guidelines care pathways represent a step beyond the *etic* approach to documentation discussed by Berkenkotter and Ravotas (1997). A care pathway tells how the professionals *should proceed* with the patient. Documentation is reserved for deviations to be corrected (Allen, 2009; Martin et al., 2017; Pinder et al., 2005).

In studies of homelessness, the notion of pathway has a different meaning. A homelessness pathway describes a *typical trajectory* into, through and possibly out of homelessness. Anderson and Tulloch defined a homelessness pathway as a description of "the route of an individual or household into homelessness, their experience of homelessness and their route out of homelessness into secure housing" (2000, p. 11).

Classifications of homelessness pathways are meant to be *descriptive,* not normative. As such, they are meant to help practitioners and policy makers to understand varieties of homelessness and to identify priorities for counteracting or reducing homelessness. Table 11.1 summarizes a few examples of classifying homelessness pathways in recent research literature.

Table 11.1. Examples of Categorization of Homelessness Pathways

Kostiainen (2015): THREE PATHWAYS: (1) transitionally homeless people whose pathways lead to stable housing after an episode of homelessness; (2) homeless people with insecure housing careers; (3) disadvantaged homeless people who rely on homeless services
Chamberlain & Johnson (2011): FIVE PATHWAYS: (1) housing crisis; (2) family breakdown; (3) substance abuse; (4) mental health; (5) youth to adult
Fitzpatrick et al. (2013): FIVE PATHWAYS: (1) mainly homeless; (2) homelessness and mental health; (3) homelessness, mental health, and victimization; (4) homelessness and street drinking; (5) homelessness, hard drugs, and high complexity
Sunikka (2016): FOUR PATHWAYS: (1) the pathway to dwelling population; (2) the pathway leading to back and forth movement between homelessness and dwelling; (3) the pathway to homelessness; (4) the pathway to death
Wiesel (2014): FOUR PATHWAYS: (1) hectic private rental pathways; (2) pathways of homelessness; (3) pathways out of homeownership; (4) repeat moves in and out of social housing

As may be seen in Table 11.1, homelessness pathways have been primarily constructed on the basis of statistical or interview data concerning "typical" background factors and critical steps or turning points of homelessness in a given population. This way pathways become categories or taxonomies of different "typical" clusters, profiles or chains of factors that often lead to homelessness. Such categories are inherently *top-down abstractions*. Real individual people seldom if ever match fully a single prototypical pathway. Pathways experienced by real people are heterogenous hybrids. This means that the predominant pathway categories are problematic if used as practitioners' tools for diagnosing, predicting, and planning steps or actions for specific clients. To use the available pathway categories this way, one has to force an individual client to match a predetermined pathway. Elements of this critique have been voiced by some scholars:

> Analyzing homelessness as subgroups or as sets of pathways provides one way to try to tackle this issue, as it breaks homelessness up into more manageable conceptual chunks. However, taxonomies always have some element of compromise; there are "boundary" cases that could go into one category or another, and decisions about the criteria used to identify each subgroup and whether it represents a robust basis for analysis are rarely straightforward . . . Building clear and consistent pathways or subgroups is likely to be difficult in a data-rich environment with a wide definition of homelessness. Recent work from the US has shown how adding new data can disrupt taxonomies that were assumed to be relatively robust. (Pleace, 2016, p. 30)

Writing for Stabilization and Writing for Possibility

Frontline work with homelessness—both preventive and rehabilitative—operates with specific individuals. Practitioners need to understand the life courses of homeless people and people at the risk of becoming homeless—as well as the courses of actions taken by service providers and professionals. For this purpose, we need a radically different type of homelessness pathways. They need to be jointly constructed by a practitioner and a client. They need to capture essential steps and features of the particular client's life course and of the courses of action taken by professionals dealing with the client. And they need to be constructed with the help of standard building blocks—a common vocabulary—so that they can be easily compared and critical phases and issues can be identified to enable intervention and transformation of practices.

This challenge was taken up in a CL intervention conducted by the research team of Annalisa Sannino in 2019 in Helsinki. In this CL, 27 homelessness professionals representing Finnish ministries, cities, and NGOs, supported by three researchers, analyzed the state of efforts to eliminate homelessness in the nation and designed an action program named *Housing First 2.0* to move these efforts to the next stage. In one of the sessions of the CL, the participants were asked to read two concise autobiographical accounts of homelessness by Mikko and Tomi, which was recently published in a book of interviews titled *Faces: Stories of Homelessness* (Pyyvaara & Timonen, 2017). The participants were asked to construct homelessness pathways for Mikko and Tomi, using a notational template given by the researchers (Figure 11.4). The participants were asked to analyze what should have been done or needs to be done differently and by whom in these cases.

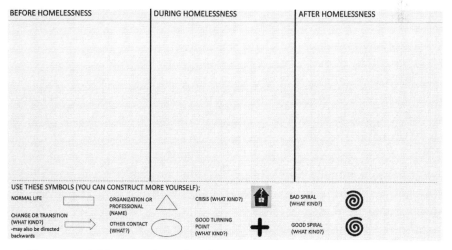

Figure 11.4. Notational template for constructing homelessness pathways for possibilization

Engeström

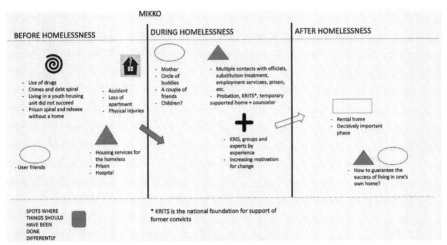

Figure 11.5. A CL participant's representation of Mikko's homelessness pathway

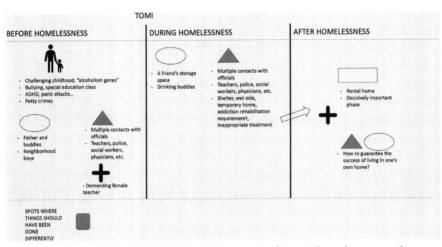

Figure 11.6. A CL participant's representation of Tomi's homelessness pathway

The template moves in time from the situation before homelessness into the situation during homelessness and after homelessness. The idea is to capture and represent a homeless person's trajectory as they experience it, including anticipated future steps and actions. In the next session of the CL, the participants presented and compared their pathway representations. Figures 11.5 and 11.6 depict one participant's pathway representations for Mikko and Tomi.

Overall, the participants found the proposed template and symbols easy to use. Many of them generated additional symbols. In Figure 11.6, the very first symbol was added by the participant. It represents Tomi's childhood and family situation.

Writing for Stabilization and Writing for Possibility

One of the participants, a manager of supported housing for formerly homeless clients run by a major NGO, took the assignment to a group of clients. These clients were residents of a supported housing unit, with a background of lengthy periods of homelessness. Working in pairs, members of this group produced their own solutions to the assignment. Figure 11.7 is a photo of one of the resulting representations.

Notable in Figure 11.7 is the detailed elaboration of symbols. The authors of this representation added symbols for the hospital, for the prison, for drugs, for social security benefits, for the adjustment of debts, and for several other components in pathways of Mikko and Tomi, including "memories of a bad adolescence."

The experience gained in the CL indicates that this kind of representation of homelessness pathways is a potentially powerful tool in the service of analysis and *forward-oriented planning* conducted in dialogue and negotiation between a client and a professional. It seems particularly apt to serve as an instrument of *criticism of past failures* or mistakes that can be turned into poignant plans for and commitments to near-future emancipatory actions.

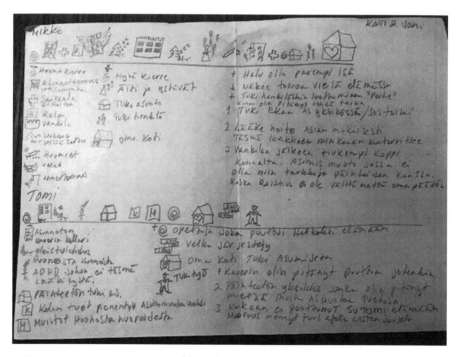

Figure 11.7. Representation of homelessness pathways produced by a pair of formerly homeless residents of a supported housing unit

The manipulability and malleability of the symbols in the template is an important characteristic of this instrument of possibilization. Writing is here intimately intertwined with pictorial representation and the possibility of playing with alternative material symbols and their positions. The pathway representation affords a degree of *decontextualization* in the sense of representing uniquely personal experiences with the help of general symbols, and *recontextualization* in the sense of building a tailor-made trajectory that is meaningful and challenging for both the client and for the system of services. The idea of this kind of a pathway representation echoes an observation made by Bazerman a few years ago: "models are for users rather than analysts and are invoked situationally and mutably" (2018, p. 301).

CONCLUSION: TOWARD A POLITICS OF DELIBERATIVE REPRESENTATIONAL SHIFTS

The idea of possibilization advocated here is based on Vygotsky's dialectical insight into human empowerment:

> The person, using the power of things or stimuli, controls his own behavior through them, grouping them, putting them together, sorting them. In other words, the great uniqueness of the will consists of man having no power over his own behavior other than the power that things have over his behavior. But man subjects to himself the power of things over behavior, makes them serve his own purposes and controls that power as he wants. He changes the environment with the external activity and in this way affects his own behavior, subjecting it to his own authority. (1997, p. 212)

We may now return to the initial distinction Berkenkotter and Ravotas (1997) made between *emic* and *etic* representation, summarized in Figure 11.1. In Figure 11.8, this summary is extended to include jointly constructed dynamic texts and models that serve possibilization.

	CLIENT'S *EMIC* ORAL ACCOUNT	PROFESSIONAL'S *ETIC* WRITTEN ACCOUNT	JOINTLY CONSTRUCTED *DYNAMIC* TEXT AND MODEL
LINGUISTIC PREFERENCE	ACTIVE VERBS	NOMINALIZATIONS, INCLUDING NUMERALLY BASED CATEGORIZATIONS	COMMISSIVES, PROJECTIONS AND TRAJECTORIES
PURPOSE AND FUNCTION	EXPRESSION OF CONCERN	STABILIZATION	POSSIBILIZATION
GENERAL QUALITY	CONTEXTUALIZED, EMIC	DECONTEXTUALIZED, ETIC	RECONTEXTUALIZED, PROSPECTIVE

Figure 11.8. Three forms of representation in professional-client interactions

Figure 11.8 implies the possibility of developing a politics of representation that does not stop with *etic* records but makes deliberate shifts to possibilization. Such a politics of representational shifts can only be accomplished in a deliberative way, understood as "involving careful thought and discussion when making decision" (*The Cambridge English Dictionary*).

It is unlikely that the shifts can be made in a linear fashion. Figure 11.9 depicts the shifts between the three kinds of representation in the case of the Mobility Agreement for home care clients, discussed earlier. In this case, the possibilization instrument is invoked as the second step, after the client's oral *emic* account. The *etic* record is commonly generated partly on the basis of the Mobility Agreement, as the third step. Most importantly, the practical implementation of the agreement involves renegotiation and often significant extension of the agreement, giving the process an iterative and cyclic pattern.

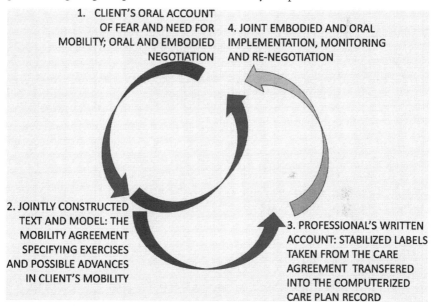

Figure 11.9. The iterative pattern of politics of representation in the case of the Mobility Agreement

Studies and practical projects of participatory and deliberative democracy (Elstub, 2018; Lafont, 2019) usually focus on relatively large collective forms of shaping policies and making decisions, participatory budgeting being a good example (Meléndez, 2021). While extremely valuable, these projects often remain exceptional deviations from life as usual. On the other hand, encounters between relatively powerless lay clients and relatively powerful professionals, often representing governmental and legal apparatuses, are very common in life as usual. When professionals start building practices of possibilization with individual clients, they will generate important groundwork and the impetus of learning for transformative agency. Such initially individual or dyadic forms of seeing and enacting possibilities can eventually translate into increasingly powerful collective initiatives toward participatory and deliberative democracy.

REFERENCES

Allen, D. (2014). Lost in translation? 'Evidence'and the articulation of institutional logics in integrated care pathways: From positive to negative boundary object? *Sociology of Health & Illness, 36*(6), 807–822.

Anderson, I. & Tulloch, D. (2000). *Pathways through homelessness: A review of the research evidence.* Scottish Homes

Bazerman, C. (1997). Discursively structured activities. *Mind, Culture, and Activity, 4*(4), 296–308.

Bazerman, C. (2018). What does a model model? And for whom? *Educational Psychologist, 53*(4), 301–318.

Berkenkotter, C. & Ravotas, D. (1997). Genre as tool in the transmission of practice over time and across professional boundaries. *Mind, Culture, and Activity, 4*(4), 256–274.

Chamberlain, C. & Johnson, G. (2011). Pathways into adult homelessness. *Journal of Sociology, 49*(1), 60–77.

Chang, S. (2021). Supporting expansive learning in preservice bilingual teachers' zone of proximal development of the activity system: An analysis of a four-field model trajectory. *Professional Development in Education.* https://doi.org/10.1080/19415257.2021.1879232.

Chang, S., Martínez-Roldán, C. M. & Torres-Guzmán, M. E. (2021). The manifestation of Chinese preservice bilingual teachers' relational agency in a Change Laboratory intervention. *Mind, Culture, and Activity.* https://doi.org/10.1080/10749039.2021.1881125.

Elstub, S. (2018). Deliberative and participatory democracy. In A. Bächtiger, J. S., Dryzek, J. Mansbridge & M. E. Warren (Eds.), *The Oxford handbook of deliberative democracy* (pp. 187–202). Oxford University Press.

Engeström, Y. (1996). Development as breaking away and opening up: A challenge to Vygotsky and Piaget. *Swiss Journal of Psychology, 55,* 126–132.

Engeström, Y. (2007). From stabilization knowledge to possibility knowledge in organizational learning. *Management Learning, 38*(3), 271–275.

Engeström, Y., Kajamaa, A. & Nummijoki, J. (2015). Double stimulation in everyday work: Critical encounters between home care workers and their elderly clients. *Learning, Culture and Social Interaction, 4,* 48–61.

Engeström, Y., Nummijoki, J. & Sannino, A. (2012). Embodied germ cell at work: Building an expansive concept of physical mobility in home care. *Mind, Culture, and Activity, 19*(3), 287–309.

Epstein, M. (2019). *A philosophy of the possible: Modalities in thought and culture.* Brill.

Fitzpatrick, S., Bramley, G. & Johnsen, S. (2013). Pathways into multiple exclusion homelessness in seven UK cities. *Urban Studies*, *50*(1), 148–168.

Grimes, M. G. & Vogus, T. J. (2021). Inconceivable! Possibilistic thinking and the sociocognitive underpinnings of entrepreneurial responses to grand challenges. *Organization Theory*, *2*(2).

Hutchins, E. (2005). Material anchors for conceptual blends. *Journal of Pragmatics*, *37*(10), 1555–1577.

Hutchins, E. (2010). Enaction, imagination, and insight. In J. Stewart, O. Gapenne & E. A. Di Paolo (Eds.), *Enaction: Toward a new paradigm for cognitive science* (pp. 425–450). MIT Press.

Kostiainen, E. (2015). Pathways through homelessness in Helsinki. *European Journal of Homelessness*, *9*(2), 63–86.

Kramer, M. (2018). Promoting teachers' agency: Reflective practice as transformative disposition. *Reflective Practice*, *19*(2), 211–224.

Kumpulainen, K., Kajamaa, A. & Rajala, A. (2018). Understanding educational change: Agency-structure dynamics in a novel design and making environment. *Digital Education Review*, (33), 26–38.

Lafont, C. (2019). *Democracy without shortcuts: A participatory conception of deliberative democracy*. Oxford University Press.

Martin, G. P., Kocman, D., Stephens, T., Peden, C. J. & Pearse, R. M. (2017). Pathways to professionalism? Quality improvement, care pathways, and the interplay of standardisation and clinical autonomy. *Sociology of Health & Illness*, *39*(8), 1314–1329.

Mehan, H. (1993). Beneath the skin and between the ears: A case study in the politics of representation. In S. Chaiklin & J. Lave (Eds.), *Understanding practice: Perspectives on activity and context* (pp. 241–268). Cambridge University Press.

Meléndez, J. W. (2021). Latino immigrants in civil society: Addressing the double-bind of participation for expansive learning in participatory budgeting. *Journal of the Learning Sciences*, *30*(1), 76–102.

Mizrahi, T. (1985). Getting rid of patients: Contradictions in the socialization of internists to the doctor-patient relationship. *Sociology of Health & Illness*, *7*(2), 214–235.

Moscrop, A. (2011). 'Heartsink' patients in general practice: A defining paper, its impact, and psychodynamic potential. *British Journal of General Practice*, *61*(586), 346–348.

Nummijoki, J. & Engeström, Y. (2009). Towards co-configuration in home care of the elderly: Cultivating agency by designing and implementing the mobility agreement. In H. Daniels, A. Edwards, Y. Engeström, T. Gallagher & S. R. Ludvigsen (Eds.), *Activity theory in practice: Promoting learning across boundaries and agencies* (pp. 49–71). Routledge.

Nummijoki, J., Engeström, Y. & Sannino, A. (2018). Defensive and expansive cycles of learning: A study of home care encounters. *Journal of the Learning Sciences*, *27*(2), 224–264.

O'Dowd, T. C. (1988). Five years of heartsink patients in general practice. *British Medical Journal*, *297*(6647), 528–530.

Pike, K. (1954). *Language in relation to a unified theory of the structure of human behavior*. Summer Institute of Linguistics.

Pinder, R., Petchey, R., Shaw, S. & Carter, Y. (2005). What's in a care pathway? Towards a cultural cartography of the new NHS. *Sociology of Health & Illness, 27*(6), 759–779.

Pleace, N. (2016). Researching homelessness in Europe: Theoretical perspectives. *European Journal of Homelessness, 10*(3), 19–44.

Pyyvaara, U. & Timonen, A. (2017). *Naamat: Tarinoita asunnottomuudesta*. Into Kustannus.

Rainio, A. P. & Hofmann, R. (2021). Teacher professional dialogues during a school intervention: From stabilization to possibility discourse through reflexive noticing. *Journal of the Learning Sciences, 30(4–5), 707–746.*

Sannino, A. (2015). The principle of double stimulation: A path to volitional action. *Learning, Culture and Social Interaction*, 6, 1–15.

Sannino, A. (2022). Transformative agency as warping: How collectives accomplish change amidst uncertainty. *Pedagogy, Culture & Society, 30*(1), 9–33.

Sannino, A. & Engeström, Y. (2018). Cultural-historical activity theory: Founding insights and new challenges. *Cultural-Historical Psychology, 14*(3), 43–56.

Sannino, A., Engeström, Y. & Lemos, M. (2016). Formative interventions for expansive learning and transformative agency. *Journal of the Learning Sciences, 25*(4), 599–633.

Smith, B. C. (1996). *On the origin of objects*. The MIT Press.

Sunikka, S. (2016). *Hietsussa yöpyneiden asunnottomuuspolut: Liikkuvuus asunnottomuuden ja asuntoväestön välillä*. Licentiate thesis. University of Helsinki, Faculty of Social Sciences.

Thuneberg, H., Hautamäki, J., Ahtiainen, R., Lintuvuori, M., Vainikainen, M. P. & Hilasvuori, T. (2014). Conceptual change in adopting the nationwide special education strategy in Finland. *Journal of Educational Change, 15*(1), 37–56.

Vygotsky, L. S. (1997). The history of development of higher mental functions, Chapter 12: Self-control. In R. W. Rieber (Ed.), *The collected works of L.S. Vygotsky: The history of the development of higher mental functions, 4* (pp. 207–219). Plenum.

Wiesel, I. (2014). Mobilities of disadvantage: The housing pathways of low-income Australians. *Urban Studies, 51*(2), 319–334.

Yasukawa, K., Brown, T. & Black, S. (2014). Disturbing practices: Training workers to be lean. *Journal of Workplace Learning, 26*(67), 392–405.

PART FIVE. WRITING RESEARCH DEVELOPMENT

CHAPTER 12.

A REVIEW ON SECOND LANGUAGE WRITING RESEARCH IN CHINA

Wu Dan and Li Zenghui
Xi'an International Studies University

Second language or SL/L2, is the language that people learn in addition to their native tongue(s) or any language whose acquisition starts after early childhood, including what is chronologically the third or subsequent language. The language to be learned is often referred to as the "target language" or "L2." From the broad sense, second language in the West includes foreign language (Ellis, 2008). From the narrow sense, second language refers to the language which is acquired in a natural condition after first language has been acquired. In China, English has been a required foreign language to be started from Grade 3 in primary schools, and when we refer to L2 in China, it means English.

Second language writing research can be dated back to the 1960s, which refers to the writer's use of their non-native language, their second language, or a foreign language to write. International second language writing research has matured in the late 20th century and has formed its own theoretical systems such as contrastive rhetoric, research objects such as writers and learners of second language, research methods such as content analysis and research teams such as second language writing teachers and writing research specialists. The study of second language writing was promoted in the US due to the rise of writing studies. And it has gradually developed into a well-defined independent discipline (Kroll, 2003; Silva & Matsuda, 2001) with its feeder disciplines, composition studies and applied linguistics (Silva & Leki, 2004).

However, in China, most L2 writing research and teaching was done by researchers and teachers trained in applied linguistics (Zou, 2016), as the major disciplines associated with L2 writing have been this due to the fact that there is not such a discipline named composition studies in foreign language studies, and the L1 writing studies in Chinese studies mainly refers to Chinese creative writing with a very small section intertwined with journalism in mass media studies. L1 writing studies have also experienced a tremendous development during the past 40 years, and researchers have had some communication and interactions with writing researchers in other countries (Yu, 2021), L1 writing researchers focus mainly on creative writing in Chinese with recent emerging

DOI: https://doi.org/10.37514/PER-B.2023.1800.2.12

areas and topics such as sci-fi, non-fiction writing, and multimedia writing (Fang, 2021). Charles Bazerman was the first international writing researcher to be invited to lecture in College of Chinese Language and Literature in Wuhan University from April 2 to 4 in 2010 and was invited to become an honorary member of The Writing Academy of China, a national Level-1 academic organization (the highest level possible in China). And the next year, 2011, Kexun Yu, the chairman of The Writing Academy of China, and some of his colleagues were invited to the fourth Writing Research Across Borders (WRAB) conference in Washington D.C. and delivered a panel on Chinese writing studies. However, L1 and L2 researchers in China have different focus interests in writing studies, while L1 researchers focus more on creative writing and L2 researchers more on English acquisition issues. The interactions between the two research areas have rarely been found in existing research and literature.

Therefore, L2 writing in China does not have the two parents (composition studies and applied linguistics) as it does in the US (Silva & Leki, 2004). From this perspective, L2 writing in China is actually single parented, which is also closely related to its research characteristics.

Second language writing is a very complicated process, as well as a major difficulty in second language learning. Therefore, it attracts attention from English researchers and teachers. Empirical research on second language writing has been carried out for early half a century, but domestic research in China in this area was started much later. After a steady development of the 1980s, second language writing experienced a period of rapid growth in the 1990s. Since stepping into the new century, the development of second language writing has been flourishing, and both the quantity and the quality of research have increased significantly (Shao, 2013). In particular, some scholars have summarized the research on second language writing of different stages from different angles, such as Yan and Cui (2011), Qin (2009), Huang and Yu (2009), Wang and Sun (2005), Yao and Cheng (2005), Wang and Wang (2004), Li and Li (2003). All these reviews have broadened the research space of the domestic writing field and promoted the further development of writing research to a certain extent.

Previous reviews on second language writing in China mainly dealt with research methods and focus entities (i.e., objects of study). These studies can be divided into four review stages. The first stage of L2 writing reviews were on studies published before 2004 (Yao & Cheng, 2005; Wang & Wang, 2004; Li & Li, 2003), and these reviews all pointed out that L2 writing research in this stage was mainly non-empirical research. The second stage reviews (Zhao et al., 2010; Qin, 2009; Huang & Yu, 2009; Guo, 2009) feature research between 2004 to 2007. Their work showed that the number of empirical studies increased significantly during that period. The third stage was from 2007 to 2010 and involved efforts of He (2013), Liu and Ling (2012), Yan and Cui (2011), Zhu (2011), and Meng (2011), in which the research subjects ended in 2010. The forth showed achievements made by Zhan and Ai (2015), Tan (2014), Zheng et al. (2014), and Luan (2012), in which the papers chosen as reviewed ones were published before 2013.

All the above scholars described the proportion changing of empirical and non-empirical studies in different journals over years. In reviews before 2003, non-empirical studies took an absolute advantage with the proportion of 72.73% (Yao & Cheng, 2005) and 66.9% (Li & Li, 2003) in different databases. Then empirical studies made a forereach with the proportion of 53.71% from 2003 to 2007 (Huang & Yu, 2009). After that, in a review on a database before 2010, empirical research took an absolute advantage with the proportion of 73.2%, and non-empirical research fell to 26.8% (Yan & Cui, 2011). Based on a longer period of reviewed publications, Zhu (2011) got a result that empirical studies (56.81%) were still leading over non-empirical studies (43.19%). Although with differences, it is still obvious that the empirical studies were started later, with a lag from the international trend, but persisted to grow with stronger development until recently.

In China, many experts and scholars have set out to define research methodology (Wang, 2000; Gao, 1999). Gao et al. (1999) classified the research methods of applied linguistics in China into three categories: quantitative studies, qualitative research, and non-empirical research. The first two, which are characterized by systematic, planned collection, and analysis of materials, are collectively referred to as empirical research. The third category, non-empirical research, is not based on the systematic collection of materials, and consists of pure theoretical discussion, including descriptions of teaching and personal experience.

After more than half a century's development, the study of second language writing began to change from non-empirical research to empirically-based research. Of course, in empirical studies qualitative and quantitative have their own characteristics. Therefore, in this study we set out to understand precisely the distribution of qualitative research and quantitative research to add clarity and detail to earlier descriptions of Chinese writing research.

However, it is notable that there are some problems with the retrospective work that is available. Firstly, in terms of research methods, only the changes of numbers of empirical and non-empirical research were counted, and nothing about the quantitative, qualitative, or the mixed methods was analyzed. Secondly, theories adopted by the researchers were not reviewed. Thirdly, as for the focus entities, the ways of the focus entities classification are various and ranges from four kinds to eight kinds. As pointed out by Wang (2013), the study of L2 writing in China is still relatively young. Its theoretical system has not yet been formed, its research methods are still immature, and the focus entities are still unbalanced. Therefore, it is necessary to further improve the quality of research, to expand the scope of research, and to optimize the methods of research.

The present study, based on international research perspectives, reviews articles on English writing published in 11 Chinese Social Sciences Citation Index (CSSCI) foreign language studies journals during 2001–2020. The present study has been conducted to explore the situation of English writing research in China in terms of research methods, research theories, and focus entities by answering the following research questions: (1) Among all of the empirical research published in the 11 surveyed foreign language studies journals during 2001–2020, how do the methods of qualitative, quantitative and mixed distribute and change over years? (2) Among all of the empirical studies, what are the content theories the authors adopted? (3) Among all of the empirical studies, what is the distribution of objects of study in terms of writers, readers, writing, and multiple entities?

METHOD

SELECTION OF PUBLICATIONS TO BE INCLUDED IN THIS STUDY

When selecting journals for reviewing, this study follows the criteria set by Nwogu (1997): representation (a representative readership holds for a particular publication), reputation (the esteem which members of an assumed readership hold for a particular publication) and accessibility (the ease with which texts that constitute the corpus can be obtained). Considering these three significant factors, the journals are chosen from the citation database: Chinese Social Sciences Citation Index (CSSCI), Chinese:中文社会科学引文索引). CSSCI is an interdisciplinary citation index program in China, which is used to search the papers that were embodied and the literature was cited in the Chinese social science field. It was developed by Nanjing University in 1997 and was established in 2000. CSSCI follows the method of bibliometrics, and it takes the method of quantitative and qualitative evaluation to select journals with precise academic and editorial characteristics from more than 2700 journals in humanities and social sciences fields in China. The selected journals can reflect the latest research results in various disciplines of the humanities and social sciences in China, which are the academic journals with the highest quality, the greatest influence, and the most standardized editing and publishing processes. Now many leading Chinese universities and institutes use CSSCI as a one of the standards for evaluating published academic achievements and faculty promotion.

Based on the previous reviews of L2 writing research, this review lays its focus on the progress in numbers of research on L2 writing, the development trends of empirical and non-empirical research, qualitative, quantitative, and mixed methods, the employment of theories adopted and the distribution of focus entities in research articles published in 11 CSSCI foreign language journals: *Foreign Language World* (《外语界》), *Computer-assisted Foreign Language Education* (《外语电化教学》), *Foreign Language Learning Theory and Practice* (《外语教学理论与实践》), *Foreign Languages in China* (《中国外语》), *Modern Foreign Languages* (《现代外语》), *Foreign Languages and Their Teaching* (《外语与外语教学》), *Foreign Language Education* (《外语教学》), *Foreign Language Teaching and Research* (《外语教学与研究》), *Foreign Languages Research* (《外语研究》), *Journal of Foreign Languages* (《外国语》) and *Chinese Translators Journal* (《中国翻译》) from 2007 to 2020.

These 11 journals are all leading journals in foreign language research in China and are considered to have high prestige in the academic community, meeting the requirements of representation and reputation. And speaking of accessibility, these 11 journals are all accessible in CNKI (China National Knowledge Infrastructure). It's necessary to point out that there are other journals that also publish articles on second language writing. The reason for selecting these 11 CSSCI journals was to obtain the results from the most representative journals in foreign language research field in China. The authors collected a total number of 30,810 articles published in these 11 CSSCI foreign language journals from 2001 to 2020. And out of these 30,810 articles, 1,012 are on or about second language writing.

RESULTS AND ANALYSIS

These 1,012 articles on second language writing were reviewed by the authors. 601 were identified as empirical studies and 411 were categorized as non-empirical studies. The authors reviewed each of the 601 empirical research by title, abstract, and methodology (and if necessary, the article in complete) to identify what method was used, what theory or theories were adopted, and what was the object of study. Out of these 601 articles, 203 were coded as "qualitative," 194 as "quantitative," and 204 as "mixed methods." All of the 601 empirical research articles were also coded by their different objects of study into 4 categories: writing (N=369), writers (N=31), readers (N=60), and multiple entities (N=141).

It can be observed from Figure 12.1 that the development of second language writing research keeps a steady range with a sudden drop in 2019. Specifically, second language writing research has experienced several significant rises during the last 20 years and has demonstrated an ascendant trend.

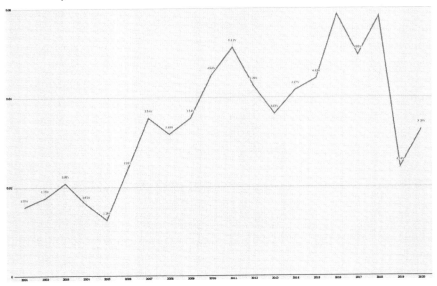

Figure 12.1. Trendline of L2 writing research articles among all published CSSCI journal articles during 2001–2020

As shown in Table 12.1 and complied with previous researchers' descriptions of the proportion changes of empirical and non-empirical research published in different journals within different periods, the development of empirical research has been quite dramatic during these 20 years. And it can be drawn from the content of the articles that, the non-empirical studies experienced some rise since 2015 with more and more studies focused on questioning the status quo of the empirical trend in the field and concerns for future theoretical and methodological developments in the field (Zhan & Ai, 2015; Xu, 2021; Ye & Duan, 2021) and also the rapid development of research overseas (Qin, 2017; Wang & Xiao, 2021). Figure 12.2 also shows the changes of empirical research and non-empirical research during these 20 years. It can be observed that the rise of empirical studies was steady before 2015, and then non-empirical studies started to come back with more theoretical evaluations and updates on international writing studies with expectations for future research in China (Qin, 2017; Wang & Xiao, 2021; Xu, 2021).

Through the analysis of the current situation of English writing research in China, it can be seen that English writing research is receiving more and more attention. Most of the research methods used in the empirical studies being reviewed are quantitative and mixed methods. Qualitative method was significantly lower than quantitative method, which shows that the qualitative method might be more challenging to researchers in the aspect of previous training and also access to publication. It is also very obvious that many researchers did not explicitly state which methodology was used in the study. Secondly, research theories often adopted by Chinese scholars are activity theory, genres, meta-cognition, and functional theory, which are very obvious influences from the North American genre theory (Hyon, 1996) and an activity theory approach to genre (Russell, 1997a). It also needs to be mentioned that over 30% of empirical research did not provide any explanation of theory which guides the research. Thirdly, the objects of study in English writing cover four aspects: writing, writers, readers, and multiple objects of study.

Table 12.1. Numbers of Empirical Research and Non-empirical Research in Surveyed Journals During 2001–2020

Year	Non-empirical Research	Empirical Research	Total
2001	11	4	15
2002	11	10	21
2003	12	11	23
2004	12	8	20
2005	11	7	18
2006	35	16	51
2007	8	18	26
2008	9	27	36
2009	10	27	37
2010	5	38	43
2011	9	30	39
2012	7	35	42
2013	4	34	38
2014	3	24	27
2015	1	39	40
2016	5	27	32
2017	60	101	161
2018	37	33	70
2019	35	36	71
2020	126	76	202
	411	601	1012

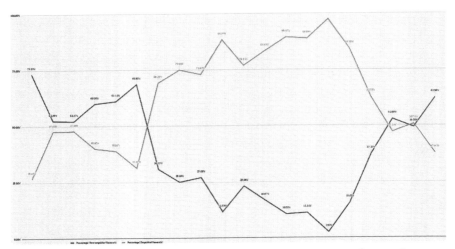

Figure 12.2. Trend of empirical research and non-empirical research

Chinese researchers are more likely to conduct research based on writing texts, which include three types of research: measures of textual characteristics, including fluency, accuracy and development, discourse features, and linguistic features; ratings of writing quality; and feedback research. Then the researchers favor multiple entities-oriented research, such as research on writer and writing, reader and writing, and teachers and textbooks, and this type of research will gain more attention in future. A small fraction of research focuses on writers as the object of study, or on writers' psychology and cognition. Attention to writers has been less common than a focus on readers, with even less research investigating the relationships between the writer and the reader (Bazerman, 2001), all of which definitely deserve more attention.

IMPLICATIONS

The present study provides a better understanding towards research methods, theories, and focus entities of English writing research in China and unveils that analyzing research methods, theories, and focus entities is a complex process. By reviewing existing research on English research articles published in 11 CSSCI foreign language journals (2001–2020) from the aspects of methods, theories, and focus entities, it can be concluded that English researchers in China in the aspect of writing research should maintain the "method" consciousness, continuing to try new writing instruction methods in practice. In addition, Chinese scholars should communicate more with international colleagues so that real dialogues are conducted concerning the research methods and focus entities of English writing research in order to promote the development of English writing.

In terms of research methods, empirical research methods continue to be used increasingly. English writing is a complex process of interaction of various variables. In order to deeply analyze the characteristics of the variables and their relationships, it needs to be noted that the mixed use of quantitative and qualitative methods is necessary. Therefore, mixed methods will become a more popular research method in the English writing research field in the future. Theories adopted in English writing will be more and more cross-disciplinary, with continuing influences from the US (Qin, 2017) and other English writing research communities. Although L2 writing studies in China has been single-parented, the influences from Rhetoric and Composition have been brought to China from the US through introductions of writing theories and research methods by various channels like journal articles (Li, 2014), books (Wu, 2013), and translated works (Bazerman, 2020). Thirdly, the research results will be more and more multi-modal. The results of writing research are emerging various forms, not only including research papers, but also a lot of new achievements, such as English writing software, English writing instruction websites, and English writing assessment platforms. It can be predicted that English writing research in the future is bound to develop in a comprehensive, scientific, and diversified way with the theorizing and standardization of English writing research methods and diversified focus entities.

REFERENCES

Bazerman, C. (2001). Writing as a development in interpersonal relations. *Journal for the Psychoanalysis of Culture and Society*, *6*(2), 298–302.

Ellis, R. (2008). *The study of second language acquisition*. Oxford University Press.

Hyon, S. (1996). Genre in three traditions: Implications for ESL. *TESOL Quarterly*, *30*(4), 693–722.

Kroll, B. (2003). *Exploring the dynamics of second language writing*. Cambridge University Press.

Nwogu, K. N. (1997). The medical research paper: Structure and functions. *English for Specific Purposes*, *16*(2), 119–138.

Reynolds, D. W. (2010). Beyond texts: a research agenda for quantitative research on second language writers and readers. *Practicing Theory in Second Language Writing*. Parlor Press.

Russell, D. (1997). Rethinking genre in school and society: An activity theory analysis. *Written Communication*, *14*(4), 504–554.

Silva, T. & Leki, I. (2004). Family matters: The influence of applied linguistics and composition studies on second language writing studies—Past, present, and future. *The Modern Language Journal*, *88*(1), 1–13.

Silva, T. & Matsuda, P. K. (Eds.). (2001). *Landmark essays on ESL writing*. Elrbaum.

Wu, D. (2013). *Introducing writing across the curriculum into China: Feasibility and adaptation*. Springer.

查尔斯·巴泽曼 (Bazerman, C.). (2020). 陈会军(译).英语写作教学与研究. 北京：北京师范大学出版社

方长安.(2021)序言.在方长安、萧映、宋时磊等主编《当代写作学40年：1980–2020》. 北京：社会科学文献出版社

高一虹, 李莉春, 吕掯. (1999). 中、西应用语言学研究方法发展趋势. 外语教学与研究 (2), 8–16.

郭姗姗. (2009). 国内二语写作研究18年述评(1991–2008). 山东外语教学, 132(5), 38–41.

何武. (2013). 中国EFL写作研究十年概览(2001–2010). 英语研究, 11(1), 66–73.

黄建滨, 于书林. (2009). 国内英语写作研究述评. 中国外语, 30(4), 60–65.

李志雪, 李绍山. (2003). 对国内英语写作研究现状的思考: 对八种外语类核心期刊十年的统计分析. 外语界, 98(6), 55–78.

李杰. (2014). 从语言技巧到社会文化功能的嬗变——美国大学写作教学范式转变述评外语教学2014(4), 51–54

刘弘, 凌雯怡. (2012). 国内外二语写作研究现状与特点的比较研究. 云南师范大学学报, 10(3), 29–40.

栾新华. (2012).《外语教学与研究》中二语写作研究综述. 海外英语(22). 120–121.

蒙梅. (2011). 近十年英语写作实证研究综述. 九江学院学报, 162(3), 122–128.

秦枫. (2017). 美国写作研究回顾与展望. 外语电化教学(2), 40–44+57.

秦朝霞. (2009). 国内大学英语写作研究现状及发展趋势分析. 现代外语, 32(2), 195–204.

覃晓琪. (2014). 我国英语写作研究现状. 长江大学学报, 37(1), 110–112.

王海龙, 萧映. (2021). 2020年海外写作学研究述略. 写作, 41(2), 119–128.

王俊菊. (2013). 国内二语写作过程研究的现状剖析. 山东外语教学, 156(5), 7–11.

王立非. (2000). 国外第二语言习得交际策略研究述评. 外语教学与研究(2), 124–131+160.

王立非, 孙晓坤. (2005). 国外第二语言写作研究的现状与取向. 外语界, 109(5), 10–16.

王文宇, 王立非. (2004). 二语写作研究: 十年回顾与展望. 外语界, 101(3), 51–58.

徐昉. (2021). 我国二语写作研究的若干重点问题. 外语教学与研究, 53(4), 571–581.

晏晓蓉, 崔沙沙. (2011). 国内二语写作研究近况及展望. 北京第二外国语学院学报, 200(12), 24–30.

姚兰, 程骊妮. (2005). 我国20世纪80年代以来英语写作研究状况之研究. 外语界, 109(5), 2–16.

叶洪, 段敏. (2021). 二语写作实证研究方法评述. 外语与翻译, 28(2), 73–80.

於可训. (2021). 我担任会长期间的二三事. 写作.2021(03)

邵春燕. (2013). 二语写作最新发展动态——第十二届国际二语写作研讨会综述. 语言学研究(1), 133–143.

展素贤, 艾丹. (2015). 我国15年来英语写作研究综述. 当代教育理论与实践, 7(2), 118–121.

赵俊峰, 郝晶, 高艳明. (2010). 大学英语写作研究现状调查. 外语学刊, 157(6), 98–100.

郑霄雯, 李熊, 赵英. (2014). 我国英语写作的研究态势分布及科研团队挖掘. 外语界, 162(3), 70–78.

朱岩岩. (2011). 对我国英语写作研究发展的调查和思考——基于我国外语类核心期刊统计分析(1980–2010). 外语界, 147(6), 56–62.

邹为诚. (2016). 教育语言学——我国外语/二语教师的精神家园. 外语与外语教学(3), 1–6+144.

CHAPTER 13.
TWENTY YEARS OF RESEARCH ON READING AND WRITING IN LATIN AMERICAN HIGHER EDUCATION: LESSONS LEARNED FROM THE ILEES INITIATIVE

Natalia Ávila Reyes
Pontificia Universidad Católica de Chile, Chile

Elizabeth Narváez-Cardona
Universidad del Valle, Colombia

Federico Navarro
Universidad de O'Higgins, Chile

Research on reading and writing in higher education has flourished as a field of study in Latin America for about two decades. Although some first-year writing courses were offered at universities in the 1990s (Pereira, 2006), various sources date the beginning of academic research on writing in higher education to the 2000s (Carlino, 2013; Navarro et al., 2016). The field is based on diverse theoretical and disciplinary traditions that conceptualize and approach reading and writing in different ways. This body of research corresponds to an emerging and interdisciplinary effort, which is characteristic of the so-called Mode 2 of knowledge production, that is, research based on contextualized and applied knowledge (Klein, 1996).

Alfabetización académica (Carlino, 2002) has been used as a term in the region to describe research on reading and writing in higher education (Navarro & Colombi, 2022), despite the fact that the discussion about the theoretical limits of this term is still open (Carlino, 2013; Lillis, 2021). The field has also experienced an accelerated process of professionalization, which is reflected in a growing number of *special issues* in academic journals in the region—eight published between 2016 and 2019—as well as local and regional conferences, and the creation of professional associations and international collaboration.

DOI: https://doi.org/10.37514/PER-B.2023.1800.2.13

This chapter represents a disciplinary research effort in which we present three lessons learnt on reading and writing studies in Latin America, which are drawn mainly from the project (*Iniciativas de Lectura y Escritura en Educación Superior*). Led by Charles Bazerman between 2012 and 2015, this project brought together Latin American scholars on writing in higher education at various stages of their careers (Bazerman et al., 2017; Navarro et al., 2016). Although the original objective of the ILEES project was the mapping of reading and writing teaching initiatives in Latin America, its participants quickly expanded this goal to include the issue of the identity and disciplinary configuration of this emerging field.

This chapter brings together different contributions to address this issue. The literature on interdisciplinarity indicates that complex and applied objects of study, such as reading and writing, frequently arouse academic interest from various disciplines. This shared interest generates a process of hybridization of knowledge (Klein, 1996) that is descriptive of the development of the field in Latin America. Emerging interdisciplinary fields are characterized by the need to analyze and establish limits, which has been described as boundary work (Klein, 1996; 2000), that is, efforts to claim the disciplinary legitimacy of an emerging field through histories, genealogies, ethnographies, bibliometric studies, and others. For Maureen Goggin (2000), one of the main historians of the archive of academic journals on the discipline of American rhetoric and composition this type of work fulfills the function of legitimizing intellectual communities to secure them a place in academia.

As is characteristic of our field, this chapter is the result of interdisciplinary collaboration between researchers from Argentina, Chile, and Colombia. Each contributes the results of their research that started with the ILEES project but was later expanded on the basis of empirical data. The lessons, which are organized chronologically and by different areas of interest, allow us to reach conclusions about the development of the field and future projections after 20 years of intensive research activity in the region.

Lesson 1: "Studies on reading and writing in higher education are a disciplinary community," by Natalia Ávila Reyes, reflects on the characteristics of the field through the first half of the 2010s based on patterns and networks, discourse analysis and triangulation with interviews. Lesson 2: "Studies on reading and writing in higher education are focused on academic settings and school genres," by Elizabeth Narváez-Cardona, analyzes studies on reading and writing in articles published between 2003 and 2015 in an influential Colombian journal. Finally, Lesson 3: "Studies on reading and writing in higher education conceptualize reading and writing as social practices," by Federico Navarro, compares and contrasts the conceptualizations of reading and writing in ten *special issues* published in the region between 2006 and 2019.

Overall, the panoramic view offered by this chapter on the disciplinary development of reading and writing studies in higher education contributes to the collective construction of meaning in our daily work as academics. As Goggin (2000) states, a more robust definition and identity of the discipline helps to promote its institutionalization, professionalization, and influence on public policies. In other words, its impact ranges from dimensions such as the awarding of scholarships, academic positions, and research funds, to governmental or institutional decisions on initiatives and policies for teaching reading and writing in higher education. In summary, promoting a better understanding of the development and configuration of the study of reading and writing in Latin America is essential to strengthen its future projections and scope.

LESSON 1: STUDIES ON READING AND WRITING IN HIGHER EDUCATION ARE A DISCIPLINARY COMMUNITY

Studies on reading and writing in higher education can be understood as a disciplinary community within the academic activity system. Interpreting these studies as part of a community, and not merely as a common area of study by academics from different disciplines, is useful for applying rhetorical and discursive analysis tools that allow a better understanding of their epistemological configuration in the region. Devitt (2004) argues that the concept of "discourse community" (Swales, 1990), although widely used in writing studies, is monolithic, since it puts discourses at the center as a cohesive element of the community. The concept of "disciplinary community" used in this chapter, on the other hand, tries to account for the group of people who make up these communities and who produce, among other things, discourses as means and products of their activity.

Consequently, the writing of a community can only be understood in relation to the activities and purposes that characterize it (Russell, 1991/2002). Texts emerge as rhetorical responses to situations that are common in the activity of this community, that is, as genres (Bazerman, 2004; Miller, 1984); therefore, the typical actions of a community can be inferred by analyzing those genres. As MacDonald explains, texts are not epiphenomena but the main source of information about the social practices of a discipline: "they help create communities, they act on us, they shape how we relate to each other as professionals" (1994, p. 9). Similarly, Devitt (1991) points to intertextuality as a practice from which the epistemologies of communities can be inferred .

Based on these premises, the results of three studies carried out within the framework of the ILEES project are presented in this section, which allow us to characterize the disciplinary community up until the mid-2010s. The data that supports this section corresponds to 50 Spanish-language publications between 2002 and 2014 that were self-reported by Latin American academics in a survey carried out by the ILEES group from 2012 to 2015; a subsample of nine articles from the most recent period (2011–2014); and interviews with academics conducted by the same team in 2013 and 2014 (see Tapia-Ladino et al., 2016). The findings allow us to identify a common attribute of emerging interdisciplinary fields: the existence of two parent disciplines. On the one hand, there is linguistics and discourse studies and, on the other, a more diffuse field that includes educational sciences, educational psychology, and, above all, a well-established tradition in Latin America that is focused on the study and teaching of reading.

The first of these studies analyzes the bibliographic references in the 50 publications in the sample and seeks to describe emerging citation patterns and co-citation networks, that is, to group the authors cited into clusters that can account for differential epistemological orientations (Ávila Reyes, 2017a). First, when analyzing the influence of different authors in the sample (that is, those authors who were cited in more articles), there is a greater influence of non-Latin American authors (62%) and the presence of a wide range of authors, including linguists (Bathia, García Negroni, Halliday, Parodi, Swales), academics mainly dedicated to the study of reading (van Dijk, Kintsch) or discourse (Arnoux), early literacy scholars (Ferreiro), and a smaller group of academics, of varied traditions, who are dedicated exclusively to the study of writing in higher education (Bazerman, Carlino, Lea, Russell). As might be expected, when breaking down the analysis by sources cited, most of the highly influential sources are not studies on writing, but linguistic or cognitive works that provide conceptual tools for the research (Ávila Reyes, 2017a).

These results are not difficult to interpret. A study on the intellectual influences present in the American journal *College Composition and Communication* identified a similar pattern when studying intervals of around 14 years of publications (Phillips et al., 1993). It found that the newer the field, the greater the influence of other well-established disciplines, such as linguistics or literature. In the early years (1950–1964), linguists such as Kenneth Pike, Noam Chomsky, and Otto Jespersen are widely cited; however, their presence declines in the following period (1965–1979) and disappears altogether in the final period, which is contemporary to the study (1980–1993). Coincidentally, many authors that are currently prominent in the field were cited for the first time during this last period. In sum, a particular theoretical core of the discipline required several decades before emerging in the citations. In both cases, it seems that, at least in its beginnings, the "new" discipline remains attached to other disciplines that provide conceptual tools for the problem being studied.

In the early 2010s, the field of writing studies in Latin America seemed to still not have a clear core group of authors and remained in a diffuse stage, consisting of authors close to the two parent disciplines that shared the aim of the study of writing in higher education. These two groups emerged by carrying out an analysis of co-citation networks, through which it was possible to identify two large clusters of references that are cited by the same sources: one group is more homogeneous, comprised almost entirely of authors from the linguistics field, and the other is more disperse, including authors on discourse, psychology, initial literacy, sociology, cognitive studies, UK academic literacies, and American rhetoric and composition (see Ávila Reyes, 2017a).

Based on the same group of 50 texts, the second study identified a subsample of the nine journal articles published most recently by academics from Argentina, Chile, and Colombia. An in-depth discursive analysis was carried out to identify the discursive characteristics of the citations. This analysis showed that the articles that cite the linguistic tradition more tend to refer to Latin American authors in the introduction, mainly to give recognition or credit (Erikson & Erlandson, 2014) to other authors who have studied writing in higher education, but they retain a theoretical or conceptual framework of foreign authors, who are frequently English-speaking and generally attached to a recognizable theoretical tradition, such as English for Academic Purposes or Systemic Functional Linguistics (Ávila Reyes, 2018). In contrast, the more hybrid group of research related to teaching and learning does not present a well-defined pattern of local and international citations.

The two studies mentioned above show, firstly, the existence of citation patterns and, secondly, practices or ways of using those citations that reinforce the idea of two traditions of studies on reading and writing in Latin American that coexisted towards the middle of the last decade. The third study (Ávila Reyes, 2017b), then, asks if there are differential discursive ways of constructing the discourse in each of these seminal clusters. To answer this question, different discourse analysis techniques were used on the aforementioned sample of nine Latin American articles.

Indeed, different rhetorical patterns were found in both groups. For example, most of the articles closest to linguistic traditions use introductions that establish their research niche by proposing a gap in research problems previously identified in the community (MacDonald, 1994), through rhetorical structures close to those described by Swales (1990), which include, for example, reviewing previous research to point out a gap.

The articles linked mainly to teaching or learning problems, on the other hand, include introductions that do not define a specific academic community and, in fact, often resort to personal narratives, such as concerns as teachers or researchers, or the "literacy crisis" (Russell, 1991/2002); what McDonald (1994) calls "anecdotal introductions." This pattern is to be expected since, as mentioned previously, the analysis of co-citation networks identified both a homogeneous linguistic tradition and a more dispersed one. It seems, then, that for the Latin American community at the beginning of the 2010s, academic literacy corresponded either to an object of study of the language sciences, or to an incipient and interdisciplinary—and, therefore, epistemologically still diffuse—intellectual effort.

In addition, the use of subjective (Kerbrat-Orecchioni, 1997) and appraisal (Martin & White, 2005) markers regarding the cited sources, that is, words that express points of view and reflect the subjectivity of the speaker, are also identified. This data was triangulated with the analysis of interviews with key Latin American scholars, which showed that these disciplinary tensions in the study of writing were apparent by 2013.

Regarding the presence of critical evaluations in the articles, in general, the analysis shows a low level of conflict, meaning that explicit positions or the opposition of ideas is infrequent. The cases in which explicit evaluations were used allowed us to identify two articles with explicit disciplinary positions. The following fragments highlight these disciplinary positions.

> **Article 1**: The method we propose in this article stems from a dilemma faced by a linguist who is also a professor of scientific writing.
>
> **Article 2**: Linguistic and psychological investigations focused on the students. . . . In these works, teaching was not usually approached as a field of study but rather as a field of application of the knowledge generated in linguistics or psychology.

The first excerpt takes an explicit disciplinary position, in which it is "a linguist" who faces the object of writing, while the second specifically criticizes the situation where the teaching of writing is limited to being an object of another discipline. Thus, at the beginning of the last decade, there were still academic publications engaging in jurisdictional disputes (Klein, 2000), that is, they make an explicit controversy regarding who should be in charge of an object of study; in short, which discipline can best respond to a social need (Abbott, 1988). This clash of jurisdictional claims indicates that there are different discursive constructions that coincide with the inferred parent disciplines.

To further investigate this hypothesis, we triangulated the textual findings with the analysis of the interviews conducted with four informants from the countries in the study (Argentina, Chile, and Colombia; cf. Tapia-Ladino et al., 2016), who, when asked about the disciplinary location of reading and writing studies, offered testimonies of how different positions emerge.

> **Informant 4**: In some cases, the research on reading and writing for teaching education is closely related to didactics and, sometimes, is unfortunately far removed from the theoretical bases.

Again, scholars engage in jurisdictional disputes; Informant 4 criticizes reading and writing studies close to didactics as "removed from the theoretical bases," creating a tacit opposition to studies of a more linguistic nature, which would be closer to theoretical support.

> **Informant 1**: Who is responsible? In other words, who and in what way is this teaching need addressed, which requires an interdisciplinary understanding and should not only be taught by linguistics and language teachers.

Informant 1 also engages in a more open dispute with linguistics specialists, claiming the need for an interdisciplinary approach that goes beyond the language sciences.

> **Informant 2**: Language specialists are in charge of most of the actions, but I do not agree with that, I think their participation is necessary but insufficient. Others think it has to be the specialist in the area and I would answer that I do not agree with that either, their participation is necessary but insufficient . . . interdisciplinary cooperation is needed.

Finally, Informant 2 also proposes interdisciplinary cooperation, with the balanced participation of language specialists and university disciplinary areas.

This data allows us to identify a specific moment in the discipline, in the early 2010s, when the epistemological discussions that have led to the broad interdisciplinary perspective we share today began.

LESSON 2: STUDIES ON READING AND WRITING IN HIGHER EDUCATION ARE FOCUSED ON ACADEMIC SETTINGS AND SCHOOL GENRES

The ILEES interregional research project (Bazerman et al., 2017) included the collection of data through an online survey of colleagues in Argentina, Brazil, Chile, Colombia, Mexico, Puerto Rico, and Venezuela, which was carried out between 2012 and 2015. One of the sections asked the respondents about which scientific journals they wanted to publish their findings in. In Colombia, the respondents frequently mentioned a Colombian journal in the field of linguistics, founded in 1972, which allowed us to characterize, among other aspects, articles published on reading and writing in higher education (Narváez-Cardona, 2017; research based on Navarro et al., 2016).

For this purpose, articles published between 2000 and 2015 were collected. The dates of the sample selection are based on the articles that document the emergence of studies and interventions on reading and writing in Colombian higher education in the early 2000s (Narváez-Cardona, 2016). Articles that were available online between 2004–2015 were accessed, and those published prior to that date were requested to the journal editor. Articles that met any of the following criteria were included: (1) articles on university, academic, and professional writing or university reading for L1 (Spanish); (2) articles on strategies and reading comprehension when linked to writing in disciplinary or professional subjects; and (3) articles on discourse analysis related to university or professional academic writing.

Here, we assume that research in the field has focused on the circulation and production of discourse as text and as social practice to offer pedagogical contributions and applications. However, such research is not only conducted in school academic contexts (e.g., classrooms and subjects), but also incorporate the analysis of texts and scientific contexts (e.g., research groups and scientific journals) and non-academic institutions (e.g., civil society, labor, religious, community, or NGO organizations). Consequently, publications that deal with the study of reading and writing as texts or practices beyond university academic contexts were also taken into account as a selection criterion for the sample.

While the number of articles analyzed corresponds to a non-representative sample, the results are used to identify trends. 17.6% of the articles in the sample (29 of 165) published between 2003 and 2015 met the selection criteria.

During this time frame, there is evidence of variation in the number of publications, with an average of 2.2 articles published per year, the lowest frequency in 2009 (no publications), and the highest in 2010 (5) and 2012 (6). Regarding the total number of authors by country affiliation, it is observed that the journal has mainly published works by authors of Colombian affiliation (21), although there are also authors based in Argentina (4), Brazil (1), Spain (2), Mexico (1), and Venezuela (2). Of the total number of publications, 14 were produced by a single author, 14 through co-authorship between two or more authors of the same national affiliation, and one through bi-national co-authorship. The distribution of the type of articles published indicates a trend of more research articles (empirical works) (22), while reflective articles (essay type) (6) and literature review articles (1) are less frequent.

A content analysis was carried out on the "introduction" and "conclusions" sections, and, in the case of research articles, the "methodology" section was also analyzed. The analysis of the introductions shows that the publications contribute to some of the following areas: a) teaching and learning of reading and writing in higher education (21), b) writing in postgraduate training (5), c) writing in professional contexts (2), and d) university teacher training (1). No publications were found that dealt with non-academic contexts. In addition, the topics of the publications were distributed as follows: a) analysis of textual and discursive phenomena (characteristics of people, *ethos*, authorship, intertextuality, audiences) in texts produced by students or in disciplinary genres (6), and b) analysis of the incidence of pedagogical interventions with students (5). Other themes identified did not receive a significant number of mentions: c) promotion of the teaching of reading and writing in the university curriculum (3); d) analysis of digital pedagogical initiatives (3); e) exploration of students' reading and writing practices (2); f) description of conceptions about reading and/or writing of teachers and/or students (2); g) literature reviews on reading (2); h) problematization of explanations about reading and writing difficulties in higher education (1); i) assessment of student' reading and writing practices (1); j) design and application of reading comprehension tests (1); k) analysis of classroom interaction in language courses (1); l) analysis of life stories of students as readers and writers (1); and, m) analysis of the incidence of pedagogical interventions with teachers (1). The relationship between the authors' country affiliation and the two themes most frequently identified in the introductions of the articles shows that Colombian authors focus more on the pedagogical dimension of reading and writing than on their textual or discursive description.

In the case of articles with empirical data, the analysis of the "methodology" section shows the following number of mentions in non-exclusive categories: a) textual analysis (qualitative and quantitative analysis of student writing, disciplinary or professional genres, or pedagogical materials) (13); b) content analysis of written productions or institutional documents (10); c) application of surveys or questionnaires (9); d) individual or group interviews with students or teachers (5); e) non-participatory observations (5); and e) reading or writing tests (3). The biographical, ethnographic, and historical methods only received one mention each. Educational levels or populations researched include undergraduate level (18) and much less so at the postgraduate level (5), professionals (2), or university professors (1). Populations of graduates or other social actors (e.g., internship coordinators, thesis tutors, directors of research offices) did not emerge from the sample, and in three cases the type of population was not a variable in the analysis.

Genres are mentioned in 14 articles in the sample of empirical studies. In these publications, academic genres for school purposes are treated as textual units of frequent interest (21 occurrences): written assignment (4), review (3), abstract (3), thesis (3), essay (2), written exam (2), essay-type exam (1), concept map (1), bibliographic record (1), and oral communication (1). In 17 articles, the publications mention the following disciplines or professions (34 occurrences): linguistics and foreign languages (6), engineering (5), health and social services (2), recreation (2), medicine (2), humanities and arts (2), business education and law (2), education (2), economics (2), social sciences (2), science (2), human rehabilitation (1), Lacanian psychoanalysis (1), literature (1), law (1), and social communication (1).

Finally, the analysis with non-exclusive categories in the "conclusions" section shows a high number of mentions related to pedagogical-curricular results to guide interventions (20) and theoretical aspects of pedagogy and learning (15). Less frequent were conclusions or emerging implications of the analyzed sample to a) propose new studies (4) and b) open methodological debates on reading and writing research (5), or theoretical debates on aspects of language, reading or writing (2).

In sum, the sample seems to indicate that the publications correspond mostly to Colombian authors, and their themes and theoretical perspectives seem to focus on reading and writing within educational settings. On the other hand, authors of non-Colombian affiliation focus on themes such as the description of discursive and textual phenomena. This contrast seems to suggest that interdisciplinary studies in the field are necessary, therefore, alliances between research groups and co-authorship between different countries in the region would bring greater theoretical and methodological complexity to the studies.

In turn, the results show that the empirical papers (22 articles analyzed) stem from an educational model focused on academic genres for school purposes. The analysis of the "methodology" section shows that the publications tend to use textual, qualitative, and quantitative analysis of student output, disciplinary or professional genres, or pedagogical materials. It could be suggested that empirical papers in this sample have a methodological influence from textual and applied linguistics and that they could be studying genres as products rather than as social practices.

Therefore, studies could be improved by incorporating a theory of genre based on the rhetorical genre studies (RGS) approach. Within RGS, activity systems theory helps to explore typical routines or interactions when reading, writing, and conversing within or between contexts (Russell, 2010). Indeed, activity systems is a useful theoretical and methodological category to explain genres, not only as textual units but also as networks between human interactions that are woven into communities, groups, and organizations. These interactions involve contradictions that arise from the social division of labor; that is, different participants who are pursuing a common objective and simultaneously seeking to fulfill personal aims while accessing—or not—resources within a collective activity (Russell, 2010).

This approach could be useful for conducting research in the region that adopts the concept of genre as a form of human interaction and intersubjectivity, beyond the material characteristics of textual products, which already seems to be a strong tradition in the region (Navarro et al., 2016). Genres stabilize and mediate human interactions over time and also promote change (Miller, 1984). Therefore, they are expectations and, at the same time, mental conventions and interactive and intersubjective material products used to anticipate and respond within certain limits (Andersen et al., 2014).

Finally, the findings suggest that academic genres for school purposes frequently emerge as textual units of analysis and are mainly associated with their formative dimension in various disciplinary and professional fields. The absence of publications outside of school and academic contexts (e.g., civil, labor, religious, community organizations, and NGOs) in the sample analyzed may also signal the need to study reading and writing in non-academic and non-school settings. This data also suggests the need for new research that focuses on exploring reading and writing in different disciplines and professions, not only in its school dimension (e.g., professional contexts), and that, in addition, incorporate the analysis of textual units and the routines or interactions pertaining reading, writing and conversation through which these textual units "travel" in the intersubjective context of collective human activities.

LESSON 3: STUDIES ON READING AND WRITING IN HIGHER EDUCATION CONCEPTUALIZE READING AND WRITING AS SOCIAL PRACTICES

Studies on reading and writing in higher education in Latin America constitute a relatively recent and heterogeneous field of interdisciplinary teaching and scientific research practice. It is an interdisciplinary field where diverse theoretical traditions and scientific sub-disciplines converge. It is a relatively new field because its institutionalization in journals, associations, and congresses only began less than two decades ago (Navarro et al., 2016). Finally, it is a heterogeneous field because the previous factors bring together diverse conceptualizations and methodologies in their approach to reading and writing.

It is interesting to consider this heterogeneity of views on reading and writing within the field, and to contrast them chronologically throughout their development in the region. To achieve this objective, the different ways of conceptualizing reading and writing are analyzed in 85 articles in 10 special issues published by Latin American scientific journals in the last two decades: Signo & Seña (Argentina, 2006); Revista Mexicana de Investigación Educativa (Mexico, 2013); Signos (Chile, 2016); Grafía (Colombia, 2016); Ilha do Desterro (Brazil,

2016); DELTA (Brazil, 2017); Lenguas Modernas (Chile, 2017); Signo y Pensamiento (Colombia, 2017); and Íkala (Colombia, 2019; two issues). As these are special issues in indexed journals, several of which have great influence in the region, the relevance of the selected articles is ensured; at the same time, the corpus in the study shows an important geographic (five countries) and temporal (14 years) distribution.

This analysis is based on a recent study (Navarro & Colombi, 2022), which investigates the ways in which reading and writing are understood through the content analysis of research published in special issues of scientific journals both in Latin America and Spain. The results show six theoretical constructs to systematically conceptualize the object of study of the field: *products, processes, learning, practices, programs,* and *teaching*.

First, reading and writing can be understood as textual and discursive *products*. These fixed products are approached through quantitative and qualitative linguistic analysis in normative, lexical-grammatical, discursive, and multimodal aspects (e.g., Oteíza, 2017, published in the special issue of *Lenguas Modernas*). The studies draw on the traditions of textual linguistics, corpus linguistics, systemic-functional linguistics, discourse studies, and genre analysis. Sometimes the analysis is complemented with surveys of writers and a description of the contexts of circulation of the texts.

Second, reading and writing can be understood as text production and comprehension *processes* that allow the generation of those textual products. The studies are based on psycholinguistics or educational psychology and focus on individual subjects (usually students). Exercises, tests, and exams are used to measure different variables (memory, comprehension, writing strategies, eye movement), sometimes with experimental designs (e.g., Parodi & Julio, 2016, published in the special issue of *Signos*).

The focus on reading and writing as a process is linked to the problem of *learning* within the framework of educational psychology, which is the third construct identified. In particular, the epistemic potential of reading and writing to facilitate student learning is of interest. Instruments such as content assessment tests and cognitive or linguistic skills are used, together with measurement of text quality, to make inferences about the underlying learning processes (e.g., Rosales and Vázquez, 2006; published in the special issue of *Signo & Seña*).

Fourth, reading and writing can be understood as *practices* or forms of participation in family, community, educational, and professional settings. This construct is especially heterogeneous because it integrates both critical and sociocultural perspectives, with an interest in what people do and value in context, as well as cognitive perspectives, with an interest in implicit and declared individual conceptions and their relationship with classic sociodemographic traits (sex, age, school level, and academic performance). The construct draws on new literacy studies, critical sociolinguistics, linguistic anthropology, critical pedagogy, as well as educational psychology, and combines quantitative and qualitative methodologies (e.g., Zavala, 2019; published in the special issue of *Íkala*). This construct shares some aspects with reading and writing as individual learning (cognitive perspectives) and as educational designs for social transformation (curricular perspectives).

Indeed, reading and writing can also be understood as *programs*, which is the fifth construct identified. The focus of interest shifts from students to higher education institutions to describe and evaluate the impact of curricular teaching devices, sometimes problematizing aspects of access, permanence, and university graduation. The studies analyze curricular designs and educational materials and interview officials and teachers, as well as providing theoretical support for the proposals (e.g., Moyano & Giudice, 2016; published in the special issue of *Grafía*). This construct shares interests and perspectives with the notion of reading and writing as practices, but it is also linked to the currents most interested in didactics and the ways of teaching and evaluating reading and writing.

Lastly, reading and writing can be understood as *teaching*, which is the sixth construct identified: specific and local interventions or activities in classroom dynamics, with a focus on teachers. Techniques and strategies for teaching, assessment criteria and methods, didactic sequences, and teaching experiences are described and evaluated in their impact and theoretical solidity, based on theories of teaching, learning, and development (e.g., Pontara & Cristóvão, 2017; published in the special issue of *DELTA*). Theoretical influences include sociodiscursive interactionism, language didactics, educational linguistics, language and second language teaching, genre-based didactics, and educational psychology.

These six constructs not only share adjoining theoretical spaces, but also, research frequently focuses on one of them, but with a broader perspective that enables coexistence with the other ways of conceptualizing reading and writing and triangulation of various data. For example, characterizations of genres (products) inscribed in sets of communities and broader activities (practices), or rather analysis of didactic interventions (teaching) based on their impact on learning, or on the quality of written texts. This heterogeneous coexistence is part of the identity of the field of the study and teaching of reading and writing in Latin America.

Next, the distribution of these six ways of conceptualizing reading and writing over two decades of special issues on the subject is analyzed. With the support of the qualitative analysis software nVivo Pro 12, a manual content analysis was performed, and the 85 articles of the corpus were classified according to prioritized construct and year (Figure 13.1). Introductions to special issues were excluded from the corpus since they do not constitute research with original contributions.

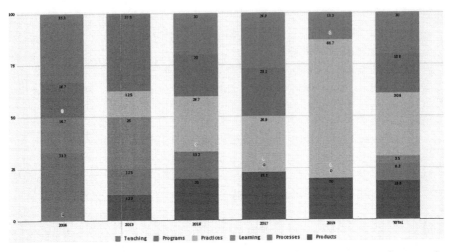

Figure 13.1. Six ways of conceptualizing reading and writing in special issues of Latin American journals (percentage per year)[1]

Most of the research papers (30.6%) focus on reading and writing practices. This construct has consistently gained predominance during the last five years, growing from 0% in the first special issue of 2006, to 12.5% in 2013, 26.7% in 2016, 26.9% in 2017, and 66.7% in the last year of the period studied. At the same time, two linked constructs show an important presence: programs (18.8%) and teaching (20%), although their distribution over time is variable in both cases.

On the other hand, the constructs on reading and writing linked to an individual cognitive perspective on reading and writing (as processes and learning) are not only less predominant (8.2% and 3.5%, respectively) but also have lost share in recent years. Indeed, the study of learning mediated by reading and writing appears only until the special issue of 2013, while the cognitive processes of reading and writing are present until the special issue of 2016, and then disappear completely. For their part, the studies that address texts as products (18.8%) show a medium level of interest, which fluctuates over time.

In sum, the main finding of this research is that the studies of reading and writing in Latin America have gradually installed at the center a conceptualization of their object of study understood as social practices. In a complementary manner, the field is supported by views interested in the teaching of this subject, the related curricular programs and the textual products derived from these practices.

---

1   The total percentage (right column) is not an average of the annualized distribution but of the distribution of the total articles. The years 2006 and 2013 only represent one issue each, while the more recent years represent two or three issues each.

The predominance of the conceptualization of reading and writing as practices is functional to a heterogeneous field, just as it was defined in the beginning: social practices necessarily integrate in the same theoretical construct other views of interest, in particular, on the texts, teaching, and curricular initiatives. In this sense, understanding reading and writing as practices allows researchers to link different dimensions and data sources. In addition, the conceptualization of reading and writing as practices can have effects on the other constructs, for example enabling genres to be understood through their role in the community or for the study of learning processes to be mediated by social interaction.

In addition, the parent disciplines that make up this interdisciplinary field have traditionally been interested in educational processes, in social groups that are largely integrated into higher education, and in the specific uses of discourse. From this point of view, the social practices construct enables a common space for communication and exchange between researchers with diverse academic backgrounds.

It is no coincidence, then, that along with the development of the field during the last two decades, the conceptualization of reading and writing as social practices is predominant today and enables the development of a field that addresses the relations between written language, education, and society.

CONCLUSIONS

At the beginning of the 21st century, the study of reading and writing in higher education constituted an emerging interdisciplinary field in Latin America, with disciplinary disputes and hybridizations similar to those of other interdisciplinary fields in their early days, such as genetics or molecular biology (Ceccarelli, 1995).

In this chapter, we have tried to show how reading and writing has been understood and investigated in higher education and what transformations have occurred over the last 20 years. On the one hand, according to Lesson 1, during the 2000s and until the mid-2010s it was still common to identify two very clear parent disciplines in research, and jurisdictional disputes even occurred between the same academics' talk on this issue. Similarly, according to Lesson 2, studies during the first 15 years of the discipline in Colombia suggest that academic genres for school purposes frequently emerge as textual units of analysis and mainly pertain to their pedagogical dimension in various disciplinary and professional fields. Lesson 3, on the other hand, shows us that the diverse constructs around writing coexist over time, but that in recent years the conceptualization of reading and writing as social practices has emerged strongly in the region.

Together, these findings lead us to assume that the regional literature on reading and writing studies in higher education has been slowly moving towards a shared broader approach. More than simply a closed epistemological option, the emergence of the concept of practices can be understood as a response that allows integrating linguistic and textual dimensions with a social perspective. However, our data also suggests that academics in the field maintain an interest in academic and school settings that could be extended in the future to other contexts (e.g., work, civil society, community, and non-formal education). Thus, given the current context of increased academic and scientific production, Latin American writing studies would benefit from more systematic literature reviews to identify new gaps and sustain epistemological debates to continue shaping the disciplinary status of the field.

In this regard, it is useful to return to a question posed by Bazerman, together with the ILEES team, about the status of regional scientific development in relation to the multiple uses of references to international scholars found in the analysis of the ILEES project up to 2014:

> The attention to scholarship from other regions and from multiple theoretical orientations can be a great strength, but it would be useful to see how these resources are being used in the Latin American region. Are the approaches from outside the region entering into a complex multi-sided discussion, in which Latin American scholars as equals are contributing new perspectives and fresh research, even as they are learning from what has gone on in other parts of the world or are the Latin American scholars only applying external approaches to local data and conditions? (Bazerman et al., 2017, p. 297)

To address this question, we need to rethink what it means to contribute to knowledge "as equals." In an influential essay published ten years ago, Donahue (2009) posits how the risk of perceiving the American development of writing studies as a role model can lead to a colonialist model of exporting this knowledge. Indeed, Donahue supports the idea that the American field "is not the sole source of writing theory in higher education" (p. 236). While Donahue calls for reorienting the authority discourse towards an "equal trade" model, the question persists as to what would be the contribution of Latin American studies in this dynamic of egalitarian exchange.

A second topic to consider is the authority with which we create our disciplinary claims. As a point of comparison with the American tradition, two decades ago Bazerman (2002) published an interesting discussion on the disciplinary status of what was then starting to be called writing studies. At the time, the study of writing seemed to be scattered and fragmented across university disciplines. Since it was not recognized as a separate discipline—such as sociology, psychology or mathematics—the study of writing seemed to have no real home: "writing is also a fundamental matter of the constitution of our world—but the organization of research and of the university itself remains consistently blind to this fact" (Bazerman, 2002, p. 33). In this text, Bazerman supports the jurisdiction of American studies of rhetoric and composition on this subject and their authority to provide an institutionalized response to a complex phenomenon, while valuing the importance of pedagogy in this task:

> Only the relatively young field of composition has paid primary attention to writing, but our core attention has tended to be narrow: on students and classes in a few courses in Universities in the United States over the last several decades, with particular attention to the underprepared student. . . . Of all disciplines, composition is best positioned to begin to put together the large, important and multidimensional history of writing. We are the only profession that makes writing its central concern. (2002, p. 33)

Almost ten years later, Bazerman (2011) refines this idea by reflecting on his own previous research. We see an important nuance in comparison to his 2002 text, that is, in the search for disciplinarity in writing studies, there is a clear risk of reducing the complexity of our object of study by opting for methods or types of data that seem more "acceptable" according to a certain disciplinary canon:

> If we choose the path to disciplinarity of narrowing the acceptable data, method, or theory, we are in danger of misunderstanding or even distorting the processes, practices and products of writing. . . . We should choose a path that finds discipline in our questions and goals, allowing us to draw on the resources of many disciplines. (Bazerman, 2011, p. 9)

This idea seems well-suited for interpreting our findings. The studies of reading and writing in higher education emerge in Latin America to a large extent as an academic response to a social need, linked both to the phenomena of university expansion (Chiroleu & Marquina, 2017) and to the adoption of student-centered pedagogical and curricular models. In this response, from the beginning of the 2000s to the mid-2010s, studies prevailed with a view on writing as a predominantly linguistic product, with well-defined problems, bibliographic discussions, and theories. However, there was an emerging need to address a more complex issue, even though the first studies tended to narrow the object of study in order to better fit previously recognizable traditions. A second more eclectic and hybridized group, which brought together traditions of great importance in the region (such as critical discourse analysis and reading studies), tried to account for a broader picture, but without much conceptual or disciplinary clarity. These tensions coexisted with calls for interdisciplinarity, that is, for the expansion of the object of study towards a more complex model of writing that, by the middle of the last decade, had not yet materialized.

On the interdisciplinary dynamics of writing studies, Bazerman continues:

> Yet each of these disciplines reduces the phenomena we are concerned with, providing monotonic accounts, and, even more seriously, monotonic approaches to the teaching of writing. If our research is narrow, our teaching and learning will follow on narrow paths. Some of the best teaching of writing has been informed by an intuitive eclecticism, addressing social, psychological, textual, and rhetorical issues as they come up in a practical way. . . . Our disciplinarity should be guided by the complexity of our subject rather than the limits of a small range of methods. (2011, p. 10)

We are interested in highlighting what Bazerman calls "an intuitive eclecticism" to answer the question about the development and use of theory by the Latin American community. Current developments in the field in Latin America, effectively born out of a hybrid and interdisciplinary approach in the early 2000s, which was driven by applied concerns typical of Mode 2 knowledge production, show a strong interest in the linguistic phenomenon, as well as in the local character and social practice of writing (see, for example, Ávila Reyes, 2021). This "intuitive eclecticism" has led scholars of the Latin American tradition to emphasize cognitive or sociolinguistic phenomena; indeed, much has been said about "sociocognitive" studies (Parodi, 2008) in seminal works in the region, and terms such as "mestizaje" (Motta-Roth, 2008) or "blend" (Bazerman, 2016) have been coined.

For this reason, the results of Lesson 3 are not surprising: while six writing constructs of different nature coexist in the same group of special issues, towards the end of the 2010s an emerging construct of social practices predominates, which appears to be broader. By the end of the decade it seems to be consensus on the fact that the examination of individual texts and cognitive processes should be complemented by activities and practices. This finding reflects the complexity of writing as claimed by Bazerman in 2011 and was not a pervasive concept in the region a decade earlier.

Finally, Bazerman points out that the main benefits of "disciplined interdisciplinarity" in writing studies lies in the possibility of accessing new questions and objects of study that allow the construction of theory based on empirical data. At the same time, the development of this theory provides the scaffolding for new areas of study: "The more I was able to articulate the theory, the more new kinds of inquiry I pursued" (Bazerman, 2011, p. 18).

Accordingly, one of the most salient reflections in our review of data on academic production in studies of reading and writing in Latin American higher education is the need to generate local theory. Indeed, we are currently investigating complex objects of study, using varieties of frameworks to unpack them, but our theoretical benchmarks for accomplishing this task remain overwhelmingly foreign. This geopolitical logic of knowledge production (Canagarajah, 2002; Lillis & Curry, 2010) puts Latin American academics at a disadvantage to "export" theories on equal terms, in Donahue's (2009) terms.

For this reason, the development of an informed interdisciplinary field, with its own development that can be understood today as a cohesive disciplinary community, must urgently focus on the local production of theory on teaching, learning, and the nature of writing. This starts with reading and citing our own authors (Navarro, 2022), and by continuing to generate epistemological discussions through, among others, comparative research and transnational co-authorship. Towards the end of the 2010s, the studies of reading and writing in higher education in Latin America are no longer an emerging field, but a multi-faceted—yet consolidated—disciplinary community, clearly oriented towards a set of problems and an object shared by the academic community. Jurisdictional disputes are no longer relevant, but rather we should focus on new discussions about the nature of our interdisciplinary knowledge.

REFERENCES

Abbott, A. D. (1988). *The system of professions: An essay on the division of expert labor*. University of Chicago Press.

Andersen, J., Bazerman, C. & Schneider, J. (2014). Beyond simple genres: Pattern mapping in global communication. In E. M. Jakobs & D. Perrin (Eds.), *Handbook of writing and text production* (pp. 305–324). De Gruyter Mouton.

Ávila Reyes, N. (2017a). Postsecondary writing studies in Hispanic Latin America: Intertextual dynamics and intellectual influence. *London Review of Education, 15*(1), 21–37. https://doi.org/10.18546/LRE.15.1.03.

Ávila Reyes, N. (2017b). *Tracing the discursive emergence of Latin American higher education writing studies* (Publication No. 10254076) [Doctoral dissertation, University of California, Santa Barbara]. ProQuest Dissertation Publishing. https://www.proquest.com/docview/1892108167.

Ávila Reyes, N. (2018). Locales, regionales y cosmopolitas: Análisis intertextual de artículos sobre escritura universitaria en América Latina Hispánica [Local, regional and cosmopolitan: Intertextual analysis of articles on university writing in Hispanic

Latin America]. In Pereira, R. C. M. (Ed.). *Escrita na universidade. Panoramas e desafios na América Latina* (pp. 45–82). UFPB.

Ávila Reyes, N. (2022). (Ed.) *Multilingual contributions to writing research: Toward an equal academic exchange.* The WAC Clearinghouse; University Press of Colorado. https://doi.org/10.37514/INT-B.2021.1404.

Bazerman, C. (2002). The case for writing studies as a major discipline. In G. Olson (Ed.), *Rhetoric and composition as intellectual work* (pp. 32–40). Southern Illinois University Press.

Bazerman, C. (2004). Speech acts, genres, and activity systems: How texts organize activity and people. In C. Bazerman & P. Prior (Eds.), *What writing does and how it does it: An introduction to analysing texts and textual practices* (pp. 309–340). Lawrence Erlbaum.

Bazerman, C. (2011). The disciplined interdisciplinarity of writing studies. *Research in the Teaching of English, 46*(1), 8–21.

Bazerman, C. (2016). The Brazilian Blend. In E. G. Lousada, A. D. O. Ferreira, L. Bueno, R. Rojo, S. Aranha & L. Abreu-Tardelli (Eds.), *Diálogos brasileiros no estudo de gêneros textuais/discursivos* (pp. 645–650). Letraria.

Bazerman, C., Ávila Reyes, N., Bork, A. V., Poliseli-Correa, F., Cristovão, V. L., Tapia Ladino, M. & Narváez Cardona, E. (2017). Intellectual orientations of studies of higher education writing in Latin America. In S. Plane, C. Bazerman, F. Rondelli, C. Donahue, A. N. Applebee, C. Boré, P. Carlino, M. Marquilló Larruy, P. Rogers & D. Russell (Eds.), *Research on writing: Multiple perspectives* (pp. 281–297). The WAC Clearinghouse; CREM. https://doi.org/10.37514/INT-B.2017.0919.2.15.

Canagarajah, S. (2002). *A geopolitics of academic writing.* University of Pittsburgh Press.

Carlino, P. (2002). Leer, escribir y aprender en la universidad: cómo lo hacen en Australia y por qué [Reading, writing and learning in higher education: How Australian universities do it and why]. *Investigaciones en Psicología, 7*(2), 43–61.

Carlino, P. (2013). Alfabetización académica diez años después [Alfabetizacion académica ten years later]. *Revista Mexicana de Investigacion Educativa, 18*(57), 355–381.

Ceccarelli, L. (1995). A rhetoric of interdisciplinary scientific discourse: Textual criticism of Dobzhansky's Genetics and the origin of species. *Social Epistemology, 9*(2), 91–111. https://doi.org/10.1080/02691729508578780.

Chiroleu, A. & Marquina, M. (2017). Democratisation or credentialism? Public policies of expansion of higher education in Latin America. *Policy Reviews in Higher Education, 1*(2), 139–160. https://doi.org/10.1080/23322969.2017.1303787.

Devitt, A. (1991). Intertextuality in tax accounting: Generic, referential, and functional. In C. Bazerman & J. Paradis (Eds.), *Textual dynamics of the professions: Historical and contemporary studies of writing in professional communities* (pp. 336–357). University of Wisconsin Press.

Devitt, A. (2004). *Writing genres.* Southern Illinois University Press.

Donahue, C. (2009). "Internationalization" and composition Studies: Reorienting the discourse. *College Composition and Communication, 61*(2), 212–243.

Erikson, M. G. & Erlandson, P. (2014). A taxonomy of motives to cite. *Social Studies of Science, 44*(4), 625–637. https://doi.org/10.1177/0306312714522871.

Goggin, M. (2000). *Authoring a discipline: Scholarly journals and the post-World War II emergence of rhetoric and composition*. Lawrence Erlbaum Associates.
Kerbrat-Orecchioni, C. (1997). *La enunciación. De la subjetividad en el lenguaje*. Edicial.
Klein, J. T. (1996). *Crossing boundaries. Knowledge, disciplinarities, and interdisciplinarities*. The University Press of Virginia.
Klein, J. T. (2000). A conceptual vocabulary of interdisciplinary science. In P. Weingart & N. Stehr (Eds.), *Practising interdisciplinarity* (pp. 3–24). University of Toronto Press.
Lillis, T. (2021). ¿Academic literacies: Intereses locales, preocupaciones globales? Academic literacies: local interests, global concerns? In N. Ávila Reyes (Ed.), *Multilingual contributions to writing research: Toward an equal academic exchange* (pp. 35–59). The WAC Clearinghouse; University Press of Colorado. https://doi.org/10.37514/INT-B.2021.1404.2.01.
Lillis, T. M. & Curry, M. J. (2010). *Academic writing in a global context: The politics and practices of publishing in English*. Routledge.
MacDonald, S. P. (1994). *Professional academic writing in the humanities and the social sciences*. Southern Illinois University Press.
Martin, J. & White, P. (2005). *The language of evaluation: Appraisal in English*. Palgrave Macmillan.
Miller, C. (1984). Genre as social action. *Quarterly Journal of Speech*, 70, 151–167.
Motta-Roth, D. (2008). Análise crítica de gêneros: contribuições para o ensino e a pesquisa de linguagem [Critical genre analysis: Contributions to language teaching and research]. *DELTA*, *24*(2), 341–383. https://doi.org/10.1590/S0102-4450 2008000200007.
Moyano, E. & Giudice, J. (2016). Un programa de lectura y escritura universitario: Lineamientos teóricos, características y resultados de aplicación [A tertiary reading and writing program: Theoretical guidelines, characteristics and application results]. *Grafía*, *13*(1), 33–59.
Narváez-Cardona, E. (2016). *Mapping expectations on writing and communication in engineering within a regional context: Accounts from a Latin-American case* [Doctoral dissertation, University of California, Santa Barbara].
Narváez Cardona, E. (2017). Las teorías de los géneros discursivos en el campo de la lectura y la escritura en la educación superior: análisis de datos emergentes de artículos publicados en una revista científica colombiana [Genre theories in the field of reading and writing in higher education: Analysis of emerging data from articles published in a Colombian scientific journal]. *Acción Pedagógica*, 26, 70–87.
Navarro, F. (2022). The unequal distribution of research roles in transnational composition: Towards illegitimate peripheral participation. In C. Donahue & B. Horner (Eds.), *Teaching and studying transnational composition*. Modern Language Association.
Navarro, F., Ávila Reyes, N., Tapia Ladino, M., Cristovão, V. L. L., Moritz, M. E. W., Narváez-Cardona, E. & Bazerman, C. (2016). Panorama histórico y contrastivo de los estudios sobre lectura y escritura en educación superior publicados en América Latina [Historical and contrastive panorama of higher education reading and writing studies published in Latin America]. *Signos*, *49*(S1), 100–126. https://doi.org/10.4067/S0718-09342016000400006.

Navarro, F. & Colombi, C. (2022). Alfabetización académica y estudios del discurso [Academic literacy and discourse studies]. In I. Carranza, T. van Dijk & C. López Ferrero (Eds.). *Handbook of Spanish discourse studies*. Routledge.

Oteíza, T. (2017). Escritura en historia: potencial de los recursos lingüísticos interpersonales e ideacionales para la construcción de la evidencia [Writing in history: Potential of the interpersonal and ideational linguistic resources to construct evidence]. *Lenguas Modernas*, 50, 193–224.

Parodi, G. (2008). Géneros del discurso escrito: hacia una concepción integral desde una perspectiva sociocognitiva [Written genres: Towards an integral conception from a sociocognitive perspective]. In G. Parodi (Ed.), *Géneros académicos y géneros profesionales: accesos discursivos para saber y hacer* (pp. 17–38). Ediciones Universitarias de Valparaíso.

Parodi, G. & Julio, C. (2016). ¿Dónde se posan los ojos al leer textos multisemióticos disciplinares? Procesamiento de palabras y gráficos en un estudio experimental con eye tracker [Where do eyes go when reading multisemiotic disciplinary texts? Processing words and graphs in an experimental study with eye tracker]. *Signos*, *49*(S1), 149–183. https://doi.org/10.4067/S0718-09342016000400008.

Pereira, C. (2006, September 28–October 1). *La lectura y la escritura en el CBC: memoria de la experiencia en la cátedra de Semiología [Reading and writing in the CBC: Memory of the experience in the chair of Semiology]* [Paper presentation]. Primer Congreso Nacional: "Leer, Escribir Y Hablar Hoy," Tandil, Argentina.

Phillips, D. B., Greenberg, R. & Gibson, S. (1993). Chronicling a Discipline's Genesis. *College Composition and Communication*, *44*(4), 443–465.

Pontara, C. L. & Cristóvão, V. L. L. (2017). Gramática/análise linguística no ensino de inglês (língua estrangeira) por meio de sequência didática: uma análise parcial [Grammar/linguistic analysis in the teaching of English as a foreign language via didactic sequence: A partial analysis]. *DELTA*, *33*(3), 873–909. https://doi.org/10.1590/0102-445024628126508654.

Rosales, P. & Vázquez, A. (2006). Escribir y aprender en la universidad. Análisis de textos académicos de los estudiantes y su relación con el cambio cognitivo [Writing and learning in college. Analysis of student' academic texts and their relationship with cognitive change]. *Signo & Seña*, 16, 47–118.

Russell, D. (2002). *Writing in the academic disciplines: A curricular history* (2nd ed.). Southern Illinois University Press.

Russell, D. (2010). Writing in multiple contexts: Vygotskian CHAT meets the phenomenology of genre. In C. Bazerman, R. Krut, K. Lunsford, S. McLeod, S. Null, P. Rogers & A. Stansell (Eds.), *Traditions of writing research* (pp. 353–364). Routledge.

Swales, J. (1990). *Genre analysis: English in academic and research settings*. Cambridge University Press.

Tapia Ladino, M., Ávila Reyes, N., Navarro, F. & Bazerman, C. (2016). Milestones, disciplines and the future of initiatives of reading and writing in higher education: An analysis from key scholars in the field in Latin America. *Ilha do desterro*, *69*(3), 189–208. https://doi.org/10.5007/2175-8026.2016v69n3p189.

Zavala, V. (2019). Justicia sociolingüística para los tiempos de hoy [Sociolinguistic justice for our times]. *Íkala*, *24*(2), 343–359. https://doi.org/10.17533/udea.ikala.v24n02a09.

PART SIX. NEW MEDIA AND TECHNOLOGY

CHAPTER 14.

RETHINKING GENRE AS DIGITAL SOCIAL ACTION: ENGAGING BAZERMAN WITH MEDIUM THEORY AND DIGITAL MEDIA

Jack Andersen
University of Copenhagen, Denmark

Writing from the point of view of a classification researcher located in information studies dealing with matters of classification in light of digital media, I have been struggling for some time with how to conceptualize specific communicative actions such as searching, tagging, or archiving as specific genres in networked media (Andersen, 2017a; 2017b; 2018; 2022); genres that are both revitalized and reinforced with digital media and their fundamental functions as storage, search, and archival media. During this research I realized three things. First, when trying to understand the forms of communication evolving with digital media, we cannot escape paying attention to the medium itself as it sets up possibilities and constraints for communication. Second, recognizing that a medium has a communicative effect on its own is not enough if we are to understand the range of communicative forms deployed by people in digital communication. These two observations together are somewhat trivial as no one would probably disagree. But what surprised me, thirdly, was that the connection between the medium itself and the forms of communication deployed was hard to trace in the literature. I was not able to find comprehensive attempts at updating genre as social action conceptually to accommodate digital media fostering specific forms of communication such as searching, archiving, or tagging. I could not find any attempt at trying to bridge media materiality and genre. Although, JoAnne Yates (1989), JoAnne Yates and Wanda Orlikowski (1992), and Inger Askehave and Anne Ellerup Nielsen (2005) began on this when they investigated the memo, e-mail, and web-mediated documents, they never fulfilled the mission completely.

Likewise, the edited works by Janet Giltrow and Dieter Stein (2009) and Carolyn Miller and Ashley Kelly (2018) are steps in these directions when looking at, respectively, internet genres and emerging genres within new media. But

DOI: https://doi.org/10.37514/PER-B.2023.1800.2.14

we cannot detect any sense or treatment of the importance of the medium as the analyses provided in these works have a point of departure in genres and not media. The two first observations may not be so trivial after all.

Charles Bazerman's contributions to writing, genre, and activity theory can be seen as key stepping-stones as to think further about how we may come to understand the communicative forms following from digital media and the habitual uses of these forms. Therefore, in this chapter, the goal is to open a discursive space in which to further think about how to understand digital forms of communication and how to rethink genre both in the light of Bazerman's work and what is broadly known as medium theory in media and communication studies. The thesis guiding this discussion is that with the permeation of digital media in society and culture, they not only become key sites for a whole range of public and private forms of communication, but they also shape our daily communicative actions along their "logics" such as searching, tagging, or archiving (Andersen, 2018). An implication of this thesis, then, is that digital media themselves are also key sites for understanding modern issues of genre and forms of communication afforded or implied by digital media.

So, what is being claimed here is that digital media is not just another kind of new media we (can) use in everyday life. Being a socio-material condition, digital media reconfigures our forms of communication and ways of being together in manners that depart from other media but of course at the same time also inherit (or remediate) aspects of previous media. Much of Bazerman's work (alongside with many other text and literary scholars) is for obvious historical reasons grounded in and tied to the print condition. I acknowledge that some of Bazerman's work is done with a view to digital media (Bazerman, 2001; 2002; 2016). But Bazerman's trajectory here seems to be more of trying to understand writing and genre in (light of) digital media simply because they are there and less the socio-material conditions afforded by digital media. For two reasons, then, it makes sense to couple ideas from medium theory with Bazerman's work. First, Bazerman can be said to be working in a social-phenomenological tradition with a substantial emphasis on activity, people, and their doings in communication, whether in a historical or contemporary setting. Such a kind of position is rarely, and for good reasons, interested in exploring material aspects of communication because of its phenomenological predisposition. Second, medium theory is rarely, and also for good reasons, interested in understanding people's doings in communication. Rather, the tradition seeks to explore a medium, its characteristics, and long-term effects on socio-cognitive aspects of human life and society at a large. I contend in this chapter that we cannot ignore neither side if we are to understand writing and genre as medium-specific and as communicative actions people accomplish due to how digital media offer particular kinds of communicative resources.

I begin with characterizing the medium theory tradition. From here I move on to characterize some of Bazerman's work on genre, writing, and activity to highlight what kind of thinking Bazerman is offering us on these matters of writing and genre. After this, I discuss how they matter to each other and how both are crucial ingredients if we are to understand modern forms of communication enacted by people in a range of situations in light of digital media saturation. I will end this discussion with an example of how search can be considered a typified social action.

MEDIUM MATTERS: A SHORT STORY OF MEDIUM THEORY

As a term symbolizing a school of thought in media and communication studies, medium theory was a term coined by Joshua Meyrowitz (1985; 1993; 1994) as an umbrella term for those kinds of studies focusing on the *medium* (in contrast to media in the plural) and its social and cognitive long-term effects on thinking, communication, and social interaction in general. In that sense, medium theory differs from the more traditional approaches in media and communication research focusing on media content or media grammar (Meyrowitz, 1993). Before being labeled by a single name, scholars as diverse as Eric Havelock, Harold Innis, Marshall McLuhan, Elisabeth Eisenstein, Jack Goody, and Walter Ong had been engaged with studies of socio-cultural effects of writing, printing, electronic media, and the whole question about orality versus writing. Meyrowitz calls them first-generation medium theorists (Meyrowitz, 1994) and places himself as second-generation medium theorist emphasizing the changing character of roles and social interaction implied by a new medium. Meyrowitz writes thus about medium theory:

> Medium theory focuses on the particular characteristics of each individual medium or of each particular type of media. Broadly speaking, medium theorists ask: What are the relatively fixed features of each means of communicating and how do these features make the medium physically, psychologically, and socially different from other media and from face-to-face interaction? (1994, p. 51)

In that sense, medium theory has a baseline of thinking that says that every medium has a set of characteristics/affordances furthering particular means and modes of communication and social interaction at the expense of others. The famous McLuhan-slogan, "The medium is the message" (McLuhan, 1964) encapsulates this kind of thinking. That is, a particular medium fosters particular forms of communication shaping the very content of that communication in terms of its format and presentation.

As such, medium theory does not pay that much attention to either the production or use side of media. Here is also where some common forms of critiques begin: you cannot estimate social and cognitive effects of media unless you study media and their use in a concrete context populated by a specific group of people. But medium theory invites us to pay particular attention to media as technologies and material configurations shaping particular forms of communication. It offers a particular gaze on media and communication, one that displaces use and users or audiences. A gaze that sensitizes us to focus on what a particular medium itself can do, and not, in terms of communication.

Regarding digital media and medium theory, some recent contributions are offered by, among others, Jay D. Bolter (2001), Lev Manovich (2001), Niels Ole Finnemann (1999, 2014), and John Durham Peters (2015). Individually and together, they update medium theory by paying attention to the specifics of digital media. For that reason, they deserve some attention here as they help us think about what is happening with digital communication and our practices with it.

Writing at a time when the internet was gaining social, cultural, and communicative impact Bolter (2001), for instance, pondered that digital media with its hypertextual bias would create a new writing space. As regards the printed book, Bolter, so far, was not right when claiming that digital media communication is dynamic and fluid in contrast to print as stable and durable. In fact, books of today are still stable and durable either in print or digital form. But books and journals, nonfiction in particular, can be linked to and shared, and its readers, views, and downloads counted, among other statistics. Social media platforms are course an example of a kind of new writing space, Bolter could not envision, yet his speculations points in that direction. Characterizing social media platforms like Twitter and Facebook is the re-birth of the author, not their death, to the extent the author has been declared dead by poststructuralists. Tweets and updates are filled with new forms of writing as an effect of digital media: hypertextual hashtags, links, posting, comments, and likes. In that sense, digital communication is fluid and dynamic as one's postings may easily disappear due to algorithmic moderation of feeds and tweets. But they are also stable and durable to the extent they archived by the platforms and by users. Search engines, too, are writing spaces. They store, circulate, and make items available by means of metadata attached to them in a database, a topical writing space, paraphrasing Bolter (2001, pp. 29–32). Thus, Bolter's idea of digital media as providing a new writing space thanks to their hypertextual and networked nature also points to their specifics.

Also, Danish medium theorist, Finnemann (1999, 2014, 2016) envisioned hypertext as a special characteristic of digital media but with a different take than

Rethinking Genre as Digital Social Action

Bolter. Finnemann (1999) regards digital media as fundamentally textual in that they are made of text (e.g., code) and they work communicatively by means of hypertext. Finnemann suggested hypertext to denote the change of modality between a reading mode and a browsing and navigation mode (Finnemann, 1999, p. 28) enabled by digital media. Avoiding making a strict dichotomy between printed forms of text and digital texts, Finnemann perceives of the differences between the two modes by pointing to how digital texts act, potentially, more like an archive with its linking, indexing, and search facilities in a single text or across texts (Finnemann, 1999, p. 16). This idea is further underscored by Finnemann when later emphasizing that digital media are always search engines as digital materials must be searched for by users to become visible:

> Digital media always convey some sort of digital material, and they are always also search engines which provide a repertoire of possible methods for analysing and presenting in a perceptible form otherwise invisible, stored digital materials. . . . Digital materials can only be accessed by means of digitally supported search and retrieval methods to establish the re-presentation of the invisible, stored content on a screen or another output device. (2014, pp. 304–306)

Digital content cannot be accessed and be made visible without search. This circumstance contributes to paving the way for perceiving search as a key communicative action in digital media and hence in digital culture.

In his book *The Language of New Media* (Manovich, 2001), Manovich launched the proposition that in digital media the database took center place at the expensive of narrative. He was asking us to pay attention to the databased forms of communication (to look up, to navigate, to search, or to list things in structured collections of items) and the way they would change our (inter)actions with and understandings of the symbolic products offered to us by means of digital media. With this argument, Manovich was trying to locate some specifics of the digital medium and how these specifics would cause changes in communicative actions. This line of thinking is also stressed by John Durham Peters when he claims that new (digital) media resemble ancient media of listing, sorting, structuring, arranging, or coordinating time, people, ideas, or information at large: "Digital media return us to the norm of data-processing devices of diverse size, shape, and format in which many people take part and polished 'content' is rare," and turning digital media into an "endless tagging, tracking, and tracing of our doings" (Peters, 2015, pp. 19, 23). What Peters here alludes to is a notion of digital media as media that primarily process and sort information (or data) at the expense of providing "content," as mass media do. That is, digital media can "contain" mass media (and they do) but fundamentally they operate on the premises of the computer as a data-processing machine making digital media different in form and function.

In sum, medium theory is a good reminder and a good tool to think with when our understandings of communication and communicative action become too focused on audience, reception, or use. Of course, people do things in and with communication. In fact, in many cases they are pretty good at it. But different media and their affordances shape how and what we can do in communication. For instance, the social and cultural force of liking is an action enacted by many people. But strictly speaking, we are not able to give a like if the particular medium setting does not provide us with that communicative opportunity. So, medium theory makes the simple, but often underestimated yet critical, remark that because individual media rely on particular technologies, they are different regarding the forms of communication they afford and how that impinge on social interaction and the formation of communities. Regarding typified forms of digital communication, the question is how digital media, and their characteristics are involved in communicative typification processes and how our social modes of recognition and expectations are correspondingly formed. With Bolter, Finnemann, Manovich, and Peters from above, we are reminded of how diverse material and technological set-ups like hypertext, the database, and data-processing configure communication in specific ways. This material aspect of communication is necessary to consider when talking about typified communication. Clearly, genres do not emerge out of the blue but out of activity and practice. Yet, they are also medium-specific although their formation and cultural uses are not determined by media only. But particular forms of media offer particular grounds for particular forms of communication to emerge.

BAZERMAN MATTERS: WRITING, GENRE, AND ACTIVITY

Of course, what follows on these pages do not do justice to the whole of Bazerman's work. But I can begin with a concrete event and place from where to get a glimpse of the work and its baseline mode of thinking. Participating in Bazerman's graduate course "History of Literacy and Social Organization" in fall 2001, Bazerman once asked us in the class 'What is it we want people to do better, when we teach them writing?' Given the course topics and readings, it was clear that the answer was not "To be better at grammar!" Writing was and is more than that. Writing does something and learning to write means learning to act in the world, learning to act with others and in particular situations with their own typifications and social and epistemological commitments. "Writing involves other people," as Bazerman wrote in the very first sentence in his textbook about writing, *The Informed Writer* (Bazerman, 1995, p. 2). Thus, researching and teaching writing is to understand the range of situations writers may be situated in and the range of conceptual tools available to writers. This little story, I think, encapsulates pretty well what kind of thinking Bazerman has been working with to unfold and strengthen during the years. There is a very consistent concern with writing in and through his work. But a concern that sees writing as empowering, shaping realities through and with others, and as a stabilizing factor in human activities where written communication plays a key role (see e.g., Bazerman, 1988; 1999).

In *Shaping Written Knowledge* (SWK) (Bazerman, 1988), comprising a range of pieces dealing with the emergence of the experimental article and its typifying force, we see how this thinking is articulated and given voice. In a footnote we are told how Bazerman distances himself from traditional literary understandings of genre and how he aligns himself with Miller's notion of genre as social action (Miller, 1984). Being dissatisfied with classic (and narrow) conceptions of genre as literary form, Bazerman had been on a hunt for a more socially oriented idea of genre and Miller offered exactly that. Still, at the end of SWK Bazerman elaborated on genre as a social-psychological category meaning a "category which we use to recognize and construct typified actions within typified situations. It is a way of creating order in the ever-fluid symbolic world" (1988, p. 319). However, perceiving genre in this manner both aligns with and differs from Miller. The emphasis on typified actions and typified situations come from Miller while the notion of genre as a social-psychological category must be interpreted as coming from Bazerman's affinity with the thinking of Lev Vygotsky and the cultural-historical school (i.e., activity theory) in psychology.

Bazerman is persistent in his attempts to understand and interrogate writing and writers as situated in "discursively structured activities" (Bazerman, 1997). Activities and contexts are structured in the sense that they are historically developed and as such were present before a concrete writing activity can take place. In that regard, they shape writing, writers, and any genre. In turn, any writing activity, writer and/or genre form the very activities and contexts by drawing on and mobilizing the rhetorical and symbolic resources offered by activities and contexts. That is, the relationship between a subject and object is never unmediated. From a genre and writing point of view, they are the tools mediating between them. This is a kind of thinking about writing, activity, and genre Bazerman is certainly not alone with (see e.g., Russell, 1997; Berkenkotter & Huckin, 1993; Spinuzzi, 2003; Winsor, 1999; Geisler, 2001) but it penetrates very consistently his thinking about these matters (for an overview see Bazerman, 2013a; 2013b) and it differentiates him from e.g., Miller (1984) and Amy Devitt (2004). In fact, the persistence with historicizing written communication to be able to explain the emergence of genres and activity contexts is also unique to Bazerman's mode of approaching topics and developing arguments (e.g., Bazerman, 1989; 1991; 1999; 2016).

It is through this line of reasoning Bazerman succeeds in establishing an understanding of written communication as localized, historical, rhetorical, political, and genred. But whereas Bazerman's focus is on these vital aspects of communication, he is less concerned with their material slants, even though his book on Thomas Alva Edison articulates a material aspect of communication (Bazerman, 1999). He is more interested in the doings of communication than with the participatory role of materiality partly enabling the doings, thereby subscribing more to pragmatic and phenomenological understandings of language and communication.

WHY DOES IT MATTER AT ALL? DISCUSSING MEDIA AS COMMUNICATIVE FORMS WITH GENRE AND ACTIVITY PERSPECTIVES

I will start the examination in this section from a point of departure that accepts the initial premise that digital media (or technologies) nowadays form the fundamental socio-material set-up for all major forms of communication, including writing, and social interaction. But digital media do not preempt what kinds of typified forms of communication people, organizations, and other collectives will enact in human activities. Nevertheless, we can observe in current digital culture forms of communication such as tagging, searching, liking, or tweeting that are promoted as prevailing exactly due to digital media performing as data-processing devices (cf., Peters, 2015). As medium theory insists on understanding the particulars of any medium it makes a good tool to think with in matters of communication and of any creation of new cultural forms and objects. Medium theory is a key to look back from particular genres and see how, and to what extent, they are specific to the medium in which they operate and are put to action by people.

Medium theory reminds us that media as socio-material configurations are communicative forms in and by themselves. They set up limits as to how and what to communicate in what ways. Television has a visual slant while radio has an audio slant. Writing is also visual but is also a storage medium in that writing stores writing (Kittler, 1999, p. 7). Digital media, too, are at one and the same time both archival and communication media that "traffic less in content, programs and opinions than in organization, power, and calculation. Digital media serve more as logistical devices of tracking and orientation than in providing unifying stories to the society at large" (Peters, 2015, p. 7). One consequence of the thinking offered to us by medium theory is that some forms of communication (i.e., genres) are relatively unique to the medium. This lead, for instance, Lev Manovich to propose that the database was a unique genre in digital media (Manovich, 1999; 2001) because digital media have a bias towards communicating "content" in terms of structured collections of items. Born-digital materials/content must be searched for to become visible for human sense-making meaning they have some form of metadata assigned to them in a database (Finnemann, 2014). This socio-material set-up implies that digital media privilege navigation, searching, and looking up as primary modes of communicative interaction as opposed to reading, viewing, or listening. But it is more than just a set-up or an infrastructural background. Also being automated media (Andrejevic, 2020), digital media collect, and process data continuously based on the actions of users and through this attempt to anticipate actions by providing e.g., recommendations, monitoring, or predictions. In other words, because of users' actions, materiality communicates through feedback, and through this shape typified forms of communication. For instance, we learn what to expect when we use Facebook or Google for locating items of information because what they return to us is determined by what, and how, they algorithmically collect. Thus, when what Miller (1984, p. 156) claimed about recurrence, that it could not be a material configuration of objects and could not be understood on material terms, is challenged with digital media, as recurrence here is part of how they communicate materially.

Bazerman and medium theory do share one thing in common: the de-emphasis on the importance of the single message/text and its socio-cognitive effect in communication. Approaching such a de-emphasis from, respectively, genre and media's technological set-up serve to underscore how we can understand human communication nevertheless without resorting to pure behavioristic explanations. However, while most of Bazerman's conceptualizations of genre, activity, and writing are pretty good at pointing at the localized, historical, and practice aspects, it is less good at providing us with a sense of why some forms of communication are appropriated in the first place. Why has Twitter and tweets succeeded in becoming powerful forms of political communication? Why has tagging suddenly gained such a social and cultural prominence? Why does search seem to be such a dominant communicative action with digital media? Answering these questions from a medium theory point of view, you would point to digital media and their cultural techniques of searching and archiving as being specific to their function as *digital* media. Then Bazerman might ask what kind of resources (symbolic, material, and social) do digital media offer to the writer? How can a writer mobilize their communicative actions through digital media? Here Johnson-Eilola argues that search engines constitute new forms of writing because one makes choices about what to include and exclude and "these choices involve responsibilities to the reader and to society, just as we do in other, more traditional forms of writing" (2004, p. 220). What Johnson-Eilola here points out is of great importance because he is reminding us that in constructing search engines, we may not write linear prose, but by means of writing, and based on our choices, we produce categories and collections with social and cultural implications.

Today, we are a bit sharper on this point. We are aware that algorithms produce categories and categorizations. But the problem remains the same as algorithms must be coded and written by someone making assumptions about the world in which the algorithm is intended to intervene in. Therefore, when Bazerman in his book, *The Informed Writer*, in the very first sentence makes it clear that "[w]riting involves other people" (1995, p. 2), this statement is still, or even more, pertinent and telling in a world of digital communication.

Of course, one can always counterargue that a one-sided focus on the medium will tell us nothing about the uses to which the medium is put and the communicative practices it fosters; that we are not able to get a sense of how and why some forms of communication become typified through their repeated uses with an emphasis on the medium only. Typification in communication obviously grow out of people's activity-based uses. True. But then again use cannot enter the picture before some means of communication, and what it affords, materializes. The stabilization of formats, titles, and page setup could not happen without printing, for instance. Let us, therefore, look at search as a typified social action as a modern example.

EXAMPLE: SEARCHING AS TYPIFIED DIGITAL ACTION

Online searching happens at the intersection of media materiality and communicative activities of humans. Materially, search engines, apps, social media, and other forms of media acting like structured collections of items turn search into a typified action. What to expect of and how to recognize the situations in which searching is called for is shaped by the role digital media play in our communicative interactions. In digital media, many cultural products, goods, movies, songs, or texts cannot be approached by feeling, touching, watching, listening, or reading them. They must be called upon, so to speak, and search is the key communicative action to be performed here. In that sense, we expect that things are coded for search in digital media. Such codification is part of the material work of digital media. Items (whether shoes, kitchen supplies, clothes) in a digital collection are all binary items and must be described by metadata and arranged in a collection. The items do only exist digitally by means of this description and arrangement activity. Thus, such codification helps to create the socially and typified forms of expectations and recognitions users, publics, audiences, or customers approach digital media in terms of searching.

Socially, searching is a communicative action in the sense that we search by typing in keywords in a search box or by talking to virtual voice assistants such as Siri. But how do we recognize situations that require of us the action of searching? What prompts us to search, with the words of Bitzer (1968)? In digital culture we constantly find ourselves in a variety of situations where we look up things but for various reasons. Some may look up recipes, some may look up the best flight ticket prices for the coming summer holidays, and some may look up things to resolve an argument (cf. Sundin et al., 2017). Searching is a form of relating to someone, or something, or looking for what is there. Searching is to look for connections and collectives and, in that sense, becomes a social space for accomplishing social action. Again, as many things in digital culture are coded for search it becomes a rather routinized, or typified, activity, we as humans are involved in when struggling with making sense of digital mediated forms of communication and social interaction. So, whereas searching has been around for centuries, the proclivity of digital media turn search into a particular genre because they perform as media of listing, arranging, or organizing items. Due to this condition, our only way of communicating with, making sense of, and using digital materials is through search.

Surely, Bazerman would resort to history and respond to this situation with asking where did search come from and how did search emerge as a particular genre in digital media? Tracing where search as a human activity come from is obviously difficult. We can speculate that hunters and gathers way back in human history would be looking for good places to find and collect food as an everyday activity. Also, rhetoric and its concept of topoi designating the place you go to and look for ideas and arguments when preparing your speech and/or production of written text, can also be understood as an awareness of search as an activity in which someone is looking for something.

The emergence of the written list in human history also occasioned a sense of looking things up and affording specific literacy skills as the content is presented in (e.g., columns and rows) but also providing the possibility of going back to the list as a recall operation (Goody, 1977). To this end, Ong argued that in primary oral cultures words are sounds and have no visual presence, meaning that "the expression 'to look up something' is an empty phrase" (1982, p. 31) as there is no material space to look. Only with writing came material memory devices such as dictionaries, indexes, commonplace books, and other reference works as places (as topoi) to go to look up things. In the library world, search has always been (and still is) considered a distinct way of communicating with materials, whether as a particular professional skill or as an activity in which patrons are involved with when seeking materials. In the libraries existing at the intersection of oral and writing cultures, it has been argued that singing in the library might have been a mode of retrieving materials (Olesen-Bagneux, 2017). Print library catalogues had three formal access points: title, author, and keyword(s); that is, the materials libraries provided access to have a title, an author, and some controlled keywords. With the online public access catalogues (OPAC's) being launched the 1960s and 70s, these access points were still in place and became defining access points as separate search boxes for each would be provided in an interface. Also, the access points could now be combined in a Boolean search with the addition that the user could also type in their own (uncontrolled) keywords in the keywords box. Although several additional access points would be added over the years (e.g., citation indexing, hypertext, or full text), the formal access points were mostly in place up until Google revolutionized the idea of search and provided only one search bar. Recalling that the first search indexes such as AltaVista, Lycos, or Yahoo provided categories and indexes to be used in search, Google did not have the idea of the book, the single journal article, or any other single item with authors and titles as the material items to be indexed. In fact, Google celebrates that everything it collects, and indexes is searchable by a variety of means (e.g., links, URL, filenames, words in full text, images). On top of that, the proliferation of social media platforms and streaming services have further spurred the idea of search, whether that includes searching for people, events, or cultural products, turning search into an everyday activity (Sundin et al., 2017). Furthermore, the prominence of the verb "to google" in everyday language use suggests an institutionalization of search.

Such a historical emphasis helps explaining how and why we can understand searching as typified digital action. While searching as a human activity has always been with us, digital media are the forms of media where search came to the forefront due to the listlike nature of most digital media forms (see e.g., Young, 2017) and because of the permeation and the domestication of digital media in almost all spheres of society, whether items are appearing as a single born-digital material or as a structured collection of hyperlinks. But contrary to the old Goody-question, "What's in a list?" (Goody, 1977) implying that we can go to a list and see what kind of content it arranges and coordinates and what power it provides to those capable of decoding a list, such a question (e.g., "What's in a search engine?") is almost nonsense in a digital media culture because we are not able to obtain a sense of what kind of content it arranges and collects as it is fairly black-boxed. It is simply not visible to us before searching for it. In that sense we can say that digital media and their materiality give search a typifying force it has not had in earlier media epochs, and with earlier media forms, because we must search in order to get in touch with digital content.

So, paraphrasing Bazerman's question to our graduate class back in 2001, we can now ask, "What is it we want people to do better, when we teach them searching?" As text and information come in various forms by means of a range of systems, platforms, and media acting like structured collections of items, people will want to know the modes of search fitting to their situations and to the particular medium they are employing for search. This is more than knowing the "right" keywords to use as these are dynamic depending on the particular medium we are employing and ours and others' previous actions. Searching involves other people (whether big tech, academia, or ordinary users) and it is a way relating to other people through search. Search is communicative in its desire for contact. Thus, learning to search is to be able to act and how to accomplish action through search.

CONCLUSION

In this chapter I have tried to add to Bazerman's thoughts about writing, genre, and activity some portion of medium theory gear. My reason for doing that is some form of discomfort with the thinking about genre, in particular, in purely phenomenological or social constructivist terms. However, to be fair, Bazerman does not see himself as a media and communication scholar (I believe), yet he is probably one of the very few, if not the only one, in writing and genre studies who is informed by some form of medium theory thinking, as we can trace references to Havelock, Ong, Eisenstein, and, not least, Goody in his work. In fact, Bazerman contributed with a piece in a book examining the implications of Goody's work (Bazerman, 2006). But what I wanted to stir attention to here is how digital media foster typified forms of communication because of their characteristics, for sure, but also because of the repeated use of these forms. In that sense, I may have made an a priori conceptualization of searching as typified action; that is, one that is not developed as a straight empirical consequence of particular activities and practices enacting search (on this matter see, Sundin et al., 2017). Yet, I have tried to associate this conceptualization as closely as possible with what we know about and can align with practices in everyday life. To this end, I have added what I consider as indispensable when trying to understand search as typified digital action: the characteristics of digital media as acting as media that list, arrange, and organize items as their raison d'être. So, whereas medium theory is good at explaining what forms of communication some media make possible, or afford, genre theory is good at explaining why and how some forms of communication become stabilized and helps accomplishing social action. But we cannot escape either of them when trying to account for the emergence and prominence of certain forms of communication in human culture.

REFERENCES

Andersen, J. (2022). Genre as digital social action: The case of archiving, tagging and searching in digital media culture. *Journal of Documentation, 78*(2), 228–241

Andersen, J. (2018). Archiving, ordering, and searching: Search engines, algorithms, databases, and deep mediatization. *Media, Culture & Society, 40*(8), 1135–1150.

Andersen, J. (2017a). Genre, organized knowledge, and communicative action in digital culture. In J. Andersen & L. Skouvig (Eds.), *The organization of knowledge: Caught between global structures and local meaning, 12* (pp. 1–16). Emerald Group Publishing.

Andersen, J. (2017b). Genre, the organization of knowledge, and everyday life. *Information Research, 22*(1). http://InformationR.net/ir/22-1/colis/colis1647.html.

Andrejevic, M. (2020). *Automated media*. Routledge.

Askehave, I. & Nielsen, A. E. (2005). Digital genres: A challenge to traditional genre theory. *Information Technology & People, 18*(2), 120–141.

Bazerman, C. (1988). *Shaping written knowledge: The genre and activity of the experimental article in science*. University of Wisconsin Press.

Bazerman, C. (1991). How natural philosophers can cooperate: The rhetorical technology of coordinated research in Joseph Priestle's History and Present State of Electricity. In C. Bazerman & J. Paradis (Eds.), *Textual dynamics of the professions: Historical and contemporary studies of writing in professional communities* (pp. 13–44). University of Wisconsin Press.

Bazerman, C. (1995). *The informed writer: Using sources in the disciplines*. Houghton Mifflin.

Bazerman, C. (1997). Discursively structured activities. *Mind, Culture, and Activity, 4*(4), 296–308.

Bazerman, C. (1999). *The languages of Edison's light*. MIT Press.

Bazerman, C. (2001). Politically wired: The changing places of political participation in the age of the internet. In J. Yates & J. van Maanen (Eds.), *Information technology and organizational transformation: History, rhetoric, and practice* (pp. 137–154). Sage.

Bazerman, C. (2002). Genre and identity: Citizenship in the age of the internet and the age of global capitalism. In R. Coe, L. Lingard & T. Teslenko (Eds.), *Rhetoric and ideology of genre: Strategies for stability and change* (pp. 13–30). Hampton Press.

Bazerman, C. (2006). The writing of social organization and the literate situating of cognition: Extending Goody's social implications of writing. In D. R. Olson & M. Cole (Eds.), *Technology, literacy, and the evolution of society implications of the work of Jack Goody* (pp. 215–239). Lawrence Erlbaum.

Bazerman, C. (2013a). *A rhetoric of literate action: Literate action volume 1*. The WAC Clearinghouse; Parlor Press. https://doi.org/10.37514/PER-B.2013.0513.

Bazerman, C. (2013b). *A theory of literate action: Literate action volume 2*. The WAC Clearinghouse; Parlor Press. https://doi.org/10.37514/PER-B.2013.4791.

Bazerman, C. (2016). Social changes in science communication: Rattling the information chain. In J. Buehl & A. Gross (Eds.), *Science and the internet: Communicating knowledge in a digital* age (pp. 267–282). Baywood.

Berkenkotter, C. & Huckin, T. N. (1993). Rethinking genre from a sociocognitive perspective. *Written Communication, 10*(4), 475–509.

Bitzer, L. F. (1968). The rhetorical situation. *Philosophy & Rhetoric, 1*(1), 1–14.

Bolter, J. D. (2001). *Writing space. Computers, hypertext and the remediation of print.* Lawrence Erlbaum.

Devitt, A. (2004). *Writing genres.* Southern Illinois University Press.

Eisenstein, E. L. (1979). *The printing press as an agent of change: Communications and cultural transformations in Early-Modern Europe.* Cambridge University Press.

Finnemann, N. O. (1999). *Hypertext and the representational capacities of the binary alphabet.* Center for Kulturforskning, Aarhus Universitet.

Finnemann, N. O. (2014). Digitization: New trajectories of mediatization? In K. Lundby (Ed.), *Mediatization of communication, Handbooks of communication science, 21(1)* (pp. 297–321). Mouton de Gruyter.

Finnemann, N. O. (2016). Hypertext configurations: Genres in networked digital media. *Journal of the Association for Information Science and Technology, 68,* 845–854.

Geisler, C. (2001). Textual objects: Accounting for the role of texts in the everyday life of complex organizations. *Written Communication, 18*(3), 296–325.

Giltrow, J. & Stein, D. (2009). *Genres in the internet: Issues in the theory of genre.* John Benjamins.

Goody, J. (1977). *The domestication of the savage mind.* Cambridge University Press.

Innis, H. (1951). *The bias of communication.* University of Toronto Press.

Johnson-Eilola, J. (2004). The database and the essay: Understanding composition as articulation. In A. F. Wysocki, J. Johnson-Eilola, C. L. Selfe & G. Sirc (Eds.), *Writing new media: Theory and applications for expanding the teaching of composition* (pp. 199–235). Utah State University Press.

Kittler, F. A. (1999). *Gramophone, film, typewriter.* Stanford University Press.

Manovich, L. (2001). *The language of new media.* MIT Press.

McLuhan, M. (1964). *Understanding media: The extensions of man.* McGraw-Hill.

Meyrowitz, J. (1985). *No sense of place. The impact of electronic media on social behavior.* Oxford University Press.

Meyrowitz, J. (1993). Images of media: Hidden ferment—and harmony—in the field. *Journal of Communication, 43*(3), 55–66.

Meyrowitz, J. (1994). Medium theory. In D. Crowley & D. Mitchell (Eds.), *Communication theory today* (pp. 50–77). Polity Press.

Miller, C. R. (1984). Genre as social action. *Quarterly Journal of Speech, 70*(2), 151–167.

Miller, C. R., Devitt, A. J. & Gallagher, V. J. (2018). Genre: Permanence and change. *Rhetoric Society Quarterly, 48*(3), 269–277.

Miller, C. R. & Kelly, A. R. (Eds.). (2017). *Emerging Genres in new media environments.* Palgrave Macmillan.

Olesen-Bagneux, O. (2017). The library before print and after the computer: The similarities between string search algorithms and mnemonic retrieval in pre-print libraries. *The Information Society, 33*(4), 205–214.

Ong, W. (1982). *Orality and literacy*. Methuen.

Peters, J. D. (2015). *The marvelous clouds. Toward a philosophy of elemental media*. University of Chicago Press.

Russell, D. R. (1997). Rethinking genre in school and society: An activity theory analysis. *Written Communication, 14*(4), 504–554.

Spinuzzi, C. (2003). *Tracing genres through organizations: A sociocultural approach to information design*. MIT Press.

Sundin, O., Haider, J., Andersson, C., Carlsson, H. & Kjellberg, S. (2016). The search-ification of everyday life and the mundane-ification of search. *Journal of Documentation, 73*(2), 224–243.

Winsor, D. A. (1999). Genre and activity systems: The role of documentation in maintaining and changing engineering activity systems. *Written Communication, 16*(2), 200–224.

Yates, J. (1989). *Control through communication: The rise of system in American management*. John Hopkins University Press.

Yates, J. & Orlikowski, W. J. (1992). Genres of organizational communication: A structurational approach to studying communication and media. *Academy of Management Review, 17*(2), 299–326.

Young, L. (2017). *List cultures: Knowledge and poetics from mesopotamia to buzzfeed*. Amsterdam University Press.

CHAPTER 15.

WHAT WRITERS DO WITH LANGUAGE: INSCRIPTION AND FORMULATION AS CORE ELEMENTS OF THE SCIENCE OF WRITING

Otto Kruse and Christian Rapp
Zurich University of Applied Sciences

The digitalization of writing, Charles Bazerman (2018) notes, moves humans into the status of intellectual cyborgs when they increasingly rely on new technologies which cover what they are less well equipped to do than the machines:

> Technology ever increasingly is taking over the work previously done by humans in the composition, distribution, storage, access, and use of communications, and is doing new tasks previously unimagined. What will the human half of the cyborg need to be able to do? (2018, p. 1)

Since writing technologies have expanded beyond offering support for lower-order activities and now, additionally, connect writing seamlessly with communication, conceptualization, visualization, calculation, and publication, writers are forced to find new roles as text workers. Bazerman's interest in human-machine interaction is clearly at the human side, when he proposes to focus on what humans can do best, not on what the machines have learned to do.

Bazerman is well aware that writing has always been a technology (Bazerman, 2000; see also Gabrial, 2008; Ong, 1982) and frequently points out that the core feature of writing is the inscription of symbols on a writing surface: "Words are the material we work with, what we inscribe to create our meanings and influence the readers. When we are done [with] writing, they are what remains on the page for others to see" (Bazerman, 2013, p. 135). What we focus on in this paper is exactly this process of bringing words into an order and putting them down on a writing surface which we address under its traditional term "formulation."

At a time, when writing technologies become knowledgeable about language and start not only to support writers but actually write and translate themselves, it seems necessary to reconsider what we know about language use in writing activities. Digital technologies change the very nature of writing (DeVoss, 2018; Haas, 1996; Williams & Beam, 2019) by supporting writers with tools such as grammar and spell checkers, hyphenation programs, word prediction software, outline generators, or structured templates. More recently, digital tools have expanded their support to higher order concerns to assist writers with their conceptual and rhetorical decisions such as focusing, coherence, and use of collocations (Allen et al., 2015; Cotos, 2014; 2015; Kruse & Rapp, 2019; 2020; 2021; Strobl et al., 2019; Williams & Beam, 2019).

Studying formulation, for us, is not an abstract endeavor but a very practical issue resulting from our work on the development of a new writing platform, called *Thesis Writer* offering linguistic support to its users (Kruse & Rapp, 2019; Rapp et al., 2020). Also, we did extensive surveys and technology reviews into digital writing (Kruse & Rapp, 2019; 2020; Strobl et al., 2019). Compared to Bazerman's position, we are clearly more on the technological side of the cyborg trying to understand what the machines do to writing. *Thesis Writer* provides a digital writing space for student writers and offers them, among other help functions, linguistic support for formulation activity. They may, for instance, consult a large phrasebook or search an attached corpus of academic texts for the usage of words and collocations.

Constructing such a tool makes it necessary to understand not only how support for formulation can be provided but also which linguistic elements are worth being supported digitally. And the answers to both questions depend on an understanding of the nature of inscription tools. What exactly is happening when writers insert letters and words into a keyboard? This question may seem trivial but is easily overlooked when writing is researched from a purely cognitive perspective. Understanding the cyborg does not start with digitalization but with writing technology itself. The aim of this paper is to sketch the outline of a formulation theory on the basis of plausible assumptions about what actually happens during inscription in digital and non-digital contexts.

A SHORT HISTORY OF FORMULATION THEORY

Even if "formulation" is not a concept currently suffering from overutilization, it has a long history that goes back into the 19th and early 20th century when language usage became both a topic in psychology and in the newly emerging discipline of linguistics as Willem Levelt (2013) in an overview on the history of psycholinguistics shows. Most research on formulation, however, is exemplified on speech (Levelt, 1989) while formulation in writing is covered only sporadically. Formulation has been treated under various labels which also refer to different theoretical approaches. A much-used term is "sentence production" focusing particularly on the generation of the linguistic part of an utterance while the content aspect remains in the background. In psycholinguistics, the term "language production" is used for both, oral and written language creation, while "language generation" is preferred in computational linguistics.

A remarkable beginning of formulation theory is contained in a textbook on "The Pathology of Language" by Adolf Kussmaul (1877/2018) which was inspired by the neurological works of Broca, Wernicke, and Lichtheim, but also contained a general theory of language usage. Levelt considers it as the "very first psycholinguistic textbook" (2013, p. 84). It also contained a stage theory of (oral) formulation in which a preparatory stage consisting of the generation of thought and mood is assumed, followed by a second stage in which the diction is created, including syntax and word selection which, in the third stage, is then articulated as speech. Levelt (2013) sees this as a precursor of his own model of formulation (Levelt, 1989).

Wilhelm Wundt (1900), the founder of modern psychology, devoted the first of his 10-volume "Ethnic Psychology" to language picturing language as a main entrance gate to an understanding of culture and thinking. Wundt was convinced that language usage is driven by "functional exercises" connecting the motor part and the images in speaking, not by an abstract grammatical faculty. He devoted a large part of "The Language" to an analysis of sentence formation and created the phrase structure tree to account for different grammatical solutions. He started with the basic question of how a sentence arises in the speaker's mind (see Levelt, 2013, p. 193), which in his view would be the basic question for the study of formulation. In Wundt's understanding (we still follow Levelt's summary) this task demands to draw the attention on a particular issue of the "total image" that a writer initially may have on their mind. Formulation would be a selection process cutting this totality down into separate parts which then are successively connected to a sentence. His solutions for sentence structures are syntactic in nature demonstrating possible expressive varieties. His starting point for this was a subject-predicate structure to which he then successively included additional parts of sentences (POS) and their various relations. For Wundt, formulation was not understandable without a concept of syntax and other "speech forms." It is not possible for us, to do justice to Wundt's language theory, in which he reacted to a century of research before him and presented an integrated psychological and linguistic view garnished with anthropological and historical ideas.

Wundt inspired more research, particularly in Germany, which expanded his theory and followed new methodological paths. The fate of this rich line of research was not very fortunate. It first started to collide with the upcoming Behaviorism in which mental concepts were banned and language usage was more or less reduced to the motor part of articulation. Then it fell victim to the Nazi take over in 1933, which forced many researchers to emigrate or be sent to one of the concentration camps.

New theory families emerged with the upcoming computer age in the 1950s. The early pioneers of the computer age, as Howard Gardner (1985) explained, were struck by the similarities between the human's logical abilities and the logical operations that computer programs were able to conduct. They tried to model the mind in analogy to computer programs. One of the roots lies in the early Artificial Intelligence (AI) research as initiated by Allen Newell and Herbert A. Simon (1976), who assumed a structural equivalence of computation and mental processing, as stated in Newell and Simon's (1976) Physical Symbol Systems Hypothesis (for discussions see, for instance; Dreyfus, 1972; 1992; Varela et al., 1991/2016; Winograd, 1991).

The most influential idea about language production came from Noam Chomsky (1965, 1999) who was one of the leading protagonists of the new cognitive sciences and helped overcoming Behaviorism. For him, the cognitive basis of the mind was a syntactic unit, allowing to combine words by syntactic rules. This approach to a "generative grammar" basically served the same function as a formulation theory, except that it also was a thinking theory. Chomsky believed in an algebraically working syntax at the bottom of human thinking. He finally arrived at the conclusion that there must be a universal grammar as a general linguistic competence shared by humans while natural languages are merely deviations of this universal capacity. This assumption was justified by the "poverty of stimulus" argument which claims that grammar must at least partly be inherited because education in general was too poor to explain the learning of a competence as complex as grammar. Exactly what cannot be explained by education, in Chomsky's argumentation, has to be inherited.

What is of particular importance in this model is that the computational grammar Chomsky was referring to cannot be a natural language. Cognitive models following Chomsky similarly proposed a computationally functioning mind as those of Jerry Fodor (1975, 2008) and Steve Pinker (1995), who both assumed that there must be a particular language for computations called "language of thought (LOT)," or "mentalese." Next to the poverty of stimulus argument, Pinker claimed that natural languages are to imperfect for computational thinking. Excluding natural languages from thinking, however, is a far-reaching decision not only for theory building, but also in terms of language education and the teaching of writing.

Currently, only the cognitive writing model in the tradition of John Hayes and Linda Flower (1980) (see also; Flower & Hayes, 1980; 1981; Hayes, 2012b) offers a theory of formulation for writing, even though formulation, in this context, is called "translation." The general structure of the model sees writing separated into several distinct but interacting "processes" which together form an iterative, goal directed activity. Writers draw materials of different kinds from memory and structure it—in accordance with a writing plan—to a message that then is translated into language. Chenoweth and Hayes describe sentence generation in the following ways:

> In many writing tasks we would expect that sentence generation would start with the proposer, which, influenced by the task goal and the text written so far, would generate prelinguistic material and pass it to the translator. The translator would then process the prelinguistic input and store its output in an articulatory buffer where it would be evaluated by the reviser. If the output is judged acceptable, then the transcriber will add it to the text written so far. If the output is deemed unacceptable, the proposer or the translator could opt to try again. (2001, p. 85)

In this description, they do not talk about processes but about processors, structural units which do the basic work of sentence generation and interact with each other fairly similar to how humans would. In their view, these processors are capable of creating "prelinguistic" material (called a "thought package") which is then checked and eventually translated into language. Even though the described process is called "sentence generation" no clue about linguistic activities such as word selection, usage of phrases, grammar, and the like are given. Linguistic specifications such as Wundt and Chomsky had offered, are omitted. Sentence planning is an overly cognitive process carried out left-handedly by a cognitive operator. In a later version of the model (Hayes, 2012a), the "translator" is completed by another cognitive processor, called "transcriber" which is assumed to bring the linguistically transformed word package into script.

Although there are several extensions and transformations of the translation idea (Alamargot & Chanquoy, 2001; Fayol et al., 2012; Galbraith, 1999; 2009; Hayes, 1996), trying to account better for the linguistic part of the emerging text, language remains excluded from thinking. Thinking, in all model variations, is done without language, obviously relying on some unspecified computational power of the mind. Chomsky assumed that it would happen on the basis of a generative grammar, Fodor assumed a "language of thought" (LOT) or a "mentalese" to think with. Hayes and Flower never disclosed what their ideas about the nature of the cognitive processes are, except that there are some memory structures containing topic knowledge, linguistic knowledge, and so on.

We have to assume that the concept of the cognitive processes follows the computational idea of the early AI research in the tradition of Newell and Simon (1976), in which Hayes had been involved (Hayes & Simon, 1974; 1976; 1979). This approach claimed that the human mind and computers process symbols in similar ways, for which they chose the term "cognition" (cf., Varela et al., 1991/2016; Winograd, 1991). To understand human thinking, they designed architectural models of the mind based on the idea of algorithmic processes as the core of human thinking. When thinking is explained in such terms then, indeed, the results of the computations then must be "translated" into natural languages while readers, in contrast, would have to re-translate text into the prelinguistic cognitive structure to understand it. We propose, in contrast to this position, that human thinking always involves words, phrases, and grammars of natural languages.

Formulation, in this paper, is not seen as an activity that sets in when the thinking is done, but we follow Wrobel's (1995, 1997, 2002) claim that formulation is the thinking itself, or, to be more precise, formulation in writing is thinking enhanced by a writing medium. In Walter Ong's words: "Writing is a technology that restructures thought" (2001). What this means, we will explain in detail in the following chapter.

THEORETICAL FRAME: INSCRIPTION AS A LINEARIZATION TECHNOLOGY

This chapter offers a new perspective on formulation theory starting with the question of what it means that, in speaking and writing, information has to be linearized to be transmitted to listeners and readers. Creating linearity is more than deciding on an order to present content because the order has to be created also linguistically by means of sentence construction, grammar, and the use of function words to organize the text. For writers, formulation means selecting the next word to be inscribed but thinking ahead to anticipate the course of the next sentences.

Formulation and Inscription: Definitions

We define "formulation" as the mental activities by which a writer selects words and phrases to create a meaningful chain of words, commonly called "text." We prefer the term "mental" over "cognitive" in order not to restrict theory building to one particular mental modality and avoid the exclusion of linguistic, emotional, or imaginative components. We neither define formulation primarily through the construction of content even if this is what formulation results in. But the construction of content is done by a broad array of thinking and reading activities before and during writing. Formulation refers only to the moment when particular thought is selected to be included in the emerging line of words in progress. What formulation theory has to explain is not content generation but the miraculously effective selection process of words and word forms to create meaningful sentences.

In written communication, formulation centers around the inscription process in which words are placed on a writing surface such as papyrus, paper, or, more recently, a digital medium. Bazerman explains that this process is far from being trivial when children have to learn it:

> The inscription of letters or characters is the first clunkiness that people learning to write encounter, whether with a stylus forming cuneiform on clay, a brush forming ideographic characters on scrolls, or a pencil forming alphabetic letters in school notebooks. Much of writing education over millennia has been devoted to teaching fine motor control and visual discrimination, manipulation of writing instruments, form and decipherment of characters, spelling, arrangement of symbols on the medium, and so on. In every child's life, five or more years are devoted to gaining reasonable competence in transcribing words and sentences. Technology has been long easing those burdens, replacing stylus and brush with pens and pencils of increasing ease and reliability, and simplifying letterforms and scripts. (2018, p. 7)

In mature writers, we assume that these difficulties are solved, and inscription is referred to as a lower-order activity as compared to the higher order activities of content development, text organization and formulation. Still, inscription is what defines writing. It may be seen as a notation procedure for letters and words (or more basically: for phonemes), which are created mentally or acoustically and then placed manually on a writing surface. Inscription is the result of formulation or, as in digital writing, it is accompanied by formulation activity.

Inscription is a manual, not a cognitive activity that always needs some form of technology (Haas, 1996; Mahlow & Dale, 2014; Ong, 1982), while formulating is a purely mental activity. In writing, however, formulation is not independent of inscription as writers usually develop their text in interaction with what they write down or have already written. They can reread it, rethink it, revise, and extend it.

Thinking during writing is thus supported by the visual control of the successively emerging language string. This control is one of the advantages of writing over speaking as it adds vision to sound while oral speech uses sound alone (de Beaugrande, 1984). The fixation of words on a surface makes language permanently visible and offers a new perspective on the writer's own thoughts. Writers can contrast two different images of their thoughts with each other: the thought as it appears when it is still purely mental, and as it appears when seen on paper or on screen as a written expression. Writers learn to match these two images of thought, and formulation means to successively align them with each other. We have to assume, that both, the mental image of the thought and its written expression, are equally changed within this process. Writing is not simply a print-out of thought but a tentative movement to understand one's own thought in the light of written language. We will have to discuss, though, what the mental image of thought is and how much or what kind of language it already contains.

LINEARITY AND SEQUENTIALITY

The most fundamental constraint of language production, both oral and written, is its strict linearity in which one word follows another and in which only one word can be placed in a certain space (or said at a certain moment of time), never two or more. Inscription, thus, may be considered a linearization technology in which letters and words are lined up one by one. Formulation, in turn, is always concerned with finding the next word to be inscribed. Similar as in chess, the writer may and must think further ahead but can do only one move at a time. Different from chess, moves can be taken back and replaced repeatedly (at least in digital writing) until the best move or word is found.

While "linearity" refers to an order in which one element follows another directly and no parallelism is possible, "sequentiality" means that the order is meaningful and that the elements are related to each other by identifiable rules. The third term, "seriality" is mostly used as a synonym to "linearity" but has in computer science additionally the meaning of command structures in programs which follow one path only and where all steps of a chain of commands have to be followed, as opposed to parallel processing structures.

In language production, grammar is such a connecting force that, to a large extent, consists of rules of managing linearity and organizing the relations of subsequent words or textual elements (de Beaugrande, 1984). Sequentiality in writing is unidirectional and the line of symbols can be created and read in one direction only. The meaning of later elements depends on what has been said earlier. This makes the difference to visual representations which can be read in several directions. Writers have to partition the information along a sequential order and then interconnect them to create coherence. For this, any language needs reference systems, called "deictic means" pointing back at things said earlier and forward at things that will be said later (anaphoric and cataphoric reference). Linearity applies not only to linguistic principles of interconnectedness but is often used to refer to thought organization as well and to the order in which content is presented (Alamargot & Chanquoy, 2001; Levelt, 1982). Even if interrelated, both kinds of linearity should be kept apart.

The question of where linearity and sequentiality in thinking come from and how we may account for them has been brought up by Karl Lashley (1951). He noticed that the behaviorist explanation of linearity as associative chains or chains of reflexes was not satisfactory as it would lead to a randomly generated connectivity. He discussed the idea that seriality of behavior may be explained by outer demands or procedural necessities, but this would not solve the question of mental seriality as it happens in thinking. The solution Lashley proposed, was that grammar may explain seriality which to him seemed a means of coordinating the spatial arrangement of memory with the temporal arrangement of language when he said, "The translation from the spatial distribution of memory traces to temporal sequence seems to be a fundamental aspect of the problem of serial order" (1951). Language, thus, transforms the rather static structure of memory into the dynamic order of speech. Chomsky (1955) picked up this idea and later made it part of his transformational grammar.

We have to be careful, though, to see grammar as the *cause* of linearity, as Chomsky did. Grammar is, if anything, the root of *sequentiality* providing the connecting rules. Grammar helps organizing it and cares for the interconnections between symbols but what creates language dynamics in first place, is its enforced linearity. Also, linearity is not created by cognitive activities. The order of causality is exactly the opposite: human cognitions are shaped by the constant need to produce linear and sequential content in both speaking and writing. Cognitions stand in the service of language production which Slobin (1996) called "thinking for speaking" and "thinking for writing" (Slobin, 2003).

We don't think that it is cognitive activity that makes memory content linear and dynamic but that it is the linearity and dynamics of language that makes the human mind progress in thinking. Cognitions such as discrimination, concept building, use of schemata, memory structures are certainly necessary to organize linearity or sequentiality but can do so only in relation to what language demands. Imagination, certainly, is a serial mental activity but it is based on visuals which cannot account for logical thinking and would not build a bridge to language production. It is the enforced successivity of word use, that makes the human mind run and that eventually makes it appear similar to a computer program, only that computer programs are driven by a pulse generator, not by the need to decide on the next word.

The deepest justification to separate formulation as a particular part of writing as well as of thinking is given by its function as a transformational agent making out of static memory content a dynamic flow of words. Formulation completely serves the generation of sequentiality and it has to account for both, its unique form as a message and its devotion to the "orderliness of language," as Bazerman (2013) said.

INSCRIPTION AS THE BOTTLE NECK OF THE WRITING PROCESS

Inscription is the basic process of word notation but may also become the bottleneck of formulation activity, an idea that Hayes (2012a) originally brought forward. Particularly in academic writing, there are usually more thoughts and preliminary formulations piled up before this bottleneck, all awaiting linearization. The congestion at this bottleneck can be the result of a slow inscription system but may also be indicative of strategies missing for the selection and integration of content for inscription. When we talk of writing blocks, we usually picture this as a kind of mental traffic jam. Keith Hjortshoj (2001) observed that blocks happen when writers have too many ideas about what to write but lack a proper strategy for selecting or linearizing them.

Once a word, phrase, or sentence has passed this bottleneck and found its place on the writing surface, the formulation process can proceed and the writer can prepare the next string of words. Owing to digital word processors, inscribed words are no longer immovable as they once were on papyrus or paper but can now be altered flexibly and with little effort or requirement for time (Baron, 2009; Bazerman, 2018; Sharples & Pemberton, 1990). This has resulted in much better ways of managing linearity in writing and interconnecting symbols. Formulation has been extended beyond the moment of inscription. After just a few words or lines, writers usually go back to read what they have written and then start revising until the text meets their expectations. When we look at screen recording of writings today, we have the impression, that writers tend to think less prior to inscription and postpone their thinking to the moment when they can see their ideas appear as words on the screen. Often, they seem to put down short notes or single words first, before they start elaborating them (Gautschi et al., 2021). Producing linear text, today, must not necessarily comply to a linear order of the text immediately, as was necessary with paper and pencil but can jump back and forth or correct something from former parts. It is as if chess players were allowed to do the third and fourth moves first and then look what the first and second ones could be.

Oral Support for Written Language

Arne Wrobel (2002) noted, that the presence of oral speech whilst trying to write something down is an essential part of formulation. Writers often are engaged in some kind of internal dialogue when formulating, as can be seen in think-aloud studies. The fact that experienced writers usually do not talk to themselves out aloud like in the experimental situation may be explained by the interiorization of external speech to inner speech in the sense of Jean Piaget (1972) and Lew Semjonowitsch Vygotski (1934/1961). If we assume that language is involved in thinking, then Vygotsky's idea of inner speech is still the one that is most convincing. Vygotsky saw inner speech markedly different form external speech: "Inner speech must not be regarded . . . as speech minus sound, but as an entirely separate speech function. Its main distinguishing trait is its peculiar syntax. Compared with external speech, inner speech appears disconnected and incomplete" (1934/1961, p. 138). Still, inner speech is sequential and can organize thought even if it would need some transformation to become written language.

An important issue of formulation is "pretext," a concept proposed by Stephen Witte (1987) that refers to the concept that formulations do not arrive all at once and are then inscribed, but that formulation is a matter of linguistic preparation in which a writer slowly approaches the textual form of what may possibly be written down. Witte defined pre-text as a "writer's tentative linguistic representation of intended meaning, that is produced in the mind, stored in the writer's memory, and sometimes manipulated mentally prior to being transcribed as written text" (1987, p. 397). In other words, writers do not simply think about the words they could use, but produce and alter several versions of interconnected words mentally. Wrobel called this "pretextual formulating" (2002, p. 93) which he considered to be a cyclical process in which wordings are created and changed successively. The quality of this iterative activity depends on the availability of linguistic resources and metalinguistic awareness. In digital writing, we observe that writers do these try-outs of possible formulations rather on screen and not in their minds. They obviously don't do the thinking before but after inscription (Gautschi et al., 2021).

Writers produce far more words, Wrobel (2002) observed, than the emerging text actually requires. While Wrobel suggested that the excess words were oral, today, they are words that are written and cut out during revision. The relation between words written and words remaining in some writers can be 2:1, meaning that 50% of the words written down are deleted again (Gautschi et al., 2021). Formulation, in this meaning could be considered as a way of testing various wordings from which the most suitable ones remain in the text. It matters to keep in mind, that the traditional sequence of thinking—inscription—revision does not seem to apply to many young writers (Gautschi et al., 2021). Rather, the sequence we found often was inscription—thinking—revision or even inscription—revision—thinking.

Moving Focus

Formulation depends not only on what a writer wants to say and an audience needs to be told, but also on what needs to be said at a certain point in the text (and sometimes also: what a genre expects from the writer at a certain part of the paper). Every formulation activity is effectively squeezed into the narrow space that opens up between what has already been written and what has been left to say in the remaining parts of the text. This is, again, a result of enforced linearity which does not allow to place elements next to each other as a diagram would do but enforces the construction of sequentiality.

De Beaugrande (1984) called this task the creation of a "moving focus" in which not only one particular thought has to be placed in the center, but in which the transition has to be managed from what has already been said to what comes next. Whatever a writer places into the text, is caught within such a transitional slot, waiting to be connected conceptually as well as linguistically with the adjacent textual elements. In linguistics, these two kinds of connectedness of text are called "coherence" (content) and "cohesion" (language) (de Beaugrande & Dressler, 1981; Halliday & Hasan, 2013; Taylor et al., 2019; van Dijk, 1977).

A moving focus refers to a principle that looks at the text from both the perspective of content organization and from the perspective of the reader who has to be guided through the text. There are many linguistic means to accomplish such a guidance, such as deixis, connectives, specifications, examples, repetitions, anaphoric and cataphoric references, topic sentences, metadiscourse, and accentuations. For long papers, the creation of a moving focus is supported by an outline which can be used to provide the necessary signs for the readers to comfortably follow the flow of ideas.

Reader Empathy

Even though our focus on formulation stresses the technological side, it should not be missed that it is always a social process, even if writer and audience are not together in the same room as in oral communication. Writing may be seen as a stretched speech situation as Konrad Ehlich (1983) said, where writer and audience are separated through time and space into the two communicative half-situations of writing and reading. Writers have to imagine their audience and assign themselves a role as the originator of a message. Slobin (1979, as cited by Clark, 2000, p. 221) referred to the fact that, in writing as in speech, most things will be left unsaid as the reader already knows them or is assumed to. A text only adds something new to what readers and listeners already have in mind and never makes a complete printout of content or thought.

Formulation, thus, also has the function of a filter which eliminates those elements that need not to be said for a particular audience because everyone is familiar with them. Here is an example of a text which does not filter information along the familiarity dimension:

> Chancellor Angela Merkel walked to the door of her office. She breathed regularly and her eyes were open except for some short moments when she blinked. She carried both of her hands with her as well as her arms and shoulders. Her feet alternatively touched the ground while walking and she never used the same foot twice. She wore clothes and most parts of her body were covered by them. Her head was placed upright in the middle of her shoulders with combed hair on it and it moved little while she walked. She also carried a purse.

This short piece of fiction demonstrates what we usually do not say. For writers not familiar with their audience, this kind of filtering information may be the harder problem than selecting what has to be said. Interestingly, computers do have great problems in understanding and using this kind of everyday knowledge (Winograd, 1972; 1991).

Slobin even doubts that there is thought at all contained in text, when he claims, that: "Language evokes ideas: it does not represent them" (1979, as cited by Clark, 2000, p. 221). It is the mental activity of the reader that reconnects written language again with cognition, emotion, and imagination in order to create thoughts out of it. Writers, in the formulation situation, need something like reader empathy that helps them to infer the audience's assumed knowledge, thoughts and feelings.

LINGUISTIC RESOURCES OF FORMULATION

The organization of information within a string of language follows the rules which languages offer and demands from the writer and speaker to comply to the conventional means by which texts are assembled. The complexity of all aspects of language creation, taken together, is overwhelming and it is or it should be one particular task of writing theory to explain how such complexity can be generated during formulation. We cannot give a complete account of this task, here, but rather intend to offer first steps into this matter to show where solutions may come from. In general, we are back in the field of psycholinguistics, here, as described in the historical part of this paper.

Words, Lexicons, and Word Usage

Words are the most natural linguistic resource of formulation. They are the basic building blocks for sentences and the basic elements of meaning-making. Writers depend on an extended mental lexicon in order to speak and write fluently and with a grammatical understanding of how words are used as different parts of speech (POS). Writers have to understand the conventional meanings of words and learn about the discipline-specific meanings of terms and definitions within academic and/or professional contexts. The mental lexicon, as Levelt explained:

> [It] plays a central role in the generation of speech. It is the repository of information about the words the speaker has available for production. This information involves, at least, the meaning of each item and its syntactic, morphological, and phonological properties. (1989, p. 232)

Words are not simply linguistic units carrying a meaning but virtually are knowledge platforms, to which more aspects are increasingly attached over time (Nagy & Scott, 2000). Also, they provide an interface between the individual mind and the society's knowledge, as Bazerman notes:

> As languages grow and cultures change their knowledges, the semantic possibilities change and extend both for individuals and members of the community. Lexicon and semantics grow through both an inward conceptual expansion and a probing outwards into the world to identify possible things to be indexed and turned into meaning through the form of words, often using shards and analogies of previous words and meanings. (2013, p. 145)

In academic or professional contexts, students have to acquire a specialized terminological knowledge in order to be able to participate in the appropriate disciplinary discourses (Bazerman, 2012). It is, as Faber (2015) pointed out, difficult to say what terminology actually is. Faber sees terms as much as units of specialized knowledge as of a specialized language and stresses their double-natured character as both cognitive and linguistic. Both appear as "access points to larger knowledge configurations" (Faber, 2015, p. 14). Terms, in this sense, should therefore be seen as a part of language crafting as much as they are parts of conceptual thinking. Common languages and their rich word treasures form the background of formulation activities and frame the use of special terminologies associated to different professional, cultural, or academic domains.

Word learning, thus, forms an essential part of intellectual and cognitive growth. Sandra Waxman noted, "Word learning stands at the very centre of the crossroad of human cognition and language (Waxman, 2004, p. 295)." Every word she sees as an invitation to learn new concepts and new concepts need words to be expressed. Linguistic and conceptual advancements, Waxman continued, are powerfully linked within child development. Literacy development, we can continue, means to be socialized in language communities and learn to use the respective symbols system not only for communicative purposes but also for thinking. This process continues at all levels of education where word learning and the acquisition of their respective conceptual and definitory background information play a major role.

CONNECTIVES

A tremendously influential linguistic element in the creation of text and thought are connectives or connectors. These function words or expressions have the ability of connecting clauses and sentence parts to more complex linguistic and conceptual units. From the word class they may be conjunctions, adverbs, or prepositions. The web-based multilingual lexical resource for connectives at connective-lex.info which collected connectives from various data bases lists 142 English, 274 German, 328 French, and 173 Italian connectives (see Stede et al., 2019 for more information). Even if the numbers do not reflect the true values for either language, they still offer an estimation of the many opportunities which languages provide to connect sentences.

Connectives achieve meaning only through their connecting capacity of indicating, for instance, that "clause A" is causally related to "clause B" if the connector "because" is used. For text production, connectives play an important role in creating cohesion (Halliday & Hasan, 2013), indicating logical relations (van Dijk, 1977), structuring reasoning and argumentation (Taylor et al., 2019), and organizing causal and temporal relationships (Halliday & Hasan, 2013).

There are far more linguistic than logical connectives. It is impossible to create meaning through the usage of logical operators alone. Similar to terms, connectors are probably as much a part of thinking as they are a part of text construction, even if we don't know for sure whether we use connectives when we think. Connectives contain human knowledge on the relations that exist between thoughts and events. Consider the following sentences: "The house is old" and "The house will be torn down." What choices do we have to connect them?

> "The house is old *and* it will be torn down." Indicates an additive relationship.
>
> "The house will be torn down *because* it is old." Indicates a causal relationship.
>
> "The house will be torn down *when* it is old." Indicates a temporal relationship.
>
> "The house will be torn down *if* it is old." Indicates a conditional relationship.
>
> "The house will be torn down *although* it is old." Indicates a contradictive relationship.
>
> "The house will be torn down *unless* it is old." Indicates an exception.
>
> "The house will be torn down *no matter* how old it is." Disregards connectedness.
>
> "The house is old, *for this*, it will be torn down." Indicates a reason.
>
> "The house is old; *therefore*, it will be torn down." Indicates a conclusion.

Relating the two clauses or bits of information to each other leads to different meanings dependent on the choice of the connector used. Each connector, by itself, is meaningless and only when it is placed between two phrases or sentence parts, it becomes a meaningful textual practice that has to be learned individually. Learning to write as much as learning to think both depend on a knowledge of their meanings and usages. If a new thought is integrated into a text, it usually requires a connective to define its place in relation to that which already has been said and what may be said next. The point being made here is that neither thinking nor language use can happen without the benefit of connectors.

Phrases and Multi-Word-Patterns

Still, words alone, along with connectives, do not provide the whole story where formulation is concerned. Formulating a sentence on the basis of connecting single words would hardly ever be successful if writers used words like domino tiles: placing one piece down and then checking what comes next. Formulation needs an overarching view of language construction and, therefore, has to rely upon word connections rather than single words. One issue of particular importance in formulation theory, therefore, is the formulaicity of language (e.g., Biber et al., 2004; Pérez-Llantada, 2014; Sinclair, 1991; Wray & Perkins, 2000) and it is no accident that the term "formula" is the root of both formulation and formulaicity. Text production makes use of fixed, multi-word formulas which may be stored mentally and later retrieved as chunks of words.

Word connections have been studied under such terms as "phrases," "recurrent multiword patterns," "formulaic language," "idioms," or "collocations" (Wray & Perkins, 2000). Britt Erman and Beatrice Warren (2000) estimated that formulaic wordings, particularly in academic discourse, may cover up to 50% of the whole text. Harald Feilke stressed the instrumental nature of phrases as "text procedures" and considers learning-to-write as a change from implicit to explicit "procedural linguistic and textual knowledge" (2014, p. 27). John Swales (1981/2011, 1990) and Ana Moreno and Swales (2018) developed a text analytical approach called "move analysis" in order to study genres with respect to their phraseological nature. They look for the rhetorical purposes which authors seek to realize when writing defined parts of the research article (or other genres), which they refer to as "moves." These moves are made up by sub-units called "steps." Both moves and steps have to be inferred from the linguistic realizations which usually have the form of fixed word connections or phrases. Swales (1981/2011, 1990) exemplified this approach in his CARS (Create A Research Space) model, which grouped the important rhetorical purposes expressed in research article introductions into three main moves, each of which contains several steps.

Collocations can be accessed through collocation dictionaries available through websites such as "Just The Word" (just-the-word.com) or "Ozdic" (ozdic.com), or Freecollocation (freecollocation.com) which all rely on the British National Corpus. However, for many purposes, these collections are considered as being too broad in what they offer, hence more focused collections such as the Manchester Academic Phrasebank (phrasebank.manchester.ac.uk) (Davis & Morley, 2015) maybe considered a more useful option. The Manchester Phrasebank offers expressions that are used mostly in academic writing, and as such demonstrates the wide array of functions, they may have for text construction. We must assume that writers not only possess mental lexica, from which they can draw upon during formulation, but also individual mental phrasebooks. These may be thought of as collections of meaningful word connections that can be reused in order to solve defined rhetorical problems during the act of writing (Swales, 1990). In digital contexts, phrases can be offered by digital phrasebooks or by corpus search tools integrated within word processors.

The Need for Grammar

Amidst the formulation process, Wrobel (2002) discussed (with reference to Levelt, 1989) the existence of a "formulator;" a mental unit which cares for the "grammatical encoding" of what is to be said. This reminds us of the fact that there must be a place for grammar in any model of formulation, without which a text could certainly not come to the point of fruition. Grammar, we have said above, to a large degree, results from the need of managing linearity. Whatever rules for this have been established, they form the backbone of any (alphabetic) language with considerable stability over time. Children learn grammar, however, without knowing about grammar. If we do not follow Chomsky's nativist idea of a generative grammar—where does grammar then come from? And how does it relate to text production?

In writing, we have to assume, grammatical encoding usually occurs automatically; grammar is not consciously constructed except, perhaps, for second-language writers at a low proficiency level. For a formulation theory, it is a great challenge to understand and study grammatical automaticity without moving into "black box" models similar to Hayes and Flower's (1980) translator. Many aspects of grammar, such as morphology, cases, declination, mode, number (singular and plural), and grammatical gender are indeed performed automatically. They are learned at an early age and are applied unintentionally and unconsciously. Other aspects of grammar may be made purposefully such as the choice of connectors, prepositions, tenses, particles, and auxiliaries. It matters that writers know or learn what to do with words and how to connect them. Grammar, we have to assume, is not an abstract rule-based system that has a fixed algorithmic structure like in today's digital text generation systems. Rather, it is individually constructed from the many operative linguistic units which are picked up successively from childhood on. Grammar, as a system, comes in when it is taught in school and even then, it seems to be a metalinguistic element, rather than an operative part of language construction.

Automaticity of Text Routines

If we cut down language use into separate procedural elements which are learned and used independently and not as an integrated grammar, then we need a learning model of how they are acquired and applied when needed. A key to understanding language learning and language usage is automaticity. Automaticity stands in contrast to controlled or attentive processing (Kahneman, 2012; Schneider, 1999). Formulation, no matter whether we look at the linguistic or cognitive side of it, is a hierarchical process in which many sub-routines are involved. Typical for automatic processes are seven qualities, as Schneider (1999) points out:

- they can be much faster than controlled processing
- they process parallel as compared to controlled processing which is serial
- they require minimal effort enabling multitask processing
- they are robust and highly reliable compared to controlled processing
- they require (constant) training and practice before they can be performed well
- subjects have reduced control over automatic processing and may have to invest time to change them if necessary
- automatic processes produce less memory modifications than controlled processes.

A large part of language learning, we have to assume, follows the path of automatization of text routines or text procedures (Feilke, 2012; 2014). A particular linguistic unit (for instance the use of a connective like "either . . . or") is applied for the first time consciously and repeated at several occasions until it is adapted to different linguistic contexts and integrated into the mental lexicon. To apply such a connective, a child must be able to make a distinction between two objects or situations which exclude each other. The cognitive task is to understand that A and non-A cannot be true at the same time and that one of them has to be chosen. We either can go to have a pizza or get ice cream but both exclude each other. We may additionally assume that the words "either . . . or" motivate the child to look for situations which are mutually exclusive and that it thus develops the cognitive skills of discrimination and logical connection to automatically detect such alternatives. Only then, the connector may be used routinely as a text procedure whenever two exclusive events have to be addressed.

Two Kinds of Language Generation

If we consider what has been said about pretext and preparation of written formulations, we have to assume that there are two different kinds of formulation going on during writing. One of them we might call "primary language production" which is still more associated with speech than with written text production even though it may be executed mentally (as inner speech). As Ann

Chenoweth and John Hayes (2001, 2003) have described, text production proceeds not at a steady pace but by chunks of words which they call "bursts." Such bursts are usually followed by a pause after which text production goes on or by a revision sequence. The question is: Where do these bursts come from? In the Hayes and Flower model there is no space, that could be associated with the production of these sentence pieces. We associate them with the primary text production which may be both, a genuine construction of a new wording or the reliance on elements from the mental phrasebook. Any mix of both, of course, is also possible. Such formulations may be kept in mind as tentative pretexts, as Witte (1987) and Wrobel (2002) have said, or written down immediately. We may assume that competent writers check these wordings mentally for their goodness of fit before they write them down.

The second kind of language production is the one happening during inscription when the text is assembled with the help of a writing tool. At this moment, a more conscious kind of language planning and decision making takes place. In digital writing, writers have more options than they had in paper-and-pencil times as they can decide to muse on a formulation first and then write it down or to start musing only when they can see the formulation appear on screen.

If we want to account for the dynamics of formulation, it is essential to separate these two language generation processes in order to understand both, the tensions between them as well as the modes of synchronizing and coordinating them. In today's flexible inscription technology, the options of coordinating them have increased and are awaiting to be analyzed in detail.

CONCLUSIONS

The aim of this paper was to re-introduce a formulation theory as a necessary part of writing studies. We have shown that such a theory needs a deeper understanding of what language is and how the enforced linearity of language determines how we structure thought. We also stressed the need to understand what inscription is and how inscription technology supports thinking and text production. We argued that cognition alone is not a sufficient concept to understand formulation but that it always needs a dialectic theory between cognitive and linguistic factors, both in human development, in individual development and in text development. Because of the limited space available, we had to omit most social and cultural factors which are not only deeply involved in writing but also in language development, literacy, education, and genre (see, for instance, Tomasello, 2003; 2008; 2014). We also find it necessary to integrate formulation research deeper into the tradition of psycholinguistic research instead of letting it start with the cognitive sciences.

Our starting point in this paper was the socio-cyborgian alliance between humans and computers which Bazerman (2018) had addressed. To fully understand how this cyborg operates, we have to become aware that the machines have started to occupy a space that until recently was completely reserved to humans: language usage. Humans, as we have argued above, do not only communicate but also think with their native languages. For this, the cyborg does not only apply to action systems but also conquers human thinking. Already by now, intellectual and literacy development are widely entangled with digital technology, and there is still more to come. We are thankful for Bazerman's metaphor of the cyborg which helped us to grasp a core element of the connection of digitalization and human development. We have expanded the metaphor slightly to "intellectual cyborgs" to account for the intrusion of the computers into our mental worlds where we have to re-arrange our own capacities with those of the machines.

REFERENCES

Alamargot, D. & Chanquoy, L. (2001). *Through the models of writing*. Kluwer. https://doi.org/10.1007/978-94-010-0804-4.

Allen, L. K., Jacovina, M. E. & McNamara, D. S. (2015). Computer-based writing instruction. In C. A. MacArthur, S. Graham & J. Fitzgerald (Eds.), *Handbook of writing research* (pp. 316–329). Guildford.

Baron, D. (2009). *A better pencil: Readers, writers, and the digital revolution*. Oxford University Press.

Bazerman, C. (2000). A rhetoric for literate society: The tension between expanding practices and restricted theories. In M. Goggin (Ed.), *Inventing a discipline: Essays in honor of Richard E. Young* (pp. 5–28). NCTE.

Bazerman, C. (2013). *A rhetoric of literate action: Literate action volume 2*. The WAC Clearinghouse; Parlor Press. https://doi.org/10.37514/PER-B.2013.4791.

Bazerman, C. (2018). What do humans do best? Developing communicative humans in the changing socio-cyborgian landscape. In S. Logan & W. Slater (Eds.), *Perspectives on academic and professional writing in an age of accountability* (pp. 187–203). Southern Illinois University Press.

Biber, D., Conrad, S. & Cortes, V. (2004). If you look at. . . .: Lexical bundles in university teaching and textbooks. *Applied Linguistics, 25*(3), 371–405. http://doi.org/10.1093/applin/25.3.371.

Chenoweth, N. A. & Hayes, J. R. (2001). Fluency in writing: Generating text in L1 and L2. *Written Communication, 18*(1), 80–98. https://doi.org/10.1177%2F0741088301018001004.

Chenoweth, N. A. & Hayes, J. R. (2003). The inner voice in writing. *Written Communication, 20*(1), 99–118. https://doi.org/10.1177%2F0741088303253572.

Chomsky, N. (1954). A review of B.F. Skinners's Verbal Behavior. *Language, 35*, 26–58.

Chomsky, N. (1965). *Aspects the theory of syntax*. MIT Press.

Chomsky, N. (1999). On the nature, use and acquisition of language. In W. C. Ritchie & T. K. Bhatia (Eds.), *Handbook of child language acquisition* (pp. 33–54). Academic Press.

Clark, E. V. (2000). Review of Michael Tomasello's "The new psychology of language: cognitive and functional approaches to language structure." *Journal of Child Language, 27*(1), 213–223. https://doi.org/10.1017/S0305000999224075.

Cotos, E. (2014). *Genre-based automated writing evaluation for L2 research writing: From design to evaluation and enhancement.* Palgrave MacMillan.

Cotos, E. (2015). Automated writing analysis for writing pedagogy: From healthy tension to tangible prospects. *Writing and Pedagogy, 7*(2–3), 197–231. https://doi.org/10.1558/wap.v7i2-3.26381.

Davis, M. & Morley, J. (2015). Phrasal intertextuality: The responses of academics from different disciplines to students' re-use of phrases. *Journal of Second Language Writing, 28*, 20–35. https://doi.org/10.1016/j.jslw.2015.02.004.

De Beaugrande, R. A. (1984). *Text production: Toward a science of composition.* Ablex.

De Beaugrande, R. A. & Dressler, W. (1981). *Introduction to text linguistics.* Longman.

DeVoss, D. N. (2018). Digital writing matters. What do we talk about when we talk about digital writing and rhetoric? In J. Alexander & J. Rhodes (Eds.), *The Routledge handbook of digital writing and rhetoric* (pp. 918–28). Routledge.

Dreyfus, H. L. (1972). *What computers can't do.* Harper.

Dreyfus, H. L. (1992). *What computers still can't do.* MIT Press.

Ehlich, K. (1983). Text und sprachliches Handeln. Die entstehung von texten aus dem bedürfnis nach überlieferung [Text and linguistic activity: The development of text from the desire to pass on]. In A. Assmann, J. Assmann & C. Hardmeier (Eds.), *Schrift und gedächtnis. Beiträge zur archäologie der literarischen kommunikation* [Writings and memory: Contributions to the archeology of literary communication] (pp. 24–43). Fink.

Erman, B. & Warren, B. (2000). The idiom principle and the open choice principle. *Text, 20*(1), 29–62. https://doi.org/10.1515/text.1.2000.20.1.29.

Faber, P. (2015). Frames as a framework for terminology. In H. J. Kockaert & F. Steuers (Eds.), *Handbook of terminology (part (1)* (pp. 14–33). Benjamin.

Fayol, M., Alamargot, D. & Berninger, V. W. (Eds.). (2012). *Translation of thought to written text while composing. Advancing theory, knowledge, research, methods, tools, and applications.* Psychology Press.

Feilke, H. (2012). Was sind Textroutinen? Zur Theorie und Methodik des Forschungsfeldes [What are text routines? Theory and methodology of a research field]. In H. Feilke & K. Lehnen (Eds.), *Schreib- und textroutinen. Theorie, erwerb und didaktisch-mediale odellierung* [Writing and text routines: Theory, acquisition, didactical and media-related modelling] (pp. 1–31). Lang.

Feilke, H. (2014). Argumente für eine didaktik der textprozeduren [Arguments for a didactic of text procedures]. In T. Bachmann & H. Feilke (Eds.), *Werkzeuge des schreibens. Beiträge zu einer didaktik der textprozeduren* [Tools of writing: Contributions to a didactic of text procedures] (pp. 11–34). Klett Fillibach.

Flower, L. S. & Hayes, J. R. (1980). The dynamics of composing: Making plans and juggling constraints. In L. W. Gregg & E. R. Steinberg (Eds.), *Cognitive processes in writing: An interdisciplinary approach* (pp. 31–50). Erlbaum.

Flower, L. S. & Hayes, J. R. (1981). A cognitive process theory of writing. *College Composition and Communication, 32*(4), 365–387. https://doi.org/10.2307/356600.

Fodor, J. A. (1975). *The language of thought.* Harvard University.

Fodor, J. A. (2008). *LOT 2. The language of thought revisited.* Clarendon Press.

Gabrial, B. (2008). History of writing technologies. In C. Bazerman (Ed.), *Handbook of research on writing* (pp. 27–39). Erlbaum.

Galbraith, D. (1999). Writing as a knowledge-constituting process. In M. Torrance & D. Galbraith (Eds.), *Knowing what to write: Conceptual processes in text production* (pp. 139–160). Amsterdam University.

Galbraith, D. (2009). Writing as discovery. *British Journal of Educational Psychology Monograph Series II, 6,* 5–26.

Gardner, H. E. (1995). *The mind's new science: A history of the cognitive revolution.* Basic Books.

Gautschi, C., Kruse, O. & Rapp, C. (2021, July 7–8). *Writing and thinking: What changes with digitalization?* [Conference presentation]. 11th European Association for the Teaching of Academic Writing, online.

Haas, C. (1996). *Writing technology. Studies on the materiality of literacy.* Routledge.

Halliday, M. A. K. & Hasan, R. (2013). *Cohesion in English.* Routledge.

Hayes, J. R. (1996). A new framework for understanding cognition and affect in writing. In C. E. Levy & S. Ransdell (Eds.), *The science of writing: Theories, methods, individual differences, and applications* (pp. 1–27). Routledge.

Hayes, J. R. (2012a). Evidence from language bursts, revision, and transcription for translation and its relation to other writing processes. In M. Fayol, D. Alamargot & V. Wiese Berninger (Eds.), *Translation of thought to written text while composing: Advancing theory, knowledge, research methods, tools, and applications* (pp. 15–25). Psychology Press.

Hayes, J. R. (2012b). Modeling and remodeling writing. *Written Communication, 29*(3), 369–388. https://doi.org/10.1177/0741088312451260.

Hayes, J. R. & Flower, L. S. (1980). Identifying the organization of writing processes. In L. W. Gregg & E. R. Steinberg (Eds.), *Cognitive processes in writing* (pp. 3–30). Erlbaum.

Hayes, J. R. & Simon, H. A. (1974). Understanding written problem instructions. In L. W. Gregg (Ed.), *Knowledge and cognition.* Erlbaum.

Hayes, J. R. & Simon, H. A. (1976). The understanding process: Problem isomorphs. *Cognitive Psychology, 8*(2), 165–190. https://doi.org/10.1016/0010-0285(76)90022-0.

Hayes, J. R. & Simon, H. A. (1979). Psychological differences among problem isomorphs. In H. A. Simon (Ed.), *Models of thought* (pp. 498–512). Yale University.

Hjortshoj, K. (2001). *Understanding writing blocks.* Oxford University.

Kahneman, D. (2012). *Thinking, fast and slow.* Penguin Books.

Kruse, O. & Rapp, C. (2019). Seamless writing: How the digitisation of writing transforms thinking, communication, and student learning. In C. K. Looi, L. H. Wong, C. Glahn & S. Cai (Eds.), *Seamless learning: Perspectives, challenges and opportunities* (pp. 191–208). Springer.

Kruse, O. & Rapp, C. (2020). Digitale schreibtechnologie: Entwicklungen, anforderungen und kompetenzen [Digital writing technology: Developments, affordances and competencies]. In B. Huemer, U. Doleschal, R. Wiederkehr, M. Brinkschulte, S. E. Dengscherz, K. Girgensohn & C. Mertlitsch (Eds.), *Schreibwissenschaft—eine neue disziplin. Diskursübergreifende perspektiven, Vol. 2* [Writing science—a new discipline. Crossdisciplinary perspectives] (pp. 227–241). Böhlau Verlag.

Kruse, O. & Rapp, C. (2021). Digital writing spaces—eine verortung digitaler schreibtechnologie in räumlichen und geographischen metaphern [Digital writing spaces: A localization of digital writing technology in spatial and geographical metaphors]. In F. Freise, M. Jacoby, L. Musumeci & M. Schubert (Eds.), *Writing spaces: Wissenschaftliches schreiben zwischen und in den disziplinen 2* [Writing Spaces: Academic writing in and between the disciplines] (pp. 69–90). wbv Media.

Kussmaul, A. (2018). Die störungen der sprache. Versuch einer pathologie der sprache [Disorders of language: Steps to a pathology of language]. In H. v. Ziemssen (Ed.), *Handbuch der speziellen pathologie und therapie, bd. 12, anhang* [Handbook of a specific pathology and therapy, vol 12, appendix]. Hanse. (Original work published 1877)

Lashley, K. S. (1951). The problem of serial order in behavior. In L. A. Jeffress (Ed.), *Cerebral mechanisms in behavior* (pp. 112–146). University of Chicago Press.

Levelt, W. J. M. (1982). Linearization in describing spatial networks. In S. Peters & E. Saarinen (Eds.), *Processes, beliefs, and questions* (pp. 199–220). Reidel. https://doi.org/10.1007/978-94-015-7668-0_7.

Levelt, W. J. M. (1989). *Speaking. From intention to articulation.* MIT Press.

Levelt, W. J. M. (2013). *A history of psycholinguistics. The pre-Chomsky era.* Oxford University Press.

Mahlow, C. & Dale, R. (2014). Production media: Writing as using tools in media convergent environments. In E. M. Jakobs & D. Perrin (Eds.), *Handbook of writing and text production* (pp. 209–230). DeGruyter Mouton.

Moreno, A. I. & Swales, J. M. (2018). Strengthening move analysis methodology towards bridging the function-form gap. *English for Specific Purposes, 50,* 40–63. https://doi.org/10.1016/j.esp.2017.11.006.

Nagy, W. E. & Scott, J. A. (2000). Vocabulary processes. In M. L. Kamil, P. Mosenthal, P. D. Pearson & R. Barr (Eds.), *Handbook of reading research, 3* (pp. 269–284). Erlbaum.

Newell, A. & Simon, H. A. (1976). Computers and science as empirical inquiry symbols and search. *Communications of the ACM, 19*(3), 116–126. https://dl.acm.org/doi/pdf/10.1145/1283920.1283930.

Ong, W. J. (1982). *Orality and literacy. The technologizing of the word.* Routledge.

Ong, W. J. (2001). Writing is a technology that restructures thought. In E. Cushman, E. Kintgen, B. Kroll & M. Rose (Eds.), *Literacy: A critical sourcebook* (pp. 19–31). St. Martins.

Pérez-Llantada, C. (2014). Formulaic language in L1 and L2 expert academic writing: Convergent and divergent usage. *Journal of English for Academic Purposes, 14,* 84–94. https://doi.org/10.1016/j.jeap.2014.01.002.

Piaget, J. (1972). *The principles of genetic epistemology.* Basic Books.

Pinker, S. (1995). *The language instinct. How the mind creates language.* Harper.
Rapp, C., Schlatter, U. & Kruse, O. (2020). The impact of writing technology on conceptual alignment in BA thesis supervision. In C. Müller Werder & J. Erlemann (Eds.), *Seamless learning—lebenslanges durchgängiges lernen ermöglichen* [Seamless learning: Enabling seamless, lifelong learning] (pp. 183–190). Waxmann.
Schneider, W. (1999). Automaticity. In R. A. Wilson & F. C. Keil (Eds.), *The MIT encyclopedia of the cognitive sciences* (pp. 63–64). MIT Press.
Sharples, M. & Pemberton, L. (1990). Starting from the writer: Guidelines for the design of user centred document processors. *Computer Assisted Language Learning (CALL), 2*(1), 37–57. https://doi.org/10.1080/0958822900020104.
Sinclair, J. (1991). *Corpus, concordance, collocation.* Harvard University.
Slobin, D. I. (1979). The role of language in language acquisition. [Invited address, University of California] 5th Annual Meeting of the Eastern Psychological Association, Philadelphia. In J. J. Gumperz & S. C. Levinsohn (Eds.), *Rethinking linguistic relativity* (pp. 70–96). Cambridge University Press.
Slobin, D. I. (2003). Language and thought online: Cognitive consequences of linguistic relativity. In D. Gentner & S. Goldin-Maedow (Eds.), *Language in mind* (pp. 157–192). MIT Press.
Stede, M., Scheffler, T. & Mendes, A. (2019). Connective-Lex: A web-based multilingual lexical resource for connectives. *Discours, 24,* Article 10098. https://doi.org/10.4000/discours.10098.
Strobl, C., Ailhaud, E., Benetos, K., Devitt, A., Kruse, O., Proske, A. & Rapp, C. (2019). Digital support for academic writing: A review of technologies and pedagogies. *Computers & Education, 131,* 33–48. https://doi.org/10.1016/j.compedu.2018.12.005.
Swales, J. M. (1990). *Genre analysis: English in academic and research settings.* Cambridge University Press.
Swales, J. M. (2011). *Aspects of article introductions.* University of Michigan Press. (Original work published 1981)
Taylor, K. S., Lawrence, J. F., Connor, C. M. & Snow, C. E. (2019). Cognitive and linguistic features of adolescent argumentative writing: Do connectives signal more complex reasoning? *Reading and Writing, 32,* 983–1007. https://doi.org/10.1007/s11145-018-9898-6.
Tomasello, M. (2003). *Constructing a language.* Harvard University Press.
Tomasello, M. (2008). *Origins of human communication.* Bradford.
Tomasello, M. (2014). *A natural history of human thinking.* Harvard University Press.
Van Dijk, T. A. (1977). Connectives in text grammar and text logic. In T. A. van Dijk & J. S. Petofi (Eds.), *Grammars and descriptions* (pp. 11–63). De Gruyter.
Varela, F. J., Thompson, E. & Rosch, E. (2016). *The embodied mind. Cognitive science and human experience* (revised). MIT Press. (Original work published 1991)
Vygotski, L. S. (1961). *Thought and language.* MIT Press. (Original work published 1934)
Waxman, S. R. (2004). Everything had a name, and each name gave birth to a new thought: Links between early word learning and conceptual organization. In D. G. Hall & S. R. Waxman (Eds.), *Weaving a lexicon* (pp. 294–334). MIT Press.

Williams, G. & Beam, S. (2019). Technology and writing: Review of research. *Computers & Education, 128*, 227–242. https://doi.org/10.1016/j.compedu.2018.09.024.

Winograd, T. (1972). *Understanding natural language*. Academic Press.

Winograd, T. (1991). Thinking machines: Can there be? Are we? In J. Sheehan & M. Sosna (Eds.), *The boundaries of humanity: Humans, animals, machines* (pp. 198–223). University of California Press.

Witte, S. P. (1987). Pretext and composing. *College Composition and Communication, 38*(4), 397–425. https://doi.org/10.2307/357634.

Wray, A. & Perkins, M. R. (2000). The functions of formulaic language: An integrated model. *Language & Communication, 20*(1), 1–28. https://doi.org/10.1016/S0271-5309(99)00015-4.

Wrobel, A. (1995). *Schreiben als handlung. Überlegungen und untersuchungen zur theorie der textproduktion* [Writing as action. Reflections and studies on a theory of text production]. Niemeyer. https://doi.org/10.1515/9783110917468.

Wrobel, A. (1997). Zur Modellierung von formulierungsprozessen [Modelling formulation processes]. In E. M. Jakobs & D. Knorr (Eds.), *Schreiben in den wissenschaften* [Writing in the sciences and humanities] (pp. 15–24). Lang.

Wrobel. A. (2002). Schreiben und formulieren. Prätext als problemindikator und lösung [Writing and formulation. Pretext as an indicator of problems and as a solution]. In D. Perrin, I. Böttcher, O. Kruse & A. Wrobel (Eds.), *Schreiben. Von intuitiven zu professionellen schreibstrategien* [Writing. From intuitive to professional writing strategies] (pp. 83–96). Westdeutscher Verlag.

Wundt, W. (1900). *Völkerpsychologie. Eine untersuchung der entwicklungsgesetze von sprache, mythos und sitte* [Ethnic psychology. A study of the developmental laws of language myths, and morals]. Engelmann.

CHAPTER 16.
GENRE FORMATION AND DIFFERENTIATION IN NEW MEDIA

Carolyn R. Miller
North Carolina State University

In a speculative paper from the year 2000, Charles Bazerman suggests that the letter as a written form "might have a special role in genre formation" (p. 15). He characterizes letters as "literate meetings" that encode direct communication "between two parties within a specific relationship in specific circumstances" (2000, pp. 15, 27), and provides evidence that letters have given rise to a panoply of more specialized and complex genres, including journalism, the novel, and the scientific report; monetary and credit instruments such as bills of exchange and paper notes; business documents such as stockholder reports; epistles, papal bulls, encyclicals, and other religious documents; patents, contracts, grants, wills, and other legal documents. I have long found this paper intriguing for the connections it reveals among seemingly disparate genres. It is also helpful in thinking about the more general questions of where genres come from and how they change, questions that have occupied me for some time (2012; 2015; 2016; 2017).

Bazerman proposes that the letter has been such a generative genre because it is "so overtly tied to particular social relations of particular writers and readers." Letters "reveal to us so clearly and explicitly the sociality that is part of all writing." They are, in his words, "self-interpreting" (2000, p. 27); that is, their social relations are both obligatory and obvious. Letters are thus a "flexible medium" that makes "new uses socially intelligible," allowing communication to develop in new directions (2000, p. 15). He concludes that letters "have helped us find the addresses of many obscure and remarkable places for literate meetings and have helped us figure out what we would do and say once we got there" (2000, p. 27).

The process of change that Bazerman tracks in this article is the classic evolutionary one of adaptive differentiation and replication. The particular affordances of the letter, as a genre, permit and perhaps encourage functional adaptations to new social circumstances and needs, and the functional utility and satisfactions of those adaptations encourage replication and typification—new genres. The story Bazerman tells is consistent with previous approaches to genre formation, such as Kathleen Jamieson's use of biological metaphors: genres have ancestors, she suggests, that convey "chromosomal imprints" (1975, p. 406). Similarly, when Tzvetan Todorov asks, "From where do genres come?" he answers, "Why, quite simply, from other genres. A new genre is always the transformation of one or several old genres: by inversion, by displacement, by combination" (1976, p. 161). Inversion, displacement, and combination are some of the resources that permit adaptive differentiation (see also my discussions of genre evolution, Miller, 2015; 2016; 2017). Furthermore, Todorov, like Bakhtin, suggests that simple genres, such as speech acts, are the origins of complex genres, such as the novel and the autobiography (Todorov, 1976, p. 165 ff), and we can see this pattern as well in Bazerman's account of the letter and its more complex progeny.

What I want to do in this space, where we are reflecting and building on the prodigious work of Charles Bazerman, is to add to his emphasis on the "social grounding of genres" some attention to the technological grounding of genres, that is, to the interplay between social relations, exigence, and medium in the formation and transformation of genres. And by taking up medium as an element of genres and their formation, I also wish to push beyond Bazerman's focus on the literate and discursive to include the auditory and the visual, that is, to emphasize the multimodality of genre.

It was in my studies of blogging with Dawn Shepherd that I became first puzzled and then intrigued by the relationship between genre and medium (Miller & Shepherd, 2004; 2009). Blogs presented an instructive case of genre formation because they appeared so suddenly and so recently, making evidence about them and those who use them easily available. It seemed clear when we began looking at blogs that they were a genre: that's how users talked and thought about blogging: it was a distinctively identifiable form of social interaction that had become typified: participants mutually recognized roles, conventions, and shared motivations. Users, or participants in blogging communities, had agreed fairly rapidly on what features blogs should have, what distinguished a good blog from a not-so-good one, and what satisfactions they could expect from the activity of blogging. These shared recognitions were based in an exigence that Shepherd and I characterized as a "widely shared, recurrent need for cultivation and validation of the self" at a time of postmodern fragmentation and mediated simulation (2004). Because we were able to apply a genre analysis to the blog, it appeared to us to be a genre. And yet, even as we finished our analysis we saw evidence that blogs had speciated, differentiating into sub-genres that responded to different exigences in different communities of use:

> Shortly after everyone thought they knew that a blog was an online diary, we started to hear about journalism blogs, team blogs, photo blogs, classroom blogs, travel blogs, campaign

> blogs, and more. The forms and features of the blog that had initially fused around the unfolding display of personal identity were rapidly put to use for purposes of political advocacy, corporate tech support, classroom interaction, and public deliberation. With a rapidity equal to that of their initial adoption, blogs became not a single discursive phenomenon but a multiplicity. (Miller & Shepherd, 2009, p. 263)

We pursued this problem further in a subsequent study. In comparing two general types of blogging, the personal blog (with which we had begun) and the public affairs blog (which came to prominence later, in the context of concern about changed media regulation, commercialized political discourse, natural disasters, and international terrorism), we saw a similar suite of technological affordances, i.e., the blogging medium, deployed to meet quite different social exigences, for different communities of users, against a background of different cultural relevancies. If there was anything singular about "*the* blog," it wasn't genre; rather, it was its nature as a technological medium, or platform. We concluded:

> When blogging technology first became widely available through hosting sites, it was perceived to fit a particular exigence arising out of the late 1990s, even helping to crystallize that exigence, and the personal blog multiplied its way into cultural consciousness. The genre and the medium, the social action and its instrumentality, fit so well that they seemed coterminous, and it was thus easy to mistake the one for the other—as we did. . . . [But] as the technology evolved, and as multiple users engaged in ceaseless experimentation and variation, the suite of affordances called blogging was discovered to fit other exigences in different ways, so other types of blogs proliferated, other genres—public affairs, corporate, tech support, team, etc.—and the coincidence between the genre and the medium dissolved. (Miller & Shepherd, 2009, p. 283)

I'll venture a hypothesis here, extrapolating from some resonances between what Bazerman found in the evolution of the letter and what Shepherd and I found with the blog: that this may be a general evolutionary process from new medium to multiple genres. Of course, the process of genre proliferation occurred much more rapidly in the case of blogging than with letter writing. But generally, the earliest use of a new technological medium will tend to be understood as the only way to engage its affordances; the recurrent exigence will be recognized simply as the use of the new tool. The technological affordances of the letter, as Bazerman tells us, were the embedded identifications of author and audience and the portability of those social relationships across time and distance; as a new medium, in particular cultural-historical situations, letters enabled the exertion of centralized authority at a time of increasing urbanization, economic exchange, and military competition between centers of authority. The medium of the letter coincided with the genre of the written, authoritative command-at-a-distance. Until it didn't. The medium, it turned out, could also address other exigences: it could be used to maintain and cultivate personal bonds, to petition authority, to promise payment, to advise or recommend peers. And, as Bazerman goes on to show, to do so much else as social, economic, religious, and legal relationships became more complex over the very long time since the first letters. Social relationships and needs evolved; the medium changed but little; the genres multiplied.

The history of communication technologies presents a series of new media, of which the letter is one of the earliest and the blog just one among many in a recent proliferation. Those who study communication media have tended, according to Joshua Meyrowitz, to understand them as conduits, as languages, or as environments (1993). As conduits, media become invisible delivery mechanisms for "content"; as languages, or grammars, media become a set of "expressive variables, or production techniques" that can alter the meaning of content (Meyrowitz, 1993, p. 58); as environments or contexts, media become a fixed suite of affordances that shape both what content and techniques can be incorporated in any given communication and how the medium relates to other media in a given socio-economic-political context. Meyrowitz contends that each perspective overlooks as much as it includes and that full understanding of any communication medium requires insights from all three. I would contend that genre, as rhetorically conceived, already incorporates all three perspectives, connecting content, grammar, and constraints into a socially recognizable cultural artifact. As I have earlier argued (1984), rhetorical genres can be characterized by their semantic features (content), syntactic features (grammars or forms), and situational contexts (see also Campbell & Jamieson, 1978). Media scholars have had little to say about genre (some major exceptions will be discussed below), and few genre scholars in rhetoric and writing studies have engaged seriously with media theory and research. As Friedrich Kittler notes, for centuries writing "functioned as a universal medium—in times when there was no concept of media" (1999, pp. 5–6). But this is no longer the case, and increased engagement between media studies and genre studies would, I believe, be of benefit in both directions.[1]

---

1   For a similar argument along these lines, see Jack Andersen's contribution to this volume.

What genre studies might gain from media studies is an appreciation for constraints and affordances offered particularly by Meyrowitz's environmental perspective, as our traditional attention to writing and print tends to overlook or obscure these. For example, Richard Altman points out that "film genre's consistent connections to the entire production—distribution—consumption process make it a broader concept than literary genre has typically been" (1999, p. 15). Understanding film as a medium requires attention to distinctive conditions such as the tools and expertise involved in production, the costs and investments required, relevant legal and regulatory frameworks, advertising practices, distribution channels, consumer behavior and habits, and much more. All these "environmental" factors of film-as-medium impinge on the development and propagation of film genres, that is, on the typified social actions that both producers and audiences find sufficiently satisfying. Likewise, understanding the blog as medium, insofar as it provided the conditions of possibility for blogging genres, requires attention to the development of Web 2.0 technologies, such as blog-hosting platforms, commenting, image editing, permalinks, web syndication, tagging, blogads, and the like, as well as to the role of legislation such as the Telecommunications Act of 1996, which affected the wider media environment, triggering the consolidation of media ownership and transforming the news industry (Miller & Shepherd, 2009, pp. 277–278).

Some media scholars have paid particular attention to the introduction of new communication technologies. Even as new tools, platforms, and machines have appeared with dramatic speed in what we call "the internet age," we are not, as Carolyn Marvin observes, "the first generation to wonder at the rapid and extraordinary shifts in the dimension of the world and human relationships it contains as a result of new forms of communication, or to be surprised by the changes those shifts occasion in the regular pattern of our lives" (1988, p. 3). Her work focuses on such shifts in the late 19th century occasioned by the early electrical communication technologies: the telegraph, telephone, phonograph, radio, and cinema—all of which "fascinated" our forebears in much the way the internet and digital media have fascinated us. She makes the case that "the history of media is never more or less than the history of their uses" (1988, p. 8), which sounds to me a lot like a history of genres. Resisting the traditional treatment of media, centered on technological artifacts, Marvin is interested, rather, in the "drama" of negotiations among social groups that ensues when a new medium transforms "old habits of transacting between groups" by altering social distance, possibilities of surveillance and exertion of authority, and modes of establishing credibility (1988, p. 5). New media, in other words, modify socially typified rhetorical situations and their historically sedimented roles and constraints (and thus their genres). And even though Marvin aims to direct our attention away from technological artifacts toward the social environments in which they are used, her approach must engage with the specifics of any given new technology *as a medium* in order to trace how it "intrudes" on and challenges established social relations.

New communication technologies do not arrive with their uses or social placement in any way obvious. As Geoffrey Pingree and Lisa Gitelman observe,

> new media, when they first emerge, pass through a phase of identity crisis, a crisis precipitated at least by the uncertain status of the given medium in relation to established, known media and their functions. In other words, when new media emerge in a society, their place is at first ill defined, and their ultimate meanings or functions are shaped over time by that society's existing habits of media use (which, of course, derive from experience with other, established media), by shared desires for new uses, and by the slow process of adaptation between the two. The "crisis" of a new medium will be resolved when the perceptions of the medium, as well as its practical uses, are somehow adapted to existing categories of public understanding about what that medium does for whom and why. (2003, p. xii)

I can't help reading "genre" into phrases here such as "habits of media use," "shared desires for new uses," and "categories of public understanding," and I see this passage as a corroboration, in alternate language, of my hypothesis that the full genrefication of a new communication technology takes place after an initial phase when the medium seems indistinguishable from genre.

While it would be difficult to discover whether the medium of letter-writing endured an "identity crisis" such as Pingree and Gitelman describe, we do have Plato's well known objections to writing in general as some indication of a process of adaptation between social habits and the uses to which the new medium of writing could be put (even as Plato expressed some of those objections in letter form!) (1961, Phaedrus 274–275, Letter VII 341c). With blogging, however, we can document the early uncertainties about what the new medium was and how it could be used: from the earliest uses by web-savvy coders in the tech industry to share links and information to the development of hosting sites that required no coding experience and thus enabled the rapid involvement of a large non-technical community engaged in mutual sharing of personal information and perceptions (Miller & Shepherd, 2004). Even in the early phase of personal blogging on the commercial blogging platforms, there was initial confusion about the relationship of blogs to older genres such as private diaries, clipping services, and newsletters. Over time, the medium and the user communities adapted to each other, as blogging platforms introduced new affordances, and users discovered shared exigences that blogging could fulfill, creating multiple new blogging genres.

During the initial period of uncertainty and confusion about which Pingree and Gitelman write, new communication technologies seem *opaque* to us, because they are unfamiliar and often un-institutionalized. It is only with use, familiarity, habituation, and institutionalization that a new technology becomes natural, obvious, transparent. A new medium is like the alphabet, which is new to each child: the child at first labors over letter shapes and sounds, focusing on this technology of writing, but with familiarity the alphabet becomes "a transparent window into conceptual thought" (Lanham, 1993, p. 4). As Gitelman writes about the telephone, "Inventing, promoting, and using the first telephones involved lots of self-conscious attention to telephony. But today, people converse through the phone without giving it a moment's thought. The technology and all of its supporting protocols (that you answer 'Hello?' and that you pay the company, but also standards like touch-tones and twelve-volt lines) have become self-evident as the result of social processes, including the habits associated with other, related media" (2006, pp. 5–6). More generally, she claims, "the success of all media depends at some level on inattention or 'blindness' to the media technologies themselves (and all of their supporting protocols) in favor of attention to the phenomena, 'the content,' that they represent for users' edification or enjoyment" (2006, p. 6). With use, we become less aware of the medium as a mediating entity and learn to operate *through* it to achieve our social ends: the medium loses its opacity and becomes transparent, a seemingly frictionless conduit.

Gitelman's point is, as she herself notes, a gloss on Marshall McLuhan's notorious dictum that "the medium is the message," or, less cryptically put, "it is only too typical that the 'content' of any medium blinds us to the character of the medium" (1964, p. 9). Jay David Bolter and Richard Grusin characterize this blinding as a "logic of transparent immediacy"—that is, a cultural imperative to erase media and mediation (1999, pp. 5, 21ff). Drawing primarily from the visual realm, they discuss examples such as the development of linear perspective in painting, photorealism in photography, and live television, but from other realms we could include stereophonic audio or "surround sound" and stylistic techniques of objectivity in prose. All these techniques have as their effect an apparent erasure of the technique and thereby of its medium in order to create the impression that what is represented (the "content") is real, is fully present—and is what matters.

Transparency is a quality that pervades discussions of prose style as a medium: the ultimate virtue of written expression becomes "clarity." The term used by Scottish Enlightenment philosopher George Campbell to describe the most essential quality of language was "perspicuity," which he defined as "transparency, such as may be ascribed to air, glass, water, or any other medium through which material objects are viewed" (1963, pp. 216, 221). And Richard Lanham has brought this ambition into the 21st century, labeling it the C-B-S model of communication, standing for clarity, brevity, and sincerity; this model, he claims, dominates our thinking about language (2006, pp. 137–138).[2] It undergirds federal requirements for government communications, written into "plain language" guidelines and the Plain Writing Act of 2010.[3] Our cultural imperative for immediacy is powerful. Lanham epitomizes the issue as a tension between "stuff and fluff," substance and style (2006), which we can see as a tension between content and mediation.

Neither Lanham nor Bolter and Grusin are satisfied with the dismissal or devaluing of media. Lanham argues that "fluff," the play of the medium—style, surface, ornament, self-consciousness—is important, and in some cases more important, more explanatory, more satisfying than the "stuff" that is purportedly transmitted by a medium. We need, he says, to learn (and teach) a dual perspective, the ability to look both *through* and *at* a text (or any communicative phenomenon), to oscillate between these two perspectives in order to understand both the expression and the medium (1993, 2006). Bolter and Grusin go on to complicate their account of immediacy by introducing a counter-imperative, the logic of "hypermediacy," which is the impulse to multiply media and mediation. This cultural "double logic" undergirds the process they call "remediation" (1999, p. 45), which is another gloss on McLuhan's claim that the "content" of a new medium is just older media. The content of writing is, supposedly, speech; the content of film is theater and photography;[4] the content of a computer's graphical interface is typewriting, or photography, or drawing, etc. Echoing Lanham's focus on "fluff," the logic of hypermediacy produces a visual style built on heterogeneity, fragmentation, and performance (Bolter & Grusin, 1999, p. 31ff). They offer many examples from various computer media and multi-windowed television screens, but also historical examples such as medieval European cathedrals, print layouts of photomontage, and modernist art.

What can these double logics and oscillations offer to genre theory? Transparency and opacity, immediacy and hypermediacy, can help us think about

---

2   See also Dilip Gaonkar's "transparency thesis," i.e., the assumption by rhetorical critics in the early 20th century that oratory is uninterestingly determined by its content, that it is a "mirror" of its object (1990, p. 298), and my discussion of the assumption that language should be a direct imitation of its object (2010, p. 26 ff).

3   plainlanguage.gov

4   Though Altman disputes this (1999, p. 30 ff).

the relations between genre and medium. Returning to the question of how genres emerge in relation to new media, I offered the hypothesis that when a new medium becomes available, its use coincides with its nature as a medium to the extent that genre and medium are indistinguishable; it is only with extensive use, experimentation, and adaptation that additional genres emerge and the medium can be distinguished from its uses. We might now say that the new medium is so opaque to its first users that it blinds us to genre. The novelty of the first telephone calls, of the first television shows, the first video conferences, the first blogs, perhaps even the first letters, is so powerful, the new illusion of presence so distracting, that the possibilities for social use are nonobvious; genre is transparent to the spell of the new technology. When it is new, a communication technology, like the letter or the blog, manifests as what we might think of as a genre-medium, a new tool, a matrix of possibilities for genre. Genre and medium are two dimensions of a new communication technology that we learn to distinguish only with time and experience, when medium becomes less opaque and genre less transparent.

Let us take one more example to test the hypothesis, and to compare with our earlier examples of the letter and the blog. My example is anchored not in the written word but in sound: the new technology of radio and radio broadcasting. According to Michele Hilmes, broadcast radio as a medium has affordances "significantly different from any preceding or subsequent medium in its ability to transcend spatial boundaries, blur the private and public spheres, and escape visual determinations while still retaining the strong element of 'realism' that sound—rather than written words—supplies" (1997, p. xvi). The development of radio is a highly complex story that is tied up with the telegraph and the telephone in the late 19th and early 20th centuries. But if, like Hilmes, "we regard radio not as a collection of wires, transmitters, and electrons but as a social practice grounded in culture, rather than in electricity" (1997, p. xiii), this history includes not only technical developments sorting wired from wireless communication, but also experiments and protocols that eventually sorted one-way from two-way communication and point-to-point from point-to-mass communication, as well as the influences of multiple inventors and amateur enthusiasts, the involvement of government regulators and the armed forces (especially during World War I), and the rapid formation of corporations that both competed and cooperated to commercialize the new technologies (with many patent disputes). All these combined to keep the social uses of radio fluid and uncertain for decades (see also Barnouw, 1966; Douglas, 1987). As Susan Douglas notes, "Sharply competing ideas about how the invention should be used, and by whom, informed the process from the start. . . . Radio broadcasting . . . was the result of battles over technological control and corporate hegemony, and of visions about who should have access to America's newly discovered frontier environment, the electromagnetic spectrum" (1987, p. 318).

So, there were grand but inchoate social expectations. The situation fits well Pingree and Gitelman's description of the "identity crisis" phase of new media emergence (2003, p. xii), mentioned earlier. It is telling that Erik Barnouw titles volume one of his three-volume history of broadcasting in the US *A Tower of Babel* (1966). As Walter Gifford, president of AT&T from 1925 to 1948, recalled in 1944:

> Nobody knew early in 1921 where radio was really headed. Everything about broadcasting was uncertain. For my own part I expected that since it was a form of telephony, and since we[5] were in the business of furnishing wires for telephony, we were sure to be involved in broadcasting somehow. Our first vague idea, as broadcasting appeared, was that perhaps people would expect to be able to pick up a telephone and call some radio station, so that they could give radio talks to other people equipped to listen. (quoted in Marvin, 1988, pp. 230–231)

In spite of the uncertainties, many of the milestone events identified by historians of radio broadcasting have a kind of proto-generic familiarity to 21st-century minds. One of the very first broadcasts, in 1906, was a Christmas eve program of music and readings. Other firsts included election returns (1916 and 1920), the World Series (1921), the opening of Congress (1923), original radio drama (1923), a Presidential campaign speech (1924), and the network series *Amos 'n' Andy* (1929). By 1921 several stations were broadcasting on announced schedules, with a typical schedule including news reading, weather, recorded music, and time signals (Barnouw, 1966, pp. 288, 285). In Chicago, "the KYW schedule for the 1921–22 season was entirely Chicago Civic Opera. All performances, afternoon and evening, six days a week, were broadcast—and nothing else" (Barnouw, 1966, p. 88) with a dramatic increase in the ownership of radio receivers in the city during that time. Later developments in the 1930s included the horror show, the variety show, the quiz show and other audience participation shows, the western, and science fiction programs (Sterling & O'Dell, 2010). Hilmes traces the development of a "framework of gradually naturalized structures and practices" (1997, p. xviii), which include personality-based shows and what she characterizes as "narratives of national definition," particularly the minstrel show and radio's "most representative textual form, the serial/series narrative," which

---

5 Gifford is referring to AT&T; before becoming president, he had served the company as chief statistician and vice-president.

originated in the *Amos 'n' Andy* series (1997, p. xix). Indeed, as Marvin observes, "Wholly invented programming . . . is a distinctive social feature of electronic mass media" (1988, p. 222). The genres of commercial radio are manufactured for the mass audience.[6] But this audience had to be equipped and constituted over a period of years, if not decades. They had to be prepared to want what radio—as it became commercial radio—would and could offer.

I think we can see a familiar pattern here: first, experimentation with the medium qua medium, where the genre-medium is just the transmission of anything, simply to demonstrate the capabilities of radio to others with the aim of impressing them; concurrently, a focus on obvious utility for urgent practical problems (military use during World War I); and later, the development and multiplication of patterns of "naturalized structures and practices," which became the genres of early radio programming. The genrification of radio is shaped in particular by its potential for commercialization, its role in the development of a mass audience and mass culture, and the economic and social conditions of that audience in the early 20th century. Like all genres, the genres of radio are both technologically and socially grounded in important and complex ways, shaped by the affordances of the medium and to the socio-historical context in which it emerged.

In the case of letters, Bazerman showed us that the combined portability and addressivity of the letter constituted a "genre-medium" in ancient cultures that transported authority across time and distance, serving practical purposes of governance, war, and commerce, and lent itself to increasingly specialized adaptations in new circumstances. Letters required few tools and supplies and little skilled labor (compared to, for example, printing, radio, or blogging, even allowing for the fact that literacy long remained an elite skill). As a genre-medium, the letter in its infancy, I am supposing, exhibits the characteristics of both a genre and a medium, and these dimensions cannot usefully be distinguished at the time. Other early written texts, with different addressivities and dissemination patterns, had different uses, giving us, for example, poetic, religious, and philosophical genres (some such texts are cast in the form of letters, but others have no apparatus of particular address). Of the early uses of writing, the letter and its specific affordances, as Bazerman has shown, had a particular fertility—and Bazerman's essay is itself a fertile exploration into the origin and evolution of genres. But I have tried to show that the pattern of adaptation and proliferation he saw is not restricted to the letter. In other words, in the history of genre formation, the letter is a particular case but not a special case.

---

6 I have earlier characterized such genres, including film genres, as "marketed" or "commercial," in contrast to administered, institutional, and vernacular genres (Miller, 2017, p. 23).

The other point I have been arguing here is that we can learn more about the nature and function of genres, and the ways they emerge and propagate, by paying attention to the media of communication in which they are embedded and which are a part of their identity as a genre; that is, we should attend to both the social and the technological grounding of genres and the historically specific interaction of these factors in any given case. All media, and the genres they subtend, involve social relationships, production and distribution conditions, and semiotic capacities and other affordances, and for "literate" communication these are distinctly different from those of other media. If we limit our scope to the written word, if we assume that writing remains the universal medium, we run the risk of blinding ourselves to the particular relationships, conditions, and capabilities that characterize written media and at the same time of ignoring the many other media in which and through which we live our lives. The increasingly pervasive digital media combine many features of older media in ways we cannot ignore. Visual and verbal, oral and written, temporal and spatial, static and dynamic—all these capacities are combined in today's digital media, in different ways, on multiple technological platforms. An exclusive focus on "writing" or "the literate" does not suffice for understanding genres, media, or their interrelationships.

REFERENCES

Altman, R. (1999). *Film/genre*. British Film Institute.

Barnouw, E. (1966). *A history of broadcasting in the United States: Vol. 1. A tower of Babel. To 1933*. Oxford University Press.

Bazerman, C. (2000). Letters and the social grounding of differentiated genres. In D. Barton & N. Hall (Eds.), *Letter writing as a social practice* (pp. 15–29). John Benjamins.

Bolter, J. D. & Grusin, R. (1999). *Remediation: Understanding new media*. MIT Press.

Campbell, G. (1963). *The philosophy of rhetoric* (Lloyd F. Bitzer, Ed.). Southern Illinois University Press.

Campbell, K. K. & Jamieson, K. H. (1978). Form and genre in rhetorical criticism: An introduction. In K. K. Campbell & K. H. Jamieson (Eds.), *Form and genre: Shaping rhetorical action* (pp. 9–32). Speech Communication Association.

Douglas, S. J. (1987). *Inventing American broadcasting: 1899–1922*. Johns Hopkins University Press.

Gaonkar, D. P. (1990). Object and method in rhetorical criticism: From Wichelns to Leff and McGee. *Western Journal of Speech Communication, 54*(3), 290–316.

Gitelman, L. (2006). *Always already new: Media, history, and the data of culture*. MIT Press.

Hilmes, M. (1997). *Radio voices: American broadcasting, 1922–1952*. University of Minnesota Press.

Jamieson, K. M. (1975). Antecedent genre as rhetorical constraint. *Quarterly Journal of Speech*, 61, 406–415.
Kittler, F. A. (1999). *Gramophone, film, typewriter* (G. Winthrop-Young & M. Wutz, Trans.). Stanford University Press.
Lanham, R. A. (1993). *The electronic word: Democracy, technology, and the arts*. University of Chicago Press.
Lanham, R. A. (2006). *The economics of attention: Style and substance in the age of information*. University of Chicago Press.
Marvin, C. (1988). *When old technologies were new: Thinking about electric communication in the late nineteenth century*. Oxford University Press.
McLuhan, M. (1964). *Understanding media: The extensions of man* (2nd ed.). New American Library.
Meyrowitz, J. (1993). Images of media: Hidden ferment—and harmony—in the field. *Journal of Communication*, 43(3), 55–66. https://doi.org/10.1111/j.1460-2466.1993.tb01276.x.
Miller, C. R. (1984). Genre as social action. *Quarterly Journal of Speech*, 70(2), 151–167. https://doi.org/10.1080/00335638409383686.
Miller, C. R. (2010). Should we name the tools? Concealing and revealing the art of rhetoric. In J. Ackerman & D. Coogan (Eds.), *The public work of rhetoric* (pp. 19–38). University of South Carolina Press.
Miller, C. R. (2012). New genres, now and then. In S. Hulan, M. McArthur & R. A. Harris (Eds.), *Literature, rhetoric, and values* (pp. 127–149). Cambridge Scholars Publishing.
Miller, C. R. (2015). Genre change and evolution. In N. Artemeva & A. Freedman (Eds.), *Genre studies around the globe: Beyond the three traditions* (pp. 154–185). Trafford Publishing.
Miller, C. R. (2016). Genre innovation: Evolution, emergence, or something else? *Journal of Media Innovations*, 3(2), 4–19. https://doi.org/10.5617/jmi.v3i2.2432.
Miller, C. R. (2017). Where do genres come from? In C. R. Miller & A. R. Kelly (Eds.), *Emerging genres in new media environments* (pp. 1–34). Palgrave Macmillan.
Miller, C. R. & Shepherd, D. (2004). Blogging as social action: A genre analysis of the weblog. In L. Gurak, S. Antonijevic, L. Johnson, C. Ratliff & J. Reymann (Eds.), *Into the blogosphere: Rhetoric, community, and the culture of weblogs*. University of Minnesota Libraries. http://hdl.handle.net/11299/172818.
Miller, C. R. & Shepherd, D. (2009). Questions for genre theory from the blogosphere. In J. Giltrow & D. Stein (Eds.), *Genres in the internet: Issues in the theory of genre* (pp. 263–290). John Benjamins.
Pingree, G. B. & Gitelman, L. (2003). Introduction: What's new about new media? In L. Gitelman & G. B. Pingree (Eds.), *New media, 1740–1915* (pp. xi–xxii). MIT Press.
Plato. (1961). *The collected dialogues*. Princeton University Press.
Sterling, C. H. & O'Dell, C. (Eds.). (2010). *The concise encyclopedia of American radio*. Routledge.
Todorov, T. (1976). The origin of genres. *New Literary History*, 8(1), 159–170.

CHAPTER 17.
CHANGE, CHANGE, CHANGE— AND THE PROCESSES THAT ABIDE

Charles Bazerman
University of California, Santa Barbara

The generous gift in this volume of such wide-ranging essays from so many friends, from so many regions is overwhelming. Their careful reading of my work here comforts me in knowing I have contributed to a dialog of possibilities for the generations to come. These essays highlight that writing has always been about change, as writing has constantly evolved in its capacities and genres; as writing has changed the forms of social organizations, activities, and communities that have drawn on its potentials; and as writing has changed people as they have become immersed in worlds saturated with writing.

CHANGING TECHNOLOGIES

Several of these essays explicitly address the opportunities new technologies afford for changing the conditions of writing and inspiring creativity in composing in multiple media. Carolyn Miller rightly points out that new technological means of production and distribution have facilitated the emergence of new genres that rapidly and widely share serially evolving information, thinking, observations, or other content, with a kind of informality consistent with its transient location in changing moments. As people engage creatively with blog opportunities, genres differentiate and proliferate. New technologies and platforms open up new potentials. Yet even as new genres emerge, the underlying processes of genre proliferation and differentiation remain as they have been since the earliest days of communication at a distance through letters.

Jack Andersen similarly looks at how genres respond to the enhanced searchability affordances of digital technologies, making texts more findable. To make texts more findable, searchability enters into the design of born digital documents, both in their production and their final form. As well, searchability creates its own genres of recognizable texts, such as hashtags. People in their communicative cleverness keep pushing the possibilities and limits of new technologies, and then designing their messages to take use of these possibilities. Yet while the texts and the practical problems to be solved in

DOI: https://doi.org/10.37514/PER-B.2023.1800.2.17

writing them are new, yet the longstanding processes of genre adaptation and proliferation remain at play.

These new technologies and the genres that explore their potentials give rise to new skills in the production, design, and distribution of the texts that come to inhabit the new media far beyond the obvious skills of learning and manipulating the technologies and the traditional skills of academic publishers. The electronic production and distribution of texts have made possible new publishing collectives, no longer dependent on the commercial or quasi-commercial presses that have attached human editorial services to industrial costs of materials, printing, and book distribution. The possibilities of such collectives are particularly striking for academic and scholarly publishing which has long relied on the voluntary labor of academics for authorship, text evaluation, and developmental editing. But creating and sustaining voluntary collectives of people to build, organize, and maintain academic publishing that will support the selection, production, and distribution of open access books, while building academic credibility that will attract authors and readers, require new sets of social, managerial, and financial skills that extend far beyond the necessary facility with the technology. Mike Palmquist offers a history of one of the most successful of such new academic publishing collaboratives and offers a guidebook for others in creating an open-access future for academic publishing.

Otto Kruse and Christian Rapp in considering how new technologies can work to support writing are led back to fundamental and longstanding psychological and psycholinguistic issues of how humans formulate words and statements. They gather together what we know about formulation theory, focusing on the relation of oral speech to inscription, the bottleneck of the inscription processes, the linearization of thought and attention into sequentially inscribed words, and projecting a role for the feeling and cognizing reader. In carrying out these formulating tasks, what writers have to work with is words, so this then directs them to consider grammar and syntax. Providing technological support for human meaning making and creativity leads us to think more deeply about the nature of writing work. Formulation at the sentence level is one piece of the larger issue of the formulation of new ideas, arguments, coherences, and tensions. Technological innovators, seeking to offload some of the work of formulating and offering what the writer needs at the right time, have cause to understand fundamental human writing processes; otherwise, the technology, no matter how clever, will find little human uptake.

CHANGING CONDITIONS AND CULTURES

Change in writing comes from sources other than technology as well. A case in point is the pandemic which has disrupted what had become a fairly stable genre system of classroom activities performed by teachers and students. Previous gradual experimentation with online learning carried out by volunteers suddenly became a pressing issue for all teachers as whole universities and school systems had to reinvent the organization and interactions of students and teachers. Administrators as well needed to find ways to support the teachers in managing the technology and redesigning their curricula. This has forced programs and teachers to rethink the nature and interactions of education in order to make it work under the new conditions. Joanne Yates in her essay documents the process by which this occurred at the Sloan School at MIT and considers what changes in classroom and faculty communication may endure past the pandemic.

Changes in conditions and relations in relatively stable scholarly communication systems may evolve in ways that are realized even at the level of word choice, as Ken Hyland documents in his corpus study of changing engagement and stance in applied linguistics, sociology, electrical engineering, and biology over five decades. Each field shows a different pattern of change suggesting different cultural changes, as some fields have become more author evacuated and others have become more author present. As well, some fields have sought higher degrees of audience engagement while others treat their audiences at greater distance. While the data do not clearly identify why this is happening, we can recognize that there are internal dynamics at work in each of the fields.

Even within a discipline each person experiences accidents of events, opportunities, and people that define how and when they engage further with their fields and what they learn to advance their knowledge. Their previous experiences and dispositions, as well, influence how they respond to these accidents. So even though each may engage with the thoughts and practices expected of their field, they develop a unique position and voice. Fatima Encinas and Nancy Keranen in their interview study find early literacy experiences and early career experiences are particularly important to opening the door to later accomplishments, and they suggest emerging scholars be aided in recognizing and taking up the opportunities that chance events offer.

CHANGING PEOPLE

Each individual working within each field also changes by entering into the practices and forms of expression of a particular field. Some of these practices may be quasi stable for generations of practitioners and represent key elements of intellectual and social enculturation. Each new practitioner needs to learn to produce credible work in their field, pursuing credible modes of reasoning supported by credible methods of data collection and use of evidence.

Montserrat Castello reviews her research program with her colleagues into how writers develop systematic regulation of their texts through self, collaborative, and social processes. Within specific situations scholars internalize increasingly sophisticated cognitive practices which help them think as scholarly writers. Her work helps us unpack the complex kinds of processes writers come to use to give direction and form to their emerging thoughts and statements.

Paula Carlino, similarly, found that master's students in education in the process of writing their theses gained new concepts of themselves as writers and as inquirers. They also gained new concepts of how to formulate research questions that can contribute to the systematic knowledge to their fields, changing their view of what they do as teachers in their classroom.

Lucia Natale in her chapter follows university trained professionals out into their workplace to see how their university-trained ways of writing disciplinary work become transformed as they enter the practical problems of the workplace with new genres. Yet they still rely on the analytic skills and professional modes of thinking developed in their university projects.

CHANGING GENRES

Changes in genres themselves can change the working and activities of groups and individuals. Genre innovations can make more visible and rearrange responsibilities, roles, regulations, and resources of different participants, aiding participants in seeing their roles and possibilities in new ways. The central role of genres for creating new possibilities runs through Yrjö Engeström's work—possibilities for new roles, new identities, new ways of working, and new senses of the self. In his first example here he considers how mobility agreements within home care fomented changes in how elderly clients conducted their lives and increased their physical activity. He then examines a graphic scheme used in multiple settings to make visible possibilities for increasing clients' responsibility in self-care and diminishing passivity. He then looks at how pathway models co-constructed with formerly homeless clients help them understand and take charge of the possibilities of their changing lives. I find the kind of work here in using genres of representations particularly poignant as it shows how abstract concepts of genres in activity system can be brought into the concrete world to help people in their own life struggles, or as Yrjö calls it "ascending from the abstract to the concrete."

Karyn Kessler and Paul Rogers also show how genres can give shape and legitimacy to a kind of work that may have occurred before, but that becomes empowered and more readily funded by documents that recognize roles, provide criteria for recognition, and create potentials for support. In short, new valued social types are brought into being, encouraged, and rewarded within an application system, enlisting people to identify with a kind of work. Potential social entrepreneurs are given identities and guidance through the categories in an application for funding. Over time as the identity emerges, the skills, criteria, accomplishments, and possibilities expand. This process suggests more broadly how social roles are formed by their naming, support, and recruitment in various documents, which in turn bring them into organizations that make their work possible. This is as true for nurses and doctors, teachers, and financiers and truck drivers as well as social entrepreneurs, although the activity and documentary systems that support these roles are longer standing and more complex, and perhaps even taken for granted. Each of these roles are given shape, regulation, training, support, sponsorship, criteria for success and failure, and organized relation to others in countless kinds of documents. The visibility and value of these roles then serve to attract new generations to fulfill these roles.

While genres evolve and new activity systems emerge, and as people experience genres new to them as they live their lives, yet the genres culturally experienced in youth and reinforced through local schooling can have enduring effect in how people engage in writing tasks throughout life. Liliana Tolchinsky and Anat Stavans examine how secondary school students in different countries (though of equivalent social economic status and given matched argumentative tasks) will write in ways particular to their region. It is unclear whether differences in curricula fully account for the patterned differences or if there are also connections between the literacy practices and ideologies in the community beyond school. In any event, the two cohorts emerge from their secondary education with distinctively different patterns of writing which they would carry with them even if they were to attend the same university in a third country. Those of us who have taught international students have seen these differences endure, even in the face of another layer of distinctively different instruction and genres, even if over time there is some accommodation and change within the more recently experienced expectations.

Two chapters here document how writing address writing education in two different parts of the world, showing the local dynamics and forces that are shaping emerging practices and institutions. Natalia Ávila Reyes, Elizabeth Narváez-Cardona, and Federico Navarro in their chapter show how writing education is particular to region and educational sector within South America. Wu Dan and Li Zenghui point out even within one country the distinctiveness of second language English writing from first language education. Writing cultures grow out of different circumstances and needs.

CHANGING KNOWLEDGE

The process of change itself concerns Clay Spinuzzi in his chapter: where change comes from and whether it is directed by inevitable dialectics or by the diversity of viewpoints that arise in dialogic processes. This question leads us not only to issues of logic and testimony which Spinuzzi raises, but also to systems of evidence, reasoning, theorizing, and credibility arising within various groups and enacted in their communications. This returns me to the issues of relativism that haunted me as a young scholar as it did many others, as we come to see the limits of our own knowledge and cultural worlds, bounded by the blindnesses, errors, interests, and limitations of practices within the systems that have taught us ways of seeing, inscribing, and conceptualizing—no matter how open we try to be. The doubts raised in undergraduate philosophizing, the dilemmas of democratic politics, or the conflicts of the science wars have only been deepened as I have come to understand the fecundity and variety of writing. Ludwik Fleck's account of thought styles of thought collectives, which in his practical analysis comes down to representational styles, I have found the most comforting, but even he has a trap door of agnosticism about the values that lie below the choice of representational styles. He characterizes scientific cultures as those that actively seek to maximize the passive constraints on discourse imposed by experience of the material world. I share with him a bet on this value preference as I think that nature will ultimately constrain our words. But since each scientific culture is particular in its practices, methods, forms of evidence, reasonings, and theories, we need to attend to all those who offer methodically gathered evidence of all sorts. This I take from Joseph Priestley. No knowledge is absolute; it is all process embedded within human communication and human activity. What we know at the present moment will influence the conditions of the future, even if those conditions raise new questions, invoke new processes, and lead us to different experiences and knowledge.

CHANGES IN OUR UNDERSTANDING OF WRITING

My whole career I have been surrounded by change in writing research. When I started teaching writing in 1971 there was no journal devoted solely to research on writing and there was only one practitioner journal focused solely on composition. Research monographs could be counted on one hand. What little research that existed was primarily linguistic, closely tied to traditional grammatical and syntactic categories and a small number of traditional school assignments. Five decades later we are aware of many more dimensions of writing and pursue many different methods. Process, genre, activity systems, WAC, WID, social networks and relationships, values, motivation, efficacy, metareflection, development, anxiety, neurological organization and diversity, affect, trauma writing, atypicality, corpora, language varieties, translanguaging and hybridity, marginalization and systematic discrimination, access, history, technology, eye-tracking, keystroke logging, FMRI, autoethnography, interviewing, participant observation, and so much more are familiar to those in the field. But we are far from the end. We have become and remain highly interdisciplinary, looking for new ways to conceive of and view writing. The chapters in this volume continue to open new doors and make new connections.

Perhaps at some point writing studies will develop a small, stable canon of issues, ideas, and methods, but we are not there now. I feel fortunate to be part of this period of proliferation and expansion, opening our eyes to the complexity of writing. It has certainly provided me the pleasure of new vistas coming into view through the haze. It at least fit my disposition to look broadly and seek underlying processes. I suspect our field will remain interesting in this way for a time to come, or at least I hope so, for it seems to me there is so much fundamental still to be discovered, beyond the reach of our current disciplinary tools and imagination. I thank my friends and colleagues, those contributing to this volume and so many others, for accompanying me on this rewarding journey into the haze of the unknown.

CHAPTER 18.

WHAT WE TEACH WHEN WE TEACH WRITING: A BIG PICTURE IN A SMALL FRAME

Charles Bazerman
University of California, Santa Barbara

Teaching writing is an immensely rewarding profession, even if the work is exhausting and institutional recognition, conditions, and recompense are regularly inadequate. We provide environments, tasks, and resources for students to become more articulate and thoughtful while they share with us their experiences, joys, traumas, and realizations in their writing. We watch them grow as people and intellects. We see students work hard to bring their thoughts and experiences into the world and escape the confines of unshared ruminations. At the same time, we prepare them for future successes no matter what subjects they study, fields they enter, or careers they launch.

The immediate personal connections of teaching writing pull us beyond ourselves and beyond the limits of our energies, often leaving us too depleted to contemplate the reach and importance of the enterprise we are engaged in, how complex and varied writing is, how it forms the ligaments and lifeblood of the modern world, and how it makes literate humans who we are today. With the luxury of a position that allows me to explore the immensity of writing, I have tried to make available to our overworked profession what I and others have found, in research publications, in edited volumes, in reference books and series, but I often feel the big picture is missing, as these publications are focused and particular, or abstract, or long. Readers may be attracted to one idea without connecting it to the big picture. James Joyce is reputed to have said that it took him seventeen years to write *Finnegan's Wake* so readers should take that long to read it. Although I appreciate the cheekiness of the remark, I do not want to consign my poor readers to a fifty-year internment just so they can share the picture my journey has led me to. After all, Nabokov in his introduction to *Lolita* said that novel was inspired by a newspaper story about a captive chimpanzee who was taught to draw, and all he drew was the bars of his cage. That portfolio of pictures might be of interest for a minute or two, but hardly longer. Let's see whether the vision of my cage can hold your attention for a few minutes more.

DOI: https://doi.org/10.37514/PER-B.2023.1800.2.18

I will tell the story as a series of discoveries, as I experienced them, given the contingencies of my life and the time I grew up in, surrounded by fellow teachers and scholars in writing and other fields, and gaining insight from their research and ideas. I have told the story of those contingencies and their impact on my development as a writer in a book-length autoethnography that I hope will be appearing soon. I have also discussed the work of my fellow scholars in many other publications, particularly my 2013 *Theory of Literate Action*. I will not cite them here, however, though you may be able to spot their thinking in what I say, because here my task is to sketch out the broad picture, rather than synthesizing relevant literatures. I want to keep the frame small so the big picture comes together. I am connecting dots without dwelling on the dots, just sketching in the connecting lines.

I first came to the power of writing through my struggle to make meanings relevant to my life while delighting in the play of language, starting with childhood puns and the syntactic fun of making complex sentences in primary school, to writing poetry and witty literary papers in college. Writing became a way of making sense of my world, values, and commitments. Many of us I think come to writing in similar ways, through our personal engagement with what we can do with writing and what meanings writing can help us discover. When I first started teaching, I simply wanted to share the power of the written word and the power of what we can make with it. Accordingly, I focused on the language itself, how it can be manipulated, and how I could share that with our students. But it didn't take me long to realize that my students didn't come through the same set of experiences and did not always find writing the means of expression, discovery, and power that I did. Many had faced obstacles and failure in their early writing education, and found writing aversive and not at all motivating. So I needed to learn what was meaningful in their lives and how writing could help them in their struggles, as well as how to help them overcome aversive, anxiety-laden writing experiences.

As I started to focus on my students' attitudes, feelings, motivations, and needs, colleagues were beginning to discuss writing processes, and how each text emerged over time requiring multiple kinds of psychological work and personal engagement. We aided student writers to become more aware of their processes and to develop the practices and commitment needed to produce good texts. I started to see the benefit of time on task and focused attention on different tasks at different moments, which needed to be coordinated over the entire process. I saw my role increasingly as stage managing sequences of activities that would both challenge and motivate, while providing explicit instruction and guidance at the point of need—which meant instruction became a dialog over writing in progress. I began thinking more concretely about the zone of proximal development and how it existed within social environments as students were addressing motivating tasks. The teacher had a role in setting engaging tasks and providing those clues or footholds as students were sorting out whatever they were trying to accomplish and make sense of within those tasks. This orientation toward engaging and supporting students' developmental tasks stayed with me as I started to understand more about the complex symbolic worlds students were learning to participate in through their writing.

Entering further into the students' writing lives, I started to learn what they wanted to become through their engagement with the university they voluntarily enrolled in. This meant seeing how writing was a means of academic success, but even more of academic discovery as they started to find meaning in their studies. Writing in my classroom became part of the entry into writing across the curriculum and then writing in their workplaces—but it was also writing as a means of knowing and learning and thinking and critical reflection on learning. Discovering how much their writing at the university was explicitly about their readings, I was led down a path of seeing how intertextual writing was, not just in the academic world, but more generally. These growing conceptions about writing were shared by a number of teachers in my generation and after.

As I started to look into writing within the curriculum, I wondered about the disciplines that lay behind the curriculum—first it was the complex relationship of classroom genres students practiced to those of disciplinary scholars and in particular their journal and book publications. As I looked more fully into social studies of science, however, I came to appreciate the many other ways writing was part of how professionals engaged with their field, whether grants, or reports, or organizational documents and everything else that was part of their activity systems and the roles they enacted. I started to see the many genres they encountered and worked in as orderly and organized to form the social ligaments and the communicative lifeblood of their worlds. This orderliness led me to look into how these genres and activity systems came to be the way they were. Even the out-sized role that money and economics take in our lives can be tied to a history of literate inventions of financial instruments, marketplaces, government financing, legal regulations, banking systems, accounting practices, commerce, communication, information technologies, and the like. I also became more self-conscious about the development and organization of the field of writing studies and how I could support continuing its growth and place within the academy, through publications that advanced areas of study and aggregated the accumulated knowledge of the field, through advancing organizations that created opportunities for communication, and for building mechanisms that raised the visibility and status of the field.

The orderly organization of genres and communications led me back to think of the classrooms as also organized activity systems, with particular histories tied to the development of educational institutions. These histories and the consequent reading and writing practices within schooling turned out to be differentiated and situated within countries, regions, cultures, and the interests of sponsoring bodies in society, whether church, state, wealthy benefactors, or communities. All this helped me understand better what was occurring in the classrooms of the universities I worked in; the range of attitude, skills, social manner, and knowledge students brought with them from the many different private, religious, home, and public school systems they experienced; and the tasks students were challenged to accomplish. Later, as I started to engage more with colleagues and universities in different countries, I became ever more aware how different organized educational systems were, how they were differently regulated, how they were guided by different ideologies, and how these educational systems arose from different histories. Practices and attitudes arising from a millennia-old system of Chinese bureaucratic examinations are still consequential for contemporary Chinese schooling. Talmudic yeshivas have distinctly different cultures and organizations than their near cousins of Islamic madrassas, even though both give supreme authority to their sacred texts. Within each system and each educational variation within any one national or religious system, writing and its teaching are differently positioned. Seeing this great variety made me realize how unusual was the tradition of college composition that developed in the US over 150 years within the equally unusual expectations of US general education. There is nothing inevitable about what we do, which is historically particular as the practices anywhere else, though we may have our reasons to prefer it and the larger way of life it supports.

As I came to see more clearly how the academy ran on documents, I came to see something similar in all spheres of society. We participate through reading and writing within large and often distant forms of social organization whether of economy, law, governance, finances, corporations, religions and belief communities, culture, and the arts. Even our most local private life is increasingly imagined and guided through ideas circulated through literacy, as our expectations and practices of personal relationships are saturated with self-help books, psychology, sociology, spiritual guidance, and literary representations. Each domain has its repertoires of symbolic meanings, knowledge, genres, communicative practices, organized roles, and communicative relations. Scholarship in history, anthropology, archeology, cultural evolution, governance, the arts, journalism, as well as of literacy and rhetorical practice, helped me see the last five thousand years since the invention of literacy as the invention of increasingly complex intertwined elements that comprise modern life—ways of thinking, communicating, relating, enacting values, creating meanings, affiliating and participating within spheres of activity. All have been mediated and held together by writing and more recent modes of recording and sharing—turning local social groups into part of larger collectives spread over space and time, increasingly global and intertwined, but also providing different locales for individuals engaged within different spheres, each located within historical and geographical moments. Although humans may be the same biological beings we were 5000 years ago, we live very different lives; do different work; are aware of, attend to, and know different things; have different identities and affiliations; and think different thoughts. Even today, people living just a few blocks away from each other in the same city, may live in very different worlds depending on their sources of information, identity, and work that draw them into worlds that extend far beyond their neighborhoods.

All along, even as I was starting to see the role of inscription in this history of the last five thousand years of human society, I remained aware that the different spheres and locations of activity and relations created different spaces for individual development. While this awareness was initially a fuzzy intuition, the more I learned about the evolving differentiated text-mediated networks of activity, the more I could see how this complex landscape created different opportunity spaces for the literacy development of individuals as they engaged with the specific reading and writing tasks they encountered. These tasks met their individual perceptions, needs, motivations, resources, and states of mind in order to create ladders for individual development, as well as to present obstacles. The opportunities and tasks became habitats for learning and formed potential zones of proximal development, while obstacles restricted the possibilities for writing development. It was a small step to move from this vision of the particularity of development within socio-historic literate locations to gain a more concrete understanding of the individuality of each person's lifespan writing trajectory and then to see the collective development of writing practices as the consequence of all the individual participations of differently developing individuals within the possibilities of their time. This ever-changing literacy environment then set the opportunities for development of future individuals and collectives. The variation and processes of lifespan development of writing along with the communal consequences for human social organization and interaction with the material environment offer possibilities for research with direct consequences for education as well as for the future of our species.

Our educational interventions are only brief episodes within the total writing development of the people who pass under our watch, and through them the literate development of the collectives they participate in. The more we understand about their individual and collective trajectories located within the historical and social space they navigate, the better we can help contribute to their lives and the lives of society. This concept reframes more robustly and crisply a more general orientation that has guided me from my earliest teaching.

The idea of lifespan development also helped integrate another dimension of ideas that had interested me, concerning emotions, anxieties, and psychological needs. People as individuals are not just motivated by rational participation in cognitive social practices; they are also driven by personal needs and desires, while constrained by aversions and anxieties. The interaction of these emotional themes with engagement with more rationally enacted social spheres could be understood more fully when seen as part of the currents that drive people along in their trajectories of developments. These emotional themes go very deeply, as I experienced when writing helped me gain bearings in my own life. More generally, the recent research on trauma writing suggests that writing can fundamentally affect our neurological organization even to the level of impacting our immune systems. It is a step further to think about the atypicality of everyone's literacy development as it becomes part of our perceptual and neurological organization in engaging with all aspects of the world. We each develop under a unique set of neurobiological conditions influenced by our unique social and material positions that we respond to. The more visible extreme of differently abled are those who have to learn to cope with written language without hearing or sight. The autism spectrum offers another recognizable set of conditions under which some learn to use symbols as part of their interaction with others. But this is true in different ways for all of us, whether or not we have an identified atypicality.

What unusual creatures we humans are. While most animals have some form of social relations, some communicate, and even a few develop cultures that pass on through generations, only humans read and write. Reading and writing has supported robust and rapid cultural evolution, making our lives change from generation to generation, as well as changing the conditions and means of our learning, thinking, and actions. Consequently, we have created highly differentiated spaces for our development as we encounter and select among the virtual world of meanings available in our time and place, making ever more complex and differentiated possibilities for individuality. We now extend far beyond the neural communication in our physical body to participate in large social bodies of knowledge, co-orientation, collaboration, and coordination.

So this brings me back to thinking about our twenty-first century students, passing through the range of educational and cultural experiences available to them in their regions and institutions. Our students are trying to make their ways in the world before them as they see it. Through education they seek to enter more fully into their chosen worlds of literate practices and knowledge, taking place in the social collective. They are trying to make meaning of those worlds and to participate in them, navigating their life trajectories during the years unfolding before them. They are no longer Mesopotamian farmers counting their sheaves of grain nor medieval monks devoting themselves to a maintaining a single set of Holy Scriptures nor even nineteenth century medical doctors, working within and contributing to the theories and knowledge of their time, using the devices and measures then current. Even the professional practices of accountants have changed radically in recent decades as computing has transformed their tools of inscription, record-keeping, and intertextual accountability; as well, the personal and civic lives of these same accountants are being played out in changing literate cultures.

The material world around us may remain pretty much the same over time (apart from what humans do to our material environment through literacy supported activities, for good and ill), but the world of meanings, knowledge, interactions, culture, and community that humans make is constantly changing. Yet this symbol-saturated communicative world is held aloft only through the attention and meaning-making of individuals, largely through reading and writing. Our communicative practices keep pumping energy into the shared world of meanings. Without that active attention and engagement the world of meanings would collapse as fast as a hologram with the plug pulled. But every bit of energy people contribute to those shared meanings changes that symbolic world, creates new meanings, interactions, organizations. As teachers of writing, we enable people to keep this theater of meaning and society alive, to maintain and evolve the built symbolic environment at a distance, to keep the human literate experiment going.

APPENDIX.
THE PUBLICATIONS OF CHARLES BAZERMAN IN CHRONOLOGICAL ORDER

Compiled by Jonathan M. Marine

PUBLICATIONS

Bazerman, C. (1970). Three Poems, *Brooklyn Poets*, Brooklyn Poets' Cooperative.
Bazerman, C., Book reviews in *The Nation*:
    Toward the End, an Effete Snob, 9/18/72, 215, 7, 215–216
    Art and the Accidents of Flesh, 11/6/72, 215, 14, 440–441
    What They Felt in Place of Joy, 11/27/72, 215, 17, 537–538
    A Fine Scheme for Criticism, 2/5/73, 216, 6, 184–186
    Building the New Jerusalem, 4/23/73, 216, 17, 537–538
    Victories of Happy Madness, 9/10/73, 217, 7, 218–219
    Serving the Larger Design, 3/9/74, 218, 10, 311–312
    Danger, Fear, and Self-Revulsion, 11/15/75, 221, 16, 502–504
Bazerman, C. (1974). Book review of J. Lievesay, *Venetian Phoenix: Paolo Sarpi* in *Seventeenth Century News*, Winter, 82–84.
Bazerman, C. (1975). Book Review of Fawcett and Sandberg, *Grassroots* in *Causes*, 2.
Bazerman, C. (1976). A Student Guide for Messing up Your First English Paper. *College Composition and Communication*, 27(3), 296–97.
Bazerman, C., Cummins, M., Liben, D., & Linn, W. (1976). Statement on the College Board's Test of Standard Written English (for the CUNY Association of Writing Supervisors). *College Composition and Communication*, 27(3), 287–89.
Bazerman, C. (1977). Help, *New Voices*, 6.
Bazerman, C. (1977). Time in Play and Film: *Macbeth* and *Throne of Blood*. *Literature/Film Quarterly*, 5(4), 333–38.
Bazerman, C. (1978). The Grant, the Scholar, and the University Community. In S. Hook, P. Kurtz, & M. Todorovich. *The University and the State* (pp. 221–226). Prometheus Books.
Wiener, H., & Bazerman, C. (1978). *English Skills Handbook*. Houghton Mifflin.
Bazerman, C. (1980). Book review of B. Latour and S. Woolgar, *Laboratory Life* in *Society for the Social Studies of Science*, 5(2) 14–19.
Bazerman, C. (1980). A Relationship between Reading and Writing: The Conversational Model. *College English*, 41(6), 656–661.
Bazerman, C. (1981). *The Informed Writer: Using Sources in the Disciplines*. Houghton Mifflin.

Appendix

Bazerman, C. (1981). What Written Knowledge Does: Three Examples of Academic Discourse. *Philosophy of the Social Sciences, 11*(3), 361–88.

Bazerman, C. (1983). Scientific Writing as a Social Act: A Review of the Literature of the Sociology of Science. In J. Anderson, J. Brockmann, & C. Miller (Eds.), *New Essays in Technical Writing and Communication* (pp. 156–184). Baywood.

Bazerman, C. (1984). Modern Evolution of the Experimental Report: Spectroscopic Articles in *Physical Review*, 1893–1980. *Social Studies of Science, 14*, 163–96.

Bazerman, C. (1984). The Writing of Scientific Non-fiction: Contexts, Choices and Constraints. *Pre/Text, 5*(1), 39–74.

Bazerman, C. (1985). Physicists Reading Physics: Schema-laden Purposes and Purpose-laden Schema. *Written Communication, 2*(1), 3–23.

Bazerman, C. (1985). Studies of Scientific Writing: E Pluribus Unum. *4S Review, 3*(2), 13–20.

Bazerman, C. (1987). Codifying the Social Scientific Style: The *APA Publication Manual* as a Behaviorist Rhetoric. In J. Nelson, A. Megill, & D. McCloskey (Eds.), *The Rhetoric of the Human Sciences* (pp. 125–144). University of Wisconsin Press.

Bazerman, C. (1987). Literate Acts and the Emergent Social Structure of Science. *Social Epistemology, 1*(4), 295–310.

Bazerman, C. (1988). *Shaping Written Knowledge: The Genre and Activity of the Experimental Article in Science*. University of Wisconsin Press.

Bazerman, C. (1989). Book Review of H. Collins, *Changing Order. Philosophy of the Social Sciences, 19*(1), 115–118.

Bazerman, C. (1989). *The Informed Reader: Contemporary Issues in the Disciplines*. Houghton Mifflin.

Bazerman, C. (1989). Rhetoricians on the Rhetoric of Science (Symposium). *Science Technology and Human Values, 14*(1), 3–6.

Bazerman, C. (1989). What Are We Doing as a Research Community? (Symposium). *Rhetoric Review, 7*(2), 223–224.

Bazerman, C. (1990). Book Review of T. Becher. *Academic Tribes and Territories. English for Specific Purposes, 9*(3), 265–266.

Bazerman, C. (1990). Comment and Response. *College English, 52*(3), 329–330.

Bazerman, C. (1990). Discourse Analysis and Social Construction. *Annual Review of Applied Linguistics, 11*, 77–83.

Bazerman, C. (1990). Reading Student Papers: Proteus Grabbing Proteus. In B. Lawson, S. Sterr, & W. R. Winterowd (Eds.), *Encountering Student Texts* (pp. 139–146). National Council of Teachers of English.

Bazerman, C. (1990). What's Interesting? *English Basics*, Winter.

Bazerman, C. (1991). Book Review. The Second Stage of Writing Across the Curriculum (Review Essay). *College English, 53*(2), 209–212.

Bazerman, C. (1991). Book Review of Greg Myers, *Writing Biology. Newsletter of the Society for Literature and Science*.

Bazerman, C. (1991). How Natural Philosophers can Cooperate: The Rhetorical Technology of Coordinated research in Joseph Priestley's *History and Present State of Electricity*. In C. Bazerman, & J. Paradis (Eds.), *Textual Dynamics of the Professions* (pp. 13–44). University of Wisconsin Press.

Bazerman, C. (1991). Theories that Help us Read and Write Better. In S. Witte (Ed.), *A Rhetoric of Doing: Festschrift for J. Kinneavy* (pp. 103–112). Southern Illinois University Press.

Bazerman, C., & Paradis, J. (Eds.). (1991). *Textual Dynamics of the Professions.* University of Wisconsin Press.

Bazerman, C. (1992). Book Review of G. Dillon, *Contending Rhetorics. Language in Society, 21*(3), 501–503.

Bazerman, C. (1992). Book Review of L. Flower et al., *Reading to write. Journal of Advanced Composition, 12*(1), 236–242.

Bazerman, C. (1992). From Cultural Criticism to Disciplinary Participation: Living with Powerful Words. In M. Moran, & A. Herrington (Eds.), *Writing, Teaching, and Learning in the Disciplines* (pp. 61–68). Modern Language Association.

Bazerman, C. (1992). The Interpretation of Disciplinary Writing. In R. H. Brown (Ed.), *Writing the Social Text* (pp. 31–38). Aldine de Gruyter.

Bazerman, C. (1992). Linguistic and Rhetorical Studies of Writing in Disciplines. *Encyclopedia of Higher Education.* Pergamon.

Bazerman, C. (1992). Where is the Classroom? *English Basics,* Winter.

Bazerman, C. (1993). Beyond the Composition Ghetto. *Literacy Across the Curriculum, 8*(3).

Bazerman, C. (1993). Book Review of Dieter Stein, *Cooperating with Written Texts. American Anthropologist, 95*(4), 1031.

Bazerman, C. (1993). A Contention over the Term Rhetoric. In T. Enos (Ed.), *Toward Defining the new Rhetorics* (pp. 3–7). Southern Illinois University Press.

Bazerman, C. (1993). Foreword. In N. Blyler, & C. Thralls (Eds.), *Professional Communication: The Social Perspective* (pp. vii–x). Sage.

Bazerman, C. (1993). Forums of Validation and Forms of Knowledge: The Magical Rhetoric of Otto von Guericke's Sulfur Globe. *Configurations, 1*(2), 201–228.

Bazerman, C. (1993). Intertextual Self-fashioning: Gould and Lewontin's Representations of the Literature. In R. Selzer (Ed.), *Understanding Scientific Prose* (pp. 20–41). University of Wisconsin Press.

Bazerman, C. (1993). Money Talks: The Rhetorical Project of Adam Smith's *Wealth of Nations.* In W. Henderson, T. Dudley-Evans, & R. Backhouse (Eds.), *Economics and Language* (pp. 173–199). Routledge.

Bazerman, C. (1993). Patent Realities: Legally Stabilized Texts and Market Indeterminacies. In J. Hultberg (Ed.), *The Narrative Construction of the Anxious Object* (pp. 5–12). University of Goteborg.

Bazerman, C. (1993). The Publicity Wizard of Menlo Park. *Electric Perspectives, 17*(6), 30–41.

Bazerman, C. (1993). Response. *Rhetoric Society Quarterly, 23*(2), 54–58.

Bazerman, C. (1993). Royal Society of London. In T. Enos (Ed.), *Encyclopedia of Rhetoric* (pp. 645–648). Southern Illinois University Press.

Bazerman, C. (1993). Writing in the Disciplines. In A. Purves (Ed.), *Encyclopedia of English Studies* (pp. 1309–1311). Scholastic Press.

Bazerman, C. (1994). Afterthoughts: Who Made Nonfiction a Negation? In V. Vitanza (Ed.), *Ten years of Pre/Text* (pp. 214–216). University of Pittsburgh Press.

Bazerman, C. (1994). *Constructing Experience*. Southern Illinois University Press.

Bazerman, C. (1994). Electrifying Words: Edison's announcement of the incandescent light. *Journal of Business and Technical Communication, 8*(1), 135–147.

Bazerman, C. (1994). Systems of Genre and the Enactment of Social Intentions. In A. Freedman, & P. Medway (Eds.), *Genre and the New Rhetoric* (pp. 79–101). Taylor & Francis.

Bazerman, C., & Russell, D. (1994). *Landmark Essays in Writing Across the Curriculum*. Hermagoras Press.

Bazerman, C. (1995). Influencing and Being Influenced: Local Acts across Large Distances. *Social Epistemology, 9*(2), 189–199.

Bazerman, C. (1995). Response: Curricular Responsibilities and Professional Definition. In J. Petraglia (Ed.), *Reconceiving Writing* (pp. 249–259). Erlbaum,

Bazerman, C. (1996). Book review of E. Hutchins, *Cognition in the Wild* in *Mind, Culture, and Activity, 3*(1), 51–54.

Bazerman, C. (1996). Editor's Introduction. In D. Winsor, *Writing like an engineer: A rhetorical education* (pp. vii–viii). Erlbaum.

Bazerman, C., & Bridwell-Bowles, L. (1996). *Students Being Disciplined: Getting Confused, Getting by Getting Rewarded, Getting Smart, Getting Real*. University of Minnesota.

Bazerman, C. (1997). Book review of A. J. Soyland, *Psychology as Metaphor* in *Theory & Psychology, 7*(1), 141–142.

Bazerman, C. (1997). Concepts in Action. *Readerly/Writerly Texts, 4*(2), 9–20.

Bazerman, C. (1997). Discursively Structured Activities. *Mind, Culture, and Activity, 4*(4), 296–308.

Bazerman, C. (1997). Editor's Introduction. In A. D. Van Nostrand, *Fundable Knowledge: The Marketing of Defense Science and Technology* (pp. ix–x). Erlbaum.

Bazerman, C. (1997). Genre and Social Science. In T. Enos (Ed.), *Making and Unmaking the Prospects for Rhetoric* (pp. 83–90). Erlbaum.

Bazerman, C. (1997). *Involved: Writing for College, Writing for Your Self*. Houghton Mifflin.

Bazerman, C. (1997). The Life of Genre, the Life in the Classroom. In W. Bishop, & H. Ostrom (Eds.), *Genre and Writing* (pp. 19–26). Boynton/Cook.

Bazerman, C. (1997). Performatives Constituting Value: The Case for Patents. In B. Gunnarsson, P. Linell, & Nordberg (Eds.), *The Construction of Professional Discourse* (pp. 42–53). Addison Wesley.

Russell, D., & Bazerman, C. (1997). *The Activity of Writing; The Writing of Activity*. Special issue of *Mind, Culture, and Activity, 4*(4).

Russell, D., & Bazerman, C. (1997). Editors' Introduction. *Mind, Culture, and Activity, 4*(4), 223.

Bazerman, C. (1998). Book Review of B. Nardi (Ed.), *Cognition and Context*. *Mind, Culture, and Activity, 5*(1), 73–75.

Bazerman, C. (1998). Book Review of G. Nunberg (Ed.), *Future of the Book*. *Written Language and Literacy, 1*(2), 297–300.

Bazerman, C. (1998). Editor's Introduction. In J. Swales, *Other Floors, Other Voices: Toward Textography and Beyond* (pp. ix–x). Erlbaum.

Bazerman, C. (1998). Editor's Introduction. In J. Petraglia-Bahri, *Reality by Design: The Rhetoric and Technology of Authenticity and Education* (pp. ix–x). Erlbaum.

Bazerman, C. (1998). Editor's Introduction. In D. Atkinson, *Scientific Discourse in Sociohistorical Context: The Philosophical Transactions of the Royal Society of London, 1675–1975* (pp. vii–ix). Erlbaum.

Bazerman, C. (1998). Editor's Introduction. In P. Prior, *Writing/Disciplinarity: A Sociohistoric Account of Literate Activity in the Academy* (pp. vii–viii). Erlbaum.

Bazerman, C. (1998). Emerging Perspectives on the Many Dimensions of Scientific Discourse. In J. Martin, & R. Veel (Eds.), *Reading Science* (pp. 15–30). Routledge.

Bazerman, C. (1998). Green Giving: Engagement, Values, Activism, and Community Life. *New Directions for Philanthropic Fundraising*, 22, 7–22.

Bazerman, C. (1998). Looking at Writing; Writing What I See. In T. Enos, & D. Roen (Eds.), *Living Rhetoric and Composition* (pp. 15–24). Erlbaum.

Bazerman, C. (1998). The Rhetoric of Technology. *Journal of Business and Technical Communication*, 12(3), 381–387.

Bazerman, C. (1998). Vygotskian Theory. In M. Kennedy (Ed.), *Theorizing Composition* (pp. 333–337). Greenwood.

Bazerman, C. (1999). Changing Regularities of Genre. *IEEE Transactions on Professional Communication*, 42(1), 1–2.

Bazerman, C. (1999). Editor's Introduction. In P. Dias, A. Pare, A. Freedman, & P. Medway. *Worlds Apart: Acting and Writing in Academic and Workplace Contexts* (pp. vii–ix). Erlbaum.

Bazerman, C. (1999). *The Languages of Edison's Light*. MIT Press.

Bazerman, C. (1999). Singular Utterances: Realizing Local Activities through Typified Forms in Typified Circumstances. In A. Trosberg (Ed.), *Analysing the Discourses of Professional Genres* (pp. 25–40). John Benjamins.

Bazerman, C. (2000). Editor's Introduction. In A. Blakeslee, *Interacting with Audiences* (pp. xi–xiii). Erlbaum.

Bazerman, C. (2000). Letters and the Social Grounding of Differentiated Genres. In D. Barton, & N. Hall (Eds.), *Letter Writing as a Social Practice* (pp. 15–30). John Benjamins.

Bazerman, C. (2000). A Rhetoric for Literate Society: The Tension between Expanding Practices and Restricted Theories. In M. Goggin (Ed.), *Inventing a Discipline* (pp. 5–28). NCTE.

Bazerman, C. (2001). Anxiety in Action: Sullivan's Interpersonal Psychiatry as a Supplement to Vygotskian Psychology. *Mind, Culture, and Activity*, 8(2), 174–186.

Bazerman, C. (2001). Book Review of E. MacPhail, *Evolution of Consciousness. Mind, Culture, and Activity*, 8(4), 315–317.

Bazerman, C. (2001). Editor's Introduction. In L. Flower, *Learning to Rival* (pp. ix–x). Erlbaum.

Bazerman, C. (2001). Nuclear Information: One Rhetorical Moment in the Construction of the Information Age. *Written Communication*, 18(3), 259–295.

Bazerman, C. (2001). Politically Wired: The Changing Places of Political Participation in the Age of the Internet. In J. Yates, & J. Van Maanen (Eds.), *IT and Organizational Transformation* (pp. 137–154). Sage.

Bazerman, C. (2001). Writing as a Development in Interpersonal Relations. *Journal for the Psychoanalysis of Culture and Society, 6*(2), 298–302.

Geisler, C., Bazerman, C., Doheny-Farina, S., Gurak, L., Haas, C., Johnson-Eilola, J., Kaufer, D., Lunsford, A., Miller, C., Winsor, D., & Yates, J. (2001). Itext: Future Directions for Research on the Relationship between Information Technology and Writing. *Journal of Business and Technical Communication, 15*(3), 269–308.

Bazerman, C. (2002). The Case for Writing Studies as a Major Discipline. In G. Olson (Ed.), *The Intellectual Work of Composition* (pp. 32–38). Southern Illinois University Press.

Bazerman, C. (2002). Distanced and Refined Selves: Educational Tensions in Writing with the Power of Knowledge. In M. Hewings (Ed.), *Academic Writing in Context* (pp. 23–29). University of Birmingham Press.

Bazerman, C. (2002). Editor's Introduction. In P. J. Salazar, *An African Athens* (pp. xi–xii). Erlbaum.

Bazerman, C. (2002). Editor's Introduction. In B. Sauer *Rhetoric Under Uncertainty* (pp. xvii–xviii). Erlbaum.

Bazerman, C. (2002). Genre and Identity: Citizenship in the Age of the Internet and the Age of Global Capitalism. In R. Coe (Ed.), *Ideologies of Genre* (pp. 13–37). Hampton Press.

Bazerman, C. (2003). Rhetorical Research for Reflective Practice: A Multi-Layered Narrative. In C. N. Candlin (Ed.), *Research & Practice in Professional Discourse* (pp. 79–94). City University of Hong Kong Press.

Bazerman, C. (2003). Statement at the Progressive Caucus. *College Composition and Communication, 55*(2), 351–354.

Bazerman, C. (2003). Textual Performance: Where the Action at a Distance Is. *JAC: Journal of Advanced Composition, 23*(2), 379–396.

Bazerman, C. (2003). What Activity Systems are Literary Genres Part Of? *Readerly/Writerly Texts, 10*, 97–106.

Bazerman, C. (2003). What is not Institutionally Visible Does Not Count: The Problem of Making Activity Assessable, Accountable, and Plannable. In C. Bazerman, & D. R. Russell (Eds.), *Writing Selves/Writing Societies: Research from Activity Perspectives* (pp. 428–483). The WAC Clearinghouse; Mind, Culture, and Activity. https://doi.org/10.37514/PER-B.2003.2317.2.13.

Bazerman, C., & Russell, D. R. (Eds.). (2003). *Writing Selves/Writing Societies: Research from Activity Perspectives.* The WAC Clearinghouse; Mind, Culture, and Activity. https://doi.org/10.37514/PER-B.2003.2317.

Bazerman, C., Little, J., & Chavkin, T. (2003). The Production of Information for Genred Activity Spaces. *Written Communication, 20*(4), 455–477.

Bazerman, C. (2004). Book review of A. G. Gross, J. E. Harmon, & M. Reidy, *Communicating science: The Scientific Article from the Seventeenth Century to the Present. Isis, 95*, 341–342.

Bazerman, C. (2004). Editor's Introduction. In J. Lauer, *Invention* (p. xv). Parlor Press; The WAC Clearinghouse. https://wac.colostate.edu/books/referenceguides/lauer-invention/.

Bazerman, C. (2004). Intertextualities: Volosinov, Bakhtin, Literary Theory, and Literacy Studies. In A. Ball, & S. W. Freedman (Eds.), *Bakhtinian Perspectives on Languages, Literacy, and Learning* (pp. 53–65). Cambridge University Press.

Bazerman, C. (2004). Intertextuality: How Texts Rely on Other Texts. In C. Bazerman, & P. Prior (Eds.), *What Writing Does and How It Does It* (pp. 89–102). Erlbaum.

Bazerman, C. (2004). Speech Acts, Genres, and Activity Systems: How Texts Organize Activity and People. In C. Bazerman, & P. Prior (Eds.), *What Writing Does and How It Does It* (pp. 314–316). Erlbaum.

Bazerman, C. & Prior, P. (Eds.). (2004). *What Writing Does and How It Does It*. Erlbaum.

Bazerman, C. (2004). Social Forms as Habitats for Action. *Journal of the Interdisciplinary Crossroads, 1*(2), 317–334.

Bazerman, C. (2004). Student Writing and Writing Education in National Contexts: Continuing a dialogue. *Revista de ABRALIN, 3*, 243–259.

Bazerman, C. (2004). A Reflective Moment in the History of Literacy. In B. Huot, B. Stroble, & C. Bazerman (Eds.), *Multiple Literacies for the Twenty-First Century* (pp. 435–440). Hampton Press.

Huot, B., Stroble, B., & Bazerman, C. (Eds.). (2004). *Multiple Literacies for the Twenty-First Century*. Hampton Press.

Bazerman, C. (2005). Communication in the Scientific Community. In S. Restivo (Ed.), *Science, Technology, and Society* (pp. 55–61). Oxford University Press.

Bazerman, C. (2005). The Diversity of Writing. *Quarterly of the National Writing Project, 24*, 2.

Bazerman, C. (2005). An Essay on Pedagogy by Mikhail M. Bakhtin and Response. Symposium in *Written Communication, 22*(3), 333–374.

Bazerman, C. (2005). *Gêneros Textuais, Tipificação e Interação*. Cortez.

Bazerman, C. (2005). A Response to Anton Fleury's "Liberal Education and Communication Against the Disciplines": A View from the World of Writing. *Communication Education, 54*(1), 86–91.

Bazerman, C. (2005). Practically Human: The Pragmatist Project of the Interdisciplinary Journal *Psychiatry*. *Linguistics and the Human Sciences, 1*(1), 15–38.

Bazerman, C., & De los Santos, R. (2005). Measuring Incommensurability: Are Toxicology and Ecotoxicology Blind to What the Other Sees? In R. Harris (Ed.), *Rhetoric and Incommensurability* (pp. 424–463). Parlor Press.

Bazerman, C., & Little, J. (2005). Knowing Academic Languages. In U. U. Melander, & H. Naslund (Eds.), *Text I Arbete/Text at Work* (pp. 261–269). Upsalla University.

Bazerman, C., Little, J., Chavkin, T., Fouquette, D., Bethel, L., & Garufis, J. (2005). *Reference Guide to Writing Across the Curriculum*. Parlor Press; The WAC Clearinghouse. https://wac.colostate.edu/books/referenceguides/bazerman-wac/.

Bazerman, C. (2006). Analyzing the Multidimensionality of Texts in Education. In J. Green, G. Camilli, & P. Elmore (Eds.), *Complementary Methods for Research in Education* (2nd ed.) (pp. 77–94). American Educational Research Association.

Appendix

Bazerman, C. (2006). Editor's Introduction. In A. Horning, & A. Becker, *Revision: History, Theory, and Practice*. Parlor Press; The WAC Clearinghouse. https://wac.colo state.edu/books/referenceguides/horning-revision/.

Bazerman, C. (2006). Foreword: Persuasive Economies. In G. Smart (Ed.), *Writing the Economy: Activity, Genre and Technology in the World of Banking* (pp. 1–5). Equinox.

Bazerman, C. (2006). *Gênero, Agencia e Escrita*. Sariava.

Bazerman, C. (2006). The Writing of Social Organization and the Literate Situating of Cognition: Extending Goody's Social Implications of Writing. In D. Olson, & M. Cole (Eds.), *Technology, Literacy and the Evolution of Society: Implications of the Work of Jack Goody* (pp. 215–240). Erlbaum.

Bazerman, C., Fouquette, D., Johnston, C., Rohrbacher, F., & De los Santos, R. A. (2006). What Schools of Education Can Offer the Teaching of Writing. In V. Anderson, & S. Romano (Eds.), *Culture Shock and the Practice of Profession* (pp. 309–324). Hampton Press.

Bazerman, C., & Herrington, A. (2006). Circles of Interest: The Growth of Research Communities in WAC and WID/WIP. In S. McLeod (Ed.), *Inventing a Profession: WAC History* (pp. 49–56). Parlor Press.

Bazerman, C. (2007). Editor's Introduction. In S. H. Macleod (Ed.), *Writing Program Administration* (pp. vii–vii). Parlor Press; The WAC Clearinghouse. https://wac.colo state.edu/books/referenceguides/mcleod-wpa/.

Bazerman, C. (2007). *Gêneros Textuais, Intertextualidade, e Atividade: Teórico Consideração*. Cortez.

Bazerman, C. (2007). WAC for Cyborgs: Discursive Thought in Information Rich Environments. In P. Takayoshi, & P. Sullivan (Eds.), *Labor, Writing Technologies, and the Shaping of Composition in the Academy* (pp. 97–110). Hampton Press.

Figueiredo, D., Bazerman, C., & Bonini, A. (Eds.). (2007). Genre and Social Identities. Special issue of *Linguistics and the Human Sciences*, 3(1).

Bazerman, C., & Prior, P. (2008). Participating in Emergent Socio-Literate Worlds: Genre, Disciplinarity, Interdisciplinarity. In J. Green & R. Beach (Eds.), *Multidisciplinary Perspectives on Literacy Research* (pp. 133–178). NCTE.

Bazerman, C. (2008). Editor's Introduction. In E. Long (Ed.), *Community Literacy and the Rhetoric of Local Publics* (pp. xiii–xiv). Parlor Press; The WAC Clearinghouse. https://wac.colostate.edu/books/referenceguides/long-community/.

Bazerman, C. (Ed.). (2008). *Handbook of Research on Writing: History, Society, School, Individual, Text*. Erlbaum.

Bazerman, C., & Rogers, P. (2008). Writing and secular knowledge apart from Modern European Institutions. In C. Bazerman (Ed.), *Handbook of Research on Writing: History, Society, School, Individual, Text* (pp. 143–156). Routledge.

Bazerman, C., & Rogers, P. (2008). Writing and Secular Knowledge within Modern European Institutions. In C. Bazerman (Ed.), *Handbook of Research on Writing: History, Society, School, Individual, Text* (pp. 157–176). Routledge.

Bazerman, C. (2008). Students Need Language Support to Write for Academic Publications. *UC Mexus News*, 44, 15–16.

Bazerman, C. (2008). Theories of the Middle Range in Historical Studies of Writing Practice. *Written Communication*, 25(3), 298–318.
Bazerman, C., Blakesley, D., Palmquist, M., & Russell, D. R. (2008). Open-Access Book Publishing in Writing Studies: A Case Study. *First Monday*, 13. http://www.uic.edu/htbin/cgiwrap/bin/ojs/index.php/fm/article/view/2088/1920.
Bazerman, C. (2009). The Diversity We Become: Education and Agency in Writing Unique Selves within Evolving Communities / a Diversidade que Viemos a Ser: Educação e Agir Autônomo na Inscrição de eus Autênticos em Comunidades Dinâmicas, *Revista Triângulo*, 2(1), 13–29.
Bazerman, C. (2009). Editor's Introduction. In J. Ramage, M. Callaway, J. Clary-Lemon, & Z. Waggoner. (2009). *Argument in composition*. Parlor Press; The WAC Clearinghouse. https://wac.colostate.edu/books/referenceguides/ramage-argument/.
Bazerman, C. (2009). How Does Science Come to Speak in the Courts? Citations, Intertexts, Expert Witnesses, Consequential Facts and Reasoning. *Law and Contemporary Problems*, 72(1), 91–120.
Bazerman, C. (2009). Prefacio. In M. Baltar (Ed.), *Radio escolar* (pp. 9–11). Editoria da Universidade de Caxias do Sul.
Bazerman, C. (2009). The Problem of Writing Knowledge. In S. Miller (Ed.), *Norton book of Composition Studies* (pp. 502–514). W. W. Norton.
Bazerman, C., Bonini, A., & Figueiredo, D. (Eds.). (2009). *Genre in a Changing World*. The WAC Clearinghouse; Parlor Press. https://doi.org/10.37514/PER-B.2009.2324.
Bazerman, C. (2009). Genre and Cognitive Development. In C. Bazerman, A. Bonini, & D. Figueiredo (Eds.), *Genre in a Changing World*. The WAC Clearinghouse; Parlor Press. https://doi.org/10.37514/PER-B.2009.2324.2.14.
Bonini, A., Figueiredo, D., & Bazerman, C. (Eds.). (2009). *Writing Education in Brazil*. Special Issue of *L1*, 8(2).
Bazerman, C. (2010) Chair's Letter. *College Composition and Communication*, 61(3), 597–601.
Bazerman, C. (2010). Continuing a Dialogue. *China Journal*, 3, 38–39.
Bazerman, C. (2010). Senior Editor's Preface. In A. Bawarshi, & M. J. Reiff, (Eds.), *Genre: An Introduction to History, Theory, Research, and Pedagogy* (pp. xi–xii). Parlor Press; The WAC Clearinghouse. https://wac.colostate.edu/books/referenceguides/bawarshi-reiff/.
Bazerman, C. (2010). Editor's Introduction. In G. Otte, & R. Mlynarczyk. *Basic Writing* (pp. xi–xiii). Parlor Press; The WAC Clearinghouse. https://wac.colostate.edu/books/referenceguides/basicwriting/.
Bazerman, C. (2010). Paying the Rent: Languaging Particularity and Novelty. *Revista Brasileira de Lingüistica Applicada*, 10(2), 459–469.
Bazerman, C. (2010). Preface. In S. Santos (Ed). *EFL Writing in Mexican Universities: Research and Experience*. Universidad Autónoma de Nayarit.
Bazerman, C. (2010). Scientific Knowledge, Public Knowledge, and Public Policy: Genred Formation and Disruption of Knowledge for Acting about Global Warming. *Linguagem em (Dis)Curso*, 10(3), 445–463.

Appendix

Bazerman, C. (2010). The Wonder of Writing. *College Composition and Communication*, *61*(3), 571–580.

Bazerman, C., & Baltar, M. (Eds.). (2010). Special Issue on Genre. *Revista Brasileira de Linguistica Aplicada*, *10*(2).

Bazerman, C., Kelly, G. J., Skukauskaite, A., & Prothero, W. (2010). Rhetorical Features of Student Science Writing in Introductory University Oceanography. In C. Bazerman, B. Krut, K. Lunsford, S. McLeod, S. Null, P. Rogers, & A. Stansell (Eds.), *Traditions of Writing Research* (pp. 265–282). Routledge.

Bazerman, C., Krut, B., Lunsford, K., McLeod, S., Null, S., Rogers, P., & Stansell, A. (Eds.). (2010). *Traditions of Writing Research*. Routledge.

Bazerman, C. (2011) Church, state, and the printing press: Conditions for autonomy of Scientific Publication in early Modern Europe. In B. L. Gunnarsson (Ed.), *Scientific Writing in the Age of Linneaus* (pp. 25–44). De Gruyter Mouton Press.

Bazerman, C. (2011). Electrons are Cheap; Society Is Dear. In D. Starke-Meyerring, A. Paré, N. Artemeva, M. Horne, & L. Yousoubova (Eds.), *Writing in knowledge societies* (pp. 75–84). The WAC Clearinghouse; Parlor Press. https://doi.org/10.37514/PER-B.2011.2379.2.04.

Bazerman, C. (2011). Genre as Social Action. In J. Gee, & M. Handford (Eds.), *The Routledge Handbook of Discourse Analysis* (pp. 226–238). Routledge.

Bazerman, C. (2011). The Orders of Documents, the Orders of Activity, and the Orders of Information. *Archival Science*, *12*(4), 377–388.

Bazerman, C. (2011). Standpoints: The Disciplined Interdisciplinarity of Writing Studies. *Research in the Teaching of English*, *46*(1), 8–21.

Bazerman, C. (2011). The Work of a Middle-Class Activist: Stuck in History. In S. Kahn (Ed.), *Activism and Rhetoric: Theories and Contexts for Political Engagement* (pp. 37–46). Routledge.

Bazerman, C. (2012). Academic Writing, Genre, and Indexicality: Evidence, Intertext and Theory. *Intercompreensao: Revista de Didactica das Linguas*, 16, 11–22.

Bazerman, C. (2012). *Géneros textuales, tipificación y actividad*. Benemérita Universidad Autónoma de Puebla.

Bazerman, C. (2012). Preface. In J. Early, & M. DeCosta-Smith (Eds.), *Real World Writing for Secondary Students: Teaching the College Admission Essay and Other Gate-Openers for Higher Education* (pp. ix–x). Teachers College Press.

Bazerman, C. (2012). Writing, Cognition, and Affect from the Perspective of Sociohistorical Studies. In V. Berninger (Ed.), *Past, Present, and Future Contributions of Cognitive Writing Research to Cognitive Psychology* (pp. 89–104). Psychology Press.

Bazerman, C. (2012). Writing with Concepts: Communal, Internalized, and Externalized. *Mind, Culture, and Activity*, *19*(3), 259–272.

Bazerman, C., Dean, C., Early, J., Lunsford, K., Null, S., Rogers, P., & Stansell, A. (Eds.) (2012). *International Advances in Writing Research: Cultures, Places, Measures*. The WAC Clearinghouse; Parlor Press. https://doi.org/10.37514/PER-B.2012.0452.

Keranen, N., Encinas, F., & Bazerman, C. (2012). Immersed in the game of science. In C. Bazerman, C. Dean, J. Early, K. Lunsford, S. Null, P. Rogers, & A. Stansell

(Eds.), *International Advances in Writing Research: Cultures, Places, Measures* (pp. 387–402). The WAC Clearinghouse; Parlor Press. https://doi.org/10.37514/PER-B.2012.0452.2.22.

Bazerman, C., Keranen, N., & Encinas, F. (2012). Facilitated Immersion at a Distance in Second Language Science Writing. In M. C. Badia, & C. Donahue (Eds.), *University writing: Selves and texts in academic societies* (pp. 235–238). Emerald.

Bazerman, C. (2013). Comprendiendo de un Viaje que Dura Toda la Vida: La Evolución de la Escritura. Understanding the Lifelong Journey of Writing Development. *Revista Infancia y Aprendizaje/Journal for the Study of Education and Development, 36*(4), 421–441.

Bazerman, C. (2013). Global and Local Communicative Networks. In A. S. Canagarajah (Ed.), *Literacy as Translingual Practice: Between Communities and Classrooms* (pp. 13–25). Routledge.

Bazerman, C. (2013). *A Rhetoric of Literate Action: Literate Action Volume 1*. The WAC Clearinghouse; Parlor Press. https://doi.org/10.37514/PER-B.2013.0513.

Bazerman, C. (2013). *A Theory of Literate Action: Literate Action Volume 2*. The WAC Clearinghouse; Parlor Press. https://doi.org/10.37514/PER-B.2013.4791.

Bazerman, C., Simon, K., Ewing, P., & Pieng, P. (2013). Domain-Specific Cognitive Development through Writing Tasks in a Teacher Education Program. *Pragmatics & Cognition, 21*(3), 530–551.

Bazerman, C. (2014). La Escritura en el Mundo del Conocimiento, Writing in the World of Knowledge. *Verbum, 9*, 11–21, 23–35.

Bazerman, C. (2014). Preface. In F. Navarro (Ed.), *Manual de Escritura para Carreras de Humanidades (Encountering Academic Writing)* (pp. 5–10). Universidad de Buenos Aires.

Bazerman, C. (2014). Sisters and Brothers of the Struggle: Teachers of Writing in their Worlds. *College Composition and Communication, 65*(4), 646–654.

Bazerman, C. (2014). Book Review of A. N. Applebee & J. Langer, *Writing Instruction that Works: Proven Methods for Middle and High School Classrooms*. *Pedagogies, 9*(2), 175–178.

Andersen, J., Bazerman, C., & Schneider, J. (2014). Beyond Single Genres: Pattern Mapping in Global Communication. In E. M. Jakobs, & D. Perrin (Eds.), *Handbook of Writing and Text Production* (pp. 305–322). Mouton De Gruyter.

Bazerman, C., & Devitt, A. (2014). Genre Perspectives in Text Production Research. In E. M. Jakobs, & D. Perrin (Eds.). *Handbook of Writing and Text Production* (pp. 257–262). Mouton De Gruyter.

Bazerman, C., Simon, K., & Pieng, P. (2014). Writing about Reading to Advance Thinking: A Study in Situated Cognitive Development. In P. Boscolo, & P. Klein (Eds.), *Writing as a Learning Activity* (pp. 249–276). Brill.

Bork, A., Bazerman, C., Poliseli-Correa, F., & Cristovão, V. (2014). Mapeamento das Initiativas de Leitura e Escrita em Lingua Materna na Educacao Superior Resultados Preliminares. *Prolingua, 9*(1), 2–14.

Bazerman, C. (2015). Five Concepts: 1c—writing expresses and shares meaning to be reconstructed by the reader (pp. 21–23) ; 2—writing speaks to situations and contexts through recognizable forms associated with those situations (pp. 34–37); 2a—writing represents the world, events, ideas, and feelings (pp. 37–39); 4a—text is an object outside of oneself that can be improved and developed (with H. Tinberg) (pp. 61–62); 5a—writing is an expression of embodied cognition (with H. Tinberg) (pp. 74–75). In L. Adler-Kassner, & E. Wardle (Eds.), *Naming What We Know*. Utah State University Press.

Bazerman, C. (2015). A Genre-Based Theory of Literate Action. In N. Artemeva, & A. Freedman (Eds.), *Genre Studies Around the Globe* (pp. 80–94). Inkshed Press.

Bazerman, C. (2015). What do Sociocultural Studies of Writing Tell Us about Learning to Write? In C. MacArthur, S. Graham, & J. Fitzgerald (Eds.), *Handbook of Writing Research* (2nd ed.) (pp. 11–23). Guilford.

Bazerman, C. (2016). Creating Identities in an Intertextual World. In A. Chik, T. Costley, & M. C. Pennington (Eds.), *Creativity and Discovery in the University Writing Class* (pp. 45–60). Equinox.

Bazerman, C. (2016). With Chapter Commentaries by D. H. Espíndola, M. P. Escudero, R. P. Carrillo, D. Rodríguez-Vergara, & A. V. Ahumada. *Escritura y Desarrollo Cognitivo en un Mundo Intertextual: Dialogos con la Obra de Charles Bazerman*. Benemerita Universidad Autonoma de Puebla.

Bazerman, C. (2016). Preface. In M. J. Braun, & G. L. Henderson (Eds.), *Managing Democracy: Propaganda and the Rhetorical Production of Economic and Political Realities* (pp. 7–10). Southern Illinois University Press.

Bazerman, C. (2016). Social Changes in Science Communication: Rattling the Information Chain. In J. Buehl, & A. Gross (Eds.), *Science and the Internet: Communicating Knowledge in a Digital Age* (pp. 267–282). Baywood.

Bazerman, C., Reyes, N., Bork, A. V., Poliseli-Corrêa, F., Cristovão, V. L., Tapia-Ladino, M., & Narváez, E. (2016). Intellectual Orientations of Studies of Higher Education Writing in Latin America. In S. Plane, C. Bazerman, P. Carlino, F. Rondelli, C. Boré, C. Donahue, Catherine Boré, M. M. Larruy, P. Rogers, & D. R. Russell (Eds.), *Writing Research from Multiple Perspectives / Recherches en Écriture: Regards Pluriels* (pp. 329–346). The WAC Clearinghouse; University of Metz. https://doi.org/10.37514/INT-B.2017.0919.2.15.

Bazerman, C., & Moritz, M. (2016). Special Issue on Writing in Latin American Higher Education. *Ilha do Desterro, 69*(3).

Navarro, F., Reyes, N., Ladino, M., Cristovão, V., Moritz, M., Narváez, E., & Bazerman, C. (2016). Panorama Histórico y Contrastivo de los Estudios sobre Lectura y Escritura en Educación Superior Publicados en América Latina. *Revista Signos: Estudios de Lingüística, 49*(1), 78–99.

Plane, S., Bazerman, C., Rondelli, F., Donahue, C., Applebee, A. N., Boré, C., Carlino, P., Larruy, M. M., Rogers, P., & Russell, D. R. (Eds.). (2017). *Research on Writing: Multiple Perspectives*. The WAC Clearinghouse; CREM. https://doi.org/10.37514/INT-B.2017.0919.

Tapia-Ladino, M., Reyes, N., Navarro, F., & Bazerman, C. (2016). Milestones, Disciplines and the Future of Initiatives of Reading and Writing in Higher Education: An Analysis from Key Scholars in the Field in Latin America. *Ilha do Desterro, 69*(3), 209–222.

Bazerman, C. (2017). The Brazilian Blend. In E. G. Lousada, A. D. O. Ferreira, L. Bueno, R. Rojo, S. Aranha, & L. Abreu-Tardelli (Eds.), *Diálogos Brasileiros no Estudo de Gêneros Textuais/Discursivos* (pp. 645–650). Araraquara Letraria.

Bazerman, C. (2017). Equity Means Having Full Voice in the Conversation. *Revista Lenguas Modernas*, *50*(2), 33–46.

Bazerman, C. (2017). The Psychology of Writing Situated within Social Action: An Empirical and Theoretical Program. In P. Portanova, M. Rifenburg, & D. Roen (Eds.), *Contemporary Perspectives on Cognition* (pp. 21–37). The WAC Clearinghouse; University Press of Colorado. https://doi.org/10.37514/PER-B.2017.0032.2.01.

Bazerman, C. (2017). What Do Humans Do Best? Developing Communicative Humans in the Changing Socio-Cyborgian Landscape. In S. Logan, & W. Slater (Eds.), *Perspectives on Academic and Professional Writing in an Age of Accountability* (pp. 187–203). Southern Illinois University Press.

Bazerman, C., Applebee, A. N., Brandt, D., Berninger, V., Graham, S., Matsuda, P., Murphy, S., Rowe, D., & Schleppegrell, M. (2017). Taking the Long View on Writing Development. *Research in the Teaching of English*, *51*(3), 51–60.

Bazerman, C., & Self, B. (2017). Writing the World to Build the World, Iteratively: Inscribing Data and Projecting New Materialities in an Engineering Design Project. In R. Durst, G. Newell, & J. Marshall (Eds.), *English Language Arts Research and Teaching: Revisiting and Extending Arthur Applebee's Contributions* (pp. 91–106). Routledge.

Bazerman, C. (2018). Commentary. In K. Hyland (Ed.), *The Essential Hyland* (pp. 100–105). Bloomsbury.

Bazerman, C. (Ed.) (2018). Lives of Writing. Special Issue on Writing Development across the Lifespan. *Writing and Pedagogy*, *10*(3), 327–331.

Bazerman, C. (2018d). What Does a Model model? And for Whom? *Educational Psychologist*, *53*(4), 301–318.

Bazerman, C., Applebee, A. N., Berninger, V., Brandt, D., Graham, S., Jeffery, J. V., Matsuda, P. K., Murphy, S., Rowe, D. W., Schleppegrell, M., & Wilcox, K. C. (2018). *Lifespan Development of Writing Abilities*. National Council of Teachers of English.

Bazerman, C. (2019a). A? Developmental? Path? To? Text? Quality? *Journal of Literacy Research*, *51*(3), 381–387.

Bazerman, C. (2018). Lifespan Longitudinal Studies of Writing Development: A Heuristic for an Impossible Dream. In C. Bazerman, A. N. Applebee, V. Berninger, D. Brandt, S. Graham, J. V. Jeffery, P. K. Matsuda, S. Murphy, D. W. Rowe, M. Schleppegrell, & K. C. Wilcox, *Lifespan Development of Writing Abilities* (pp. 326–365). National Council of Teachers of English.

Bazerman, C. (2019). Development Makes History, Where Inside Meets Outside. In S. A. Daghé, E. B. Bronckart, G. S. Cordeiro, J. Dolz, I. Leopoldoff, A. Monnier, C. Ronveaux, & B. Vedrines (Eds.), *La Construction de la Didactique du Français comme Discipline Scientifique* (pp. 83–92). Presses Universitaires du Septentrion (University of Lille).

Bazerman, C. (2019). Inscribing the world into knowledge: Data and evidence in Disciplinary Academic Writing. In C. Bazerman, B. Gonzalez, Russell, D., Rogers, P.,

Appendix

Pena, L., Narvaez, E., Carlino, P., Castello, M., & Tapia-Ladino, M (Eds.), *Conocer la Escritura: Investigación más allá de las Fronteras; Knowing Writing: Writing Research across Borders* (pp. 279–294). Universidad Javeriana.

Bazerman, C., Gonzalez, B., Russell, D., Rogers, P., Pena, L., Narvaez, E., Carlino, P., Castello, M., & Tapia-Ladino, M. (Eds.). (2019). *Conocer la Escritura: Investigación más allá de las Fronteras; Knowing Writing: Writing Research Across Borders*. Universidad Javeriana.

Fahler, V., & Bazerman, C. (2019). Data Power in Writing: Assigning Data Analysis in a General Education Linguistics Course to Change Ideologies of Language. *Across the Disciplines, 16*(4), 4–25. https://doi.org/10.37514/ATD-J.2019.16.4.18.

Bazerman, C. (2020). Always Already in Flux: A Response to Anne Freadman. *Canadian Journal for Studies in Discourse and Writing/Redactologie, 30*(152). http://journals.sfu.ca/cjsdw.

Bazerman, C. (2020). Preface. In R. J. Dippre, & T. Phillips (Eds.), *Approaches to Lifespan Writing Research: Generating an Actionable Coherence* (pp. xxi–xxiii). The WAC Clearinghouse; University Press of Colorado. https://doi.org/10.37514/PER-B.2020.1053.1.3.

Bazerman, C. (2021). Emergent Learning in the Emergency/Aprendizagem Emergente na Pandemia. *Revista Triangulo, 14*(1). https://doi.org/10.18554/rt.v14i1.5469.

Bazerman, C. (2021). The Ethical Poetry of Academic Writing. *Educação, Sociedade E Culturas,* (58), 185–188. https://doi.org/10.24840/esc.vi58.152.

Bazerman, C. (2021). The Puzzle of Conducting Research on Lifespan Development of Writing. In K. Blewett, C. Donahue, & C. Monroe (Eds.), *The Expanding Universe of Writing Studies: Higher Education Writing Research* (pp. 403–416). Peter Lang.

Bazerman, C. (2021). Scientific Knowledge, Public Knowledge, and Public Policy: How Genres Form and Disrupt Knowledge for Acting about Anthropogenic Climate Change. In S. Auken, & C. Sunesen (Eds.), *Genre in the Climate Debate* (pp. 34–50). De Gruyter Open Poland. https://doi.org/10.1515/9788395720499-004.

Bazerman, C. (2021). The Value of Empirically Researching a Practical Art. In N. Ávila Reyes (Ed.), *Multilingual Contributions to Writing Research: Toward an Equal Academic Exchange* (pp. 103–124). The WAC Clearinghouse; University Press of Colorado. https://doi.org/10.37514/INT-B.2021.1404.2.04.

Bazerman, C., & Kuntzman, J. (2021). How the US Congress Knows and Evades Knowing about Anthropogenic Climate Change: The Record Created in Committee Hearings, 2004–2016. In S. Auken, & C. Sunesen (Eds.), *Genre in the Climate Debate* (pp. 51–84). De Gruyter Open Poland. https://doi.org/10.1515/9788395720499-005.

Bazerman, C. (2022). Won't You Be My Neighbor? In G. Giberson, M. Schoen, & C. Weisser (Eds.), *Behind the Curtain of Scholarly Publication: Editors in Writing Studies* (pp. 213–228). Utah State University Press.

Bazerman, C. (2022). Escolarizando para la vida, todas las vidas: oportunidad, dilema, desafío y pensamiento crítico. In M. Vergara Fregoso, R. García Reynaga, & S. Ayala Ramírez (Eds.), *Literacidad crítica, formación e inclusión* (pp. 87–107). Guadalajara, Jalisco: Editorial Universidad de Guadalajara.

Bazerman, C. (in press). Revisiting the Early Uses of Writing in Society Building: Cuneiform Culture and the Chinese Imperium. *Literatura y Linguistica.*

Bazerman, C. (in press). *How I Became the Kind of Writer I Became: An Experiment in Autoethnography.* The WAC Clearinghouse; University Press of Colorado.

Bazerman, C. (in press). Reproduction, Critique, Expression, and Cooperation: The Writer's Dance in an Intertextual World. *Revista de Educaccion a la Distancia.*

Bazerman, C. (in press). Longtime Writing Teacher; Latecomer to ELA. *Leaders in English Language Arts Educational Studies: Intellectual Self Portraits.* Brill.

INTERVIEWS

Writing is Motivated Participation: An Interview with Charles Bazerman. (1995). *Writing on the Edge, 6*(2), 7–20. Reprinted in Boe, J., Masiel, D., Schroeder, E., & Sperber, L. (Eds.). (2017). *Teachers on the Edge: The WOE Interviews, 1989–2017* (pp. 181–193). Routledge.

Crawford, T. H., & Smout, K. S. (1995). An Interview with Charles Bazerman. *Composition Studies* 23(1), 21–36.

Charles Bazerman on John Swales. (1998). *English for Special Purposes, 17*(1), 105–112.

Kairos. (1999, March). *An Interview with Professor Bazerman: Interdisciplinary Perspectives on Writing, 1,* 5–8.

Working Inside and Outside Composition Studies (with Richard Lloyd Jones, Charles Cooper and Lee O'Dell.). (1999). In M. Rosner, B. Boehm, & D. Journet (Eds.), *History, Reflection, and Narrative: The Professionalization of Composition, 1963–1983,* Vol. 3 (pp. 331–341). Greenwood Publishing Group.

UCTelevision. (2008, January 31). *50 Years of Research on Writing: What Have We Learned?* Panel with George Hillocks and Peter Elbow. YouTube. http://www.youtube.com/watch?v=mrcq3dzt0Uk.

Roth, D. M., & Bazerman, C. (2015). Literate action, writing and genre studies: Interview with Charles Bazerman. *Calidoscópio, 13*(3), 452–461.

Waigandt, D. M., & Bazerman, C. (2016). The inevitability of teaching writing: An interview with Charles Bazerman. *Argentinian Journal of Applied Linguistics, 4*(2), 23–38.

Jacob Craig, Matt Davis, Christine Martorana, Josh Mehler, Kendra Mitchell, Anthony N. Ricks, Bret Zawilski, & Kathleen Blake Yancey. (2016). *Against the Rhetoric and Composition Grain: A Microhistorical View. Microhistories of Composition* edited by Bruce McComiskey, 284–306. Utah State University Press.

Interview with Charles Bazerman/Entrevisa com Charles Bazerman. (2016). In Sweder Souza & Adail Sobral (Eds.), Gêneros, entre o texto e o discurso: Questões Conceituais e Metodológicas. Mercado de Letras.

Entrevista de Charles Bazerman con el group relif. (2021). https://www.estudiosdelaescritura.org/noticias/entrevista-de-charles-bazerman-con-el-group-relif-disponible-online.

Wood, Shane. Pedagogue. Episode 13: Interview with Charles Bazerman. https://www.pedagoguepodcast.com/episodes.html.

The Built Symbolic Environment. (2022, February 9). Room 42. Episode 15. https://room42.castos.com/episodes/the-built-symbolic-environment.

Appendix

EDITOR, BOOK SERIES

Series: Rhetoric, Knowledge, and Society

Publisher: Lawrence Erlbaum Associates

Dorothy Winsor. *Writing Like an Engineer: A Rhetorical Education.* 1996.
A. D. Van Nostrand. *Fundable Knowledge: The Marketing of Defense Science and Technology.* 1997.
Paul Prior. *Writing/Disciplinarity: A Sociohistoric Account of Literate Activity in the Academy.* 1998.
Joseph Petraglia-Bahri. *Reality by Design: The Rhetoric and Technology of Authenticity and Education.* 1998.
John Swales. *Other Floors, Other Voices: Toward Textography and Beyond.* 1998.
Dwight Atkinson. *Scientific Discourse in Sociohistorical Context: The Philosophical Transactions of the Royal Society of London, 1675–1975.* 1998.
Patrick Dias, Anthony Pare, Aviva Freedman, & Peter Medway. *Worlds Apart: Working and Writing in Academic and Workplace Contexts.* 1999.
Linda Flower, Elenore Long, & Lorraine Higgins, *Learning to Rival: A Literate Practice for Intercultural Inquiry.* 2000.
Ann Blakeslee. *Interacting with Audiences: Social and Rhetorical Practice in Ordinary Science.* 2000.
Phillippe-Joseph Salazar, *An African Athens: Rhetoric and the Shaping of Democracy in South Africa.* 2002.
Beverly Sauer. *Rhetoric Under Uncertainty.* 2002.

Series: Reference Guides to Rhetoric and Composition

Publisher: Parlor Press and The WAC Clearinghouse

Janice Lauer. *Invention.* 2004.
Charles Bazerman, Joseph Little, Teri Chavkin, Danielle Fouquette, Lisa Bethel, and Janet Garufis. *Reference Guide to Writing Across the Curriculum.* 2005.
Alice Horning et al. *Revision.* 2006.
George Otte and Rita Mlynarczyk. *Basic Writing,* 2010.
Susan McLeod, *Writing Program Administration,* 2007.
Elenore Long, *Community Literacy and the Rhetoric of Local Publics,* 2008.
John Ramage, Micheal Callaway, Jennifer Clary-Lemon, and Zachary Waggoner. *Reference Guide to Argument.* 2009.
Anis Bawarshi and JoAnne Reiff. *Genre.* 2010.
Alice Horning and Elizabeth Kraemer. *Reconnecting Reading and Writing.* 2012.
Brian Ray. Style: *An Introduction to History, Theory, Research, and Pedagogy.* 2015.

REPRINTS

Wiener, H., & Bazerman, C. (1978). *English Skills Handbook.* Houghton Mifflin. Revised and reissued in parts as

English Skills Handbook. Longman: 1982, 1985, 1988, 1991, 1994, 1997, 2000, 2006.
Basic Reading Skills Handbook. Longman: 1988, 1991, 1994, 1997, 2000, 2006.
Writing Skills Handbook. 1983, 1988, 1993, 1998, 2003.
All of Us: Cross-Cultural Reading Skills Handbook. 1992, 1995, 1999.
Reading College Textbooks: A Skills Handbook. 1997.
A Reader's Guide. 1999.
Side by Side: A Multi-Cultural Anthology. Houghton Mifflin, 1993, 1996.

Bazerman, C. (1980). A relationship between reading and writing: The conversational model. *College English, 41*(6), 656–661. Reprinted in
MacDonald, J. (Ed.). (1996). *Allyn & Bacon Sourcebook for College Writing Teachers*. Allyn & Bacon.
MacDonald, J. (Ed.). (2000). *Allyn & Bacon Sourcebook for College Writing Teachers* (2nd edition). Allyn & Bacon.

Bazerman, C. (1981). *The Informed Writer: Using Sources in the Disciplines*. Houghton Mifflin. Revised in 1985; 1989; 1992; 1995.

Bazerman, C. (1981). What Written Knowledge Does: Three examples of Academic Discourse. *Philosophy of the Social Sciences, 11*(3), 361–88. Reprinted in
Bazerman, C., & Russell, D. (1994). *Landmark Essays in Writing Across The Curriculum*. Hermagoras Press.
Susan Miller (Ed.). (2009). *Norton Book of Composition Studies*. Norton.
Atkinson, P., & Delamont, S. (Eds.). (2008). *Ethnographic Discourse*. SAGE.

Bazerman, C. (1984). The writing of scientific non-fiction: Contexts, choices and constraints. *Pre/Text, 5*(1), 39–74. Reprinted in V. Vitanza (Ed.), *Ten Years of Pre/Text*. University of Pittsburgh Press.

Bazerman, C. (1991). How natural philosophers can cooperate: The rhetorical technology of coordinated research in Joseph Priestley's History and Present State of Electricity. In C. Bazerman, & J. Paradis (Eds.), *Textual Dynamics of the Professions* (pp. 13–44). University of Wisconsin Press. Reprinted in T. Kynell, & M. Moran (Eds.), *Three Keys to the Past*. Ablex.

Bazerman, C. (1992). From Cultural Criticism to Disciplinary Participation: Living with Powerful Words. In M. Moran, & A. Herrington (Eds.), *Writing, Teaching, and Learning in the disciplines* (pp. 61–68). Modern Language Association. Reprinted in R. Jones (Ed.), *Harcourt Brace Guide to Writing in the Disciplines*. Harcourt Brace.

Bazerman, C. (1992). Where is the Classroom? English Basics, Winter. Reprinted in A. Freedman, & P. Medway (Eds.), *Learning and Teaching Genre* (pp. 25–30). Boynton-Cook.

Bazerman, C. (1994). Systems of Genre and the Enactment of Social Intentions. In A. Freedman, & P. Medway (Eds.), *Genre and the New Rhetoric* (pp. 79–101). Taylor & Francis. Reprinted in C. Miller, & A. Devitt (Eds.), *On rhetorical genre studies* (pp. 113–134). Routledge.

Bazerman, C. (2011). The Work of a Middle-Class Activist: Stuck in History. In S. Kahn (Ed.), *Activism and Rhetoric: Theories and Contexts for Political Engagement* (pp. 37–46). Routledge. Reprinted in Lee, J., & Kahn, S. (Eds.), *Activism and Rhetoric: Theories and Contexts for Political Engagement* (2nd edition) (pp. 190–200). Routledge.

Appendix

TRANSLATIONS

Bazerman, C. (1988a). *Shaping Written Knowledge: The Genre and Activity of the Experimental Article in Science.* University of Wisconsin Press, 1988.
Italian translation: *Le Origini della Scrittura Scientifica. Il Lavoro Editorale* in the series, History of Mentality, 1991.
Chapter 2 reprinted in R. Harris (Ed.), *Landmark Essays in the Rhetoric of Science* (pp. 263–279). Erlbaum, Routledge.

Bazerman, C. (2004). Social Forms as Habitats for Action. *Journal of the Interdisciplinary Crossroads, 1*(2), 317–334. Also in Portuguese translation: *Formas Socais como Habitats para Ação. Investigações Lingüística e Teoria Literária, 16*(2), 123–142.

Bazerman, C., Little, J., Chavkin, T., Fouquette, D., Bethel, L., & Garufis, J. (2005). *Reference Guide to Writing across the Curriculum.* Parlor Press; The WAC Clearinghouse. Spanish translation: *Escribir a Través del Currículum. Una Guía de Referencia.* Córdoba, Argentina, 2016.

Bazerman, C. (2006). The Writing of Social Organization and the Literate Situating of Cognition: Extending Goody's Social Implications of Writing. In D. Olson, & M. Cole (Eds.), *Technology, Literacy and the Evolution of Society: Implications of the Work of Jack Goody* (pp. 215–240). Erlbaum. French translation: *Pratiques, 113*(1), 95–115. Spanish translation: *Revista Signos Estudios de Linguistica, 41*(68), 355–380.

Bazerman, C. (2009). Genre and Cognitive Development: Beyond Writing to Learn. In C. Bazerman, A. Bonini, D. Figueiredo (Eds.), *Genre in a Changing World* (pp. 283–298). The WAC Clearinghouse; Parlor Press. French translation: *Écrire pour Apprendre: La Maîtrise des Genres et le Développement Sociocognitif du Scripteur* (pp. 143–144).

Bazerman, C. (2010). Paying the Rent: Languaging Particularity and Novelty. *Revista Brasileira de Lingüística Applicada, 10*(2), 459–469. Spanish translation: "Pagando o Aluguel: Particularidade e Inovação na Produção da Linguagem," in C. Lemos Vóvio, L. Soares Sito, & P. Baracat De Grande (Eds.), *Letramentos: Rupturas, Deslocamentos e Repercussões de Pesquisas em Linguística Aplicada* (pp. 163–178). Editora Mercado de Letras.

Bazerman, C. (2013). *A Rhetoric of Literate Action: Literate Action, Volume 1.* The WAC Clearinghouse; Parlor Press. Translated into Portuguese: *Retórica da Ação Letrada.* Parabola.

Bazerman, C. (2016). Creating Identities in an Intertextual World. In A. Chik, T. Costley, & M. C. Pennington (Eds.), *Creativity and Discovery in the University Writing Class* (pp. 45–60). Equinox. Portuguese translation: Criando Identidades em um Mundo Textual. In Messias Dieb (Ed.) *A Aprendizagem e o Ensina da Escrita* (pp. 115–132). Pontes.

Bazerman, C. (2019). *Teaching and Studies of Writing in English*, translation of previously published essays into Chinese by Dr. Huijun Chen (陈会军). Beijing, Normal University Press.

EDITORS

Paul M. Rogers is Associate Professor of Writing Studies at the University of California, Santa Barbara. He is a co-founder and former chair of the International Society for the Advancement of Writing Research (ISAWR) and a co-editor of seven collections.

David R. Russell is Professor Emeritus of English in Rhetoric and Professional Communication at Iowa State University. He has published widely on writing across the curriculum (WAC), international writing instruction, activity theory, and genre theory. He is the author of Writing in the Academic Disciplines: A Curricular History, numerous articles, and co-editor of four collections.

Paula Carlino, Ph.D. in Psychology, is Research Professor with the National Council of Scientific and Technical Research (CONICET) at the University of Buenos Aires, where she leads the multidisciplinary team GICEOLEM (Group for an Inclusive and Quality Education by Taking Care of Reading and Writing in all Subjects). She is also a Professor at the Universidad Pedagógica Nacional, Argentina.

Jonathan Marine is a doctoral student in George Mason University's Writing & Rhetoric Program, where his research centers on the life, theory, and work of James Moffett. He was named the 2020 recipient of the National Council of Teachers of English ELATE James Moffett Award and is the Corresponding Secretary for the International Society for the Advancement of Writing Research.

INDEX

A

academic publishing 332
  open access books 217
  partnerships 216, 220
academic writing 79, 81, 84, 99, 102, 144, 147
  cultural differences in 145
activity system(s) 135, 138, 229, 256, 329, 417
activity theory 129, 195, 206, 208, 212, 268, 273, 336
affect 113
analytical writing 143
Applebee, A. 32
applied linguistics 317
apprenticeship 114
argument 12, 80, 81, 94, 95, 143, 207
  patterns 86, 104
argumentation 143, 381
  studies 149
Ashoka Fellow Profile 234
assignments 39
Association for Business Communication 9
Association of Teachers of Technical Writing 9

B

Bakhtinian 265
Bakhtin, M. 101, 268, 269, 394
blogs 395

C

career development 115
Change Laboratory 286, 303
Chomsky, N. 330, 370
College Composition and Communication (CCC) 13
composition
  field of 147, 328, 331, 343
  processes. *See* writing process(es)
computers 216
Conference on College Composition and Communication (CCCC) 4, 201, 211
context. *See* institutional context
context(s) 81
corpus linguistics 82
COVID-19 pandemic 170
Cultural Historical Activity Theory (CHAT) 53
curriculum 128, 148
  Hebrew 152
  Spanish 151

D

Dartmouth 4
degree qualifications profiles 126
dialectic(s) 265, 270
  Marxist 272
dialogic(s) 148, 265
dialogue 107
disciplinary identity 329
disciplinary knowledge 61
disciplinary practices 53
disciplinary writing 44, 98
  changes in 97, 105
distributed cognition 229, 267

E

empathy 379
enculturation 52, 61, 75
Engeström, Y. 34, 216, 266, 276, 286, 410

F

feedback 113, 134
festschrifts 3
first-year composition (FYC) 4
first-year students 127
formulation 372
funding proposals 234

G

genre 125, 140, 282, 329, 335, 352, 393, 404
  analysis 394

442

assemblages 287
change 191, 244, 267
classroom 417
cognition 35, 36, 38, 50, 53
emergence 357
knowledge 50, 135, 140, 141
learning 34, 35, 39, 50, 51, 52, 102, 134, 137, 141, 265, 276
repertoire 190
set(s) 129, 169
social action 34, 227, 254, 267, 351
studies 237, 397
system(s) 129, 131, 169, 170, 173, 189
theory 267, 323, 400
genre change 229
genre repertoire 170
Gere, A. 52, 214
Goody, J. 5, 33, 353
graduate students 35, 59, 104, 109, 112, 115
grammar 370, 372, 374, 375, 384

H

hyflex 180

I

identity 39, 106, 112, 116, 128, 237, 251
  transformation 249
inequalities 126
inscription 373, 419
instruction 51, 115, 162, 173
interaction 81
International Society for the Advancement of Writing Research (ISAWR) 16
intertextuality 137
intervention(s) 53, 73, 74, 296, 300

K

keystroke logging 112
knowledge
  production 31
  tacit 62

L

leadership 213
learning to write 115, 382

Leontiev, A. 276
lifespan development of writing 419
literacy 5
  academic 332
  activities 162
  consequences of 33, 53
literacy development 61, 68, 69, 102, 381, 387
longitudinal 53, 109

M

mediation 129, 131, 132, 227, 253, 256, 337, 419
medium 394
metacognition 109
meta-genre(s) 244
Miller, C. 34, 129, 169, 267, 351, 357
mobility agreement 297

N

National Council of Teachers of English (NCTE) 13
new media 170, 351, 396, 398

P

pedagogy 37, 141
peer response 110
politics 5, 6, 7
possibilization 294
professional development 59, 177, 183, 192
publishing
  digital 196, 197
  open-access 195, 197, 209
publishing collaborative(s) 202, 219

R

reading and writing 7
  research 25
remote teaching 38, 171, 177
rhetoric 3, 9, 10, 102
  contrastive 144, 146, 148, 162
rhetorical genre studies (RGS) 33, 36, 265, 268, 336
rhetorical genre theory 228
rhetorical situation 49
Rhetorical Structure Theory (RST) 146

Index

rhetorical traditions 145
roles 39, 49, 129, 136, 139, 367, 410
Russell, D. 200, 266

S

scientific writing 12, 79, 101, 147
 changes in 99
second language writing 317
social entrepreneurship 227, 230, 232
socialization 52, 114, 144
social media 197, 287, 354
Spanish 36, 65
stabilization 294
strategies 69, 72, 109, 113
 career development 74
 persuasion 148
 regulation 111, 112

T

teachers 35, 41
teaching genres 173, 178
teaching writing 36, 162, 412
textbooks 6, 7, 8
text(s)
 reader responsible 150
The Sweetland Digital Rhetoric Collaborative 201
tools 209, 256, 276, 329, 357
Toulmin model 149, 154

U

universities
 Argentina 125, 126
 Chinese 320
 Latin American 125
 publishing 220
 social entrepreneurship programs 230
 United States 343
 USSR 272

V

Voloshinov, V. 265, 267
Vygotskian 34, 265. *See* Vygotsky, L.
Vygotsky, L. 52, 101, 267, 268, 274, 310, 357, 377

W

WAC Clearinghouse 16, 24, 199
Wertsch, J. 280
writing 310, 368
 cognition 31
 practices 131
 school sponsored 148
 social change 228
 task(s) 33, 44
 workplace 126, 131, 132, 138, 140
writing across the curriculum (WAC) 6, 417
writing development 107, 112, 114, 116, 117
 second language writing 73
writing in the disciplines (WID) 6, 144
writing practices 36
writing process(es) 10, 53, 85, 105, 107, 112, 416
 online 108
writing regulation 106, 111
 processes 102
 social 107
writing research 16, 317
 Latin American 327
 second language 317
writing studies 3, 195, 208, 265, 266, 317, 328, 341, 342, 343, 417
 Chinese 318
 Latin American 331
writing teachers 6
writing to learn 32

Z

zone of proximal development 296, 417

444